Fodor's 2000

Europe's Great Cities

The complete guide, thoroughly up-to-date

Packed with details that will make your trip

What to see, what to skip

City strolls, countryside adventures

Smart dining options

Transportation tips, distances and directions

Key contacts, savvy travel tips

When to go, what to pack

Clear, accurate, easy-to-use maps

Excerpted from *Fodor's Europe '99*

Fodor's Travel Publications, Inc. • New York, Toronto, London, Sydney, Auckland
www.fodors.com

Europe's Great Cities

EDITOR: Nancy van Itallie

Editorial Contributors: Barbara Walsh Angelillo, Toula Bogdanos, David Brown, Jacqueline Brown, Peter Collis, Nancy Coons, Fionn Davenport, Martha de la Cal, Bonnie Dodson, Debbie Ebanks, Jon Eldan, Judith Glynn, Brent Gregston, Kay Hammond, Nancy Hart, Simon Hewitt, Alannah Hopkin, Beth Ingpen, Nicola Keegan, Suzanne Rowan Kelleher, Ky Krauthamer, Martha Lagace, Mark Little, Alexander Lobrano, Andrew May, Dan Navid, Ian Phillips, Ian Plenderleith, Robert Rigney, Rich Rubin, Patricia Rucidlo, Jurgen Scheunemann, Helayne Schiff, Marshall Schwartzmann (Gold Guide editor), Kate Sekules, George Semler, Katherine Semler, Eric Sjogren, Gilbert Summers, Robert Tilley, Julie Tomasz, Susan Tuttle-Laube

Editorial Production: Melissa Klurman

Maps: David Lindroth, *cartographer*; Steven Amsterdam and Bob Blake, *map editors*

Design: Fabrizio La Rocca, *creative director*; Guido Caroti, *art director*; Jolie Novak, *photo editor*

Production/Manufacturing: Robert B. Shields

Cover Photograph: Bob Krist

Copyright

ISBN 0–679–00660–5

Although all prices, opening times, and other details in this book are based on information supplied to us at press time, changes occur all the time in the travel world, and Fodor's cannot accept responsibility for facts that become outdated or for inadvertent errors or omissions. So **always confirm information when it matters,** especially if you're making a detour to visit a specific place.

Special Sales

Fodor's Travel Publications are available at special discounts for bulk purchases for sales promotions or premiums. Special editions, including personalized covers, excerpts of existing guides, and corporate imprints, can be created in large quantities for special needs. For more information, contact your local bookseller or write to Special Markets, Fodor's Travel Publications, 201 East 50th Street, New York, NY 10022. Inquiries from Canada should be directed to your local Canadian bookseller or sent to Random House of Canada, Ltd., Marketing Department, 2775 Matheson Boulevard East, Mississauga, Ontario L4W 4P7. Inquiries from the United Kingdom should be sent to Fodor's Travel Publications, 20 Vauxhall Bridge Road, London SW1V 2SA, England.

PRINTED IN THE UNITED STATES OF AMERICA

10 9 8 7 6 5 4 3 2 1

CONTENTS

*Italic entries are maps.

ON THE ROAD WITH FODOR'S

On Your Way with EF and How to Use This Book

Organization

The section following this one, **New and Noteworthy,** cues you in on trends and happenings. Following that is Chapter 1, the **Gold Guide,** with Smart Travel Tips arranged alphabetically by topic. Under each listing you'll find tips and information that will help you accomplish what you need to in Europe. You'll also find addresses and telephone numbers of organizations and companies that offer destination-related services and detailed information and publications.

Chapters in *Europe's Great Cities* are in alphabetical order by city. Each covers the city's essential information, exploring, dining, nightlife and the arts, and shopping. Sites in major cities accompanied by maps are arranged alphabetically, but they are numbered on the maps according to the suggested sequence of a walk or tour. The Essentials section that ends all chapters covers getting there and getting around. It also provides helpful contacts and resources.

Icons and Symbols
★ Our special recommendations
✕ Restaurant
☺ Good for kids (rubber duck)
☞ Sends you to another section of the guide for more information

✉ Address
☎ Telephone number
☉ Opening and closing times
💲 Admission prices for attractions that charge more than $10 or the equivalent (those we give apply to adults; substantially reduced fees are almost always available for children, students, and senior citizens); we indicate if the attraction does not charge admission.

Numbers in black circles ❸ that appear on the maps, in the margins, and within the tours correspond to one another.

Dining
The restaurants we list are the cream of the crop in each price range. Price charts appear in the Dining section of each chapter.

Restaurant Reservations and Dress Codes
Reservations are always a good idea; we mention them only when they're essential or are not accepted. Book as far ahead as you can, and reconfirm as soon as you arrive. Unless otherwise noted, the restaurants listed are open daily for lunch and dinner. We mention dress only when men are required to wear a jacket or a jacket and tie.

Credit Cards
The following abbreviations are used: **AE,** American Express; **DC,** Diners Club; **MC,** MasterCard; and **V,** Visa.

NEW AND NOTEWORTHY

A NEW MONETARY CURRENCY will make its debut on January 1, 1999 when the conversion to the euro (€) begins for all members of the European Union. Some payment systems (mainly in trade) will begin using the euro immediately. The rates of conversion between the euro and local currencies will be irrevocably fixed, which should eliminate commission charges when exchanging currency. Consumers will continue to use chiefly their own national currency because euro banknotes and coins will not yet be available, but the gradual introduction of dual pricing of goods and services will enable people to slowly get used to the new money. Eventually, the euro will become a currency in its own right and participating national currencies will no longer be listed on foreign exchange markets. By January 1, 2002 at the latest, new euro banknotes and coins will be put into circulation and the old national currencies will be withdrawn. In Austria this will be done over a period of three months, after which euro banknotes and coins alone will have legal tender status.

Amsterdam

Amsterdam's central **Museumplein,** once a major artery for traffic, is being transformed into a landscaped recreation area with stunning modernistic waterscapes as a backdrop for the extensions to both the Van Gogh Museum and the Stedelijk Museum of Modern Art that are currently being built. The **Rembrandt's House** museum has also just been given a new wing, making it possible to display more of the old master's works, as well as providing space for multimedia presentations. **Exhibitions** to watch for in 1999 include 17th- and 18th-century still lifes from June to September at the Rijksmuseum.

Barcelona

In Catalonia the Spanish Ministry of Tourism is now operating a **Dali triangle,** which includes not only the world-famous Museu Dalí, in Figueres, but the artist's fishing shack in Port Lligat, near Cadaqués, and his castle in Pubol. Starting from Barcelona, the triangular tour of Dali's personal world covers roughly 140 miles and crosses some of the most beautiful countryside in Catalonia.

Brussels

In Brussels, the permanent **Magritte Museum** opens at 138 Esseghemstraat in the borough of Jette. This is the house where the artist lived until 1954 with the studio and living room restored and an exhibition of his paintings on the upper two floors. A new **Booking Office** (☎ 0800/ 21 22 1) has opened in Brussels covering events all over the country. There is no charge for its services, and callers can enquire about what's on and prices before deciding to book. Payment is by direct debit or (for visitors) by major credit cards.

Budapest

Grand old Budapest is seeing more and more improvements and development, from private restoration of crumbling, once-elegant buildings to city-funded infrastructure projects, such as the construction of a fourth metro line through southern Buda, begun in late 1998. More pedestrian-only zones are appearing, and new restaurants and shops are sprouting around the city.

Dublin

The expansion of Dublin continues without any sign of abating. Amid all the new cafés, restaurants, and hotels in Ireland's capital, the most important cultural attraction is the new **Collins Barracks,** which now houses the decorative arts exhibits of the National Museum, part of an ongoing expansion project. For 1999, the city has unveiled the **Arthouse,** one of the world's first multimedia centers for the arts and home to a comprehensive database of many of Ireland's up-and-coming artists. Dublin's newest swanky hotel, the Merrion, is just one of many new hostelries meeting the tourist boom.

London

London's renaissance continues at full blast, with Tony Blair, the dynamic, young(ish) Labour Prime Minister and the National Lottery—which funds exciting projects—leading the way. London's art, style, dining, and fashion scenes are sizzling. England is in the grip of Millennium fever, which will only intensify as the numbers creep toward the big 2000. Among the several buildings due to open on or around the big day is the **Millennium Dome,** at Greenwich. This multimillion-pound multi-football-field-size structure designed by architect-provocateur Richard Rogers is to house a cornucopia of architectural installations.

The new **BBC Experience** is a guided tour of the Broadcasting House of the British Broadcasting Corporation, including the Marconi Collection of early audiovisual equipment and interactive bits where you can play at directing *EastEnders,* the popular Cockney TV soap, or cast yourself in a role on *Desert Island Discs.* Islington's first major museum, the new **Estorick Collection of Italian Art,** displays those naughty Futurists in a renovated Georgian building on Cannonbury Square. The new **British Library** won't be completely operational until mid-1999, but some services were available in 1998.

The performing arts Muses seem to be, for all intents and purposes, practically homeless in London these days. The world-renowned **Royal Opera House** is still shuttered, owing to an ongoing renovation. Its resident troupes are taking up temporary shelter, gypsylike, at other theaters in the interim. The English National Opera (**ENO**) has abandoned the Coliseum, its home since 1968. Possible sites for a new house, funded by the Lottery, include several places along the South Bank, King's Cross, or the sadly disused yet magisterial Battersea Power Station. In addition, the **Royal Shakespeare Theatre** will no longer offer a summer season, and the Vic theater may close, with the resultant eviction of some of London's livelier theater troupes.

Madrid

A timeless Madrid landmark has been revived after nearly a decade of disuse. Closed intermittently for almost 70 years due to successive disasters, such as fire and faulty engineering, the capital's **Teatro Real** underwent a massive refurbishment to open grandly in October 1997 with a performance of Manual de Falla's *La Vida Breve.* Now replete with golden balconies, plush seats, and state-of-the-art stage equipment for operas and ballets, the theater is a modern concert hall with its vintage appeal intact.

Paris

Not content with being the world's largest museum, the **Louvre** continues to expand: 11 new rooms of Persian and Arab antiquities opened in October 1997, followed in December by an extra-large exhibit space devoted to Greek, Roman, Egyptian, Etruscan, and Coptic art. The **Centre Pompidou** closed in October 1997 for a $120-million renovation program and will not reopen till the last day of the century—December 31, 1999. In the meantime, you can visit the **Atelier Brancusi** in front of the center—the reconstituted studios of avant-garde sculptor Constantin Brancusi. The **Bibliothèque Nationale François-Mitterrand,** the new national library building in Paris (which replaced the old national library, the Bibliothèque Nationale Richelieu, on rue Richelieu), has proved a popular addition to the southeast section of the city. The Tolbiac district around the new library was due to be united to central Paris by the express **Météor** métro line by late 1998.

Paris is gearing up for **L'An 2000** (The Year 2000) with a host of special events planned to celebrate the millennium. A digital clock on the Eiffel Tower is counting down the days to the end of the century and, more frenetically, the Genitron on place de la Bastille is ticking down the seconds.

Prague

A spacious and spiffy **new terminal** at Prague's Ruzyně airport has made traveling through it a pleasure rather than an exercise in crowd tolerance. The arrival of visitors and long-term residents from all over the world has brought forth **new restaurants** offering Cajun, Indian, vegetarian, and other exotic fare alongside the traditional ones serving pork and dumplings.

Prague's cultural life as a European capital continues to thrive, and the city in particular is a dream for classical-music lovers and opera fans. The annual mid-May–early June **Prague Spring Music Festival,** which even before the collapse of the Communist government was one of the great events on the European calendar, is attracting record numbers of music lovers. The less-hyped **Prague Autumn festival** has begun to bring in equally strong performers and orchestras, and the State Opera's annual **Verdi Festival** in August is gaining popularity.

Rome

During 1999 in Rome the rush to finish public works and infrastructure planned for the **Jubilee Year of 2000** is evident in road works in progress and in the number of public buildings still covered with shrouds of restoration scaffolding. Among the Vatican facilities being constructed to handle the millions of pilgrims is an entirely new entrance to the Musei Vaticani, which will be near the former one on Viale Vaticano.

Rome loses one obelisk and gains another: The **Obelisk of Axum,** a victory trophy brought from Ethiopia by Mussolini and placed near the Circo Massimo, has been returned to that country as a gesture of reconciliation. U.S. architect Richard Meier is putting up a new obelisk as part of his refurbishing of **Piazza dell'Augusteo** and the building containing the **Ara Pacis.**

Vienna

The year opens with the annual **New Year's Day concert** by the Vienna Philharmonic, conducted by Lorin Maazel, with the musical selection for the gala event a secret until 10 days before the performance. The main musical event of 1999 is the 100th anniversary of the death of the king of the waltz, **Johann Strauss the Younger,** and the 150th anniversary of the death of his father. Austria plans to mark the year with a celebration of Strauss operettas and waltzes, and both the Vienna State Opera and the Volksoper will host performances of several of both composers' works. Getting tickets to the glamorous **Opernball** in Vienna depends on luck and speed. Earmark February 2, 1999, to take part in this quintessentially Viennese event.

New in the **Vienna art world** is the transformation of the rambling Messepalast building, near the Kunsthistorisches Museum, into a museum for post-1918 art, with works by Egon Schiele forming the nucleus of the collection.

Near the United Nations center in Vienna a massive new complex called **Donau City,** or Danube City, is under construction. When it's completed, it will house restaurants, shops, and movie theaters. The new four-star Forum Hotel, part of the Inter-Continental Hotel Group, is scheduled to open there by press time.

A new addition to Vienna's Stephansplatz is the **Jewish Welcome Center,** at Number 10. Along with trying to keep in touch with emigrants all over the world, the Welcome Center provides information on where to visit important Jewish landmarks and former Jewish neighborhoods in the city.

EF OFFICES AND INTERNATIONAL LANGUAGE SCHOOLS

Dublin **EF**

EF Cambridge

London **EF**

Brighton **EF** **EF** Hastings

EF Amsterdam

Co

Brussels **EF**

EF Reims

Paris **EF**

Lucerne **EF**

Turin **EF**

Nice **EF**

Bilbao **EF**

Barcelona **EF**

Madrid **EF**

EF Valencia

Lisbon **EF**

EF Oslo

Helsinki EF

EF St. Petersburg

EF Stockholm

EF Göteburg

Moscow EF

hagen EF EF Malmö

Hamburg

EF Berlin

EF Warsaw

EF Dresden

eidelberg

EF Munich

EF Vienna

rich

Milan

EF Florence

Rome EF

Istanbul EF

EF Malta

World Time Zones

Numbers below vertical bands relate each zone to Greenwich Mean Time (0 hrs.).
Local times frequently differ from these general indications,
as indicated by light-face numbers on map.

Algiers, **29**	Berlin, **34**	Delhi, **48**	Jerusalem, **42**
Anchorage, **3**	Bogotá, **19**	Denver, **8**	Johannesburg, **44**
Athens, **41**	Budapest, **37**	Dublin, **26**	Lima, **20**
Auckland, **1**	Buenos Aires, **24**	Edmonton, **7**	Lisbon, **28**
Baghdad, **46**	Caracas, **22**	Hong Kong, **56**	London
Bangkok, **50**	Chicago, **9**	Honolulu, **2**	(Greenwich), **27**
Beijing, **54**	Copenhagen, **33**	Istanbul, **40**	Los Angeles, **6**
	Dallas, **10**	Jakarta, **53**	Madrid, **38**
			Manila, **57**

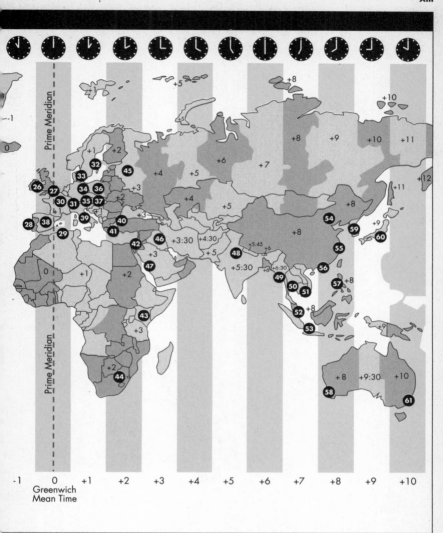

Mecca, **47**
Mexico City, **12**
Miami, **18**
Montréal, **15**
Moscow, **45**
Nairobi, **43**
New Orleans, **11**
New York City, **16**

Ottawa, **14**
Paris, **30**
Perth, **58**
Reykjavík, **25**
Rio de Janeiro, **23**
Rome, **39**
Saigon (Ho Chi Minh City), **51**

San Francisco, **5**
Santiago, **21**
Seoul, **59**
Shanghai, **55**
Singapore, **52**
Stockholm, **32**
Sydney, **61**
Tokyo, **60**

Toronto, **13**
Vancouver, **4**
Vienna, **35**
Warsaw, **36**
Washington, D.C., **17**
Yangon, **49**
Zürich, **31**

On Your Way with EF

ON YOUR WAY TO THE GLOBAL CLASSROOM

These pages will help you and your students get ready for your upcoming EF Educational Tour. A world of discovery awaits you, and making sure your group is well prepared and knows what to expect enables everyone to make the most of the experience. Following, you'll find practical details, reminders, a list of books and movies about your destination, and helpful tips from experienced EF travelers. Have a wonderful trip!

PRE-TOUR ACTIVITIES

Topics for pre-tour meetings

Practice some key phrases and words in the language of the countries you'll be visiting. "Please," "thank you," and "excuse me" should be in everyone's vocabulary! You can also find basic foreign language vocabulary at www.eftours.com.

Discuss the use of foreign currency. Gather exchange rates from the newspaper, on the web at www.eftours.com or at a local bank; have students practice converting dollars into foreign currency and vice versa.

Contact the national tourist offices of your destination countries for informational materials and maps.

Review the optional excursions available on your itinerary, and discuss which ones to sign up for (whether individually or as a group). Most of our optional excursions are available at a discounted rate for pre-enrollment. Prepare the telephone chain chart supplied by EF. Every household should receive a copy, and a copy must be sent to your EF Tour Consultant no later than 14 days before you leave. This will prove invaluable if, for instance, your flight is delayed and families must be notified.

Fundraisers

Many groups use the months and weeks leading up to their tour to organize fundraising activities. Fundraisers serve not only to defray the costs of your tour, but also to build enthusiasm and team spirit among your participants.

CULTURAL DIFFERENCES ABROAD

Hotels

Except where noted, EF uses first-class, superior tourist-class, or tourist-class hotels, as defined by the OHG (Official Hotel Guide). Hotels are representative of the country you are visiting. Every room will have a private bathroom. Hotel rooms abroad are often less modern, less standardized, and smaller than those in North America. As is customary in some countries, not all hotel bathrooms have face towels (students may wish to bring one) and many do not have elevators.

Meals

Most EF itineraries include continental breakfast and dinner daily. In much of the world, breakfasts are traditionally not as large as what your students may be accustomed to. Your breakfast while on tour will typically include bread or rolls, juice, and coffee. For dinner, groups dine in restaurants or hotel dining rooms selected and personally visited by EF's Operations Department. Meals are generally chosen to appeal to students, and to offer a taste of the local cuisine whenever possible. Because of the challenges of serving a large group, you will usually receive a pre-set meal rather than ordering from a menu.

Smoking

Although public smoking is decreasing in Europe, it is still much more common than in North America. Smoking in restaurants is fairly common.

Public transportation

Public transportation is more commonly used abroad than it is in many parts of North America. To travel to local activities or free-time options, EF groups generally find it easy to use public transportation. Your tour director will help you to learn the maps and routes. It's also a good idea to research the public transportation systems of the cities you'll be visiting before your tour.

GROUP DYNAMICS: IT'S A TEAM EFFORT!

Punctuality

No matter where you travel, there's a tremendous amount to see and do—and a limited time in which to cover it. For that reason, most EF itineraries are packed with activities. It is crucial that everyone makes punctuality a priority—for wake-up calls, sightseeing tours, meals, meeting times, etc. It takes just one person showing up late to throw off a whole day's schedule. Please be sure that all your participants understand how imperative it is that they keep track of time and follow instructions. Remind your students to wear watches if possible!

Making the most of your time as a group

Depending on your itinerary, you may have one or more bus transfers of several hours. There are many informal activities that can make the time pass quickly while also enhancing the educational value of your tour. Experienced EF Group Leaders have suggested that students use this time to:

- Share impressions of the tour with other students—comparing favorite stops, most interesting excursions, etc.
- Learn from the tour director about daily life for teenagers in the countries they are visiting.

- Design a question-and-answer game related to the sights seen so far.
- If traveling with a group from another part of the United States or Canada, compare notes on life at home—classes, school activities, after-school jobs, social concerns.

PRACTICAL TRAVEL TIPS

Passports and visas

Nearly all EF destinations require that each participant has a passport, valid for the entire duration of the trip. If your participants have not already begun the process of obtaining all required documentation, they should do so immediately. (Students should make one copy of their passport for themselves and one copy for you.)

Inoculations

Travelers should check with their family doctor or contact a local doctor or hospital to find out what vaccinations are needed (if any) for the country to which they plan to travel. At the time of printing, no inoculations are required for any EF destinations, but many are recommended.

Insurance

We strongly recommend that all students protect themselves by obtaining travel insurance. EF offers medical and baggage insurances as well as an extended tour cancellation/interruption plan to all participants.

Phoning home

Chances are, your participants will want to call home at least once in a while on tour—to keep parents up-to-date on their travels or simply to speak with a familiar voice. Telephone calls abroad are generally very costly, particularly if made from the hotel. This, in addition to time differences, sometimes makes it difficult to contact home. Any calls to home should be dialed collect, or made with a calling card. For your participants' convenience, EF offers prepaid international calling cards with simple printed instructions. Your group members may purchase them before departure or during the tour.

Time differences and the busy pace of EF tours often make it difficult for students to phone home at the exact times that their parents may have requested before departure. You might want to reassure parents before the trip not to worry if they don't hear from their child right away. Some groups even plan ahead of time to activate their telephone chain upon arrival to say that they've safely arrived. This way only one traveler needs to call home in order for every family to feel reassured.

PACKING TIPS

Special packing considerations

It is advised that your travelers carry valuables, medicines, cameras, toiletries, and an extra change of clothes in their EF backpack and bring this with them on planes, buses, trains, and ferries, when applicable. Stress to your group members that they should leave nonessential valuables, such as jewelry, at home, and that passports and money should always be carried with them, rather than packed in suitcases.

Students who require prescription medicine should give you a copy of the prescription for safekeeping. Students who wear contact lenses or glasses should bring a backup pair and a copy of their prescription.

Customs officials may want to verify that a medicine container's contents match its label. Therefore, every medication (whether it is prescription, over-the-counter, or even vitamins) should be carried in its original container, not consolidated.

Luggage and clothing

Your group members should pack as lightly as possible, including only essential items for the tour—as much as will fit in one suitcase and an EF backpack. Please make it clear to all your participants (students and adults alike) that they will be responsible for loading their luggage on and off buses and trains, through airports, and into hotels (which often do not have elevators). Every bag should have a personal identification tag attached to it, and the name of the traveler should be clearly written on the inside.

Because many tours include extensive walking, students should pack their most comfortable shoes. Regardless of the season, an umbrella or raincoat is also essential. Advise your travelers that at some religious sites they will be required to wear clothing that covers their shoulders and upper arms, and at those same sites shorts are not permitted.

Electrical appliances

Electrical current in most European countries is 220V, as opposed to 110V in the United States, Canada, and Mexico. Still, other voltages are used in Africa, Asia, the South Pacific, and Latin America. This means that travelers will need a converter to use hair dryers, electric razors, contact lens sterilizers, etc. In addition, the configuration of the plug needed will differ from country to country. Special travel kits, with a selection of electric converter plugs, can usually be found in major department or luggage stores. Encourage students to share appliances such as hair dryers, and remind them to charge cordless appliances before departing.

CASH, CHECK OR CHARGE

Spending money

The safest way to carry money is in the form of traveler's checks. We suggest one of the universally popular brands, such as Thomas Cook or American Express. Before departure, have students record in duplicate the identification numbers of their checks, giving one copy to you for safekeeping. Each student should also give you $20 in traveler's checks to hold in case of emergency.

As a general guideline, EF recommends your participants bring with them at least $30-$50 U.S./$45-$75 Canadian per day for most destinations. This amount may vary depending on how many gifts and souvenirs they intend to purchase, and on the length and destinations of the tour. On most programs, however, students must remember to allocate a certain amount for lunches, beverages, optional excursions (if they did not pre-pay for them), and public transportation, in addition to their shopping budget. Urge your students to bring enough money to cover all likely expenses, as transferring money from home can be extremely inconvenient as well as time-consuming and costly.

Many parents choose to let their child take a credit card to use with discretion as the need arises. (Should they wish, students may enroll for optional excursions during the tour with their credit card.)

Additionally, most European ATMs accept a wide number of bank cards as well as Visa and Master-Card for cash withdrawals. Travelers will need to know their PIN password in number form because international machines often do not have letters on the keys.

Changing money and safety

Many stores will accept traveler's checks for payment, but your group will receive the best value for their money by exchanging checks into the local currency. Local banks often offer the best exchange rate and the lowest fee. When banks are closed, checks can be changed at a money-exchange booth. Your EF Tour Director will point out the nearest bank or exchange booth and explain the different currencies as you travel. Coins are usually not convertible from one currency to another, so be sure to use them before leaving the country.

Changing money at hotels or retail shops is not recommended as the exchange fees are generally much higher. Under no circumstances should money be exchanged on the black market, as this is illegal and can result in severe penalties in many countries!

Unfortunately, travelers are often easy targets for thieves and pickpockets. Please remind students to take great care of all their possessions, especially cameras, cash, traveler's checks, credit cards, and passports, throughout the trip.

Most luggage stores sell a variety of money belts and security wallets designed specifically for travelers' security.

Please note: Before leaving for tour, participants should change $30–$40 in the currency of the first country visited, in case there is a delay before they can change money upon arrival.

SUGGESTED BOOKS AND FILMS

Austria
Austria
Sacheverell Sitwell

The Land and People of Austria
Raymond Wholrabe

Films: The Sound of Music, Amadeus

Belgium and the Netherlands
The Land and the People of Holland
A.J. Barnouw

The Diary of Anne Frank
Anne Frank

The Land and the People of Belgium
Dorothy Loder

Rembrandt
G. Schmidt

Central and Eastern Europe

Fresh From the Laundry
L. Chase

Hungary: A Guide with a Difference
Z. Halasz

The Metamorphosis
Franz Kafka

My First Loves
Ivan Klima

The Book of Laughter and Forgetting Milan Kundera

Century in Scarlet
L. Zilahy

Films: The Unbearable Lightness of Being, Kolya

France

France
Pierre Broden

Memoirs of a Dutiful Daughter
Simone de Beauvoir

A Tale of Two Cities
Charles Dickens

A Moveable Feast
Ernest Hemingway

Les Misérables
Victor Hugo

A Year in Provence
Peter Mayle

The Scarlet Pimpernel
Baroness Orczy

Shadow of a Man
May Sarton

Films: Jean de Florette, Manon of the Spring, Au Revoir les Enfants, The Return of Martin Guerre, Cyrano de Bergerac, Les Misérables, Grand Illusion, Mon Oncle d'Amerique, May Fools, Story of Adele H, Small Change

Germany

Badenheim, 1939
Aharon Appelfeld

The Blue Flower
Penelope Fitzgerald

The Berlin Wall
P. Gallante

The Tin Drum
Günter Grass

Stones from the River
Ursula Hegi

The Magic Mountain
Thomas Mann

All Quiet on the Western Front
Erich Maria Remarque

The Land and People of Germany
Raymond Wholrabe

Night
Elie Wiesel

Films: Das Boot, Cabaret, Triumph of the Will, Das Versprechen (The Promise), Wings of Desire

Great Britain and Ireland

Pride and Prejudice
Jane Austen

Oliver Twist
Charles Dickens

Literary Tour Guide of England and Scotland
E.C. Harting

Dubliners
James Joyce

Angela's Ashes
Frank McCourt

Down and Out in Paris and London
George Orwell

Kingdom by the Sea
Paul Theroux

Trinity
Leon Uris

Films: My Left Foot, American Werewolf in London, Emma, Orlando, Local Hero, Cal, Hope and Glory, Remains of the Day, Anne of the Thousand Days, Another Country, Henry IV, Nicholas Nickelby, Wuthering Heights, Shadowlands, The Commitments, In the Name of the Father

Greece

The Greek Islands
Lawrence Durrell

Greek Gods and Heroes
Robert Graves

Zorba the Greek
Nikos Kazantzakis

Mythology
Edith Hamilton

The Republic
Plato, as translated by Allan Bloom

The King Must Die
Mary Renault

Films: Zorba the Greek, Never on Sunday

Italy
The Italians
Luigi Barzini

The Last Days of Pompeii
Edward Bulwer-Lytton

Death in Venice
Thomas Mann

The Stones of Florence
Mary McCanlly

The Agony and the Ecstasy
Irving Stone

Films: Cinema Paradiso, La Dolce Vita, The Agony and the Ecstasy, Il Postino, Only You, A Month by the Lake, Life is Beautiful

Russia
Crime and Punishment
Fyodor Dostoevsky

The Girl from Petrovka
George Feifer

Land of the Firebird
Suzanne Massey

Russians as People
Wright Miller

Pale Fire
Vladimir Nabokov

The Russians
Hedrick Smith

And Quiet Flows the Don
Mikhail Solokov

The Gulag Archipelago
Alexander Solzhenitsyn

Anna Karenina
Leo Tolstoy

Films: Dr. Zhivago, Moscow Does Not Believe in Tears, Dark Eyes, The Russians are Coming, Battleship Potemkin, End of the St. Petersburg

Scandinavia
Winter's Tales
Isak Dinesen

Smilla's Sense of Snow
Peter Hoeg

Scandinavian Legends and Folk Tales
Gwyn Jones

Sweden: The Nation's History
Franklin Scott

The Land and People of Denmark
Raymond Wholrabe

Films:: My Life as a Dog, Fanny and Alexander, Pelle the Conqueror

Spain and Portugal
A Concise History of Portugal
David Birmingham

Don Quixote
Miguel de Cervantes

For Whom the Bell Tolls
Ernest Hemingway

The Sun Also Rises
Ernest Hemingway

Tales of the Alhambra
Washington Irving

Iberia
James Michener

Portugal
Richard Moore

Homage to Catalonia
George Orwell

The Franco Years
Jose Yglesias

Films: El Cid, Carmen

Switzerland
The Visit
Friedrich Dürrenmatt

Heidi
Johanna Spyri

Turkey
The Wind from the Plains
Yasar Kemal

The Ottoman Centuries
Lord Kinross

The Emergence of Modern Turkey
Bernard Lewis

DEPARTURE AND ARRIVAL PROCEDURES

Before you leave for the airport

As you prepare to set off for the airport, be certain that all members of your group have any documentation they need (such as passports and visas) with them. Plan to arrive at the airport at least three hours in advance of the scheduled departure time of your flight. (Airlines may legally "bump" passengers who have not checked in for an international flight two hours prior to departure.) Keep all airline tickets (which you have already counted and checked) in your possession. Obtaining a replacement for a lost ticket can be both inconvenient and costly.

Please ensure that your group members have signed their passports beforehand, and that they are carrying their passports in an easily accessible place (such as a purse or secure jacket pocket). They will need to present passports at airport check-in. Remind participants never to pack their passports in suitcases!

Flight check-in

If your group, including you, numbers fewer than ten travelers, follow normal check-in procedures. Simply have your group join the line at the counter.

If your group numbers ten or more travelers, do not join the passenger line. Instead, go to the counter and request a "group check." The airline personnel will then instruct you as to the most efficient procedure.

Baggage and boarding

In many cases, you will be able to check your baggage through to your final flight destination. Collect all group boarding passes from the airline staff, and distribute these to your group as they board the plane. This will prevent the possibility of loss and will enable you to verify that the entire group is safely aboard.

On the flight

Of course your students will be excited once the trip is under way, but encourage them to relax: getting some sleep now (if it's an overnight flight) will help them to conquer their jet lag faster once they arrive. Other recommendations for a comfortable flight are to avoid caffeine but drink plenty of water and juice to ward off dehydration.

Arrival

Upon arrival at your destination, go to the baggage claim. When your entire group has claimed its belongings, proceed through customs. Your tour director will be waiting for you on the other side of the customs gate. (Alternatively, a local EF representative might meet your flight and assist with the transfer to your first hotel, where you'll meet your tour director.) In the event that no EF staff member appears immediately, please wait right outside the customs gate; he or she may have had to meet a flight elsewhere in the airport and will be there shortly.

Your tour director will then direct you to your motorcoach. In some cases, your group might wait briefly at the airport for another group who will be joining your tour. Once the whole group is aboard the bus, you will transfer to your hotel. If it is too early for hotel check-in, the hotel will probably provide common space to store your belongings until room keys are available.

You're on your way—have a wonderful time!

Dealing with jet lag

There are almost as many "remedies" for jet lag as there are world travelers. However, the best and easiest guideline is simply to adapt your behavior to the time of day it is at your destination—starting as soon as you board your flight. Relax and try to sleep if your flight is overnight. Upon arriving, encourage your students to put their energy into the day's activities, even if they are tired.

Try to avoid long naps during the day, but don't stay up too late in the evening. After a full night's sleep, everyone will be on their way back to normal!

IN CASE OF EMERGENCY WHEN ON TOUR

EF Tour Directors are fully trained to handle any emergency that might arise on tour, and have access to local EF offices worldwide.

In the event that an emergency arises when your tour director is not available (such as before you reach your destination), group leaders may contact an EF representative at the following offices 24 hours a day.

Boston, Massachusetts
(617) 619–2913

Dallas, Texas
(972) 383–8700

Santa Barbara, California
(805) 963–9171

Toronto, Ontario
(416) 927–1911

**Vancouver,
British Columbia**
(604) 687–5566

1 The Gold Guide

SMART TRAVEL TIPS A TO Z

Basic Information on Traveling in Europe's Great Cities, Savvy Tips to Make Your Trip a Breeze, and Companies and Organizations to Contact

AIR TRAVEL

CHECK IN & BOARDING

Airlines routinely overbook planes, assuming that not everyone with a ticket will show up, but sometimes everyone does. When that happens, airlines ask for volunteers to give up their seats. In return these volunteers usually get a certificate for a free flight and are rebooked on the next flight out. If there are not enough volunteers, the airline must choose who will be denied boarding. The first to get bumped are passengers who checked in late and those flying on discounted tickets, so **get to the gate and check in as early as possible,** especially during peak periods.

Although the trend on international flights is to drop reconfirmation requirements, many airlines still ask you to reconfirm each leg of your international itinerary. Failure to do so may result in your reservation being canceled.

Always **bring a government-issued photo ID to the airport.** You may be asked to show it before you are allowed to check in.

For scheduled international flights, **arrive in time to check in one hour before departure**; for charter flights, allow two hours. If you just have hand luggage, you may be able to check in as late as 30 minutes before takeoff. If you're traveling Business Class, **ask about special deals,** such as check-in at designated hotels, or telephone check-in.

ENJOYING THE FLIGHT

For better service, **fly smaller or regional carriers,** which often have higher passenger-satisfaction ratings. Sometimes you'll find leather seats, more legroom, and better food.

For more legroom, **request an emergency-aisle seat.** Don't sit in the row in front of the emergency aisle or in front of a bulkhead, where seats may not recline.

If you don't like airline food, **ask for special meals when booking.** These can be vegetarian, low-cholesterol, or kosher, for example.

When flying internationally, try to maintain a normal routine, to help fight jet-lag. At night, **get some sleep.** By day, **eat light meals, drink water (not alcohol), and move around the cabin** to stretch your legs.

Many carriers have prohibited smoking on all of their international flights; others allow smoking only on certain routes or certain departures, so **contact your carrier regarding its smoking policy.**

AIRPORTS

ARRIVALS

Passport control has become a perfunctory affair within most of the European Union (EU). The nine signatories to the Schengen Agreement (Austria, Belgium, France, Germany, Italy, Luxembourg, The Netherlands, Portugal and Spain) have abolished passport controls for travelers within that area, but individual countries can temporarily suspend it.

The most notable exception is Great Britain, which has no intention of waiving its border controls. When a number of flights from the U.S. arrive at Heathrow or Gatwick close together in the morning, **be prepared for a longish wait** (though rarely as long as Europeans have to wait at JFK in New York).

The Green Channel/Red Channel customs system in operation at most Western European airports and other borders is basically an honor system. If you have nothing to declare, walk through the Green Channel, where there are only spot luggage checks; if in doubt, go through the Red Channel. If you fly between two EU-member countries, go through the new **Blue Channel,** where there are no customs officers except the one who glances at baggage labels to make sure only people off EU flights get through. On average, you need to **count on at least half an hour from deplaning to getting out of the airport.**

DUTY-FREE SHOPPING

If you're looking for good deals associated with duty-free airport shopping, **check out liquor and beauty products,** although prices vary considerably. The amount of liquor you may buy is restricted, generally to two bottles. Duty-free sales will cease within the EU on June 30, 1999, but will continue to be allowed for non-EU destinations.

Some airport concourses, notably in Amsterdam, Copenhagen, and Shannon, have practically been transformed into shopping malls, selling everything from electronics and chocolates to fashion and furs. These are tax-free rather than duty-free shops; if this is your last stop before leaving the EU there's no VAT and you can **avoid the tax-refund rigmarole.**

CAMERAS & COMPUTERS

EQUIPMENT PRECAUTIONS

Always **keep your film, tape, or computer disks out of the sun.** Carry an extra supply of batteries, and **be prepared to turn on your camera, camcorder, or laptop** to prove to security personnel that the device is real. Always **ask for hand inspection of film,** which becomes clouded after successive exposure to airport X-ray machines, and **keep videotapes and computer disks away from metal detectors.**

TRAVEL PHOTOGRAPHY

➤ PHOTO HELP: **Kodak Information Center** (☎ 800/242–2424). *Kodak Guide to Shooting Great Travel Pictures,* available in bookstores or from Fodor's Travel Publications (☎ 800/533–6478; $16.50 plus $4 shipping).

CUSTOMS & DUTIES

When shopping, **keep receipts** for all of your purchases. Upon reentering the country, **be ready to show customs officials what you've bought.** If you feel a duty is incorrect, appeal the assessment. If you object to the way your clearance was handled, get the inspector's badge number. In either case, first ask to see a supervisor, then write to the appropriate authorities, beginning with the port director at your point of entry.

IN EUROPE

Since the EU's 1992 agreement on a unified European market, the same customs regulations apply to all 15 member states (Austria, Belgium, Denmark, Finland, France, Germany, Great Britain, Greece, Ireland, Italy, Luxembourg, the Netherlands, Portugal, Spain, and Sweden). If you arrive from another EU country, you do not have to pass through customs.

Duty-free allowances for visitors from outside the EU are the same whatever your nationality (but you have to be over 17): 200 cigarettes or 50 cigars or 100 cigarillos or 250 grams of pipe tobacco; 1 liter of spirits or 2 liters of fortified or sparkling wine or liqueurs; 2 liters of still table wine; 60 milliliters of perfume; 250 milliliters of toilet water (note: 1 U.S. quart equals 0.946 liters); plus $200 worth of other goods, including gifts and souvenirs. Unless otherwise noted in individual city chapters, there are no restrictions on the import or export of currency. These limits will continue in force after June 30, 1999, when duty-free shopping for travel within the EU will be abolished.

Duty-free shopping for travel **within** the EU until June 30, 1999, has been considerably relaxed: 300 cigarettes, or 400 cigarillos, or 200 cigars, or 1 kg of pipe tobacco; 10 liters of spirits, or 90 liters of wine, or 110 liters of beer.

See individual city chapters on non-EU countries for information on their import limits.

IN AUSTRALIA

Australia residents who are 18 or older may bring back $A400 worth of souvenirs and gifts (including jewelry), 250 cigarettes or 250 grams of tobacco, and 1,125 ml of alcohol (including wine, beer, and spirits). Residents under 18 may bring back $A200 worth of goods.

➤ INFORMATION: **Australian Customs Service** (Regional Director, ✉ Box 8, Sydney, NSW 2001, ☎ 02/9213–2000, FAX 02/9213–4000).

IN CANADA

Canadian residents who have been out of Canada for at least seven days may bring in C$500 worth of goods duty-free. If you've been away less than seven days but more than 48 hours, the duty-free allowance drops to C$200; if your trip lasts 24–48 hours, the allowance is C$50. You may not pool allowances with family members. Goods claimed under the C$500 exemption may follow you by mail; those claimed under the lesser exemptions must accompany you. Alcohol and tobacco products may be included in the seven-day and 48-hour exemptions but not in the 24-hour exemption. If you meet the age requirements of the province or territory through which you reenter Canada, you may bring in, duty-free, 1.14 liters (40 imperial ounces) of wine or liquor *or* 24 12-ounce cans or bottles of beer or ale. If you are 16 or older you may bring in, duty-free, 200 cigarettes and 50 cigars.

You may send an unlimited number of gifts worth up to C$60 each duty-free to Canada. Label the package UNSOLICITED GIFT—VALUE UNDER $60. Alcohol and tobacco are excluded.

➤ INFORMATION: **Revenue Canada** (✉ 2265 St. Laurent Blvd. S, Ottawa, Ontario K1G 4K3, ☎ 613/993–0534, 800/461–9999 in Canada).

IN NEW ZEALAND

Although greeted with a "Haere Mai" ("Welcome to New Zealand"), homeward-bound residents with goods to declare must present themselves for inspection. If you're 17 or older, you may bring back $700 worth of souvenirs and gifts. Your duty-free allowance also includes 4.5 liters of wine or beer; one 1,125-ml bottle of spirits; and either 200 cigarettes, 250 grams of tobacco, 50 cigars, or a combo of all three up to 250 grams.

➤ INFORMATION: **New Zealand Customs** (✉ Custom House, ✉ 50 Anzac Ave., Box 29, Auckland, New Zealand, ☎ 09/359–6655, ☎ 09/309–2978).

IN THE U.K.

If you are a U.K. resident and your journey was wholly within the European Union (EU), you won't have to pass through customs when you return to the United Kingdom. If you plan to bring back large quantities of alcohol or tobacco, check EU limits beforehand. From countries outside the EU, you may import, duty-free, 200 cigarettes or 50 cigars; 1 liter of spirits or 2 liters of fortified or sparkling wine or liqueurs; 2 liters of still table wine; 60 milliliters of perfume; 250 milliliters of toilet water; plus £136 worth of other goods, including gifts and souvenirs.

➤ INFORMATION: **HM Customs and Excise** (✉ Dorset House, ✉ Stamford St., London SE1 9NG, ☎ 020/7202–4227).

IN THE U.S.

U.S. residents may bring home $400 worth of foreign goods duty-free if they've been out of the country for at least 48 hours (and if they haven't used the $400 allowance or any part of it in the past 30 days).

U.S. residents 21 and older may bring back 1 liter of alcohol duty-free. In addition, regardless of your age, you are allowed 200 cigarettes and 100 non-Cuban cigars. Antiques, which the U.S. Customs Service defines as objects more than 100 years old, enter duty-free, as do original works of art done entirely by hand, including paintings, drawings, and sculptures.

You may also send packages home duty-free: up to $200 worth of goods for personal use, with a limit of one parcel per addressee per day (and no alcohol or tobacco products or perfume worth more than $5); label the package PERSONAL USE, and attach a list of its contents and their retail value. Do not label the package UNSOLICITED GIFT, or your duty-free exemption will drop to $100. Mailed items do not affect your duty-free allowance on your return.

➤ INFORMATION: **U.S. Customs Service** (Inquiries, ✉ Box 7407, Washington, DC 20044, ☎ 202/927–6724; complaints, Office of Regulations and Rulings, ✉ 1301 Constitution Ave. NW, Washington, DC 20229; registration of equipment, Resource Management, ✉ 1301 Constitution Ave. NW, Washington DC 20229, ☎ 202/927–0540).

DISABILITIES & ACCESSIBILITY

ACCESS IN EUROPE

Getting around in many European cities can be difficult if you're using a wheelchair, as cobblestone-paved streets and sidewalks are common in older, historic districts.

MAKING RESERVATIONS

When discussing accessibility with an operator or reservations agent, **ask hard questions.** Are there any stairs, inside *or* out? Are there grab bars next to the toilet *and* in the shower/tub? How wide is the doorway to the room? To the bathroom? For the most extensive facilities meeting the latest legal specifications, **opt for newer accommodations,** which are more likely to have been designed with access in mind. Older buildings or ships may have more limited facilities. Be sure to **discuss your needs before booking.**

TRANSPORTATION

➤ COMPLAINTS: **Disability Rights Section** (✉ U.S. Department of Justice, Civil Rights Division, ✉ Box 66738, Washington, DC 20035–6738, ☎ 202/514–0301 or 800/514–0301, TTY 202/514–0383 or 800/514–0383, FAX 202/307–1198) for general complaints. **Aviation Consumer Protection Division** (☞ Air Travel, *above*) for airline-related problems.

HEALTH

MEDICAL PLANS

No one plans to get sick while traveling, but it happens, so **consider signing up with a medical-assistance company.** Members get doctor referrals, emergency evacuation or repatri-

ation, 24-hour telephone hot lines for medical consultation, cash for emergencies, and other personal and legal assistance. Coverage varies by plan, so **review the benefits of each carefully.**

➤ MEDICAL-ASSISTANCE COMPANIES: **International SOS Assistance** (✉ 8 Neshaminy Interplex, Suite 207, Trevose, PA 19053, ☎ 215/245–4707 or 800/523–6586, FAX 215/244–9617; ✉ 12 Chemin Riantbosson, 1217 Meyrin 1, Geneva, Switzerland, ☎ 4122/785–6464, FAX 4122/785–6424; ✉ 10 Anson Rd., 14-07/08 International Plaza, Singapore, 079903, ☎ 65/226–3936, FAX 65/226–3937).

PACKING

LUGGAGE

How many carry-on bags you can bring with you is up to the airline. Most allow two, but the limit is often reduced to one on certain flights. Gate agents will take excess baggage—including bags they deem oversize—from you as you board and add it to checked luggage. To avoid this situation, make sure that everything you carry aboard will fit under your seat. Also, get to the gate early, and request a seat at the back of the plane; you'll probably board first, while the overhead bins are still empty. Since big, bulky baggage attracts the attention of gate agents and flight attendants on a busy flight, make sure your carry-on is really a carry-on. Finally, a carry-on that's long and narrow is more likely to remain unnoticed than one that's wide and squarish.

If you are flying internationally, note that baggage allowances may be determined not by piece but by weight—generally 88 pounds (40 kilograms) in first class, 66 pounds (30 kilograms) in business class, and 44 pounds (20 kilograms) in economy.

Airline liability for baggage is limited to $1,250 per person on flights within the United States. On international flights it amounts to $9.07 per pound or $20 per kilogram for checked baggage (roughly $640 per 70-pound bag) and $400 per passenger for unchecked baggage. You can buy additional coverage at check-in for about $10 per $1,000 of coverage, but it excludes a rather extensive list of items, shown on your airline ticket.

Before departure, **itemize your bags' contents** and their worth, and label the bags with your name, address, and phone number. (If you use your home address, cover it so that potential thieves can't see it readily.) Inside each bag, **pack a copy of your itinerary.** At check-in, **make sure that each bag is correctly tagged** with the destination airport's three-letter code. If your bags arrive damaged or fail to arrive at all, file a written report with the airline before leaving the airport.

PACKING LIST

You should **pack more for the season than for any particular dress code.** In general, northern and central Europe have cold, snowy winters, and the Mediterranean countries have mild winters, though parts of southern Europe can be bitterly cold, too. On the Mediterranean, **bring a warm jacket for mornings and evenings,** even in summer. The mountains usually are warm on summer days, but the weather is unpredictable, and the nights are generally cool.

For European cities, **pack as you would for an American city;** formal outfits for first-class restaurants and nightclubs, casual clothes elsewhere. Jeans are perfectly acceptable for sightseeing and informal dining. Sturdy walking shoes are appropriate for the cobblestone streets and gravel paths that fill many of the parks and surround some of the historic buildings. For visits to churches, cathedrals, and mosques, **avoid shorts and revealing outfits.** In Italy, women cover their shoulders and arms (a shawl will do). Women, however, no longer need to cover their heads in Roman Catholic churches.

To discourage purse snatchers and pickpockets, **take a handbag with long straps** that you can sling across your body, bandolier-style, and with a zippered compartment for money.

If you stay in budget hotels, **take your own soap.**

In your carry-on luggage **bring an extra pair of eyeglasses or contact lenses** and **enough of any medication you take** to last the entire trip. You may also want your doctor to write a spare prescription using the drug's generic name, since brand names may vary from country to country. **Never put prescription drugs or valuables in luggage to be checked.** To avoid customs delays, carry medications in their original packaging. And don't forget to copy down and carry addresses of offices that handle refunds of lost traveler's checks.

PASSPORTS & VISAS

When traveling internationally, **carry a passport even if you don't need one** (it's always the best form of I.D.), and make **two photocopies of the data page** (one for someone at home and another for you, carried separately from your passport). If you lose your passport, promptly call the nearest embassy or consulate and the local police.

ENTERING EUROPE

Citizens of the US, Canada, UK, Ireland, Australia, and New Zealand need passports for travel in Europe. Visas may also be required for visits to or through Hungary and the Czech Republic even for short stays or train trips, and in some cases must be obtained before you'll be allowed to enter. Check with the nearest consulate of the country you'll be visiting for visa requirements. Rather than visas, Austria and Italy require that you register with the local police shortly after arriving.

PASSPORT OFFICES

The best time to apply for a passport or to renew is during the fall and winter. Before any trip, be sure to check your passport's expiration date and, if necessary, renew it as soon as possible. (Some countries won't allow you to enter on a passport that's due to expire in six months or less.)

➤ AUSTRALIAN CITIZENS: **Australian Passport Office** (☎ 131–1232).

➤ CANADIAN CITIZENS: **Passport Office** (☎ 819/994–3500 or 800/567–6868).

➤ NEW ZEALAND CITIZENS: **New Zealand Passport Office** (☎ 04/494–

0700 for information on how to apply, 0800/727–776 for information on applications already submitted).

➤ U.K. CITIZENS: **London Passport Office** (☎ 0990/21010), for fees and documentation requirements and to request an emergency passport.

➤ U.S. CITIZENS: **National Passport Information Center** (☎ 900/225–5674; calls are charged at 35¢ per minute for automated service, $1.05 per minute for operator service).

TAXES

VALUE-ADDED TAX (V.A.T.)

Global Refund is a V.A.T. refund service that makes getting your money back hassle-free. Global Refund services are offered in more than 130,000 shops worldwide. In participating stores, **ask for a Global Refund Cheque when making a purchase**— this Cheque will clearly state the amount of your refund in local currency, with the service charge already incorporated (the service charge equals approximately 3%–4% of the purchase price of the item). Global Refund can also process other customs forms, though for a higher fee. When leaving the European Union, get your Global Refund Cheque and any customs forms stamped by the customs official. You can take them to the cash refund office at the airport, where your money will be refunded right there in cash, by check, or a refund to your credit card. Alternatively, you can mail your validated Cheque to Global Refund, and your credit card account will automatically be credited within three billing cycles. Global Refund has a fax-back service further clarifying the process.

➤ VAT REFUNDS: **Global Refund** (✉ 707 Summer St., Stamford, CT 06901, ☎ 800/566–9828).

TELEPHONES

COUNTRY CODES

When dialing a European number from abroad, drop the initial 0 from the local area code.

INTERNATIONAL CALLS

Consult individual city chapters for information on dialing international calls.

AT&T, MCI, and Sprint international access codes make calling the United States relatively convenient, but you may find the local access number blocked in many hotel rooms. First ask the hotel operator to connect you. If the hotel operator balks, ask for an international operator, or dial the international operator yourself. One way to improve your odds of getting connected to your long-distance carrier is to travel with more than one company's calling card (a hotel may block Sprint, for example, but not MCI). If all else fails, call from a pay phone in the hotel lobby. Check individual city chapters for local access numbers or call your carrier for the number before you go.

➤ TO OBTAIN ACCESS CODES: **AT&T Direct** (☎ 800/435–0812). **MCI WorldPhone** (☎ 800/444–4141). **Sprint International Access** (☎ 913/624–5336).

LONG-DISTANCE CALLS

Check individual city chapters for information on calling long-distance within a country.

U.S. GOVERNMENT

Government agencies can be an excellent source of inexpensive travel information. When planning your trip, **find out what government materials are available.**

➤ ADVISORIES: **U.S. Department of State** (✉ Overseas Citizens Services Office, ✉ Room 4811 N.S., Washington, DC 20520; ☎ 202/647–5225 or FAX 202/647–3000 for interactive hot line; ☎ 301/946–4400 for computer bulletin board); enclose a self-addressed, stamped, business-size envelope.

➤ PAMPHLETS: **Consumer Information Center** (✉ Consumer Information Catalogue, Pueblo, CO 81009, ☎ 719/948–3334 or 888/878–3256) for a free catalog that includes travel titles.

VISITOR INFORMATION

For general information before you go, contact the national tourism offices below.

➤ AUSTRIAN NATIONAL TOURIST OFFICE: **U.S.** (✉ Box 1142, Times Square Station, New York, NY 10108-1142,

☎ 212/944–6880, ℻ 212/730–4568). **Canada** (✉ 2 Bloor St. E, Suite 3330, Toronto, Ontario M4W 1A8, ☎ 416/967–3381, ℻ 416/967–4101); ✉ 1010 Ouest Rue, Sherbrooke, Ste. 1410, Montréal, Québec, H3A 2R7, ☎ 514/849–3709, ℻ 514/849–9577; ✉ Granville Sq., 200 Granville St., Ste. 1380, Vancouver, British Columbia, V6C 1S4, ☎ 604/683–5808, ℻ 604/662–8528). **U.K.** (✉ 14 Cork St., London, W1X 1PF, ☎ 020/7629–0461, ℻ 020/7499–6038). **Australia and New Zealand** (✉ 36 Carrington St., 1st floor, Sydney, NSW 2000, ☎ ☎ 2/9299–3621, ℻ 2/92993808). **Ireland** (✉ Merrion Hall, Strand Rd., Sandymount, P.O. Box 2506, Dublin, ☎ ☎ 283–0488, ℻ 283–0531).

➤ Belgian National Tourist Office: **U.S.** (✉ 780 3rd Ave., New York, NY 10017, ☎ 212/758–8130, ℻ 212/355–7675). **Canada** (✉ Box 760 NDG, Montréal, Québec H4A 3S2, ☎ 514/484–3594, ℻ 514/489–8965). **U.K.** (✉ 29 Prince St., London W1R 7RG, ☎ 0891/887–799, ℻ 020/7629–0454). Calls cost 50p per minute peak rate or 45p per minute cheap rate.

➤ British Tourist Authority: **U.S.:** Nationwide (✉ 551 5th Ave., Suite 701, New York, NY 10176, ☎ 212/986–2200 or 800/462–2748, ℻ 212/986–1188); 24-Hour Fax information line (℻ 818/441–8265); Chicago (✉ 625 N. Michigan Ave., Suite 1510, 60611; walk-in service only). **Canada** (✉ 111 Avenue Rd., Suite 450, Toronto, Ontario M5R 3J8, ☎ 416/961–8124, ℻ 416/961–2175). **U.K.** British Travel Centre (✉ 12 Regent St., London SW1Y 4PQ [no information by phone] or ✉ Thames Tower, Black's Rd., London W6 9EL, ☎ 020/8846–9000). **Australia** (✉ Level 16, Gateway, 1 Macquarie Place, Sydney, NSW 2000, ☎ ☎ 2/9377–4400, ℻ 2/9377–4499). **New Zealand** (✉ Dilworth Bldg., Suite 305, 3rd floor, Corner of Queen & Customs Streets, Auckland 1, ☎ ☎ 9/303–1446, ℻ 9/377–6965). **Ireland** (✉ 18-19 College Green, Dublin 2, ☎ ☎ 1670–8000, ℻ 1670–8244).

➤ Czech Center: **U.S. and Canada** (✉ 1109 Madison Ave., New York,

NY 10028, ☎ 212/288–0830). **U.K.** (✉ 49 Southwark St., London SE1 1RU, ☎ 020/7378–6009, ℻ 020/7403–2321; ✉ 30 Kensington Palace Gardens, London W8 4QY, ☎ 020/7243–7981, ℻ 020/7727–9589).

➤ Danish Tourist Board: **U.S. and Canada** Scandinavia Tourism Inc. (✉ Box 4649 Grand Central Station, New York, NY 10163–4649, ☎ 212/949–2333, ℻ 212/885–9710). **U.K.** ✉ 55 Sloane St., London SW1X 9SY, ☎ 020/7259–5959 or ☎ 0891/600–109 for 24-hour brochure line, ℻ 020/7259–5955). Calls to the brochure line cost 50p per minute peak rate or 45p per minute cheap rate.

➤ French Government Tourist Office: **U.S.** Nationwide (☎ 900/990–0040; costs 50¢ per minute); New York City (✉ 444 Madison Ave., 10022, ☎ 212/838–7800); Chicago (✉ 676 N. Michigan Ave., 60611, ☎ 312/751–7800); Beverly Hills (✉ 9454 Wilshire Blvd., 90212, ☎ 310/271–6665, ℻ 310/276–2835). **Canada** (✉ 1981 Ave., McGill College, Suite 490, Montréal, Québec H3A 2W9, ☎ 514/288–4264, ℻ 514/845–4868; ✉ 30 St. Patrick St., Suite 700, Toronto, Ontario M5T 3A3, ☎ 416/491–7622, ℻ 416/979–7587). **U.K.** (✉ 178 Piccadilly, London W1V OAL, ☎ 0891/244–123, ℻ 020/7493–6594). Calls cost 50p per minute peak rate or 45p per minute cheap rate.

➤ German National Tourist Office: **U.S.** Nationwide (✉ 122 E. 42nd St., New York, NY 10168, ☎ 212/661–7200, ℻ 212/661–7174). **Canada** (✉ 175 Bloor St. E, Suite 604, Toronto, Ontario M4W 3R8, ☎ 416/968–1570, ℻ 416/968–1986). **U.K.** (✉ Nightingale House, 65 Curzon St., London W1Y 8NE, ☎ 020/7493–0081 or 0891/600–100 for brochures, ℻ 020/7495–6129). **Australia** (✉ P.O. Box A980, Sydney, NSW 1235, ☎ 9267–8148, ℻ 9267–9035). Calls to the brochure-line cost 50p per minute peak rate or 45p per minute cheap rate.

➤ Greek National Tourist Organization: **U.S.:** Nationwide (✉ 645 5th Ave., New York, NY 10022, ☎ 212/421–5777, ℻ 212/826–6940); Los Angeles (✉ 611 W. 6th St., Suite 2198,

90017, ☎ 213/626–6696, FAX 213/489–9744); Chicago (✉ 168 N. Michigan Ave., Suite 600, 60601, ☎ 312/782–1084, FAX 312/782–1091). **Canada** (✉ 1233 Rue de la Montagne, Suite 101, Montréal, Québec H3G 1Z2, ☎ 514/871–1535, FAX 514/871–1498); ✉ 1300 Bay St., Toronto, Ontario M5R 3K8, ☎ 416/968–2220, FAX 416/968–6533). **U.K.** (✉ 4 Conduit St., London W1R 0DJ, ☎ 020/7734–5997, FAX 020/7287–1369). **Australia** (✉ 51-57 Pitt St., Sydney, NSW 2000, ☎ ☎ 9241–1663, FAX 9235–2174.

➤ HUNGARIAN NATIONAL TOURIST OFFICE: **U.S. and Canada** (✉ 150 E. 58th St., New York, NY 10155, ☎ 212/355–0240, FAX 212/207–4103). **U.K.** (✉ Embassy of the Republic of Hungary, Commercial Section, 46 Eaton Pl., London SW1X 8AL, ☎ 020/7823–1032 or 020/7823–1055, FAX 020/7823–1459).

➤ IRISH TOURIST BOARD: **U.S.** (✉ 345 Park Ave., New York, NY 10154, ☎ 212/418–0800 or 800/223–6470, FAX 212/371–9052). **Canada** (✉ 160 Bloor St. E, Suite 1150, Toronto, Ontario M4W 1B9, ☎ 416/487–3335, FAX 416/929–6783). **U.K.** (✉ Ireland House, 150 New Bond St., London W1Y 0AQ, ☎ 020/7493–3201, FAX 020/7493–9065). **Australia** (✉ 5th floor, 36 Carrington St., Sydney, NSW 2000, ☎ ☎ 2929–9677, FAX 9299–6323). **Ireland** (✉ Baggot Street Bridge, Dublin 2, ☎ 3531/605–7700 FAX 3531/605–7749).

➤ ITALIAN GOVERNMENT TOURIST BOARD (ENIT): **U.S.** Nationwide (✉ 630 5th Ave., New York, NY 10111, ☎ 212/245–4822, FAX 212/586–9249); Chicago (✉ 401 N. Michigan Ave., 60611, ☎ 312/644–0990, FAX 312/644–3019); Los Angeles (✉ 12400 Wilshire Blvd., Suite 550, 90025, ☎ 310/820–0098, FAX 310/820–6357). **Canada** (✉ 1 Pl. Ville Marie, Suite 1914, Montréal, Québec H3B 3M9, ☎ 514/866–7667, FAX 514/392–1429). **U.K.** (✉ 1 Princes St., London W1R 8AY, ☎ 020/7408–1254, FAX 020/7493–6695).

➤ NETHERLANDS BOARD OF TOURISM: **U.S. and Canada** (✉ 225 N. Michi-

gan Ave., Suite 1854, Chicago, IL 60601, ☎ 312/819–1500, FAX 312/819–1740; for brochures, ☎ 888/464–6552). **Canada** (✉ 25 Adelaide St. E, Suite 710, Toronto, Ontario M5C 1Y2; mailing address only). **U.K.** (✉ 25–28 Buckingham Gate, London SW1E 6LD, ☎ 0891/717–777, FAX 020/7828–7941). Calls cost 50p per minute peak rate or 45p per minute cheap rate.

➤ TOURIST OFFICE OF SPAIN: **U.S.:** Nationwide (✉ 666 5th Ave., 35th floor, New York, NY 10103, ☎ 212/265–8822, FAX 212/265–8864); Chicago (✉ 845 N. Michigan Ave., 60611, ☎ 312/642–1992, FAX 312/642–9817); Los Angeles (✉ 8383 Wilshire Blvd., Suite 960, 90211, ☎ 213/658–7188, FAX 213/658–1061); Miami (✉ 1221 Brickell Ave., Suite 1850, 33131, ☎ 305/358–1992, FAX 305/358–8223). **Canada** (✉ 2 Bloor St. W, 34th floor, Toronto, Ontario M4W 3E2, ☎ 416/961–3131, FAX 416/961–1992). **U.K.** (✉ 57–58 St. James's St., London SW1A 1LD, ☎ 020/7499–0901 or 0891/669–920 [24-hour brochure line], FAX 020/7629–4257); calls to the brochure line cost 50p per minute peak rate or 45p per minute cheap rate.

➤ SWISS NATIONAL TOURIST OFFICE: **U.S.:** New York (✉ 608 5th Ave., 10020, ☎ 212/757–5944, FAX 212/262–6116; El Segundo, CA (✉ 222 N. Sepulveda Blvd., Suite 1570, 90245, ☎ 310/335–5980, FAX 310/335–5982); Chicago (✉ 150 N. Michigan Ave., Suite 2930, 60601, ☎ 312/630–5840, FAX 312/630–5848). **Canada** (✉ 926 The East Mall, Etobicoke, Ontario M9B 6KI, ☎ 416/695–2090, FAX 416/695–2774). **U.K.** (✉ Swiss Centre, 1 New Coventry St., London W1V 8EE, ☎ 020/7734–1921, FAX 020/7437–4577).

WEB SITES

Do check out the World Wide Web when you're planning. You'll find everything from up-to-date weather forecasts to virtual tours of famous cities. Fodor's website, www.fodors.com, is a great place to start your online travels.

2 Amsterdam

*A*msterdam is a gem of a city for the visitor. Small and densely packed with fine buildings, many dating from the 17th century or earlier, it is easily explored on foot or by bike.

EXPLORING AMSTERDAM

The old heart of the city consists of canals, with narrow streets radiating out like the spokes of a wheel. The hub of this wheel and the most convenient point to begin sight-seeing is Centraal Station. Across the street, in the same building as the Old Dutch Coffee House, is a tourist information office. The Rokin, once an open canal, is the main route from Centraal Station via the Dam to the Muntplein. Amsterdam's key points of interest can be covered within two or three days, including visits to one or two of the important museums and galleries. The city center is broken up into districts that are easily covered on foot.

Around the Dam

Numbers in the margin correspond to points of interest on the Amsterdam map.

★ **14** **Anne Frankhuis** (Anne Frank House). Immortalized by the poignant diary kept by the young Jewish girl from 1942 to 1944, when she and her family hid here from the German occupying forces, it also holds a small exhibition on the Holocaust. ⊠ *Prinsengracht 263,* ☎ *020/5567100.* ☉ *June–Aug., Mon.–Sat. 9–7, Sun. 10–7; Sept.–May, Mon.–Sat. 9–5, Sun. 10–5.*

10 **Beurs van Berlage** (Berlage's Stock Exchange). This impressive building, completed in 1903, dominates the Damrak between Centraal Station and the Dam. It was designed by Hendrik Petrus Berlage (1856–1934), whose principles were to guide modernism; the building's function was fundamental to the design. The sculpture and rich decoration of the plain brick interior are among modernism's embryonic masterpieces. It now houses two concert halls, a large exhibition space, and its own museum, which also offers the chance to climb the 39-m- (138-ft-) high tower for its superb views. ⊠ *Damrak 277,* ☎ *020/6265257.* ☉ *Museum: Tues.–Sun. 10–4.*

1 Centraal Station (Central Station). The flamboyant redbrick and stone portal was designed by P. J. H. Cuijpers (1827–1921) and built in 1884–89. It provides an excellent viewpoint for both the Beurs van Berlage and the Scheepvaartshuis, two of the city's best examples of early 20th-century architecture. Compare it with Cuijpers's other significant contribution to Amsterdam's architectural heritage—the Rijksmuseum (☞ *below*). ✉ *Stationsplein.*

11 Dam (Dam Square). This is the broadest square in the old section of the town. Fishermen used to come here to sell their catch. Today it is a busy crossroads, circled with shops and bisected by traffic; it is also a popular spot for outdoor performers. At one side of the square stands a simple monument to Dutch victims of World War II. Eleven urns contain soil from the 11 provinces of the Netherlands, while a 12th contains soil from the former Dutch East Indies, now Indonesia. ✉ *Jct. Rokin, Damrak, Moses en Aaronstraat, and Paleisstraat.*

6 De Waag (The Weighhouse). Dating from 1488, this turreted, redbrick monument dominates the Nieuwmarkt (New Market) in the oldest part of Amsterdam. Once the headquarters for ancient professional guilds, the building now is home to the Society for Old and New Media, which hosts occasional exhibitions in the magnificently restored **Theatrum Anatomicum,** up the winding stairs. ✉ *Nieuwmarkt,* ☏ *020/5579844.*

13 Het Koninklijk Paleis te Amsterdam (Royal Palace in Amsterdam). The vast, well-proportioned classical structure dominating the Dam was completed in 1655. It is built on 13,659 pilings sunk into the marshy soil. The great pediment sculptures are an allegorical representation of Amsterdam surrounded by Neptune and mythological sea creatures. Filled with opulent 18th- and early 19th-century furnishings, it is the official royal residence but is used only on high state occasions. ✉ *Dam,* ☏ *020/6248698.* ☉ *Tues.–Thurs. 1–4 in winter; daily 12:30–5 in summer. Sometimes closed for state events.*

9 Museum Amstelkring. The facade carries the inscription "*Ons Lieve Heer Op Solder*" ("Our Lord in the Attic"). In 1578 Amsterdam embraced Protestantism and outlawed the church of Rome. The municipal authorities were so tolerant that secret Catholic chapels were allowed to exist; at one time there were 62 in Amsterdam alone. One such chapel was established in the attics of these three neighboring canalside houses, built around 1661. The lower floors were used as ordinary dwellings, while services were held in the attics regularly until 1888, the year the St. Nicolaaskerk was consecrated for Catholic worship. Of interest are the Baroque altar with its revolving tabernacle, the swinging pulpit that can be stowed out of sight, and the upstairs gallery with its displays of religious artifacts. ✉ *Oudezijds Voorburgwal 40,* ☏ *020/6246604.* ☉ *Mon.–Sat. 10–5, Sun. 1–5.*

3 NewMetropolis (Science and Technology Museum). This stunning, modern science and technology center was designed by Renzo Piano, architect of the Pompidou Center in Paris. The building's colossal, copper-clad volume rises from the harbor waters like the hull of a ship. Hands-on exhibits for young and old range from elementary physics to the latest technological gadgets. The rooftop terrace offers a superb panoramic view across the city. ✉ *Oosterdok 2, Prins Hendrikkade,* ☏ *020/5313233.* 🎫 *Fl. 23.50.* ☉ *Mon.–Thurs. 10–6, Fri.–Sun. 10–9.*

12 Nieuwe Kerk (New Church). This huge Gothic structure stands next to the royal palace, in a corner of the Dam. It was gradually expanded until 1540, when it reached its present size. Gutted by fire in 1645, it was reconstructed in an imposing Renaissance style, as interpreted by strict Calvinists. The superb oak pulpit, the 14th-century nave, the stained-glass windows, and the great organ (1645) are all shown to great effect on national holidays, when the church is bedecked with flowers. As befits the Netherlands' national church, the Nieuwe Kerk is the site of all coronations, most recently that of Queen Beatrix in 1980. In democratic Dutch spirit, the church is also used as a meeting place and has a lively café, temporary exhibitions, and concerts. ⊠ *Dam,* ☎ *020/6268168.* 🎫 *Free, except for special exhibitions.* ⊙ *Daily 11–5; exhibitions daily 10–6.*

❽ **Oude Kerk** (Old Church). The city's oldest house of worship dates from the early 14th century but it was badly damaged by iconoclasts after the Reformation. The church still retains its original bell tower and a few remarkable stained-glass windows. The tower overlooks a typical view of Old Amsterdam. Rembrandt's wife, Saskia, is buried here. ⊠ *Oudekerksplein 23,* ☎ *020/6258284.* ⊙ *Mon.–Sat. 11–5, Sun. 1–5.*

❺ **Rijksmuseum Nederlands Scheepvaart** (State Museum of Netherlands Shipping). This former naval warehouse maintains a collection of restored vessels, including a replica of a three-masted VOC (Verenigde Oostindische Compagnie—Dutch East India Company) trading ship from 1749. The museum explains the whole history of Dutch shipping, from dugout canoes right through to modern container ships, with maps, paintings, and models. The Prins Hendrikkade and the Eastern Harbor were the hub of shipping activity during the Netherlands' Golden Age. ⊠ *Kattenburgerplein 1,* ☎ *020/5232222.* ⊙ *Mon.–Sat. 10–5, Sun. 1–5.*

❼ **Rosse Buurt** (red-light district). This area is defined by two of the city's oldest canals. Although the area is generally safe, midnight walks down dark side streets are not advised. If you do explore the area, watch for purse snatchers and pickpockets. ⊠ *Bordered by Oudezijds Voorburgwal and Oudezijds Achterburgwal.*

❹ **Scheepvaartshuis** (Shipping Offices). Designed (1911–16) by J. M. der Mey and the Van Gendt brothers, this office building is the earliest example of the Amsterdam School's unique building style. The fantastical facade is richly decorated in brick and stone, with lead and zinc roofing that seems to pour from on high. ⊠ *Prins Hendrikkade 108–119.*

❷ **Schreierstoren** (Weepers' Tower). Facing the harbor stands a lookout tower, erected in 1480, for women whose men were out at sea. A tablet marks the point from which Henrik (a.k.a. Henry) Hudson set sail on the *Half Moon* on April 4, 1609, on a voyage that eventually took him to what is now New York and the river that still bears his name. ⊠ *Prins Hendrikkade 94–95.*

❿❺ **Westerkerk** (West Church). The church's 279-ft tower is the city's highest; it also has an outstanding carillon. Rembrandt (1606–1669) and his son Titus are buried in the church, which was completed as early as 1631. In summer you can climb to the top of the tower for a fine view over the city. ⊠ *Prinsengracht (corner of Westermarkt),* ☎ *020/6247766.* ⊙ *Tower: June–Sept., Tues.–Wed. and Fri.–Sat. 2–5.*

South of the Dam

❶❻ **Amsterdam Historisch Museum** (Amsterdam Historical Museum). The museum traces the city's history from its origins as a fishing village through the 17th-century Golden Age of material and artistic wealth to the decline of the trading empire during the 18th century. A display of old maps, documents, and paintings, often aided by a commentary in English tells the story. In the courtyard off Kalverstraat a striking

22

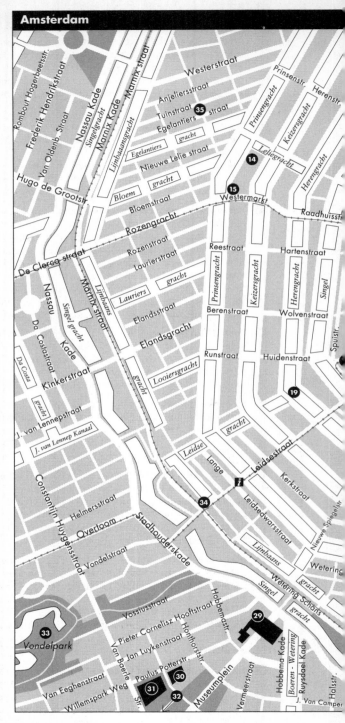

Amsterdam

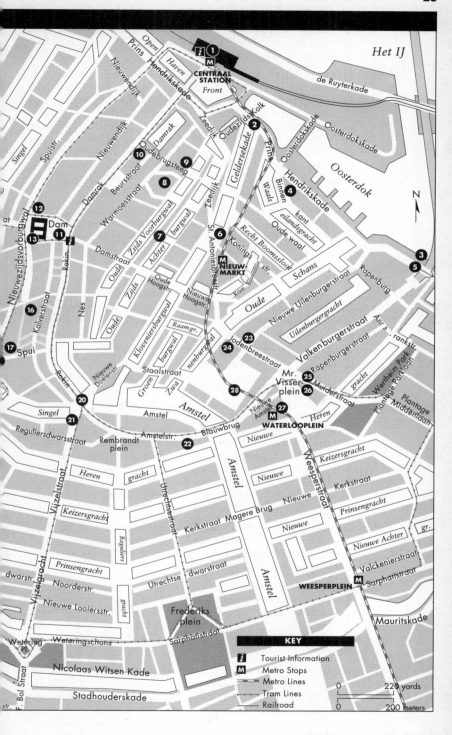

Het IJ

CENTRAAL
STATION
Front

de Ruyterkade

Open
Haven
Front

Prins Hendrikskade

Nieuwendijk

Singel
Spuistr.

Nieuwendijk

Damrak
Beursstraat
Warmoesstraat

Oudebrugsteeg
Damrak

Oudezijds Voorburgwal

Dam

Nieuwezijdsvorburgwal

Rokin

Damstraat
Oude Zijds Voorburgwal

Achter
burgwal

St. Antoniesbr.str.

Zeedijk

Gelderskade

Oudezijds Kolk

Prins
Hendrikskade

Binnen
Waals
kant
eilandsgracht
Oude waal

Oosterdokskade

Oosterdokskade

Oosterdok

Recht Boomssloot

Koningstr.

Koning

Schans

Oude

Nieuwe Uilenburgerstraat

Uilenburgergracht

Valkenburgerstraat

Rapenburgerstraat

Rapenburg

Anne Franksr.

Wertheim Park
plantage Parklaan

Plantage
Middenlaan

Plantage
Middenlaan

NIEUW-
MARKT

Oude
Hoogstr.

Nieuwe
Hoogstr.

Kram

Oude
Hoogstr.

Nes

Kloveniersburgwal

Raamgr.
nieuwburgwal

Oude

Zijds

Kalverstraat

Spui

Nieuwe
Doelenstr.

Groen
Zua

Staalstraat

Jodenbreestraat

Mr.
Visser-
plein

Munderstraat

Amstel

Amstel

Singel

Rokin

Reguliersdwarsstraat

Rembrandt
plein

Amstelstr.

Blauwbrug

Nieuwe
Amstel

WATERLOOPLEIN

Heren

Heren

gracht

Keizersgracht

Vijzelstraat

Keizersgracht

Prinsengracht

Noorderstr.

Nieuwe Looiersstr.

Regulers

gracht

Utrechtsestraat

Kerkstraat Magere Brug

Utrechtse dwarstraat

Frederiks
plein

Sarphatistraat

Nieuwe

Nieuwe

Nieuwe

Nieuwe

Amstel

Amstel

Weesperstraat

Kerkstraat

Prinsengracht

Nieuwe Achter

Valckenierstraat

Sarphatistraat

WEESPERPLEIN

Mauritskade

Wetering
Pl.

Weteringschans

dwarstr.

Vijzelgracht

F. Bol Straat
str.

Nicolaas Witsen Kade

Stadhouderskade

KEY

🛈 Tourist Information
Ⓜ Metro Stops
═══ Metro Lines
┈┈┈ Tram Lines
──── Railroad

0   220 yards
0   200 meters

Renaissance gate (1581) guards a series of tranquil inner courtyards. In medieval times, this area was an island devoted to piety. Today the bordering canals are filled in. ✉ *Kalverstraat 92,* ☎ *020/5231822.* ◷ *Weekdays 10–5, weekends 11–5.*

★ ⓱ **Begijnhof** (Beguine Court). This is an enchanting, enclosed square of almshouses founded in 1346 that is a surprising oasis of peace just a stone's throw from the city's hectic center. The Beguines were women who chose to lead a form of convent life, often taking the vow of chastity. The last Beguine died in 1974 and her house, Number 26, has been preserved as she left it. Number 34, dating from the 15th century, is the oldest house, and the only one to retain its wooden Gothic facade. A small passageway and courtyard link the Begijnhof to the Amsterdam Historisch Museum (☞ *above*). ✉ *Begijnhof 29,* ☎ *020/6233565.* ▦ *Free.* ◷ *Daily 9–dusk.*

㉑ **Bloemenmarkt** (Flower Market). Here, floating stalls carry a bright array of freshly cut flowers and foliage, as well as an enviable variety of bulbs and plants. ✉ *Along Singel Canal, from Muntplein to Koningsplein.* ◷ *Mon.–Sat. (occasionally Sun.) 9:30–5.*

⓱ **Engelse Kerk** (English Church). This church was given to Amsterdam's English and Scottish Presbyterians early in the 17th century. On the church wall and in the chancel are tributes to the Pilgrim Fathers who sailed from Delftshaven (present-day Delfshaven, in Rotterdam) to the New World in 1620. Opposite the church is another of the city's secret Catholic chapels, whose exterior looks as though it were two adjoining houses, built in 1671. ✉ *Begijnhof (☞ above).*

★ ⓲ **Gouden Bocht** (Golden Bend). The Herengracht (Gentlemen's Canal) is the city's most prestigious canal. The stretch of the canal from Leidsestraat to Huidenstraat is named for the sumptuous patrician houses with double staircases and grand entrances that line it. Seventeenth-century merchants moved here from the Amstel River to escape the byproducts of their wealth: noisy warehouses, unpleasant brewery smells, and the risk of fire in the sugar refineries. These houses display the full range of Amsterdam architectural detailing, from gables in a variety of shapes to elaborate Louis XIV–style cornices and frescoed ceilings. They are best seen from the east side of the canal. For more gables turn down Wolvenstraat into the Keizersgracht (the Emperor's Canal). ✉ *Herengracht—Leidsestraat to Huidenstraat.*

⓴ **Munttoren** (Mint Tower). Built in 1620 at this busy crossroads, the graceful tower that was later added to this former royal mint has a clock and bells that still seem to mirror the Golden Age. There are frequent carillon recitals. ✉ *Muntplein.*

㉒ **Museum Willet-Holthuysen.** Built in 1690, the elegant residence was bequeathed to the city of Amsterdam, on condition that it be retained as a museum. It provides a peek into the lives of the city's well-heeled merchants. The rooms are elegantly furnished in an opulent Louis XVI style. ✉ *Herengracht 605,* ☎ *020/5231870.* ◷ *Weekdays 10–5, weekends 11–5.*

⓲ **Spui** (sluice). In the heart of the university area, the lively square was a center for revolutionary student rallies in 1968. Now you'll find bookstores and bars, including cozy brown cafés. ✉ *Jct. Nieuwe zijds Voorburgwal, Spuistraat, and Singel Canal.*

Jewish Amsterdam

The original settlers in the Jodenbuurt (old Jewish Amsterdam) were wealthy Sephardic Jews from Spain and Portugal, later followed by poorer Ashkenazic refugees from Germany and Poland. At the turn of the century this was a thriving community of Jewish diamond polishers, dyers, and merchants.

㉓ **Jodenbreestraat.** During World War II this street marked the southwestern border of the *Joodse wijk* (Jewish neighborhood), by then an imposed ghetto. The character of the area was largely destroyed by highway construction in 1965 and more recently by construction of both the Metro and the Muziektheater/Stadhuis complex (☞ *below*).

㉗ **Joods Historisch Museum** (Jewish Historical Museum). A complex of three ancient synagogues, places of worship that once served a community of 100,000 Jews, shrunk to fewer than 10,000 after 1945, is now a museum. Founded by American and Dutch Jews, it displays religious treasures in a clear cultural and historical context. As the synagogues lost most of their treasures in the war, their architecture and history are more compelling than the exhibits. ⊠ *Jonas Daniël Meijerplein 2–4,* ☏ *020/6269945.* ⊙ *Daily 11–5.*

㉕ **Muiderstraat.** This pedestrianized area east of Waterlooplein retains much of the neighborhood's historic atmosphere. Notice the gateways decorated with pelicans, symbolizing great love; according to legend, the pelican will feed her starving young with her own blood. ⊠ *Muiderstraat/Waterlooplein.*

★ ㉔ **Museum het Rembrandthuis** (Rembrandt's House). From 1639 to 1658, Rembrandt (1606–1669) lived at Jodenbreestraat 4. For more than 20 years the ground floor was used by the artist as living quarters; the sunny upper floor was his studio. It contains a superb collection of his etchings as well as work by his contemporaries. The modern new wing next door houses a multimedia auditorium, two new exhibition spaces, and a shop. From St. Antonies Sluis bridge, just by the house, there is a canal view that has barely changed since Rembrandt's time. ⊠ *Jodenbreestraat 4–6,* ☏ *020/6249486.* ⊙ *Mon.–Sat. 10–5, Sun. 1–5.*

㉘ **Muziektheater/Stadhuis** (Music Theater/Town Hall complex). Amsterdammers come to the town hall section of the building by day to obtain driver's licenses, pick up welfare payments, and get married. They return by night to the rounded, marble-clad facade overlooking the Amstel river to see opera and ballet performed by the Netherlands' finest companies. You can wander into the town hall for a look at some interesting sculptures and other displays. A guided tour of the Muziektheater takes you around the dressing rooms, dance studios, backstage, and even to the wig department. ⊠ *Amstel 3,* ☏ *020/5518054.* ⊙ *Guided tours Wed. and Sat. at 3.*

★ ㉖ **Portugese Israelitische Synagoge** (Portuguese Israelite Synagogue). As one of Amsterdam's four neighboring synagogues, this was part of the largest Jewish religious complex in Europe. The beautiful, austere interior of the 17th-century building is still intact, even if the building itself is marooned on a traffic island. ⊠ *Mr. Visserplein 3,* ☏ *020/6245351.* ⊙ *Apr.–Oct., Sun.–Fri. 10–12:30 and 1–4; Nov.–Mar., Mon.–Thurs. 10–12:30 and 1–4, Fri. 10–12:30 and 1–3, Sun. 10–noon.*

The Museum Quarter

㉜ **Concertgebouw** (Concert Hall). The sounds of the country's foremost orchestra, the world-famous Concertgebouworkest, resonate in this imposing, classical building. The smaller of the two auditoriums is used for chamber music and solo recitals. The main hall hosts world-class concerts. ⊠ *Concertgebouwplein 2–6,* ☏ *020/6718345.*

㉞ **Leidseplein.** This lively square is the pulsing heart of the city's nightlife. During the summer you can enjoy the entertainment of street performers on the many café terraces.

★ ㉙ **Rijksmuseum** (State Museum). Allow at least an hour or two to explore the main collection of Dutch paintings at the most important of Dutch museums, and a whole morning or afternoon if you want to visit other sections. It was founded in 1808, but the current, rather lavish building dates from 1885, designed by the architect of Centraal Station, P. J. H. Cuijpers. As well as Italian, Flemish, and Spanish paintings, there are also vast collections of furniture, textiles, ceramics, sculpture, and prints. The museum's fame, however, rests on its unrivaled collection of Dutch 16th- and 17th-century masters. Of Rembrandt's masterpieces, *The Nightwatch*, concealed during World War II in caves in Maastricht, was misnamed because of its dull layers of varnish; in reality it depicts the Civil Guard in daylight. Also worth searching out are Frans Hals's family portraits, Jan Steen's drunken scenes, Van Ruysdael's romantic but menacing landscapes, and Vermeer's glimpses of everyday life bathed in his limpid light. The recently refurbished Zuid Vleugel (South Wing) houses an impressive treasure trove of Eastern art. ⊠ *Stadhouderskade 42,* ☎ *020/6732121.* ☉ *Daily 10–5.*

★ ㉚ **Rijksmuseum Vincent van Gogh** (Vincent van Gogh State Museum). This museum contains the world's largest collection of the artist's works—200 paintings and nearly 500 drawings—as well as works by some 50 of his contemporaries. There are usually very well presented temporary exhibitions. The modern, airy building was designed by Gerrit Rietvelt (1888–1964) and completed in 1972. The low entrance foyer opens into a high, skylit exhibition space. From September 1998 through the end of 1999 the museum is being extended and renovated. Van Gogh's most important works will be exhibited in the South Wing of the Rijksmuseum (☞ *above*). ⊠ *Paulus Potterstraat 7,* ☎ *020/ 5705200.* ☉ *Daily 10–5.*

㉛ **Stedelijk Museum** (Municipal Museum). The museum has a stimulating collection of modern art and ever-changing displays of the works of contemporary artists. Before viewing the paintings of Cézanne, Chagall, Kandinsky, and Mondriaan, check the list of temporary exhibitions in Room 1. Museum policy is to trace the development of the artist rather than merely to show a few masterpieces. Don't forget the museum's restaurant overlooking a garden filled with modern sculptures. ⊠ *Paulus Potterstraat 13,* ☎ *020/5732911.* ☉ *Daily 11–5.*

㉝ **Vondelpark.** Amsterdam's central park is an elongated rectangle of paths, lakes, and pleasant, shady greenery. A monument honors the 17th-century epic poet Joost van den Vondel, after whom the park is named. There is also an open-air sculpture by Picasso. In-line skaters duck and weave around Sunday strollers, and there are special children's areas with paddling pools and sandboxes. From June through August, free outdoor concerts and plays are performed in the park from Wednesday through Sunday. ⊠ *Stadhouderskade.*

The Jordaan

㉟ **Jordaan.** In this old part of Amsterdam the canals and side streets are named for trees, flowers, and plants. When it was the French quarter of the city, the area was known as *le jardin* (the garden), a name that over the years has become Jordaan. The best time to explore the district is on a Sunday morning or in the evening. The Jordaan has attracted many artists and is something of a bohemian quarter, where run-down buildings are being converted into restaurants, antiques shops, boutiques, and galleries. ⊠ *Bordered by Prinsengracht, Lijn-baansgracht, Brouwersgracht, and Raadhuisstraat.*

DINING

Amsterdammers are less creatures of habit than are the Dutch in general. Even so, health-conscious citizens prefer set menus and early dinners. The blue-and-white TOURIST MENU sign in a restaurant guarantees an economical (Fl. 25) yet imaginative set menu created by the head chef. For traditionalists the NEDERLANDS DIS soup tureen sign is a promise of regional recipes and seasonal ingredients. "You can eat in any language" is the city's proud boast, so when Dutch restaurants are closed, Indonesian, Chinese, and Turkish restaurants are often open.

RATINGS

Prices are per person including three courses (appetizer, main course, and dessert), service, and sales tax but not drinks. For budget travelers, many restaurants offer a tourist menu at an officially controlled price, currently Fl. 25.

CATEGORY	COST
$$$$	over Fl. 100
$$$	Fl. 70–Fl. 100
$$	Fl. 40–Fl. 70
$	under Fl. 40

$$$$ ★ ✕ **La Rive.** This world-class restaurant is fit for royalty. The French cuisine, with an awe-inspiring "truffle menu" of dishes prepared with exotic (and expensive) ingredients, can be tailored to meet your every whim. Epicureans should inquire about the "chef's table": With a group of six you can sit at a table alongside the open kitchen and watch chefs prepare and describe each of your courses. ⊠ *Amstel Inter-Continental hotel, Professor Tulpplein 1,* ☎ *020/6226060. Jacket and tie. AE, DC, MC, V.*

$$$$ ★ ✕ **'t Swarte Schaep.** The Black Sheep is named after a proverbial 17th-century sheep that roamed the area. With its creaking boards and array of copper pots, the interior is reminiscent of a ship's cabin. The Dutch chef uses seasonal ingredients to create classical, gastronomic dishes with regional flourishes. Choices include scallops wrapped in bacon for starters and fillet of beef with hazelnuts as a filling main course. ⊠ *Korte Leidsedwarsstraat 24,* ☎ *020/6223021. Reservations essential. Jacket and tie. AE, DC, MC, V.*

$$$–$$$$ ★ ✕ **Excelsior.** The restaurant at the Hôtel de l'Europe (☞ *below*) offers a varied menu of French cuisine based on local ingredients prepared by chef Jean Jacques Menanteau. There is a splendid selection of no less than 15 set menus. Service is discreet and impeccable, and the view over the Amstel River, to the Muntplein on one side and the Muziektheater on the other, is the best in Amsterdam. ⊠ *Hôtel de l'Europe, Nieuwe Doelenstraat 2–4,* ☎ *020/6234836. Reservations essential. Jacket and tie. AE, DC, MC, V. No lunch Sat.*

$$$ ★ ✕ **De Silveren Spiegel.** In an alarmingly crooked 17th-century house, you can have an outstanding meal while you enjoy the personal attention of the owner at one of just a small cluster of tables. Local ingredients such as Texel lamb and wild rabbit are cooked with subtlety and flair. ⊠ *Kattengat 4–6,* ☎ *020/6246589. Jacket and tie. AE, MC, V.*

$$$ ✕ **Le Tout Court.** This small, meticulously appointed restaurant serves seasonal specialties (spring lamb, summer fruits, game in autumn and winter) personally prepared by owner-chef John Fagel, who mixes gen-

erous Dutch helpings with rich sauces. Lighter main courses include poached turbot. The restaurant is popular with Amsterdam's media set. ⊠ *Runstraat 13,* ☎ *020/6258637. AE, DC, MC, V. Closed Sun.–Mon.*

$$–$$$ ✕ **Dynasty.** Surrounded by luxurious oriental furniture and murals, you can savor subtly spiced Pan-Asian dishes from Thailand, Malaysia, and China. Main-course delicacies include mixed seafood in banana leaves and succulent duck and lobster on a bed of watercress. In one of the city's most active nightlife areas, it can get very busy, but service is always impeccable. ⊠ *Reguliersdwarsstraat 30,* ☎ *020/6268400. Jacket required. AE, DC, MC, V. Closed Tues. No lunch.*

$$–$$$ ✕ **Eerste Klas.** Amsterdam's best-kept secret is in the most obvious of places: the former first-class waiting lounge of the central train station. Classic dark-wood paneling and soft interior lighting create the perfect hideaway from the city's hustle and bustle. A continental brasserie-like menu includes tasty salads, steaks, and fish dishes. ⊠ *Stationsplein 15, Spoor 2b,* ☎ *020/6250131. Jacket and tie. AE, DC, MC, V.*

$$–$$$ ✕ **Lonny's.** Lonny Gerungan's family have been cooks on Bali for gen-
★   erations—even preparing banquets for visiting Dutch royals. His plush restaurant in Amsterdam, draped in silky fabrics, serves the finest authentic Indonesian cuisine. Staff are dressed in exuberant traditional Balinese costumes. Even the simplest rijsttafel is a feast of more than 15 delicately spiced dishes. ⊠ *Rozengracht 46–48,* ☎ *020/6238950. Reservations essential. AE, DC, MC, V.*

$$–$$$ ✕ **Lucius.** Outstanding fish and seafood are simply served in an informal brasserie setting. Choices range from grilled lobster to more adventurous creations such as sea bass with buckwheat noodles and mushrooms. This may not be the place for the queasy, though—as you tuck into your fish, its live cousins eye you from a tank along the wall. ⊠ *Spuistraat 247,* ☎ *020/6241831. AE, DC, MC, V. Closed Sun. No lunch.*

$$–$$$ ✕ **Oesterbar.** The Oyster Bar specializes in seafood, grilled, baked, or fried. The upstairs dining room is more formal than the downstairs bistro, but prices don't vary. The sole is prepared in four different ways, or you can try the local specialties such as halibut and eel; oysters are a stimulating, if pricey, appetizer. ⊠ *Leidseplein 10,* ☎ *020/6232988. AE, DC, MC, V.*

$$–$$$ ✕ **Pier 10.** Perched on the end of a pier behind Centraal Station, this
★   intimate restaurant was built in the '30s as a shipping office. Water laps gently just beneath the windows, and the harbor lights twinkle in the distance. The chef's special salads are lavish affairs, and the vegetable side orders are carefully steamed to perfection. Other culinary adventures might include a handsome platter of dove, duck, and partridge with cranberry sauce. ⊠ *De Ruyterkade Steiger 10,* ☎ *020/ 6248276. Reservations essential. AE, MC, V. No lunch.*

$$ ✕ **De Knijp.** Traditional Dutch food is served here in a traditional Dutch environment. The mezzanine level is especially cozy. Alongside tamer dishes, there are seasonal game specialties including wild boar ham with red cabbage and fillet of hare. After-midnight dinner draws concert goers from the neighboring Concertgebouw. ⊠ *Van Baerlestraat 134,* ☎ *020/6720077. AE, DC, MC, V.*

$$ ✕ **De Waag.** The lofty, beamed interior below the Theatrum Anatomicum (☞ De Waag *in* Exploring Amsterdam, *above*) has been converted into a grand café and restaurant. The reading table harbors computer terminals for Internet enthusiasts. Dinnertime brings a seasonal selection of generous, French-influenced continental cuisine to be savored by candlelight. ⊠ *Nieuwmarkt 4,* ☎ *020/5579844. AE, MC, V.*

$$ ✕ **Kantjil en de Tijger.** This lively Indonesian restaurant is a favorite with the locals and close to the bars on the Spui. The menu is based on three different rijsttafel, with a profusion of meat and vegetable dishes varying in flavor from coconut-milk sweetness to peppery hot. ⊠ *Spuistraat 291/293,* ☎ *020/6200994. AE, DC, MC, V. No lunch.*

$$ ✕ **Rose's Cantina.** A perennial favorite of the sparkling set, it offers spicy Tex-Mex food, lethal cocktails, and a high noise level. Pop in for a full meal or a late afternoon drink. ⊠ *Reguliersdwarsstraat 38,* ☎ *020/6259797. Weekend reservations essential. AE, DC, MC, V.*

$$ ✕ **Toscanini.** This cavernous, noisy Italian restaurant has superb cui-
★ sine. Try antipasti followed by fresh pasta or the simple fish and meat dishes, all expertly prepared with the day's best fresh produce. Top it off with a sumptuous dessert. ⊠ *Lindengracht 75,* ☎ *020/6232813. Reservations essential. No credit cards. No lunch.*

$ ✕ **Het Gasthuys.** In this bustling restaurant you'll be served handsome portions of traditional Dutch home cooking, choice cuts of meat with excellent fries and piles of mixed salad. Sit at the bar or take a table high up in the rafters at the back. In summer there is an enchanting terrace on the canal side.⊠ *Grimburgwal 7,* ☎ *020/6248230. No credit cards.*

$ ✕ **Pancake Bakery.** Here's a chance to try a traditionally Dutch way of keeping eating costs down. The name of the game is pancakes—laden with savory cheese and bacon or fruit and liqueur. The Pancake Bakery is not far from the Anne Frankhuis (☞ Exploring Amsterdam, *above*). ⊠ *Prinsengracht 191,* ☎ *020/6251333. Reservations not accepted. AE, MC, DC, V.*

NIGHTLIFE AND THE ARTS

The Arts

The arts flourish in cosmopolitan Amsterdam. The best sources of information about performances are the *Time Out Amsterdam* listings on the Internet (http://www.timeout.nl). *De Uit Krant* is available in Dutch and covers practically every event. The biweekly *What's On in Amsterdam* is published by the tourist office, where you can also secure tickets for the more popular events. Tickets must be booked in person from Monday through Saturday, 10–4. You can also book at the **Amsterdam Uit Buro** (⊠ Stadsschouwburg, Leidseplein 26, ☎ 020/6211211).

CLASSICAL MUSIC

The **Concertgebouw** (⊠ Concertgebouwplein 2–6, ☎ 020/6718345) is the home of one of Europe's finest orchestras. A smaller auditorium in the same building is used for chamber music, recitals, and even jam sessions. While ticket prices for international orchestras are fairly high, most concerts are good value, and the Wednesday lunchtime concerts are free.

FILM

The largest concentration of movie theaters is around Leidseplein and near Muntplein. Most foreign films are subtitled rather than dubbed, which makes Amsterdam a great place to catch up on movies you missed at home. The largest theater (seven screens) in the city is the **City 1–7** (⊠ Kleine Garmanplantsoen 13–25, ☎ 020/6234579). The Art Deco–era **Tuschinski** (⊠ Reguliersbreestraat 26, ☎ 020/6262633) is the most beautiful cinema house.

OPERA AND BALLET

The Dutch national ballet and opera companies are housed in the **Muziektheater** (⊠ Waterlooplein, ☎ 020/6255455). Guest companies from other countries perform here during the three-week Holland Festival in June. The country's smaller regional dance and opera companies usually include performances at the **Stadsschouwburg** (Municipal Theater; ⊠ Leidseplein 26, ☎ 020/624 2311) in their schedules.

Young American comedians living in Amsterdam have created **Boom Chicago** (✉ Leidspleintheater, Leidseplein 12, ☎ 020/5307300), improvised comedy with a local touch. You can munch pizzas and salad during performances. For experimental theater, dance, and colorful cabaret in Dutch, catch the shows at **Felix Meritis House** (✉ Keizersgracht 324, ☎ 020/6231311). Along the **Nes** you'll find a phenomenal selection of performance spaces for theater and dance. The main theater ticket booking office is at the **De Brakke Grond** (✉ Nes 45, ☎ 020/6229014), which is also the Flemish Cultural Center.

Nightlife

Amsterdam has a wide variety of dance clubs, bars, and exotic shows. The more respectable—and expensive—after-dark activities are in and around Leidseplein and Rembrandtsplein; fleshier productions are on Oudezijds Achterburgwal and Thorbeckeplein. Most bars and clubs are open every night from 5 PM to 2 AM or 5 AM. On weeknights very few clubs charge admission, though the more lively ones sometimes ask for a "club membership" fee of Fl. 20 or more.

CAFÉS AND BARS

Amsterdam, and particularly the Jordaan (☞ Exploring Amsterdam, *above*), is renowned for its brown cafés, so named because of the rich wooden furnishings and—some say—the centuries-old pipe-tobacco stains on the ceilings. There are also a variety of grand cafés, with spacious interiors, snappy table service, and well-stocked reading tables. Two other variants of Amsterdam's buzzing bar are the *proeflokalen* (tasting houses) and *brouwerijen* (breweries). "When in Rome, do as the Romans do," could be applied to the Dutch tolerance of the dreaded weed, to be enjoyed in one of the many "coffee shops" with the green leaves of the marijuana plant showing in the window.

At the **Rooie Nelis** (✉ Laurierstraat 101, ☎ 020/6244167), you can spend a rainy afternoon chatting with friendly strangers over homemade meatballs and a beer or apple tart and coffee. **De Gijs** (✉ Lindegracht 249, ☎ 020/6380740) is a characterful example of the brown café. More fashionable cafés include **Caffe Esprit** (✉ Spui 10, ☎ 020/6221967), serving delicious burgers and fine lunches. It is often used as a venue for radio and television interviews. **De Jaren** (✉ Nieuwe Doelenstraat 20, ☎ 020/6255771), a spacious café with a canal-side terrace, attracts smart young businesspeople, arts and media workers, and trendy types. The beamed interior of **De Admiraal Proeflokaal en Spijhuis** (✉ Herengracht 319, ☎ 020/6254334) is an intimate setting to enjoy the head-warming selection of award-winning *genevers* (gins). If Continental lagers no longer tickle your fancy, then the home-brewed selection of beers at **Maximiliaan Amsterdams Brouwhuis** (✉ Kloveniersburgwal 6, ☎ 020/6266280) are well worth sampling. **Tweede Kamer** (✉ Heisteeg 6, just off the Spui, ☎ no phone), named for parliament's lower house, offers draughts, chess, and backgammon in a convivial, civilized atmosphere permeated with the smoke of hemp.

CASINO

Holland Casino (✉ Max Euweplein 62, ☎ 020/6201006), just off Leidseplein, has blackjack, roulette, and slot machines in elegant, canal-side surrounds. There are also glamorous, but pricey, cabaret dinner arrangements. You'll need your passport to get in; the minimum age is 18.

DANCE CLUBS

Dance clubs tend to fill up after midnight. The cavernous **Escape** (✉ Rembrandtsplein 11–15, ☎ 020/6221111) has shrugged off its mainstream image and taken on a much hipper mantle. The **It** (✉ Amstelstraat 24, ☎ 020/6250111) is gay on Saturday. It's primarily straight on Thursday, Friday, and Sunday—but could never be accused of being straitlaced. **RoXY** (✉ Singel 465, ☎ 020/6200354) is the current hot spot, though you need to be a member or impressively dressed to get in. **Seymour Likely Too** (✉ Nieuwezijd Voorburgwal 161, ☎ 020/4205663) was opened by a group of artists in the wake of their success with the Seymour Likely Lounge, a popular bar across the road. This club is guaranteed to have a lively, trendy crowd hopping to the latest music.

GAY AND LESBIAN BARS

Amsterdam has a vibrant gay and lesbian community, concentrated principally on Warmoesstraat, Reguliersdwarsstraat, Amstelstraat, and Kerkstraat near Leidseplein. The **Gay & Lesbian Switchboard** (☎ 020/6236565, ⊙ 10–10) has friendly operators who provide information on the city's nightlife and other advice for gay or lesbian visitors. The **COC** (✉ Rozenstraat 14, ☎ 020/6263087), the Dutch lesbian and gay political organization, operates a coffee shop and weekend discos.

JAZZ CLUBS

Café Meander (✉ Voetboogsteeg 5, ☎ 020/6258430) caters to a younger crowd with traditional jazz to the latest in hip-hop and experimental crossover streams. The **Bimhuis** (✉ Oude Schans 73–77, ☎ 020/6233373, ⊙ Thurs.–Sat. from 9 PM), in a converted warehouse, has long offered the best jazz and improvised music in town. Ticket holders can sit in the adjoining BIM café and enjoy a magical view across the Oude Schans canal.

ROCK CLUBS

Melkweg (✉ Lijnbaansgracht 234, ☎ 020/6248492), a big draw in the flower-power era, is making a comeback as a major rock and pop venue with its large, new auditorium; it also has a gallery, theater, cinema, and café. The **Paradiso** (✉ Weteringschans 6–8, ☎ 020/6264521), converted from a church, has become a vibrant venue for rock, New Age, and even contemporary classical music.

SHOPPING

Amsterdam is a cornucopia of interesting markets, quirky specialty shops, antiques, art, and diamonds.

Department Stores

De Bijenkorf (✉ Dam 1), the city's number-one department store, is excellent for contemporary fashions and furnishings. **Maison de Bonneterie en Pander** (✉ Rokin 140–142; ✉ Beethovenstraat 32) is the Queen Mother of department stores—gracious, genteel, and understated. The well-stocked departments of **Vroom and Dreesmann** (✉ Kalverstraat 201) carry all manner of goods.

Gift Ideas

DIAMONDS

Since the 17th century, "Amsterdam cut" has been synonymous with perfection in the quality of diamonds. You can see this craftsmanship at any of the diamond-cutting houses. The cutters explain how the diamond's value depends on the four cs—carat, cut, clarity, and color—before encouraging you to buy. There is a cluster of diamond houses on the Rokin.

PORCELAIN

The Dutch have been producing Delft, Makkum, and other fine porcelain for centuries. **Focke and Meltzer** (✉ P. C. Hooftstraat 65–67, ☎ 020/6642311) stores have been selling it since 1823. Available pieces range from affordable, newly painted tiles to expensive Delft blue-and-white pitchers.

Markets

Antiekmarkt de Looier (⊠ Elandsgracht 109; ⊙ Sun.–Wed. 11–5, Thurs. 11–9) is a bustling covered market that's great for antiques, especially silver and toys. In summer, you'll find etchings, drawings, and watercolors at the Sunday **art markets** on Thorbeckeplein and the Spui. On Saturday the Noordermarkt and Nieuwmarkt host an **organic farmers' market,** with essential oils and other New Age fare alongside oats, pulses, and vegetables. Amsterdam's lively **Waterlooplein flea market** (⊙ Mon.–Sat. 9:30–4) next to the Muziektheater is the ideal spot to rummage for secondhand clothes, inexpensive antiques, and other curiosities. The **Bloemenmarkt** (flower market) on the Singel has bulbs and cut flowers. A small but choice **stamp market** (⊙ Wed. and Sat. 1–4) is held on the Nieuwezijds Voorburgwal.

Shopping Districts

The Jordaan and the quaint streets crisscrossing the main ring of old canals are a treasure trove of trendy small boutiques and unusual crafts shops. Leidsestraat, Kalverstraat, Utrechtsestraat, and Nieuwendijk are Amsterdam's chief shopping districts, which have largely been turned into **pedestrian-only areas.** The imposing new **Kalvertoren** shopping mall (⊠ Kalverstraat, near Munt) offers covered shopping and a rooftop restaurant with magnificent views of the city. **Magna Plaza** shopping center (⊠ Nieuwezijds Voorburgwal 182), built inside the glorious old post office behind the Royal Palace, is *the* place for A-to-Z shopping in a huge variety of stores. The **Spiegelkwartier** (⊠ Nieuwe Spiegelstraat and Spiegelgracht), just a stone's throw from the Rijksmuseum, is Amsterdam's antiques center, with galleries for wealthy collectors, as well as old curiosity shops. **P. C. Hooftstraat,** and also Van Baerlestraat and Beethovenstraat, are the homes of haute couture and other fine goods. **Rokin** is hectic with traffic and houses a cluster of boutiques and renowned antiques shops selling 18th- and 19th-century furniture, antique jewelry, Art Deco lamps, and statuettes. **Schiphol Airport** tax-free shopping center is often lauded as the world's best.

AMSTERDAM ESSENTIALS

Arriving and Departing

BY PLANE

Most international flights arrive at Amsterdam's Schiphol Airport. Immigration and customs formalities on arrival are relaxed, with no forms to be completed.

Between the Airport and Downtown. The best transportation between the airport and the city center is the direct rail link to the central train station, where you can get a taxi or tram to your hotel. The train runs every 10 to 15 minutes throughout the day and takes about a half hour. Make sure you buy a ticket before boarding: ruthless conductors will happily impose a fine. Second-class single fare is Fl. 6.25. Taxis from the airport to central hotels cost about Fl. 60.

BY TRAIN

The city has excellent rail connections with the rest of Europe, including the high-speed **Thalys** service to Brussels and Paris (☎ 0900/9228, 50¢ per minute) with a journey time of just over four hours. Other fast links include Cologne and Hannover. It is now possible to travel by train to London, by either the Eurostar channel tunnel link or the High Speed Sea service, in less than seven hours. Centraal Station (⊠ Stationsplein; international service information, ☎ 0900/9296, 50¢ per minute, long wait) is in the center of town.

Getting Around

BY BICYCLE
Rental bikes are widely available for around Fl. 10 per day with a Fl. 50–Fl. 200 deposit. Several rental companies are close to the central train station, or ask at tourist offices for details. Lock your bike whenever you park it, preferably to something immovable. Also, check with the rental company to see what your liability is under their insurance terms.

BY BOAT
The **Canalbus** (⌨ Fl. 19.50 for a hop-on, hop-off day card) travels between the central train station and the Rijksmuseum. The **Museum Boat** (⌨ Fl. 22; ☞ Guided Tours, *below*) makes seven stops near major museums.

BY CAR
The city's concentric ring of canals, one-way systems, and lack of parking facilities continue to plague drivers. It's best to put your car in one of the parking lots on the edge of the old center and abandon it for the rest of your stay.

BY METRO, TRAM, AND BUS
A zonal fare system is used. Tickets (starting at Fl. 3) are available from automatic dispensers on the Metro or from the drivers on trams and buses; or buy a money-saving strippenkaart. Even simpler is the dagkaart, which covers all city routes for Fl. 12. These discount tickets can be obtained from the main GVB ticket office (weekdays 7–7, weekends 8–7) in front of Centraal Station and from many newsstands, along with route maps of the public transportation system. A new alternative for visitors is the Circle Tram 20, which goes both ways around a loop that passes close to most of the main sights and offers a hop-on, hop-off ticket for one–three days.

BY TAXI
Taxis are expensive: A 5-km (3-mi) ride costs around Fl. 15. Taxis are not usually hailed on the street but are picked up at stands near stations and other key points. Alternatively, you can dial 020/6777777. Water taxis (☎ 020/6222181) are more expensive: Standard-size water taxis—for up to eight people—cost Fl. 90 for a half hour, including pick-up charge, and Fl. 30 per 15 minutes thereafter.

ON FOOT
Amsterdam is a compact city of narrow streets and canals, ideal for exploring on foot. The tourist office issues seven excellent guides in English that detail walking tours around the center. The best are "The Jordaan," a stroll through the lively canal-side district; and "Jewish Amsterdam," a walk past the symbolic remains of Jewish housing and old synagogues.

Money Matters

CURRENCY
The unit of currency in the Netherlands is the guilder, written as NLG (for Netherlands guilder), Fl., or simply F. (from the centuries-old term for the coinage, florin). Each guilder is divided into 100 cents. Bills are in denominations of 10, 25, 50, 100, 250, and 1,000 guilders. Denominations over Fl. 100 are rarely seen, and many shops refuse to change them. Coins are 1, 2.5, and 5 guilders and 5, 10, and 25 cents. Don't confuse the 1- and 2.5-guilder coins and the 5-guilder and 5-cent coins. Bills have a code of raised dots that can be identified by touch.

At press time (spring 1998), the exchange rate for the guilder was Fl. 2 to the U.S. dollar, Fl. 1.39 to the Canadian dollar, Fl. 3.32 to the pound sterling, Fl. 1.29 to the Australian dollar, and Fl. 1.10 to the New Zealand dollar.

Telephoning

COUNTRY CODE

The country code for the Netherlands is 31. When dialing a number in the Netherlands from outside the country, drop the initial 0 from the local area code.

Contacts and Resources

CONSULATES

United States (⊠ Museumplein 19, ☎ 020/6645661). **Canadian** (⊠ 7 Sophialaan, The Hague, ☎ 070/3614111). **United Kingdom** (⊠ Koningslaan 44, ☎ 020/6764343).

EMERGENCIES

Police (☎ 112). **Ambulance** (☎ 112). **Central Medical Service** (☎ 0900/35032042, Fl. 1 per minute), will give you names and opening hours of pharmacists and dentists as well as doctors.

ENGLISH-LANGUAGE BOOKSTORES

American Book Center (⊠ Kalverstraat 185, ☎ 020/6255537). **Athenaeum Boekhandel** (⊠ Spui 14, ☎ 020/6233933). **English Bookshop** (⊠ Lauriergracht 71, ☎ 020/6264230). **Waterstone's** (⊠ Kalverstraat 152, ☎ 020/6383821).

GUIDED TOURS

Bike. From April through October, guided bike tours are an excellent way to discover Amsterdam. There are also supervised tours to the idyllic countryside and quaint villages just north of the city. The three-hour city tour costs Fl.30, and the 6½-hour countryside tour costs Fl.42.50, arranged by **Yellow Bike Guided Tours** (⊠ Nieuwezijds Kolk 29, ☎ 020/6206940).

Boat. The most enjoyable way to get to know Amsterdam is on a boat trip along the canals. Departures are frequent from points opposite Centraal Station, along the Damrak, and along the Rokin and Stadhouderskade (near the Rijksmuseum). For a tour lasting about an hour, the cost is around Fl. 12.50, but the student guides expect a small tip for their multilingual commentary. A candlelight dinner cruise costs upward of Fl. 39.50. Trips can be booked through the tourist office.

At **Canal-Bike** locations (⊠ corner Leidsestraat and Keizersgracht, Leidsekade, Stadhouderskade opposite Rijksmuseum, Prinsengracht opposite Westerkerk; ☎ 020/6239886), a pedal boat for four costs FL. 20.50 per hour.

The **Museum Boat** (⊠ Stationsplein 8, ☎ 020/6222181) combines a scenic view of the city with seven stops near 20 museums. Tickets, good for the entire day, are Fl. 22.

Bus. Guided bus tours also provide an excellent introduction to Amsterdam. A bus-and-boat tour includes the inevitable trip to a diamond factory. Costing Fl. 25–Fl. 35, the comprehensive 3½-hour tour can be booked through **Lindbergh** (⊠ Damrak 26–27, ☎ 020/6222766) or **Key Tours** (⊠ Dam 19, ☎ 020/6235051).

Travel Agencies

American Express (⊠ Damrak 66, ☎ 020/5207777; ⊠ Van Baerlestraat 39, ☎ 020/6738550). **Holland International** (⊠ Leidseplein 23, ☎ 020/6262660). **Key Tours** (⊠ Dam 19, ☎ 020/6235051). **Reisburo**

Arke (✉ Damrak 90, ☎ 020/5550888). **Thomas Cook** (Bureau de Change, ✉ Leidseplein 31a, ☎ 020/6267000; ✉ Damrak 1, ☎ 020/6203236).

Visitor Information

VVV Amsterdam Tourist Office (✉ Stationsplein 10, in front of Centraal Station in Old Dutch Coffee House; ☎ 0900/4040400, Fl. 1 per minute—electronic queue—you may end up paying for a long wait).

3 Athens

Athens is essentially a village that outgrew itself, spreading outward from the original settlement at the foot of the Acropolis. Back in 1834, when it became the capital of modern Greece, the city had a population of fewer than 10,000. Now it houses more than a third of the entire Greek population—around 4.3 million. A modern concrete city has engulfed the old village and now sprawls for 388 square km (244 square mi), covering almost all the surrounding plain from the sea to the encircling mountains. The city is crowded and overwhelmingly hot during the summer. It also has an air-pollution problem, caused mainly by traffic fumes; in an attempt to lessen the congestion, it is forbidden to drive private cars in central Athens on alternate workdays. Still, Athens is an experience not to be missed.

Although Athens covers a huge area, the major landmarks of the ancient Greek, Roman, and Byzantine periods are conveniently close to the modern city center. You can easily stroll from the Acropolis to the other sites, taking time to browse in shops and relax in cafés and tavernas along the way. From many quarters of the city one can glimpse "the *glory that was Greece" in the form of the Acropolis looming above the horizon, but only by actually climbing that rocky precipice can you feel the impact of the ancient settlement. The Acropolis and Filopappou, two craggy hills sitting side by side; the ancient Agora (marketplace); and Kerameikos, the first cemetery, form the core of ancient and Roman Athens.*

EXPLORING ATHENS

Numbers in the margin correspond to points of interest on the Athens map.

The central area of modern Athens is small, stretching from the Acropolis to Mt. Lycabettus, with its small white church on top. The layout is simple: Three parallel streets—Stadiou, Venizelou (a.k.a. Panepistimiou), and Akademias—link two main squares—Syntagma and Omonia. Try to wander off this beaten tourist track: Seeing the Athenian butchers in the central market near Monastiraki sleeping on their cold marble slabs during the heat of the afternoon siesta may give you more of a feel for the city than looking at hundreds of fallen pillars.

In summer closing times often depend on the site's available personnel, but throughout the year, arrive at least 30 minutes before the official closing time to ensure you can buy a ticket. Flash photography is forbidden in museums.

❻ Agios Eleftherios. What's fascinating about the city's former cathedral is that the walls of this 12th-century Byzantine church incorporate reliefs— fanciful figures and zodiac signs—from buildings that date back to the Classical period. The church is also known as Little Mitropolis and Panagia Gorgoepikoos (Virgin Who Answers Prayers Quickly), based on its 13th-century icon, said to perform miracles. ⊠ *Mitropolis Sq.,* ☎ *No phone.* ☜ *Free.* ☉ *Hours depend on services, but usually open daily 8–1.*

★ ❶ Akropolis. After a 30-year building moratorium at the time of the Persian wars, the Athenians built this complex during the 5th century BC to honor the goddess Athena, patron of the city. It is now undergoing conservation as part of an ambitious 20-year rescue plan launched with international support in 1983 by Greek architects. The first ruins you'll see are the **Propylaia,** the monumental gateway that led worshipers from the temporal world into the spiritual world of the sanctuary; now only the columns of Pentelic marble and a fragment of stone ceiling remain. Above, to the right, stands the graceful **Naos Athenas Nikis** or **Apterou Nikis** (Wingless Victory). The temple was mistakenly called the latter because common tradition often confused Athena with the winged goddess Nike. Athenians claimed the sculptor had purposely omitted the wings on the temple's statue to ensure Victory would never fly away from the city. The elegant and architecturally complex **Erechtheion,** most sacred of the shrines of the Acropolis and later turned into a harem by the Turks, has finally emerged from extensive repair work. Dull, heavy copies of the Caryatids (draped maidens) now support the roof. The **Acropolis Museum** (☞ Museo Akropoleos, *below*) houses five of the six originals, their faces much damaged by acid rain. The sixth is in the British Museum in London.

38

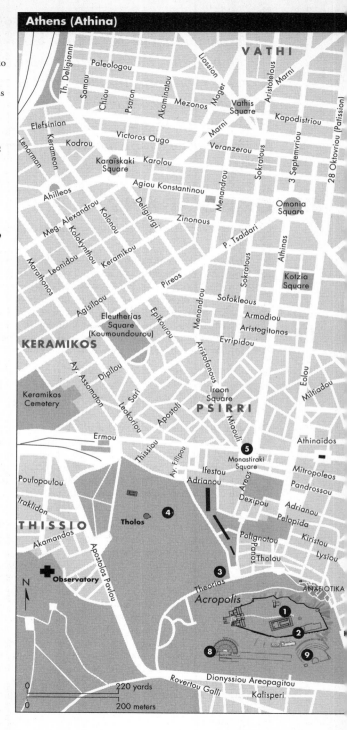

Athens (Athina)

NEAPOLIS

Strefi

Tossitsa

Stournara

Solomou

Kapodistriou

Kaningos
Square

Themistokleous

Em. Benaki

Zoodohou Pigis

Hariloou Trikoupi

Mavromichali

Navarinou

Ippokratous

Methonis

Eressou

Dervenion

Arachovis

Kallidromiou

Tsimiski

Isavron

Smolenski

Voulgaroktonou

Valatzi

Laskareos

Tsimiski

Sarantapichou

N. Ouranou

Dafnomili

N. Ouranou

Chersonos

LIKAVITOS

Agios
Giorgos

15

Panepistimiou (Venizelou)

Stadiou

Akademias

Asklepiou

Skoufa

Massalias

Solonos

Sina

Omirou

Didotou

Lykavitou

Anagnostopoulou

**Municipal
Cultural
Center**

17

Aristippou

Loukianou

Kleomenous

Spefsipou

Marasli

Korai

Klafthmonos
Sq.

Ch. Lada

Dragatsaniou

Paparigopoulou

Praxitelous

Kolokotroni

Karageorgi
Servias

Perikleos

Ermou

Pendeli

Voulis

Georgiou I

Amerikis

Dimokritou

Voukourestiou

Pindarou

Schliemann's
Mansion

Kanari

Merlin

KOLONAKI

Kolonaki
Square

Koumbari

Patriarhou Ioakim

Alopekis

Irodotou

Karneadou

Ypsilantou

Ploutarchou

14

13

PLAKA

Apollonos

Nikodimou

Mitropoleos

Nikis

Filellinon

Souri

Amalias

Vasilissis Sofias

Syntagma
Square

16

Parliament

Herod Atticus

Rigilis

Vasileos Georgiou B

**National
Gardens**

Vasileos Konstantinou

Patsaniou

Arianou

Vasileos Georgiou B

Adrianou

Scholiou

Tripodon

Kidathineon

Thespidos

7

Amalias Ave.

Zappion

Eratosthenous

Vasileos Konstantinou

Simenidou

Vironas

Goura

Lysikratous

Pitakou

Vasilissis Olgas

10

11

Vasilissis Olgas

Arditos
Hill

Agras

12

Plastira
Square

6

18

The **Parthenonas** (Parthenon) dominates the Acropolis and indeed the Athens skyline. Designed by Ictinus, with Phidias as master sculptor, it was completed in 438 BC and is the most architecturally sophisticated temple of that period. Even with hordes of tourists wandering around the ruins, you can still feel a sense of wonder. The architectural decorations were originally painted vivid red and blue, and the roof was of marble tiles, but time and neglect have given the marble pillars their golden-white shine, and the beauty of the building is all the more stark and striking. The British Museum houses the largest remaining part of the original 532-ft frieze (the Elgin Marbles). The building has 17 fluted columns along each side and 8 at the ends, and these were cleverly made to lean slightly inward and to bulge, counterbalancing the natural optical distortion. The Parthenon has had a checkered history: It was made into a brothel by the Romans, a church by the Christians, and a mosque by the Turks. The Turks also stored gunpowder in the Propylaia. When this was hit by a Venetian bombardment in 1687, 28 columns of the Parthenon were blown out and a fire raged for two days, leaving the temple in its present condition. ⊠ *Top of Dionyssiou Areopagitou,* ☎ *01/321–4172.* ☉ *Weekdays 8– 6:30 (8–4:30 in winter), weekends 8:30–2:30.*

❹ Archaia Agora (Ancient Agora). Now a sprawling confusion of stones, slabs, and foundations, this was the civic center and focal point of community life in ancient Athens, where Socrates met with his students while merchants haggled over the price of olive oil. It is dominated by the best-preserved Doric temple in Greece, the **Hephaisteion,** built during the 5th century BC. Nearby, the impressive Stoa Attalou (Stoa of Attalos II), reconstructed by the American School of Classical Studies in Athens with the help of the Rockefeller Foundation, houses the **Museo tis Agoras** (Museum of Agora Excavations). The museum offers a fascinating glimpse of everyday life in ancient Athens, its objects ranging from a terra-cotta chamber pot to the shards used in secret ballots to recommend banishment of powerful citizens (*ostraka,* from which the word "ostracism" is derived). ⊠ *Three entrances: from Monastiraki, on Adrianou St.; from Thission, on Apostolos Pavlou St.; from Acropolis, on descent along Ag. Apostoli,* ☎ *01/321–0185.* ☉ *Tues.–Sun. 8:30–2:45.*

❸ Areios Pagos (Areopagus). From this rocky outcrop, ancient Athens's supreme court, you can view the Propylaia, the Agora, and the modern city. Legend claims it was here that Orestes was tried for the murder of his mother, and much later St. Paul delivered his Sermon to the Unknown God, so moving that a senator named Dionysius was converted and became the first bishop of Athens. ⊠ *Opposite Acropolis entrance.* ▣ *Free.* ☉ *Always open.*

★ ⓲ Ethniko Archaiologiko Museo (National Archaeological Museum). Though it's somewhat off the tourist route, a good 10-minute walk north of Omonia Square, this is a must for visitors. It houses one of the most exciting collections of antiquities in the world, including sensational archaeological finds made by Heinrich Schliemann at Mycenae; 16th-century BC frescoes from the Akrotiri ruins on Santorini; and the 6½-ft-tall bronze sculpture *Poseidon,* an original work of circa 470 BC, possibly by the sculptor Kalamis, which was found in the sea off Cape Artemision in 1928. ⊠ *28 Oktovriou (Patission) 44,* ☎ *01/ 821–7717.* ☉ *Mon. 12:30–7 (10:30–4:45 in winter), Tues.–Fri. 8– 7 (8:30–3 in winter), weekends and holidays 8:30–3.*

★ ⓮ Goulandri Museo Kikladikis ke Archaias Technis (Goulandris Museum of Cycladic and Ancient Art). The collection spans 5,000 years, with nearly 100 exhibits of the Cycladic civilization (3000–2000 BC), including many of the slim marble figurines that so fascinated such artists as Picasso and Modigliani. ✉ *Neofitou Douka 4 or Irodotou 1,* ☎ *01/722–8321.* ⊙ *Mon. and Wed.–Fri. 10–4, Sat. 10–3.*

⑧ Irodion (Odeon of Herod Atticus). This hauntingly beautiful 2nd-century AD theater was built Greek-style into the hillside but with typical Roman archways in its three-story stage building and barrel-vaulted entrances. Now restored, it hosts Athens Festival performances (☞ The Arts, *below*). ✉ *Dionyssiou Areopagitou St. across from Propylaia St.,* ☎ *01/323–2771.* ⊙ *Open only to Athens Festival audiences.*

★ **⑮ Likavitos** (Mt. Lycabettus). Athens's highest hill is only a 10-minute walk northeast of Syntagma. It borders fashionable Kolonaki, a residential quarter worth a visit if you enjoy window-shopping and people-watching. A steeply inclined funicular climbs to the summit, crowned by whitewashed Agios Giorgios chapel. The view from the top—pollution permitting—is the finest in Athens. ✉ *Funicular every 10 min from Ploutarchou 1 at Aristippou (take minibus 060 from Kolonaki Sq.),* ☎ *01/722–7065.* ⊙ *Fri.–Wed. 8:45 AM–midnight (12:30 AM in summer), Thurs. 10:30 AM–midnight (12:30 AM in summer).*

⑤ Monastiraki. The old Turkish bazaar area takes its name from Panayia Pantanassa Church, commonly called Monastiraki (Little Monastery); it once flourished as an extensive convent, perhaps dating from the 10th century. Near the church stands the Tzistarakis Mosque (1759), exemplifying the East-West paradox that characterizes Athens. But the district's real draw is the Sunday flea market, centered on tiny Abyssinia Square and running along Ifestou and Kynetou streets. Watching the interplay between Greeks, complete with wildly gesturing hands and dramatic facial expressions, will provide hours of entertainment. Everything's for sale, from gramophone needles to old matchboxes, from nose rings sold by young nomads to lacquered eggs and cool white linens from former USSR emigres. ✉ *South of intersection of Ermou and Athinas Sts.*

★ **② Museo Akropoleos** (Acropolis Museum). Tucked into one corner of the Acropolis, this institution contains superb sculptures, including the Caryatids and a collection of colored *korai* (statues of women dedicated by worshipers to Athena, patron of the ancient city). ☎ *01/323–6665.* ⊙ *Mon. 11–6:30 (11–4:30 in winter), Tues.–Fri. 8:30–6:30 (8:30–4:30 in winter), weekends 8:30–2:30.*

⑫ Panathinaiko Stadio (Panathenaic Stadium). A reconstruction of the ancient Roman stadium in Athens, this gleaming white marble structure was built for the first modern Olympic Games in 1896 and seats 80,000 spectators. ✉ *Near intersection Vas. Konstantinou and Vas. Olgas,* ☎ *No phone.* ⊡ *Free.* ⊙ *Daily 9–2 but can be viewed in its entirety from entrance.*

⑩ Pili tou Adrianou (Hadrian's Arch). Built in AD 131–32 by Emperor Hadrian to delineate ancient and imperial Athens, the Roman archway with Corinthian pilasters bears an inscription on the side facing the Acropolis, which reads, THIS IS ATHENS, THE ANCIENT CITY OF THESEUS. But the side facing the Temple of Olympian Zeus proclaims, THIS IS THE CITY OF HADRIAN AND NOT OF THESEUS. ✉ *Intersection Vas. Amalias and Dionyssiou Areopagitou.* ⊡ *Free.* ⊙ *Always open.*

★ **⑦ Plaka.** Stretching east from the Agora, this is almost all that's left of 19th-century Athens, a lovely quarter with winding walkways, neoclassical houses, and such sights as the **Museo Ellinikis Laikis Technis** (Greek Folk Art Museum; ✉ Kidathineon 17, ☎ 01/322–9031, ⊙ Tues.–Sun. 10–2), with a collection dating from 1650, and the Roman Agora's **Aerides** (Tower of the Winds; ✉ Pelopidas and Aeolou, ☎ 01/324–5220, ⊙ Tues.–Sun. 8:30–2:45), a 1st-century BC water clock.

The **Mnimeio Lysikratous** (Monument of Lysikrates; ✉ Herefondos and Lysikratous Sts.) is one of the few surviving tripods on which stood the award given to the producer of the best play in the Dionyssia festival. Above Plaka, at the northeastern base of the Acropolis is **Anafiotika,** the closest thing you'll find to a village in Athens. Take time to wander among its whitewashed, bougainvillea-framed houses and tiny churches, away from the city's bustle.

⓫ **Stiles Olymbiou Dios or Olymbion** (Temple of Olympian Zeus). This famous temple was begun during the 6th century BC, and, when it was finally completed 700 years later, it exceeded in magnitude all other temples in Greece. It was destroyed during the invasion of the Goths in the 4th century; only a few towering, sun-browned columns remain. ✉ *Vas. Olgas 1,* ☏ *01/922–6330.* ⊘ *Tues.–Sun. 8:30–3.*

⓰ **Syntagma** (Constitution Square). At the top of the square stands the **Vouli** (Parliament), formerly the royal palace, completed in 1838 for the new monarchy. From the Parliament you can watch the changing of the Evzone honor guard at the **Mnimeio Agnostou Stratiotou** (Tomb of the Unknown Soldier), with its text from Pericles's famous funeral oration and a bas-relief of a dying soldier modeled after a sculpture on the Temple of Aphaia in Aegina. The guard changes every few hours depending on the weather, but the most elaborate ceremony takes place on Sunday, when these sturdy young men don their *foustanellas* (kilts) with 400 pleats, one for each year of the Ottoman occupation. The procession usually arrives in front of Parliament at 11:15 AM. On the square's southern side sits the lush **Ethniko Kipo** (National Garden), offering a quick escape from the center's bustle. ✉ *Corner of Vas. Sofias and Vas. Amalias.*

⓿ **Theatro Dionyssou** (Theater of Dionyssos). In this theater dating from about 330 BC, the famous ancient dramas and comedies were performed in conjunction with bacchanalian feasts. The throne in the center was reserved for the priest of Dionyssos: It is adorned with regal lions' paws, and the back is carved with reliefs of satyrs and griffins. ✉ *Dionyssiou Areopagitou opposite Mitsaion St.,* ☏ *01/322–4625.* ⊘ *Daily 8:30–2:45.*

⓱ **Vivliothiki, Panepistimio, Akademia** (Old University complex). These three dramatic buildings belong to the University of Athens, designed by the Hansen Brothers in the period after independence and built of white Pentelic marble, with tall columns and decorative friezes. In the center is the Senate House of the university; on the right is the Academy, flanked by statues of Athena and Apollo; and on the left is the National Library. ✉ *Panepistimiou 28,* ☏ *Library 01/361–4413, Panepistimio 01/361–4301, Akademia 01/360–0207.* ▣ *Free.* ⊘ *Library weekdays 9–9, others weekdays 9–2. Closed Aug.*

⓭ **Vizantino Museo** (Byzantine Museum). Housed in an 1848 mansion built by an eccentric French aristocrat, the museum is undergoing renovation. Not all its pieces are on display, but it has a unique collection of icons, re-creations of Greek churches throughout the centuries, and the very beautiful 14th-century Byzantine embroidery of the body of Christ, in gold, silver, yellow, and green. Sculptural fragments provide an excellent introduction to Byzantine architecture. ✉ *Vas. Sofias 22,* ☏ *01/721–1027.* ⊘ *Tues.–Sun. 8:30–2:50.*

DINING

Search for places with at least a half dozen tables occupied by Athenians—they're discerning customers.

RATINGS

Prices are per person and include a first course, main course, dessert, VAT, and service charge. They do not include drinks or tip.

CATEGORY	COST
$$$$	over 13,000 dr.
$$$	9,000 dr.–13,000 dr.
$$	4,500 dr.–9,000 dr.
$	under 4,500 dr.

$$$$ ★ ✕ **Bajazzo.** If you can splurge only once in Greece, this is the place, the only restaurant in Athens that has been accorded international praise. Chef Klaus Feuerbach changes the menu often, creating imaginative, beautifully presented dishes. The beef fillets with Metaxa sauce grilled in tobacco leaves, simple but flawless pork tenderloin with brie, intense smoked duck breast with foie gras and cherry froth, and the venison with bittersweet chocolate sauce are just some of the mouth-watering dishes. Try the herbed ice cream (rosemary, tarragon, dill) or the meringues filled with amaretto and crème anglaise for dessert. ✉ *Anapafseos 14, Mets,* ☎ *01/921–3013. Reservations essential. AE, DC, V. Closed Sun. No lunch.*

$$$$ ✕ **Vardis.** This grand restaurant is sometimes compared to the five-star Taillevent in Paris and a meal here is obviously worth the ride to the northern suburb of Kifissia. The award-winning chef is committed to the classics and to quality ingredients—he brings in sweetwater crayfish from Orhomenos and tracks down rare large shrimp from Thassos island. The clientele may be a little sedate, but the food is heavenly. Especially good are the warm foie gras with dried fig purée, the superb crayfish linguini, and the tournedos Rossini served with a demiglace enriched with foie gras. ✉ *Diligianni 66 in Pentelikon Hotel, Kefalari, Kifissia,* ☎ *01/623–0650. Reservations essential. AE, DC, MC, V. Closed Sun. and Aug. No lunch.*

$$$–$$$$ ★ ✕ **Varoulko.** Acclaimed chef Lefteris Lazarou has joined forces with Fabrizio Buliani, and the results are magnificent as they try to outdo each other. Customers wait in line to sample such appetizers as sturgeon-filled phyllo triangles or carpaccio made from *petrobarbouno* (a kind of rock fish). Although the restaurant is most famous for its creative presentations of monkfish, there is a mind-boggling array of other seafood dishes. ✉ *Deligeorgi 14, Piraeus,* ☎ *01/411–2043,* ☎ FAX *01/411–1283. Reservations essential. AE, DC, V. Closed Sun. and Aug. No lunch.*

$$$ ★ ✕ **Boschetto.** The restaurant pampers diners with its park setting, expert maître d', and creative Italian nouvelle. The specialty here is fresh pasta, such as papardelle with wild mushrooms and quail-parmesan ragout, airy capellini with crab and sautéed tomatoes, or ravioli with crayfish, foie gras, and poppy seeds. End your meal with an unusual dessert of cream and chicken, followed by the finest espresso in Athens (cigars available). The tables tend to be close together; reserve near the window or in the courtyard during summer. ✉ *Alsos Evangelismos, Hilton area,* ☎ *01/721–0893. Reservations essential. AE, V. Closed Sun. and 2 wks in Aug. No lunch weekends.*

$$$ ✕ **Spondi.** You may feel like you're dining in a medieval wine cellar in this vaulted stone-interior restaurant with heavy candlesticks and massive wood furniture, but the cuisine is delightfully contemporary. Savor the grilled fresh foie gras with caramelized endive in mavrodafni sauce, together with a red wine chosen by the award-winning sommelier. When weather permits, diners sit in the bougainvillea-draped courtyard. ✉ *Pirronos 5, Pangrati,* ☎ *01/726–4021. Reservations essential. V. No lunch.*

$$-$$$ ✕ **Kollias.** Friendly owner Tassos Kollias creates his own dishes, ranging from the humble to the aristocratic: grilled scorpion fish flavored with mastic; lobster with lemon, balsamic vinegar, and a shot of honey; mussels stuffed with rice, grapes, and pine nuts. The large mixed salads include one with white beets, arugula, parsley, caper leaves, endive, and radishes. A fitting end to the meal: *loukoumades* (sweet fritters), best with the kumquat liqueur. ⊠ *Stratigou Plastira 3, Piraeus,* ☎ *01/461–9150. Reservations essential weekends. AE, DC, MC, V. Closed Sun. and Aug. No lunch.*

$$ ✕ **Ta Tria Tetarta.** A bit more upscale than most mezedopolia, Tria Tetarta serves a large variety of unusual appetizers in a tri-level stone and wood house, decorated with eye-catching *objets* and antiques. Try the spicy feta sprinkled with red pepper and roasted in foil; spinach crepes with tomato, basil, and yogurt; skewered *seftalies* (seasoned meat dumplings); and the seafood pie. ⊠ *Oikonomou 25, Exarchia,* ☎ *01/823–0560. Reservations essential. No credit cards. Closed Aug. No lunch Mon.–Sat.*

$$ ✕ **Vitrina.** From the stenciled bread baskets to the door handles on the
★ chair backs, it's obvious this restaurant concentrating on Aegean-inspired cooking is the creation of a fashion photographer. The combinations are bold: crayfish with coffee and coriander, scallops sautéed in mastic and lemon, grilled lamb ribs with grapefruit, honey, and buttermilk. If it's in season, sample the delicate chestnut mousse for dessert. Seating upstairs is best; downstairs is a bit claustrophobic. ⊠ *Navarchou Apostoli 7, Psirri,* ☎ *01/321–1200. Reservations essential. No credit cards. Closed Mon. and mid-June–Sept. No lunch Tues.–Sat.; no dinner Sun.*

$$ ✕ **Vlassis.** Relying on recipes from Thrace, Roumeli, Thessaly, and the
★ islands, the chefs whip up Greek home cooking in generous portions. Musts are the *pastitsio* (baked minced lamb and macaroni) with bits of liver, the *lahanodolmades* (cabbage rolls), and the octopus *stifado* (stew), tender and sweet with lots of onions. The king-size *galaktobouriko* (custard in phyllo) will leave you with a smile on your face. ⊠ *Paster 8, Platia Mavili (near American embassy),* ☎ *01/646–3060. Reservations essential. No credit cards. Closed Sun. and late July–mid-Sept. No lunch.*

$$ ✕ **Xynos.** Enter a time warp in this Plaka taverna: Athens in the '50s. The excellent food is still the same. Start with stuffed grape leaves, then move on to the taverna's forte, such cooked dishes as *tsoutsoukakia,* spicy meat patties with cinnamon. Nightly, a guitar duo drops by to charm the crowd with old Greek ballads. ⊠ *Aggelou Geronta 4, Plaka (entrance down walkway next to Kafenion Glikis),* ☎ *01/322–1065. No credit cards. Closed weekends and July. No lunch.*

$ ✕ **Karavitis.** A neighborhood favorite, this taverna near the Olympic Stadium has warm-weather garden seating and a winter dining room decorated with huge wine casks. Classic Greek cuisine is well prepared here, including pungent *tzatziki* (yogurt-garlic dip), *bekri meze* (lamb chunks in a spicy red sauce), and *stamnaki* (beef baked in a clay pot). ⊠ *Arktinou 35 and Pausaniou 4, Pangrati,* ☎ *01/721–5155. No credit cards. Closed a few days around Aug. 15. No lunch.*

$ ✕ **O Platanos.** Set in a picturesque courtyard, this is one of Plaka's old-
★ est yet least touristy tavernas. Don't miss the oven-baked potatoes, roast lamb, and exceptionally cheap but delicious barrel retsina. Although the waiters are helpful, not much English is spoken. ⊠ *Diogenous 4, Plaka,* ☎ *01/322–0666. No credit cards. Closed Sun. and 2 wks in Aug.*

$ ✕ **Sigalas-Bairaktaris.** Run by the Bairaktaris family for more than a century, this is the best place to eat in Monastiraki Square. Order the tiny *tiropites* (cheese pies) sprinkled with sesame seeds and fried zucchini with garlicky dip for appetizers, then go to the window case to view the day's *magirefta* (stove-top cooked dish, usually made earlier) or sample the gyro platter. ⊠ *Platia Monastiraki 2, Monastiraki,* ☎ *01/321–3036. AE, V.*

$ ✕ **To Ouzadiko.** If you're exploring Kolonaki's boutiques and museums, stop at this mezedopolion for the cozy interior (old posters, abundant wood, small marble tables), the friendly service, and the enticing mezedes. Depending on what the owner bought at market that morning, you may find delicious Thessaloniki mini meat pies called *tsigerosarmadakia* and juicy rooster with onions. Ouzadiko lives up to its name, serving 110 kinds of ouzo and tsipouro. ⊠ *Karneadou 25–29 in Lemos shopping mall, Kolonaki,* ☎ *01/729–5484. Reservations essential. No credit cards. Closed Sun. and Aug. 10–31.*

NIGHTLIFE AND THE ARTS

The Arts

The **Athens Festival** (box office, ⊠ Arcade at Stadiou 4, ☎ 01/322–1459) runs from late June through September with concerts, opera, ballet, folk dancing, and drama. Performances are in various locations, including the theater of Herod Atticus (Irodion) below the Acropolis and Mt. Lycabettus. Tickets range in price from 4,000 dr. to 20,000 dr. and are available a few days before the performance.

Though rather corny, the **sound-and-light shows** (⊠ Pnyx theater box office off Dionyssiou Areopagitou opposite Acropolis, ☎ 01/922–6210) beautifully display the Acropolis with dramatic lighting and a brief narrated history. Performances are given nightly from April through October, in English, at 9 PM, and admission is about 1,500 dr.

CONCERTS AND OPERAS

Greek and world-class international orchestras perform September through June at the **Megaron Athens Concert Hall** (⊠ Vas. Sofias and Kokkali, ☎ 01/728–2333, FAX 01/728–2300). Information and tickets are available from the Megaron weekdays 10–4; prices range from 2,500 dr. to 20,000 dr. The Megaron also has a downtown box office (⊠ Arcade at Stadiou 4).

DANCE

The lively **Dora Stratou Troupe** (⊠ theater, Filopappou Hill, ☎ 01/921–4650; 01/324–4395 offices, FAX 01/324–6921; ☉ performances mid-May–Sept., Tues.–Sun. 10:15 PM, also 8:15 PM Wed. and Sun.) performs Greek and Cypriot folk dances in authentic costumes. Tickets cost 3,000 dr. and are available from the box office before the show.

FILM

Almost all Athens cinemas now show foreign films; *The Athens News* and *Hellenic Times* list them in English. Tickets run about 1,800 dr.

Nightlife

Athens has an active nightlife: even at 3 AM the central squares and streets are crowded with revelers. In summer many downtown night spots move to the seaside. Ask your hotel for recommendations and check ahead for summer closings. For a uniquely Greek evening visit a club featuring *rembetika* music, a type of blues, or the popular *bouzoukia* (clubs with live bouzouki music). In the larger venues, where the food tends to be overpriced and second-rate, there is usually a per-person minimum or a prix-fixe menu; a bottle of whiskey costs about 29,000 dr.

BARS

Balthazar (⊠ Tsoha 27, Ambelokipi, ☎ 01/644–1215 or 01/645–2278), in a neoclassical house, has a lush garden courtyard and subdued music. To enjoy Greek *kefi* (high spirits), visit the always-packed **Vare-**

ladiko (⊠ Distomou and E. Zanni 1, Piraeus, ☎ 01/422–7500) where you'll see some frenzied table dancing to Greek hits. Of the new bars for the under-40 crowd, **Kingsize** (⊠ Amerikis 3, Syntagma, ☎ 01/323–2500) and **Plus Soda** (⊠ Ermou 161, Thissio, ☎ 01/345–6187) are the most popular, playing techno, progressive, and house. With low-key music and a romantic park setting, **Parko** (⊠ Eleftherias Park, Ilisia, ☎ 01/722–3784) is a summer favorite. **Folie** (⊠ Eslin 4, Ambelokipi, ☎ 01/646–9852) has a friendly crowd of all ages dancing to jazz, blues, funk, and ethnic music. Ensconced in a 1940s arcade, **Stoa Cooper** (⊠ Patission 101 and Kodrigtonos 19, ☎ 01/825–3932) lets you enjoy a quiet conversation in the glass-roofed hall or step into the fray of the split-level bar and dance to everything from rock to rembetika.

BOUZOUKIA

Diogenes Palace (⊠ Syngrou 259, Nea Smyrni, ☎ 01/942–4267) is currently the "in" place with Athenians who want to hear Greece's singing stars, such as Antonis Vardis and Kaiti Garbi; it's also the most expensive. Decadence reigns at **Posidonio** (⊠ Posidonios 18, Elliniko, ☎ 01/894–1033) as diners dance the seductive *tsifteteli* (the Greek version of a belly dance) with enthusiasm.

LIVE ROCK, JAZZ, BLUES

Most big names in popular music perform at the informal **Rodon Live** (⊠ Marni 24, Platia Vathis, ☎ 01/524–7427). Smaller groups play the sophisticated **Half Note** (⊠ Trivonianou 17, Mets, ☎ 01/921–3310), the laid-back **Blues Hall** (⊠ Ardittou 44, Mets, ☎ 01/924–7448), and the lively **Hi-Hat Cafe** (⊠ Dragoumi and Krousovou 1, Hilton, ☎ 01/721–8171), which has hosted such artists as Guitar Shorty and Louisiana Red.

REMBETIKA CLUBS

Rembetika, the blues sung by Asia Minor refugees who came to Greece in the 1920s, still enthralls Greeks. At **Stathmos** (⊠ Mavromateon 22, Pedion Areos, ☎ 01/883–2392), the band featuring the popular rembetis Bobis Goles usually starts off slowly, but by 1 AM is wailing to a packed dance floor. At **Stoa Athanaton** (⊠ Sofokleous 19, Central Market, ☎ 01/321–4362 or 01/321–0342), in a renovated warehouse, the authentic music is enhanced by an infectious mood and the enthusiastic participation of the audience.

SHOPPING

Antiques

Pandrossou Street in Monastiraki is especially rich in shops selling small antiques and icons. Keep in mind that there are many fakes, and that you must have permission from the government to export objects from the Classic, Hellenistic, Roman, or Byzantine periods. Serious antiques collectors should head for **Martinos** (⊠ Pandrossou 50, ☎ 01/321–2414). **Motakis** (⊠ Abyssinia Sq. 3 in basement, ☎ 01/321–9005), run by members of the same family for more than 90 years, sells antiques and other beautiful old objects. At **Nasiotis** (⊠ Ifestou 24, ☎ 01/321–2369) you may uncover interesting finds in a basement stacked with engravings, old magazines, and books, including first editions.

Flea Markets

The **Sunday morning flea market** (⊠ Pandrossou and Ifestou Sts.) sells everything from secondhand guitars to Russian caviar. However little it costs, you should haggle. **Ifestou,** where coppersmiths have their shops, is interesting on weekdays; you can pick up copper wine jugs, candlesticks, and cookware for next to nothing.

Gift Ideas

Better tourist shops sell copies of traditional Greek jewelry; silver filigree; Skyrian pottery; onyx ashtrays and dishes; woven bags; attractive rugs, including flokatis; worry beads in amber or silver; and blue-and-white amulets to ward off the *mati* (evil eye). Reasonably priced natural sponges from Kalymnos also make good gifts. **George Goutis** (⊠ Pandrossou 40, Monastiraki, ☎ 01/321–3212) has an eclectic assortment of costumes, embroidery, and old, handcrafted silver items. At **Riza** (⊠ Voukourestiou 35 and Skoufa, Kolonaki, ☎ 01/361–1157) you can pick up wonderful handmade lace in romantic designs, unusual fabric at good prices, and such decorative items as handblown glass bowls. **Mati** (⊠ Voukourestiou 20, Syntagma, ☎ 01/362–6238) has finely designed amulets to battle the evil eye, as well as a collection of monastery lamps and candlesticks. **Karamichos Mazaraki** (⊠ Voulis 31–33, Syntagma, ☎ 01/323–9428) offers a large selection of flokatis that they will insure and ship to your home. **Pylarinos** (⊠ Stadiou 6, Syntagma, ☎ 01/321–0384) carries Greek coins and stamps, as well as catalogs for collectors. For an inexpensive gift pick up some freshly ground Greek coffee at **Misseyiannis** (⊠ Levendis 7, Kolonaki, ☎ 01/721–0136).

Handicrafts

The **National Welfare Organization** (⊠ Vas. Sofias 135, across from Athens Tower, ☎ 01/646–0603; ⊠ Ipatias 6 and Apollonos, Plaka, ☎ 01/321–8272) displays work by Greek craftspeople—stunning handwoven carpets, flat-weave kilims, tapestries from original designs, hand-embroidered tablecloths, ceramics, and flokatis. The **Center of Hellenic Tradition** (⊠ Mitropoleos 59 or Pandrossou 36, Monastiraki, ☎ 01/321–3023) is another outlet for quality handicrafts. The Greek cooperative **EOMMEX** (⊠ Mitropoleos 9, Syntagma, ☎ 01/323–0408) operates a showroom with folk and designer rugs made by more than 30 weavers around the country.

Jewelry

Prices for gold and silver are much lower in Greece than in many Western countries, and jewelry is of high quality. Many shops in Plaka carry original-design pieces available at a good price if you bargain hard enough. The more expensive **LALAoUNIS** (⊠ Panepistimiou 6, Syntagma, ☎ 01/362–4354) showcases pieces by the world-famous Ilias Lalaounis, who takes his ideas from nature, biology, and ancient Greek pieces. **Zolotas** (⊠ Pandronou 8, Plaka, ☎ 01/323–2413; ⊠ Stadiou 9, Syntagma, ☎ 01/322–1222) is noted for its superb museum copies. The **Benaki Museum gift shop** (⊠ Koumbari and Vas. Sofias, Kolonaki, ☎ 01/362–7367) has finely rendered copies of classical jewelry. The **Goulandris Cycladic Museum** (⊠ Neofitou Douka 4, Kolonaki, ☎ 01/724–9706) carries good jewelry reproductions.

SIDE TRIPS

Mikrolimano

The pretty, crescent-shape harbor of Mikrolimano is famous for its many seafood restaurants. Although it has become increasingly touristy, its delightful atmosphere remains intact, and the harbor is crowded with elegant yachts. If you don't like seafood, you'll still be enchanted by the terraces of lovely houses tucked up against the hillsides. Take the Metro from Monastiraki Square to the Neo Faliron train station; it's only five minutes' walk from there.

Moni Kaisarini

★ Outside central Athens, on the slopes of Mt. Ymittos (ancient Mt. Hymettus), stands Moni Kaisarini (Kaisarini Monastery), one of the city's most evocative Byzantine remains. The well-restored 11th-century monastery, built on the site of a sanctuary of Aphrodite, has some beautiful frescoes dating from the 17th century. Nearby is a basilica and a picnic site with a superb panorama of the Acropolis and Piraeus. Take a taxi or bus 224 (in front of the Byzantine museum) to the end of the line, then walk 35 minutes along the paved road that climbs Mt. Ymittos. ⊠ *Ethnikis Antistaseos,* ☎ *01/723–6619.* ⊙ *Monastery, Tues.–Sun. 8:30–2:45; grounds, daily sunrise–sunset.*

ATHENS ESSENTIALS

Arriving and Departing

BY BOAT

Most ships from the Greek islands dock at Piraeus (port authority ☎ 01/422–6000, 01/451–1311), 10 km (6 mi) from the center. From the main harbor you can take the nearby Metro right into Omonia Square. The trip takes 25 minutes and costs 150 dr. Alternatively, you can take a taxi, which takes longer because of traffic and costs around 1,700 dr. Often the driver will wait until he fills the taxi with several passengers headed in the same direction. It's faster to walk to the main street and hail a cab from there. If you arrive by hydrofoil in the smaller port of Zea Marina, take Bus 905 or Trolley 20 to the Metro. At Rafina port (☎ 0294/22–300), which serves some of the closer Cyclades, you will have difficulty finding a taxi. Take a KTEL bus instead (slightly uphill from the port); they leave every 30 minutes from 5:40 AM until 9:30 PM, ☎ 460 dr.

BY BUS

Greek buses arrive either at Terminal A (⊠ Kifissou 100, ☎ 01/512–4910) or Terminal B (⊠ Liossion 260, you must call each regional counter for information; EOT provides a phone list ☞ Visitor Information, *below*). From Terminal A, take Bus 051 to Omonia Square; from Terminal B, take Bus 24 downtown. To get to the stations, catch Bus 051 at Zinonos and Menandrou off Omonia Square and Bus 024 on Amalias Avenue in front of the National Gardens. International buses drop their passengers off on the street, usually in the Omonia or Syntagma Square areas or at Stathmos Peloponnisos.

BY CAR

Whether you approach Athens from the Peloponnese or from the north, you enter by the Ethniki Odos (or National Road, as the main highways going north and south are known) and then follow signs for the center. Leaving Athens, routes to the National Road are well marked; signs usually name Lamia for the north and Corinth or Patras for the southwest.

BY PLANE

All travel visitors arrive by air at **Ellinikon Airport** (⊠ Vas. Georgiou B' 1, ☎ 01/936–3363 for West Terminal, ☎ 01/969–4466 for East Terminal). The airport lies about 10 km (6 mi) from the city center. Olympic Airways flights, international and domestic, use the West Terminal, and all other flights arrive and depart from the East Terminal.

Between the Airport and Downtown. A **bus** service connects the two air terminals, Syntagma Square, Omonia Square, and Piraeus. Between the terminals and Athens, the express bus (No. 091) runs around the clock, about every 30 minutes during the day, hourly at night. You can catch the bus on Syntagma Square in front of McDonalds or off

Omonia Square on Stadiou and Aeolou. From the airport terminals to Piraeus (Karaiskaki Sq.), the express bus (No. 019) leaves about every hour, day and night. The fare is 200 dr., 400 dr. after midnight (check with EOT, ☞ *below,* for night schedules). It's easier to take **taxis**: about 2,000 dr. to Piraeus; 1,000 dr. between terminals; 2,200 dr. to the center, more if there is traffic. The price goes up by about two thirds between midnight and 5 AM.

BY TRAIN

Athens has two railway stations, side by side, not far from Omonia Square. International trains from the north use **Stathmos Larissis** (☎ 01/823–7741). Take Trolley 1 from the terminal to Omonia Square. Trains from the Peloponnese use the marvelously ornate **Stathmos Peloponnisos** (☎ 01/513–1601). To Omonia and Syntagma squares take Bus 057. As the phones are almost always busy, it's easier to get departure times from the main information phone service (☞ By Train *in* Transportation, *above*) or buy tickets at a **railway office** downtown. ✉ *Sina 6,* ☎ *01/362–4402 through 01/362–4406;* ✉ *Filellinon 17,* ☎ *01/323–6747 or 01/323–6273; or* ✉ *Karolou 1,* ☎ *01/522–4302 for the Peloponnese, 01/522–2491 for northern Greece.*

Getting Around

Many of the sights and most of the hotels, cafés, and restaurants are within a fairly small central area. It's easy to walk everywhere, though sidewalks are often obstructed by cars parked by desperately frustrated drivers.

BY BUS

EOT (☞ Visitor Information, *below*) can provide bus information, as can the Organization for Public Transportation (✉ Metsovou 15, ☎ 01/883–6076, ◷ weekdays 7:30–3, and Metsovou 185, ◷ weekdays 7:30–3 and 7 PM–9 PM). The fare on buses and trolleys is 100 dr., and monthly passes are sold at the beginning of each month for 6,000 dr. (bus and trolley). Purchase tickets beforehand at curbside kiosks or from booths at terminals. Validate your ticket in the orange machines when you board to avoid a fine. Buses run from the center to all suburbs and nearby beaches from 5 AM until about midnight. For suburbs beyond central Kifissia, change at Kifissia. Most buses to the east Attica coast, including those for Sounion (☎ 01/823–0179; ▭ 1,150 dr. inland route, 1,200 dr. on coastal road) and Marathon (☎ 01/821–0872; ▭ 700 dr.), leave from the KTEL terminal (✉ Platia Aigyptiou, corner Mavromateon St. and Alexandras Ave.).

BY METRO

An electric (partially underground) railway runs from Piraeus to Omonia Square and then on to Kifissia, with downtown stops at Thission, Monastiraki, Omonia, and Platia Victorias (near the National Archaeological Museum). The standard fare is 100 dr. or 150 dr., depending on the number of zones traveled. You can buy a monthly pass covering the Metro, buses, and trolleys for 8,000 dr. at the beginning of each month. Validate your ticket by stamping it in the orange machines at the entrance to the platforms, or you will be fined.

BY TAXI

Although you will eventually find an empty taxi, it's often faster to call out your destination to one already carrying passengers; if the taxi is going in that direction, the driver will pick you up. Most drivers speak basic English. The meter starts at 200 dr., and even if you join other passengers, you must add this amount to your final charge. There is a basic charge of 66 dr. per km (½ mi); this increases to 130 dr. between midnight and 5 AM. There are surcharges for holidays (100 dr.), pickups from, not to, the airport (300 dr.) and from the port, train stations, and bus terminals (160 dr.) There is also a 55 dr. charge for each suitcase over 10 kilograms (22 pounds). Waiting time is 2,200 dr. per hour. Some drivers overcharge foreigners; make sure they turn on the meter and use the high tariff ("Tarifa 2") only after midnight. You can also call a radio taxi, which charges an additional 400 dr. for the pickup. Some reliable services are Kosmos (☎ 1300), Ermis (☎ 01/411–5200 and 01/411–5660), and Parthenon (☎ 01/581–4711 and 01/582–1292).

Money Matters

CURRENCY

The Greek monetary unit is the drachma (dr.). Banknotes are in denominations of 100, 200, 500, 1,000, 5,000, and 10,000 dr.; coins, 5, 10, 20, 50, and 100. At press time (spring 1998), there were approximately 307 dr. to the U.S. dollar, 213 dr. to the Canadian dollar, 510 dr. to the pound sterling, 197 dr. to the Australian dollar, and 170 dr. to the New Zealand dollar. Daily exchange rates are prominently displayed in banks.

Telephoning

COUNTRY CODE

The country code for Greece is 30. When dialing Greece from outside the country, drop the first zero in the regional telephone code.

Contacts and Resources

EMBASSIES

United States (✉ Vasilissis Sofias 91, ☎ 01/721–2951). **Canadian** (✉ Gennadiou 4, ☎ 01/725–4011). **United Kingdom** (✉ Ploutarchou 1, ☎ 01/723–6211).

EMERGENCIES

Police: Tourist police (✉ Dimitrakopoulou 77, Koukaki, ☎ 171); for auto accidents call city police (☎ 100). **Fire** (☎ 199). **Ambulance** (☎ 166, but a taxi is often faster). Not all hospitals are open nightly (☎ 106 for a Greek listing); ask your hotel to check for you. **Doctor:** Most hotels will call one for you; or contact your embassy. A Greek recording (☎ 105) lists doctors available 2 PM–7 AM, Sunday, and holidays. **Dentist:** Ask your hotel or embassy. **Pharmacy:** Many pharmacies in the central area have someone who speaks English. Try **Mantika** (✉ Stadiou 41 between Omonia and Syntagma, ☎ 01/331–2060, –2061). For information on late-night pharmacies dial 107 (Greek) or check the *Athens News.*

ENGLISH-LANGUAGE BOOKSTORES

Booknest (✉ Folia tou Bibliou, Panepistimiou 25–29, ☎ 01/322–9560). **Compendium** (✉ Nikis 28, upstairs, ☎ 01/322–1248). **Eleftheroudakis** (✉ Nikis 4, near Syntagma, ☎ 01/322–9388; and their main store at ✉ Panepistimiou 17, ☎ 01/331–4180). **Pantelides** (✉ Amerikis 9–11, ☎ 01/362–3673).

GUIDED TOURS

Excursions. The choice is almost unlimited. A one-day tour to Delphi will cost 19,500 dr., with lunch included, 17,000 without lunch; a two-day tour to Mycenae, Nauplion, and Epidaurus, around 30,400 dr., including half board in first-class hotels; and a full-day cruise from Piraeus, visiting the islands of Aegina, Poros, and Hydra costs around 18,000 dr., including buffet lunch on the ship.

Orientation. All tour operators offer a four-hour morning bus tour of Athens, including a guided tour of the Acropolis and its museum (9,300 dr.). Make reservations at your hotel or at a travel agency; many are situated around Filellinon and Nikis streets off Syntagma Square.

Personal Guides. All the major tourist agencies can provide English-speaking guides for personally organized tours, or call the **Union of Guides** (✉ Apollonas 9A, ☎ 01/322–9705, FAX 01/323–9200). Hire only those licensed by the EOT.

Special-Interest. For folk dancing take a four-hour evening tour (April–October; 9,000 dr.) that begins with a sound-and-light show of the Acropolis and then goes on to a performance of Greek folk dances in the open-air theater nearby. Another tour offers a dinner show at a taverna in the Plaka area, after the sound and light, for around 12,500 dr. Any travel agency can arrange these tours for you, but for the most efficient service, go first to **CHAT Tours**(☞ Travel Agencies, *below*). For those who want organized adventure travel, contact **Trekking Hellas** and **F-Zein**(☞ Travel Agencies, *below*).

Travel Agencies

American Express (✉ Ermou 2, ☎ 01/324–4975, FAX 01/322–7893). **CHAT Tours** (✉ Stadiou 4, ☎ 01/322–2886, FAX 01/323–5270). **Condor Travel** (✉ Stadiou 43, ☎ 01/321–2453 or 01/321–6986, FAX 01/321–4296). **Key Tours** (✉ Kallirois 4, ☎ 01/923–3166, FAX 01/923–2008). **Travel Plan** (✉ Christou Lada 9, ☎ 01/323–8801, FAX 01/322–2152). **Trekking Hellas** (✉ Fillelinon 7, 3rd floor, ☎ 01/331–0323, FAX 01/323–4548; offices also in Thessaloniki and Kalambaka). **F-Zein** (✉ Syngrou 132, 5th floor, ☎ 01/921–6285, FAX 01/922–9995).

Visitor Information

EOT (✉ Amerikis 2, near Syntagma, ☎ 01/331–0561; ✉ East Terminal—Arrivals—of Ellinikon Airport, ☎ 01/961–2722 and 01/969–4500; ✉ Piraeus, EOT Building, 1st floor, Zea Marina, ☎ 01/452–2591).

4 Barcelona

Barcelona, capital of Catalunya (Catalonia), thrives on its business acumen and industrial muscle. The hardworking citizens of this thriving metropolis are proud to have and use their own language—street names, museum exhibits, newspapers, radio programs, and movies are all in Catalan. An important milestone here was the city's long-awaited opportunity to host the Olympic Games, in summer 1992; the Olympics were of singular importance in Barcelona's modernization. Their legacy includes a vastly improved ring road and several other highways; four new beaches; and an entire new neighborhood in what used to be the run-down industrial district of Poble Nou. In addition, the promontory of Montjuïc has a new sports stadium, several swimming pools, and an adjoining marina. Few cities can rival the medieval atmosphere of the Gothic Quarter's narrow alleys, the elegance and distinction of the Moderniste (Art Nouveau) Eixample, or the many fruits of Gaudí's whimsical imagination. Extraordinarily endowed with 2,000 years of art and architecture, Barcelona remains a world center for design.

EXPLORING BARCELONA

Numbers in the margin correspond to points of interest on the Barcelona map.

It should take you two full days of sightseeing to complete the following tour. The first part covers the Gothic Quarter, the Picasso Museum, and the Rambla. The second part takes you to Passeig de Gràcia and the church of the Sagrada Família; and the third, to Montjuïc.

The Barri Gòtic (Gothic Quarter) and La Rambla

★ ❶ **Catedral de la Seu** (Cathedral). Citizens of Barcelona gather on Sunday morning to dance the *sardana,* a symbol of Catalan identity, on Plaça de la Seu, in front of the cathedral. The elaborate Gothic structure was built between 1298 and 1450, though the spire and Gothic facade were not added until 1892. Inside, highlights are the beautifully carved **choir stalls;** Santa Eulàlia's tomb, in the crypt; the battle-scarred crucifix from Don Juan's galley in the naval battle of Lepanto, in the **Capella de Lepanto** (Lepanto Chapel); and the cloisters. ⊠ *Plaça de la Seu,* ☎ *93/315–1554.* ⊞ *Free.* ☉ *Daily 7:45–1:30 and 4–7:45.*

❶❷ **Gran Teatre del Liceu.** Barcelona's famous opera house was tragically gutted by fire in 1994 and is scheduled to reopen in early 1999. Built between 1845 and 1847, the Liceu claims to be the world's oldest opera house and was also one of the world's most beautiful, with ornamental gilt and plush red-velvet fittings. Anna Pavlova danced here in 1930, and Maria Callas sang here in 1959. If the theater is still closed, you can arrange a visit to the rooms that were not damaged. ⊠ *Rambla, corner of C. de Sant Pau,* ☎ *93/318–9122.*

❾ **Monument a Colom** (Columbus Monument). You can ride an elevator to the top for a commanding view of the city and port. Columbus faces out to sea, pointing, ironically, east toward Naples. Nearby you can board the cable car to cross the harbor to Barceloneta or catch it in the other direction up Montjuïc. ⊠ *Bottom of the Rambla.* ☉ *Tues.– Sat. 10–2 and 3:30–6:30, Sun. 10–7.*

❶❺ **Museu d'Art Contemporani** (MACBA; Museum of Contemporary Art). Designed by American Richard Meier, the new contemporary-art museum is an important addition to Barcelona's treasury of art and architecture. Located in the city's once (and still) rough-and-tumble Raval district, it and the neighboring **Centre de Cultura Contemporània** (CCCB; Center for Contemporary Culture) have reclaimed important buildings and spaces as part of the city's renewal of its historic quarters and traditional neighborhoods. ⊠ *Plaça dels Àngels 1,* ☎ *93/ 412–0810.* ☉ *Tues.–Fri. noon–8, weekends 10–3.*

❷ **Museu Frederic Marès.** Here you can browse for hours among the miscellany assembled by sculptor/collector Frederic Marès, including everything from polychrome crucifixes to hat pins, pipes, and walking sticks. ⊠ *Plaça Sant Iu 5,* ☎ *93/310–5800.* ⊞ *Free 1st Sun. of month.* ☉ *Tues.–Sat. 10–5, Sun. 10–2.*

❶❶ **Museu Marítim** (Maritime Museum). Housed in the 13th-century Drassanes Reiales (Royal Shipyards), this museum is packed with ships, figureheads, and nautical paraphernalia. You can pore over early navigation charts, including a map by Amerigo Vespucci and the 1439 chart of Gabriel de Valseca, the oldest chart in Europe. ⊠ *Plaça Portal de la Pau 1,* ☎ *93/318–3245.* ⊞ *Free 1st Sun. of every month.* ☉ *Tues.– Sat. 10–2 and 4–7, Sun. 10–2.*

54

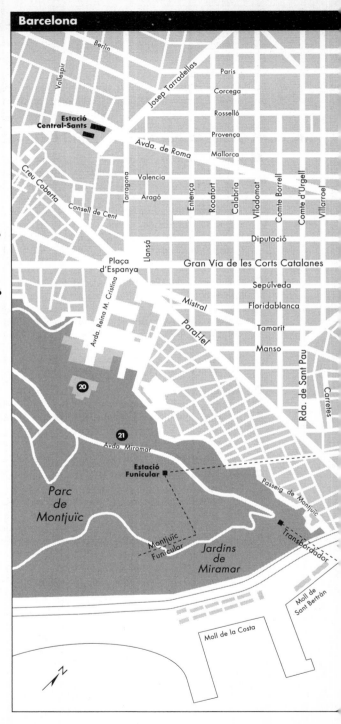

Barcelona

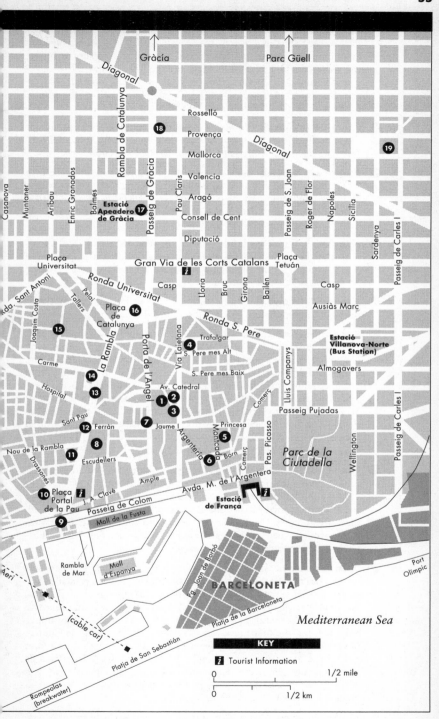

★ ❺ **Museu Picasso.** Two 15th-century palaces provide a striking setting for these collections of Picasso's early art, donated in 1963 and 1970 by Picasso's secretary and then by the artist himself. The works range from childhood sketches to exhibition posters done in Paris shortly before the artist's death. In rare abundance are the Rose Period and Blue Period paintings and the variations on Velázquez's *Las Meninas.* ✉ *Carrer Montcada 1519,* ☎ *93/319–6310.* 🎫 *Free 1st Sun. of the month.* ⊙ *Tues.–Sat. 10–8, Sun. 10–3.*

★ ❹ **Palau de la Música** (Palace of Music). Attend a performance at Domènech i Montaner's fantastic Moderniste concert house. ✉ *Sant Francesc de Paula 2, off Via Laietana,* ☎ *93/268–1000.*

⓮ **Palau de la Virreina.** Built by a one-time Spanish viceroy to Peru in 1778, this building is now a major exhibition center. Check to see what's showing while you're in town. ✉ *Rambla de les Flors 99,* ☎ *93/301– 7775.* ⊙ *Tues.–Sat. 10–2 and 4:30–9, Sun. 10–2, Mon. 4:30–9. Last entrance 30 min before closing.*

★ ⓫ **Palau Güell.** Gaudí built this mansion between 1885 and 1890 for his patron, Count Eusebi de Güell. It's the only Gaudí house open to the public and one of the highlights on the Ruta Modernista. ✉ *Nou de la Rambla 3.* ⊙ *Tues.–Sat. 10–1:30 and 4–7:30.*

⓰ **Plaça de Catalunya.** This intersection is the business center and transport hub of the modern city. ✉ *Top of the Rambla.*

❸ **Plaça del Rei.** Several historic buildings surround what is widely considered the most beautiful square in the Gothic Quarter. Following Columbus's first voyage to America, the Catholic Kings received him in the **Saló de Tinell,** a magnificent banquet hall built in 1362. Other ancient buildings around the square are the **Palau del Lloctinent** (Lieutenant's Palace); the 14th-century **Capella de Santa Àata** (Chapel of St. Agatha), built right into the Roman city wall; and the **Palau Padellàs** (Padellàs Palace), which houses the **Museu d'Historia de la Ciutat** (City History Museum). ✉ *Plaça del Rei,* ☎ *93/315–1111,* ⊙ *Tues.–Sat. 10–2 and 4–8, Sun. 10–2.*

❽ **Plaça Reial.** In this splendid 19th-century square, arcaded houses overlook the wrought-iron **Font de les Tres Gràcies** (Fountain of the Three Graces) and lampposts designed by a young Gaudí in 1879. Despite the preponderance of substance users, abusers, and peddlers here, Plaça Reial retains its elegance; the most colorful time to come is Sunday morning, when crowds gather at the stamp and coin stalls and listen to soapbox orators. ✉ *C. Colom, off Rambla.*

❼ **Plaça Sant Jaume.** This impressive square in the heart of the Gothic Quarter was built in the 1840s, but the two imposing buildings facing each other across it are much older. The 15th-century **ajuntament** (city hall), has an impressive black and gold mural (1928) by Josep María Sert (who also painted the murals in New York's Waldorf-Astoria) and the famous **Saló de Cent,** the first European parliament, from which the Council of One Hundred ruled the city from 1372 to 1714. To visit the interior, you'll need to arrange permission in the protocol office. The **Palau de la Generalitat,** seat of the Autonomous Catalonian Government, is a 15th-century palace open to the public on special days or by arrangement. ✉ *Meeting of C. de Ferràn and C. Jaume I.*

⓭ **Rambla St. Josep.** This stretch of the boulevard is one of the most fascinating. The colorful paving stones on the Plaça de la Boquería were designed by Joan Miró. Glance up at the swirling Moderniste dragon and the Art Nouveau street lamps; then take a look inside the bustling **Boquería Market** and the **Antiga Casa Figueras,** a vintage pastry shop on the corner of Petxina, with a splendid mosaic facade. ⊠ *Between Pl. de la Boquería and Rambla de les Flors.*

★ ❻ **Santa Maria del Mar** (St. Mary of the Sea). Simply the best example of Mediterranean Gothic architecture, this church is widely considered Barcelona's loveliest. It was built between 1329 and 1383 in fulfillment of a vow made a century earlier by James I to build a church for the Virgin of the Sailors. The structure's simple beauty is enhanced by a stunning rose window and magnificent soaring columns. ⊠ *Plaça Santa Maria.* ☉ *Weekdays 9–12:30 and 5–8.*

Eixample

Above the Plaça de Catalunya you enter modern Barcelona and an elegant area known as the Eixample, built during the late 19th century as part of the city's expansion scheme. Much of the building here was done at the height of the Moderniste movement, a Spanish and mainly Catalan version of Art Nouveau, whose leading exponents were the architects Luís Domènech i Montaner, Josep Puig i Cadafalch, and Antoni Gaudí. The principal thoroughfares are the Rambla de Catalunya and the Passeig de Gràcia, on which stand some of the city's most elegant shops and cafés. Moderniste houses are among Barcelona's special drawing cards. For the Ruta Modernista tour of the city's main Art Nouveau sights, stop at the Casa Lleó Morera (⊠ Passeig de Gràcia 35, 3rd floor).

★ ⓲ **Casa Milà** (⊠ Passeig de Gràcia 92). This Gaudí house is known as **La Pedrera** (stone quarry). Its remarkable curving stone facade, with ornamental balconies, ripples its way around the corner of the block. In the attic of La Pedrera is the superb **Espai Gaudí,** Barcelona's only museum dedicated exclusively to the architect's work. ⊠ *Provença 261,* ☎ *93/484–5995.* ☉ *Tues.–Sun. 10–8; guided tours Tues.–Fri. 6 PM.*

⓱ **Mançana de la Discòrdia** (Block of Discord). The name is a pun on the word *mançana,* which means both "block" and "apple." The houses here are quite fantastic: the floral **Casa Lleó Morera** (No. 35) is by Domènech i Montaner, the pseudo-Gothic **Casa Amatller** (No. 41) is by Puig i Cadafalch, and No. 43 is Gaudí's **Casa Batlló.** ⊠ *Passeig de Gràcia, between Consell de Cent and Aragó.*

★ ⓳ **Temple Expiatori de la Sagrada Família** (Expiatory Church of the Holy Family). Barcelona's most eccentric landmark, designed by Gaudí, was far from finished at his death in 1926, when he was run over by a tram and died unrecognized in a pauper's hospital. This striking creation causes consternation, wonder, shrieks of protest, and cries of rapture. In 1936, during the Spanish Civil War, Barcelona's Anarchists loved their crazy temple enough to spare it from the flames that engulfed so many of the city's other churches. An elevator takes visitors to the top of one of the towers for a magnificent view of the city. Gaudí is buried in the crypt. ⊠ *C. de Sardenya between C. de Mallorca and C. de Provença,* ☎ *93/ 455–0247.* ☉ *Sept.–May, daily 9–7; June–Aug., daily 9–9.*

Montjuïc

The hill of Montjuïc is thought to have been named for the Jewish cemetery once located there. Montjuïc has a fortress, an amusement park, delightful gardens, a model Spanish village, an illuminated fountain, the recently rebuilt Mies van der Rohe Pavilion, and a cluster of museums—all of which could keep you busy for several days. Montjuïc was the principal site of the 1992 Olympics.

★ ㉑ **Fundació Miró** (Miró Foundation). A gift from the artist Joan Miró to his native city, this is one of Barcelona's most exciting galleries, with many of its exhibition spaces devoted to Miró's droll, colorful works. ⊠ *Av. de Miramar,* ☎ *93/329–1908.* ⊘ *Tues., Wed, Fri., Sat. 11–7, Thurs. 9:30–7, Sun. 10:30–2:30.*

★ ⑳ **Museu Nacional d'Art de Catalunya** (National Museum of Catalan Art). In the **Palau Nacional** atop a long flight of steps up from the Plaça Espanya, the collection of Romanesque and Gothic art treasures, medieval frescoes, and altarpieces—most from small churches and chapels in the Pyrenees—is simply staggering. The museum's last renovation was directed by architect Gae Aulenti, who also remodeled the Musée d'Orsay, in Paris. ⊠ *Montjuïc,* ☎ *93/423–7199.* ⊘ *Tues–Sat. 10–7; Thurs. 10–9; Sun. 10–2:20.*

Elsewhere in Barcelona

★ **Parc Güell.** This park at the north end of town is Gaudí's magical attempt at creating a garden city. ⊠ *C. D'Olot s/n,* ⊘ *May–Aug., daily 10–9; Sept.–Apr., daily 10–7.*

Gràcia. This small, once-independent village within the city is a warren of narrow streets whose names change at every corner. Here you'll find tiny shops that sell everything from old-fashioned tin lanterns to feather dusters. ⊠ *Around C. Gran de Gràcia above Diagonal.*

Barceloneta. Take a stroll around the old fishermen's quarter, built in 1755. There are no-frills fish restaurants on the Passeig Joan de Borbó. Hike out to the end of the *rompeolas* (breakwater), extending 4 km (2½ mi) southeast into the Mediterranean, for a panoramic view of the city and a few breaths of fresh air. The modernized port is home to the Aquarium, one of Europe's best; the Maregmagnum shopping center; the IMAX wide-format cinema; the newly opened World Trade Center; and numerous bars and restaurants. The 1992 Olympic Village, now a hot tapas and nightlife spot, is up the beach to the north and is easily identifiable by the enormous, gold, Frank Gehry–designed fish sculpture next to the Hotel Arts. ⊠ *Below Estació de França and Ciutadella Park.*

BULLFIGHTING

Barcelona's bullring is the **Monumental** (⊠ Gran Via and Carles I), where bullfights are held on Sunday between March and October; check the newspaper for details. For tickets with no markup, go to the official ticket office (⊠ Muntaner 24, near Gran Via, ☎ 93/453–3821). There's a **Bullfighting Museum** at the ring (⊘ Mar.–Oct., daily 10–1 and 5:30–7).

DINING

RATINGS

Spanish restaurants are officially classified from five forks down to one fork, with most places earning two or three forks. In our rating system, prices are per person and include a first course, main course, and dessert, but not wine or tip. Sales tax (IVA) is usually included in the menu price; check the menu for *IVA incluído* or *IVA no incluído.* When it's not included, an additional 7% will be added to your bill. Most restaurants offer a prix-fixe menu called a *menú del día;* however, this is often offered only at lunch, and dinner tends to be a reheated version of the same. *Menús* are usually the cheapest way to eat; à la carte dining is more expensive. Service charges are never added to your bill; leave around 10%, less in $ restaurants and bars. Major centers such as Madrid, Barcelona, Marbella, and Seville tend to be a bit more expensive.

CATEGORY	COST
$$$$	over 9,000 ptas.
$$$	6,000 ptas.–9,000 ptas.
$$	3,000 ptas.–6,000 ptas.
$	under 3,000 ptas.

$$$$ ✕ **Beltxenea.** There's an air of intimacy in this redecorated Eixample apartment, now converted into a series of elegant dining rooms. In summer you can dine outside, in the formal garden. Chef Miguel Ezcurra's excellent cuisine makes for one of Barcelona's top Basque dining opportunities; a specialty is his *merluza con kokotxas y almejas* (hake and clams fried in garlic, then simmered in stock). ⊠ *Mallorca 275*, ☎ 93/215–3024. *AE, DC, MC, V. Closed Sun. and July–Aug. No lunch Sat.*

$$$$ ✕ **Jean Luc Figueras.** Every restaurant that Jean Luc Figueras has touched has shot straight to the top of the charts, so it's no surprise that the first to bear his name has done likewise. This one, installed in a Gràcia town house that was once couturier Cristóbal Balenciaga's studio, may be the best of all. For an extra $20 or so, the taster's menu is the best choice. ⊠ *C. Santa Teresa 10*, ☎ 93/415–2877. *Reservations essential. AE, DC, MC, V. Closed Sun. No lunch Sat.*

$$$ ✕ **Agut d'Avignon.** This venerable Barcelona institution takes a bit of finding; it's near the junction of Ferràn and Avinyó, in the Gothic Quarter. The ambience is rustic, the clientele often businesspeople and politicians from the nearby Generalitat. The cuisine is traditional Catalan; try one of the game specialties in season. ⊠ *Trinitat 3*, ☎ 93/317–3693. *Reservations essential. AE, DC, MC, V.*

$$$ ✕ **La Cuineta.** This intimate restaurant, in a 17th-century house just off Plaça Sant Jaume, has a sister behind the cathedral; both specialize in Catalan nouvelle cuisine. The decor is elegant and traditional; the service, professional; and the cuisine, impeccable. ⊠ *Paradis 4*, ☎ 93/315–0111; ⊠ *Pietat 12*, ☎ 93/315–4156. *AE, DC, MC, V. Closed Mon.*

$$$ ✕ **Quo Vadis.** Just off the Rambla, near the Bogueria Market and Betlem Church, is an unimpressive facade camouflaging one of Barcelona's most respected restaurants. The much-praised cuisine includes such delicacies as *hígado de ganso con ciruelas* (goose liver with plums). ⊠ *Carme 7*, ☎ 93/317–7447. *AE, DC, MC, V. Closed Sun.*

$$$ ✕ **Tram-Tram.** With chef Isidro Soler at the helm in the kitchen and
★ Reyes Lizán as hostess and pastry chef, Tram-Tram is one of Barcelona's culinary highlights. The excursion northwest to the villagelike suburb of Sarrià is a delight. Order the taster's menu and let Isidro take care of you—you won't regret it. ⊠ *Major de Sarrià 121*, ☎ 93/204–8518. *AE, MC, V. Closed Sun. and Dec. 24–Jan. 6.*

$$ ✕ **Can Culleretes.** This picturesque old restaurant began life as a pastry shop in 1786; today it's one of the most atmospheric and reasonably priced restaurants in Barcelona. Tucked into an alley between Ferràn and Bogueria, it has three dining rooms decorated with photos of visiting celebrities; the kitchen serves real Catalan cooking and is very much a family concern. Don't be put off by the street life that might be raging outside. ⊠ *Quintana 5*, ☎ 93/317–3022. *AE, MC, V. Closed Mon. No lunch Sun.*

$$ ✕ **Los Caracoles.** Just below the Plaça Reial is Barcelona's best-known tourist haunt, crawling with Americans having a terrific time. Its walls are hung thick with photos of bullfighters and visiting celebrities; its specialties are mussels, paella, and of course, *caracoles* (snails). ⊠ *Escudellers 14*, ☎ 93/309–3185. *AE, DC, MC, V.*

$$ ✕ **Set Portes.** With plenty of Old-World charm, this delightful restau-
★ rant near the waterfront has been going strong since 1836. The cook-

ing is Catalan, the portions enormous, and specialties are paella *de pescado* (with seafood) and *zarzuela Set Portes* (a mixed grill of seafood). The restaurant serves nonstop from 1 PM to 1 AM. ✉ *Passeig Isabel II 14,* ☎ *93/319–3033. AE, DC, MC, V.*

$$ ✕ **Sopeta Una.** Dining in this delightful, small restaurant, with old-fashioned decor and intimate atmosphere, is more like eating in a private home—and you're right near the Palau de la Música. All the dishes are Catalan, and the atmosphere is genteel and middle-class. For dessert try the traditional Catalan *música,* a plate of raisins, almonds, and dried fruit served with a glass of muscatel. ✉ *Verdaguer i Callis 6,* ☎ *93/319–6131. V. Closed Sun.*

$ ✕ **Agut.** Simple, hearty Catalan fare awaits you in this unpretentious ★ restaurant in the lower reaches of the Gothic Quarter. Founded in 1924, Agut has kept its popularity. There's plenty of wine to go with the traditional home cooking, along with a family warmth that always makes the place exciting. ✉ *Gignàs 16,* ☎ *93/315–1709. AE, MC, V. Closed Mon. and July. No dinner Sun.*

$ ✕ **Egipte.** This small, friendly restaurant hidden behind the Boquería ★ Market is a real find, known better to locals than to visitors. Its traditional Catalan home cooking, huge desserts, and swift, personable service all make it a good value. ✉ *Jerusalem 12,* ☎ *93/301–6208. Reservations not accepted. AE, DC, MC, V. Closed Sun.*

$ ✕ **La Fonda.** This is one of three Camós family restaurants that offer top dining value. The other two locations are in neighboring Plaça Reial: Les Quinze Nits (✉ Plaça Reial 6) and Hostal de Rita (✉ Carrer Arago 279, near the corner of Arago and Pau Claris). Be early (1 for lunch, 8 for dinner), as long lines tend to form. ✉ *Escudellers 10,* ☎ *93/301–7515. Reservations not accepted. AE, DC, MC, V.*

NIGHTLIFE AND THE ARTS

The Arts

To find out what's on, look in the daily papers or the weekly *Guía del Ocio,* available at newsstands all over town. *Actes a la Ciutat* is a weekly list of cultural events published by the *ajuntament* and available from its information office on Plaça Sant Jaume, or at the Palau de la Virreina (☞ Exploring, *above*). The daily *El Pais* lists all events of interest on its *agenda* page.

CONCERTS

Catalans are great music lovers. Their main concert hall is the **Palau de la Música** (☞ Exploring, *above*), whose ticket office is open weekdays 11–1 and 5–8 and Saturday 5–8 only. You can usually buy tickets just before the concert. Sunday-morning concerts (11 AM) are a local tradition. Musical events are also held (free) in the Town Hall's Saló de Cent on Thursday at 8, as well as in some of Barcelona's best architectural venues, such as the church of Santa Maria del Mar and others. Barcelona's opera house, the newly rebuilt **Liceu,** should open in early 1999.

DANCE

L'Espai de Dansa i Mùsica de la Generalitat de Catalunya (✉ Travessera de Gràcia 63, ☎ 93/414–3133), usually listed simply as "L'Espai" (The Space), is now Barcelona's prime venue for ballet and contemporary dance. **El Mercat de les Flors** (✉ Lleida 59, ☎ 93/426–1875), not far from Plaça d'Espanya, always has a rich program of modern dance and theater. The **Teatre Victoria** (✉ Avda. Parallel 67, ☎ 93/443–2929) also has a good selection of dance and theater, as does the **Teatre Nacional de Catalunya** (Plaça de les Arts 1, ☎ 93/306–5706), in the Olympic Port.

FILM

More and more theaters in Barcelona regularly show foreign movies in their original languages—indicated by "v.o.," or *versión original*. Some of the most important are the Olympic Port's 15-screen **Icaria Yelmo** (Salvador Espriu 61, 93/221–7585), **Capsa** (Pau Claris 134, 93/215–7393), or the happening Gràcia neighborhood's **Verdi** (✉ Verdi 32, Gràcia, ☎ 93/237–0516).

THEATER

Most plays are in Catalan, but Barcelona is also known for its experimental theater and its mime troupes. The best-known modern theaters are the **Teatre Lliure** (✉ Montseny 47, Gràcia, ☎ 93/218–9251), **El Mercat de les Flors** (☞ Dance, *above*), **Teatre Romea** (✉ Hospital 51, ☎ 93/317–7189), **Teatre Tívoli** (✉ Casp 10, ☎ 93/412–2063), **Teatre Poliorama** (✉ Rambla Estudios 115, ☎ 93/317–7599), and **Teatre Nacional de Catalunya** (Plaça de les Arts 1, ☎ 93/900–121133).

Nightlife

BARS

Champagne Bars. *Xampanyerías* (champagne bars), serving sparkling Catalan *cava*, are something of a Barcelona specialty. **El Xampanyet** (✉ Montcada 22, ☎ 93/319–7003), just down from the Picasso Museum, has cider, cava, and tapas in a lively setting. **La Cava del Palau** (✉ Verdaguer i Callis 10, ☎ 93/310–0938), near the Palau de la Música, has a wide selection of cavas, wines, and cocktails. **La Folie** (✉ Bailén 169, ☎ 93/457–4449) is one of the best.

Cocktail Bars. The **Passeig del Born,** near the Picasso Museum, is lined with bars. **Dry Martini** (✉ Aribau 162, ☎ 93/217–5072) has more than 80 different gins. **El Copetín** (✉ Passeig del Born 19) has exciting decor and good cocktails. **El Paraigua** (Plaça Sant Miquel, Gothic Quarter, behind City Hall, ☎ 93/217–3028), serves cocktails in a stylish setting with classical music. **Ideal Cocktail Bar** (✉ Aribau 89, ☎ 93/453–1028) has good malt whiskeys. **Miramelindo** (✉ Passeig del Born 15, ☎ 93/319–5376) offers a large selection and often jazz.

Tapas Bars. Cal Pep (✉ 8 Plaça de les Olles, ☎ 93/319–6183), near Santa Maria del Mar, is a popular spot, with the best and freshest selection of tapas. **Euskal Etxea** (✉ Placeta Montcada 13, ☎ 93/310–2185), a Basque bar, has excellent tapas and atmosphere. **Carrer de la Mercé** is all tapas bars, just across from the Moll de la Fusta, from Correos (the post office) down to the Iglesia de la Mercé. **Alt Heidelberg** (✉ Ronda Universitat 5, ☎ 93/318–1032) has German beer on tap and German sausages. **Casa Tejada** (Tenor Viñas, near Plaça Francesc Macià, ☎ 93/200–7341) has some of the finest tapas in Barcelona. The tapas establishments along Passeig de Gràcia look inviting, but serve mainly prepared and microwaved fare. **Tramoia,** at the corner of Rambla de Catalunya and Gran Via, is a happy exception.

CABARET

Barcelona City Hall (✉ Rambla de Catalunya 2-4 [access through New Canadian Store], ☎ 93/317–2177) offers sophisticated shows in a beautifully decorated music hall. **Starlets** (✉ Av. Sarrià 44, ☎ 93/430–9156) has cabaret nightly.

CAFÉS AND TEAROOMS

Carrer Petritxol (from Portaferrissa to Plaça del Pi) is famous for its *chocolaterías* (serving hot chocolate, tea, coffee, and pastries) and tearooms. The **Café de l'Opera** (✉ Rambla 74, ☎ 93/317–7585; ☉ daily 10AM–2AM), across from the Liceu opera house, is a perennial hangout. **Els Quatre Gats** (✉ Montsió 3, ☎ 93/302–4140) draws a devoted crew of regulars. The traditional **Salón de Té Libre i Serra** (✉ Ronda

Sant Pere 3, ☎ 93/318–9183) has a good selection of pastries. **Salón de Té Mauri** (✉ corner of Rambla de Catalunya and Provença, ☎ 93/215–8146) is a traditional tearoom. Near the Picasso Museum, don't miss the hip **Textil Café** (✉ Montcada 1214, ☎ 93/268–2598), in the Museu Textil's lovely medieval courtyard.

DISCOS AND NIGHTCLUBS

At **Luz de Gas** (✉ Muntaner 246, ☎ 93/209–7711), guitar and soul performances are followed by wild abandon. **Otto Zutz** (✉ Lincoln 15, just below Via Augusta, ☎ 93/238–0722) is a top-ranked spot. **Up and Down** (✉ Numancia 179, ☎ 93/280–2922), pronounced "pendow," is a lively classic. **Oliver and Hardy** (✉ Diagonal 593, next to Barcelona Hilton, ☎ 93/419–3181), **La Tierra** (✉ Aribau 230, ☎ 93/200–7346), and **El Otro** (✉ Valencia 166, ☎ 93/323–6759) welcome all ages, even those over 35.

FLAMENCO

El Patio Andaluz (✉ Aribau 242, ☎ 93/209–3378) is a solid option but rather expensive. **Los Tarantos** (✉ Plaça Reial 17, ☎ 93/318–3067) was the most happening flamenco spot at press time. **Tablao del Carmen** (✉ Arcs 9, Poble Espanyol, ☎ 93/325–6895) is a solid runner-up.

JAZZ CLUBS

The **Barcelona Pipa Club** (✉ Plaça Reial 3, ☎ 93/302–4732) hosts such visiting artists as Jordi Rossy and Billy McHenry. The Gothic Quarter's **Harlem Jazz Club** (✉ Comtessa Sobradiel 8, ☎ 93/310–0755) veritably sizzles. **Jamboree** (✉ Plaça Reial 17, ☎ 93/301–7564), downstairs from Los Tarantos (☞ Flamenco, *above*), has regular jazz performances. **La Cova del Drac** (✉ Vallmajor 33, ☎ 93/200–7032) is still hot.

PORTS AND BEACHES

The Barcelona waterfront has undergone a major overhaul since 1992. The **Port Vell** (Old Port) now includes an extension of the Rambla, the **Rambla de Mar,** crossing the inner harbor from just below the Columbus Monument. This boardwalk connects the Rambla with the **Moll d'Espanya,** which comprises a shopping mall, a dozen restaurants, an aquarium, a cinema complex, and Barcelona's two yacht clubs. A walk around the Port Vell leads past the marina to Passeig Joan de Borbó, both lined with restaurants and their outdoor tables. From here you can go south out to sea along the *rompeolas,* a 3-km (2-mi) excursion, or north (left) down the San Sebastián beach to the Passeig Marítim, which leads to the **Port Olímpic.** Except for the colorful inner streets of Barceloneta, the traditional fisherman's quarter, this new construction is largely devoid of local character. Take the Golondrinas boat (☞ Getting Around, By Boat, *below*) to the end of the breakwater and walk into Barceloneta for some paella.

Beaches

Barcelona's beaches have improved and proliferated. Starting at the southern end of the city (to the right looking out to sea) is the **Platja (Beach) de Sant Sebastià,** a nudist enclave, followed by **La Barceloneta, Passeig Marítim, Port Olímpic, Nova Icaria, Bogatell,** and, at the northern tip, the **Mar Bella.** Topless bathing is the rule. Water quality is officially tested and rated as acceptable, but you should still have a careful look before you dive; some days are better than others.

SHOPPING

Elegant shopping districts are the Passeig de Gràcia, Rambla de Catalunya, and the Diagonal. For more affordable, old-fashioned, and typically Spanish-style shops, explore the area between the Rambla and Via Laietana, especially around Carrer de Ferràn. The area around Plaça del Pi from Boquería to Portaferrisa and Canuda is well stocked with youthful fashion stores and imaginative gift shops.

Barcelona has several shopping plazas: **Les Glories** (⊠ Avda. Diagonal 208, Plaça de les Glories, ☎ 93/486–0639), **L'Illa** (⊠ Diagonal 545, between Numancia and Entenza, ☎ 93/444–0000), and **Maremagnum** (⊠ Moll d'Espanya s/n, Port Vell, ☎ 93/225–8100). Try **Carrer Tuset,** north of Diagonal between Aribau and Balmes, for small boutiques.

Antiques
Carrer de la Palla and Banys Nous, in the Gothic Quarter, are lined with antiques shops where you'll find old maps, books, paintings, and furniture. An **antiques market** is held every Thursday in front of the Cathedral. The **Centre d'Antiquaris** (⊠ Passeig de Gràcia 57, ☎ 93/215–4499), has some 75 antiques stores. **Gothsland** (⊠ Consell de Cent 331, ☎ 93/488–1922) specializes in Moderniste designs.

Boutiques
Fashionable boutiques line Passeig de Gràcia and Rambla de Catalunya. Others are on Gran Via between Balmes and Pau Claris, and on the Diagonal between Ganduxer and Passeig de Gràcia. **Adolfo Domínguez** (⊠ Passeig de Gràcia 89, Valencia 245, ☎ 93/487–3687) is one of Spain's top clothing designers. **Loewe** (⊠ Passeig de Gràcia 35, Diagonal 570, ☎ 93/216–0400) is Spain's top leather store. **Joaquín Berao** (⊠ Rosselló 277, ☎ 93/218–6187) and **Zapata** (⊠ Buenos Aires 64, at Diagonal, ☎ 93/430–4785) are top jewelry dealers.

Department Stores
El Corte Inglés (⊠ Plaça de Catalunya 14, ☎ 93/302–1212; ⊠ Diagonal 617, near the María Cristina metro stop, ☎ 93/419–2828) is Barcelona's—and Spain's—great consumer emporium. L'Illa (☞ *above*) contains a **Marks & Spencer** and an **FNAC.**

Food and Flea Markets
The **Boquería Market** (⊠ on Rambla between Carme and Hospital) is a superb, colorful food market, held every day except Sunday. **Els Encants** (⊠ end of Dos de Maig, on the Plaça Glòries Catalanes), Barcelona's wild-and-woolly flea market, is held every Monday, Wednesday, Friday, and Saturday, 8–7. **Sant Antoni Market** (⊠ end of Ronda Sant Antoni) is an old-fashioned food and clothes market, best on Sunday when there's a secondhand **book market** with old postcards, press cuttings, lithographs, and prints. There's a **stamp and coin market** (⊠ Plaça Reial) on Sunday morning. An **artists' market** (⊠ Placeta del Pi, just off Rambla and Boquería) sets up on Saturday morning.

Gift Ideas
No special handicrafts are associated with Barcelona, but you'll have no trouble finding typical Spanish goods anywhere in town. **Xavier Roca i Coll** (⊠ Sant Pere mes Baix 24, off Via Laietana, ☎ 93/215–1052) specializes in silver models of Barcelona's buildings.

If your friends back home are into fashion and jewelry, you're in the right city—Barcelona makes all the headlines on Spain's booming fashion front. Barcelona and Catalonia passed along a playful sense of design even before Antoni Gaudí began creating shock waves over a century ago. A number of stores and boutiques specialize in design items (jewelry, furnishings, knickknacks). **Bd** (Barcelona Design; ⊠ Mallorca 291293, ☎ 93/458–6909) offers reproduction furniture from many designers. **Dos i Una** (⊠ Rosselló 275, ☎ 93/217–7032) is a good source of clever gifts. **Vinçon** (⊠ Passeig de Gràcia 96, ☎ 93/215–6050) has a huge selection of stylish housewares.

BARCELONA ESSENTIALS

Arriving and Departing

BY BUS

Barcelona has no central bus station, but all buses operate either from the old Estació Vilanova, generally known as **Estació del Norte** (⊠ end of Av. Vilanova, ☎ 93/893–5312) or from the **Estació Autobuses de Sants** (⊠ C. Viriato, next to Sants Central train terminal, ☎ 93/490–0202). **Julià** (⊠ Ronda Universitat 5, ☎ 93/317–6454) runs buses to Zaragoza and Montserrat. **Alsina Graëlls** (⊠ Ronda Universitat 4, ☎ 93/265–6866) runs to Lérída and Andorra.

BY PLANE

All international and domestic flights arrive at **El Prat de Llobregat** airport (☎ 93/478–5000 or 93/478–5032), 14 km (8½ mi) south of Barcelona just off the main highway to Castelldefels and Sitges. For information on arrival and departure times, call the airport or Info-Iberia (☎ 93/412–5667).

Between the Airport and Downtown. The airport-to-city **train** leaves every 30 minutes between 6:30 AM and 11 PM, costs about 350 ptas., and reaches the Barcelona Central (Sants) Station in 15 minutes and Plaça de Catalunya, in the heart of the old city (at the head of La Rambla), in 20–25 minutes. From there a short taxi hop of 350–500 ptas. will take you from Plaça Catalunya to most of central Barcelona's hotels. The **Aerobus** service connects the airport with Plaça Catalunya every 15 minutes between 6:25 AM and 11 PM; the fare of 475 ptas. can be paid with all international credit cards. RENFE also provides a bus service to the Central Station during the night hours. A **taxi** from the airport to your hotel, including airport and luggage surcharges, will cost about 3,000 ptas.

BY TRAIN

The **Sants Central Station** (⊠ Plaça Països Catalans, ☎ 93/490–0202, 24-hr RENFE information line) is Barcelona's main train station, serving international and national destinations as well as suburban areas. The old and elegant **Estació de França** (⊠ Av. Marquès de l'Argentera, ☎ 93/490–0202, 24-hr RENFE information) now serves as the main terminal for certain trains to France and some express trains to points in Spain. Inquire at the tourist office (☞ Visitor Information, *in* Contacts and Resources, *below*) for current travel information and to find out which station you need. Many trains also stop at the **Passeig de Gràcia underground station** (⊠ Passeig de Gràcia and C. Aragó, ☎ 93/488–0236); this station is closer to the Plaça de Catalunya and Rambla area than Sants. Tickets and information are available here, but luggage carts are not.

Getting Around

Modern Barcelona, the Eixample—above the Plaça de Catalunya—is built on a grid system, but there's no helpful numbering scheme. The Gothic Quarter from the Plaça de Catalunya to the port is a warren of narrow streets. You'll need a good street map to get around. Almost all sightseeing can be done on foot, but you may need to use taxis, the metro, or buses to link certain sightseeing areas, depending on how much time you have. From mid-May to mid-October look for **Bus Turistic 100** for low-cost transport to Barcelona's main sites.

Golondrinas boats operate short harbor trips from the Portal de la Pau near the Columbus Monument daily 10–8 in summer, 10 AM–1:30 PM, weekends only, in winter. A one-way ticket lets you off at the end of the breakwater for a 4-km (2½-mi) stroll, surrounded by the Mediterranean, back into Barceloneta.

BY BUS
City buses run from about 5:30 or 6 AM to 10:30 PM, though some stop earlier. There are also night buses to certain destinations. The flat fare is 155 ptas. Route plans are displayed at bus stops. You can purchase a **tarjeta multiviatge,** good for 10 rides, at the transport kiosk on Plaça de Catalunya (750 ptas.).

BY CABLE CAR AND FUNICULAR
Montjuïc Funicular (✆ summer, noon–2:45 and 4:30–9:25; winter, 11–8:15) is a cog railroad that runs from the junction of Avenida Parallel and Nou de la Rambla to the Miramar Amusement Park on Montjuïc. A **teleferic** (cable car; summer, daily noon–8; winter, weekends 11–7:30) runs from the amusement park up to Montjuïc Castle.

The **Transbordador Aeri Harbor Cable Car** (🎫 1,500 ptas.; ✆ Oct.–June, weekdays noon–5:45, weekends noon–6:15; June–Oct., daily 11–9) runs from Miramar on Montjuïc to the Torre de Jaume I across the harbor on Barcelona *moll* (quay), and on to the Torre de Sant Sebastià at the end of Passeig Joan de Borbó in Barceloneta. You can board at either stage.

To reach Tibidabo summit, take either Bus 58 or the Ferrocarrils de la Generalitat train from Plaça de Catalunya to Avenida Tibidabo, then the *tramvía blau* (blue tram) to Peu del Funicular, and the **Tibidabo Funicular** from there to the Tibidabo Fairground. The funicular runs every half hour from 7:15 AM to 9:45 PM.

BY METRO
The subway is the fastest and easiest way to get around. You can pay a flat fare of 150 ptas. or buy a **tarjeta multiviatge,** good for 10 rides (780 ptas.). Maps of the system are available at main metro stations and branches of the Caixa savings bank.

BY TAXI
Taxis are black and yellow. When available for hire, they show a LIBRE sign in the daytime and a green light at night. The meter starts at 315 ptas., and there are supplements for luggage (100 ptas. per case), and for rides from the airport, a station, or the port (varies according to zone). There are cab stands all over town; cabs may also be flagged down on the street. Taxi drivers in Barcelona are nearly always pleasant, helpful, and fair, and don't care much about tips one way or the other.

Money Matters
CURRENCY
Spain's unit of currency is the peseta (pta.). Bills are worth 10,000, 5,000, 2,000, and 1,000 ptas.; coins are worth 500, 200, 100, 50, 25, 10, 5, and 1 pta. At press time (spring 1998), Europe's currency markets were rather unstable; the Spanish exchange rate was about 150 ptas. to the U.S. dollar, 105 ptas. to the Canadian dollar, and 250 ptas. to the pound sterling.

CURRENCY REGULATIONS
Visitors may take any amount of foreign currency in bills or traveler's checks into Spain, as well as any amount of pesetas. When leaving Spain you may take out only 100,000 ptas. per person in Spanish banknotes

and foreign currency up to the equivalent of 500,000 ptas., unless you can prove you declared the excess at customs on entering the country.

Telephoning

COUNTRY CODE

The country code for Spain is 34. When calling Spain from outside the country, drop the initial 9 from the regional code.

Contacts and Resources

CONSULATES

United States (⊠ Pg. Reina Elisenda 23, ☎ 93/280–2227). **Australia** (⊠ Gran Viá Carles III 98, ☎ 93/330–9496). **Canada** (⊠ Via Augusta 125, ☎ 93/209–0634). **New Zealand** (⊠ Travessera de Gràcia 64, ☎ 93/209–0399). **United Kingdom** (⊠ Diagonal 477, ☎ 93/419–9044).

EMERGENCIES

112 is the **general emergency number** in all EU nations (akin to 911 in the U.S.). **Police** (National Police, ☎ 091; Municipal Police, ☎ 092). **Medical emergencies** (☎ 061). **Pharmacies** (☎ 010). **Tourist Attention** (⊠ La Rambla 43, ☎ 93/317–7016, 24-hour assistance for crime victims).

ENGLISH-LANGUAGE BOOKSTORES

BCN Books (⊠ Aragó 277, ☎ 93/487–3123) is one of Barcelona's top spots for books in English. **Come In** (⊠ Provença 203, ☎ 93/253–1204) is another good option for English books. **El Corte Inglés** (☞ Department Store, *in* Shopping, *above*) sells English guidebooks and novels, but the selection is limited. For variety, try **The English Bookshop** (⊠ Entençan 63, ☎ 93/425–4466). The bookstore at the **Palau de la Virreina** (☞ Exploring, *above*) has good books on art, design, and Barcelona.

GUIDED TOURS

Orientation. City sightseeing tours are run by **Julià Tours** (⊠ Ronda Universitat 5, ☎ 93/317–6454). **Pullmantur** (⊠ Gran Viá de les Corts Catalanes 635, ☎ 93/318–5195) also has city sightseeing. Tours leave from the above terminals, though you may be able to arrange a pickup at your hotel. Both agencies offer the same tours at the same prices. A morning sightseeing tour visits the Gothic Quarter and Montjuïc; an afternoon tour concentrates on Gaudí and the Picasso Museum. You can visit Barcelona's Olympic sites from May through October.

Excursions. Trips out of town are run by **Julià Tours** and **Pullmantur** (☞ *above*). The principal attractions are a half-day tour to Montserrat to visit the monastery and shrine of the famous Black Virgin; a full-day trip to the Costa Brava resorts, including a boat cruise to the Medes Isles; and, from June through September, a full-day trip to Andorra for tax-free shopping.

SPECIAL-INTEREST AND WALKING TOURS

La Ruta del Modernismo (the Route of Modernism), created by Barcelona's *ayuntamiento*, connects some 50 key sites in the city's rich trove of Art Nouveau architecture. Everything from Gaudí's first lamppost to the colossal Sagrada Família to the odd Moderniste pharmacy or bakery is included, along with guided visits of key sites not open to the general public. The Palau Güell (⊠ Carrer Nou de Rambla 3–5, ☎ 93/317–3974) is "kilometer zero" for the tour; you can also buy the multiple ticket at the Casa Lleó Morera (⊠ Passeig de Gràcia 35, 3rd floor, ☎ 93/488–0139). Tickets are 1,500 ptas. adults, 800 ptas. students and seniors. Both offices are open Monday–Saturday 10–7.

TRAVEL AGENCIES

American Express (⊠ Rosselló 257, corner of Passeig de Gràcia, ☎ 93/217–0070). **Bestours** (⊠ Diputación 241, ☎ 93/487–8580). **Viajes**

Iberia (✉ Rambla 130, ☎ 93/317–9320). **Wagons-Lits Cook** (✉ Passeig de Gràcia 8, ☎ 93/317–5500).

VISITOR INFORMATION

Information on Barcelona: Centre d'Informació Turistic de Barcelona (Plaça de Catalunya 17, lower level, ☎ 93/304–3135, FAX 93/304–3155). **Sants** train station (☎ 93/491–4431). **França** train station (☎ 93/319–5758). **El Prat Airport** (☎ 93/478–4704). **Ajuntament** (✉ Plaça Sant Jaume, ☎ 93/402–7000, ext. 433). **Palau de la Virreina** (cultural information; ✉ Rambla 99, ☎ 93/301–7775). **Palau de Congressos** (during special events and conferences; ✉ Avda. María Cristina, ☎ 93/423–3101, ext. 8356). **Information on Catalonia and Spain: El Prat Airport** (☎ 93/478–4704). **Centre d'Informació Turística** (Palau Robert, Passeig de Gràcia 107, at Diagonal, ☎ 93/238–4000). **General information:** ☎ 010.

5 Berlin

The year 1999 will establish Berlin's role as capital of Germany, as the Federal Parliament moves to the city. Due to burgeoning building development, the city is still the Continent's largest construction site. As ever, life here is literally on the razor's edge.

EXPLORING BERLIN

Visiting Berlin is still a bittersweet experience, as so many of the triumphs and tragedies of the past are tied up with the bustling present. The result can be either dispiriting or exhilarating. By European standards, Berlin isn't too old. Although already a royal residence during the 15th century, Berlin really came into its own 3 centuries later, under the rule of King Friedrich II—Frederick the Great—whose liberal reforms and artistic patronage led the way as the city developed into a major cultural capital.

What Berlin was forced to endure during the 20th century would have crushed the spirit of most other cities. Hitler and his supporters destroyed the city's reputation for tolerance and plunged Berlin headlong into the war that led to the wholesale destruction of monuments and houses. And after World War II, Berlin was still to face the bitter division of the city and the construction of the infamous Wall in 1961.

Downtown Berlin

Numbers in the margin correspond to points of interest on the Downtown Berlin map.

★ ⑬ **Ägyptisches Museum** (Egyptian Museum). This small but outstanding museum is home to the beautiful portrait sculpture head of Nefertiti. The 3,300-year-old queen is the centerpiece of a fascinating collection of Egyptian antiquities that includes some of the finest preserved mummies outside Cairo. ⊠ *Schloss-Str. 70,* ☎ *030/320–911.* ☼ *Mon.–Thurs. 9–5, weekends 10–5.*

★ **❾** **Berliner Mauer** (Berlin Wall). One of only four still-standing sections of the Berlin Wall has been left here, in the city's historic heart. ⊠ *Along Niederkirchnerstr.*

★ **❻** **Brandenburger Tor** (Brandenburg Gate). Berlin's premier historic landmark was built in 1788 to celebrate the triumphant Prussian armies. The monumental gate was cut off from West Berlin by the Wall, and it became a focal point of celebrations marking the reunification of Berlin and of all Germany. The square behind the gate, the **Pariser Platz**, has regained its pre-war design. Among the new buildings erected here between 1996 and 1998 is the American Embassy. You'll reach the gate by walking along Strasse des 17. Juni (June 17th Street). ⊠ *Under den Linden at Pariser Pl.*

⓮ **Dahlemer Museen** (Dahlem Museums). This unique complex of six museums includes the **Museum für Völkerkunde** (Ethnographic Museum), internationally famous for its arts and artifacts from Africa, Asia, the South Seas, and the Americas, and the **Skulpturensammlung** (Sculpture Collection), which houses Byzantine and European sculpture from the 3rd through the 18th centuries. *Please note:* Due to the reorganization of Berlin's major state museums, both the Museum für Völkerkunde and the Skulpturensammlung, as well as parts of the other four museums at the Dahlem location, will be closed in 1999. ⊠ *Lansstr. 8 and Arnimalle 23–27, subway line U-2 to Dahlem-Dorf station,* ☎ *030/83011.* ⊙ *Tues.–Fri. 9–5, weekends 10–5.*

⓯ **Grunewald** (Green Forest). Together with its Wannsee lakes, this splendid forest is the most popular green retreat for Berliners, who come out in force, swimming, sailing their boats, tramping through the woods, and riding horseback. In winter a downhill ski run and even a ski jump operate on the modest slopes of Teufelsberg hill. Excursion steamers ply the water wonderland of the Wannsee, the Havel River, and the Müggelsee (☞ Guided Tours *in* Berlin Essentials, *below*). ⊠ *Southwest of downtown western Berlin.*

★ **⓫** **Haus am Checkpoint Charlie** (House at Checkpoint Charlie–The Wall Museum). The history of the events leading up to the Wall's construction can be followed in the museum that arose at its most famous crossing point, at Friedrichstrasse, the second cross street heading east. Checkpoint Charlie, as it was known, disappeared along with the Wall. ⊠ *Friedrichstr. 44,* ☎ *030/251–1031.* ⊡ *DM 7.50.* ⊙ *Daily 9 AM–10 PM.*

★ **❷** **Kaiser-Wilhelm-Gedächtniskirche** (Kaiser Wilhelm Memorial Church). This landmark had come to symbolize West Berlin, and it still is a dramatic reminder of the futile destructiveness of war. The shell of the tower is all that remains of the church that was built at the end of the 19th century and dedicated to Kaiser Wilhelm I. Surrounding the tower are the new church and bell tower. ⊠ *Breitscheidpl.,* ☎ *030/218–5023.* ⊡ *Free.* ⊙ *Old Tower, Mon.–Sat. 10–4; Memorial Church, daily 9–7. Closed holidays.*

★ **❽** **Kulturforum** (Cultural Forum). With its unique ensemble of museums, galleries, and libraries, the complex is considered one of Germany's cultural jewels. It includes the **Philharmonie** (Philharmonic Hall), home of the Berlin Philharmonic orchestra. ⊠ *Matthäikirchstr. 1,* ☎ *030/ 2548–8132.* ⊙ *Box office: weekdays 3:30–6, weekends 11–2.*

The **Kunstgewerbemuseum** (Museum of Decorative Arts) displays arts and crafts of Europe from the Middle Ages to the present. ⊠ *Matthäikirchpl. 10,* ☎ *030/266–2911.* ⊡ *DM 8 (day card covers 1-day admission to all museums at Kulturforum and is available at all museums.* ⊙ *Tues.–Fri. 9–5, weekends 10–5.*

Downtown Berlin

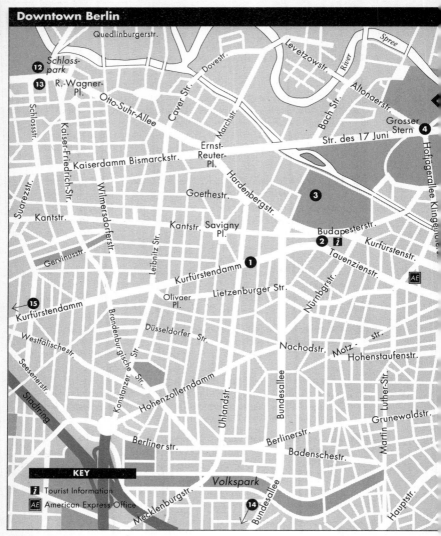

KEY

i Tourist Information

AE American Express Office

Ägyptisches
Museum, **13**

Berliner Mauer, **9**

Brandenburger
Tor, **6**

Dahlemer Museen, **14**

Grunewald, **15**

Haus am Checkpoint
Charlie, **11**

Kaiser-Wilhelm-
Gedächtniskirche, **2**

Kulturforum, **8**

Kurfürstendamm, **1**

Potsdamer Platz, **7**

Prinz-Albrecht-
Gelände, **10**

Reichstag, **5**

Schloss
Charlottenburg, **12**

Siegessäule, **4**

Zoologischer
Garten, **3**

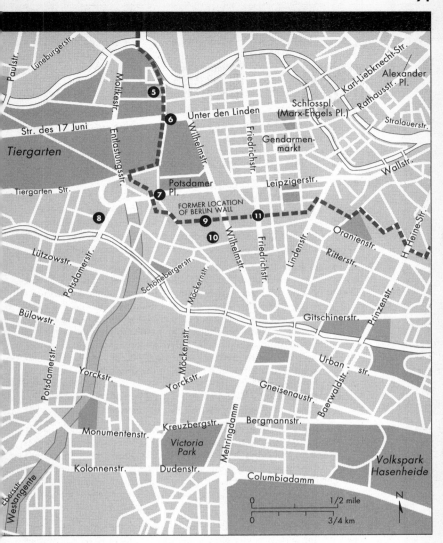

Paulstr.

Lüneburgerstr.

Maliikstr.

⑤

⑥ Unter den Linden

Str. des 17 Juni

Tiergarten

Entlastungsstr.

Wilhelmstr.

Tiergarten Str.

Potsdamer
Pl.

⑦

⑧

FORMER LOCATION
OF BERLIN WALL

⑨

⑩

⑪

Wilhelmstr.

Lützowstr.

Potsdamerstr.

Schöneber/gerstr.

Möckernstr.

Bülowstr.

Potsdamerstr.

Yorckstr.

Yorckstr.

Möckernstr.

Monumentenstr.

Kreuzbergstr.

Victoria
Park

Kolonnenstr.

Dudenstr.

Columbiadamm

Mehringdamm

überestr.
Westtangente

Friedrichstr.

Friedrichstr.

Gendarmen-
markt

Schlosspl.
(Marx-Engels Pl.)

Karl-Liebknecht-Str.

Rathausstr.

Alexander
· Pl.

Stralauerstr.

Wallstr.

Leipzigerstr.

Lindenstr.

Oranienstr.

Ritterstr.

Prinzenstr.

H Heine-Str.

Gitschinerstr.

Urban - str.

Baerwaldstr.

Gneisenaustr.

Bergmannstr.

Volkspark
Hasenheide

N

0   1/2 mile

0   3/4 km

The **Gemäldegalerie** (painting gallery) reunites formerly separated collections from eastern and western Berlin. One of Germany's finest art galleries, it houses an extensive selection of European paintings from the 13th through the 18th centuries, among them works by Dürer, Cranach the Elder, and Holbein, as well as of the Italian masters—Botticelli, Titian, Giotto, Lippi, and Raphael. ⊠ *Matthäikirchpl.,* ☏ *030/ 266–2002.* ✆ *DM 8 (☞ above).* ⊗ *Tues.–Fri. 9–5, weekends 10–5.*

The **Neue Nationalgalerie** (New National Gallery), a modern glass-and-steel building designed by Mies van der Rohe and built in the mid-1960s, presents paintings, sculptures, and drawings from the 19th and 20th centuries. ⊠ *Potsdamer Str. 50,* ☏ *030/266–2662.* ✆ *DM 8 (☞ above).* ⊗ *Tues.–Fri. 9–5, weekends 10–5.*

★ ❶ **Kurfürstendamm.** Ku'damm, as the Berliners call it, is one of Europe's busiest thoroughfares, throbbing with activity day and night. Today the boulevard is undergoing a vigorous face-lift as some of the 1950s buildings are being replaced by modern, futuristic-looking skyscrapers. Still, the **Europa Center,** a shopping center dating back to the early '60s, and the bustling square in front of it, are not to be missed.

★ ❼ **Potsdamer Platz** (Potsdam Square). This huge square was Europe's busiest plaza before World War II. Today Sony, Mercedes Benz, Asea Brown Boveri, and Hertie are building their new company headquarters here. The **Potsdamer Platz Arkaden,** Berlin's new and most elegant shopping and entertainment mecca covering 40,000 square yards, houses close to 150 upscale shops, a musical theater, a variety stage, cafés, a movie complex with a 3D-IMAX cinema, and even a casino. The best overview of the ongoing constructions can be found at a futuristic, bright-red **Information Center,** at the square's eastern end. ⊠ *Infobox, Leipziger Pl. 21,* ☏ *030/2266–2424.* ✆ *Free, observation deck DM 2.* ⊗ *Mon.–Wed. and Fri. 9–7, Thurs. 9–9, weekends 9– 7. English-language tours of exhibit by appointment.*

❿ **Prinz-Albrecht-Gelände** (Prince Albrecht Grounds). The buildings that once stood here housed the headquarters of the Gestapo, the secret security police, and other Nazi security organizations from 1933 until 1945. After the war, they were leveled; in 1987 what was left of the buildings was excavated and an exhibit, "Topography of Terrors," documenting their history and Nazi atrocities, was opened. ⊠ *Stresemannstr. 110,* ☏ *030/254–509.* ✆ *Free.* ⊗ *Daily 10–6.*

❺ **Reichstag** (German Parliament). The monumental and rather grim-looking building served as Germany's seat of parliament from its completion in 1894 until 1933, when it was gutted by fire under suspicious circumstances. The Bundestag, the lower house of parliament, will again convene here. The building opens to the public in late 1998. ⊠ *Pl. der Republik.*

★ ⓬ **Schloss Charlottenburg** (Charlottenburg Palace). Built at the end of the 17th century by King Frederick I for his wife, Queen Sophie Charlotte, this grand palace and its magnificent gardens were progressively enlarged for later royal residents and now include museums. ⊠ *Luisenpl., U-7 subway line to Richard-Wagner-Pl. station. From the station walk east along Otto-Suhr-Allee,* ☏ *030/320–911.* ⊗ *Tues.–Fri. 9–5, weekends 10–5.*

❹ **Siegessäule** (Victory Column). The memorial erected in 1873 to commemorate four Prussian military campaigns, is at the center of the 630-acre **Tiergarten** (Animal Park), the former hunting grounds of the Great Elector. From its 285 steps to its 213-ft summit, you'll be rewarded with a fine view of Berlin. ⊠ *Am Grossen Stern,* ☎ *030/391–2961.* ⊙ *Mon. 1–6, Tues.–Sun. and holidays 9–6.*

★ ❸ **Zoologischer Garten** (Zoological Gardens). Berlin's zoo has the world's largest variety of individual types of fauna along with a fascinating aquarium. ⊠ *Hardenbergpl. 8 and Budapester Str. 34,* ☎ *030/254–010.* 🖰 *Zoo DM 11, aquarium DM 11, combined ticket DM 18.* ⊙ *Zoo, daily 9–6:30 or until dusk in winter; aquarium, daily 9–6.*

Historic Berlin

Numbers in the margin correspond to points of interest on the Historic Berlin map.

㉒ **Berliner Dom** (Berlin Cathedral). The impressive 19th-century cathedral with its enormous green copper dome is one of the great ecclesiastical buildings in Germany. Its main nave was reopened in June 1993 after a 20-year renovation. More than 80 sarcophagi of Prussian royals are on display in the cathedral's catacombs. ⊠ *Am Lustgarten,* ☎ *030/202–69136.* 🖰 *Balcony DM 5, museum free.* ⊙ *Church Mon.– Sat. 9–6:30, Sun. 11:30–6:30; balcony Mon.–Sat. 10–6, Sun. 11:30– 6; museum Wed.–Sun. 10–6.*

㉕ **Berliner Rathaus** (Berlin City Hall). After the city's reunification this pompous symbol of Berlin's 19th-century urban pride again became the seat of the city government. ⊠ *Jüdenstr. at Rathausstr.,* ☎ *030/ 24010.* 🖰 *Free.* ⊙ *Weekdays 9–6.*

㉓ **Deutsches Historisches Museum** (German Historical Museum). The one-time Prussian Zeughaus (arsenal), a magnificent Baroque building constructed in 1695–1730, houses Germany's National History Museum, a compendium of German history from the Middle Ages to the present. ⊠ *Unter den Linden 2,* ☎ *030/215–020.* 🖰 *Free.* ⊙ *Thurs.–Tues. 10–6. Tours by appointment only. English-speaking guides available for DM 60.*

㉔ **Fernsehturm** (TV Tower). At 1,198 ft high, eastern Berlin's TV tower is 710 ft *taller* than western Berlin's. Its observation deck affords the best view of Berlin; the city's highest café, which revolves, is also up here. ⊠ *Alexanderpl.,* ☎ *030/242–3333.* ⊙ *Daily 9 AM–midnight.*

★ ⑯ **Friedrichstrasse** (Frederick Street). For a sense of times past and new, head south on historic Friedrichstrasse, where you'll pass various new business and shopping buildings, including the **Friedrichstadtpassagen,** a gigantic shopping and business complex. At the corner of Französische Strasse is the French department store **Galeries Lafayette.** ⊠ *Französische Str. 23,* ☎ *030/209–480.*

⑰ **Gendarmenmarkt** (Gendarme Market). With its beautifully reconstructed **Schauspielhaus** (Theatre)—built in 1818, and now one of the city's main concert halls—and twin **Deutscher** (German) and **Französischer** (French) cathedrals, this historic square is one of Europe's finest piazzas. The French cathedral houses a museum displaying the history of Huguenot immigrants in Berlin while the German cathedral showcases an official exhibit on German history. ⊠ *Deutscher Dom, Gendarmenmarkt 1,* ☎ *030/2273–2141.* 🖰 *Free.* ⊙ *Tues.–Sun. 10– 5.* ⊠ *Französischer Dom, Gendarmenmarkt,* ☎ *030/229–1760.* ⊙ *Tues.–Sat. noon–5, Sun. 11–5.*

★ ㉘ **Hamburger Bahnhof** (Hamburg Train Station). Berlin's newest museum for contemporary art is housed in an early 19th-century structure, once a major train station. Remodeled and given a huge and spectacular new wing—a stunning interplay of glass, steel, color, and sunlight—it displays

74

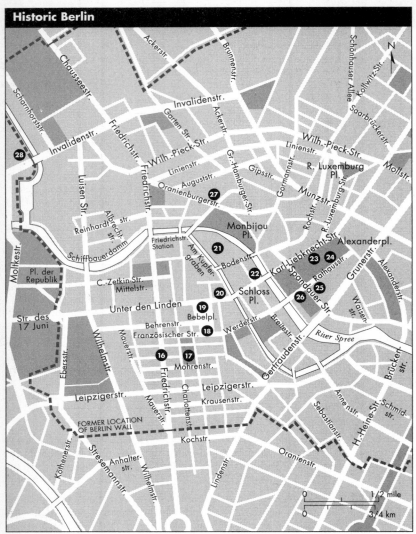

Berliner Dom, **22**

Berliner Rathaus, **25**

Deutsches
Historisches
Museum, **20**

Fernsehturm, **24**

Friedrichstrasse, **16**

Gendarmenmarkt, **17**

Hamburger
Bahnhof, **28**

Museumsinsel, **21**

Neue Synagoge, **27**

Nikolaiviertel, **26**

St. Hedwigs-
kathedrale, **18**

St. Marienkirche, **23**

Staatsoper Unter den
Linden, **19**

an outstanding private collection of works by German artists Joseph Beuys and Anselm Kiefer as well as paintings by Andy Warhol, Cy Twombly, Robert Rauschenberg, and Robert Morris. ⊠ *Invalidenstr. 50–51,* ☎ *030/397–8340.* ⊡ *DM 12.* ⊘ *Tues.–Fri. 10–6, weekends 11–6.*

★ ㉑ **Museumsinsel** (Museum Island). This unique complex contains four world-class museums. The **Altes Museum** (Old Museum; entrance on Lustgarten) is an austere neoclassical building, decorated with red marble. The collections here include postwar art from some of Germany's most prominent artists and numerous works by the old masters. The **Alte Nationalgalerie** (Old National Gallery; Bodestrasse) displays 19th- and 20th-century paintings and sculptures. The **Pergamonmuseum** (Am Kupfergraben), one of Europe's greatest museums, takes its name from its principal exhibit, the Pergamon Altar, a monumental Greek sculpture dating from 180 BC that occupies an entire city block. To the north is the **Bodemuseum** (Am Kupfergraben; entrance on Monbijoubrücke), with an outstanding collection of early Christian, Byzantine, and Egyptian art. *Please note:* Due to reconstruction and a major reorganization of the Museum Island's collections, the Bodemuseum and parts of the Alte Nationalgalerie are closed to the public through the year 2001. ⊠ *Museumsinsel; right from Unter den Linden along Spree Canal via Am Zeughaus and Am Kupfergraben;* ☎ *030/209–050 for all museums.* ⊡ *DM 8, free 1st Sun. of month.* ⊘ *Tues.–Sun. 10–6.*

㉗ **Neue Synagoge** (New Synagogue). Completed in 1866, in Middle Eastern style, this was one of Germany's most beautiful synagogues until it was seriously damaged on *Kristallnacht,* November 9, 1938, when synagogues and Jewish stores across Germany were vandalized, looted, and burned. Today the outside is perfectly restored, and the interior is connected to the **Centrum Judaicum** (Jewish Center)—an institution of Jewish culture and learning that frequently stages exhibitions and other cultural events. ⊠ *Oranienburger Str. 28/30,* ☎ *030/2840–1316.* ⊘ *Sun.–Thurs. 10–6, Fri. 10–2.*

㉖ **Nikolaiviertel** (Nikolai Quarter). Berlin's oldest historic quarter has been handsomely rebuilt and is now filled with delightful shops, cafés, and restaurants. On the quarter's Nikolaikirchplatz is Berlin's oldest building, the **Nikolaikirche** (St. Nicholas Church), dating from 1230. ⊠ *Nikolaikirchpl.,* ☎ *030/238–0900.* ⊡ *DM 3.* ⊘ *Tues.–Sun. 10–6.*

⑱ **St. Hedwigskathedrale** (St. Hedwig's Cathedral). When Berlin's premier Catholic church was erected in 1747, it was the first to be built in resolutely Protestant Berlin since the Reformation of the 16th century. ⊠ *Hinter der Katholischen Kirche 3,* ☎ *030/203–4810.* ⊘ *Weekdays 10–5, Sun. 1–5.*

㉓ **St. Marienkirche** (Church of St. Mary). This medieval church, one of the finest in Berlin, is worth a visit for its late-Gothic fresco *Der Totentanz* (*Dance of Death*). ⊠ *Karl-Liebknecht-Str. 8,* ☎ *030/242–4467.* ⊘ *Mon.–Thurs. 10–noon and 1–5, Sat. noon–4:30, Sun. noon–5. Free tours Mon.–Thurs. at 1, Sun. at 11:45.*

⑲ **Staatsoper Unter den Linden** (German State Opera). This lavishly restored hall is Berlin's prime opera house. ⊠ *Unter den Linden 7,* ☎ *030/2035–4555.* ⊘ *Box office: weekdays 10–6, weekends 2–6. Reservations by phone: weekdays 10–8, weekends 2–8.*

DINING

Dining in Berlin can mean sophisticated nouvelle creations in upscale restaurants or hearty local specialties in atmospheric and inexpensive inns. Typical are *Eisbein mit Sauerkraut,* (knuckle of pork with sauerkraut), *Spanferkel* (suckling pig), *Berliner Schüsselsülze* (potted meat in aspic), *Schlachterplatte* (mixed grill), and *Currywurst* (chubby and very spicy frankfurters sold at wurst stands).

RATINGS

The following chart gives price ranges for restaurants in the western part of Germany. Food prices in the former East Germany are still somewhat unstable, although in the bigger cities many of the better-quality restaurants already mimic rates in western Germany. Generally speaking, the prevailing price structure in the eastern part of the country, except for restaurants in the priciest hotels, falls into the $ to $$$ categories listed below. Bills in simple restaurants in country areas of the eastern region will, however, still come well below DM 35. Prices are per person and include a first course, main course, dessert, and tip and 10% tax.

CATEGORY	COST
$$$$	over DM 100
$$$	DM 75–DM 100
$$	DM 50–DM 75
$	under DM 50

$$$$ ✕ **Bamberger Reiter.** At one of the city's best restaurants, Tyrolean chef
★   Franz Raneburger relies heavily on fresh market produce for his *Neue Deutsche Küche* (new German cuisine), so the menu changes from day to day. ⊠ *Regensburger Str. 7,* ☎ *030/218–4282. Reservations essential. AE, DC, V. Closed Sun., Mon., Jan. 1–15.*

$$$ ✕ **Borchardt.** At this fashionable meeting place, columns, red plush
★   benches, and an Art Nouveau mosaic create the impression of a 1920s salon. Entrées are prepared with a French accent. ⊠ *Französische Str. 47,* ☎ *030/2039–7117. Reservations essential. AE, V.*

$$$ ✕ **Paris Bar.** This trendy restaurant in Charlottenburg attracts a polyglot clientele of film stars, artists, entrepreneurs, and executives. The cuisine is high-powered, but medium-quality French. ⊠ *Kantstr. 152,* ☎ *030/313–8052. AE.*

$$$ ✕ **Rockendorf's.** The city's premier restaurant has only fixed-price
★   menus, some with up to nine courses. Exquisitely presented, the mainly nouvelle specialties are sometimes fused with classic German cuisine. The wine list—with 800 choices—has the appropriate accompaniment to any menu. ⊠ *Düsterhauptstr. 1,* ☎ *030/402–3099. Reservations essential. AE, DC, MC, V. Closed Sun., Mon., 3–4 wks in summer, and Dec. 25–Jan. 6.*

$$$ ✕ **VAU.** Still a newcomer to Berlin's hip restaurant scene, the VAU serves
★   excellent German fish and game dishes prepared by chef Kolja Kleeberg. Among his creations are combinations such as *Lammhaxe mit Schmorgemüse* (leg of lamb with braised vegetables) or *Steinbutt mit Kalbbries auf Rotweinschalotten* (turbot with veal sweetbread on shallots in red wine). The VAU's cool interior is all style and modern art. ⊠ *Jägerstr. 54/55,* ☎ *030/202–9730. Reservations essential. AE, DC, MC, V. Closed Sun.*

$$ ✕ **Reinhard's.** Berliners of all stripes meet here in the Nikolai Quar-
★   ter to enjoy the carefully prepared entrées and to sample spirits from the amply stocked bar. *Adlon* (honey-glazed breast of duck) is one of the house specialties. Due to its success, Reinhard's has opened a second restaurant on the Ku'damm. It's much smaller but more elegant and one of the trendiest places in town. ⊠ *Poststr. 28,* ☎ *030/242–5295;* ⊠ *Kurfürstendamm 190,* ☎ *030/881–1621. Reservations essential on weekends. AE, DC, MC, V. Closed Dec. 24.*

$$ ✕ **Turmstuben.** Tucked away below the cupola of the French Cathedral on the north side of the beautiful Gendarmenmarkt, this restaurant is approached by a long, winding staircase. At the top of the stairs is one of Berlin's most original and attractive restaurants. The menu is short, but there's an impressive wine list. ✉ *Gendarmenmarkt 5,* ☎ *030/204–4888. Weekend reservations essential. AE, MC, V.*

$ ✕ **Alt-Cöllner Schankstuben.** A tiny restaurant and pub are contained within this charming, historic Berlin house. The menu is relatively limited, but the quality, like the service, is good. ✉ *Friedrichsgracht 50,* ☎ *030/201–1299. AE, DC, MC, V.*

$ ✕ **Blockhaus Nikolskoe.** Prussian King Frederick Wilhelm III built this Russian-style wooden lodge for his daughter Charlotte, wife of Russia's Tsar Nicholas I. It's on the eastern edge of Glienicke Park, with an open terrace (in summer) overlooking the Havel River. The Blockhaus features game dishes. ✉ *Nikolskoer Weg 15,* ☎ *030/805–2914. DC, MC, V. Closed Thurs.*

$ ✕ **Café Oren.** This popular vegetarian eatery is next to the Neue Syn-
★ agoge, not far from Friedrichstrasse. The restaurant buzzes with loud chatter all evening, and the atmosphere and service are welcoming and friendly. The extensive menu offers mostly Israeli and Middle Eastern fare—including delicious, filled "Moroccan Cigars." ✉ *Oranienburger Str. 28,* ☎ *030/282–8228. AE, MC, V.*

$ ✕ **Zur Letzten Instanz.** Established in 1621, Berlin's oldest restaurant combines the charming atmosphere of old-world Berlin with a limited (but tasty) choice of dishes. The emphasis here is on beer, both in the recipes and in the mug. Service can be erratic, though engagingly friendly. ✉ *Waisenstr. 14–16,* ☎ *030/242–5528. AE, DC, MC, V.*

NIGHTLIFE AND THE ARTS

The Arts

The quality of opera and classical concerts in Berlin is high. Tickets are available at the theaters' own box offices, either in advance or an hour before the performance, at many hotels, and at numerous ticket agencies: **Showtime Konzert- und Theaterkassen** at the KaDeWe (✉ Tauentzienstr. 21, ☎ 030/217–7754); **Wertheim** (✉ Kurfürstendamm 181, ☎ 030/882–2500); **Theaterkonzertkasse City Center** (✉ Kurfürstendamm 16, ☎ 030/882–6563); and **Hekticket office** at Alexanderplatz (✉ Rathausstr. 1 and Kurfürstendamm 14, ☎ 030/2431–2431). Detailed information about what's going on in Berlin can be found in *Berlin–the magazine,* an English-language monthly cultural magazine published by Berlin's Tourism Board; *Berlin Programm,* a monthly tourist guide to Berlin arts, museums, and theaters; and the magazines *prinz, tip,* and *zitty,* which appear every two weeks and provide full arts listings.

CONCERTS

The Berlin Philharmonic, one of the world's leading orchestras, performs in the **Philharmonie** (✉ Matthäikirchstr. 1, ☎ 030/254–880 or 030/2548–8132). A more historic venue is the **Konzerthaus Berlin** (✉ Gendarmenmarkt, ☎ 030/2030–92101).

MUSICALS

For **musicals** check out: **Estrel Festival Center** (✉ Sonnenallee 225/Ziegrastr. 21–29, ☎ 030/6831–6831); **Theater des Westens** (✉ Kantstr. 12, ☎ 030/882–2888); **Metropol Theater** (✉ Friedrichstr. 101, ☎ 030/2024–6117); **Schiller-Theater** (✉ Bismarckstr. 110, ☎ 030/3111–3111); and **Space Dream Musical Theater** (✉ Tempelhof Airport, Clumbiadamm 2–6, ☎ 030/6951–2802).

Please note: Berlin's largest musical theater is likely to open in 1999 at the Potsdamer Platz Arkaden. At press time, however, information was still unavailable. Contact Berlin tourist information office (☞ Berlin Essentials, *below*) for more details.

OPERA AND BALLET

The **Deutsche Oper** (German Opera House; ⊠ Bismarckstr. 35, ☎ 030/ 343−8401), by the U-bahn stop of the same name, is home to both opera and ballet. The grand **Staatsoper Unter den Linden** (German State Opera; ⊠ Unter den Linden 7, ☎ 030/2035−4555) is Berlin's main opera venue. **Komische Oper** (Comic Opera House; ⊠ Behrenstr. 55−57, ☎ 030/4702−1000) schedules opera performances regularly.

VARIETY SHOWS

During the past few years Berlin has become Germany's prime hot spot for variety shows. The world's largest circus is at the **Friedrichstadt-palast** (⊠ Friedrichstr. 107, ☎ 030/2326−2474). Small but classy in style is the **Wintergarten** (⊠ Potsdamer Str. 96, ☎ 030/2308−8230 or 030/2500−8863), a romantic homage to the '20s. Equally intimate and intellectually entertaining is the **Bar jeder Vernuft** (⊠ Schaperstr. 24, ☎ 030/883−1582). More than hilarious and constantly sold out are the shows at the **Chamäleon Varieté** (⊠ Rosenthaler Str. 40/41, ☎ 030/ 282−7118).

Nightlife

With more than 6,000 Kneipen (pubs), bars, and clubs, nightlife in Berlin is no halfhearted affair. It starts late (from 9 PM) and runs until breakfast. Almost 50 Kneipen have live music of one kind or another, and there are numerous small cabaret clubs and discos. The heart of this nocturnal scene used to be the Kurfürstendamm, but today most of the best bars and Kneipen can be found around Savignyplatz in Charlottenburg, Nollendorfplatz and its side streets in Schöneberg, and along Oranienstrasse and Wienerstrasse in Kreuzberg. In eastern Berlin nighthawks come together around Kollwitzplatz in the Prenzlauer Berg district, along Oranienburger Strasse, and around Rosenthaler Platz and Hackesche Höfe in Mitte.

Berlin is a major center for jazz in Europe. If you're visiting in the fall, call the tourist office (☞ Berlin Essentials, *below*) for details on the annual international Jazz Fest. Throughout the year a variety of jazz groups appear at the **A-Trane** (⊠ Pestalozzistr. 105, ☎ 030/313−2550), **Eierschale** (⊠ Podbielskiallee 50, ☎ 030/832−7097), and **Quasimodo** (⊠ Kantstr. 12a, ☎ 030/312−8086).

SHOPPING

Antiques

On weekends from 10 to 5, the colorful and lively antiques and handicrafts fair on **Strasse des 17. Juni** swings into action. Not far from **Wittenbergplatz,** several streets are strong on antiques, including Eisenacher Strasse, Fuggerstrasse, Keithstrasse, Kalckreuthstrasse, Motzstrasse, and Nollendorfstrasse.

Department Stores

One of Berlin's classiest department stores is the **Kaufhaus des Westens** (KaDeWe; ⊠ Tauentzienstr. 21, ☎ 030/21210); be sure to check out the food department, which occupies the whole sixth floor. Downtown Berlin's **Wertheim** (⊠ Kurfürstendamm 181, ☎ 030/8800−3206) is neither as big nor as attractive as KaDeWe, but it nonetheless has a large selection of fine wares. The popular **Galeries Lafayette** (⊠

Französische Str. 23, ☎ 030/209–480) carries almost exclusively French products, including designer clothes, perfume, and French produce. The main department store in eastern Berlin is **Kaufhof** (✉ north end of Alexanderpl., ☎ 030/247–430).

Gift Ideas

Fine porcelain is still produced at the former Royal Prussian Porcelain Factory, now called **Staatliche Porzellan Manufaktur** (State Porcelain Factory) or KPM. This delicate, handmade, hand-painted china is sold at KPM's store (✉ Kurfürstendamm 26A, ☎ 030/886–7210), but it may be more fun to visit the factory salesroom (✉ Wegelystr. 1, ☎ 030/ 390–090), where seconds are sold at reduced prices. If you long to have the Egyptian queen Nefertiti on your mantelpiece at home, try the **Gipsformerei der Staatlichen Museen Preussicher Kulturbesitz** (Plaster Sculpture of the Prussian Cultural Foundation State Museums; ✉ Sophie-Charlotte-Str. 17, ☎ 030/321–7011), which sells plaster casts of this and other museum treasures.

Shopping Districts

The liveliest and most famous shopping area in west Berlin is the **Kurfürstendamm** and its side streets, especially between Breitscheidplatz and Olivaer Platz. The **Europa Center** at Breitscheidplatz encompasses more than 100 stores, cafés, and restaurants—but this is not a place to bargain hunt. Running east from Breitscheidplatz is **Tauentzienstrasse,** another shopping street. The **Potsdamer Platz Arkaden,** the city's newest shopping mall on Potsdamer Platz, is also its fanciest. **Eastern Berlin** has major shopping districts along **Friedrichstrasse, Unter den Linden,** and in the area around **Alexanderplatz.**

BERLIN ESSENTIALS

Arriving and Departing

BY BUS

Long-distance bus services link Berlin with numerous other German and European cities. For travel details, if you're in Berlin, call the main bus station (✉ Messedamm, ☎ 030/301–8028); if you're in other parts of Germany, inquire at the local tourist office.

BY CAR

The eight roads linking the western part of Germany with Berlin have been incorporated into the country-wide autobahn network, but be prepared for large traffic jams, particularly on weekends.

BY PLANE

Tegel (☎ 030/41010) airport is only 7 km (4 mi) from downtown. Air France, British Airways, Delta, Deutsche BA, Lufthansa, United, and some charter specialists regularly fly to Tegel. Because of increased air traffic at Tegel following unification, the former military airfield at **Tempelhof** (☎ 030/691–510), even closer to downtown, is used for commuter plane traffic. **Schönefeld** (☎ 030/60910) airport is about 24 km (15 mi) outside the downtown area; it is used primarily for charter flights to Asia and southern and eastern Europe.

Between the Airports and Downtown. Buses 109 and X09 run every 10 minutes between **Tegel** airport and downtown. The journey takes 30 minutes; the fare is DM 3.90 and covers all public transportation throughout Berlin. A taxi costs about DM 25. If you're driving from the airport, follow signs for the STADTAUTOBAHN (City Freeway). **Tempelhof** is right on the U-6 subway line, in the center of the city. A shuttle bus leaves **Schönefeld** airport every 10–15 minutes for the nearby

S-bahn station. S-bahn trains leave every 20 minutes for the Friedrich-strasse and Zoologischer Garten stations. The trip takes about 30 minutes, and you can get off at whatever stop is nearest your hotel; The fare is DM 3.60. Taxi fare to your hotel is about DM 40–DM 55, and the trip takes about 40 minutes. By car follow the signs for BERLIN–ZENTRUM (Downtown Berlin).

BY TRAIN

There are six major rail routes to Berlin from the western part of the country (from Hamburg, Hannover, Köln, Frankfurt, Munich, and Nürnberg), and the network has expanded considerably, making the rest of eastern Germany more accessible. For information call **Deutsche Bahn** (☎ 030/19419) or inquire at the local main train station.

Getting Around
BY PUBLIC TRANSPORTATION

The city has an excellent **public transportation system**: a combination of U-bahn and S-bahn lines, buses, and streetcars (in eastern Berlin only). For DM 3.60, you can buy a ticket that covers travel on the entire downtown system (fare zones A and B) for two hours. If you are just making a short trip, buy a **Kurzstreckentarif.** It allows you to ride six bus stops or three U-bahn or S-bahn stops for DM 2.50. The **Day Card,** for DM 7.50 (no children's discount), is valid until 3 AM of the day following validation. The **Group Day Card,** for DM 20, offers the same benefits for two adults and up to three children.

If you're staying for more than a few days, the **Tourist Pass,** valid for a week and costing DM 40, is the best bargain. The **BerlinWelcome-Card,** at DM 16 for a day (DM 29 for two days), entitles one adult and up to three children to unlimited travel as well as free or reduced sightseeing trips and admission to museums, theaters, and other events and attractions. If you're caught without a ticket, the fine is DM 60. Tickets are available from vending machines at U-bahn and S-bahn stations or from bus drivers. For information call the **Berliner Verkehrs-betriebe** (BVG; Berlin Public Transportation; ☎ 030/19449) or go to the information office on Hardenbergplatz, directly in front of the Bahnhof Zoo train station.

Please note: Subway fares quoted above were those available in spring 1998. Fares are likely to rise during the latter half of 1998, and ticket regulations will likely be different in 1999.

BY TAXI

The base rate is DM 4, after which prices vary according to a complex tariff system. If your ride will be short, ask in advance for the special Kurzstreckentarif, which is DM 5 for rides of less than 2 km (1 mi) or five minutes. Figure on paying around DM 15 for a ride the length of the Kurfurstendamm. Hail cabs in the street or at taxi stands, or order one by calling 030/9644, 030/210–202, 030/691–001, or 030/261–026. U-bahn employees will call a taxi for passengers after 8 PM.

A new service offered in the downtown areas is *Velotaxis*, a rickshaw service system operating along Kurfürstendamm and Unter den Linden. Just hail one of the orange- or red-color bicycle cabs on the street or look for the VELOTAXI STAND signs along the boulevards mentioned. The fare is DM 2 (for up to 1 km/½ mi), DM 5 for a tour between sightseeing landmarks (for example, Europa Center to the Brandenburger Tor), and DM 15 for 30 minutes of individual travel. Velotaxis operate from April through October, 1 PM–8 PM only. For more information call 030/4435–8990.

Money Matters

CURRENCY

Although the new European monetary unit, the Euro, officially makes its appearance in 1999, it won't replace the Deutschmark as a currency until the year 2002. In 1999 Deutschmark banknotes and coins will still be the means of exchange. The Deutschmark, written DM and generally referred to as the mark, is divided into 100 pfennige. There are bills of 5 (rare), 10, 20, 50, 100, 200, 500, and 1,000 marks and coins of 1, 2, 5, 10, and 50 pfennige and 1, 2, and 5 marks. At press time (spring 1998), the mark stood at DM 1.80 to the U.S. dollar, DM 1.26 to the Canadian dollar, and DM 2.98 to the pound sterling.

Telephoning

COUNTRY CODE

Germany's country code is 49. When dialing a number in Germany from outside the country, drop the initial 0 in the regional code.

Contacts and Resources

CONSULATES

United States (⊠ Neustädtische Kirchstr. 4–5, ☎ 030/238–5174). **Canadian** (⊠ International Trade Center, Friedrichstr. 95, ☎ 030/261–1161). **United Kingdom** (⊠ Unter den Linden 32–34, ☎ 030/201–840). **Ireland** (⊠ Ernst-Reuter-Pl. 10, ☎ 030/3480–0822).

Please note: The embassies listed above are branch offices of the embassies' head offices in Bonn. By the year 2000, the United States, among other nations, will have moved their main offices to new facilities in Berlin. Phone numbers and addresses shown above are likely to change in 1999.

EMERGENCIES

Police (☎ 030/110). **Ambulance** (☎ 030/112). **Ambulance and emergency medical attention** (☎ 030/310–031). **Dentist and emergency pharmaceutical assistance** (☎ 030/01141).

ENGLISH-LANGUAGE BOOKSTORES

Hugendubel (⊠ Tauentzienstr. 13, ☎ 030/214–060), **Dussmann Kulturkaufhaus** (⊠ Friedrichstr. 90, ☎ 030/20250), **Marga Schoeller** (⊠ Knesebeckstr. 33, ☎ 030/881–1112), and **Buchhandlung Kiepert** (⊠ Hardenbergstr. 4–5, ☎ 030/311–0090) sell English-language publications.

GUIDED TOURS

Orientation. Severin & Kühn (⊠ Kurfürstendamm 216, ☎ 030/880–4190); **Berliner Bären Stadtrundfahrt** (BBS, ⊠ Seeburgerstr. 19b, ☎ 030/3519–5270); **Berolina Stadtrundfahrten** (⊠ Kurfürstendamm 22, corner Meinekestr., ☎ 030/8856–8030); and **Bus Verkehr Berlin (BVB,** ⊠ Kurfürstendamm 225, ☎ 030/885–9880) offer more or less identical tours in English, covering all the major sights in Berlin, as well as day tours to Potsdam and Dresden. The Berlin tours cost DM 25–DM 45, those to Potsdam and Sanssouci Palace, the favorite residence of Frederick the Great, DM 54.

Boat. Berlin is a city of waterways, and boat trips can be made on the Spree River, on the canals that connect the city's network of big lakes, and on the lakes themselves. For details contact the main city tourist office (☞ Visitor Information, *below*).

TRAVEL AGENCIES

American Express Reisebüro (⊠ at Wittenbergpl., Bayreuther Str. 37, ☎ 030/2149–8363; ⊠ Uhlandstr. 173, ☎ 030/882–7575; ⊠ Friedrichstr. 172, ☎ 030/238–4102). **American Lloyd** (⊠ Kurfürstendamm 209, ☎ 030/20740).

The **Berlin Tourismus Marketing GmbH** (main tourist office; Europa Center; Brandenburger Tor; Tegel Airport; by mail, Berlin Tourismus Marketing ⊠ Am Karlsbad 11, D-10785 Berlin).

Berlin-Hotline (☏ 030/250–025, FAX 030/2500–2424).

6 Brussels

Brussels remains at heart a comfortable provincial city. It is remarkably unaffected by its status as "the capital of Europe" and by the influx of international experts who staff the institutions of the European Union and NATO. A stone's throw away from steel and glass towers are cobbled streets, where the demands of modern life have had little impact. Away from the winding alleys of the city center, parks and squares are plentiful, and the park of the Bois de la Cambre at the end of fashionable Avenue Louise leads straight into a forest as large as the city itself. In Brussels, Art Nouveau flourished as nowhere else, and its spirit lives on. Town houses are gloriously different from one another, which makes walking down most any residential street a joyous adventure.

EXPLORING BRUSSELS

You need to give yourself at least two days to explore the many riches of Brussels, devoting one day to the Old Town (whose cobblestones call for comfortable walking shoes), and the other to the great museums and uptown shopping streets.

Around the Grand'Place

Numbers in the margin correspond to points of interest on the Brussels map.

9 **Cathédrale St-Michel et Ste-Gudule.** The names of the archangel and an obscure 7th-century local saint have been joined together for the cathedral of Brussels. Begun in 1226, it combines architectural styles from the Romanesque to full-blown Gothic. The chief treasures are the stained-glass windows designed by Bernard van Orley, an early 16th-century court painter. In summer the great west window is flood-lighted from within to reveal its glories. The ornately carved pulpit (1699) depicts Adam and Eve being expelled from the Garden of Eden. In the crypt are remnants of the original church. The huge construction is again gleaming white after the removal of centuries of grime. The interior restoration of the nave is complete, but the choir is not yet accessible. ⊠ *Parvis Ste-Gudule,* ☎ *02/217–8345.* ◯ *Nov.–Mar., Mon.–Sat. 7–7, Sun. 8–6; Apr.–Oct., Mon.–Sat. 7–7, Sun. 8–7.*

★ ❼ **Centre Belge de la Bande Dessinée** (Belgian Comic-Strip Center). This unique museum celebrates the comic strip, focusing on such famous Belgian graphic artists as Hergé, Tintin's creator; Morris, the progenitor of Lucky Luke; and many others. Temporary exhibitions feature other practitioners of the "seventh art." There's also a lending library and bookshop. The display is housed in a splendid Art Nouveau building from 1903, designed down to the smallest detail by that movement's leading figure, Victor Horta (1861–1947). ⊠ *Rue des Sables 20,* ☎ *02/219–1980.* ◯ *Tues.–Sun. 10–6.*

❺ **Galeries St-Hubert.** This oldest and most elegant of covered shopping arcades was constructed in 1847 and is filled with upscale shops, restaurants, and theaters. Recently spruced up and renovated, it is now particularly attractive. Diffused daylight penetrates the gallery from the glassed arches high above, flags of many nations billow ever so slightly, and neoclassical gods and heroes in their sculpted niches look down on the crowded shopping scene below. Midway through the gallery, it is traversed by the **Rue des Bouchers,** which, with its side streets, forms the main restaurant area in the heart of the tourist maelstrom. Caveat: The more lavish the display of food outside, the poorer the cuisine inside. ⊠ *Between Rue du Marché-aux-Herbes and Rue d'Arenberg.*

★ ❶ **Grand'Place.** In one of his more pointless military exercises, France's "Sun King," Louis XIV, had the Grand'Place bombarded with red-hot cannon balls in 1695. The resulting fires destroyed all but the Town Hall. The ornate Baroque guild houses of the Grand'Place, with their burnished facades, were built shortly after the French bombardment. They are topped by gilded statues of saints and heroes so vividly rendered that they seem to call out to each other. Thus the end result of Louis XIV's folly is Europe's most sumptuous market square, the jewel of Brussels. There is a daily flower market from spring to fall and a Sunday-morning bird market. On summer nights, music and colored light flood the entire square. Shops and taverns occupy most ground floors, but one serves its original purpose. This is the Maison des Brasseurs, which houses the **Brewery Museum** (⊠ Grand'Place 10, ☎ 02/511–4987). The Grand'Place comes enchantingly alive during local festivals, such as the *Ommegang,* a magnificent historical pageant re-creating Emperor Charles V's reception in the city (first Tuesday and Thursday in July) and the European Christmas Market, with stalls representing many different nations and a life-size crèche with real animals.

❷ **Hôtel de Ville** (Town Hall). Dominating the Grand'Place, the Town Hall is 500 years older than the guild houses that line the square. Over the gateway are statues of the prophets and effigies of long-gone dukes and duchesses. The slender central tower, combining boldness and light, is topped by a statue of St. Michael crushing a figure of the devil under his feet. During the current restoration, the weather-worn St. Michael

was airlifted off the top of the tower and another archangel flown in
to replace him. The halls are embellished with some of the finest examples of Brussels and Mechelen tapestries. ⊠ *Grand'Place,* ☎ *02/
279–4365.* ☉ *English-speaking tours Tues. 11:30 and 3:15, Wed.
3:15, Sun. 12:15. No individual visits.*

❸ **Maison du Roi** (King's House). Despite the name, no king ever lived in
the 16th-century palace facing the Town Hall on the Grand'Place. It
contains the **Musée de la Ville de Bruxelles** (City Museum), whose collections include Gothic sculptures, porcelain, and silverware, as well
as a number of paintings, such as Bruegel's *Marriage Procession.* On
the top floor is an extravagant wardrobe of more than 600 costumes
for Manneken Pis, Brussels's naughty trademark, starting with one donated by the self-same Louis XIV who destroyed the original Grand'-
Place. ⊠ *Grand'Place,* ☎ *02/279–4355.* ☉ *Mon.–Thurs. 10–12:30
and 1:30–5 (Oct.–Mar. until 4), weekends 10–1.*

❹ **Manneken Pis.** Originally this was one of many public fountains. The
first mention of him dates from 1377, but the present version, a small
bronze statue of a chubby little boy peeing, was made by Jerome
Duquesnoy in 1619. The statue of "Brussels's Oldest Citizen" is in fact
a copy; the original was kidnapped by 18th-century French soldiers.
⊠ *3 blocks southwest of Grand'Place, corner of Rue de l'Etuve and
Rue du Chêne.*

❻ **Théâtre de Marionettes Toone** (Toone Marionette Theater). Brussels folklore lives in this tiny puppet theater, with an adjoining pub and a small
museum. The puppeteers irreverently tackle anything from *Hamlet* to
the *Three Musketeers* in the broadest of Brussels dialect. For the ben-
efit of visitors, there are occasional performances in more widely un-
derstood languages, such as French, Dutch, and even English. ⊠
L'Impasse Schuddeveld off Petite Rue des Bouchers, ☎ *02/511–7137.*
▣ *BF400.* ☉ *Daily; performances Fri. and Sat. 8:30 PM.*

❽ **Vismet** (Fish Market). The river has been channeled underground, but
the many seafood restaurants remain, making this a pleasantly animated
area, highly popular with the *Bruxellois* (residents of Brussels). There's
one seafood restaurant after the other on both of the former wharves,
and when the weather is good they all set up tables and chairs on the
wide promenade that separates them. ⊠ *Quai au Bois-à-Brûler and
Quai aux Briques.*

Around the Place Royale

★ ⓱ **Grand Sablon.** The city's most sophisticated square is alive with cafés,
restaurants, art galleries, and antiques shops. At the upper end of the
square stands the church of **Notre Dame du Sablon,** built in flamboyant Gothic style by the crossbowmen who used to train here. The stained-
glass windows are illuminated from within at night, creating an
extraordinary effect of kindly warmth. A much-needed restoration
program has begun. Weekend mornings, more than 100 stall holders
participate in a lively antiques market below the church. Downhill from
the Grand Sablon stands the **Eglise Notre-Dame de la Chapelle** (⊠ Pl.
de la Chapelle). Its Gothic exterior and surprising Baroque belfry have
been splendidly restored. This was the parish church of Pieter Bruegel
the Elder (1520–69), and he is buried here in an imposing marble tomb
amid much statuary.

⓭ **Musée d'Art Ancien** (Museum of Ancient Art). The collection of old masters focuses on Flemish and Dutch paintings from the 15th to the 19th
centuries. In the Bruegel Room is one of the finest collections of his works,
including the *Fall of Icarus;* The Rubens Room contains paintings by

86

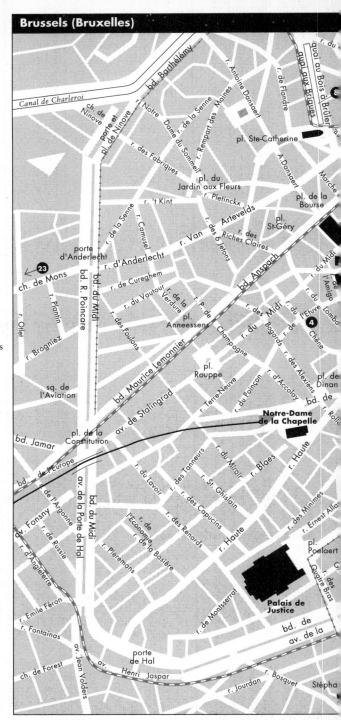
Brussels (Bruxelles)

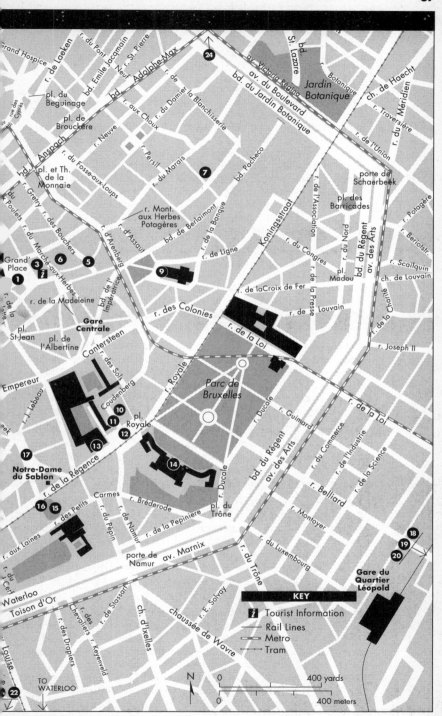

Grand Hospice
r. de Laeken
r. du Pont
bd. Emile Jacqmain
r. Neuve r. St. Pierre
Adolphe-Max
r. du Damier
la Blanchisserie
av. Victoria Regina
St. Lazare
bd. du Jardin Botanique
av. du Boulevard
Botanique
ch. de Haecht
Jardin Botanique
r. du Méridien
r. Traversière
②④
pl. du Beguinage
pl. de Brouckère
bd. Anspach
r. Neuve
r. aux Choux
r. Persil
r. du Marais
bd. Pacheco
r. de l'Union
r. de l'Association
porte de Schaerbeek
pl. des Barricades
r. Potagère
r. Bériotstr.
r. des Cyprès
rue des mali
pl. et Th. de la Monnaie
bd. Grétry
r. du Fossé-aux-Loups
r. des Bouchers
r. Mont. aux Herbes Potagères
bd. de Berlaimont
r. d'Assaut
r. de la Banque
Koningsstraat
bd. du Régent
av. des Arts
r. Scailquin
ch. de Louvain
r. du Marché aux Herbes
⑥
r. d'Arenberg
⑤
r. de Ligne
r. du Congres
r. du Nord
pl. Madou
Grand' Place
③
i
①
r. de la Madeleine
bd. de l'Impératrice
⑨
r. des Colonies
r. de laCroix de Fer
r. de la Presse
r. de Louvain
ch. de Louvain
r. de la Charité
r. de la lenta
pl. St-Jean
Gare Centrale
Cantersteen
r. des Sols
r. de la Loi
r. Joseph II
pl. de l'Albertine
Empereur
r. J. Lebeau
Coudenberg
⑩
⑪
r. Royale
Parc de Bruxelles
r. Ducale
r. Guimard
r. de la Loi
r. du Commerce
r. de l'Industrie
r. de la Science
k
pl. Royale
⑫
⑬
⑭
bd. du Régent
av. des Arts
r. Belliard
Notre-Dame du Sablon
⑰
r. de la Régence
Carmes
r. Bréderode
r. Ducale
r. Montoyer
⑯ ⑮
r. des Petits
r. du Pépin
r. de Namur
r. de la Pepinière
pl. du Trône
r. aux Laines
porte de Namur
av. Marnix
r. du Luxembourg
⑱
⑲
⑳
Gare du Quartier Léopold
Waterloo
Toison d'Or
r. de Stassart
r. du Trône
r. E. Solvay
chaussée de Wavre
r. du Cerf
r. des Chevaliers
r. des Drapiers
r. de Keyenveld
r. d'Ixelles

KEY

ℹ Tourist Information
— Rail Lines
⊢⊣ Metro
······ Tram

r. Louise
②②
TO WATERLOO

N

0 _____ 400 yards

0 _____ 400 meters

that master. The museum displays paintings by Hieronymus Bosch, Matsys, Van Dyck, and others. An underground passage links the museum with the adjacent Museum of Modern Art. The two have staggered lunch hours so as not to inconvenience visitors. ✉ *Rue de la Régence 10,* ☎ *02/508–3211.* 🎫 *Free.* ☉ *Tues.–Sun. 10–noon and 1–5.*

★ ⓫ **Musée d'Art Moderne** (Museum of Modern Art). Housed in an exciting feat of modern architecture, it descends seven floors into the ground around a central light well. There are some excellent paintings by modern French artists, but the surprise lies in the quality of Belgian modern art: not only Magritte's luminous fantasies, Delvaux's nudes in surrealist settings, and James Ensor's hallucinatory carnival scenes, but also the works of several artists who deserve much wider recognition, such as Spilliaert, Permeke, Brusselmans, and Wouters from the first half of the century; the post-war COBRA group, including Pierre Alechinsky and Henri Michaux; and on to contemporary works. Note: entrance is via the ☞ **Musée d'Art Ancien.** ✉ *Pl. Royale 1,* ☎ *02/508–3211.* 🎫 *Free.* ☉ *Tues.–Sun. 10–1 and 2–5.*

⓰ **Musée Instrumental** (Musical Instruments Museum). Six thousand instruments, from the Bronze Age to today, make up this extraordinary collection. The saxophone family is well represented, as befits the country of its inventor, Adolphe Sax (1814–94). The museum is scheduled to move at the end of 1999 to the Old England building, a few blocks away. ✉ *Pl. du Petit Sablon 17,* ☎ *02/511–3595.* 🎫 *Free.* ☉ *Tues.–Sat. 9:30–4:45 (Sat. from 10 AM).*

★ ⓾ **Old England.** This is one of the masterpieces of Art Nouveau. The glass-and-steel building, with a fanciful corner turret, was designed by Paul Saintenoy (1862–1952) for the British-owned department store, Old England, in 1899. Renovation of the facade has been completed, and the Musical Instruments Museum will move in toward the end of 1999; until then, the interior cannot be visited. ✉ *Rue Montagne-de-la-Cour 94.*

⓮ **Palais Royal** (Royal Palace). The palace was rebuilt in 1904 to suit the expansive tastes of Leopold II (1835–1909). The king's favorite architect, Alphonse Balat, achieved his masterpiece with the monumental stairway and the Throne Hall. ✉ *Pl. des Palais,* ☎ *02/551–2020.* 🎫 *Free.* ☉ *July 22–mid-Sept., Tues.–Sun. 9:30–3:30.*

⓯ **Petit Sablon.** The benches in this peaceful garden square offer welcome respite after the busy Grand Sablon. Statues of the counts Egmont and Hoorn, who were executed by the Spanish in 1568, hold pride of place. The square is surrounded by a magnificent wrought-iron fence, topped by 48 small statues representing Brussels's medieval guilds. Each craftsman carries an object that reveals his trade: The furniture maker holds a chair; the wine merchant, a goblet. ✉ *Rue de la Régence.*

⓬ **Place Royale.** This white, symmetrical square is neoclassical Vienna transposed to Brussels during the Austrian reign in the late 18th century. From here you have a superb view over the lower town. The Coudenberg Palace once stood here. Underneath the square, excavations have revealed the "Aula Magna" (soon to become accessible to the public), where the Flanders-born King of Spain and Holy Roman Emperor Charles V (1500–58) was crowned and where he also announced his abdication two years before his death. The name of the palace lives on in the 18th-century church, St-Jacques-sur-Coudenberg. In the center of the square stands the equestrian statue of Godefroy de Bouillon (1060–1100), leader of the First Crusade and ruler of Jerusalem.

Elsewhere in Brussels

⑱ Autoworld. This mecca for vintage car aficionados comprises a collection of 450 vehicles. The surprise star of the show is the Belgian-made Minerva, a luxury car from the early '30s. ⊠ *Parc du Cinquantenaire 11,* ☎ *02/736–4165.* ⊙ *Daily 10–6 (Nov.–Mar. until 5).*

⑲ European Union Institutions. The various offices of the European Commission are centered on Rond Point Schuman (Metro: Schuman.) The rounded glass summit of the new **European Parliament** building (⊠ Rue Wiertz 43) looms behind the Gare de Luxembourg.

㉑ Hôtel Hannon (Hannon Mansion). The flowering of Art Nouveau produced this handsome and original town house by Jules Brunfaut (1903). In the interior note the staircase with its romantic fresco, and the stained glass. ⊠ *Av. de la Jonction 1,* ☎ *02/538–4220.* ⊙ *Tues.–Sun. 1–6; closed July 15–Aug. 15. Near Musée Horta; trams 91 and 92 from Place Louise.*

★ **㉓ Maison d'Erasme** (The Erasmus House). The remarkable redbrick 15th-century house where Erasmus (1466–1536), the great humanist, lived in 1521 stands in the middle of a nondescript neighborhood. Every detail is authentic, with period furniture, paintings by Holbein and Hieronymus Bosch, prints by Albrecht Dürer, and early editions of Erasmus's works, including *In Praise of Folly.* ⊠ *Rue du Chapitre 31,* ☎ *02/521–1383.* ⊙ *Wed.–Thurs. and Sat.–Mon., 10–noon and 2–5. Metro: St-Guidon.*

㉔ Mini-Europe. This highly popular family attraction comprises 300 models (on a 1:25 scale) of famous European buildings, monuments, and technical achievements. ⊠ *Bd. du Centenaire 20,* ☎ *02/478–0550.* ☜ *BF390.* ⊙ *Apr.–Dec., daily 10–6 (July–Aug. until 8). Metro: Heysel.*

★ **㉒ Musée Horta** (Horta Museum). Victor Horta (1861–1947), the Belgian master of Art Nouveau, designed this building for himself and lived and worked here until 1919. From cellar to attic—the staircase is a great work of art—every detail of the house displays the exuberant curves of the Art Nouveau style. It was Horta's aim to put nature and light back into daily life, and here his floral motifs give a sense of opulence and spaciousness where in fact space is very limited. ⊠ *Rue Américain 25,* ☎ *02/537–1692.* ⊙ *Tues.–Sat. 2–5:30. Bus 91 or 92 from Place Louise.*

⑳ Musée Royal de l'Afrique Centrale (Royal Museum of Central Africa). King Leopold II (1835–1909) didn't do things by halves. He was sole owner of the Congo, later Zaire, and now the Republic of Congo—in hindsight an unfortunate colonial adventure, which brought great wealth to the exploiters and untold misery to the exploited. He built a museum outside Brussels to house some 250,000 objects emanating from his domain, as well as an avenue leading to the attractive site. The museum has since become a leading research center for African studies, with 13 specialized libraries. ⊠ *Leuvensesteenweg 13, Tervuren,* ☎ *02/ 769–5211.* ⊙ *Tues.–Sun. 10–5. Tram 44 from Square Montgomery.*

DINING

You can eat as well in Brussels as anywhere else in the world, but one restaurant meal a day is as much as most can manage. Brussels's 3,000-odd restaurants are supplemented by a multitude of fast-food establishments and snack bars, and most cafés also offer *petite restauration* (light meals)—omelets, pastas, and the like. It is *always* advisable to check out prix-fixe menus, especially in top-dollar restaurants. They sometimes cost only half of what you would pay dining à la carte. There's much less smoking than in the past, but dedicated no-smoking areas are rare.

RATINGS

Prices are per person, à la carte, and include a first course, main course, dessert, 16% service, and a whopping 21% value added tax, but no wine. Look for fixed-price menus; if you sacrifice choice, you can eat for less than BF500 in many good restaurants. Restaurant prices are roughly the same in Brussels and other cities.

CATEGORY	COST
$$$$	over BF3,500
$$$	BF2,500–BF3,500
$$	BF1,500–BF2,500
$	under BF1,500

$$$$ ✕ **Comme Chez Soi.** Pierre Wynants, with his second-in-command, Li-
★ onel Rigolet, runs a restaurant where the kitchen is larger than the Art Nouveau dining room. One all-time favorite, fillet of sole with a white wine mousseline and shrimp, is always on the menu. A new creation is warm oysters with Belgian endives and bacon. Many dishes are served for a minimum of two persons. You'll be happier here if you can go as a party of four; tables for two are too close for comfort. Be sure to reserve well ahead of time. ⊠ *Pl. Rouppe 23,* ☎ *02/512–2921. Reservations essential. Jacket and tie. AE, DC, MC, V. Closed Sun., Mon., July.*

$$$$ ✕ **Maison du Cygne.** With decor to match its classical cuisine, this restau-
rant is set in a 17th-century guildhall on the Grand'Place. The formal dining room upstairs has paneled walls hung with old masters, and a small room on the mezzanine floor contains two priceless Bruegels. Service is flawless in the grand old manner. The food is dependable but not the main attraction; rack of lamb and braised turbot are special-ties. ⊠ *Rue Charles Buyls 2,* ☎ *02/511–8244. Reservations essential. Jacket and tie. AE, DC, MC, V. Closed Sun. and 3 wks in Aug. No lunch Sat.*

$$$$ ✕ **Sea Grill.** Gigantic etched-glass murals convey the cool of the Arc-
★ tic fjords that provide many of the ingredients for this seafood restau-rant, one of Belgium's best. The young chef, Yves Mattagne, has gone from strength to strength with such dishes as ravioli stuffed with smoked langoustines and served with sun-dried tomato butter. Clas-sics include whole sea bass baked in salt and Brittany lobster pressed at your table. ⊠ *Radisson SAS Hotel, Rue du Fossé-aux-Loups 47,* ☎ *02/227–3120. Jacket and tie. AE, DC, MC, V. Closed Sun., Easter wk, and 4 wks in July/Aug. No lunch Sat.*

$$$ ✕ **Ogenblik.** With green-shade lamps over marble-top tables, saw-
★ dust on the floor, ample servings, and a great ambience, Ogenblik is a true (but expensive) bistro. The long and imaginative menu changes frequently but generally includes such specialties as mille-feuille with lobster and salmon, and saddle or leg of lamb with fresh, young veg-etables. ⊠ *Galerie des Princes 1,* ☎ *02/511–6151. Reservations not accepted after 8 PM. AE, DC, MC, V. Closed Sun.*

$$ ✕ **Aux Armes de Bruxelles.** This restaurant is one of the few to escape the "tourist trap" label in this hectic little street. The three rooms have a lively atmosphere: The most popular section overlooks the street the-ater outside, but locals prefer the cozy rotunda. Among the specialties are tomatoes stuffed with freshly peeled shrimps, waterzooi, and mus-sels in white wine. ⊠ *Rue des Bouchers 13,* ☎ *02/511–2118. AE, DC, MC, V. Closed Mon. and June.*

$$ ✗ **L'Idiot du Village.** Walls and ceiling in the front room are cornflower blue and in the back room oxblood red; the paintings are surrealist and the chandelier multicolored in this old-town eatery, vastly popular with a young clientele. Goose liver marbled with prunes, salmon-stuffed cannelloni, and roast suckling pig are popular items on the menu. ⊠ *Rue Notre-Seigneur 19,* ☎ *02/502–5582. Reservations essential. AE, MC, V. Closed weekends and mid-July–mid-Aug.*

$ ✗ **Au Vieux St-Martin.** When neighboring eateries on Grand Sablon are empty, this one remains busy, and you're equally welcome whether you order a full meal or a cup of coffee. Belgian specialties dominate the menu, and portions are generous. The restaurant claims to have invented the now ubiquitous *filet américain,* the well-seasoned Belgian version of steak tartare. The walls are hung with bright contemporary paintings, and picture windows face the pleasant square. ⊠ *Pl. du Grand Sablon 38,* ☎ *02/512–6476. Reservations not accepted. No credit cards.*

$ ✗ **Chez Jean.** This old-timer next to the Grand'Place is celebrating 65 years of serving good, honest Belgian food: shrimp croquettes, waterzooi, salmon-and-endives cooked with a dash of beer. Waitresses in black and white provide friendly service. ⊠ *Rue des Chapeliers 6,* ☎ *02/511– 9815. AE, DC, MC, V.*

$ ✗ **Falstaff.** Some things never change, and Falstaff used to be one of
★ them. There is now an up-market Falstaff Gourmand (Rue des Pierre 38) where the food is fancier and prices higher. But old-timers stick with the original, a huge tavern, with an Art Nouveau interior, that fills up for lunch and keeps going until 5 AM, with an ever-changing crowd, from students to pensioners. Cheerful waitresses take your orders for onion soup, filet mignon, salads, and other straightforward dishes. ⊠ *Rue Henri Maus 19,* ☎ *02/511–8789. AE, DC, MC, V.*

$ ✗ **Léon de Bruxelles.** Even though prices have been edging upward lately, Léon continues to do a land-office business and has over the years expanded into a row of eight old houses. Heaping plates of mussels and other Belgian specialties, such as eels in a green sauce, are served nonstop from noon to midnight, accompanied by what may be the best french fries in town. ⊠ *Rue des Bouchers 18,* ☎ *02/511–1415. Reservations not accepted. AE, DC, MC, V.*

$ ✗ **Le Pain Quotidien.** These bakeries-cum-snack bars have spread like wildfire all over Brussels (and even to New York and Boston in the U.S.) with the same formula: copious salads and delicious open sandwiches on farm-style bread, served at a communal table from 7 AM to 7 PM. Service at peak hours tends to be slow. ⊠ *Rue des Sablons 11,* ☎ *02/ 513–5154;* ⊠ *Rue Antoine Dansaert 16,* ☎ *02/502–2361; and other locations. Reservations not accepted. No credit cards.*

$ ✗ **Les Salons de Wittamer.** The elegant upstairs rooms at Brussels's best-
★ known patisserie have been converted into a stylish breakfast and lunch restaurant, topped off with the establishment's celebrated pastry or ice-cream concoctions. ⊠ *Pl. du Grand Sablon 12,* ☎ *02/511– 9339. AE, DC, MC, V. Closed Mon.*

NIGHTLIFE AND THE ARTS

The Arts

The best way to find out what's going on is to buy a copy of the English-language weekly magazine, the *Bulletin.* It's published every Thursday and sold at newsstands for BF85.

FILM

Movies are mainly shown in their original language. Complete listings appear in the *Bulletin.* The Acropole (⊠ Galeries de la Toison d'Or), the new UCG complex (⊠ Pl. de Brouckère), and the multiscreen

Kinepolis (⊠ Av. du Centenaire 1) have comfortable armchairs and **first-run movies.** For unusual movies or screen classics, visit the **Musée du Cinéma** (Cinema Museum; ⊠ Rue Baron Horta 9, ☎ 02/507–8370, 🖃 BF90 [BF60 if bought 24 hrs in advance]), where three movies with sound and two silents are shown daily.

Major symphony concerts and recitals are held at the **Palais des Beaux-Arts** (⊠ Rue Ravenstein 23, ☎ 02/507–8200). Chamber music is best enjoyed at the intimate **Conservatoire Royal de Musique** (⊠ Rue de la Régence 30, ☎ 02/507–8200). Free Sunday morning and lunchtime concerts take place at various churches, including the Cathédrale St-Michel et Ste-Gudule (☞ Exploring Brussels, *above*) and the Petite Eglise des Minimes (⊠ Rue des Minimes 62). **Forest National** (⊠ Av. du Globe 36, ☎ 02/347–0355) hosts rock and pop concerts.

The national opera company, based at the handsome **Théâtre Royal de la Monnaie** (⊠ Pl. de la Monnaie, ☎ 02/218–1202), stages productions of international quality under up-and-coming music director Antonio Pappano. Tickets cost BF300–BF3,100. Touring dance and opera companies often perform at the **Cirque Royal** (⊠ Rue de l'Enseignement 81, ☎ 02/218–2015).

The most attractive theater in town is the **Théâtre Royal du Parc** (⊠ Rue de la Loi 3, ☎ 02/512–2339), which stages productions of Molière and other French classics. Avant-garde theater is performed at: **Théâtre Varia** (⊠ Rue du Sceptre 78, ☎ 02/640–8258) and at the recently refurbished **Théâtre de Poche** (⊠ Chemin du Gymnase, in Bois de la Cambre, ☎ 02/649–1727).

Nightlife

There's a café on virtually every corner in Brussels, and all of them serve beer from morning to late at night. Some of the most authentic, with old-style Flemish wooden furniture and fittings, are around the Grand'-Place. **Le Cerf** (⊠ Grand'Place 20, ☎ 02/511–4791) is particularly pleasant. An appealing uptown outpost is **Nemrod** (⊠ Bd. de Waterloo 61, ☎ 02/511–1127). **La Fleur en Papier Doré** (⊠ Rue des Aléxiens 53, ☎ 02/511–1659) is a quiet bar with surrealist decor that attracts an artsy crowd. **Cirio** (⊠ Rue de la Bourse 18, ☎ 02/512–1395) is a pleasant old Art Nouveau bar. **Rick's Café Américain** (⊠ Av. Louise 344, ☎ 02/647–7530), a favorite with the American and British expat community, packs them in three deep at the bar at lunch. It serves great burgers and Tex-Mex fare. **Henry J. Bean's** (⊠ Rue du Montagne-aux-Herbes-Potagères 40, ☎ 02/219–2828), a 1950s-style bar and grill, attracts mostly the young.

In all the clubs the action starts after midnight. **Griffin's** (⊠ Rue Duquesnoy 5, ☎ 02/505–5555), at the Royal Windsor Hotel, appeals to young adults and business travelers. The trendy favor **Jeux d'Hiver** (⊠ Chemin du Croquet 1A, ☎ 02/649–0864), a members-only club in the Bois de la Cambre; you'll be admitted if you look the part. **Le Garage** (⊠ Rue Duquesnoy 16, ☎ 02/512–6622) draws a young crowd (Sun. gays only). **Le Mirano Continental** (⊠ Chaussée de Louvain 38, ☎ 02/218–5772) attracts a self-styled jet set.

Most of Brussels's dozen or so jazz haunts lead a double life and feature live music only on certain nights; check before you go. **New York**

Café Jazz Club (⊠ Chaussée de Charleroi 5, ☎ 02/534–8509) is an American restaurant by day and a modern jazz hangout by night. **Sounds** (⊠ Rue de la Tulipe 28, ☎ 02/512–9250), a big café, emphasizes jazz rock and other modern trends. **Travers** (⊠ Rue Traversière 11, ☎ 02/218–4086), a café-cum-jazz club, has sounds from swing to modern jazz.

SHOPPING

Gift Ideas

Belgium is where the *praline*—rich chocolate filled with flavored creams, liqueur, or nuts—was invented. Try Godiva, Neuhaus, or the lower-priced Leonidas, available at shops throughout the city. Exclusive handmade pralines can be bought at **Wittamer** (⊠ Pl. du Grand Sablon 16, ☎ 02/512–3742). **Le St. Aulaye** (Rue Jean Chapelie 4, ☎ 02/345–7785) is an excellent pâtisserie with a sideline in superb chocolates. **Mary** (Rue Royal 73, ☎ 02/217–4500) is devoted exclusively to the art of the chocolatier.

Only the Val-St-Lambert mark guarantees handblown, hand-carved **crystal** tableware. Many stores sell crystal, including **Art and Selection** (⊠ Rue Marché-aux-Herbes 83, ☎ 02/511–8448) near the Grand'Place.

In shopping for **lace,** be sure to ask the store assistant outright whether it is handmade Belgian or made in East Asia. **Maison F. Rubbrecht** (⊠ Grand'Place, ☎ 02/512–0218) sells authentic Belgian lace. For a large choice of old and modern lace, try **Manufacture Belge de Dentelles** (⊠ Galerie de la Reine 6–8, ☎ 02/511–4477).

Markets

On Saturday (9–5) and Sunday (9–1), the upper end of the Grand Sablon square becomes an **antiques market** with well over 100 stalls. The **Vieux Marché** (Old Market; ⊠ Place du Jeu de Balle) is a flea market worth visiting for the authentic atmosphere of the working-class Marolles district. The market is open daily 7–2. If you hope to make real finds, get there early in the morning.

Shopping Districts

The shops in the **Galeries St-Hubert** sell mostly luxury goods or gift items. **Rue Neuve** and the **City 2** mall are good for less expensive boutiques and department stores. Avant-garde clothes by the recently famous Antwerp Six and their followers are sold in boutiques in the **Rue Antoine Dansaert.**

Uptown, **Avenue Louise,** with the arcades **Galerie Louise** and **Espace Louise,** counts a large number of boutiques selling expensive men's and women's wear, accessories, leather goods, and jewelry. The **Boulevard de Waterloo** is home to the same fashion names as Bond Street and Rodeo Drive. The **Grand Sablon** has more charm; this is the center for antiques and oriental carpets and for art galleries.

SIDE TRIP

Waterloo, where Napoléon was finally defeated by the British and German armies on June 18, 1815, lies 19 km (12 mi) to the south of the city; take a bus from Place Rouppe or a train from Gare Centrale to Waterloo station. The **Waterloo Tourist Office** (⊠ Chaussée de Bruxelles 149, ☎ 02/354–9910) is in the center of town.

The **Wellington Museum,** in the building where the general established his headquarters, displays maps and models of the battle and military memorabilia. ⊠ *Ch. de Bruxelles 147, ☎ 02/354–7806.* ☉ *Apr.–Sept., daily 9:30–6:30; Oct.–Mar., daily 10:30–5.*

Just south of town is the actual battlefield. Start at the **Visitors' Center,** which has an audiovisual presentation that shows scenes of the battle. You can also book guides to take you around the battlefield. ✉ *Rte. du Lion 252–254, Braine–l'Alleud,* ☎ *02/385–1912.* 🖃 *BF300.* ☉ *Apr.–Oct., daily 9:30–6:30; Nov.–Mar., daily 10:30–4. Guides 1815:* ✉ *Rte. du Lion 250,* ☎ *02/385–0625.* 🖃 *BF1,400, 1 hr; BF2,200, 3 hrs.*

Overlooking the battlefield is the **Butte de Lion,** a pyramid-shape monument erected by the Dutch. After climbing 226 steps, you will be rewarded with a great view of the site, especially the quadrangular fortified farms where British troops broke the French assault.

BRUSSELS ESSENTIALS

Arriving and Departing

BY BUS

Eurolines (✉ Place de Brouckère 50, ☎ 02/217–0025) operates up to three daily express services from and to Amsterdam, Berlin, Frankfurt, Paris, and London. The Eurolines Coach Station (✉ Rue du Progrès 80, ☎ 02/203–0707) in Brussels adjoins the Gare du Nord.

BY CAR

If you use Le Shuttle under the English Channel or a ferry arriving in Calais, note that the E40 (via Oostende and Brugge) now connects with the French expressway, cutting driving time from Calais to Brussels to under two hours.

BY FERRY

Holyman Hoverspeed (☎ 01304/240–241 in the U.K.; ☎ 059/559–955 in Belgium) operates catamaran and ferry services between Dover and Oostende, carrying cars and foot passengers. Travel time by catamaran is less than two hours, by ferry about four hours. Trains at either end connect with London and Brussels.

P&O North Sea Ferries (☎ 01482/377–177 in the U.K.; ☎ 050/543–430 in Europe) operates an overnight conventional ferry service between Hull and Zeebrugge.

BY PLANE

All international flights arrive at Brussels National Airport at Zaventem (sometimes called simply Zaventem), about a 30-minute drive or a 16-minute train trip from the city center. For flight information, call 0900/00747.

Between the Airport and Downtown. Trains depart from the airport for the Gare du Nord (North Station) and the Gare Centrale (Central Station) every 20 minutes. The trip takes 16 minutes and costs BF110 (first class) and BF85 (second class). A taxi to the city center takes about a half hour and costs about BF1,000.

BY TRAIN

Ten **Eurostar** (☎ 02/555–2525 for information; ☎ 0900/10177 for telephone sales, MC and V only) passenger trains a day link Brussels's Gare du Midi with London's Waterloo station via the Channel Tunnel in two hours, 40 minutes. A one-way trip costs BF6,700 in business class, BF4,200 in economy; rail pass holders qualify for 50% discounts.

All rail services between Brussels and Paris are now operated with new **Thalys** high-speed trains, which have slashed travel time between the two cities to one hour, 25 minutes. A one-way trip costs BF2,990 in "Confort 1", BF1,900 in "Confort 2." Reservations are required (☎ 0800/95777 for information, ☎ 0900/10177 for reservations). Thalys trains, traveling at lower speeds on conventional tracks, also link Brussels with Amsterdam and Cologne.

Getting Around

BY METRO, TRAM, AND BUS

The metro (subway), trams (streetcars), and buses run as parts of the same system. All are clean and efficient, and a single ticket costs BF50. The best buy is a 10-trip ticket for BF330 or a one-day card costing BF130. Tickets are sold in any metro station or at newsstands. Single tickets can be purchased on the bus.

BY TAXI

To call a cab, phone **Taxis Verts** (☎ 02/349–4949) or catch one at a cab stand. It's not possible to hail cruising taxis. Typical downtown rides cost BF250–BF500. Tips are included in the fare.

Money Matters

CURRENCY

The unit of currency in Belgium is the franc (BF). There are bills of 100, 200, 500, 1,000, 2,000, and 10,000 francs, and coins of 1, 5, 20, and 50 francs. At press time (spring 1998), the exchange rate was BF37 to the U.S. dollar, BF25 to the Canadian dollar, BF60 to the pound sterling, BF23 to the Australian dollar, and BF20 to the New Zealand dollar.

Telephoning

COUNTRY CODE

The country code for Belgium is 32. When dialing Belgium from outside the country, drop the first zero in the regional telephone code.

Contacts and Resources

EMBASSIES

U.S. (✉ Bd. du Régent 27, 1000 Brussels, ☎ 02/513–3830). **Canadian** (✉ Av. de Tervuren 2, 1040 Brussels, ☎ 02/741–0611). **U.K.** (✉ Rue d'Arlon 85, 1040 Brussels, ☎ 02/287–6211). **Australian** (Rue Guimard 6–8, 1040 Brussels, ☎ 02/286–0500). **New Zealand** (Bd. du Régent 47, 1000 Brussels, ☎ 02/512–1040).

EMERGENCIES

Police (☎ 101). **Ambulance and Fire Brigade** (☎ 100). **Doctor** (☎ 02/479–1818). **Dentist** (☎ 02/426–1026). **Pharmacy:** For information about all-night and weekend services, call ☎ 02/479–1818.

ENGLISH-LANGUAGE BOOKSTORES

Librairie de Rome (✉ Av. Louise 50b, ☎ 02/511–7937. **Sterling Books** (✉ Rue du Fossé-aux-Loups 38, ☎ 02/223–6223). **W. H. Smith** (✉ Bd. Adolphe Max 71–75, ☎ 02/219–2708).

GUIDED TOURS

Orientation. De Boeck Sightseeing (✉ Rue de la Colline 8, Grand'Place, ☎ 02/513–7744) operates city tours (BF750) with multilingual cassette commentary. Passengers are picked up at major hotels and at the tourist office in the Grand'Place. More original tours are run by **Chatterbus** (✉ Rue des Thuyas 12, ☎ 02/513–8940 for reservations). Tours include visits on foot or by minibus to the main sights (BF600) and a walking tour with a visit to a bistro (BF250). Tours are operated early June–September. **Walking Tours** organized by the tourist office (BF350) depart from the T.I.B. in the Town Hall (May–Sept., Mon.–Sat. at 10).

Side Trips. De Boeck Sightseeing Tours (☞ *above*) visits Antwerp, the Ardennes, Brugge, Ghent, Ieper, and Waterloo.

Special-Interest Bus Tours. Expertly guided half-day English-language coach tours are organized by **ARAU** (⊠ Bd. Adolphe Max 55, ☎ 02/219–3345, information and reservations; ☑ BF600) from March through November, including "Brussels 1900: Art Nouveau" (every Sat. AM) and "Brussels 1930: Art Deco" (every 3rd Sat.). Tours begin in front of Métropole hotel on Place Brouckère.

TRAVEL AGENCIES

American Express (⊠ Bd. du Souverain 100, 1170 Brussels, ☎ 02/676–2727). **Carlson Wagonlit Travel**(⊠ Bd. Clovis 53, 1040 Brussels, ☎ 02/287–8110).

VISITOR INFORMATION

Tourist Information Brussels (T.I.B.; ⊠ Hôtel de Ville, Grand'Place, ☎ 02/513–8940); here you can buy a **Tourist Passport** (BF300)—a one-day transport card and BF1,000 worth of museum admissions.

7 Budapest

Budapest, lying on both banks of the Danube, unites the hills of Buda and the wide boulevards of Pest. Though it was the site of a Roman outpost during the 1st century, the modern city was not actually created until 1873, when the towns of Óbuda, Pest, and Buda were joined. The resulting capital is the cultural, political, intellectual, and commercial heart of the nation; for the 20% of the nation's population who live here, anywhere else is just "the country."

Much of the charm of a visit to Budapest consists of unexpected glimpses into shadowy courtyards and long vistas down sunlit cobbled streets. Although some 30,000 buildings were destroyed during World War II and in 1956, the past lingers on in the often crumbling architectural details of the antique structures that remain in the memories and lifestyles of Budapest's citizens.

The principal sights of the city fall roughly into three areas, each of which can be comfortably covered on foot. The Budapest hills are best explored using public transportation. Many street names have been changed since 1989 to purge all reminders of the communist regime—you can sometimes still see

*the old name, negated with a victorious red "X,"
next to the new. The 22 districts of Budapest are
referred to in addresses with Roman numerals,
starting with I for the Várhegy (Castle Hill) district;
V, VI, and VII indicate the main downtown areas.*

EXPLORING BUDAPEST

Várhegy (Castle Hill)

*Numbers in the margin correspond to points of interest on the Budapest
map.*

Most of Buda's main sights are on Várhegy (Castle Hill), a long, narrow plateau laced with cobblestone streets, clustered with beautifully
preserved Baroque, Gothic, and Renaissance houses, and crowned by
the stately Royal Palace. Painstaking reconstruction work has been in
progress here since the area was nearly leveled during World War II.

❺ Hadtörténeti Múzeum (Museum of Military History). The collection
here includes uniforms and regalia, many belonging to the Hungarian
generals who took part in the abortive uprising against Austrian rule
in 1848. Other exhibits trace the military history of Hungary from the
original Magyar conquest in the 9th century up to the middle of this
century. English-language tours can be arranged in advance. ✉ *I, Tóth
Árpád sétány 40,* ☎ *1/356–9522.* ⊙ *Apr.–Sept., Tues.–Sun. 10–6;
Oct.–Mar., Tues.–Sun. 10–4.*

★ ❸ Halászbástya (Fishermen's Bastion). This wondrous porch overlooking Pest and the Danube was built at the turn of the century as a lookout tower to protect what was once a thriving fishing settlement. Its
neo-Romanesque columns and arches frame views over the city and
the river. ✉ *I, Behind Mátyás templom.*

★ ❶ Királyi Palota (Royal Palace, also known as Buda Castle). The Nazis
made their final stand here and left it a blackened wasteland. Under
the rubble archaeologists discovered the medieval foundations of the
palace of King Matthias Corvinus, who, during the 15th century,
presided over one of the most splendid courts in Europe. The rebuilt
palace is now a vast museum complex and cultural center. ✉ *I, south
of Szent György tér.*

In the castle's northern wing, the **Ludwig Múzeum** (Ludwig Museum)
houses a collection of more than 200 pieces of Hungarian and contemporary world art, including works by Picasso and Lichtenstein. ✉
I, Buda Castle (Wing A), Dísz tér 17, ☎ *1/375–7533.* 🎟 *Free Tues.*
⊙ *Tues.–Sun. 10–6.*

The central section of the palace houses the **Magyar Nemzeti Galéria**
(Hungarian National Gallery), which exhibits a wide range of Hungarian
fine art. Names to look for are Munkácsy, a 19th-century Romantic
painter, and Csontváry, an early Surrealist admired by Picasso. Tours
for up to five people with an English-speaking guide can be booked in
advance. ✉ *I, Buda Castle (Wing C), Dísz tér 17,* ☎ *1/175–7533.* ⊙
*Mid-Mar.–Oct., Tues.–Sun. 10–6; Nov.–mid-Mar., Tues.–Sun. 10–4.
(Note: mid-Jan.–mid-Mar., may reduce hours to Fri.–Sun. 10–4.)*

The **Budapesti Történeti Múzeum** (Budapest History Museum), the southern block of the palace, displays a fascinating new permanent exhibit

of the city's history from Buda's liberation from the Turks in 1686 through the 1970s. The 19th- and 20th-century photos and videos of the castle, the Chain Bridge, and other Budapest monuments here can provide a helpful orientation to the city. Down in the cellars are the original medieval vaults of the palace, a palace chapel, and more royal relics. ✉ *I, Buda Castle (Wing E), Szt. György tér 2,* ☎ *1/375–7533.* ☉ *Mar.–mid-May, Wed.–Mon. 10–6; mid-May–mid-Sept., daily 10–6; mid-Sept.–Oct., Wed.–Mon. 10–6; Nov.–Feb., Wed.–Mon. 10–4.*

★ ➋ **Mátyás templom** (Matthias Church). This venerable church with its distinctive roof of colored, diamond-pattern tiles and skeletal Gothic spire dates from the 13th century. Built as a mosque by the Turks, it was destroyed and reconstructed during the 19th century, only to be bombed during World War II. Only the south porch survives from the original structure. The Hapsburg emperors were crowned kings of Hungary here, the last of them, Charles IV, in 1916. High mass is held every Sunday at 10 AM with an orchestra and choir, and organ concerts are often held in the summer on Friday at 8 PM. Visitors are asked to remain at the back of the church during services (it's least intrusive to come after 9:30 AM weekdays and between 1 PM and 5 PM Sunday and holidays). Saturday is a popular wedding day; visitors are asked to be respectful. ✉ *I, Szentháromság tér 2,* ☎ *1/355–5657.* ▣ *Free, except during concerts.*☉ *Church: Daily 7 AM–8 PM; Treasury: Daily 9:30–5:30.*

➍ **Zenetörténeti Múzeum** (Museum of Music History). The handsome, 18th-century gray-stone palace that once belonged to the noble Erdődy family hosts intimate recitals of classical music and displays rare manuscripts and antique instruments. ✉ *I, Táncsics Mihály u. 7,* ☎ *1/214–6770.* ☉ *Mid-Nov.–late Dec. and 1st 2 wks of Mar., Tues.–Sun. 10–5; mid-Mar.–mid-Nov., Tues.–Sun. 10–6.*

The Heart of the City

Pest fans out from the Belváros (Inner City), which is bounded by the Kiskörút (Little Ring Road). The Nagykörút (Grand Ring Road) describes a wider semicircle from the Margaret Bridge to the Petőfi Bridge.

⓫ **Belvárosi plébánia templom** (Inner-City Parish Church). The oldest church in Pest dates from the 12th century. The structure incorporates a succession of Western architectural styles as well as preserving a Muslim prayer niche from the time when the Turks ruled the country. Liszt, who lived only a few yards away, often played the organ here. ✉ *V, Március 15 tér 2.*

★ **Korzó.** This elegant promenade runs south along the river, providing views of Castle Hill, the Chain Bridge, and Gellért Hill on the other side of the Danube. ✉ *V, from Eötvös tér to Március 15 tér.*

★ ⓱ **Magyar Állami Operaház** (Hungarian State Opera House). Flanked by a pair of marble sphinxes, this 19th-century neo-Renaissance treasure was the crowning achievement of architect Miklós Ybl. It has been restored to its original ornate glory—particularly inside. The best way to view the inside is to attend a ballet or opera, but there are no performances from around mid-July to late September, except for the week-long BudaFest international opera and ballet festival in mid-August. ✉ *VI, Andrássy út 22,* ☎ *1/331–2550, ext. 156 for tours. Foreign-language tours (45 min.) daily, 3 PM and 4 PM, meet in front of opera house.*

⓬ **Magyar Nemzeti Múzeum** (Hungarian National Museum). The stern, classical edifice was built between 1837 and 1847. On its steps, on March 15, 1848, Petőfi Sándor recited his revolutionary poem, the *"Nemzeti*

100

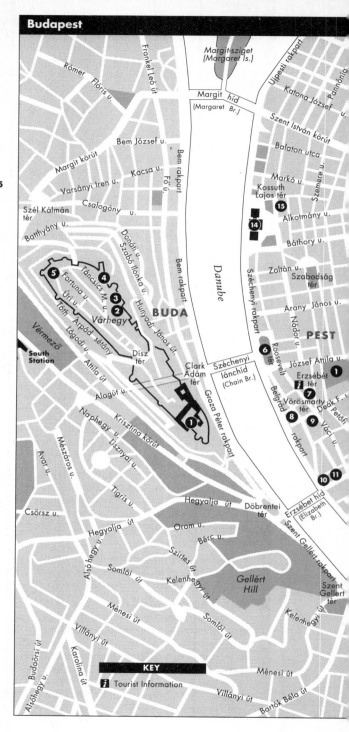

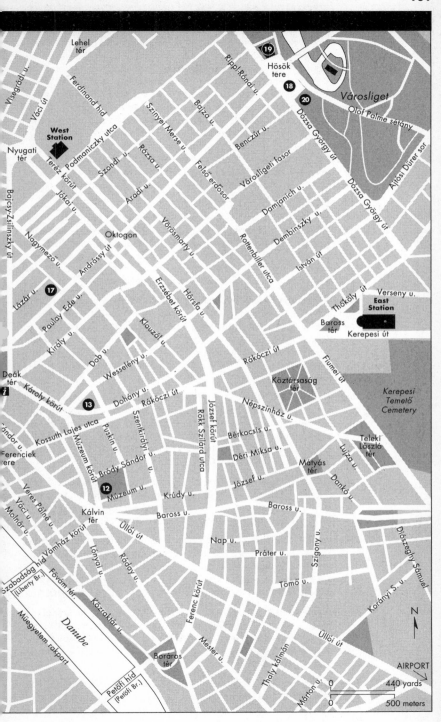

Dal" ("National Song"), declaring "By the God of Magyar, / Do we swear, / Do we swear, chains no longer / Will we wear." This poem, along with the "12 Points," a formal list of political demands by young Hungarians, called upon the people to rise up against the Hapsburgs. Celebrations of the national holiday—long banned by the communist regime—are now held here (and throughout the city) every year on March 15. The museum's most sacred treasure, the Szent Korona (Holy Crown)—the one that looks like a great golden soufflé resting on a Byzantine band of enamel, pearls, and other gems—lies with a host of other royal relics in the domed Hall of Honor. The museum's epic Hungarian history exhibition includes exhibits chronicling the end of communism and the much-celebrated exodus of the Russian troops. ⊠ *IX, Múzeum körút 14–16,* ☎ *1/338–2122.* ⊙ *Mid-Mar.–mid-Oct., Wed.– Sun. 10–6; mid-Oct.–mid-Mar., Wed.–Sun. 10–5. Museum may open Tues. also; call ahead to confirm.*

🔟 **Március 15 tér** (March 15 Square). This square is not particularly picturesque, but it commemorates the 1848 struggle for independence from the Hapsburgs with a statue of the poet Petőfi Sándor, who died in a later uprising. On March 15, the national holiday commemorating the revolution, the square is packed with patriotic Hungarians. ⊠ *V, end of Apácai Csere János u. just north of Erzsébet Bridge.*

⑬ **Nagy Zsinagóga** (Great Synagogue). Europe's largest synagogue was built between 1844 and 1859 in a Byzantine-Moorish style. Desecrated by German and Hungarian Nazis, it underwent years of massive restorations, completed in fall of 1996. Liszt and Saint-Saëns are among the great musicians who have played the synagogue's grand organ. ⊠ *VII, Dohány u. 2–8,* ☎ *1/342–1335.* ⊙ *Weekdays 10–3, Sun. 10–1. Closed Jewish holidays.*

★ ⑮ **Néprajzi Múzeum** (Museum of Ethnography). Elegant both inside and out, this museum has impressive, exhaustive exhibits—captioned in English—of folk costumes and traditions. These are the authentic pieces you can't see in tourist shops. ⊠ *V, Kossuth Lajos tér 12,* ☎ *1/332–6340.* ▭ *Free Tues.* ⊙ *Mid-Mar.–mid-Oct., Tues.–Sun. 10–6; mid-Oct.–mid-Mar., Tues.–Sun. 10–4.*

⑭ **Országház** (Parliament). The riverfront's most striking landmark is the imposing neo-Gothic Parliament, now minus the red star on top. Still a workplace for the nation's legislators, it is open for tours only. ⊠ *V, Kossuth Lajos tér. For tours: IBUSZ Tours,* ☎ *1/319–7520.*

❻ **Roosevelt tér** (Roosevelt Square). On this picturesque square opening onto the Danube you'll find the 19th-century neoclassical **Magyar Tudományos Akadémia** (Hungarian Academy of Sciences), and the 1907 **Gresham Palota** (Gresham Palace), a crumbling temple to the age of Art Nouveau. ⊠ *V, at Pest end of Széchenyi lánchíd (Chain Bridge).*

★ **Széchenyi lánchíd** (Chain Bridge). The most beautiful of the Danube's eight bridges, the Széchenyi lánchíd was built twice: once in the 19th century and again after it was destroyed by the Nazis. Luckily, its classic, symmetrical design was left unchanged. ⊠ *Spanning the Danube between I, Clark Ádám tér, and V, Roosevelt tér.*

⑯ **Szent István Bazilika** (St. Stephen's Basilica). Dark and massive, the 19th-century basilica is one of the chief landmarks of Pest. It was planned early in the 19th century as a neoclassical building, but by the time it was completed more than 50 years later, it was decidedly neo-Renaissance. During World War II the most precious documents from the municipal archives were placed in the basilica's bombproof cellar. The mummified right hand of St. Stephen, Hungary's first king and patron saint, is preserved in the Szent Jobb chapel; the guard will illuminate it for you for a minimal charge. A climb up to the cupola (or a lift on the elevator) affords a sweeping city view. As restorations are under way, with a target completion date of 2010, some part of the structure is likely to be under scaffolding when you visit. ⊠ *V, Szt. István tér,* ☎ *1/317–2859.* ⌨ *Free.* ☉ *Church: Mon.–Sat. 7–7, Sun 1–7. Szt. Jobb Chapel: Apr.–Sept., Mon.–Sat. 9–5, Sun. 1–5; Oct.–Mar., Mon.–Sat. 10–4, Sun. 1–4. Cupola: Apr. and Sept.–Oct., daily 10– 5; May–Aug., daily 9–6.*

❾ Váci utca (Váci Street). Lined with expensive boutiques and dozens of souvenir shops, this pedestrian-only thoroughfare is Budapest's most upscale shopping street, and one of its most touristy areas. Váci utca's stretch south of Kossuth Lajos utca was recently transformed into another pedestrian-only zone, making the total length extend from Vörösmarty tér to the Szabadság Bridge. ⊠ *V, south from Vörösmarty tér.*

❽ Vigadó tér (Vigadó Square). This square, opening onto a grand Danube view, is named for the **Vigadó concert hall** (☞ Nightlife and the Arts, *below*). The hall was built in an eclectic mix of Byzantine, Moorish, and Romanesque styles; the façade even draws upon the ceremonial knots from the uniforms of the Hungarian hussars. Liszt, Brahms, and Bartók all performed here. Completely destroyed during World War II, it has been faithfully rebuilt. ⊠ *V, off the Korzó, between Vigadó u. and Deák Ferenc u.*

❼ Vörösmarty tér (Vörösmarty Square). In this handsome square in the heart of the Inner City, street musicians and sidewalk cafés combine to make one of the liveliest, albeit sometimes too touristy, atmospheres in Budapest. It's a great spot to sit and relax—but prepare to be approached by caricature artists and money changers. ⊠ *V, at northern end of Váci u.*

Hősök tere (Heroes' Square) and Városliget (City Park)

⓱ Hősök tere (Heroes' Square). Budapest's grandest boulevard of music and mansions, Andrássy út, ends appropriately at this sweeping piazza flanked by the Szépművészeti Múzeum (☞ *below*) and the Műcsarnok (☞ *below*). In the center stands the 120-ft bronze **Millenniumi Emlékmű** (Millennium Monument), begun in 1896 to commemorate the 1,000th anniversary of the Magyar Conquest and now newly shining in celebration of yet another 100 years. Statues of Árpád and six other founders of the Magyar nation occupy the base of the monument, while Hungary's greatest rulers and princes stand between the columns on either side. ⊠ *VI, Andrássy út at Dózsa György út.*

⓴ Műcsarnok (Palace of Exhibitions). This striking 1895 structure on Heroes' Square schedules exhibitions of contemporary Hungarian and international art and a rich series of films, plays, and concerts. ⊠ *XIV, Dózsa György út 37,* ☎ *1/343–7401.* ⌨ *Free Tues.* ☉ *Tues.– Sun. 10–6.*

★ ⓳ Szépművészeti Múzeum (Fine Arts Museum). An entire section of this Heroes' Square museum is devoted to Egyptian, Greek, and Roman artifacts, including many rare pieces of Greco-Roman ceramics. The institution's collection of Spanish paintings is among the best of its kind outside Spain. ⊠ *XIV, Dózsa György út 41,* ☎ *1/343–9759.* ☉ *Tues.– Sun. 10–5:30.*

★ Városliget (City Park). Just behind Heroes' Square, this 1-square-km (⅓-square-mi) park harbors Budapest's zoo, the state circus, an amusement park, and the outdoor swimming pool of the Széchenyi mineral baths. Inside is **Vajdahunyad Vár** (Vajdahunyad Castle), an art historian's Disneyland, created for the millennial celebration in 1896 and incorporating architectural elements typical of various periods of Hungary's history all in one complex. ✉ *XIV, between Dózsa György út and Hungária körút, and Vágány u. and Ajtósi Dürer sor.*

ELSEWHERE IN THE CITY

Aquincum. The reconstructed remains of the capital of the Roman province of Pannonia, dating from the 1st century AD, lie in northern Budapest's Óbuda district. A varied selection of artifacts and mosaics have been unearthed, giving a tantalizing inkling of what life was like on the northern fringes of the Roman empire. The on-site **Aquincum Museum** displays the dig's most notable finds. ✉ *III, Szentendrei út 139,* ☎ *1/250–1650. Grounds:* ☉ *Mid-Apr.–end Apr. and Oct., Tues.–Sun. 9–5; May–Sept., Tues.–Sun. 9–6.*

Jánoshegy (János Hill). A *libegő* (chairlift) will take you to the summit, the highest point in Budapest, where you can climb a lookout tower for the best view of the city. ✉ *Take Bus 158 from Moszkva tér to last stop, Zugligeti út,* ☎ *1/395–6494 or 1/376–3764.* ☉ *Mid-May–mid-Sept., daily 9–5; mid-Sept.–mid-May (depending on weather), daily 9:30–4. Closed alternate Mon.*

Szobor Park (Statue Park). For a look at Budapest's too-recent Iron Curtain past, make the 30-minute trip out to this open-air exhibit cleverly nicknamed "Tons of Socialism." Forty-two communist statues and memorials that once dominated the city have been exiled here since the political changes in 1989. You can wander among mammoth figures of Lenin and Marx while listening to songs from the Hungarian and Russian workers' movement blaring from loudspeakers. ✉ *XXII, Balatoni út, corner of Szabadkai út,* ☎ FAX *1/227–7446.* ☉ *Mid-Apr.–Oct., daily 8–8; Nov.–mid-Apr., weekends 10–dusk.*

DINING

Private restaurateurs are breathing excitement into the Budapest dining scene. You can choose from Chinese, Mexican, Italian, French, Indian, or various other cuisines—there are even vegetarian restaurants. Or you can stick to solid, traditional Hungarian fare. Be sure to check out the less expensive spots favored by locals. If you get a craving for sushi or tortellini, consult the restaurant listings in *The Budapest Sun* or *Budapest Week* (☞ Visitor Information *in* Budapest Essentials, *below*).

RATINGS

Prices are per person and include a first course, main course, and dessert, but no wine or tip. Prices in Budapest tend to be a good 30% higher than elsewhere in Hungary.

CATEGORY	COST
$$$$	over 3,200 Ft.
$$$	2,300 Ft.–3,200 Ft.
$$	1,400 Ft.–2,300 Ft.
$	under 1,400 Ft.

$$$$ ✕ **Vadrózsa.** The name means "wild rose," and there are always fresh ones on the table at this restaurant in a romantic old villa in Buda's exclusive Rózsadomb district. It's elegant to the last detail—even the service is white-glove—and the garden is delightful in summer. Kitchen fortés include venison and a variety of grilled fish, and the house spe-

cialty, grilled goose liver, is exquisite. ✉ *II, Pentelei Molnár u. 15,* ☎ *1/326–5817. Reservations essential. AE, DC, MC, V.*

$$$–$$$$ ✗ **Kacsa.** Hungarian and international dishes with a focus on duck are done with a light touch, with quiet chamber music in the background, in this small, celebrated restaurant just a few steps from the river. Try the crisp wild duck stuffed with plums. ✉ *II, Fő u. 75,* ☎ *1/201–9992. Reservations essential. AE, DC, MC, V. Dinner only.*

$$$–$$$$ ✗ **Múzeum.** Named for its location just steps from the National Museum, this elegant salon with mirrors, mosaics, and swift-moving waiters serves authentic Hungarian cuisine with a lighter touch. The salads are generous, the Hungarian wines excellent, and the chef dares to be creative. ✉ *VIII, Múzeum körút 12,* ☎ *1/267–0375. AE. Closed Sun.*

$$$ ✗ **Gundel.** George Lang, Hungary's best-known restaurateur, show-
★ cases his country's cuisine at this lauded turn-of-the-century palazzo in City Park. Dark-wood paneling, rich navy-blue and pink fabrics, paintings by exemplary Hungarian artists, and tables set with Zsolnay porcelain make the oversize dining room plush and handsome. Violinist György Lakatos, of the Lakatos Gypsy musician dynasty, strolls from table to table playing folk music, adding to the sensory extravagance. Waiters in black tie serve traditional favorites such as tender veal in a paprika-and-sour-cream sauce and carp *Dorozsma* (panfried with mushrooms). ✉ *XIV, Állatkerti út 2,* ☎ *1/321–3550. Reservations essential. AE, DC, MC, V.*

$$$ ✗ **Kisbuda Gyöngye.** This Budapest favorite, hidden away on a small street in Óbuda, is filled with mixed antique furniture, and its walls are covered with a patchwork of antique carved wooden cupboard doors. Try the fresh trout smothered in cream sauce with mushrooms and capers. ✉ *III, Kenyeres u. 34,* ☎ *1/368–6402 or 1/368–9246. Reservations essential. AE, DC, MC, V. Closed Sun.*

$$$ ✗ **Lou Lou.** Since it opened in 1995, this convivial bistro tucked onto
★ a side street near the Danube has been the hottest restaurant in Budapest. Framed prints, low lighting, and candles conjure a tasteful, elegantly romantic atmosphere. Blending local and Continental cuisines, the menu includes excellent rack of lamb—flown in fresh from New Zealand, and succulent fresh salmon with lemongrass; the Dijon-spiced venison fillets with wild berry sauce are a standout. At press time, Lou Lou was planning to relocate to a larger venue; check with Tourinform (☞ Visitor Information *in* Budapest Essentials, *below*) for the latest information. ✉ *V, Vigyázó Ferenc u. 4,* ☎ *1/312–4505. Reservations essential. AE. Closed daily 3–7, Sat. lunch, and Sun.*

$$$ ✗ **Művészinas.** Walls hung with framed vintage prints and photos, antique vitrines filled with old books, and tall slender candles on the tables create a romantic, old-world ambience in this bustling, bistrolike restaurant in the heart of Pest. Dozens of Hungarian specialties fill the long menu; beef, veal, and poultry are each prepared a half-dozen ways, from sirloin "Budapest style" (smothered in a goose-liver, mushrooms, and sweet-pepper ragout) to spinach-stuffed turkey breast in fragrant garlic sauce. Poppy-seed crepes with plum sauce are a sublime dessert. ✉ *VI, Bajcsy-Zsilinszky út 9,* ☎ *1/268–1439. Reservations essential. AE, MC, V.*

$$ ✗ **Bagolyvár.** George Lang opened this restaurant next door to his gastronomic palace, Gundel (☞ *above*), in 1993. The immaculate dining room with soaring beamed ceilings has a familial yet professional atmosphere, and the kitchen produces first-rate daily menus of home-style Hungarian specialties. Soups, served in shiny silver tureens, are particularly good. Musicians entertain with cimbalom music nightly from 7 PM. In warm weather there is outdoor dining on a roomy back patio. ✉ *VI, Állatkerti körút 2,* ☎ *1/343–0217. AE, DC, MC, V.*

$$ ✕ **Náncsi Néni.** "Aunt Nancy's" restaurant is a perennial favorite, despite its out-of-the-way location. Irresistibly cozy, the dining room feels like a country kitchen: Chains of paprikas and garlic dangle from the low wooden ceiling and shelves along the walls are crammed with jars of home-pickled vegetables, which you can purchase to take home. On the home-style Hungarian menu (large portions!), turkey dishes are given a creative flair, such as breast fillets stuffed with apples, peaches, mushrooms, cheese, and sour cream. Special touches include an outdoor garden in summer and free champagne for all couples in love. ✉ *II, Ördögárok út 80,* ☎ *1/397–2742. AE, MC, V.*

$ ✕ **Fészek.** Hidden away inside the 100-year-old Fészek Artists' Club in downtown Pest is this large, neoclassical dining room. In summer, you can dine outdoors in a Venetian-style courtyard. The extensive menu proffers heavy Hungarian classics such as turkey stuffed with goose liver and a variety of game dishes; the venison stew with tarragon is outstanding. Guests must pay a 150-Ft. Artists' Club cover charge upon arrival; if you've reserved a table in advance, the fee will be added to your bill instead. ✉ *VII, Kertész u. 36 (corner of Dob u.),* ☎ *1/322–6043. AE, DC, MC, V.*

$ ✕ **Tüköry Söröző.** At this traditional Hungarian spot, courageous car-
★ nivores can sample the beefsteak tartar, topped with a raw egg; many say it's the best in town. ✉ *V, Hold u. 15,* ☎ *1/269–5027. MC, V. Closed weekends.*

NIGHTLIFE AND THE ARTS

The Arts

The English-language *The Budapest Sun* and *Budapest Week* list the week's entertainment and cultural events. Hotels and tourist offices distribute the monthly *Programme,* which contains details of all cultural events in the city. The monthly *Where Budapest,* free at most hotels, is another good resource in English. Buy tickets at venue box offices, your hotel desk, many tourist offices, or ticket agencies, among them the **National Philharmonic Ticket Office** (✉ V, Vörösmarty tér 1, ☎ 1/318–0281) and the **Central Theater Booking Office** (✉ VI, Andrássy út 18, ☎ 1/312–0000).

Arts festivals begin to fill the calendar in early spring. The season's first and biggest, the **Budapest Spring Festival** (early to mid-March), showcases Hungary's best opera, music, theater, fine arts, and dance, as well as visiting foreign artists. The weeklong **BudaFest** opera and ballet festival (mid-August) takes place at the Opera House. Information and tickets are available from ticket agencies (☞ *above*).

CONCERTS AND MUSICALS

Several excellent orchestras, such as the Budapest Festival Orchestra, are based in Budapest. Concerts frequently include works by Hungarian composers Bartók, Kodály, and Liszt. **Liszt Ferenc Zeneakadémia** (Franz Liszt Academy of Music; ✉ VI, Liszt Ferenc tér 8, ☎ 1/342–0179) is Budapest's premier classical concert venue; orchestra and chamber music performances take place in its splendid main hall. Classical concerts are also held at the **Pesti Vigadó** (Pest Concert Hall; ✉ V, Vigadó tér 2, ☎ 1/318–9167). The **Régi Zeneakadémia** (Old Academy of Music; ✉ VI, Vörösmarty u. 35, ☎ 1/322–9804) is a smaller venue for chamber music. The 1896 **Vígszínház** (Comedy Theater; ✉ XIII, Pannónia út 1, ☎ 1/269–5340) presents mostly musicals. Operettas and Hungarian renditions of popular Broadway musicals are staged at the **Operett Színház** (Operetta Theater; ✉ VI, Nagymező u. 19, ☎ 1/332–0535).

OPERA AND DANCE

Budapest has two opera houses, one of which is the gorgeous neo-Renaissance **Magyar Állami Operaház** (Hungarian State Opera House; ⊠ VI, Andrássy út 22, ☎ 1/331–2550). There's also the plainer **Erkel Színház** (Erkel Theater; ⊠ VIII, Köztársaság tér, ☎ 1/333–0540).

Displays of Hungarian folk dancing take place at the **Folklór Centrum** (Folklore Center; ⊠ XI, Fehérvári út 47, ☎ 1/203–3868). The Hungarian State Folk Ensemble performs regularly at the **Budai Vigadó** (⊠ I, Corvin tér 8, ☎ 1/201–5846). There are regular participatory folk-dance evenings—with instructions for beginners—at district cultural centers; consult the entertainment listings of *The Budapest Sun* or *Budapest Week* for schedules and locations, or check with a hotel concierge.

Nightlife

Budapest is a lively city by night. Establishments stay open well past midnight and Western European–style bars and British-style pubs have sprung up all over the city. For quiet conversation, hotel bars are a good choice, but beware of the inflated prices. Expect to pay cash for your night on the town. The city also has its share of seedy go-go clubs and "cabarets," some of which have been shut down for scandalously excessive billing and physical intimidation and assault. Avoid places where women lingering nearby "invite" you in, and never order without first seeing the price.

BARS

The most popular of Budapest's Irish pubs and a favorite expat watering hole is **Becketts** (⊠ V, Bajcsy-Zsilinszky út 72, ☎ 1/311–1035), where Guinness flows freely amid polished-wood and brass decor. A hip, low-key crowd mingles at the stylish **Café Incognito** (⊠ VI, Liszt Ferenc tér 3, ☎ 1/351–9428), with low lighting and funky music kept at a conversation-friendly volume by savvy DJs. **Café Pierrot** (⊠ I, Fortuna u. 14, ☎ 1/375–6971), an elegant café and piano bar on a small street on Castle Hill, is well suited for a secret rendezvous.

CASINOS

Most casinos are open daily from 2 PM until 4 or 5 AM and offer gambling in hard currency—usually dollars—only. Sylvester Stallone is alleged to be an owner of the popular **Las Vegas Casino** (⊠ V, Roosevelt tér 2, ☎ 1/317–6022), in the Atrium Hyatt Hotel. The **Gresham Casino** (⊠ V, Roosevelt tér 5, ☎ 1/317–2407) is in the Gresham Palace at the Pest end of the Chain Bridge. In an 1879 building designed by prolific architect Miklós Ybl, who also designed the Hungarian State Opera House, the **Várkert Casino** (⊠ I, Miklós Ybl tér 9, ☎ 1/202–4244) is the most attractive in the city.

JAZZ AND ROCK CLUBS

Established Hungarian jazz headliners and young up-and-comers play nightly at **The Long Jazz Club** (⊠ VII, Dohány u. 22–24, ☎ 1/322–0006; closed Sun.). **Made Inn** (⊠ VI, Andrássy út 112, ☎ 1/311–3437), in an old stone mansion near Heroes' Square, has elaborate decor, a large outdoor bar, and a disco dance floor packed with local and international beautiful people. With wrought-iron and maroon-velvet decor, the stylish but unpretentious **Fél 10 Jazz Club** (⊠ VIII, Baross u. 30, ☎ 06/60–318–467) has a dance floor and two bars on three open levels.

SHOPPING

You'll find plenty of expensive boutiques, folk art and souvenir shops, and classical record shops on or around **Váci utca,** Budapest's pedestrian-only promenade. Browsing among some of the smaller, less touristy, more typically Hungarian shops in Pest—on the **Kiskörút** (Small Ring Boulevard) and **Nagykörút** (Great Ring Boulevard)—may prove more interesting and less pricey. Artsy boutiques are springing up in the section of district V south of Ferenciek tere toward the Danube and around Kálvin tér. **Falk Miksa utca,** north of Parliament, is home to some of the city's best antiques stores. You'll also encounter Transylvanian women dressed in colorful folk costume standing on busy sidewalks selling their own handmade embroideries and ceramics at rock-bottom prices. Look for them at **Moszkva tér, Jászai Mari tér,** outside the **Kossuth tér Metro,** and around **Váci utca.**

The popular, modern **Skála-Metro** department store (✉ VI, Nyugati tér 1–2) near the Nyugati train station sells a little bit of not entirely everything; its Buda branch, Skála-Budapest (✉ XI, Október 23 u. 6–10), is larger and usually has a large open-air market out front.

Markets

The magnificent, cavernous, three-story **Vásárcsarnok** (Central Market Hall; ✉ IX, Vámház körút 1–3) teems with shoppers browsing among stalls packed with salamis, red paprika chains, and other enticements. Upstairs you can buy folk embroideries and souvenirs.

A good way to find bargains (and adventure) is to make an early morning trip out to **Ecseri Piac** (✉ IX, Nagykőrösi út—take Bus 54 from Boráros tér), a vast, colorful, chaotic flea market on the outskirts of Budapest. Try to go Saturday morning when by far the most vendors are out. Foreigners are a favorite target for overcharging, so prepare to be tough when bargaining.

BUDAPEST ESSENTIALS

Arriving and Departing

BY BUS

Most buses to Budapest from the western region of Hungary and from Vienna arrive at **Erzsébet tér station** (✉ V, Erzsébet tér, ☎ 1/317–2318) downtown.

BY CAR

The main routes into Budapest are the M1 from Vienna (via Győr), the M5 from Kecskemét, the M3 from near Gyöngyös, and the M7 from the Balaton region.

BY PLANE

The only nonstop service between Budapest and the United States is aboard **Malév** (☎ 1/235–3535; 06/80–212–121 toll free or 1/235–3804 for tickets).

Hungary's international airport, **Ferihegy** (☎ 1/296–9696), is about 22 km (14 mi) southeast of the city. All Lufthansa and Malév flights operate from the newer Terminal 2; other airlines use Terminal 1. For same-day flight information call the airport authority (☎ 1/296–7155), where operators theoretically speak some English.

Between the Airport and Downtown. Minibuses marked LRI CENTRUM-AIRPORT-CENTRUM leave every half hour from 5:30 AM to 9:30 PM for the Erzsébet tér station (Platform 1) in downtown Budapest. The trip takes 30–40 minutes and costs around 700 Ft. The modern minivans of the reliable **LRI Airport Shuttle** (☎ 1/296–8555 or 1/296–6283) take you to any destination in Budapest, door to door, for around 1,300 Ft., even less than the least expensive taxi—and most employees speak English. At the airport buy tickets at the LRI counter in the arrivals hall near baggage claim; for your return trip call ahead for a pick-up. There are also approved **Airport Taxi** (☎ 1/282–2222) stands outside both terminals, with fixed rates based on which district you are going to. The cost to the central districts is about 3,500 Ft. Going to the airport, the cost is 1,999 Ft.; call one day ahead to arrange for a pick-up.

BY TRAIN
There are three main train stations in Budapest: **Keleti** (Eastern; ⊠ VII, Rákóczi út, ☎ 1/313–6835), **Nyugati** (Western; ⊠ V, Nyugati tér, ☎ 1/331–5346), and **Déli** (Southern; ⊠ XII, Alkotás u., ☎ 1/375–6593). Trains for Vienna usually depart from Keleti station, those for Lake Balaton from Déli.

Getting Around
Budapest is best explored on foot. The maps provided by tourist offices are not very detailed, so arm yourself with one from any of the bookshops in Váci utca or from a stationery shop or newsstand.

BY BICYCLE
On Margaret Island in Budapest, **Bringóhintó** (⊠ Hajós Alfréd sétány 1, across from the Thermal Hotel, ☎ 1/329–2072) rents four-wheeled pedaled contraptions called *Bringóhintós,* as well as traditional two-wheelers; standard bikes cost about 450 Ft. per hour, 600–1,000 Ft. for 24 hours. For more information about renting in Budapest, contact **Tourinform** (⊠ V, Sütő u. 2, ☎ 1/317–9800).

BY PUBLIC TRANSPORTATION
The Budapest Transportation Authority (BKV) runs the public transportation system—the Metro (subway) with three lines, buses, streetcars, and trolleybuses—and it's cheap, efficient, and simple to use. Most of it closes down around 11:30 PM, but certain trams and buses run on a limited schedule all night. A *napijegy* (day ticket) costs about 600 Ft. (three-day "tourist ticket," around 1,200 Ft.) and allows unlimited travel on all services within the city limits. Metro stations or newsstands sell single-ride tickets for about 70 Ft. You can travel on all trams, buses, and on the subway with this ticket, but you can't change lines or direction.

Bus, streetcar, and trolleybus tickets must be canceled on board—watch how other passengers do it. Metro tickets are canceled at station entrances. Plainclothes agents wearing red armbands do frequent spot checks, often targeting tourists, and you can be fined several hundred forints if you don't have a canceled ticket.

BY TAXI
Taxis are plentiful and are a good value, but make sure that they have a working meter. The average initial charge is 50 Ft.–75 Ft., to which is added about 110 Ft. per km (½ mi) plus 30 Ft. per minute of waiting time. Avoid unmarked "freelance" taxis; stick with those affiliated with an established company. Your safest bet is to do what the locals do and order a taxi by phone. Simply provide the phone number you're calling from and they will know where you are; a car will arrive in about 5 to 10 minutes. The best rates are offered by **Citytaxi** (☎ 1/211–1111), **Fötaxi** (☎ 1/222–2222) and **6 X 6** (☎ 1/266–6666).

Money Matters
CURRENCY
The unit of currency is the forint (Ft.). There are bills of 200, 500, 1,000, 2,000, 5,000, and 10,000 forints and coins of 1, 2, 5, 10, 20, 50, 100, and 200 forints. Note that a redesigned, small, two-tone 100-forint coin is now in co-circulation with the much larger, earlier version. At press time (spring 1998) the exchange rate was approximately 209 Ft. to the U.S. dollar, 145 Ft. to the Canadian dollar, 347 Ft. to

the pound sterling, 134 Ft. to the Australian dollar, and 116 Ft. to the New Zealand dollar. Note that official exchange rates are adjusted at frequent intervals.

There is still a black market in hard currency, but changing money on the street is risky and illegal, and the bank rate almost always comes close. Stick with banks and official exchange offices.

Telephoning

COUNTRY CODE
The country code for Hungary is 36.

Contacts and Resources

EMBASSIES
United States (✉ V, Szabadság tér 12, ☎ 1/267–4400). **Canadian** (✉ Mailing address: XII, Budakeszi út 32; ✉ street address: XII, Zugligeti út 51–53, ☎ 1/275–1200). **United Kingdom** (✉ V, Harmincad u. 6, ☎ 1/266–2888). **Australian** (✉ XII, Királyhágó tér 8–9, ☎ 1/201–8899).

EMERGENCIES
Police (☎ 107). **Ambulance** (☎ 104 or 1/200–0100 private, English-speaking). **Doctor** (☎ 1/325–9999 private, English-speaking). **24-hour pharmacies** (**Gyógyszertár,** in Pest, ☎ 1/311–4439; in Buda, ☎ 1/355–4691).

ENGLISH-LANGUAGE BOOKSTORES
Bestsellers (✉ V, Október 6 u. 11, ☎ 1/312–1295). **Central European University Academic Bookshop** (✉ V, Nádor u. 9, ☎ 1/327–3096).

GUIDED TOURS
Boat. From late March through October boats leave from the quay at Vigadó tér on 1½-hour cruises between the railroad bridges north and south of the Árpád and Petőfi bridges, respectively. The trip, organized by **MAHART Tours** (☎ 1/318–1704), runs only on weekends and holidays until late April, then once or twice a day, depending on the season; the trip costs around 800 Ft.

Excursions. Excursions farther afield include day-long trips to the *Puszta* (Great Plain), the Danube Bend, and Lake Balaton. **IBUSZ Travel** (☞ Visitor Information, *below*) offers trips to the Buda Hills and stays in many of Hungary's historic castles and mansions.

Orientation. Year-round, **IBUSZ Travel** (☞ Visitor Information, *below*) sponsors three-hour bus tours of the city that cost about 4,000 Ft. Starting from Erzsébet tér, they take in parts of both Buda and Pest. **Gray Line Cityrama** (✉ V, Báthori u. 22, ☎ 1/302–4382) also offers a three-hour city bus tour (about 4,000 Ft. per person).

Special-Interest. IBUSZ Travel (☞ Visitor Information, *below*), Gray Line Cityrama (☞ Orientation, *above*), and Budapest Tourist (☞ Visitor Information, *below*) organize a number of unusual tours, including horseback riding, bicycling, and angling, as well as visits to the National Gallery. These tour companies will provide personal guides on request. Also check at your hotel's reception desk.

The Chosen Tours (✉ XII, Zolyomi lépcső 27, ☎ 1/319–3427 or ☎ FAX 1/319–6800) offers a three-hour combination bus and walking tour (about 3,400 Ft.), "Budapest Through Jewish Eyes," highlighting the sights and cultural life of the city's important Jewish community.

TRAVEL AGENCIES
American Express (✉ V, Déak Ferenc u. 10, ☎ 1/266–8680). **Getz International** (✉ V, Falk Miksa u. 5, ☎ 1/269–3728 or 1/312–0649). **Vista** (✉ VI, Andrássy út 1, ☎ 1/269–6032, 1/269–6033, or 1/267–8603).

Tourinform (⊠ V, Sütő u. 2, ☎ 1/317–9800. **Tourism Office of Budapest** (⊠ V, Március 15 tér 7, ☎ 1/117–5964, 1/266–0479; ⊠ VI, Nyugati pályaudvar, ☎ 1/302–8580). **IBUSZ Travel** (main branch, ⊠ V, Ferenciek tere 10, ☎ 1/318–6866; tours and programs, ⊠ Rubin Aktiv Hotel, XI, Dajka Gábor u. 3, Budapest, ☎ 1/319–7510 main, 1/319–7520 program information). **IBUSZ Welcome Hotel Service** (⊠ V, Apáczai Csere János u. 1, ☎ 1/318–3925 or 1/118–5776). **Budapest Tourist** (⊠ V, Roosevelt tér 5, ☎ 1/317–3555).

The English-language weeklies *The Budapest Sun* and *Budapest Week* cover news, business, and culture and carry tips for visitors.

The Tourism Office of Budapest (☞ *above*) has developed the **Budapest Card,** which entitles holders to unlimited travel on public transportation; free admission to many museums and sights; and discounts on various purchases, entertainment events, tours, meals, and services from participating businesses. The cost is 2,000 Ft. for two days, 2,500 Ft. for three days; one card is valid for an adult plus a child under 14.

8 Copenhagen

*I*f you arrive in Copenhagen Airport on the isle *of Amager, as you taxi into the city you are met with no startling skyline, no seething metropolis. Instead, elegant spires and cobbled streets characterize Scandinavia's most populous capital and one of its oldest towns. It is not divided like most other cities into single-purpose districts; instead it is a rich, multilayered capital where people work, play, shop, and live throughout its central core. Surrounded by water, be it sea or canal, and connected by bridges and drawbridges, it has a maritime atmosphere that is indelible.*

EXPLORING COPENHAGEN

Numbers in the margin correspond to points of interest on the Copenhagen map.

When Denmark ruled Norway and Sweden during the 15th century, Copenhagen was the capital of all three countries. Today it is still a lively northern capital, with about 1 million inhabitants. It's a city meant for walking, the first in Europe to recognize the value of pedestrian streets in fostering community spirit. As you stroll through the cobbled streets and squares, you'll find that Copenhagen combines the excitement and variety of big-city life with a small-town atmosphere. If there's such a thing as a cozy metropolis, this is it.

In Copenhagen you're never far from water, whether sea or canal. The city itself is built upon two main islands, Slotsholmen and Christianshavn, connected by drawbridges. The ancient heart of the city is intersected by two heavily peopled walking streets—part of the five such streets known collectively as Strøget—and around them curls a maze of cobbled streets packed with tiny boutiques, cafés, and restaurants—

all best explored on foot. In summer, when Copenhagen moves outside, the most engaging views of city life are from sidewalk cafés in the sunny squares. Walk down Nyhavn Canal, formerly haunted by a fairly salty crew of sailors, now gentrified and filled with chic restaurants.

16 **Amalienborg** (Amalia's Castle). During the fall and winter, when the royal family has returned to its principal residence since 1784, the Royal Guard and band march through the city at noon to change the palace guard. Amelienborg's other main attraction is the second division of the Royal Collection (the first is at Rosenborg), housed inside the **Amalienborg Museum.** Among the collection's offerings are the study of King Christian IX (1818–1906) and the drawing room of his wife, Queen Louise. Also included are a set of Rococo banquet silver, highlighted by a bombastic Viking ship centerpiece, and a small costume exhibit. Afterward, you can view visiting yachts along the castle's harbor, as well as the modern sculptures and manicured flower beds of **Amalienhaven** (Amalia's Gardens). ☒ *Amalienborg Pl.,* ☎ *33/12–21–86.* ☉ *May–late Oct., daily 11–4; late Oct.–Apr., Tues.–Sun. 11–4.*

10 **Børsen** (the Stock Exchange). This edifice is believed to be the oldest such structure still in use, though it functions only on special occasions. It was built by the 16th-century monarch King Christian IV, a scholar and warrior, and the architect of much of the city. The king is said to have had a hand in twisting the tails of the four dragons that form the structure's distinctive green copper spire. With its steep roofs, tiny windows, and gables, the building is one of Copenhagen's treasures. ☒ *Christiansborg Slotspl. Not open to the public.*

25 **Botanisk Have** (Botanical Garden). Copenhagen's 25-acre botanical gardens, with a rather spectacular Palm House containing tropical and subtropical plants, upstages the palatial gardens of ☞ **Rosenborg Slot** (Rosenborg Castle). Also on the grounds are an observatory and a geological museum. ☒ *Gothersg. 128,* ☎ *33/32–22–40.* ☒ *Free.* ☉ *Grounds: May–Aug., daily 8:30–6; Sept.–Apr., daily 8:30–4. Palm House: daily 10–3.*

32 **Carlsberg Bryggeri** (Carlsberg Brewery). Four giant Bornholm granite elephants guard the entrance to this world-famous brewery; a tour of the draft-horse stalls and **Carlsberg Museum** begins at the front gate. ☒ *Ny Carlsbergvej 140,* ☎ *33/27–13–14.* ☉ *Tours: weekdays at 11 and 2 or by arrangement for groups.*

★ **5** **Christiansborg Slot** (Christiansborg Castle). This massive gray complex contains the Folketinget (Parliament House) and the Royal Reception Chambers. It is on the site of the city's first fortress, built by Bishop Absalon in 1167. While the castle was being built at the beginning of the 20th century, the National Museum excavated the ruins beneath the site. ☒ *Christiansborg. Christiansborg ruins:* ☎ *33/92–64–92;* ☉ *May–Sept., daily 9:30–3:30. Closed Oct.–Apr., Mon., Wed., and Sat. Folketinget:* ☎ *33/37–55–00;* ☒ *Free;* ☉ *Tour times vary; call ahead. Reception chambers:* ☎ *33/92–64–92.* ☉ *Hrs and tour times vary; call ahead.*

20 **Den Lille Havfrue** (The Little Mermaid). In 1913 this statue was erected to commemorate Hans Christian Andersen's lovelorn creation, now the subject of hundreds of travel posters. On Sunday **Langelinie,** the lick of land you follow to reach the famed nymph, is thronged with promenading Danes and tourists—the pack of which are often much more absorbing to watch than the somewhat overrated sculpture. She has been mysteriously decapitated a couple of times since she was set on her perch; the most recent incident took place in early 1998, and though her head was returned within a week, she gained much more publicity without it. ☒ *Langelinie promenade.*

114

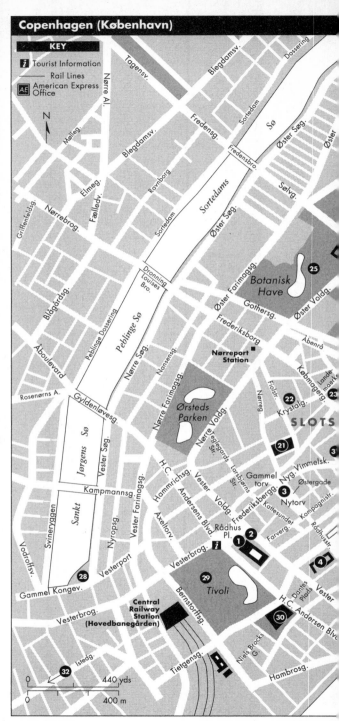

Copenhagen (København)

KEY

i Tourist Information
Rail Lines
AE American Express
Office

Tarimagsg.

Dag Hammarskjölds Al.

Kristianiag.

Langeliniebrd.

Østbaneg.

Folke Bernadottes Al.

Østerport Station

Oslo Plads

Stockholmsg.

Øster Anlæg

Øster

27

26

Sølvg.

Rigensg.

Fredericiag.

St. Kongensg.

Grønningen

Churchill-parken

19

Forbindelsesv.

Langelinie

Yderhavn

20

18

Esplanaden

Bredg.

Amalieg.

17

24

Kongens Have

Kronprincesseg.

Store Kongensg.

Dronningens Tværg.

15

Bredg.

16

Amalieg.

Toldbodg.

Sankt Annæ Plads

Adelg.

Borgerg.

Vognmagerg. Gammelmønt

Gothersg.

Pilestræde

Ny Østerg.

Kr. Berniig.

Bremerholm

Kongens Nytorv

14 Nyhavn

OLMEN

Østerg.

Højbro

13

Heibergsg.

Holmenskanal

Nyhavn

Canal

Inderhavn

AE

12

Amagertorv

Lædersfr.

Gammel Strand

Holbergsg.

Havnegade

Vindelbrog

6

Christiansborg Slotsplads

Holmenskanal

Chr. IV's Bro

5

10

Børsg.

8

Tøjhusgade

7

Knippelsbro

Sankt Annæ.

CHRISTIANSHAVN

9

Frederiksholms Kanal

Christians Brygge

11

oldg.

Torveg.

Dronningensg.

Princessg.

Valdb.

Langebro

Langerbrog.

Christianshavns

Amagerbrog.

Amager Blvd.

Stadsgraven

Vermlandsg.

⑱ Frihedsmuseet (Liberty Museum). Evocative displays commemorate the heroic World War II Danish resistance movement, which saved 7,000 Jews from the Nazis by hiding them and then smuggling them across to Sweden. ✉ *Churchillparken,* ☎ *33/13–77–14.* 🎫 *Free.* ⊙ *Sept. 16– Apr., Tues.–Sat. 11–3, Sun. 11–4; May–Sept. 15, Tues.–Sat. 10–4, Sun. 10–5.*

㉛ Helligånds Kirken (Church of the Holy Ghost). This church on Strøget contains a marble font by the sculptor Bertel Thovaldsen (1770–1844) in its 18th-century choir. ✉ *Niels Hemmingsensg. 5, Amagertorv section,* ☎ *33/12–95–55.* 🎫 *Free.* ⊙ *Weekdays 9–1, Sat. 10–noon.*

㉗ Hirschsprungske Samling (Hirschprung Collection). This cozy museum displays works from the Golden Age, as well as a collection of paintings by the late-19th-century artists of the Danish Skagen school. It also contains interiors with furnishings from the artists' homes. ✉ *Stockholmsg. 20,* ☎ *31/42–03–36.* 🎫 *Free.* ⊙ *Thurs.–Mon. 11–4, Wed. 11–9.*

⑲ Kastellet (The Citadel). Once surrounded by two rings of moats, this building was the city's main fortress during the 18th century, but, in a grim reversal during World War II, the Germans used it as their headquarters during their occupation of Denmark. The lovely green area around it, cut throughout with walking paths, is a favorite among the Danes, who flock here on weekends. If you have time, walk past the spired **St. Alban's,** an English church that stands at Churchillparken's entrance. ✉ *Churchillparken. Grounds:* ⊙ *Daily 6 AM–sunset.*

㉒ Københavns Synagoge (Copenhagen Synagogue). This synagogue was designed by the contemporary architect Gustav Friedrich Hetsch, who borrowed from the Doric and Egyptian styles in creating the arklike structure. ✉ *Krystalg. 12.* ⊙ *Daily services 4:15.*

⑬ Kongelig Teater (Royal Theater). The home of Danish opera and ballet as well as theater occupies the southeast side of Kongens Nytorv. The Danish Royal Ballet remains one of the world's great companies, with a repertory ranging from classical to modern. On the western side of the square you'll see the stately facade of the **D'Angleterre,** the grandest of Copenhagen's hotels. ✉ *Tordenskjoldsg. 3,* ☎ *33/69–69– 69. Not open for tours.*

❼ Kongelige Bibliotek (Royal Library). This library houses the country's largest collection of books, newspapers, and manuscripts. Look for early records of the Viking journeys to America and Greenland and the statue of the philosopher Søren Kierkegaard in the garden. A marble annex next door, which opens in the fall of 1999, has special reading rooms, a ground-floor performance space, and a bookstore. ✉ *Christians Brygge 8,* ☎ *33/47–47–47.* 🎫 *Free.* ⊙ *June–Aug., weekdays 9–7, Sat. 10–7; Sept.–May, Mon. 9–7, Tues.–Thurs. 9–9, Fri. 9–7, Sat. 10–7.*

⑰ Kunstindustrimuseet (Museum of Decorative Art). The highlights of this museum's collection are a large selection of European and Asian handicrafts, as well as ceramics, silver, and tapestries. The quiet library full of design tomes and magazines doubles as a primer for Danish functionalism with its Le Klint paper lamp shades and wooden desks. ✉ *Bredg. 68,* ☎ *33/14–94–52.* ⊙ *Permanent exhibition: Tues.–Sun. 1–4; special exhibitions: Tues.–Sat. 10–4, Sun. 1–4.*

❷ Lurblæserne (Lur Blower Column). Topped by two Vikings blowing an ancient trumpet called a *lur,* this column displays a good deal of artistic license—the lur dates from the Bronze Age, 1500 BC, whereas the Vikings lived a mere 1,000 years ago. The monument is a starting point for sightseeing tours of the city. ⊠ *East side of Rådhus Pl.*

⑮ Marmorkirken (The Marble Church). The ponderous Frederikskirke, commonly called the Marmorkirken, is a Baroque church begun in 1749 in high-priced Norwegian marble that lay unfinished (because of budget constraints) from 1770 to 1874. It was finally completed and consecrated in 1894. Perched around the exterior are 16 statues of various religious leaders from Moses to Luther, and below them stand sculptures of outstanding Danish ministers and bishops. ⊠ *Frederiksgade 4,* ☎ *33/15– 01–44.* ◻ *Free.* ⊙ *Weekdays 11–2, Sat. 11–4, Sun. noon–4, with service at 10:30.*

④ Nationalmuseet (National Museum). On Ny Vestergade you'll find the entrance to this museum with extensive collections chronicling Danish cultural history to modern times and displays of Egyptian, Greek, and Roman antiquities. You can see Viking Runic stones in the Danish cultural history section. ⊠ *Ny Vesterg. 10,* ☎ *33/13–44–11.* ⊙ *Tues.–Sun. 10–5.*

⑫ Nikolaj Kirken (St. Nicholas Church). In Østergade, the easternmost of the streets that make up Strøget, you cannot miss the green spire of St. Nicholas Church. The present structure was built in the 20th century; the previous one, dating from the 13th century, was destroyed by fire in 1728. Today the building is no longer a church but an art gallery and exhibition center. ⊠ *Nikolaipl.,* ☎ *33/93–16–26.* ◻ *Changing admission for special exhibitions.* ⊙ *Daily noon–5.*

★ **㉚ Ny Carlsberg Glyptotek** (New Carlsberg Sculpture Museum). This elaborate neoclassical building houses an impressive collection of works by Gauguin, Degas, and other Impressionists. The French, Egyptian, Greek, and Roman sculpture is one of the most impressive collections of antiquities and sculpture in northern Europe. ⊠ *Dantes Pl. 7,* ☎ *33/41–81–41.* ◻ *Free Wed. and Sun.* ⊙ *Tues.–Sun. 10–4.*

★ **⑭ Nyhavn** (New Harbor). After a long tour, relax with a beer in one of the most gentrified parts of the city, longtime haunt of sailors. Now restaurants and cafés outnumber tattoo shops. The name refers to both the street and the canal leading southeast out of Kongens Nytorv— but to Danes, it could as well mean the general feeling of tipsy euphoria that erupts here every warm, sunny day. Long into the hot summer nights, the area still gets rowdy, with Scandinavians reveling against the backdrop of a fleet of old-time sailing ships and well-preserved 18th-century buildings. Hans Christian Andersen lived at numbers 18 and 20. Nearer to the harbor are old shipping warehouses, including two—Nyhavn 71 and the Admiral—that have been converted into comfortable hotels. ⊠ *East of Kongens Nytorv.*

★ **① Rådhus Pladsen** (City Hall Square). This hub of Copenhagen's commercial district is the best place to start a stroll. The Renaissance-style building dominating it is the **Rådhus** (City Hall), completed in 1905. A statue of Copenhagen's 12th-century founder, Bishop Absalon, sits atop the main entrance. Inside, you can see the first World Clock, an astrological timepiece invented and built by Jens Olsen and set in motion in 1955. If you're feeling energetic, take a guided tour partway up the 350-ft **tower** for a panoramic view. ⊠ *Square in Strøget at eastern end of Vesterbrog, and western end of Frederiksbergg.,* ☎ *33/66– 25–82.* ⊙ *Rådhus Pl.: Mon.–Wed., Fri. 9:30–3, Thurs. 9:30–4, Sat. 9:30–1. Tours in English, weekdays at 3, Sat. at 10. Tower tours: Mon.– Sat. at noon; additionally June–Sept. at 10 and 2. Call to confirm hrs.*

★ **㉔** **Rosenborg Slot** (Rosenborg Castle). This Renaissance palace—built by jack of all trades Christian IV—houses the Crown Jewels, as well as a collection of costumes and royal memorabilia. Don't miss Christian IV's pearl-studded saddle. ⊠ *Øster Voldg. 4A,* ☎ *33/15–32–86.* ☉ *Castle: late-Oct.–Apr., Tues., Fri., and Sun. 11–2; treasury: Tues.–Sun. 11–3; both: May, Sept.–late-Oct., daily 11–3; June–Aug., daily 10–4.*

㉓ **Rundetårn** (Round Tower). It is said that Peter the Great of Russia drove a horse and carriage up the 600 ft of the inner staircase of this round tower, built as an observatory in 1642 by Christian IV. It's a formidable walk, but the view is worth it. At the base of the tower is the university church, Trinitas; halfway up the tower you can take a break at the tower's art gallery. ⊠ *Købmagerg. 52A,* ☎ *33/93–66–60.* ☉ *Tower: Sept.–May, Mon.–Sat. 10–5, Sun. noon–4; June–Aug., Mon.–Sat. 10–8, Sun. noon–8. Observatory and telescope, with astronomer on hand to answer questions, mid-Oct.–mid-Mar., Tues.–Wed. 7 PM–10 PM.*

☼ **㉖** **Statens Museum for Kunst** (National Art Gallery). This museum reopens in the fall of 1999 with a complete refurbishment of the original 100-year-old building and a new, modern building that doubles the exhibition space. Though the collection remains the same—including works of Danish art from the Golden Age (early 19th century) to the present, as well as paintings by Rubens, Dürer, the Impressionists, and other European masters—the space also includes a children's museum, an amphitheater, a documentation center and study room, a bookstore, and a restaurant. ⊠ *Sølvg. 48–50,* ☎ *33/91–21–26.* ☉ *Tues.–Sun. 10–4:30, Wed. until 9.*

❸ **Strøget.** Frederiksberggade is the first of the five pedestrian streets that make up Strøget, Copenhagen's shopping district and promenade area. Walk past the cafés and trendy boutiques to the double square of **Gammeltorv** and **Nytorv**, where, farther along, the street is paved with mosaic tiles. Outside the posh displays of the fur and porcelain shops the sidewalks have the festive aura of a street fair. **Kongens Nytorv** (King's New Market) is the square marking the end of Strøget.

❽ **Teatermuseum** (Theater Museum). Built in 1767 in the Royal Court, this museum is devoted to exhibits on theater and ballet history. You can wander around the boxes, stage, and dressing rooms to see where it all happened. ⊠ *Christiansborg Ridebane 18,* ☎ *33/11–51–76.* ☉ *Wed. 2–4, weekends noon–4.*

★ **❻** **Thorvaldsen Museum.** The 19th-century Danish sculptor Bertel Thorvaldsen, whose tomb stands in the center of the museum, was greatly influenced by the statues and reliefs of classical antiquity. In addition to his own works, the collection includes paintings and drawings by other artists illustrating the influence of Italy on the artists of Denmark's Golden Age. ⊠ *Porthusg. 2,* ☎ *33/32–15–32.* 🎫 *Free.* ☉ *Tues.–Sun. 10–5.*

★ ☼ **㉙** **Tivoli.** In the 1840s the Danish architect Georg Carstensen persuaded King Christian VIII that an amusement park would be the perfect opiate for the masses, arguing that "when people amuse themselves, they forget politics." In the season from May through September, about 4 million people come through the gates. Tivoli is more sophisticated than a mere funfair: It offers a pantomime theater and an open-air stage, elegant restaurants, and frequent classical, jazz, and rock concerts in addition to a museum chronicling its own history. On weekends there are elaborate fireworks displays. Try to see Tivoli at least once by night, when the trees are illuminated along with the Chinese Pagoda and the main fountain. In recent years Tivoli has also been opened a month before Christmas with a gift and decorations market and a children's theater, albeit in Danish. Most of the restaurants are also open. ⊠ *Vester-brog. 3,* ☎ *33/15–10–01.* ⊙ *May–mid-Sept., daily 11 AM–midnight.*

⑨ Tøjhusmuseet (Royal Armory). The Renaissance structure was built by King Christian IV, a scholar and a warrior as well as the architect of much of the city. It houses impressive displays of uniforms, weapons, and armor in an arched hall 200 yards long. ⊠ *Tøjhusg. 3,* ☎ *33/11–60–37.* ⊙ *Tues.–Sun. 10–4.*

㉘ Tycho Brahe Planetarium. This modern cylindrical building is filled with astronomy exhibits and an Omnimax theater that takes visitors on a simulated journey up into space and down into the depths of the seas. Because these films can be disorienting, planetarium officials do not recommend them for children under 7. ⊠ *Gammel Kongevej 10,* ☎ *33/12–12–24.* 🖾 *Exhibition and theater Dkr65. Reservations advised for theater.* ⊙ *Daily 10:30–9.*

⑪ Vor Frelsers Kirken (Our Savior's Church). Local legend has it the staircase encircling the fantastic green-and-gold spire of this 1696 Gothic structure was built curling the wrong way around and that when its architect reached the top and saw what he had done, he jumped. ⊠ *Skt. Annæg. 9,* ☎ *31/57–63–25.* 🖾 *Free.* ⊙ *Weekdays 9–1. Closed during services and special functions; call ahead.*

㉑ Vor Frue Kirken (Church of Our Lady). Though this has been Copenhagen's cathedral since 1924, the site itself has been a place of worship since the 13th century, when Bishop Absalon built a chapel here. The spare, neoclassical facade is a 19th-century innovation repairing damage suffered during Nelson's bombing of the city in 1801. If the church is open, you can see Thorvaldsen's marble sculptures of Christ and the Apostles. Afterwards, if you're on your way to the Nørreport train station, you'll pass the stoic, columned **Copenhagen University**. It was built during the 19th century on the site of the medieval bishops' palace. ⊠ *Pilestræde 67,* ☎ *33/14–41–28.* ⊙ *Irregular hrs; call ahead.*

DINING

Food remains one of the great pleasures in Copenhagen, a city with more than 2,000 restaurants. Traditional Danish fare spans all the price categories: You can order a light lunch of smørrebrød, snack from a store kolde bord, or dine out on lobster and Limfjord oysters. If you are strapped for cash, you can enjoy fast food Danish style, in the form of *pølser* (hot dogs) sold from trailers on the street. Team any of this with some pastry from a bakery (the shops displaying an upside-down gold pretzel), and you've got yourself a meal on the go. Many restaurants close for Christmas, roughly from December 24 through December 31.

RATINGS

Meal prices vary little between town and country. While approximate price ranges are given below, remember that careful ordering, especially when it comes to beer, wine, and liquor, can get you a moderate ($$) meal at a very expensive ($$$$) restaurant. Prices are per person and include a first course, main course, and dessert, plus taxes and tip, but not wine.

CATEGORY	COST
$$$$	over DKr400
$$$	DKr200–DKr400
$$	DKr120–DKr200
$	under DKr120

$$$$ ✕ **Kong Hans Kaelder.** Five centuries ago this was a Nordic vineyard,
 ★   but now it's one of Scandinavia's finest restaurants—though change
is afoot. After 17 years as the restaurant's head chef, Daniel Letz is
passing the torch to Thomas Rode Andersen. No major restructuring
is planned; rather the staff promises to continue serving superb, French-
inspired dishes. The setting is subterranean and mysterious, with whitewashed, arching ceilings, candles, and wood carvings. ⊠ *Vingårdstr.
6,* ☎ *33/11–68–68. AE, DC, MC, V. Closed Sun. last 2 wks in July,
and Easter week. No lunch.*

$$$$ ✕ **Krogs.** This elegant canal-front restaurant commands a loyal clientele, both foreign and local. It's decorated with pale green walls and
paintings of old Copenhagen. The menu (printed in five languages) lists
such specialties as a rich, dark bouillabaisse and a generous cold platter heaped with sea scallops, lobster, and local fish. ⊠ *Gammel Strand
38,* ☎ *33/15–89–15. Reservations essential. AE, DC, MC, V.*

$$$$ ✕ **Sct. Gertruds Kloster.** The history of this monastery goes back 700
 ★   years. The dining room, bedecked with hundreds of icons, is illuminated by 2,000 candles. The extensive French menu lists such specials
as fillet of halibut with lobster glacé and duck breast in tarragon sauce.
⊠ *Hauser Pl. 32,* ☎ *33/14–66–30. Reservations essential. AE, DC,
MC, V. No lunch.*

$$$ ✕ **Els.** When it opened in 1853, the intimate Els was the place to be
 ★   seen before the theater, and the painted Muses on the walls still watch
diners rush to make an 8 o'clock curtain. Antique wooden columns
and Royal Copenhagen tile tables complement a nouvelle Danish and
French menu that changes daily, offering game, fish, and market-fresh
produce. ⊠ *Store Strandstr. 3,* ☎ *33/14–13–41. Reservations essen-
tial. AE, DC, MC, V.*

$$$ ✕ **L'Alsace.** In the cobbled courtyard of Pistolstraede and hung with paint-
ings by Danish surrealist Wilhelm Freddie, this restaurant is peaceful
and quiet, attracting such diverse diners as Queen Margrethe and Pope
Paul II. The hand-drawn menu includes a hearty *choucroute* (sauerkraut)
with sausage and pork, plus superb fruit tarts and cakes for dessert. ⊠
Ny Østerg. 9, ☎ *33/14–57–43. AE, DC, MC, V. Closed Sun.*

$$$ ✕ **Pakhuskælderen.** Surrounded by thick white walls and raw tim-
bers, the Nyhavn 71 hotel's intimate restaurant attracts a mix of busi-
ness and holiday guests. In recent years it has moved away from being
exclusively of the seafood school and now is known for its fresh, clas-
sically prepared range of Danish-French specialties. ⊠ *Nyhavn 71,* ☎
*33/11–85–85. Reservations essential. AE, DC, MC, V. Closed Sun.
No lunch.*

$$ ✕ **Copenhagen Corner.** Diners here are treated to a superb view of the
Rådhus Pladsen, as well as to a terrific store kolde bord, both of which
compensate for the often harried staff. Specialties include fried veal with
bouillon gravy and fried potatoes; entrecôte in garlic and bordelaise
sauce, served with creamed potatoes; and a herring plate with three
types of spiced and marinated herring and boiled potatoes. ⊠ *Rådhus
Pl.,* ☎ *33/91–45–45. AE, DC, MC, V.*

$$ ✕ **El Meson.** Ceiling-hung pottery, knowledgeable waiters, and a top-
notch menu make this Copenhagen's best Spanish restaurant. Choose
carefully for a moderately priced meal, which might include beef spiced
with spearmint, lamb with honey sauce, or paella for two. ⊠ *Hauser
Pl. 12,* ☎ *33/11–91–31. AE, DC, MC, V. Closed Sun. No lunch.*

$$ ✕ **Havfruen.** A life-size wooden mermaid swings decorously from the
ceiling in this small, rustic fish restaurant in Nyhavn. Natives love the
maritime-bistro ambience and the daily evolving French and Danish
menu. ⊠ *Nyhavn 39,* ☎ *33/11–11–38. DC, MC, V. Closed Sun.*

$$ ✕ **Ida Davidsen.** Five generations old (counting Ida's children Oscar
 ★   and Ida Maria), this world-renowned lunch spot has become synony-

mous with smørrebrød. Choose from these creative open-face sand-wiches, piled high with such ingredients as pâté, bacon, and steak tartare, or even kangaroo, or opt for smoked duck served with a beet salad and potatoes. ⊠ *St. Kongensg. 70,* ☎ *33/91–36–55. Reservations essential. AE, DC, MC, V. Closed weekends and July. No dinner.*

$$ ✕ **Peder Oxe.** This countrified, lively bistro welcomes you with rus-tic antiques, 15th-century Portuguese tiles, and damask-covered tables set with heavy cutlery. Grilled steaks and fish—and some of the best burgers in town—come with an excellent salad bar. ⊠ *Gråbrødretorv 11,* ☎ *33/11–00–77. DC, MC, V.*

$$ ✕ **Victor.** This French-style corner café has great people-watching and bistro fare. It's best during weekend lunches, when Danes gather for such specialties as rib roast, homemade pâté, smoked salmon, and cheese platters. Careful ordering here can get you an inexpensive meal. Un-fortunately, the waiters can be obnoxious. ⊠ *Ny Østerg. 8,* ☎ *33/13–36–13. AE, DC, MC, V.*

$ ✕ **Flyvefisken.** Silvery stenciled fish swim along blue-and-yellow sten-ciled walls in this funky Thai eatery. Among the city's more experi-mental (and spicy) restaurants, it offers chicken with cashews, spicy shrimp soup with lemongrass, and herring shark in basil sauce. A less-expensive health-food café is in the basement. ⊠ *Larsbjørnsstr. 18,* ☎ *33/14–95–15. AE, DC, MC, V. Closed Sun.*

$ ✕ **Quattro Fontane.** On a corner west of the lakes, one of Copenhagen's busiest Italian restaurants is a noisy, two-story affair, packed tight with marble-top tables and a steady flow of young Danes. Chatty Ital-ian waiters serve cheese or beef ravioli, cannelloni, linguine with clam sauce, and thick pizzas. ⊠ *Guldbersg. 3,* ☎ *31/39–39–31. Reserva-tions essential weekends. No credit cards.*

$ ✕ **Riz Raz.** On a corner off Strøget, this Middle Eastern restaurant packs
★   in young and old, families, and singles every night and on weekends. The very inexpensive all-you-can-eat buffet is heaped with healthy dishes, in-cluding lentils, falafel, bean salads, and occasionally pizza. ⊠ *Kompagnistr. 20,* ☎ *33/15–05–75. Reservations essential weekends. DC, MC, V.*

NIGHTLIFE AND THE ARTS

Copenhagen This Week has good information on musical and theatri-cal happenings, as well as on special events and exhibitions. Concert and festival information is available from the **Dansk Musik Informa-tion Center** (DMIC; ⊠ Gråbrødretorv 16, ☎ 33/11–20–66). Copen-hagen's main theater and concert season runs from September through May, and tickets can be obtained either directly from theaters and con-cert halls or from ticket agencies; ask your hotel concierge for advice. **Billetnet** (⊠ Main post office: Tietgensg. 37, ☎ 38/88–70–22), a box-office service available at all large post offices, has tickets for most major events. Keep in mind that same-day purchases at the box office **ARTE** (⊠ near Nørreport station) are half price. There is no phone number, so you must show up in person.

The Arts

FILM AND TELEVISION
Copenhagen natives are avid **movie** buffs, and as the Danes rarely dub films or television imports, you can often see original American and British movies and TV shows with Danish subtitles.

MUSIC
Tivoli Concert Hall (⊠ Vesterbrog. 3, ☎ 33/15–10–12) offers more than 150 concerts each summer, presenting a host of Danish and foreign soloists, conductors, and orchestras.

The **Royal Theater** (✉ Kongens Nytorv, ☎ 33/14−10−02) regularly holds theater, ballet, and opera performances. For English-language theater, try to catch a performance of the professional **London Toast Theatre** (☎ 31/22−86−86).

Nightlife

Many of the city's restaurants, cafés, bars, and clubs stay open after midnight, some as late as 5 AM. Copenhagen is famous for jazz, but you'll find nightspots catering to musical tastes ranging from bop to ballroom music. In the inner city most discos open at 11 PM, have a cover charge (about DKr40), and pile on steep drink prices. A few streets behind the railway station is Copenhagen's red-light district, where sex shops share space with grocers. Although the area is fairly well lighted and lively, women may feel uncomfortable here alone at night.

JAZZ

Many of Copenhagen's sophisticated jazz clubs have closed in the past couple of years. **La Fontaine** (✉ Kompagnistr. 11, ☎ 33/11−60−98) is Copenhagen's quintessential jazz dive, with sagging curtains, impenetrable smoke, crusty lounge lizards, and the random barmaid nymph; for jazz lovers the bordello mood and Scandinavian jazz talent make this a must. **Copenhagen Jazz House** (✉ Niels Hemmingsensg. 10, ☎ 33/15−26−00) is infinitely more upscale than La Fontaine, attracting European and some international talent to its chic, modern barlike ambience. **Tivoli Jazzhouse Mantra** (✉ Vesterbrog. 3, ☎ 33/11−11−13), Tivoli's jazz club, lures some of the biggest names in the world.

NIGHTCLUBS AND DANCING

The young set gets down on the disco floor in the fashionable **Park Café** (✉ Østerbrog. 79, ☎ 35/26−63−42). The mellower folks come for brunch when the place transforms back to its Old World roots, or to check out the movie theater next door. **Rosie McGees** (✉ Vesterbrog. 2A, ☎ 33/32−19−23) is a very popular English-style pub with Mexican food and dancing. **Sabor Latino** (✉ Vester Voldg. 85, ☎ 33/11−97−66) is the UN of discos, with an international crowd dancing to salsa and other Latin beats. Among the most enduring clubs is **Woodstock** (✉ Vesterg. 12, ☎ 33/11−20−71), where a mixed audience grooves to '60s classics.

SHOPPING

Strøget's pedestrian streets are synonymous with shopping.

Specialty Shops

Just off Østergade street is **Pistolstræde,** a typical old courtyard filled with intriguing boutiques. Farther down the street toward the town hall square is a compound that includes several important stores: **Georg Jensen** (✉ Amagertorv 4 and Østerg. 40, ☎ 33/11−40−80), one of the world's finest silversmiths, gleams with a wide array of silver patterns and jewelry. Don't miss the **Georg Jensen Museum** (✉ Amagertorv 6, ☎ 33/14−02−29), which showcases glass and silver creations ranging from tiny, twisted-glass shot glasses to an $85,000 silver fish dish. **Royal Copenhagen Porcelain** (✉ Amagertorv 6, ☎ 33/13−71−81) carries both old and new china, plus porcelain patterns and figurines.

A. C. Bang (✉ Østerg. 27, ☎ 33/15−17−26) upholds its Old World, old-money aura with impeccable quality; midsummer and after-Christmas fur sales offer real savings. **Bang & Olufsen** (✉ Østerg. 3−5, ☎ 33/15−04−22) offers reasonable prices on high-end stereos in its own upscale

shop. Along Strøget, at furrier **Birger Christensen** (⊠ Østerg. 38, ☎ 33/
11–55–55), you can peruse designer clothes and chic furs. **FONA** (⊠
Østerg. 47, ☎ 33/15–90–55) carries stereo equipment, including the superior design and sound of Bang & Olufsen. **Illum** (⊠ Østerg. 52, ☎ 33/
14–40–02) is a department store that has a fine basement grocery store
and eating arcade. Don't confuse Illum with **Illums Bolighus** (⊠ Amagertorv 10, ☎ 33/14–19–41), where designer furnishings, porcelain,
quality clothing, and gifts are displayed in near-gallery surroundings.
Magasin (⊠ Kongens Nytorv 13, ☎ 33/11–44–33), one of the largest
department stores in Scandinavia, offers all kinds of clothing and gifts,
as well as an excellent grocery department.

SIDE TRIPS

Helsingør
Shakespeare immortalized both the town and the castle when he chose
Helsingør's **Kronborg Slot** (Kronborg Castle) as the setting for *Hamlet*. Completed in 1585, the present gabled and turreted structure is
about 600 years younger than the fortress we imagine as the setting
of Shakespeare's tragedy. Inside are a 200-ft-long dining hall, the luxurious chapel, and the royal chambers. The ramparts and 12-ft-thick
walls are a reminder of the castle's role as a coastal bulwark—Sweden
is only a few kilometers away. Helsingør town—about 47 km (29 mi)
north of Copenhagen—possesses a number of picturesque streets with
16th-century houses. Frequent trains stop at Helsingør station, and then
it's a 20-minute walk around the harbor to the castle. ⊠ *Kronborg
Slot*, ☎ *49/21–30–78*. ☉ *Easter and May–Sept., daily 10:30–5; Oct.
and Apr., Tues.–Sun. 11–4; Nov.–Mar., Tues.–Sun. 11–3.*

Humlebæk
★ ☾ **Louisiana** is a world-class modern art collection housed in a spectacular building in Humlebæk—part of the "Danish Riviera" on the
North Sjælland coast. Even if you can't tell a Rauschenberg from a Rembrandt, you should make the 35-km (22-mi) trip to see the setting: It's
an elegant, rambling structure set in a large park with views of the sound,
and, on a clear day, Sweden. The children's wing houses pyramid-shape
chalkboards, kid-proof computers, and weekend activities under the
guidance of an artist or museum coordinator. It's a half-hour train ride
from Copenhagen to Humlebæk. A 10-minute walk from the station,
the museum is also accessible by the E4 highway and the more scenic
Strandvejen, or coastal road. ⊠ *Gammel Strandvej 13*, ☎ *49/19–07–
19.* 🖃 *Combined train fare (from Copenhagen) and admission DKr94
available from DSB (☞ Arriving and Departing by Train in Copenhagen Essentials, below); prices higher for special exhibitions.* ☉ *Daily
10–5, Wed. 10–10.*

Roskilde
For a look into the past, head 30 km (19 mi) west of Copenhagen to
the bustling market town of Roskilde. A key administrative center during Viking times, it remained one of the largest towns in northern Europe through the Middle Ages. Today the legacy of its 1,000-year
history lives on in its spectacular cathedral. Built on the site of one of
Denmark's first churches, the **Domkirke** (cathedral) has been the burial
place of Danish royalty since the 15th century. The combined effect of
their tombs is striking—from the magnificent shrine of Christian IV
to the simple brick chapel of Frederik IX. ⊠ *Domkirkepl.*, ☎ *46/35–
27–00.* ☉ *Subject to change; call ahead.*

A 10-minute walk south and through the park takes you to the water
★ and to the **Vikingeskibshallen** (Viking Ship Museum). Inside are five

exquisitely reconstructed Viking ships, discovered at the bottom of Roskilde Fjord in 1962. Detailed placards in English chronicle Viking history. There are also English-language films on the excavation and reconstruction. ⊠ *Strandengen,* ☎ *46/35–65–55.* ⊙ *Apr.–Oct., daily 9–5; Nov.–Mar., daily 10–4.*

COPENHAGEN ESSENTIALS

Arriving and Departing

BY PLANE

The main airport for both international and domestic flights is Copenhagen Airport, 10 km (6 mi) southeast of town.

Between the Airport and Downtown. Bus service to the city is frequent. The airport bus to the central station leaves every 15 minutes: The trip takes about 25 minutes; the fare is about DKr39 (pay on the bus). Public buses cost about DKr16 and run as often but take longer. Bus 250S takes you to Rådhus Pladsen, the city hall square. A taxi ride takes 15 minutes and costs about DKr120.

BY TRAIN

Copenhagen's clean and convenient central station, **Hovedbanegården** (⊠ Just south of Vesterbrog., ☎ 33/14–88–00), is the hub of the country's train network. Intercity express trains leave hourly, on the hour, from 6 AM to 10 PM for principal towns in Fyn and Jylland. Find out more from DSB Information (☎ 70/13–14–15) at the central station. You can make reservations at the central station as well as most other stations, and through travel agents. Public shower facilities at the central station are open 4:30 AM–2 AM and cost DKr15.

Getting Around

BY BICYCLE

More than half the 5 million Danes are said to ride bikes, which visitors use as well. Bike rental costs DKr25 to DKr60 a day, with a deposit of DKr100 to DKr200. Contact **Københavns Cykler** (⊠ Central Station, ☎ 33/33–86–13) or **Østerport Cykler** (⊠ Oslo Plads, ☎ 33/33–85–13).

BY BUS AND SUBURBAN TRAIN

The best bet for visitors is the **Copenhagen Card,** affording unlimited travel on buses and suburban trains (S-trains), admission to some 60 museums and sights around metropolitan Copenhagen, and a reduction on the ferry crossing to Sweden. Buy the card, which costs about DKr140 (24 hours), Dkr255 (48 hours), or DKr320 (72 hours)—half price for children ages 5 to 11—at tourist offices or hotels or from travel agents.

Buses and suburban trains operate on the same ticket system and divide Copenhagen and environs into three zones. Tickets are validated on the time system: On the basic ticket, which costs DKr10 for an hour, you can travel anywhere in the zone in which you started. You can buy a discount *klip cort* (clip card), equivalent to 10 basic tickets, for DKr70. Call the 24-hour information service for zone information: ☎ 36/45–45–45 for buses, ☎ 70/13–14–15 for S-trains (wait for the Danish message to end and a live operator will answer). Buses and S-trains run from 5 AM (6 AM on Sunday) to 12:30 AM. A reduced network of buses drives through the night.

BY CAR

Copenhagen is a city for walkers, not drivers. The charm of its pedestrian streets is paid for by a complicated one-way road system and difficult parking. Leave your car in the garage: Attractions are relatively close together, and public transportation is excellent.

BY TAXI
The computer-metered Mercedes and Volvos are not cheap. The base charge is DKr15, plus DKr8–DKr10 (DKr 11 at night) per km (½ mi). A cab is available when it displays the sign FRI (free); you can either hail a cab (though this can be difficult outside the center), pick one up at a taxi stand, or call ☎ 31/35–35–35 (surcharge of DKr20).

Money Matters
CURRENCY
The monetary unit in Denmark is the krone (kr., DKr, or DKK), which is divided into 100 øre. At press time (spring 1998), the krone stood at DKr6.8 to the U.S. dollar, DKr4.7 to the Canadian dollar, DKr11.2 to the pound sterling, DKr4.3 to the Australian dollar, and DKr3.7 to the New Zealand dollar. Most well-known credit cards are accepted in Denmark, though the American Express card is accepted less frequently than others. Traveler's checks can be cashed in banks and in many hotels, restaurants, and shops.

Telephoning
COUNTRY CODE
The country code for Denmark is 45.

Contacts and Resources
EMBASSIES
United States (✉ Dag Hammarskjöldsallé 24, ☎ 35/55–31–44). **Canadian** (✉ Kristen Benikowsg. 1, ☎ 33/44–52–00). **United Kingdom** (✉ Kastelsvej 40, ☎ 35/26–46–00).

EMERGENCIES
Police, fire, ambulance (☎ 112). **Auto Rescue/Falck** (☎ 31/14–22–22). **Doctor** (Weekdays 8–4, ☎ 33/936300; daily after 4 PM, ☎ 38/84–00–41; fees payable in cash only; night fees around DKr120–DKr350). **Dentist:** Dental Emergency Service (✉ Tandlægevagten 14, Oslo Pl., near Østerport station, ☎ no phone; emergencies only; cash only). **Pharmacies** open 24 hours: **Steno Apotek** (✉ Vesterbrog. 6C, ☎ 33/14–82–66); **Sønderbro Apotek** (✉ Amagerbrog. 158, Amager area, ☎ 32/58–01–40).

ENGLISH-LANGUAGE BOOKSTORES
Boghallen (✉ Rådhus Pl. 37, ☎ 33/11–85–11, ext. 309). **Arnold Busck** (✉ Købmagerg. 49, ☎ 33/12–24–53).

GUIDED TOURS
Orientation. The boat "Harbor and Canal Tour" leaves from Gammel Strand and the east side of Kongens Nytorv; it runs from May through mid-September, daily every half hour from 10 to 5. The following bus tours, conducted by **Copenhagen Excursions** (☎ 31/54–06–06), leave from the Lur Blowers' Column in Rådhus Pladsen: "City Tour" (mid-June–mid-Sept., daily at 9:30, 1, and 3); "Grand Tour of Copenhagen" (daily at 11; Apr.–Sept., additional tour daily at 1:30; Oct.–Mar., Sat. at 1:30); "Royal Tour of Copenhagen" (June–mid-Sept., Tues. and Sat. at 10); "City and Harbor Tour" (combined bus and boat; mid-May–mid-Sept., daily at 9:30; mid-June–mid-Sept., additional tour daily at 3). Tickets are available aboard the bus and boat or from travel agencies.

Personal Guides. The Danish Tourist Board (☞ Visitor Information, *below*) can recommend multilingual guides for individual needs; travel agents have details on hiring a limousine and guide.

Regional. The Danish Tourist Board (☞ Visitor Information, *below*) has full details relating to excursions outside the city, including visits to castles (such as Hamlet's castle), the Viking Ship Museum, and Sweden.

Special-Interest. The "Royal Copenhagen Porcelain" tour (⊠ Smalleg. 45, ☎ 31/86–48–59) is given on weekdays at 9, 10, and 11. If you're a beer aficionado, try the "Carlsberg Brewery Tour" (☞ Exploring Copenhagen, *above*).

Walking. The Danish Tourist Board (☞ Visitor Information, *below*) supplies maps and brochures and can recommend a walking tour.

TRAVEL AGENCIES
American Express (⊠ Amagertorv 18, ☎ 33/12–23–01). **Spies** (⊠ Nyropsg. 41, ☎ 33/32–15–00) arranges charter flights and accommodations all over Europe.

VISITOR INFORMATION
Danish Tourist Board (⊠ Danmarks Turistråd, Bernstoffsg. 1, Tivoli Grounds, DK 1577 KBH V, ☎ 33/11–13–25).

9 Dublin

Today, Europe's most intimate capital has become a boom town—the soul of the new Ireland is in the throes of what may be the nation's most dramatic period of transformation since the Georgian era. Dublin is riding the back of the Celtic Tiger (as the roaring Irish economy has been nicknamed) and massive construction cranes are hovering over both shiny new hotels and old Georgian houses. Irish culture is hot: patriot Michael Collins has become a Hollywood box-office star, Frank McCourt's Angela's Ashes *has conquered American best-seller lists, and* Riverdance *has become a worldwide tearjerking old Irish mass-jig. Because of these and other attractions, travelers are coming to Dublin in ever-greater numbers, so don't be surprised if you stop to consult your map in Temple Bar—the city's most happening neighborhood—and are swept away by the ceaseless flow of bustling crowds. Dublin has become a colossally entertaining, engaging city—all the more astonishing considering its gentle size.*

EXPLORING DUBLIN

Numbers in the margin correspond to points of interest on the Dublin map.

Originally a Viking settlement, Dublin is situated on the banks of the River Liffey, which divides the city north and south. The liveliest round-the-clock spots, including Temple Bar and Grafton Street, are both on the south side, although a variety of construction projects on the north side are helping to reinvigorate areas that have not typically been on visitors' paths. The majority of the city's most notable buildings date from the 18th century—the Georgian era—and, although many of its finer Georgian buildings disappeared in the redevelopment of the '70s, enough remain, mainly south of the river, to recall the elegant Dublin of centuries past. Literary Dublin can still be recaptured by those who follow the footsteps of Leopold Bloom's progress, as described in James Joyce's *Ulysses*. Trinity College, alma mater of Oliver Goldsmith, Jonathan Swift, and Samuel Beckett, among others, is a green, Georgian oasis, alive with young students scurrying to and fro, just like generations of aspiring scholars before them.

Trinity and St. Stephen's: The Georgian Heart of Dublin

"In Dublin's fair city—where girls are so pretty" went the centuries-old ditty about Ireland's historic capital. If Dublin is still one of the most charming cities in Europe, redolent in parts of the dignity and elegance of the 18th century, it is due to the elegant Georgian style of art and architecture, which flowered in the city between 1714 and 1820 during the English reigns of the three Georges. South of the Liffey are graceful squares and fashionable terraces from Dublin's elegant heyday and, interspersed with some of the city's leading sights, this area is perfect for an introductory city tour. Many travelers begin at O'Connell Bridge—as Dublin has no central focal point, most natives regard it as the city's Piccadilly Circus or Times Square—then head south down Westmoreland Street to Parliament House. When you pass 12 Westmoreland Street, drop in on **Bewley's Coffee House,** an institution that has been supplying Dubliners with coffee and buns since 1842. Open Monday–Saturday 9–5:30, its historic interior evokes the Dublin of everyone's dreams. Continue on to Trinity College—the Book of Kells, Ireland's greatest artistic treasure, is on view here—then eastward to Merrion Square and the National Gallery, south to St. Stephen's Green and Fitzwilliam Square, then head west to Dublin's two beautiful cathedrals— Christ Church and St. Patrick's—before heading back north for supper in a Temple Bar restaurant overlooking the Liffey.

② **Bank of Ireland.** With a grand facade that is a veritable forest of marble columns, the Bank of Ireland is one of Dublin's most striking buildings. Located across the street from the front entrance to Trinity College, the Georgian structure was once the home of the Irish Parliament. Built in 1729, it was bought by the Bank of Ireland in 1803. Hurricane-shape rosettes adorn the coffered ceiling in the pastel-hued, colonnaded, clerestoried main banking hall, once the Court of Requests where citizens' petitions were heard. Just down the hall is the original House of Lords, with tapestries, an oak-panel nave, and a 1,233-piece Waterford glass chandelier; ask a guard to show you in. Visitors are welcome during normal banking hours; a brief guided tour is given every Tuesday at 10:30, 11:30, and 1:45. ⊠ *2 College Green,* ☎ *01/677–6801.* ⊙ *Weekdays 10–4; Thurs. until 5.*

㉗ **Christ Church Cathedral.** Although St. Patrick's Cathedral is Dublin's grandest house of worship, Christ Church is actually the flagship of the Church of Ireland—it, not St. Paddy's, stood initially within the walls of the city. Construction was begun in 1172 by Strongbow, a Norman baron and conqueror of Dublin for the English crown, but an 1875 renovation to the exterior gave Christ Church much the look it has today. The vast, sturdy **crypt**, with its 12th- and 13th-century vaults, is Dublin's oldest surviving architecture and the building's most notable feature. ⊠ *Christ Church Pl. and Winetavern St.,* ☎ *01/677–8099.* ☉ *Mon., Tues., and Fri.–Sat. 10–5; Wed.–Thurs., and Sun. 10–6.*

⑬ **City Hall.** Prominently situated facing the Liffey from the top of Parliament Street, this grand Georgian municipal building (1769–79), once the Royal Exchange, has a central rotunda encircled by 12 columns, a fine mosaic floor, and 12 frescoes depicting Dublin legends and ancient Irish historical scenes. Just off the rotunda is a gently curving staircase, a typical feature of most large Dublin town houses. ☎ *01/679–6111.* ☉ *Weekdays 9–1, 2:15–5.*

⑮ **Civic Museum.** Built in 1765–71 as an assembly house for the Society of Artists, the museum displays drawings, models, maps of Dublin, and other civic memorabilia. ⊠ *58 S. William St.,* ☎ *01/679–4260.* ⊡ *Free.* ☉ *Tues.–Sat. 10–5:45, Sun. 11–2.*

⑭ **Dublin Castle.** Neil Jordan's film *Michael Collins* captures this structure's near-indomitable status in the city. Just off Dame Street behind City Hall, the grounds of the Castle encompass a number of buildings, including the **Record Tower,** a remnant of the original 13th-century Norman castle that was the seat of English power in Ireland for almost 7½ centuries, as well as various 18th- and 19th-century additions. The lavishly furnished **state apartments** are now used to entertain visiting heads of state. Guided tours are offered every half hour, but the rooms are closed when in official use, so phone first. ⊠ *Castle St.,* ☎ *01/677–7129.* ☉ *Weekdays 10–5, weekends 2–5.*

⑱ **Genealogical Office.** The reference library here is a good place to begin your ancestor-tracing efforts. It also houses the **Heraldic Museum** (⊠ Free. ☉ Mon.–Wed, 10–8:30, Thurs.–Fri. 10–4:30, Sat. 10–12:30), where displays of flags, coins, stamps, silver, and family crests highlight the uses and development of heraldry in Ireland. ⊠ *2 Kildare St.,* ☎ *01/661–8811.* ☉ *Weekdays 10–12:30, 2–4:30. Guided tours by appointment.*

★ ⑯ **Grafton Street.** Open only to pedestrians, brick-lined Grafton Street is one of Dublin's vital spines: the most direct route between the front door of Trinity College and Stephen's Green; the city's premier shopping street, off which radiate smaller streets that house stylish shops and pubs; and home to many of the city's singing and strumming buskers, or street musicians. Browse through the Irish and international designer clothing and housewares at **Brown Thomas,** still Ireland's most elegant department store despite its recent move from its quaint old building to a newly designed store across the street. The **Powerscourt Town House** is a shopping arcade installed in the covered courtyard of one of Dublin's most famous Georgian mansions.

㉑ **Leinster House.** When it was built in 1745 it was the largest private residence in Dublin. Today it is the seat of Dáil Eireann (pronounced dawl Erin), the Irish House of Parliament. The building has two facades: the one facing Merrion Square is designed in the style of a country house; the other, in Kildare Street, is in the style of a town house. ⊠ *Kildare St.,* ☎ *01/678–9911.* ☉ *Tours: Mon. and Fri. by prior ar-*

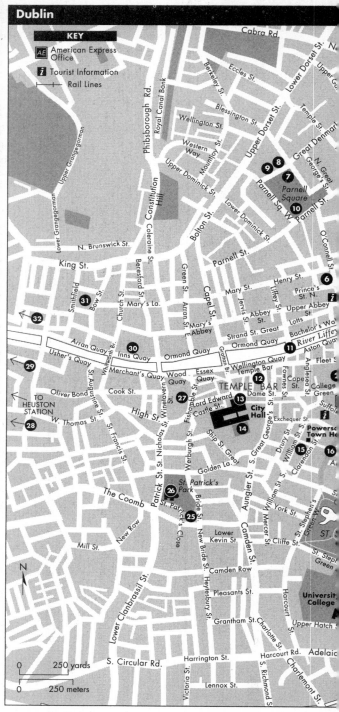

Dublin

KEY

AE American Express
    Office

i   Tourist Information

⊢—⊢ Rail Lines

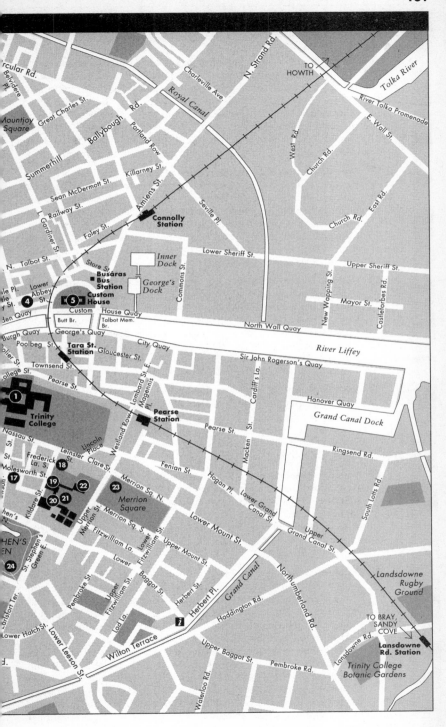

rangement (when Parliament is not in session). Dáil visitors' gallery: Access with an introduction from a member of Parliament.

㉕ Marsh's Library. A short walk west from Stephen's Green and accessed through a tiny but charming cottage garden lies a gem of old Dublin: the city's—and Ireland's—first public library, opened in 1701 to "All Graduates and Gentlemen." Its interior has been left practically unchanged since it was built—it still contains "cages" into which scholars who wanted to peruse rare books were locked. (The cages were to discourage students who, often impecunious, may have been tempted to make the books their own.) ⊠ *St. Patrick's Close,* ☎ *01/454–3511.* ⊙ *Mon. and Wed.–Fri. 10–12:45 and 2–5, Sat. 10:30–12:45.*

★ ㉓ Merrion Square. This tranquil Georgian square is lined on three sides by some of Dublin's best-preserved Georgian town houses, many of which have brightly painted front doors over which sit intricate fanlights. Even when the flower gardens are not in bloom, the vibrant green grounds, dotted with sculpture and threaded with meandering paths, are worth a walk-through. **No. 1,** at the northwest corner, was the home of Sir William and Speranza Wilde, Oscar's parents. ⊠ *East end of Nassau St.* ⊙ *Daily sunrise–sunset.*

★ ㉒ National Gallery of Ireland. On the west side of Merrion Square, this 1854 building contains the country's finest collection of old masters— great treasures include Vermeer's incomparable *Woman Writing a Letter* (twice stolen from Sir Alfred Beit and now safe at last), Gainsborough's *Cottage Girl,* and Caravaggio's recently rediscovered *The Arrest of Christ.* The gallery's restaurant is one of the city's best spots for an inexpensive, top-rate lunch. ⊠ *Merrion Sq. (W),* ☎ *01/661–5133.* ⊡ *Free.* ⊙ *Mon.–Sat 10–5:30, Thurs. until 8:30, Sun. 2–5.*

⑲ National Library. The collections here include first editions of every major Irish writer. Temporary exhibits are held in the entrance hall, off the colonnaded rotunda. The recently renovated main reading room, opened in 1890, has a dramatic dome ceiling. ⊠ *Kildare St.,* ☎ *01/661–8811.* ⊡ *Free.* ⊙ *Mon. 10–9, Tues.–Wed. 2–9, Thurs.–Fri. 10–5, Sat. 10–1.*

⑳ National Museum. Situated on the other side of Leinster House from the National Library, the museum is most famous for its spectacular collection of Irish artifacts from 6000 BC to the present, including the Tara Brooch, the Ardagh Chalice, the Cross of Cong, and a fabled hoard of Celtic gold jewelry. There is also an important collection of Irish decorative arts. ⊠ *Kildare St.,* ☎ *01/660–1117.* ⊡ *Free.* ⊙ *Tues.– Sat. 10–5, Sun. 2–5.*

❸ O'Connell Bridge. Strange but true: the main bridge spanning the Liffey is wider than it is long. The north side of the bridge is dominated by an elaborate memorial to Daniel O'Connell, "The Liberator," erected as a tribute to the great 19th-century orator's achievement in securing Catholic Emancipation in 1829. Today **O'Connell Street** is less a street to loiter in than to pass through on your way to elsewhere. **Henry Street,** to the left just beyond the General Post Office, is, like Grafton Street, a busy pedestrian thoroughfare where you'll find throngs of Dubliners out doing their shopping. A few steps down Henry Street off to the right is the colorful **Moore Street Market,** where street vendors recall their most famous ancestor, Molly Malone, by singing their wares—mainly flowers and fruit—in the traditional Dublin style.

⑰ Royal Irish Academy. The country's leading learned society houses important manuscripts in its 18th-century library. Just below the academy is the **Mansion House,** the official residence of the Lord Mayor of Dublin. Its Round Room, the site of the first assembly of Dáil Eireann in January 1919, is now used mainly for exhibitions. ✉ *19 Dawson St.,* ☎ *01/676–2570.* 🖼 *Free.* ⊘ *Weekdays 9:30–5.*

㉖ **St. Patrick's Cathedral.** Legend has it that St. Patrick baptized many converts at a well on the site of the cathedral during the 5th century. The building dates from 1190 and is mainly early English Gothic in style. At 305 ft, it is the longest church in the country. During the 17th century Oliver Cromwell, dour ruler of England and no friend of the Irish, had his troops stable their horses in the cathedral. It wasn't until the 19th century that restoration work to repair the damage was begun. St. Patrick's is the national cathedral of the Anglican church in Ireland and has had many illustrious deans. The most famous was Jonathan Swift, author of *Gulliver's Travels,* who held office from 1713 to 1745. Swift's tomb is in the south aisle; a corner at the top of the north transept commemorates him. Memorials to many other celebrated figures from Ireland's past line the walls. ✉ *Patrick St.,* ☎ *01/475–4817.* ⊘ *Weekdays 9–5:15, weekends 9–5.*

㉔ **St. Stephen's Green.** Dubliners call it simply Stephen's Green; green it is—strikingly so, year-round (you can even spot a palm tree or two). The north side is dominated by the magnificent Shelbourne Hotel, which lives up to its billing as "the best address in Dublin." A drink in one of its two bars, thronged after work, or afternoon tea in the elegant Lord Mayor's Room (IR£9 per person, including sandwiches and cakes), is the most financially painless way to soak in the old-fashioned luxury and genteel excitement.

★ **⑫** **Temple Bar.** Dublin's hippest neighborhood—bordered by Dame Street to the south, the Liffey to the north, Fishamble Street to the west, and Westmoreland Street to the east—is the city's version of the Latin Quarter, the playing ground of "young Dublin." Representative of the improved fortunes of the area, with its narrow, winding pedestrian-only cobblestone streets, is the **Clarence** (✉ 6–8 Wellington Quay, ☎ 01/670–9000), a favorite old Dublin hotel now owned and understatedly renovated in 1996 by Bono and the Edge of U2. The area is chock-full of small, hip stores, art galleries, and inexpensive restaurants and pubs. The **Irish Film Centre** (✉ 6 Eustace St., ☎ 01/679–5744), with a full program of new independent films and revivals, is emblematic of the area's vibrant mix of high and alternative culture.

★ **❶** **Trinity College.** A must for every visitor, Ireland's oldest and most famous college is the heart of college-town Dublin. Trinity College, Dublin (familiarly known as TCD), was founded by Elizabeth I in 1592 and offered a free education to Catholics—providing they accepted the Protestant faith. As a legacy of this condition, until 1966 Catholics who wished to study at Trinity had to obtain a dispensation from their bishop or face excommunication. Today more than 70% of Trinity's students are Catholics, an indication of how far away those days seem to today's generation.

The pedimented, neoclassical Georgian facade, built between 1755 and 1759, consists of a magnificent portico with Corinthian columns. The design is repeated on the interior, so the view from outside the gates and from the quadrangle inside is the same. On the quad's lawn are statues of two of the university's illustrious alumni—statesman Edmund Burke and poet Oliver Goldsmith. Other famous students include the philosopher George Berkeley (who gave his name to the northern California city), Jonathan Swift, Thomas Moore, Oscar Wilde, John Millington Synge, Bram Stoker, Edward Carson, and Samuel Beckett.

The 18th-century building on the left, just inside the entrance, is the chapel. There's an identical building opposite, the **Examination Hall.** The oldest buildings are the library in the far right-hand corner and a row of redbrick buildings known as the **Rubrics,** which contain student apartments; both date from 1712.

Ireland's largest collection of books and manuscripts is housed in **Trinity College Library,** entered through the library shop. Its principal treasure is the Book of Kells, generally considered the most striking manuscript ever produced in the Anglo-Saxon world. Only a few pages from the 682-page, 9th-century gospel are displayed at a time, but there is an informative exhibit that reproduces many of them. At peak hours you may have to wait in line to enter the library; it's less busy early in the day. Don't miss the grand and glorious Long Room, an impressive 213 ft long and 42 ft wide, which houses 200,000 volumes in its 21 alcoves. ☎ *01/677–2941.* ☉ *Mon.–Sat. 9:30–4:45, Sun. noon–4:30.*

In the Thomas Davis Theatre in the Arts Building, the **"Dublin Experience"** is an audiovisual presentation devoted to the history of the city over the last 1,000 years. ☎ *01/677–2941.* ☉ *May–Oct., daily 10–5; shows every hr on the hr.*

NORTH OF THE LIFFEY

The Northside city center is a mix of densely thronged shopping streets and run-down sections of once genteel homes. Nevertheless, there are some classic sights here, including some gorgeous Georgian monuments—the Custom House, the General Post Office, Parnell Square, and the Hugh Lane Gallery—and two landmarks of literary Dublin, the Dublin Writers Museum and the James Joyce Cultural Center, hub of Bloomsday celebrations. Most travelers begin heading up O'Connell Street to Parnell Square and the heart of James Joyce Country.

❹ Abbey Theatre. Ireland's national theater was founded by W. B. Yeats and Lady Gregory in 1904. The original building was destroyed in a fire in 1951; the present theater was built in 1966. It has some noteworthy portraits and mementos in the foyer. Seats are usually available for about IR£8–12; all tickets are IR£8 for Monday performances. ✉ *Lower Abbey St.,* ☎ *01/878–7222*

❺ Custom House. Extending 375 ft on the north side of the Liffey, this is the city's most spectacular Georgian building, the work of James Gandon, an English architect who arrived in Ireland in 1781 when construction commenced here (it continued for 10 years). The central portico is linked by arcades to the pavilions at each end. A statue of Commerce tops the graceful copper dome; statues on the main facade are based on allegorical themes. Republicans set the building on fire in 1921, but it was completely restored; it now houses government offices but there is a visitors center that is open to the public. ✉ *Custom House Quay,* ☎ *01/679–3377.* ▣ *IR£2.* ☉ *Weekdays 9:30–4, weekends 2–5.*

★ ❽ Dublin Writers Museum. Two restored 18th-century town houses on the north side of Parnell Square, an area rich in literary associations, lodge one of Dublin's finest cultural sights. Rare manuscripts, diaries, posters, letters, limited and first editions, photographs and other mementos commemorate the lives and works of the nation's greatest writers (and there are *many* of them, so leave plenty of time) including Joyce, Shaw, Wilde, Yeats, and Beckett. Readings are held in the upstairs drawing rooms, gorgeously decorated with paintings and bas-relief wall decorations. The bookshop and café make this an ideal place to spend a rainy afternoon. ⊠ *18–19 Parnell Sq. N,* ☎ *01/872–2077.* ☼ *Mon.–Sat. 10–5, Sun. 11–5.*

㉚ Four Courts. Today the seat of the High Court of Justice of Ireland, the Four Courts are James Gandon's second Dublin masterpiece, built between 1786 and 1802. Like the Custom House and other buildings lining the north side of the Liffey, the courts were destroyed during the "Troubles" of the '20s and restored by 1932. Its distinctive copper-covered dome atop a colonnaded rotunda makes this one of Dublin's most instantly recognizable buildings. Visitors are allowed to listen in on court proceedings, which can often be interesting, educational, even scandalous. ⊠ *Inns Quay,* ☎ *01/872–5555.* ☼ *Daily 10:30–4.*

❻ General Post Office. The GPO (1818) is one of the great civic buildings of Dublin's Georgian era, but its fame derives from the role it played during the Easter Rising. Here, on Easter Monday, 1916, the Republican Forces stormed the building and issued the Proclamation of the Irish Republic. After a week of shelling, the GPO lay in ruins; 13 rebels were ultimately executed. Most of the original building was destroyed; only the facade—in which you can still see the scars of bullets on its pillars—remained. It is still a working post office, with an attractive two-story central gallery. ⊠ *O'Connell St.,* ☎ *01/872–8888.* ☼ *Mon.–Sat. 8–8, Sun. 10:30–6:30.*

⓫ Ha'penny Bridge. This heavily trafficked footbridge crosses the Liffey at a prime spot: Temple Bar is on the south side, and the bridge provides the fastest route to the thriving Mary and Henry Street shopping areas to the north. Until early in this century, a half-penny toll was charged to cross it. Yeats was one among many Dubliners who found this too high a price to pay—more a matter of principle than of finance—and so made the detour via O'Connell Bridge.

★ ❾ Hugh Lane Municipal Gallery of Modern Art. The imposing Palladian facade of this town house, once the home of the Earl of Charlemont, dominates the north side of Parnell Square. Sir Hugh Lane, a nephew of Lady Gregory (Yeats's patron), collected Impressionist paintings and 19th-century Irish and Anglo-Irish works. Among them are canvases by Jack Yeats (W. B.'s brother) and Paul Henry. ⊠ *Parnell Sq.,* ☎ *01/874–1903.* 🎟 *Free.* ☼ *Tues.–Thurs. 9:30–6, Fri.–Sat. 9:30–5, Sun. 11–5.*

㉛ Old Jameson Distillery. The birthplace of one of Ireland's best whiskeys has been fully restored and offers a fascinating insight into the making of *uisce batha,* or "holy water," as whiskey is known in Irish. There is a guided tour of the old distillery, an audiovisual tour, and a complimentary tasting where you get to sample five top-name Irish whiskeys. ⊠ *Bow St.,* ☎ *01/872–5566.* ☼ *Tours: May–Oct., weekdays 11, 2:30, and 3:30, Sat. 2:30 and 3:30, Sun. 3:30; Nov.–Apr., weekdays 3:30. Also by appointment.*

❼ Parnell Square. This is the north side's most notable Georgian square and one of Dublin's oldest. Because the first-floor reception rooms of the elegant brick-face town houses on the square were designed as reception rooms—fashionable hostesses liked passersby to be able to peer in and admire the distinguished guests at their luxurious, candlelit soireés—their windows are much larger than the others.

❿ Rotunda Hospital. Founded in 1745 as the first maternity hospital in Ireland or Britain, it is now most worth a visit for its **chapel,** with elaborate plasterwork, appropriately honoring motherhood. The **Gate Theater** (☞ Nightlife and the Arts, *below*), housed in an extension, attracts large crowds to its fine repertoire of classic Irish and European drama. ⊠ *Parnell St.,* ☎ *01/873—0700*

Dublin West

If you're not an enthusiastic walker, hop a bus or find a cab to take you to these sights in westernmost Dublin.

★ ㉘ **Guinness Brewery.** Founded by Arthur Guinness in 1759, Ireland's all-dominating brewery is situated on a 60-acre spread to the west of Christ Church Cathedral; it is the most popular tourist destination in town. The brewery itself is closed to the public, but the **Hop Store,** part museum and part gift shop, puts on an 18-minute audiovisual show. After the show visitors get two complimentary glasses (or one pint) of the famous black stout. ⊠ *Crane St.,* ☎ *01/453–3645.* ⊙ *Apr.–Sept., Mon.–Sat. 9:30–5, Sun. 10:30–4:30; Oct.–Mar., Mon.–Sat. 9:30–4, Sun. noon–4.*

★ ㉜ **Phoenix Park.** Europe's largest public park, extending about 3 mi along the Liffey's north bank, encompasses 1,752 acres of verdant lawns, woods, lakes, playing fields, a zoo, a flower garden (the **People's Garden,** to the right as you enter the park on Chesterfield Avenue), and two residences—those of the president of Ireland and the American ambassador. A 210-ft-tall obelisk, built in 1817, commemorates the Duke of Wellington's defeat of Napoléon. It is a jogger's paradise, but Sunday is the best time for everyone to visit: Games of cricket, soccer, polo, baseball, hurling—a combination of lacrosse, baseball, and field hockey—or Gaelic football are likely to be in progress.

★ ㉙ **Royal Hospital Kilmainham.** A short ride by taxi or bus from the city center, this is regarded as the most important 17th-century building in Ireland. Completed in 1684 as a hospice for soldiers, it survived into the 1920s as a hospital. The ceiling of the Baroque chapel is extraordinary. It now houses the **Irish Museum of Modern Art,** opened in 1991, which displays works by such non-Irish greats as Picasso and Miró but concentrates on the work of Irish artists. ⊠ *Kilmainham La.,* ☎ *01/612–9900.* ⊡ *Free.* ⊙ *Exhibitions: Tues.–Sat. 10–5:30, Sun. noon–5:30; museum tours: Wed., Fri. 2:30, Sat. 11:30; historical tours: Sun. 2–4:30.*

DINING

Dublin's restaurateurs are key players in the Irish food revolution now under way. You can still order up a traditional John Dory fillet, but more and more diners are opting for such nouvelle novelties as Dublin Bay prawns with Japanese sushi rice, pear, and a sweet soy chilli sauce. In dozens of spots adventurous young chefs are challenging older establishments on price and quality; many are taking advantage of the magnificent fresh livestock and fish that Ireland has in such abundance. If you want to browse beyond the restaurants recommended here, the area between Grafton Street and South Great George's Street has many to offer, as does Temple Bar, just across Dame Street. You'll find a pub—if not two or three—on virtually every block (☞ Nightlife and the Arts, *below,* for additional pub listings).

RATINGS

Prices are per person and include an appetizer, main course, and dessert, but no wine or tip. Many restaurants also have à la carte menus allowing you to select only the main course or even two appetizers. Sales tax is included in the price. Many places add a 10%–15% service charge—if not, a 10% tip is fine.

CATEGORY	COST
$$$$	over IR£25
$$$	IR£20–IR£25
$$	IR£15–IR£20
$	under IR£15

$$$$ ✕ **Le Coq Hardi.** John Howard has been running one of Dublin's best
★ restaurants here for many years. He has one of the most extensive wine
lists in the country. Service is friendly and relaxed, and there is an air
of quiet elegance about the Georgian dining room. Appetizer "smok-
ies" are served in a ramekin of smoked haddock with a sauce of
tomato, double cream, and cheese. A house speciality is the bacon-
wrapped Coq Hardi chicken, with potatoes, apples, and ham, all in
an Irish whiskey sauce. ✉ *35 Pembroke Rd., Ballsbridge,* ☎ *01/668–
9070. AE, DC, MC, V. Closed Sun.*

$$$$ ✕ **Patrick Guilbaud.** Everything is French here, including the epony-
mous owner, his chef, the maître d' and the two Michelin stars that
make it Ireland's highest-rated restaurant. Guillaume Le Brun's cooking is a fluent expression of modern French cuisine—not particularly
flamboyant, but coolly professional. Expect superb foie gras, confit of
Landaise duck in a delicate phyllo pastry, roe deer with junipers—and
also some homage to Irish dishes, from Connemara lobster in season
to braised pig's trotters. ✉ *Hotel Merrion, Merrion St.,* ☎ *01/676–
4192. AE, DC, MC, V. Closed Sun., Mon., and Dec. 24–Jan. 14.*

$$$$ ✕ **Peacock Alley.** Ireland's most bravura chef-owner is Conrad Gal-
★ lagher, who ran away from school at 12 to be a cook. By 18 he was
sous chef at the Plaza in New York, and at 19 *chef de cuisine* at the
Waldorf-Astoria's Peacock Alley. Elegantly set white-linen-covered tables set the stage for the dazzling fare; Gallagher builds up the food
on the plate and dabs multicolor oils and garnishes with painterly pre-
cision. His strikingly inventive dishes include an appetizer of smoked
salmon with basmati rice, pear, preserved ginger, soy sauce, and que-
sadilla; an intensely flavored roast chestnut soup; deep-fried crab cakes
with *katifi* (shredded phyllo pastry); daube of pot-roasted beef; and
pan-seared red snapper with purée of pumpkin. ✉ *47 South William
St.,* ☎ *01/662–0760. AE, DC, MC, V. Closed Sun.*

$$$$ ✕ **Thornton's.** Chef-owner Kevin Thornton is as restrained and clas-
★ sical in his approach as Conrad Gallagher is flamboyant, yet like Gallagher, he is a naturally gifted chef. Thornton's is in a renovated house
with pine floors on the north bank of the Grand Canal, a long walk
or short ride southwest of Stephen's Green. Service is French and quite
formal. The cooking style is light, and the dishes are small masterpieces
of structural engineering. In season Thornton marinates legs of partridge and cooks them separately, then removes the insides of the bird
and purées them before stuffing and reforming the bird with the
deboned breasts presented as a crown. ✉ *1 Portobello Rd.,* ☎ *01/454–
9067. AE, DC, MC, V. Closed Sun. No lunch.*

$$$ ✕ **The Commons Restaurant.** This is a large elegant room with French
windows in the basement of Newman House, where James Joyce was
a student at the original premises of University College Dublin. The
seasonal menu offers a light treatment of classical themes—steamed
sea bass with Sevruga caviar in an oyster emulsion; panfried foie gras
in ginger bread crumbs, accompanied by a glass of walnut wine; and
venison cutlet with red-wine mashed pototoes and blueberry pudding.
✉ *85–86 St. Stephen's Green,* ☎ *01/478–0530. AE, DC, MC, V. Closed
Sun. No lunch Sat.*

$$$ ✕ **Cooke's Café.** Johnny Cooke has turned this city-center, Californian–
Mediterranean-style bistro into a cool spot for visiting movie stars. Spe-
cialties tend toward fresh seafood (except Monday) and game: Cooke

does a crab salad with spinach, coriander, mango salsa, and lime dressing; lobster grilled with garlic herb butter; and in season, a selection of roast game including wild mallard and teal, sliced venison, and wood pigeon. It's busy and service can be slow; the outdoor seating on nice summer days is a consolation. ⊠ *14 S. William St.,* ☎ *01/679–0536. AE, DC, MC, V. No lunch.*

$$$ ✕ **L'Ecrivain.** Chef-owner Derry Clarke's sense of humor is sometimes
★ tested by tipsy patrons who fall over a life-size sculpture of the writer Brendan Behan on their way out of his elegant restaurant. Paintings of Beckett and other Irish writers hang on the walls. The food is serious—disciplined and restrained, with the emphasis on fresh Irish produce. Starters may include grilled goat cheese with eggplant and charcoal-grilled Mediterranean vegetables. Cured, marinated lamb with prune stuffing is superb. ⊠ *109a Lower Baggot St.,* ☎ *01/661– 1919. AE, DC, MC, V. Closed Sun.*

$$ ✕ **Adrian's.** When Adrian Holden's daughter Catriona is in the kitchen, this unpretentious waterfront restaurant in the fishing village of Howth (30 minutes north of Dublin by commuter train or taxi) really starts to sing. A specialty are six varieties of spiced seafood—from the nearby fishing pier, of course—over cous-cous. ⊠ *3 Abbey St., Howth,* ☎ *01/ 839–0231. AE, DC, MC, V.*

$$ ✕ **Chapter One.** Housed in the vaulted, stone-walled basement of the engrossing Dublin Writers Museum, just down the street from the Hugh Lane Municipal Gallery (☞ *above*), this is one of the most notable restaurants in north-side Dublin. Dishes include pressed duck and black pudding terrine with a pear chutney; grilled black sole with poached ravioli stuffed with salmon mousse; and pork with a confit of spiced pork belly. ⊠ *18–19 Parnell Sq.,* ☎ *01/873–2266. AE, DC, MC, V. Closed Sun. No lunch Sat., no dinner Mon.*

$–$$ ✕ **La Mére Zou.** Eric Tydgadt is Belgian and his wife Isabelle is from Paris, so it's not surprising that their basement restaurant is Continental in emphasis. The menu includes six king-size plates; one of them, "La Belge," has a 6-ounce charcoal-grilled rump steak with french fries, and a salad with salami, country ham, chicory, and mayonnaise. ⊠ *22 St. Stephen's Green,* ☎ *01/661–6669. AE, DC, MC, V. Closed Jan. 1–10. No lunch weekends.*

$ ✕ **Caviston's.** The Cavistons have been dispensing recipes for years from their fish counter and delicatessen in Sandycove, just south of the ferry port of Dun Laoghaire, 30 minutes by taxi or DART train south of Dublin. The fish restaurant next door is a lively and intimate place, with appetizers such as a phyllo pastry basket with prawns and twice-baked gorgonzola soufflé with a green salad. Typical entrées include panfried scallops served in the shell with a Thermidor sauce, and steamed Dover sole with mustard sauce. ⊠ *59 Glasthule Rd., Dun Laoghaire,* ☎ *01/280–9120. MC, V. Closed Sun., Mon., and Dec. 23– Jan. 2. No dinner.*

$ ✕ **Milano.** This is a well-designed room with lots of brio and a tempting array of flashy pizzas. Expect to find thinner pizza crust than in the United States, with such combinations as tomato and mozzarella, ham and eggs, Cajun with prawns and tabasco, spinach and egg, or ham with anchovies. The owners opened a second restaurant in Temple Bar in late 1997. ⊠ *38 Dawson St.,* ☎ *01/670–7744. AE, MC, V.*

$ ✕ **The Side Door.** The five-star Shelbourne Hotel has a stylish budget restaurant with oak floors, cream walls, and art deco–style tables and chairs. You can start off with a bowl of Thai soup, a grilled chicken risotto, or Mediterranean vegetable pizza. Main dishes include supreme of chicken marinated in honey, or charcoal-grilled rib eye of beef. Designer beers and a good wine list complement the food nicely. ⊠ *27 St. Stephen's Green,* ☎ *01/676–6471. AE, DC, MC, V.*

Pub Food

Most pubs serve food at lunchtime, some throughout the day. The pub is at the heart of Irish social life—a center of good *craic,* good talk, and general fun. Food ranges from hearty soups and stews to chicken curries, smoked salmon salads, and sandwiches. Expect to pay IR£4–IR£5 for a main course. Many pubs do not take credit cards.

✕ **Davy Byrne's.** James Joyce immortalized Davy Byrne's in his sprawling novel *Ulysses.* Nowadays it's more akin to a cocktail bar than a Dublin pub, but it's good for fresh and smoked salmon, salads, and a hot daily special. Food is available at lunchtime and in the early evening. ✉ *21 Duke St.,* ☎ *01/671–1298.*

✕ **John M. Keating.** For a real Irish pub lunch, this old-timer at the corner of Mary and Jervis streets can't be beat. Upstairs you can sit at a low table and chat with locals as you warm up with a bowl of soup and nibble on a sandwich. ✉ *14 Mary St./23 Jervis St.,* ☎ *01/873–1567.*

✕ **Kitty O'Shea's.** Kitty O'Shea's cleverly, if a little artificially, re-creates the atmosphere of old Dublin. ✉ *23–25 Grand Canal St.,* ☎ *01/660–9965.*

✕ **Old Stand.** Located conveniently close to Grafton Street, the Old Stand offers grilled food, including steaks. ✉ *37 Exchequer St.,* ☎ *01/677–0823.*

✕ **Porterhouse.** Ireland's first brew pub has an open kitchen and offers a dazzling range of beers—from pale ales to dark stouts. ✉ *16–18 Parliament St.,* ☎ *01/679–8847.*

✕ **Stag's Head.** Recognized by Egon Ronay as serving the best pub lunch in the city, the Stag's Head is a favorite of Trinity students and businesspeople alike. ✉ *1 Dame Court,* ☎ *01/679–3701.*

Cafés

While Dublin has nowhere near as many cafés as pubs, it's easier than ever to find a good cup of coffee at most hours of the day or night.

✕ **Bewley's Coffee House.** The granddaddy of the capital's cafés, Bewley's has been supplying Dubliners with coffee and buns for more than a century. The aroma of coffee is irresistible, and the dark interior—with marble-top tables, original wood fittings, and stained-glass windows—evokes a more leisurely Dublin of the past. The Grafton Street location houses a museum. ✉ *78 Grafton St., 13 S. Great George's St., and 12 Westmoreland St.; all* ☎ *01/677–6761.*

✕ **Kaffe Moka.** One of Dublin's hottest haunts for the caffeine-addicted, this spot has three hyper-stylish floors and a central location in the heart of the city center. ✉ *39 S. William St.,* ☎ *01/679–8475.*

✕ **Thomas Read's.** By day it's a café, by night a pub. Its large windows overlooking a busy corner in Temple Bar make it a great spot for people-watching. The menu includes hot bagels, danishes, and baguette sandwiches. The coffees are particularly good. ✉ *123 Parliament St.,* ☎ *01/677–1487.*

NIGHTLIFE AND THE ARTS

Dublin has undergone a small nightlife revolution. Sophisticated, internationally acclaimed dance clubs have taken the place of discos. The bar-pub scene has also gone upmarket, with bright, European-style café-bars nestling side by side with older, more traditional pubs. Still, Dublin's pub scene retains its celebrated charm and camaraderie.

The fortnightly magazine *In Dublin* (at newsstands) contains comprehensive details of upcoming events, including ticket availability. *The Event Guide* also lists events, and is given away free at many pubs and cafés. In peak season consult the free Bord Fáilte leaflet "Events of the Week."

Cabarets

The following all offer Irish cabaret. They are open only in peak season (roughly May–October; call to confirm):

Burlington Hotel (⊠ Upper Leeson St., ☎ 01/660–5222). **Jurys Hotel** (⊠ Ballsbridge, ☎ 01/660–5000). **Abbey Tavern** (⊠ Howth, Co. Dublin, ☎ 01/839–0307).

Music

The **National Concert Hall** (⊠ Earlsfort Terrace, ☎ 01/475–1666), just off Stephen's Green, is the place to go for classical concerts.

Nightclubs

Lillie's Bordello (⊠ Grafton St., ☎ 01/679–9204) is a favorite with celebs and their admirers. **The Kitchen** (⊠ Essex St., ☎ 01/677–6635) is part-owned by U2 and attracts a young, vibrant clientele.

Velure (⊠ The Gaiety, South King St., ☎ 01/677–1717) attracts crowds every Saturday night to this elegant theater-cum-nightclub.

Pubs

Check advertisements in evening papers for "sessions" of folk, ballad, Irish traditional or jazz music. Listings below with telephone numbers offer some form of musical entertainment. For details on pubs that serve food, *see* Dining *in* Dublin, *above*.

The **Brazen Head** (⊠ 20 Lower Bridge St., ☎ 01/677–9549)—Dublin's oldest pub, dating from 1688—has music every night. President Bill Clinton dropped in at **Cassidy's** (⊠ 42 Lower Camden St.) for a pint of stout during his visit to Dublin. **Doheny & Nesbitt's** (⊠ 5 Lower Baggot St., ☎ 01/676–2945) is frequented by local businesspeople, politicians, and legal eagles. In the **Horseshoe Bar** (⊠ Shelbourne Hotel, St. Stephen's Green) you can eavesdrop on Dublin's social elite and their hangers-on. **Kehoe's** (⊠ 9 S. Anne St.) is popular with students, artists, and writers. Locals and visitors bask in the theatrical atmosphere of **Neary's** (⊠ 1 Chatham St.). **O'Donoghue's** (⊠ 15 Merrion Row, ☎ 01/661–4303) features some form of musical entertainment on most nights. The **Palace Bar** (⊠ 21 Fleet St.) is a journalists' haunt. William Ryan's (⊠ 28 Parkgate St.) is a beautifully preserved Victorian gem.

Theaters

Ireland has a rich theatrical tradition. The **Abbey Theatre** (⊠ Marlborough St., ☎ 01/878–7222) is the home of Ireland's national theater company, its name forever associated with J. M. Synge, W. B. Yeats, and Sean O'Casey. The **Peacock Theatre** (same address and phone) is the Abbey's more experimental small stage. The **Gate Theatre** (⊠ Cavendish Row, Parnell Sq., ☎ 01/874–4045) is an intimate spot for modern drama and plays by Irish writers. The **Gaiety Theatre** (⊠ South King St., ☎ 01/677–1717) features musical comedy, opera, drama, and revues. The **Olympia Theatre** (⊠ Dame St., ☎ 01/677–7124) has seasons of comedy, vaudeville, and ballet. The **Project Arts Centre** (⊠ 39 E. Essex St., ☎ 01/679–6622) is an established fringe theater.

SHOPPING

Although the rest of the country is well supplied with crafts shops, Dublin is the place to seek out more specialized items—antiques, traditional sportswear, haute couture, designer ceramics, books and prints, silverware and jewelry, and designer hand-knit items.

Department Stores

The shops north of the river—many of them chain stores and lackluster department stores—tend to be less expensive and less design-conscious. Things may be changing, though, with the recent opening of the **Jervis Shopping Center** (⊠ Jervis St. at Mary St., ☎ 01/878–1323), the city's newest major shopping center. Also on the north side, **Clery's** (⊠ O'Connell St., directly opposite the GPO, ☎ 01/878–6000) was once the city's most fashionable department store and is still worth a visit, despite its rapidly aging decor.

In the heart of Grafton Street is **Brown Thomas** (⊠ Grafton St., ☎ 01/605–6666), Dublin's most elegant department store, offering many international and Irish designers. **Arnotts** (⊠ Henry St., ☎ 01/805–0400) is Dublin's largest department store and has a good range of cut crystal.

Shopping Districts

Grafton Street is the most sophisticated shopping area in Dublin city center. **Molesworth** and **Dawson streets** are the places to browse for antiques. **Nassau** and **Dawson streets** are for books; the smaller side streets for jewelry, art galleries, and old prints. The pedestrianized **Temple Bar** area, with its young, offbeat ambience, has a number of small art galleries, specialty shops (including music and books), and inexpensive and adventurous clothes shops. The area is further enlivened by buskers (street musicians) and street artists. **St. Stephen's Green Center** contains 70 stores, large and small, in a vast Moorish-style glass-roof building. ⊠ *St. Stephen's Green,* ☎ *01/478–0888.* ☉ *Mon.–Sat. 9–6, Sun. noon–6.*

Books

Fred Hanna's (⊠ 29 Nassau St., ☎ 01/677–1255) sells old and new books, with a good choice of books on travel and Ireland. **Hodges Figgis** (⊠ 56–58 Dawson St., ☎ 01/677–4754) is Dublin's leading independent, with a café on the first floor. **Waterstone's** (⊠ 7 Dawson St.,☎ 01/679–1415) is the Dublin branch of the renowned British chain.

Crystal, Ceramics, Jewelry, and Housewares

Kilkenny Shop (⊠ Nassau St., ☎ 01/677–7066) is good for contemporary Irish-made ceramics, pottery, and silver jewelry. **McDowell** (⊠ 3 Upper O'Connell St., ☎ 01/874–4961), in business for over 100 years, is a jewelry shop popular among Dubliners.

Tweeds and Woolens

Kevin & Howlin (⊠ Nassau St., ☎ 01/677–0257) has ready-made tweeds for men. The **Blarney Woollen Mills** (⊠ Nassau St., ☎ 01/671–0068) has a good selection of tweed, linen, and woolen sweaters in all price ranges. The **Dublin Woolen Mills** (⊠ Metal Bridge Corner, 41 Lower Ormond Quay, ☎ 01/677–0301) at Ha'penny Bridge, has a good selection of hand-knit and other woolen sweaters at competitive prices.

DUBLIN ESSENTIALS

Arriving and Departing

BY BUS

The central bus station, **Busaras,** is at Store Street near the Custom House. Some buses terminate near O'Connell Bridge. Call 01/873–4222 for information on city services (Dublin Bus); dial 01/836–6111 for express buses and provincial services (Bus Eireann).

The main access route from the north is N1; from the west, N4; from the south and southwest, N7; from the east coast, N11. On all routes there are clearly marked signs indicating the center of the city: AN LÁR. The new M50 motorway encircles the city from Dublin Airport in the north to Tallaght in the south.

BY PLANE

All flights arrive at Dublin Airport, 10 km (6 mi) north of town.

Between the Airport and Downtown. Buses leave every 20 minutes from outside the Arrivals door for the central bus station in downtown Dublin. The ride takes about 30 minutes, depending on the traffic, and the fare is IR£2.50. A taxi ride into town will cost from IR£10 to IR£14, depending on the location of your hotel; be sure to ask in advance if the cab has no meter (☞ Getting Around By Taxi *below*).

BY TRAIN

There are three main stations: **Heuston Station** (⊠ at Kingsbridge) is the departure point for the south and southwest; **Connolly Station** (⊠ at Amiens St.), for Belfast, the east coast, and the west; and **Pearse Station** (⊠ on Westland Row), for Bray and connections via Dun Laoghaire to the Liverpool/Holyhead ferries. Call 01/836−6222 for information.

Getting Around

Dublin is small as capital cities go—the downtown area is compact—and the best way to see the city and soak in the full flavor is on foot.

BY BUS

Most city buses originate in or pass through the area of O'Connell Street and O'Connell Bridge. If the destination board indicates AN LÁR, that means that the bus is going to the city center. Timetables (IR£2.50) are available from the **Dublin Bus** office (⊠ 59 Upper O'Connell St., ☎ 01/873−4222) and give details of all routes, times of operation, and price codes. The minimum fare is 55p.

BY TAXI

Official licensed taxis, metered and designated by roof signs, do not cruise; they are beside the central bus station, at train stations, at O'Connell Bridge, Stephen's Green, College Green, and near major hotels. The initial charge is IR£2; the fare is displayed in the cab. (Make sure the meter is on.) A 1-mi trip in city traffic costs about IR£3.50. Hackney cabs, which also operate in the city, have neither roof signs nor meters, and will sometimes respond to hotels' requests for a cab. Negotiate the fare before your journey begins.

BY TRAIN

An electric train commuter service, **DART,** serves the suburbs out to Howth, on the north side of the city, and to Bray, County Wicklow, on the south side. Fares are about the same as for buses. Street-direction signs to DART stations read STAISIUN/STATION. The **Irish Rail** office is at 35 Lower Abbey Street; for rail inquiries, call 01/836−6222.

Money Matters

CURRENCY

The unit of currency in Ireland is the pound, or punt (pronounced poont), written as IR£ to avoid confusion with the pound sterling. The currency is divided into the same denominations as in Britain, with IR£1 divided into 100 pence (written *p*). There is likely to be some variance in the rates of exchange between Ireland and the United Kingdom (which includes Northern Ireland). Change U.K. pounds at a bank when you get to Ireland (pound coins not accepted); change Irish pounds before you leave.

Although the Irish pound is the only legal tender currency in the Republic, U.S. dollars and British currency are often accepted in large hotels and shops licensed as bureaux de change. Banks give the best rate of exchange. The rate of exchange at press time (spring 1998) was 70 pence to the U.S. dollar, 48 pence to the Canadian dollar, IR£1.17 to the British pound sterling, 45 pence to the Australian dollar, and 39 pence to the New Zealand dollar.

Telephoning
COUNTRY CODE
The country code for the Republic of Ireland is 353.

Contacts and Resources
EMBASSIES
United States (✉ 42 Elgin Rd., Ballsbridge, ☎ 01/668–8777). **Canadian** (✉ 65 St. Stephen's Green, ☎ 01/478–1988). **United Kingdom** (✉ 29 Merrion Rd., ☎ 01/205–3700).

EMERGENCIES
Police (☎ 999). **Ambulance** (☎ 999). **Doctor** (☎ 01/679–0700). **Dentist** (☎ 01/662–0766). **Pharmacy** (✉ Hamilton Long, 5 Upper O'Connell St., ☎ 01/874–8456).

GUIDED TOURS
Orientation. Both Dublin Bus (☎ 01/873–4222) and **Gray Line Sightseeing** (☎ 01/661–9666) offer bus tours of Dublin and its surrounding areas. Both also offer three- and four-hour tours of the main sights in the city center. In summer Dublin Bus has a daily three-hour city-center tour using open-top buses in fine weather (IR£8). From mid-April through September Dublin Bus runs a continuous guided open-top bus tour (IR£5) that allows you to hop on and off the bus as often as you wish and visit some 15 sights along its route.

Special-Interest. Elegant Ireland (☎ 01/475–1665) organizes tours for groups interested in architecture and the fine arts; these include visits with the owners of some of Ireland's stately homes and castles.

Walking. Most tourist offices have leaflets giving information on a selection of walking tours, including "Literary Dublin," "Georgian Dublin," and "Pub Tours." **Bord Fáilte** (☞ *below*) has a "Tourist Trail" walk, which takes in the main sites of central Dublin and can be completed in about three hours, and a "Rock 'n Stroll" tour, which covers the city's major pop and rock music sites.

Excursions. Bus Eireann (☎ 01/836–6111) and **Gray Line Sightseeing** (☎ 01/661–9666) offer daylong tours into the surrounding countryside and longer tours elsewhere; the price includes accommodations, breakfast, and admission costs. **CIE Tours International** (☎ 01/703–1888) offers vacations lasting from 5 to 10 days that include touring by luxury coach, accommodations, and main meals. Costs range from about IR£299 (IR£400 including round-trip airfare from London) to IR£580 (IR£680 from London) for an eight-day tour in July and August.

TRAVEL AGENCIES
American Express (✉ 116 Grafton St., ☎ 01/677–2874). **Thomas Cook** (✉ 118 Grafton St., ☎ 01/677–1721).

VISITOR INFORMATION
There are visitor information offices in the entrance hall of the **Bord Fáilte** headquarters (✉ Baggot St. Bridge, ☎ 01/676–5871; ☉ weekdays 9:15–5:15); **Dublin Tourism** also has visitor information at the airport (arrivals level, ☉ daily 8 AM–10 PM); and at the Ferryport, Dun Laoghaire (☉ daily 10 AM–9 PM).

10 Edinburgh

S cotland and England are *different—and let no Englishman tell you otherwise. Although the two nations have been united in a single state since 1707, Scotland retains its own marked political and social character, with, for instance, legal and educational systems quite distinct from those of England (a division that will become even greater, now that Edinburgh is once again to be the seat of a Scottish Parliament). And by virtue of its commanding position on top of a long-dead volcano and the survival of a large number of outstanding stone buildings carrying echoes of the nation's history, Edinburgh ranks among the world's greatest capital cities.*

EXPLORING EDINBURGH

Numbers in the margin correspond to points of interest on the Edinburgh map.

The key to understanding Edinburgh is to make the distinction between the Old and New Towns. Until the 18th century the city was confined to the rocky crag on which its castle stands, straggling between the fortress at one end and the royal residence, the Palace of Holyroodhouse, at the other. In the 18th century, during a civilizing time of expansion known as the "Scottish Enlightenment," the city fathers fostered the construction of another Edinburgh, one a little to the north. In 1767 the competition to design the New Town was won by a young and unknown architect, James Craig. His plan was for a grid of three east–west streets, balanced at each end by a grand square. The plan survives today, despite all commercial pressures. Princes, George, and Queen streets are the main thoroughfares, with St. Andrew Square at one end and Charlotte Square at the other. The mostly residential New Town, with elegant squares, classical facades, wide streets, and harmonious proportions, remains largely intact and lived-in today.

⑬ Arthur's Seat. The open grounds of Holyrood Park enclose Arthur's Seat, Edinburgh's distinctive, originally volcanic minimountain, with steep slopes and miniature crags. ⊠ *Holyrood Park.*

★ **⑯ Calton Hill.** Steps and a road lead up to splendid views north across the Firth (estuary) of Forth to the Lomond Hills of Fife, and south to the Pentland Hills. Among the various monuments on Calton Hill are a partial reproduction of Athens's **Parthenon,** begun in 1824 but left incomplete because the money ran out; the **Nelson Monument;** and the **Royal Observatory.** ⊠ *North side of Regent Rd.*

⑪ Canongate Kirk. In the graveyard of this church, built in 1688, are buried some notable Scots, including the economist Adam Smith and the poet Robert Fergusson. ⊠ *Canongate.*

⑱ Charlotte Square. The centerpiece of the New Town opens out at the western end of George Street. The palatial facade of the north side was designed by the great Scottish neoclassical architect, Robert Adam. The rooms of the elegant **Georgian House** are furnished to show the domestic arrangements of a prosperous late-18th-century Edinburgh family. ⊠ *7 Charlotte Sq.,* ☎ *0131/225–2160.* ☑ *£4.20.* ۞ *Apr.–Oct., Mon.–Sat. 10–5, Sun. 2–5 (last admission 4:30).*

★ **❶ Edinburgh Castle.** The brooding symbol of Scotland's capital and the nation's martial past, the castle dominates the city center. Its attractions include the city's oldest building—the 11th-century **St. Margaret's Chapel;** the **Crown Room,** where the Regalia of Scotland are displayed; **Old Parliament Hall;** and **Queen Mary's Apartments,** where Mary, Queen of Scots, gave birth to the future King James VI of Scotland (who later became James I of England). In addition military features of interest include the **Scottish National War Memorial** and the **Scottish United Services Museum.** The **Castle Esplanade,** the wide parade ground at the entrance to the castle, hosts the annual Edinburgh Military Tattoo—a grand military display staged during a citywide festival every summer (☞ The Arts, *below*). ⊠ *Castlehill,* ☎ *0131/668–8800.* ☑ *£6.* ۞ *Apr.–Sept., daily 9:30–5:15; Oct.–Mar., daily 9:30–4:15.*

❸ Gladstone's Land. This six-story tenement dates from 1620. It has an arcaded front and first-floor entrance typical of the period and is furnished in the style of a merchant's house of the time; there are magnificent painted ceilings. ⊠ *377B Lawnmarket,* ☎ *0131/226–5856.* ☑ *£3.* ۞ *Easter–Oct., Mon.–Sat. 10–5, Sun. 2–5 (last entrance 4:30).*

❻ High Kirk of St. Giles. Often called St. Giles's Cathedral, this historic structure dates back to the 12th century; the impressive choir was built during the 15th century. ⊠ *High St.* ☑ *Suggested donation: £1.* ۞ *Mon.–Sat. 9–5 (7 in summer), Sun. 1–5 and for services.*

⑩ Huntly House. Built in 1570, this museum presents Edinburgh history and social life. ⊠ *142 Canongate,* ☎ *0131/529–4143.* ☑ *Free.* ۞ *Mon.–Sat. 10–5, Sun. during festival 2–5.*

❼ John Knox House. Its traditional connections with Scotland's celebrated religious reformer are tenuous, but this 16th-century dwelling gives a flavor of life in the Old Town during Knox's time. ⊠ *45 High St.,* ☎ *0131/556–2647.* ۞ *Mon.–Sat. 10–5 (last admission 4:30).*

❾ Museum of Childhood. Even adults may well enjoy this celebration of toys. The museum was the first in the world to be devoted solely to

Edinburgh

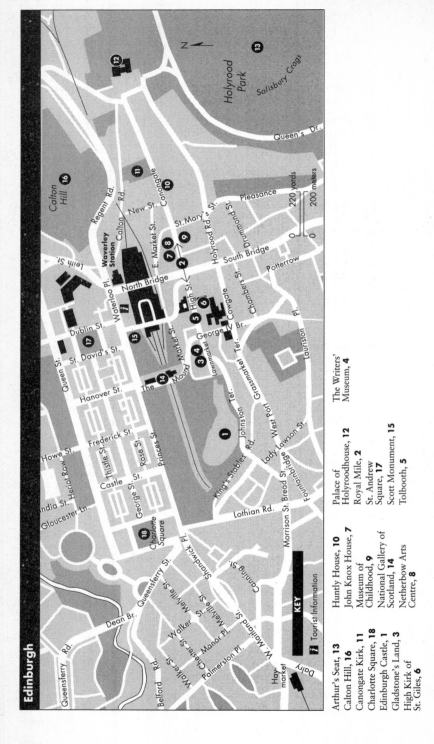

Arthur's Seat, **13**
Calton Hill, **16**
Canongate Kirk, **11**
Charlotte Square, **18**
Edinburgh Castle, **1**
Gladstone's Land, **3**
High Kirk of
St. Giles, **6**

Huntly House, **10**
John Knox House, **7**
Museum of
Childhood, **9**
National Gallery of
Scotland, **14**
Netherbow Arts
Centre, **8**

Palace of
Holyroodhouse, **12**
Royal Mile, **2**
St. Andrew
Square, **17**
Scott Monument, **15**
Tolbooth, **5**

The Writers'
Museum, **4**

KEY

i Tourist Information

the history of childhood. ⊠ *42 High St.,* ☎ *0131/529–4142,* ⅩⅩ *0131/ 558–3103.* ☞ *Free.* ☉ *Mon.–Sat. 10–5, Sun. during festival 2–5.*

★ ⓮ **National Gallery of Scotland.** Works by the old masters and the French Impressionists and a good collection of Scottish paintings make this one of Britain's best national galleries. It is small enough to be taken in easily on one visit. There may be a charge for special exhibitions. ⊠ *The Mound,* ☎ *0131/556–8921.* ☞ *Free.* ☉ *Mon.–Sat. 10–5, Sun. 2–5. Print Room, weekdays 10–noon, 2–4, by arrangement.*

⓼ **Netherbow Arts Centre.** In addition to the art gallery there are a theater and a café here. ⊠ *43 High St.,* ☎ *0131/556–9579.* ☞ *£1.95.* ☉ *Mon.–Sat. 10–5 (last admission 4:30).*

★ ⓬ **Palace of Holyroodhouse.** Still the Royal Family's official residence in Scotland, the palace came into existence originally as a guest house for the Abbey of Holyrood, founded in 1128 by Scottish king David I. It was extensively remodeled by Charles II in 1671. The state apartments, with their collections of tapestries and paintings, can be visited. ⊠ *East end of Cannongate,* ☎ *0131/556–7371, 0131/556–1096 (recorded information).* ☉ *Apr.–Oct., daily 9:30–5:15; Nov.–Mar., daily 9:30– 3:45; closed during royal and state visits.*

⓶ **Royal Mile.** The backbone of the Old Town, the Royal Mile starts immediately below the Castle Esplanade (☞ **Edinburgh Castle,** *above*). It consists of a number of streets running into one another—Castlehill, Lawnmarket, High Street, and Canongate—leading downhill to the **Palace of Holyroodhouse.** The many original Old Town "closes," narrow alleyways enclosed by high tenement buildings, reward exploration with a real sense of the former life of the city. ⊠ *Between Edinburgh Castle and the Palace of Holyroodhouse.*

⓱ **St. Andrew Square.** The most notable building on this square at the eastward termination of George Street is the Georgian headquarters of the **Royal Bank of Scotland,** with a lavishly decorated central banking hall. ⊠ *St. Andrew Sq.,* ☎ *0131/556–8555.* ☉ *Mon., Wed.–Fri. 9:15–4:45, Tues. 10–4:45.*

⓯ **Scott Monument.** This unmistakable 200-ft-high Gothic spire was built in the 1840s to commemorate Sir Walter Scott (1771–1832), the celebrated novelist of Scots history. The monument is undergoing renovation, so it's best to call to make sure it's open. ⊠ *Princes St.,* ☎ *0131/529–4068.* ☉ *Apr.–Sept., Mon.–Sat. 9–6; Oct.–Mar., Mon.–Sat. 9–3.*

⓹ **Tolbooth.** A heart shape set in the cobbles of High Street marks the site of the 15th-century Tolbooth, the center of city life—and original inspiration for Sir Walter Scott's novel *The Heart of Midlothian*—until its demolition in 1817. ⊠ *High St.*

⓸ **The Writers' Museum.** Housed in Lady Stair's House, a town dwelling of 1622, this museum recalls Scotland's literary heritage with exhibits on Sir Walter Scott, Robert Louis Stevenson, and Robert Burns. ⊠ *Lady Stair's Close, Lawnmarket,* ☎ *0131/529–4901.* ☞ *Free.* ☉ *Mon.–Sat. 10–5, Sun. during festival 2–5.*

DINING

Food in the British Isles used to be put down for its lack of imagination and its mediocrity. The problem today may be not so much bad food as expensive food—you might want to check prices on the menu, which, by law, must be displayed outside the restaurant, before stepping inside. The best of traditional cooking, deeper into the country, uses top-quality, fresh, local ingredients: wild salmon; spring lamb; distinctive handmade cheeses; myriad, almost forgotten, fruit varieties; and countless types of seasonal vegetables. Nearly all restaurant menus include vegetarian dishes, and interesting ethnic cuisines, especially Asian, can be found in the main street of even the smaller towns and villages.

MEALTIMES

These vary somewhat, depending on the region of the country you are visiting. But in general breakfast is served between 7:30 and 9 and lunch between noon and 2 (in the North the latter meal is called dinner). Tea—a famous British tradition and often a meal in itself—is generally served between 4 and 5:30. Dinner or supper is served between 7:30 and 9:30, sometimes earlier, but rarely later outside the metropolitan areas. High tea, at about 6, replaces dinner in some areas—especially in Scotland—and in large cities, pre- and after-theater suppers are often available. Note that many upscale restaurants close for 10 days during Easter and/or Christmas and for several weeks in July, August, or September. Call ahead.

RATINGS

Prices quoted here are per person and include a first course, a main course, and dessert, but not wine or service.

CATEGORY	COST
$$$$	OVER £40
$$$	£25–£40
$$	£15–£25
$	UNDER £15

Edinburgh's restaurants make the most of Scotland's excellent game, fish, shellfish, beef, and lamb.

$$$$　✕ **Le Pompadour.** The decor in this hotel-restaurant, with its subtle plasterwork and rich murals, is inspired by the France of Louis XV. A sophisticated French menu is accented with Scottish delicacies. ✉ *Caledonian Hotel, Princes St.,* ☎ *0131/459–9988. Reservations essential. Jacket and tie. AE, DC, MC, V. No lunch weekends.*

$$$　✕ **Jackson's Restaurant.** Set in the historic Old Town halfway down
★　the Royal Mile, this intimate and candlelit spot offers good Scots fare. Aberdeen Angus steaks and Border lamb are excellent; there are vegetarian and seafood specialties, too. ✉ *2 Jackson Close, 209–213 High St.,* ☎ *0131/225–1793. Reservations essential. AE, MC, V.*

$$　✕ **The Dome.** The splendid interior of this former bank—splendid is the word, thanks to the painted plasterwork and central dome—provides an elegant backdrop for relaxed dining. Or you just might opt for a drink at the central bar, a favored spot for sophisticates to wind down after work. The toasted BLT sandwiches are almost big enough for two, but if you're even more ravenous, the eclectic menu offers many other options. ✉ *14 George St. EH2 2PF,* ☎ *0131/624–8624. AE, MC, V.*

$$　✕ **Howie's.** Howie's is a simple neighborhood bistro. The steaks are tender Aberdeen beef, the Loch Fyne herring are sweet-cured to Howie's own recipe, and the clientele is lively. ✉ *75 St. Leonard's St.,* ☎ *0131/668–2917, MC, V, No lunch Mon.;* ✉ *63 Dalry Rd.,* ☎ *0131/313–3334, MC, V, No lunch Mon.;* ✉ *208 Bruntsfield Pl.,* ☎ *0131/221–1777, MC, V, No lunch Mon.*

$–$$ ✕ **Pierre Victoire.** An Edinburgh success story with five in-town branches and franchises as far as London and Bristol, this bistro chain serves tasty, unpretentious French cuisine in excellent set menus, with especially good value at lunch. ✉ *38 Grassmarket,* ☎ *0131/226–2442, MC, V;* ✉ *10 Victoria St.,* ☎ *0131/225–1721, MC, V;* ✉ *8 Union St.,* ☎ *0131/557–8451, MC, V, Closed Mon.;* ✉ *17 Queensferry St.,* ☎ *0131/226–1890, MC, V, Closed Sun.;* ✉ *5 Dock Pl., Leith,* ☎ *0131/555–6178, MC, V, No dinner Sun.*

$ ✕ **Beehive Inn.** One of the oldest pubs in the city, the Beehive snuggles
★ in the Grassmarket, under the majestic shadow of the castle. The upstairs Rafters restaurant lies hidden in an attractive and spacious attic room, crammed with weird and wonderful junk. Open only for dinner, it features mostly steaks and fish: Try the charcoal-grilled trout with Drambuie. ✉ *18/20 Grassmarket,* ☎ *0131/225–7171. AE, DC, MC, V.*

NIGHTLIFE AND THE ARTS

The Arts

EDINBURGH FESTIVAL

The **Edinburgh International Festival,** a celebration of music, dance, and drama staged each summer (Aug. 15–Sept. 4 in 1999), draws international artists of the highest caliber. The **Festival Fringe** (information: ✉ 180 High St., ☎ 0131/226–5257or 0131/226–5259, ℻ 0131/220–4205), the unruly child of the official festival, spills out of halls and theaters all over town, offering visitors a cornucopia of theatrical and musical events of all kinds—some so weird that they defy description. At the official festival you'll see top-flight performances by established artists, while at a Fringe event you might catch a new star, or a new art form, or a controversial new play. Advance information, programs, and ticket sales for the festival are available from the **Edinburgh International Festival Office** (✉ 21 Market St., ☎ 0131/226–4001, ℻ 0131/225–1173).

The **Edinburgh Military Tattoo** (information: Edinburgh Military Tattoo Office, ✉ 32 Market St., EH1 1QB, ☎ 0131/225–1188, ℻ 0131/225–8627) may not be art, but it is certainly entertainment. This celebration of martial music and skills (in 1999, held Aug. 6–28) is set on the Castle Esplanade. Dress warmly for late-evening shows. Even if it rains, the show most definitely goes on! Away from the August–September festival overkill, **Shoots and Roots** (☎ 0131/554–3092), the Edinburgh Folk Festival, takes place over Easter weekend (1999: April 2–5) and also the third weekend in November (in 1999: Nov. 18–22). This is the premier festival for Scottish folk music and folk/rock crossover.

The List, available from newsagents throughout the city; *The Day by Day List;* and *Events 1999,* available from the Information Centre, carry the most up-to-date details about cultural events. *The Scotsman,* an Edinburgh daily, also carries reviews in its arts pages on Monday and Wednesday.

EDINBURGH ESSENTIALS

Arriving and Departing

BY BUS

Regular service is operated by **National Express** (☎ 0990/808080, ℻ 0141/332–8055) between Victoria Coach Station, London, and St. Andrew Square bus station, Edinburgh, twice a day. The journey takes approximately eight hours.

BY CAR

London and Edinburgh are 656 km (407 mi) apart; allow a comfortable nine hours for the drive. The two principal routes to the Scottish border are A1 (mostly a small but divided road) or the eight-lane M1, then M6. From there, the choice is between the four-lane highway A74, which can be unpleasantly busy, followed by A701 or A702, or the slower but much more scenic A7 through Hawick. All the main car-rental agencies have offices in Edinburgh.

BY PLANE

British Airways (☎ 0345/222111) operates a shuttle service from London's Heathrow Airport to Edinburgh; reservations are not necessary, and you are guaranteed a seat. Flying time from London is one hour, 15 minutes. **British Midland** (☎ 0345/554554) also flies from Heathrow. **Air UK** flies from Gatwick (☎ 01293/535353) and Stansted (☎ 01279/680500) to Edinburgh (☎ 0345/666777). **EasyJet** (☎ 0990/292929) offers bargain fares from London Luton to Edinburgh. Transatlantic flights direct to Scotland use Glasgow Airport, with regular rail connections to Glasgow city center and on to Edinburgh.

BY TRAIN

Regular trains run from London's King's Cross Station (☎ 0345/484950) to Edinburgh Waverley (☎ 0131/557–3000 for recorded information); the fastest journey time is just over four hours.

Getting Around

BY BUS

Lothian Regional Transport (✉ 27 Hanover St., ☎ 0131/555–6363; ✉ Waverley Bridge, ☎ 0131/554–4494), operating dark-red-and-white buses, is the main operator within Edinburgh. A **Day Saver Ticket** (£2.20), allowing unlimited one-day travel on the city's buses, can be purchased in advance.

BY CAR

Driving in Edinburgh has its quirks and pitfalls, but competent drivers should not be intimidated. Metered parking in the center city is scarce and expensive, and the local traffic wardens are alert. Note that illegally parked cars are routinely wheel-clamped and towed away, and getting your car back will be expensive. After 6 PM the parking situation improves considerably, and you may manage to find a space quite near your hotel, even downtown. If you park on a yellow line or in a resident's parking bay, be prepared to move your car by 8 AM the following morning, when the rush hour gets under way.

BY TAXI

Taxi stands can be found throughout the downtown area, most conveniently at the west end of Princes Street, South St. David Street, and North St. Andrew Street (the latter two just off St. Andrew Sq.), Waverley Market, Waterloo Place, and Lauriston Place. You can also hail any taxi displaying an illuminated FOR HIRE sign.

Contacts and Resources

CONSULATE

U.S. Consulate General (✉ 3 Regent Terr., ☎ 0131/556–8315).

EMERGENCIES

Police, ambulance, fire (☎ 999). **Pharmacy. Boots** (✉ 48 Shandwick Pl., west end of Princes St., ☎ 0131/225–6757).

GUIDED TOURS

Orientation. Lothian Regional Transport (☞ Getting Around By Bus, *above*) operates tours in and around the city.

Walking. The Cadies and Witchery Tours (⊠ 352 Castlehill, 3rd floor, ☎ 0131/225–6745) offers a highly popular murder and mystery tour, and historical and other special-interest tours.

VISITOR INFORMATION

Edinburgh and Scotland Information Centre (⊠ 3 Princes St., ☎ 0131/557–1700, ℻ 0131/473–3881) is adjacent to Waverley Station.

11 Florence

O ne of Europe's preeminent treasures, Florence draws visitors from all over the world. Its architecture is predominantly Early Renaissance and retains many of the implacable, fortresslike features of pre-Renaissance palazzi, whose facades were mostly meant to keep intruders out rather than to invite sightseers in. With the exception of a very few buildings, the classical dignity of the High Renaissance and the exuberant invention of the Baroque are not to be found here. The typical Florentine exterior gives nothing away, as if obsessively guarding secret treasures within. The treasures, of course, are very real. And far from being a secret, they are famous the world over. The city is an artistic treasure trove of unique and incomparable proportions. A single historical fact explains the phenomenon: Florence gave birth to the Renaissance.

EXPLORING FLORENCE

Numbers in the margin correspond to points of interest on the Florence map.

Founded by Julius Caesar, Florence was built in the familiar grid pattern common to all Roman colonies that makes it easy to explore. Except for the major monuments, which are appropriately imposing, the buildings are low and unpretentious and the streets are narrow. At times Florence can be a nightmare of mass tourism. Plan, if you can, to visit the city in late fall, early spring, or even in winter, to avoid the crowds. For 15,000 lire you can purchase a special museum ticket valid for six months at six city museums, including the Palazzo Vecchio and the Museum of Santa Maria Novella. Inquire at any city museum.

Piazza del Duomo and Piazza della Signoria

★ ❸ **Battistero** (Baptistery). In front of the Duomo is the octagonal baptistery, one of the city's oldest and most beloved edifices, where since the 11th century Florentines have baptized their children. The interior dome mosaics are famous but cannot outshine the building's renowned gilded bronze east portal (facing the Duomo). Crafted by Lorenzo Ghiberti (1378–1455), it is the most splendid of the Baptistery's three portals. They were dubbed the "Gates of Paradise" by Michelangelo. A gleaming copy replaces the original, removed to the Museo dell'Opera del Duomo (☞ *below*). ⊠ *Piazza del Duomo.* ⊘ *Mon.–Sat. 1:30–6:30, Sun. 8:30–1:30.*

❷ **Campanile** (Bell tower). Giotto (1266–1337) designed the early 14th-century bell tower, richly decorated with colored marbles and sculpture reproductions (the originals are in the Museo dell'Opera del Duomo (☞ *below*). The 414-step climb to the top is less strenuous than that to the cupola. ⊠ *Piazza del Duomo.* ⊘ *Apr.–Oct., daily 9–7:30; Nov.–Mar., daily. 9–5.*

★ ❶ **Duomo.** Cattedrale di Santa Maria del Fiore is dominated by a cupola representing a touchstone in the history of architecture. The cathedral itself was begun by master sculptor and architect Arnolfo di Cambio in 1296, and its construction took 140 years to complete. Gothic architecture predominates; the facade was added in the 1870s but is based on Tuscan Gothic models. Inside, the church is cool and austere, a fine example of the architecture of the period. Take a good look at the frescoes of equestrian figures on the left wall; the one on the right is by Paolo Uccello (1397–1475), the one on the left by Andrea del Castagno (1421–57). The dome frescoes by Vasari take second place to the dome itself, Brunelleschi's greatest architectural and technical achievement. It was also the inspiration behind such later domes as the one Michelangelo designed for St. Peter's in Rome and even the Capitol in Washington. You can visit early medieval and ancient Roman remains of previous constructions excavated under the cathedral. And you can climb to the cupola gallery, 463 exhausting steps up between the two layers of the double dome for a fine view. ⊠ *Piazza del Duomo.* ⊘ *Weekdays 10–5 (1st Sat. of month 10–3:30), Sun. 1–5. Cupola (entrance in left aisle of cathedral):* ⊘ *Weekdays 8:30–6:20, Sat. 9:30– 5 (1st Sat. of month 9:30–3:20).*

★ ❾ **Galleria degli Uffizi** (Uffizi Gallery). The Uffizi Palace was built to house the administrative offices of the Medici, onetime rulers of the city. Later their fabulous art collection was arranged in the Uffizi Gallery on the top floor, which was opened to the public in the 17th century—making this the world's first modern public gallery. It houses Italy's most important collection of paintings. The emphasis is on Italian art of the Gothic and Renaissance periods. Make sure you see the works by Giotto, and look for the Botticellis (1445–1510) in Rooms X–XIV, Michelangelo's *Holy Family* in Room XXV, and the works by Raphael next door. In addition to its art treasures, the gallery offers a magnificent close-up view of the Palazzo Vecchio tower from the little coffee bar at the end of the corridor. Notoriously long lines can be avoided by purchasing tickets in advance from Consorzio ITA. ⊠ *Loggiato Uffizi 6,* ☎ *055/23885; advance tickets, Consorzio ITA 055/2347941.* ⊘ *Tues.–Sat. 8:30–6:50, Sun. 8:30–1:50.*

154

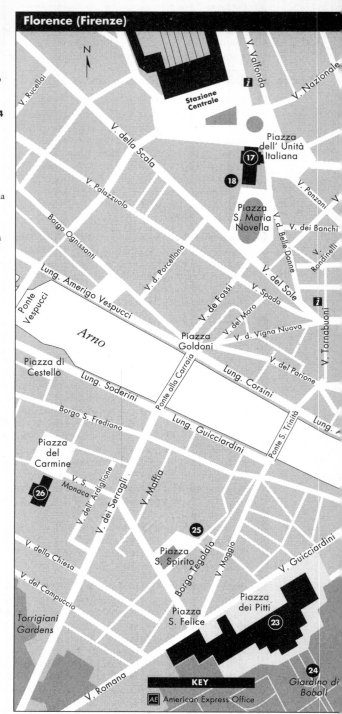

Florence (Firenze)

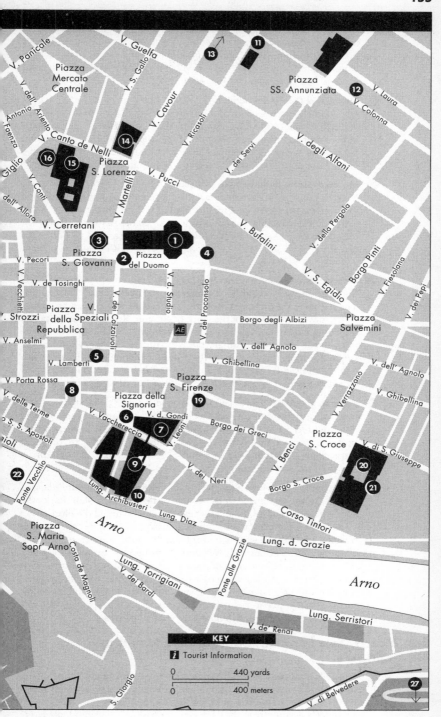

⑧ Loggia del Mercato Nuovo (Loggia of the New Market). Tiers of souvenirs and straw and leather goods are crammed into this historic open-air marketplace. Along with the goods, a main attraction is Pietro Tacca's bronze Porcellino (Piglet) fountain, a 17th-century copy of an ancient Roman work now in the Uffizi. Rubbing its snout is said to bring good luck. ⊠ *Via Calimala.* ⊘ *Mon.–Sat. 8–7 (closed Mon.* AM*).*

★ **④ Museo dell'Opera del Duomo** (Cathedral Museum). The museum contains some superb sculptures by Donatello (c.1386–1466) and Luca della Robbia (1400–82)—especially their *cantorie,* or singers' galleries—and an unfinished *Pietà* by Michelangelo, which was intended for his own tomb. ⊠ *Piazza del Duomo 9,* ☎ *055/2302885.* ⊘ *Mar.–Oct., Mon.–Sat. 9–7:30; Nov.–Feb., Mon.–Sat. 9–7.*

⑩ Museo di Storia della Scienza (Museum of Science History). You don't have to know a lot about science to appreciate the antique scientific instruments presented here in informative, eye-catching exhibits. From astrolabes and armillary spheres to some of Galileo's own instruments, the collection is one of Florence's lesser-known treasures. ⊠ *Piazza dei Giudici 1,* ☎ *055/2398876.* ⊘ *Mon., Wed., Fri. 9:30–1 and 2–5; Tues., Thurs., Sat. 9:30–1.*

⑤ Orsanmichele. For centuries this was an odd combination of first-floor church and second-floor granary of one of Florence's craft guilds. The statues in the niches on the exterior (many of which are now copies) constitute an anthology of the work of eminent Renaissance sculptors, including Donatello, Ghiberti, and Verrocchio (1435–88). The tabernacle inside is an extraordinary piece by Andrea Orcagna. Some of the original statues can be seen in the Museo Nazionale del Bargello (☞ *below*) and the Palazzo della Signoria (☞ *below*). ⊠ *Via Calzaiuoli.* ⊘ *Daily 9–noon and 4–6.Closed 1st and last Mon. of month.*

⑦ Palazzo Vecchio (Old Palace). Also called Palazzo della Signoria, this massive, fortresslike city hall was begun in 1299 and was taken over, along with the rest of Florence, by the Medici family. Inside, the impressive, frescoed salons and the Medici *Studiolo* (Study) are the main attractions. ⊠ *Piazza della Signoria,* ☎ *055/2768465.* 🎫 *Free Sun.* ⊘ *Mon.–Wed. and Fri.–Sat. 9–7, Sun. 8–1.*

⑥ Piazza della Signoria. This is the heart of Florence and the city's largest square. In the pavement in the center of the square a slab marks the spot where Savonarola, the reformist monk who urged the Florentines to burn their pictures, books, musical instruments, and other worldly objects, was hanged and then burned at the stake as a heretic in 1498. The square, the Fontana di Nettuno (Neptune) by Ammanati (1511–92), and the surrounding cafés are popular gathering places for Florentines and for tourists who come to admire the Palazzo della Signoria, the copy of Michelangelo's *David* standing in front of it, and the sculptures in the 14th-century Loggia dei Lanzi, including a copy of Cellini's famous bronze *Perseus Holding the Head of Medusa.*

San Marco, San Lorenzo, Santa Maria Novella, Santa Croce

★ **⑯ Cappelle Medicee** (Medici Chapels). These extraordinary chapels, part of the San Lorenzo complex, contain the tombs of practically every member of the Medici family, and there were a lot of them, for they guided Florence's destiny from the 15th century to 1737. Cosimo I, a Medici whose acumen made him the richest man in Europe, is buried in the crypt beneath the Chapel of the Princes, and Donatello's tomb is next to that of his patron. The **Cappella dei Principi** upstairs displays a dazzling array of colored marble panels. Michelangelo's **Sagrestia Nuova** tombs of Giuliano and Lorenzo de' Medici are adorned with the justly famed sculptures of *Dawn* and *Dusk, Night* and *Day.* ⊠ *Piazza Madonna degli Aldobrandini, San Lorenzo,* ☎ *055/2388602.* ⊙ *Daily 8:30–1:50. Closed 1st, 3rd, and 5th Mon. of month.*

★ ⑪ **Galleria dell'Accademia** (Accademia Gallery). Michelangelo's *David* is a tour de force of artistic conception and technical ability, for he was using a piece of stone that had already been worked on by a lesser sculptor. Take time to see the forceful *Slaves,* also by Michelangelo; their rough-hewn, unfinished surfaces contrast dramatically with the highly polished, meticulously carved *David.* Michelangelo left the *Slaves* "unfinished," it is often claimed, to accentuate the figures' struggle to escape the bondage of stone. He simply abandoned them because his patrons changed their minds about the tomb monument for which they were planned. Try to be first in line at opening time or go shortly before closing time so you can get the full impact without having to fight your way through the crowds. ⊠ *Via Ricasoli 60,* ☎ *055/2388609.* ⊙ *Tues.–Sat. 8:30–6:50, Sun. 8:30–1:50.*

⑫ **Museo Archeologico** (Archaeological Museum). Fine Etruscan and Roman antiquities and a pretty garden are the draw here. ⊠ *Via della Colonna 36,* ☎ *055/2478641.* ⊙ *Tues.–Sat. 9–2, and 1st, 3rd, and 5th Mon. and 2nd and 4th Sun. of the month 9–1.*

⑬ **Museo di San Marco.** A former Dominican monastery houses this museum, a memorial to Fra Angelico (1400–55). Within the same walls where the unfortunate Savonarola, the monastery's prior, contemplated the sins of the Florentines, Fra Angelico went humbly about his work, decorating many of the otherwise austere cells and corridors with brilliantly colored frescoes on religious subjects. Look for his masterpiece, the *Annunciation.* Together with many of his paintings arranged on the ground floor, just off the little cloister, they form a fascinating collection. ⊠ *Piazza San Marco 1,* ☎ *055/2388608.* ⊙ *Daily 8:30–1:40. Closed 1st, 3rd, and 5th Sun. and 2nd and 4th Mon. of month.*

⑱ **Museo di Santa Maria Novella.** Adjacent to the church, this museum is worth a visit for its serene atmosphere and the faded Paolo Uccello frescoes from Genesis. ⊠ *Piazza Santa Maria Novella 19,* ☎ *055/ 282187.* ⊙ *Mon.–Thurs. and Sat. 9–2, Sun. 8–1.*

★ ⑲ **Museo Nazionale del Bargello.** This grim, fortresslike palace served in medieval times as a residence of Florence's chief magistrate and later as a prison. It is now a treasure trove of Italian Renaissance sculpture. In this historic setting you can see masterpieces by Donatello, Verrocchio, Michelangelo, and other major sculptors amid an eclectic array of arms and ceramics. For Renaissance enthusiasts this museum is on a par with the Uffizi. ⊠ *Via del Proconsolo 4,* ☎ *055/2388606.* ⊙ *Daily 8:30–1:50. Closed 1st, 3rd, and 5th Sun. and 2nd and 4th Mon. of month.*

⑭ **Palazzo Medici-Riccardi.** Few tourists get to see Benozzo Gozzoli's (1420–97) glorious frescoes in the tiny second-floor chapel of this palace, built in 1444 for Cosimo de' Medici. Gleaming with gold, they represent the journey of the Magi as a spectacular cavalcade with Lorenzo Il Magnifico (1449–1492) on a charger. ⊠ *Via Cavour 1,* ☎ *055/ 2760340.* ⊙ *Mon.–Tues., Thurs.–Sat. 9–1 and 3–6, Sun. 9–1.*

⑮ **San Lorenzo.** The facade of this church was never finished, but the Brunelleschi (1377–1446) interior is elegantly austere. Stand in the middle of the nave at the entrance, on the line that stretches to the high altar, and you'll see what Brunelleschi wanted to achieve with the grid of inlaid marble in the pavement. Every architectural element in the church is placed to achieve a dramatic effect of single-point perspective. The **Sagrestia Vecchia,** decorated with stuccoes by Donatello, is attributed to Brunelleschi. ⊠ *Piazza San Lorenzo.*

★ ❷⓿ **Santa Croce.** The mighty church of Santa Croce was begun in 1294 and has become a kind of pantheon for Florentine greats; monumental tombs of Michelangelo, Galileo (1564–1642), Machiavelli (1469–1527), and other Renaissance luminaries line the walls. Inside are two chapels frescoed by Giotto and another painted by Taddeo Gaddi (c. 1330–66), as well as an *Annunciation* and crucifix by Donatello. But it is the scale of this grandiose church that proclaims the power and ambition of medieval Florence. ⊠ *Piazza Santa Croce,* ☎ *055/244619.* ◷ *Apr.–Sept., Mon.–Sat. 8–6:30, Sun. 3–5; Oct.–Mar., Mon.–Sat. 8–12:30 and 3–6:30, Sun. 3–5.*

❶❼ **Santa Maria Novella.** A Tuscan interpretation of the Gothic style, this handsome church should be viewed from the opposite end of Piazza Santa Maria Novella for the best view of its facade. Inside are some famous paintings, especially Masaccio's (1401–28) *Trinity,* a Giotto crucifix in the sacristy, and Ghirlandaio's frescoes in the choir chapel. ⊠ *Piazza Santa Maria Novella,* ☎ *055/210113.* ◷ *Sun.–Fri. 7–12:15 and 3–6, Sat. 7–12:15 and 3–5.*

Oltrarno

❷❹ **Giardino di Boboli** (Boboli Garden). The main entrance to this garden on a landscaped hillside is in the right wing of Palazzo Pitti. The garden was laid out in 1550 for Cosimo de' Medici's wife, Eleanor of Toledo, and was further developed by later Medici dukes. ⊠ *Piazza dei Pitti,* ☎ *055/213440.* ◷ *Daily 9–1 hr before sunset. Closed 1st and last Mon. of month.*

❷❶ **Museo dell'Opera di Santa Croce e Cappella dei Pazzi** (Museum of Santa Croce and Pazzi Chapel). From the cloister of the monastery adjacent to Santa Croce you can visit the small museum and see what remains of the Giotto crucifix irreparably damaged by a flood in 1966, when water rose to 16 ft in parts of the church. The **Cappella dei Pazzi** in the cloister is an architectural gem by Brunelleschi. The interior is a lesson in spatial equilibrium and harmony. ⊠ *Piazza Santa Croce,* ☎ *055/244619.* ◷ *Apr.–Sept., Thurs.–Tues. 10–12:30 and 2:30–6:30; Oct.–Mar., Thurs.–Tues. 10–12:30 and 3–5.*

❷❸ **Palazzo Pitti.** This enormous palace is a 15th-century extravaganza the Medici acquired from the Pitti family shortly after the latter had gone deeply into debt to build the central portion. The Medici enlarged the building, extending its facade along the immense piazza. Solid and severe, it looks like a Roman aqueduct turned into a palace. The palace houses several museums: The **Museo degli Argenti** (Silver Museum) displays the fabulous Medici collection of objects in silver and gold; another has the collections of the **Galleria d'Arte Moderna** (Gallery of Modern Art). The most famous museum, though, is the **Galleria Palatina** (Palatine Gallery), with an extraordinary collection of paintings, many hung frame-to-frame in a clear case of artistic overkill. Some are high up in dark corners, so try to go on a bright day. ⊠ *Piazza Pitti,* ☎ *055/ 210323. Museo degli Argenti and Galleria d'Arte Moderna:* ◷ *Daily 8:50–1:50. Closed 2nd and 4th Sun. and 1st, 3rd, and 5th Mon. of month. Galleria Palatina:* ◷ *Tues.–Sat. 8:50–6:50, Sun. 8:30–1:50.*

★ ❷❷ **Ponte Vecchio** (Old Bridge). Florence's oldest bridge appears to be just another street lined with goldsmiths' shops until you get to the middle and catch a glimpse of the Arno below. Spared during World War II by the retreating Germans (who blew up every other bridge in the city), it also survived the 1966 flood. It leads into the **Oltrarno dis-**

trict, where the atmosphere of old-time Florence is preserved amid fascinating crafts workshops. ⊠ *East of Ponte Santa Trinita and west of Ponte alle Grazie.*

㉗ San Miniato al Monte. One of Florence's oldest churches, this charming green-and-white marble Romanesque edifice is full of artistic riches, among them the gorgeous Renaissance chapel where a Portuguese cardinal was laid to rest in 1459 under a ceiling by Luca della Robbia. ⊠ *Viale Michelangelo, or take stairs from Piazzale Michelangelo.*

㉖ Santa Maria del Carmine. The church is of little architectural interest but of immense significance in the history of Renaissance art. It contains the celebrated frescoes painted by Masaccio in the **Cappella Brancacci.** The chapel was a classroom for such artistic giants as Botticelli, Leonardo da Vinci (1452–1519), Michelangelo, and Raphael, since they all came to study Masaccio's realistic use of light and perspective and his creation of space and depth. ⊠ *Piazza del Carmine,* ☎ *055/2382195.* ☉ *Mon. and Wed.–Sat. 10–5, Sun. 1–5.*

㉕ Santo Spirito. Its plain, unfinished facade is less than impressive, but this church is important as one of Brunelleschi's finest architectural creations. It contains some superb paintings, including a *Madonna* by Filippo Lippi. Santo Spirito is the hub of a colorful, trendy neighborhood of artisans and intellectuals. An outdoor market enlivens the square every morning except Sunday; in the afternoon, pigeons, pet owners, and pensioners take over. ⊠ *Piazza Santo Spirito.* ☉ *Thurs.–Tues. 8–noon and 4–6, Wed. 8–noon.*

DINING

Mealtimes in Florence are 12:30 to 2 and 7:30 to 9 or later. Many $$ and $ places are small, and you may have to share a table. Reservations are always advisable; to find a table at inexpensive places, get there early.

RATINGS

Prices are per person and include first course, main course, dessert or fruit, and house wine, where available.

CATEGORY	COST
$$$$	over 120,000 lire
$$$	70,000 lire–120,000 lire
$$	40,000 lire–70,000 lire
$	under 40,000 lire

$$$$ ✕ Enoteca Pinchiorri. A sumptuous Renaissance palace with high, fres-
★ coed ceilings and bouquets in silver vases is the setting for this restaurant, one of the best and most expensive in Italy. A Tuscan menu and a special degustation menu, plus a variety of fish, game, and meat dishes à la carte are always on offer. Of the splendid combinations, a favorite is the *ignudi*—ricotta and cheese dumplings with a lobster and coxcomb fricassee. ⊠ *Via Ghibellina 87,* ☎ *055/242777. Reservations essential. AE, MC, V. Closed Sun., Aug., and 10 days during Christmas. No lunch Mon. or Wed.*

$$$ ✕ Alle Murate. This sophisticated restaurant features creative versions of classic Tuscan food, along with such specialties as *lasagne con mozzarella al pomodoro fresco* (lasagna with mozzarella and fresh tomatoes). In the smaller room called the *vineria,* the menu and service are simpler and prices lower. ⊠ *Via Ghibellina 52/r,* ☎ *055/240618. AE, DC, MC, V. Closed Mon. No lunch.*

$$ ✕ Cammillo. This bustling trattoria just on the other side of the Arno has been in the capable hands of the Masiero family for three generations, and in its present venue since 1945. Their farm in the country supplies the olive oil and wines for the restaurant, which marry nicely with the wide-ranging list of Tuscan specialities on the menu. Reservations are advised. ✉ *Borgo Sant'Jacopo 57/r,* ☎ *055/212427. AE, DC, MC, V. Closed Wed., 15 days in Aug., and 15 days Dec.–Jan.*

$$$ ✕ **Cibrèo.** The food here is fantastic, from the first bite of seamless,
★ creamy *crostini di fegatini* (savory Tuscan chicken liver spread on grilled bread) to the last bite of one of the melt-in-your-mouth-good desserts. If you thought you'd never try tripe, let alone like it, this is the place to lay any doubts to rest: the cold tripe salad with parsley and garlic is an epiphany. ✉ *Via dei Macci 118/r,* ☎ *055/2341100. Reservations essential. AE, DC, MC, V. Closed Sun., Mon., July 25– Sept. 5, and Dec. 31–Jan. 7.*

$$ ✕ **La Giostra.** La Giostra, which means "carousel" in Italian, serves un-
★ usually good pastas requiring some explanation from Dimitri or Soldano, the owner's good-looking twin sons. In perfect English they'll describe a favorite dish, delicious *gnocchetti alla tibetana,* little potato dumpling morsels with mint and basil pesto. Leave room for dessert: this might be the only show in town with a sublime tiramisu and a wonderfully gooey Sacher torte. ✉ *Borgo Pinti 12/r,* ☎ *055/241341. AE, MC, V.*

$$ ✕ **Le Fonticine.** This restaurant is a welcome oasis in the culinary Siberia near the train station. The cheery interior is filled with the Brucis' painting collection, and you dine very well on Tuscan and Emilia-Romagnan dishes. Start with the mixed vegetable antipasto before moving on to their *osso buco alla fiorentina* (veal shanks in a hearty tomato sauce). ✉ *Via Nazionale 79/r,* ☎ *055/282106. AE, DC, MC, V. Closed Sun., Mon., and July 25–Aug. 25.*

$$ ✕ **Pallottino.** With its tile floor, photograph-filled walls, and wooden tables, Pallottino is the quintessential Tuscan trattoria, with such hearty, heartwarming classics as *pappa al pomodoro* (a tomato and bread soup) to *peposo alla toscana* (beef stew laced with black pepper). Their lunch special—*primo, secondo,* and *dolce* (first, second, and dessert courses)—could be, at 13,000 lire, the best bargain in town. ✉ *Via Isola delle Stinche 1/r,* ☎ *055/289573. AE, DC, MC, V. No credit cards at lunch. Closed Mon. and Aug. 1–20.*

$$ ✕ **Toscano.** A small table attractively set in a shop window identifies this restaurant near Palazzo Medici-Riccardi. It lives up to its name with Tuscan ambience and food, beamed ceilings, and a cold-cuts counter at the entrance. The kitchen prides itself on top-quality meat; try *spezzatino peposo* (beef stew with black pepper and a wine sauce). The prix-fixe menu is a good value. ✉ *Via Guelfa 70/r,* ☎ *055/215475. AE, DC, MC, V. Closed Tues. and Aug.*

$ ✕ **Baldovino.** This lively, brightly hued trattoria across the street from Santa Croce is the brainchild of David Gardner and Catherine Storrar, two Scottish expats. In addition to turning out fine, thin-crust pizzas, Baldovino offers some tasty antipasti (like their plate of smoked salmon and tuna), *insalatone* ("big salads"), as well as various pasta dishes and grilled meats—and they do it till the wee hours. It's a good idea to reserve ahead. ✉ *Via S. Guiseppe, 22/r,* ☎ *055/241 773, AE, DC, MC, V. Closed Mon. and last week Nov.–first week Dec.*

$ ✕ **La Maremmana.** The owners and chef here have been working together for 18 years, and it shows. The space is light and cheery—with white walls, tile floor, and pink tablecloths, giving the place a warm glow. Dead center is an impressive array of antipasti, which whet the taste buds for the glories that follow, such as spaghetti *alla vongole* (with tiny clams) and grilled meats. ✉ *Via dei Macci 77/r,* ☎ *055/241226. MC, V. Closed Sun.*

NIGHTLIFE AND THE ARTS

The Arts

FILM

English-language films are shown Tuesday through Sunday evenings at the **Cinema Astro** (✉ Piazza San Simone near Santa Croce), and on Monday at the **Odeon** (✉ Piazza Strozzi) and the **Goldoni** (✉ Via dei Serragli).

MUSIC

Most major musical events are staged at the **Teatro Comunale** (✉ Corso Italia 16, ☎ 055/2779236). The box office (closed Sunday and Monday) is open from 9 to 1, and a half hour before performances. It's best to order your tickets by mail, however, as they're difficult to come by at the last minute. Amici della Musica (Friends of Music) puts on a series of concerts at the **Teatro della Pergola** (✉ Box office, Via della Pergola 10a/r, ☎ 055/2479652). For program information contact the **Amici della Musica** (✉ Via Sirtori 49, ☎ 055/608420) directly.

Nightlife

BARS

The bar in the lobby of the **Excelsior** (✉ Piazza Ognissanti 3, ☎ 055/264201) attracts locals as well as business travelers and tourists. **The Jazz Club** (✉ Via Nuova dei Caccini 3, ☎ 055/2479700) offers good live jazz in a surprisingly well-ventilated club near the Duomo.

NIGHTCLUBS

The River Club (✉ Lungarno Corsini 8, ☎ 055/282465; closed Sun.) has winter-garden decor and a large dance floor. **Meccanò** (✉ in the Cascine park at Viale degli Olmi 1, ☎ 055/331371; closed Sun.) offers a multimedia experience, with videos, art, and music in a high-tech disco with a late-night restaurant, the Pomodoro d'Acciaio. **Hurricane Roxy** (✉ Via Il Prato 58/r, ☎ 055/2103999) serves a light lunch during the day but in the evening there's a deejay, good music, and welcoming atmosphere. **Jackie O** (✉ Via dell'Erta Canina 24a, ☎ 055/2342442; closed Wed.) is a glittering art deco disco with lots of mirrors and marble and a trendy clientele. **Space Electronic** (✉ Via Palazzuolo 37, ☎ 055/2393082; closed Mon., except Mar.–Sept.) is exactly what its name implies: ultramodern and psychedelic. **Yab** (✉ Via Sassetti 5/r, ☎ 055/282018; closed Sun. and Mon.) is another futuristic disco popular with the young jet set.

SHOPPING

Markets

The **Mercato di San Lorenzo** (✉ Piazza San Lorenzo and Via dell'Ariento; ⊙ Tues.–Sat. 8–7, Sun. in summer) is a fine place to browse for buys in leather goods and souvenirs. Don't miss the indoor, two-story **Mercato Centrale** (✉ Piazza del Mercato Centrale), near San Lorenzo, open in the morning Monday–Saturday.

Shopping Districts

Via Tornabuoni is the high-end shopping mecca. **Via della Vigna Nuova** is just as fashionable. Goldsmiths and jewelry shops can be found on and around the **Ponte Vecchio** and in the **Santa Croce area,** where there is also a high concentration of leather shops and inconspicuous shops selling gold and silver jewelry at prices much lower than those of the elegant jewelers near Ponte Vecchio. The monastery of **Santa Croce** (✉ entrances at Via San Giuseppe 5/r and Piazza Santa Croce 16) houses a leather-working school and showroom. Antiques dealers can be found in and around the center, but are concentrated on **Via Maggio** in the Oltrarno area. **Borgo Ognissanti** is also home to shops selling period decorative objects.

FLORENCE ESSENTIALS

Arriving and Departing

BY PLANE

The airport that handles most arrivals is **Aeroporto Galileo Galilei** (✉ Pisa, ☎ 050/500707), more commonly known as **Aeroporto Pisa-Galilei.** Some domestic and European flights use Florence's **Aeroporto Vespucci** (✉ Peretola, ☎ 055/333498).

Between the Airport and Downtown. Pisa-Galilei Airport is connected to Florence by train direct to the Stazione Centrale di Santa Maria Novella. Service is hourly throughout the day and takes about 60 minutes. When departing, you can buy train tickets for the airport and check in for all flights leaving from Aeroporto Pisa-Galilei at the Florence Air Terminal at Track 5 of Stazione Centrale di Santa Maria Novella. Aeroporto Vespucci is connected to downtown Florence by SITA bus.

BY TRAIN

The main station is **Stazione Centrale di Santa Maria Novella** (☎ 1478/88088 toll free). Florence is on the main north–south route between Rome, Bologna, and Milan or Venice. High-speed Eurostar trains reach Rome in less than two hours and Milan in less than three.

Getting Around

BY BICYCLE

Alinari (✉ Via Guelfa 85/r, ☎ 055/280500). **Motorent** (✉ Via San Zanobi 9/r, ☎ 055/490113).

BY BUS

Bus maps and timetables are available for a small fee at the Azienda Transporti Autolinee Fiorentine (ATAF, ✉ near Stazione Centrale di Santa Maria Novella; Piazza del Duomo 57/r) city bus information booths. The same maps may be free at visitor information offices. **ATAF** city buses run from about 5:15 AM to 1 AM. Buy tickets before you board the bus; they are sold at many tobacco shops and newsstands. The cost is 1,500 lire for a ticket good for one hour, 2,500 lire for 2 hours, and 5,800 lire for four one-hour tickets, called a *multiplo.* A 24-hour tourist ticket (*turistico*) costs 6,000 lire. For excursions outside Florence, for instance, to Siena, you take **SITA** (bus terminal, ✉ Via Santa Caterina da Siena 17, near the Stazione Centrale di Santa Maria Novella). The **CAP** bus terminal (✉ Via Nazionale 13) is also near the train station.

BY CAR

The north–south access route to Florence is the Autostrada del Sole (A1) from Milan or Rome. The Florence–Mare autostrada (A11) links Florence with the Tyrrhenian coast, Pisa, and the A12 coastal autostrada. Parking in Florence is severely restricted.

BY MOPED

Try **Alinari** or **Motorent** (☞ By Bicycle, *above*).

BY TAXI

Taxis wait at stands and you can call them (☎ 055/4798 or 055/4390). Use only authorized cabs, which are white with a yellow stripe or rectangle on the door. The meter starts at 4,500 lire, with extra charges for nights, holidays, or radio dispatch.

ON FOOT
It is easy to find your way around in Florence with the help of the many landmarks. Major sights can be explored on foot, as they are packed into a relatively small area. Wear comfortable shoes. The system of street addresses is unusual, with commercial addresses (those with an *r* in them, meaning *rosso,* or red) and residential addresses numbered separately (32/r might be next to or a block away from plain 32).

Money Matters
CURRENCY
The unit of currency in Italy is the lira (plural, lire). There are bills of 1,000, 2,000, 5,000, 10,000, 50,000, 100,000, and 500,000 lire (impossible to change, except in banks); coins are worth 50, 100, 200, and 500 lire. In 1999 the euro will be used as a banking currency, but the lire will still be the currency in use on a day-to-day basis. At press time (spring 1998) the exchange rate was about 1,798 lire to the U.S. dollar, 1,266 lire to the Canadian dollar, and 2,943 lire to the pound sterling.

When your purchases run into hundreds of thousands of lire, beware of being shortchanged, a dodge that is practiced at ticket windows, toll booths, and cashiers' desks, as well as in shops and even in banks. *Always count your change before you leave the counter.* Always carry some smaller-denomination bills for sundry purchases; you're less likely to be shortchanged, and you won't have to face the eye-rolling dismay of cashiers reluctant to change large-denomination bills.

Credit cards are generally accepted in shops and hotels, but may not always be welcome in restaurants, so always look for card logos displayed in windows or ask when you enter to avoid embarrassing situations. When you wish to leave a tip beyond the 15% service charge that is usually included with your bill (☞ Tipping, *below*), leave it in cash rather than adding it to the credit card slip.

Telephoning
COUNTRY CODE
The country code for Italy is 39.

Contacts and Resources
CONSULATES
United States (✉ Lungarno Vespucci 38, ☎ 055/2398276). **Canadian** (citizens should refer to their embassy in Rome). **United Kingdom** (✉ Lungarno Corsini 2, ☎ 055/284133).

EMERGENCIES
Police (☎ 113). **Ambulance** (☎ 118 or 055/212222). **Tourist Medical Service** (✉ Viale Lorenzo Il Magnifico, ☎ 055/475411). **Pharmacies** are open Sunday and holidays by rotation. Signs posted outside pharmacies list those open all night and on weekends. The pharmacy at Santa Maria Novella train station is always open.

ENGLISH-LANGUAGE BOOKSTORES
Seeber (✉ Via Tornabuoni 68, ☎ 055/215697). **Paperback Exchange** (✉ Via Fiesolana 31/r, near Santa Croce, ☎ 055/2478154). **BM Bookshop** (✉ Borgo Ognissanti 4/r, ☎ 055/294575).

GUIDED TOURS
Excursions. Operators offer a half-day excursion to Pisa, usually in the afternoon, costing about 48,000 lire, and a full-day excursion to Siena and San Gimignano, costing about 68,000 lire. Pick up a timetable at ATAF information offices near the train station, at SITA (✉ Via Santa Caterina da Siena 17, ☎ 055/214721), or at the APT tourist office (☞ *below*).

Orientation. A bus consortium (through hotels and travel agents) offers tours in air-conditioned buses covering the important sights in Florence with a trip to Fiesole. The cost is about 48,000 lire for a three-hour tour, including entrance fees, and bookings can be made through travel agents.

Special-Interest. Inquire at travel agents or at **Agriturist Regionale** (⊠ Piazza San Firenze 3, ☏ 055/287838) for visits to villa gardens around Florence from April through June, or for visits to farm estates during September and October.

TRAVEL AGENCIES

American Express (⊠ Via Guicciardini 49/r, ☏ 055/288751; ⊠ Via Dante Alighieri 20/r, ☏ 055/50981). **CIT** (⊠ Via Cavour 54/r, ☏ 055/294306). **Wagons-Lits** (⊠ Via del Giglio 27/r, ☏ 055/218851).

VISITOR INFORMATION

Azienda Promozione Turistica (APT; ⊠ Via Manzoni 16, 50121, ☏ 055/2346284).

12 Istanbul

*I*stanbul *is noisy, chaotic, and exciting. Spires and domes of mosques and medieval palaces dominate the skyline. At dawn, when the muezzin's call to prayer rebounds from ancient minarets, many people are heading home from the nightclubs and bars, while others are kneeling on their prayer rugs, facing Mecca.*

Day and night, Istanbul has a schizophrenic air. Women in jeans, business suits, or elegant designer outfits pass women wearing the long skirts and head coverings that villagers have worn for generations. Donkey-drawn carts vie with old Chevrolets and Pontiacs or shiny Toyotas and BMWs for dominance of the loud, narrow streets. The world's most fascinating Asian bazaar competes with Western boutiques for your time and attention.

EXPLORING ISTANBUL

Ironically, Istanbul's Asian side is filled with Western-style sprawling suburbs, while its European side contains Old Istanbul—an Oriental wonderland of mosques, opulent palaces, and crowded bazaars. The Golden Horn, an inlet 6½ km (4 mi) long, flows off the Bosporus on the European side, separating Old Istanbul from New Town. The center of New Town is Beyoğlu, a district filled with a combination of modern and turn-of-the-century hotels, banks, and shops grouped around Taksim Square. There are three bridges spanning the Golden Horn: the Atatürk, the Galata, and the Haliç.

The historic Galata Bridge (the original structure has been replaced by a modern drawbridge) is a central landmark and a good place to get your bearings. From here, you can see the city's layout and its seven hills. The bridge will also give you a taste of Istanbul's frenetic street life. It's filled with peddlers selling everything from pistachio nuts and spices to curly-toed slippers fancy enough for a sultan; fishermen grill their catch on coal braziers and sell them to passersby. None of this sits well with motorists, who blast their horns constantly, usually to no avail. If you want to orient yourself in a quieter way, take a boat trip from the docks on the Eminönü side of the Galata Bridge up the Bosporus.

Old Istanbul (Sultanahmet)

Numbers in the margin correspond to points of interest on the Istanbul map.

★ ❷ **Arkeoloji Müzesi** (Archaeological Museum). This museum houses a fine collection of Greek and Roman antiquities, including finds from Ephesus and Troy. Admission to the Archaeological Museum is also good for entrance to the **Eski Şark Eserleri Müzesi** (Museum of the Ancient Orient), with Sumerian, Babylonian, and Hittite treasures; and the **Çinili Kösk** (Tiled Pavilion), which houses ceramics from the early Seljuk and Osmanli empires. ⊠ *Gülhane Park,* ☎ *212/520–7740.* ☉ *Tues.–Sun. 9:30–5.*

★ ❸ **Hagia Sophia** (Church of the Divine Wisdom; Aya Sofya in Turkish). One of the world's greatest examples of Byzantine architecture, it was built in AD 532 under the supervision of Emperor Justinian. The third church on the site, it took 10,000 men five years to complete it. The first was built in 360; both it and its successor were destroyed by fire. The dome of the current church was the world's largest until the dome at St. Peter's Basilica was built in Rome 1,000 years later. Hagia Sophia was the cathedral of Constantinople for nearly 1,000 years, surviving earthquakes and looting Crusaders until 1453, when it was converted into a mosque by Mehmet the Conqueror. Minarets were added by succeeding sultans. Hagia Sophia originally had many mosaics depicting Christian scenes, which were plastered over by Süleyman I, who felt they were inappropriate for a mosque. In 1935 Atatürk converted Hagia Sophia into a museum. Shortly after that American archaeologists discovered the mosaics, which were restored and are now on display. According to legend, the Sacred Column in the north aisle "weeps water" that can work miracles. It's so popular that over the centuries believers have worn a hole through the marble and brass column. You can stick your finger in it and make a wish. ⊠ *Ayasofya Meyd., Sultanahmet,* ☎ *212/522–1750.* ☉ *Tues.–Sun. 9:30–4.*

❺ **Hippodrome.** Once a Byzantine stadium with 100,000 seats, it was the focal point for city life, including chariot races, circuses, and public executions. Disputes between rival groups of supporters of chariot teams often degenerated into violence. In AD 531, 30,000 people died in the Hippodrome in what came to be known as the Nike riots. The original shape of the Hippodrome is still clearly visible. The monuments that can be seen today—the **Dikilitas** (Egyptian Obelisk), the **Örme Sütun** (Column of Constantinos), and the **Yilanli Sütun** (Serpentine Column) taken from the Temple of Apollo at Delphi in Greece—formed part of the central barrier around which the chariots raced. ⊠ *Meyd., Sultanahmet.* ☎ *Free.* ☉ *All hrs.*

❾ **İstanbul Üniversitesi** (Istanbul University). The main campus of one of Istanbul's leading universities is worth visiting for its magnificent Ottoman gateway and quiet walkways. ⊠ *Fuatpaşa Cad., Beyazit.* ☜ *Free.* ⊘ *Open dawn–dusk.*

★ ❽ **Kapalı Çarşısı** (Grand Bazaar, also known as the Covered Bazaar). This maze of 65 winding, covered streets hides 4,000 shops, tiny cafés, and restaurants, believed to be the largest number under one roof anywhere in the world. Originally built by Mehmet the Conqueror in the 1450s, it was ravaged by two modern-day fires, one in 1954 that nearly destroyed it, and a smaller one in 1974. In both cases the bazaar was quickly rebuilt. It's filled with thousands of curios, including carpets, fabrics, clothing, brass ware, furniture, icons, and gold jewelry. ⊠ *Yeniçeriler Cad. and Fuatpaşa Cad.* ☜ *Free.* ⊘ *Apr.–Oct., Mon.–Sat. 8:30–7; Nov.–Mar., Mon.–Sat. 8:30–6:30.*

★ ⑪ **Mısır Çarşısı** (Egyptian Bazaar). Built during the 17th century to provide rental income for the upkeep of the Yeni Mosque, the Egyptian Bazaar was once a vast pharmacy, filled with burlap bags overflowing with herbs and spices for folk remedies. Today, you're more likely to see bags full of fruit, nuts, royal jelly from the beehives of the Aegean coast, and white sacks spilling over with culinary spices. Some shopkeepers will offer you tastes of energizing pastes, such as *macun,* as well as dried fruits or other Turkish delights. Nearby are equally colorful fruit and fish markets. ⊠ *Sabunchanı Sok., Eminönü.* ⊘ *Mon.– Sat. 8–7.*

★ ⑩ **Süleymaniye Cami** (Mosque of Süleyman). Sinan, the 16th-century architectural genius who masterminded more than 350 buildings and monuments under the direction of Süleyman the Magnificent, designed this mosque. It is his grandest and most famous monument. The mosque serves as the burial site of both Sinan and his patron, Süleyman. ⊠ *Süleymaniye Cad., near Istanbul University's north gate.* ☜ *Free.* ⊘ *Daily except prayer hrs.*

❹ **Sultan Ahmet Cami** (Blue Mosque). With its shimmering blue tiles, 260 stained-glass windows, and six minarets, Sultan Ahmet is as grand and beautiful a monument to Islam as Hagia Sophia was to Christianity. Mehmet Ağa, also known as Sedefkar (Worker of Mother of Pearl) built the mosque during the reign of Sultan Ahmet I in eight years, beginning in 1609, nearly 1,100 years after the completion of Hagia Sophia. His goal was to surpass Justinian's masterpiece, and some believe he succeeded. Press through the throngs and enter the mosque at the side entrance that faces Hagia Sophia. Remove your shoes and leave them at the entrance. Immodest clothing is not allowed, but an attendant will lend you a robe if he feels you are not dressed appropriately. **Hünkar Kasrı** (the Carpet and Kilim Museum; ☏ 212/518–1330; call for hours) is in the mosque's stone-vaulted cellars and upstairs at the end of a stone ramp, where the sultans rested before and after their prayers. ⊠ *Sultanahmet Meyd.* ☜ *Free.* ⊘ *Daily 9–5.*

★ ❶ **Topkapı Saray** (Topkapı Palace). The number-one attraction in Istanbul stands on Seraglio Point in Old Istanbul, known as Sultanahmet. The palace, which dates from the 15th century, was the residence of a number of sultans and their harems until the mid-19th century. To avoid the crowds try to get there by 9 AM, when the gates open. If you're arriving by taxi, tell the driver you want the *Topkapı Saray* in Sultanahmet, or you could end up at the remains of the former Topkapı bus terminal on the outskirts of town.

Sultan Mehmet II built the first palace during the 1450s, shortly after the Ottoman conquest of Constantinople. Over the centuries, sultan after sultan added ever more elaborate architectural fantasies, until the palace eventually ended up with more than four courtyards and some

168

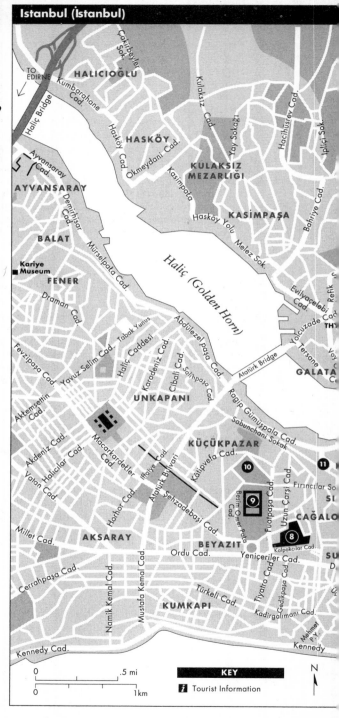

Istanbul (İstanbul)

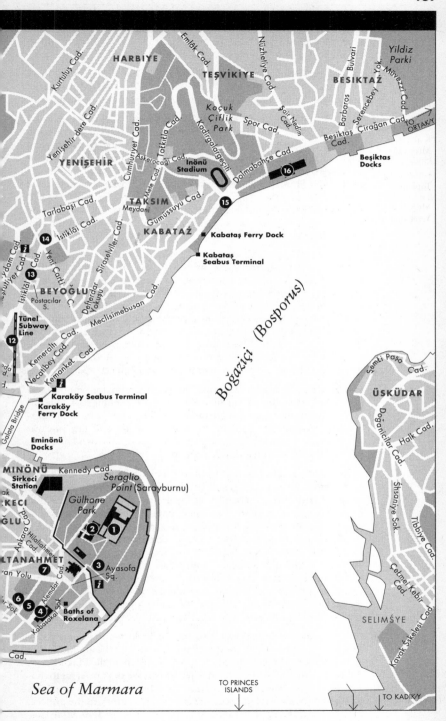

HARBIYE

Emlâk Cad.

Nüzhetiye Cad.

Yildiz Parki

Bulvari

TEŞVİKİYE

Şair Nedim Cad.

Barbaros

Serencebey

BEŞIKTAŞ

Kurtuluş Cad.

Yenişehir dere Cad.

Koçuk Çiflik Park

Spor Cad.

Beşiktaş Cad.

Çirağan Cad.

TO ORTAKÖY

Kadirgalargeçiti

Dolmabahçe Cad.

Beşiktaş Docks

YENİŞEHİR

Cumhuriyet Cad.

Askerocaği Cad.

Tatkitla Cad.

İnönü Stadium

Mete Cad.

16

Tarlabaşi Cad.

İstiklâl Cad.

Siraselviler Cad.

Gümüssuyu Cad.

TAKSİM
Meydani

15

14

KABATAŞ

Kabataş Ferry Dock

Yeni Çarti

Kabataş Seabus Terminal

i

ı Cad.

13

BEYOĞLU

Postacılar S.

İstiklâl Cad.

Defterdar Yokuşu

Meclisimebusan

Boğaziçi (Bosporus)

Tünel Subway Line

ÜSKÜDAR

12

Kemeralti Cad.

Necatibey Cad.

Kemanket Cad.

Şemi Paşa Cad.

Karaköy Seabus Terminal

Galata Bridge

i

Karaköy Ferry Dock

Doğancilar Cad.

Halk Cad.

Eminönü Docks

MİNÖNÜ

Kennedy Cad.

Seraglio Point (Sarayburnu)

Sirkeci Station

Şhsaniye Sok.

ak

KECİ

Gülhane Park

Tibbiye Cad.

ĞLU

Ankara Hilalfahmet Cad.

2

1

Çetmet Kebir Cad.

LTANAHMET

an Yolu

7

3

Ayasofa Sq.

i

SELİMŞYE

6

5

Alemdar Cad.

4

Baths of Roxelana

Kabasakal Sok.

Yavak Eskelesi Cad.

r Sok.

Cad.

Sea of Marmara

TO PRINCES ISLANDS

TO KADIKÖY

5,000 residents, many of them concubines and eunuchs. Topkapı was the residence and center of bloodshed and drama for the Ottoman rulers until the 1850s, when Sultan Abdül Mecit moved with his harem to the European-style Dolmabahçe Palace farther up the Bosporus coast.

In Topkapı's outer courtyard are the **Aya Irini** (Church of St. Irene), open only during festival days for concerts, and the **Merasim Avlusu** (Court of the Janissaries), originally for members of the sultan's elite guard.

Adjacent to the ticket office is the **Bab-i-Selam** (Gate of Salutation), built in 1524 by Süleyman the Magnificent, who was the only person allowed to pass through it. In the towers on either side, prisoners were kept until they were executed beside the fountain outside the gate in the first courtyard. In the second courtyard, amid the rose gardens, is the **Divan-i-Humayun**, the assembly room of the council of state, once presided over by the *grand vizier* (prime minister). The sultan would sit behind a latticed window, hidden by a curtain so no one would know when he was listening, although occasionally he would pull the curtain aside to comment.

One of the most popular sections of Topkapı is the **Harem,** a maze of nearly 400 halls, terraces, rooms, wings, and apartments grouped around the sultan's private quarters on the west side of the second courtyard. Forty rooms are restored and open to the public. Next to the entrance are the quarters of the eunuchs and about 200 of the lesser concubines, who were lodged in tiny cubicles, as cramped and uncomfortable as the main rooms of the Harem are large and opulent. Tours begin every half hour. Only a limited number are taken on each tour. During the height of the tourist season it is advisable to try to buy a ticket for the harem tour soon after you enter the palace.

In the third courtyard is the **Hazine Dairesi** (Treasury), four rooms filled with jewels, including two uncut emeralds, each weighing 3½ kilograms (7.7 pounds), that once hung from the ceiling. Here, too, is the dazzling emerald dagger used in the movie *Topkapı* and the 84-carat "Spoonmaker" diamond that, according to legend, was found by a pauper and traded for three wooden spoons.

In the fourth and last courtyard of the Topkapı Palace are small, elegant summer houses, mosques, fountains, and reflecting pools scattered amid the gardens on different levels. Here you will find the **Rivan Köşk,** built by Murat IV in 1636 to commemorate the successful Rivan campaign. In another kiosk in the gardens, called the **Iftariye** (Golden Cage), the closest relatives of the reigning sultan lived in strict confinement under what amounted to house arrest. The custom began during the 1800s after the old custom of murdering all possible rivals to the throne had been abandoned. The confinement of the heirs apparently helped keep the peace, but it deprived them of any chance to prepare themselves for the formidable task of ruling a great empire. ⊠ *Topkapı Palace,* ☎ *212/512–0480.* ⊙ *Wed.–Mon. 9:30–5.*

❻ Türk Ve Islâm Eserleri Müzesi (Museum of Turkish and Islamic Arts). The museum is housed in Ibrahim Paşa Palace, once the grandiose residence of the son-in-law and grand vizier of Süleyman the Magnificent, Ibrahim Paşa, who was executed when he became too powerful for Süleyman's liking. The collection gives a superb insight into the lifestyles of Turks of every level of society, from the 8th century to the present. ⊠ *Şifahane Sok., opposite Blue Mosque, in line with Serpentine Column,* ☎ *212/518–1385 or 212/518–1805.* ⊙ *Tues.–Sun. 9:30–5.*

★ ❼ Yerebatan Sarnıcı (the Sunken Palace, also known as the Cistern Basilica). This underground cistern was probably first excavated by Emperor

Constantine in the 4th century and then enlarged by Emperor Justinian in the 6th century. It has 336 marble columns rising 8 meters (26 ft) to support Byzantine arches and domes. The cistern was always kept full as a precaution against long sieges. Its echoing vastness and the reflections of the columns in the dark water give it a haunting, cathedral-like beauty, and it is a welcome relief from the heat and noise above ground. ⊠ *Yerebatan Cad.,* ☎ *212/522–1259.* ⊙ *Daily 9–4:30.*

New Town

New Town is the area on the northern shore of the Golden Horn, the waterway that cuts through Istanbul on the European side of the Bosporus.

⑭ Çiçek Pasajı (Flower Arcade). Here you'll find a lively blend of tiny restaurants, bars, and street musicians. ⊠ *Çiçek Pasajı, off İstiklâl Cad., Galatasaray.*

★ **⑮ Dolmabahçe Cami** (Dolmabahçe Mosque). Founded by Valide Sultan Bezmialem, mother of Abdül Mecit I, it was completed in 1853; the 88-ft-tall clock tower was built a year later. ⊠ *Dolmabahçe Cad.* 🎟 *Free.* ⊙ *Daily except prayer hrs.*

⑯ Dolmabahçe Sarayi (Dolmabahçe Palace). Built in 1853, it was, until the declaration of the modern republic in 1923, the residence of the last sultans of the Ottoman Empire. It was also the residence of Atatürk, who died here in 1938. The palace, floodlit at night, is an extraordinary mixture of Hindu, Turkish, and European styles of architecture and interior design. Queen Victoria's contribution to the lavishness was a chandelier weighing 4½ tons. Guided tours of the palace take about 80 minutes. ⊠ *Gümüssuyu Cad.,* ☎ *212/258–5544.* ⊙ *Apr.–Oct. 9–4; Nov.–Mar. 9–3. Closed Mon. and Thurs.*

⑫ Galata Kulesi (Galata Tower). It was built by the Genoese in 1349 as part of the fortifications for their quarter of the Byzantine city. In this century it served as a fire lookout until 1960. Today it houses a restaurant and nightclub (☞ Nightlife, *below*), and a viewing tower. ⊠ *Büyük Hendek Cad., Galata.* ⊙ *Daily 9–8.*

⑬ İstiklâl Caddesi. Formerly known as La Grande Rue de Pera, İstiklâl Caddesi was the most fashionable street in the city during the 19th and early 20th centuries. Pedestrianized and lined with shops, restaurants, banks, and cafés in turn-of-the-century buildings, the street teems with every human element in Turkey's cultural melting pot, dodging the restored 19th-century tram that runs from Tünel to Taksim Square. In the side streets you'll find Greek and Armenian churches, bars, and other establishments; in the narrow, poorer residential alleys, you'll see children playing and laundry hanging between the old buildings. ⊠ *İstiklâl Cad., Beyoğlu.*

DINING

The Turkish people are justly proud of their cuisine. In addition to the blends of spices used, the food is also extremely healthy, full of fresh vegetables, yogurt, legumes, and grains, not to mention fresh seafood, roast lamb, and kebabs made of lamb, beef, or chicken. Because Turkey is predominantly Muslim, pork is not readily available. But there's plenty of alcohol, including local beer and wine, which are excellent and inexpensive. Particularly good wines are Villa Doluca and Kavaklidere, available in *beyaz* (white) and *kırmızı* (red). The most popular local beer is Efes Pilsen. The national alcoholic drink, *rakı,* is made from grapes and aniseed. Turks mix it with water or ice and sip it through-out their meal or serve it as an aperitif.

Many hotel restaurants have English-language menus and usually serve a bland version of Continental cuisine. Far more adventurous and tasty are meals in *restorans* and in *lokantas* (Turkish restaurants). Most lokantas do not have menus because they serve only what's fresh and in season, which varies daily. At lokantas you simply sit back and let the waiter bring food to your table, beginning with a tray of mezes (appetizers). You point to the dishes that look inviting and take as many as you want. Then you select your main course from fresh meat or fish—displayed in glass-covered refrigerated units—which is then cooked to order, or from a steam table laden with casseroles and stews. For lighter meals there are *kebabcıs,* tiny restaurants specializing in kebabs served with salad and yogurt, and *pidecis,* selling *pides,* a pizzalike snack of flat bread topped with butter, cheese, egg, or ground lamb and baked in a wood-burning oven.

MEALTIMES

Lunch is generally served from noon to 3 and dinner from 7 to 10. In cities you can find restaurants or cafés open almost any time of day or night, but in villages, finding a restaurant open at odd hours can be a problem. In more conservative areas restaurants often close during day-light hours in the Islamic holy month of Ramadan, when many Mus-lims fast.

PRECAUTIONS

Although tap water is heavily chlorinated, it is often not safe to drink in cities and resorts. It's best to play it safe and drink *maden suyu* (bot-tled mineral water) or regular *şişe suyu* (bottled water), which is bet-ter tasting and inexpensive.

RATINGS

Prices are per person and include an appetizer, main course, and dessert. Wine and gratuities are not included.

CATEGORY	COST
$$$$	over $40
$$$	$25–$40
$$	$12–$25
$	under $12

Most major hotels have dining rooms serving bland international cui-sine. It's far more rewarding to eat in Turkish restaurants.

$$$$ ✕ **Körfez.** The specialty here is seafood dishes such as bass baked in salt. The garden setting on the waterfront is very romantic. The restau-rant has a boat that ferries you across the Bosporus from Rumeli Hisarı. ⊠ *Körfez Cad. 78, Kanlıca,* ☎ *216/413–4098 or 216/413–1881. AE, MC, V. Closed Mon.*

$$$$ ✕ **Tuğra.** This spacious and luxurious restaurant in the historic Çira-ğan Palace serves the most delectable of long-savored Ottoman recipes, including slices of tender beef cooked in paper, air-dried beef cooked in vine leaves, and desserts such as quince tart in cinnamon syrup. The Bosporus view is framed by the palace's marble columns; the high ceil-ings support dazzlingly crafted glass chandeliers. ⊠ *Çirağan Cad. 84, Beşiktaş,* ☎ *212/258–3377, ext. 7684. AE, DC, MC, V.*

$$$$ ✕ **Ulus 29.** Seafood is the specialty at this chic restaurant tucked away in a park in the upscale Ulus district. The terrace has spectacular views spanning both Bosporus bridges. In summer, guests are ferried across to the Bosporus site, Çubuklu 29, which is reminiscent of a Roman villa. ⊠ *Ahmet Adnan Saygun Cad., Kireçhane Sok. 1, Ulus,* ☎ *212/ 265–6181 in spring, fall, and winter;* ⊠ *Paşabahçe Yolu, Çubuklu,* ☎ *216/322–3888 in summer. Reservations essential. AE, DC, MC, V.*

\$\$\$ ✕ **Develi Restaurant.** Established in 1912, the Develi specializes in dishes from southeast Anatolia, which are traditionally more spicy than those from the west of the country. Try the *patlıcan kebap* (kebab with egg- plants) or the *fıstıklı kebap* (kebab with pistachios). ⊠ *Balıkpazarı, Gümüşyüzük Sok. 7, Samatya,* ☎ *212/529–0833. AE, MC, V.*

\$\$\$ ✕ **Divan.** Enjoy Turkish and international haute cuisine, elegant sur- roundings, and excellent service at this restaurant in the Divan hotel. Specialties include *islim kebap* (lamb covered with eggplant and served with Turkish rice). ⊠ *Cumhuriyet Cad. 2, Elmadağ,* ☎ *212/231–4100. AE, DC, MC, V. Closed Sun. No lunch Sat.*

\$\$\$ ✕ **Gelik.** This restaurant in a two-story, 19th-century villa is usually packed, often with people who want to savor its specialty: various meats cooked in deep pits. ⊠ *Sahil Yolu, Ataköy,* ☎ *212/560–7282. AE, DC, MC, V.*

\$\$ ✕ **Borsa Lokantası.** This unpretentious restaurant serves some of the ★ best food in Turkey. The baked lamb in eggplant purée and the stuffed artichokes are not to be missed. A second branch is in Kalamış on the Asian side of Istanbul. ⊠ *Yaliköskü Cad., Yaliköskü Han 60–62, Em- inönü,* ☎ *212/522–4173. No credit cards.* ⊠ *Fener Kalamış Cad. 87, Fenerbahçe,* ☎ *216/348–7700. DC, MC, V.*

\$\$ ✕ **Çatı.** On the seventh floor of a building in a Beyoğlu side street, this place serves a range of excellent hot and cold Turkish cuisine and a good open buffet. Its lofty location provides a rare opportunity to ap- preciate the architectural splendors of İstiklâl Caddesi. ⊠ *Orhan Apaydın Sok. 20/7, İstiklâl Cad., Beyoğlu,* ☎ *212/251–0000. MC, V.*

\$\$ ✕ **Dört Mevsim** (Four Seasons). The restaurant, in a large Victorian build- ing, is noted for its blend of Turkish and French cuisine and for its own- ers, Gay and Musa, an Anglo-Turkish couple who opened it in 1965. On any given day you'll find them in the kitchen overseeing such de- lights as shrimp in cognac sauce and baked marinated lamb. ⊠ *İstik- lâl Cad. 509, Beyoğlu,* ☎ *212/293–3941. AE, DC, MC, V. Closed Sun.*

\$\$ ✕ **Dünya.** The busy traffic of the adjacent Ortaköy Square and wait- ers balancing appetizer trays is countered by the picturesque Bosporus view, which on summer nights includes many passing pleasure boats. The grilled *cupra* (bream) is a must, and the mezes are always fresh and delicious. ⊠ *Salhane Sok. 10, Ortaköy,* ☎ *212/258–6385. V.*

\$\$ ✕ **Pandeli.** Indulge in savory food underneath domed alcoves at this frenetic restaurant up two flights of stairs over the arched gateway to the Egyptian Bazaar. Try the *kağıtta levrek* (paper-wrapped grilled sea bass) and *patlıcan böreği* (eggplant pastry). ⊠ *Mısır Çarsışı, Eminönü,* ☎ *212/527–3909. AE, DC, MC, V. Closed Sun. No dinner.*

\$ ✕ **Hacıbaba.** This large, cheerful-looking place has a summer terrace ★ overlooking an old Greek church. Fish, meat, and a wide variety of vegetable dishes are on display for your selection. Before you choose your main course, you'll be offered a tray of mezes that can be a meal in themselves. ⊠ *İstiklâl Cad. 49, Taksim,* ☎ *212/244–1886 or 212/ 244–0419. AE, DC, MC, V.*

\$ ✕ **Hacı Salih.** This tiny, family-run restaurant has only 10 tables, so you ★ may have to line up and wait—but it's worth it. Traditional Turkish food is the fare, with special emphasis on vegetable dishes and lamb. Alcohol is not served. ⊠ *Anadolu Pasajı 201, off İstiklâl Cad., Beyoğlu,* ☎ *212/ 243–4528. No credit cards. Closed Sun. No dinner.*

\$ ✕ **Rejans.** Founded by two Russians and a Crimean fleeing the Bolshevik revolution, and now run by their widows, this restaurant has excellent Russian food and lemon vodka, as well as Turkish dishes. The decor has remained basically unchanged since the 1930s. ⊠ *İstiklâl Cad., Olivo Gecidi 15, Galatasaray,* ☎ *212/244–1610 or 212/243–3882. V.*

$ ✕ **Yakup.** This cheerful hole-in-the-wall is smoky and filled with locals rather than tourists. It can get loud, especially if there is a soccer game on TV. From the stuffed peppers to the *tereyağlı börek* (buttered pastries) and octopus salad, the mezes are above average. ⊠ *Asmali Mescit Sok. 35–37, Beyoğlu,* ☎ *212/249–2925 or 212/251–3181. AE, MC, V.*

NIGHTLIFE AND THE ARTS

The Arts

Entertainment in Istanbul ranges from the Istanbul International Festival—held late-June through mid-July and attracting internationally renowned artists and performers—to local folklore and theatrical groups, some amateur, some professional. Because there is no central ticket agency, ask your hotel for help getting tickets. You can also get them at the box office or through a local tourist office. For tickets to the **Istanbul International Festival,** contact the Istanbul Foundation for Culture and Arts (⊠ Kültür ve Sanat Vakfı, İstiklâl Cad., Luvr Apt. 146, Beyoğlu, 80070, ☎ 212/293–3133). Tickets can also be purchased at the Marmara Hotel (⊠ Taksim Sq., ☎ 212/251–4696). Performances, which include modern and classical music, ballet, opera, and theater, are given throughout the city in historic buildings, such as the Church of St. Irene and Rumeli Castle. The season at the city of Istanbul's **Cemal Resit Rey Concert Hall** (☎ 212/248–1061) runs from September through May and includes classical, jazz, and rock music, as well as ballet performed by visiting and local groups.

CONCERTS

From October through May, the Istanbul State Symphony gives performances at the main concert hall, **Atatürk Kültür Merkezi** (⊠ box office, Taksim Sq., ☎ 212/251–5600; tickets are also available here for concerts at Cemal Resit Rey Concert Hall). Ballet and dance companies perform at this hall, too.

Nightlife

BARS

Bebek Bar (⊠ Bebek Ambassadeurs Hotel, Cevdet Paşa Cad. 113, Bebek, ☎ 212/263–3000) has views over the Bosporus and draws locals from the neighborhood and nearby Bosporus University. Sophisticated **Beyoğlu Pub** (⊠ İstiklâl Cad. 140/7, Beyoğlu, ☎ 212/252–3842), behind an arcade off İstiklâl Caddesi, has a pleasant first-story garden and a discreet indoor bar. **Hayal Kahvesi** (⊠ Büyük Parmakkapı Sok. 19, Beyoğlu, ☎ 212/244–2558) is a bohemian side-street bar with wooden furniture, lace curtains, and live music. The loud and lively three-story **Kemancı Rock-Bar** (⊠ Taksim Sitesi, Sıraselviler 69, ☎ 212/245–3048 or 212/251–3015) has live rock and blues bands. The fin de siècle decor of the **Orient Express Bar** (⊠ Pera Palace Hotel, Meşrutiyet Cad. 98, Tepebaşı, ☎ 212/251–4560) distills the atmosphere of old Istanbul with the lingering presence of the rich, powerful, and famous who once played here. **Tribunal** (⊠ İstiklâl Cad. Muammer Karaca Cikmazi 3, ☎ 212/249–7179) once served as a French court and retains the original inlaid brick ceiling.

DANCE CLUBS

Çubuklu 29 (⊠ Bahçeburun, Çubuklu, ☎ 216/322–2829), by the Bosporus on the Asian side, is open mid-June through September. **Hayal Kahvesi** (⊠ Burunbahçe, Çubuklu, ☎ 216/413–6880), a huge, restaurant/bar/disco complex on the Asian shore of the Bosporus, has dancing to live jazz or rock on Friday or Saturday (summer only). **Memo's** (✉ Salhane Sok. 10, Ortaköy, ☎ 212/261–8304 or 212/260–8491), near hopping Ortaköy Square, is home to a faithful yuppie clientele. **Şaziye** (✉ Abdi İpekçi Cad. 24–26, Maçka, ☎ 212/232–4155 or 212/231–1401) turns into a popular disco after 11:30 PM. **2019** (✉ Abdülhakhamit Cad. Talimhane 75, Taksim, ☎ 212/235–6197), a crowded disco-bar, draws a young, affluent crowd.

JAZZ CLUBS

Q Jazz Bar (✉ Çırağan Cad. 84, Beşiktaş, ☎ 212/236–2489 or 212/236–2131), the Çırağan Hotel's luxurious jazz bar, has some of the classiest music in town—at equally classy prices. **Tepe Bar Lounge** (✉ Marmara Hotel, Taksim Sq., ☎ 212/251–4696), on the top floor the Marmara Hotel, has a 360-degree view of Istanbul, as well as local and visiting musicians.

NIGHTCLUBS

Galata Tower (✉ Kuledibi, ☎ 212/245–1160) serves dinner followed by a Turkish show and dancing. **Kervansaray** (✉ Cumhuriyet Cad. 30, Elmadağ, ☎ 212/247–1630) has dining, dancing, and belly-dancing shows. The revue at **Regine's** (✉ Cumhuriyet Cad. 16, Elmadağ, ☎ 212/247–1630) is the spot for some of Istanbul's best-known belly dancers and big dance production numbers.

SHOPPING

Districts and Malls

In New Town, stores and boutiques line İstiklâl Caddesi, which runs off Taksim Square, and Rumeli, Halaskargazi, and Valikonaği Caddeleri, north of the Hilton Hotel. Two streets in the Kadiköy area with good shops are Bağdat and Bahariye Caddeleri. **Akmerkez,** the newest of the malls in Etiler, has luxury and designer wear. **Ataköy Shopping and Tourism Center** is a large mall near the airport. In Altunizade on the Asian side, the slick **Capitol** mall has movies and entertainment, too.

Gift Ideas

The **Grand Bazaar** (☞ Exploring Istanbul, *above*) is what it sounds like: a smattering of all things Turkish—carpets, brass, copper, jewelry, textiles, and leather goods. **Tünel Square,** a quick Metro ride up from Karaköy, is a quaint group of stores with old prints, books, and artifacts.

Markets

Balıkpazarı (fish market) is in Beyoğlu Caddesi, off İstiklâl Caddesi. A bustling clutter of narrow covered streets, **Balıkpazarı** contains stalls and tiny stores, selling everything from spices, vegetables, and fruit to fish, cooked meats, and even pork. Turkish traders are joined by new arrivals from the former Soviet Union at a flea market held in **Beyazit Square,** near the Grand Bazaar, every Sunday starting at about 10 AM; here you can find everything from cheap electronic goods to Soviet army boots and hats. A crafts market, with street entertainment, is open on Sunday along the Bosporus at **Ortaköy.** A weekend crafts market takes place on **Bekar Sokak,** off İstiklâl Caddesi.

ISTANBUL ESSENTIALS

Arriving and Departing

BY BUS

Esenler terminal, northwest of the city center, is the destination for buses arriving in Istanbul. From the terminal, the major bus companies offer free minibus service to centers such as Sultanahmet, Taksim, and Aksaray. The Hızlı Tren (rapid train) also connects the terminal to Aksaray, though it is often very crowded and can be extremely hot in summer. A few buses from Anatolia arrive at **Harem terminal,** on the eastern shore of the Bosporus. If you arrive with baggage, it is much easier to take a taxi, which will cost about $8 to Taksim from the Esenler terminal and about $5 to Old Istanbul.

BY CAR

If you drive in from the west, take the busy E5 highway, also called Londra Asfaltı, which leads from Edirne to Atatürk Airport and on through the city walls at Cannon Gate (Topkapı). E5 heading out of Istanbul leads into central Anatolia and on to Iran and Syria. You can also take one of the numerous car ferries that ply the Sea of Marmara and the Dardanelles from Kabataş Dock, or try the overnight ferry to İzmir, which leaves from Sarayburnu.

BY PLANE

All international and domestic flights arrive at Istanbul's **Atatürk Airport.** For arrival and departure information call the individual airline or the airport's information desk (☎ 212/663–6400).

Between the Airport and Downtown. Shuttle buses run from the airport's international and domestic terminals to the Turkish Airlines (THY) terminal in downtown Istanbul, at Cumhuriyet Caddesi, near the THY Taksim office. Buses depart for the airport at the same address on the hour every hour from 7 AM to 11 PM. After that, departure time depends on demand. Allow at least 45 minutes for the bus ride. Plan to be at the airport two hours before your international flight because of the lengthy security and check-in procedures. The ride from the airport into town takes from 30 to 40 minutes, depending on traffic. Taxis charge about $15 to Taksim Square and $11 to Sultanahmet.

BY TRAIN

Trains from the west arrive at **Sirkeci Station** (☎ 212/527–0050 or 0051) in Old Istanbul. Eastbound trains to Anatolia depart from **Haydarpasa station** (☎ 216/336–0475) on the Asian side.

Getting Around

The best way to get to the various magnificent monuments in Sultanahmet in Old Istanbul is to walk. They're all within easy distance of one another, along streets filled with peddlers, children playing, and craftsmen working. Dolmuş vehicles and taxis are plentiful, inexpensive, and more comfortable than city buses. A tram system runs from Topkapı, via Sultanahmet, to Sirkeci. The Tünel, a tiny underground train, is handy for getting up the steep hill from Karaköy to the bottom of İstiklâl Caddesi. It runs every 10 minutes and costs about 25¢. Nostalgic trams run the length of İstiklâl Caddesi from Taksim to Tünel and cost about 25¢.

BY BOAT

Many ferries run between the Asian and European continents. *Deniz otobüsü* (sea buses; ☎ 216/362–0444) run between the continents, as well as to destinations such as the Princes' Islands; they are fast and efficient. For an inexpensive ride take the boat in the direction of *Anadolu Kavağı,* along the Bosporus to its mouth at the Black Sea. The boat leaves year-round from the Eminönü Docks, next to the Galata Bridge on the Old Istanbul side, at 10:30 AM and 1:30 PM, with two extra trips on weekdays and four extra trips on Sunday from April through September. The fare is $6 (round-trip). The trip takes 1¾ hours one way. You can disembark at any of the stops and return by land if you wish. Regular ferries depart from Kabataş Dock, near Dolmabahçe Palace on the European side, to Üsküdar on the Asian side;

and also from Eminönü Docks 1 and 2, near Sirkeci station (☎ 212/
244–4233).

BY BUS
You need to buy a ticket before boarding a bus. Individual tickets or
books of 10 can be purchased at ticket stands around the city. Shoe-
shine boys or men on the street will also sell them to you for a few
cents more. Fares are about 25¢ per ride. On the city's orange priva-
tized buses (Halk Otobüsü), you pay for tickets on the bus. The Lon-
don-style double-deckers operate along a scenic route between
Sultanahmet and Emigran on the Bosporus and between Europe and
Asia and cost about $1 one-way.

BY DOLMUŞ
These are shared taxis operating between set destinations throughout
the city. Dolmuş stops are indicated by a blue and white sign with a
large D. The destination is shown on either a roof sign or a card in the
front window. Until the mid-1990s all the dolmuş were classic American cars from the 1950s, but they have now been nearly all been replaced by modern yellow minibuses.

BY TAXI
Taxis are inexpensive and metered. As most drivers do not speak English and may not know the street names, write down the street you want,
the nearby main streets, and the name of the area. Although tipping is
not expected, you should round off the fare to the nearest 50,000 TL.

Contacts and Resources
CONSULATES
Canadian (⊠ Büyükdere Cad. 107/3, Bengün Han, 80300, Gayrettepe,
☎ 212/272–5174). **United Kingdom** (⊠ Meşrutiyet Cad. 34, Tepebaşı
80050, Beyoğlu, ☎ 212/293–7540). **United States** (⊠ Meşrutiyet
Cad. 104–108 Tepebaşi, 80050, Beyoğlu, ☎ 212/251–3602).

EMERGENCIES
Tourism Police (☎ 212/527–4503). **Ambulance** (☎ 112). **Doctors:**
American Hospital (⊠ Güzelbahçe Sok. 20, Nişantaşı 80200, ☎ 212/
231–4050/69); **International Hospital** (Yesilyurt, ☎ 212/663–3000).
Pharmacies (☎ 118, for 24-hour pharmacy in each neighborhood; notice in window of every pharmacy lists name and address of nearest
all-night shop); in center, **Taksim** (⊠ İstiklâl Cad. 17, Taksim 80060,
☎ 212/249–2252).

ENGLISH-LANGUAGE BOOKSTORES
ABC Bookshop (⊠ İstiklâl Cad. 461, Tünel 80050, ☎ 212/249–2414).
Dünya Aktuel Bookshop (⊠ İstiklâl Cad. 469, Tünel 80050, ☎ 212/
249–1006). **Net** (⊠ Şifa Hamamı Sokak 18/2, Sultanahmet 34410, ☎
212/516–8467). **Robinson Crusoe** (⊠ İstiklâl Cad. 389, Tünel 80060,
☎ 212/293–6968 or 212/293–6977).

GUIDED TOURS
Tours can be arranged through travel agencies (☞ Travel Agencies,
below). Most companies have a half- or full-day "Classical Tour." The
half-day tour includes Hagia Sophia, the Museum of Turkish and Islamic
Arts, the Hippodrome, Yerebatan Saray, and the Blue Mosque; the full-
day tour, in addition to the above sights, includes Topkapı Palace, the
Süleymaniye Mosque, the Covered or Egyptian Bazaar, and lunch. The
"Bosporus Tour" includes lunch at Sariyer and visits to the Dolmabahçe
and Beylerbeyi palaces. The "Night Tour" includes dinner and drinks
at Kervansaray or Galata for a show.

Fest (⌧ Barbaros Bulvarı 85, A Daire 13, Beşiktaş 80690, ☎ 212/258–2589 or 212/258–2573). **Intra** (⌧ Halaskargazi Cad. 111/2, Harbiye 80230, ☎ 212/247–8174 or 212/240–3891). **Plan Tours** (⌧ Cumhuriyet Cad. 131/1, Elmadağ 80230, ☎ 212/230–2272 or 212/230–8118). **Setur** (⌧ Cumhuriyet Cad. 107, Harbiye 80230, ☎ 212/230–0336). **Türk Express** (American Express Travel Service representative; ⌧ Hilton Hotel, Cumhuriyet Cad., Harbiye 80200, ☎ 212/241–0248 or 212/241–0249). **Vip Tourism** (⌧ Cumhuriyet Cad. 269/2, Harbiye 80230, ☎ 212/241–6514).

VISITOR INFORMATION
Official tourist information offices: **Atatürk Airport** (☎ 212/663–6400); the **Hilton Hotel** (☎ 212/233–0592); **Karaköy Yolcu Salonu,** International Maritime Passenger Terminal (☎ 212/249–5776); **pavilion,** Sultanahmet district of Old Istanbul (⌧ Divan Yolu Cad. 3, ☎ 212/518–1802 or 212/518–8754).

13 London

If London contained only its famous land-marks—Buckingham Palace, Big Ben, Parlia-ment, the Tower of London—it would still rank as one of the world's great destinations. It is a vast city of living history, whose story is still emerging in big events, like the death of Princess Diana in 1997, and small, like the opening of what seems like the millionth new restaurant. A city that loves to be explored, London beckons with great museums, royal pageantry, and his-tory-steeped houses. Marvel at the Duke of Wellington's house, track Jack the Ripper's shadow in Whitechapel, then get Beatle-ized at Abbey Road. East End, West End, you'll find London is a dickens of a place.

EXPLORING LONDON

Traditionally London has been divided between the City, to the east, where its banking and commercial interests lie, and Westminster, to the west, the seat of the royal court and of government. It is in these two areas that you will find most of the grand buildings that have played a central role in British history: the Tower of London and St. Paul's Cathedral, Westminster Abbey and the Houses of Parliament, Buck-ingham Palace, and the older royal palace of St. James's.

Visitors who restrict their sightseeing to the well-known tourist areas miss much of the best the city has to offer. Within a few minutes' walk of Buckingham Palace, for instance, lie St. James's, and Mayfair, two neighboring quarters of elegant town houses built for the nobility dur-ing the 17th and early 18th centuries and now notable for the shopping opportunities they house. The same lesson applies to The City, where, tucked away in quiet corners, stand many of the churches Christopher Wren built to replace those destroyed during the Great Fire of 1666.

Other parts of London worth exploring include Covent Garden, a former fruit and flower market converted into a lively shopping and entertainment center where you can wander for hours enjoying the friendly bustle of the streets. Hyde Park and Kensington Gardens, by contrast, offer a great swath of green parkland across the city center, preserved by past kings and queens for their own hunting and relaxation. A walk across Hyde Park will bring you to the museum district of South Kensington, with three major national collections: the Natural History Museum, the Science Museum, and the Victoria & Albert Museum, which specializes in the fine and applied arts.

The south side of the River Thames has its treats as well. A short stroll across Waterloo Bridge brings you to the South Bank Arts Complex, which includes the National Theatre, the Royal Festival Hall, the Hayward Gallery (with changing exhibitions of international art), the National Film Theatre, and the Museum of the Moving Image (MOMI)—a must for movie buffs. Here also are the exciting reconstruction of Shakespeare's Globe theater and its sister museum; and the future home, at Bankside Power Station, of the Tate Gallery of Modern Art—due for completion for the millennium. The views from the South Bank are stunning—to the west are the Houses of Parliament and Big Ben; to the east the dome of St. Paul's is just visible on London's changing skyline. London, although not simple of layout, is a rewarding walking city, and this remains the best way to get to know its nooks and crannies. The infamous weather may not be on your side, but there's plenty of indoor entertainment to keep you amused if you forget the umbrella!

Westminster

Numbers in the margin correspond to points of interest on the London map.

Westminster is the royal backyard—the traditional center of the royal court and of government. Here, within 1 km (½ mi) or so of one another, are nearly all London's most celebrated buildings, and there is a strong feeling of history all around you. Generations of kings and queens have lived here since the end of the 11th century—including the current monarch. The Queen resides at Buckingham Palace through most of the year; during summer periods when she visits her country estates, the palace is partially open to visitors.

⑰ Banqueting House. On the right side of the grand processional avenue known as Whitehall—site of many important government offices—stands this famous monument of the English Renaissance period. Designed by Inigo Jones in 1625 for court entertainments, it is the only part of Whitehall Palace, the monarch's principal residence during the 16th and 17th centuries, that was not burned down in 1698. It has a magnificent ceiling by Rubens, and outside is an inscription that marks the window through which King Charles I stepped to his execution. ✉ *Whitehall,* ☎ *020/7930–4179.* 💷 *£3.25.* ☉ *Tues.–Sat. 10–5, Sun. 2–5.*

❽ Buckingham Palace. Supreme among the symbols of London, indeed of Britain generally, and of the royal family, Buckingham Palace tops many must-see lists—although the building itself is no masterpiece and has housed the monarch only since Victoria moved here from Kensington

Palace at her accession in 1837. Located at the end of the Mall, the palace is the London home of the Queen and the administrative hub of the entire royal family. When the Queen is in residence (normally on weekdays except in January, August, September, and part of June), the royal standard flies over the east front. Inside are dozens of ornate 19th-century-style state rooms used on formal occasions. The private apartments of Queen Elizabeth and Prince Philip are in the north wing. Parts of Buckingham Palace are now open to the public during August and September; during the entire year, the former chapel, bombed during World War II, rebuilt in 1961, is the site of the **Queen's Gallery** (☞ *below*), which shows treasures from the vast royal art collections. The ceremony of the **Changing of the Guard** takes place in front of the palace at 11:30 daily, April through July, and on alternate days during the rest of the year. It's advisable to arrive early, as people are invariably stacked several deep along the railings, whatever the weather. ✉ *Buckingham Palace Rd.,* ☎ *020/7839–1377;* ☎ *020/7321–2233 credit-card pre-booking reservations line (AE, MC, V).* 🎫 *£9.* ☉ *Early Aug.–early Oct. (confirm specific dates, which are subject to the Queen's mandate), daily 9:30–4.*

⑫ **Cabinet War Rooms.** It was from this small maze of 17 bomb-proof underground rooms—located in back of the hulking Foreign Office—that Britain's World War II fortunes were directed. During air raids the Cabinet met here—the Cabinet Room is still arranged as if a meeting were about to convene. Among the rooms are the Prime Minister's Room, from which Winston Churchill made many of his inspiring wartime broadcasts, and the Transatlantic Telephone Room, from which he spoke directly to President Roosevelt in the White House. ✉ *Clive Steps, King Charles St.,* ☎ *020/7930–6961.* 🎫 *£4.40.* ☉ *Daily 10–5:15.*

❻ **Carlton House Terrace.** This architectural showpiece of the Mall (☞ *below*) is a Regency-era masterpiece, built in 1827–32 by John Nash in imposing white-stucco and with massive Corinthian columns. It is home to the Institute of Contemporary Arts.

⑱ **Horse Guards Parade.** The former tiltyard of Whitehall Palace is the site of the annual ceremony of Trooping the Colour, when the Queen takes the salute in the great military parade that marks her official birthday on the second Saturday in June (her real one is on April 21). Demand for tickets is great, but happily there are Queenless rehearsals on the previous two Saturdays, the later one presided over by Prince Charles; for information, call 020/7414–2497. There is also a daily guard-changing ceremony outside the guard house, on Whitehall, at 11 AM (10 on Sunday)—one of London's best photo-ops. ✉ *Whitehall, opposite Downing St.*

⑮ **Houses of Parliament.** The Houses of Parliament are among the city's most famous and photogenic sights. The Clock Tower keeps watch on Parliament Square, in which stand statues of everyone from Richard the Lionhearted to Abraham Lincoln, and, across the way, Westminster Abbey. Also known as the **Palace of Westminster,** this was the site of the monarch's main residence from the 11th century until 1512; the court then moved to the newly built Whitehall Palace. The only parts of the original building to have survived are the Jewel Tower and **Westminster Hall,** which has a fine hammer-beam roof. The rest of the structure was destroyed in a disastrous fire in 1834 and was rebuilt in the newly popular mock-medieval Gothic style to the delight of millions. The architect, Augustus Pugin, designed the entire place, right down to the Gothic umbrella stands. This newer part of the palace contains the debating chambers and committee rooms of

182

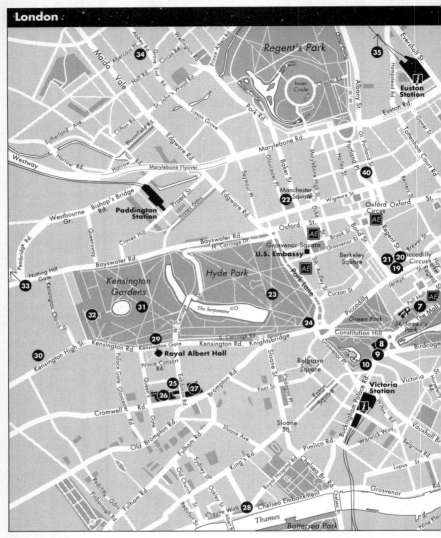

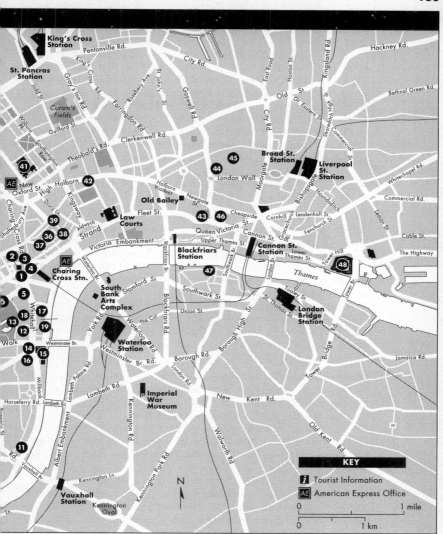

the two Houses of Parliament—the Commons (whose members are elected) and the Lords (whose members are appointed or inherit their seats). There are no tours of the palace, but the public is admitted to the Public Gallery of each House; expect to wait in line for several hours (the line for the Lords is generally much shorter than that for the Commons). The most famous features of the palace are its towers. At the south end is the 336-ft **Victoria Tower.** At the other end is **St. Stephen's Tower,** or the Clock Tower, better known, but inaccurately so, as **Big Ben;** that name properly belongs to the 13-ton bell in the tower on which the hours are struck. Big Ben himself was probably Sir Benjamin Hall, commissioner of works when the bell was installed in the 1850s. A light shines from the top of the tower during a night sitting of Parliament. ⊠ *St. Stephen's Entrance, St. Margaret St., SW1,* ☎ *020/7219–3000.* 🎫 *Free.* ☉ *Commons: Mon.–Thurs. 2:30–10, Fri. 9:30–3; Lords: Mon.–Thurs. 2:30–10.*

❺ **The Mall.** The splendid and imperial **Admiralty Arch** guards the entrance to The Mall, the noted ceremonial way that leads alongside **St. James's Park** to Buckingham Palace. The Mall takes its name from a game called *palle maille,* a version of croquet that James I imported from France, and Charles II popularized during the late 1600s. The park was developed by successive monarchs, most recently by George IV in the 1820s, having originally been used for hunting by Henry VIII. Join office workers relaxing with a lunchtime sandwich, or stroll here on a summer's evening when the illuminated fountains play and Westminster Abbey and the Houses of Parliament are floodlit. Toward Buckingham Palace, along The Mall, you'll pass the foot of the imposing **Carlton House Terrace** (☞ *above*).

★ ❷ **National Gallery.** Generally ranked right after the Louvre, the National Gallery is one of the world's greatest museums. Occupying the long neoclassical building on the north side of Trafalgar Square (☞ *below*), it contains works by virtually every famous artist and school from the 14th to the 19th centuries. Its galleries overflow with masterpieces, including Jan van Eyck's *Arnolfini Marriage,* Leonardo da Vinci's *Burlington Virgin and Child,* Velásquez's *The Toilet of Venus* (known as "The Rokeby Venus"), and Constable's *Hay Wain.* The gallery is especially strong on Flemish and Dutch masters, Rubens and Rembrandt among them, and on Italian Renaissance works. The museum's Brasserie is an excellent spot for lunch. ⊠ *Trafalgar Sq.,* ☎ *020/7839–3321; 020/7839–3526 (recorded general information).* 🎫 *Free; admission charge for special exhibitions.* ☉ *Mon.–Sat. 10–6, Sun. 2–6; June– Aug., also Wed. until 8.*

❸ **National Portrait Gallery.** This fascinating collection contains portraits of well-known (and not so well-known) Britons, including monarchs, statesmen, and writers. ⊠ *2 St. Martin's Pl., at foot of Charing Cross Rd.,* ☎ *020/7306–0055.* 🎫 *Free.* ☉ *Weekdays 10–5, Sat. 10– 6, Sun. 2–6.*

❾ **Queen's Gallery.** This is the former chapel at the south side of Buckingham Palace (☞ *above*). On display here are smaller shows drawn from the royal collections, such as Michelangelo drawings; call for information on current exhibits. ⊠ *Buckingham Palace Rd.,* ☎ *020/7 799–2331.* 🎫 *£3.50; combined ticket for Queen's Gallery and Royal Mews: £6.20.* ☉ *Tues.–Sat. 10–5, Sun. 2–5.*

❿ **Royal Mews.** Unmissable children's entertainment, this museum is the home of Her Majesty's Coronation Coach. Here, some of the queen's horses are stabled and the elaborately gilded state coaches are on view. ⊠ *Buckingham Palace Rd.,* ☎ *020/7799–2331.* 🎫 *£3.70; combined* *ticket with Queen's Gallery: £6.* ☉ *Oct. 7–Dec. 23 and Jan. 6–Mar. 24, Wed. noon–4; Apr. 1–Sept. 30, Tues.–Thurs. noon–4.*

❹ St. Martin-in-the-Fields. Soaring above Trafalgar Square, this landmark church may seem familiar to many Americans because James Gibbs's classical-temple-with-spire design became a pattern for churches in early Colonial America. Built in about 1730, the distinctive neoclassical church is the site for regular lunchtime music recitals. ✉ *Trafalgar Sq.,* ☎ *020/7930–0089, 020/7839–8362 credit-card bookings for evening concerts.* ☉ *Church daily 8–8; crypt Mon.–Sat. 10–8, Sun. noon–6.*

⓫ Tate Gallery. By the river to the north of Chelsea, on traffic-laden Millbank, the Tate Gallery of Modern British Art is the greatest museum devoted to British painting and sculpture. "Modern" is slightly misleading, as one of the three collections here consists of British art from 1545 to the present, including works by William Hogarth, Thomas Gainsborough, Sir Joshua Reynolds, and George Stubbs from the 18th century; and by John Constable, William Blake, and the Pre-Raphaelite painters from the 19th century (don't miss Sir John Everett Millais' unforgettable *Ophelia*). Also from the 19th century is the second of the Tate's collections, the incredible Turner Bequest, consisting of the personal collection of England's greatest romantic painter, J. M. W. Turner. About a 20-minute walk south of the Houses of Parliament, the Tate is also accessible if you tube it to the Pimlico stop, then take a five-minute walk through Chelsea to the museum. ✉ *Millbank, SW1,* ☎ *020/7821–1313 or 020/7821–7128.* ✆ *Free; special exhibitions £3– £7.* ☉ *Mon.–Sat. 10–5:50, Sun. 2–5:50.*

⓭ Ten Downing Street. As you walk along Whitehall, past government offices, you'll note, on the north side of the street, the entrance to Downing Street, a row of unassuming 18th-century houses. The prime minister's office is at No. 10 (with a private apartment on the top floor). The chancellor of the exchequer, the finance minister, occupies No. 11. The street is now gated off from the main thoroughfare. Not far away in the middle of Whitehall is the **Cenotaph,** a stone national memorial to the dead of both world wars. At 11 AM on the Sunday closest to the 11th day of the 11th month, the Queen and other dignitaries lay flowers in tribute here.

❶ Trafalgar Square. This is the center of London, by dint of a plaque on the corner of the Strand and Charing Cross Road from which distances on U.K. signposts are measured. It is the home of the **National Gallery** (☞ *above*) and of one of London's most distinctive landmarks, **Nelson's Column,** a tribute to one of England's favorite heroes, Admiral Lord Horatio Nelson, who routed the French at the Battle of Trafalgar in 1805. Permanently alive with Londoners and tourists alike, roaring traffic, and pigeons, it remains London's "living room"—great events, such as New Year's, royal weddings, elections, sporting triumphs—will always see the crowds gathering in the city's most famous square.

★ ⓰ Westminster Abbey. This is the most ancient of London's great churches and the most important, for it is here that Britain's monarchs are crowned. Most of the abbey dates largely from the 13th and 14th centuries. The main nave is packed with atmosphere and memories, as it has witnessed many splendid coronation ceremonies, royal weddings, and more recently, the funeral of Diana, Princess of Wales. It is also packed with crowds—so many, in fact, that the Abbey has now started to charge admission to the main nave (always free, of course, for participants in religious services). **Henry VII's Chapel,** an exquisite example of the heavily decorated late-Gothic style, was not built until the early 1600s, and the twin towers over the west entrance are an 18th-century addition. There is much to see inside, including the tomb of the Unknown Warrior, a nameless World War I soldier buried, in memory of the war's victims, in earth brought with his corpse from France; and the famous Poets' Corner, where England's great writers—Milton, Chaucer, Shakespeare, et al—are memorialized, and some are actually buried. Behind the high altar are the royal tombs, including those of Queen Elizabeth I; Mary, Queen of Scots; and Henry V. In the Chapel of Edward the Confessor stands the Coronation Chair. Among the royal weddings that have taken place here are those of the present queen and most recently, in 1986, the (ill-starred) duke and duchess of York. It is all too easy to forget, swamped by the crowds trying to see the abbey's sights, that this is a place of worship. Early morning is a good moment to catch something of the building's atmosphere. Better still, take time to attend a service. Note that photography is not permitted except Wednesday 6 PM–8 PM. ⊠ *Broad Sanctuary,* ☎ *020/7222–5152.* 🖃 *£5.* ☉ *Mon., Tues., Thurs., and Fri. 9–4; Wed. 9–7:45; Sat. 9–2 and 3:45–5; Sun. all day for services only. Undercroft, Pyx Chamber, Chapter House, and Treasury daily 10:30–4. Closed Sun. except for religious services; Henry VII Chapel closed Sun.*

St. James's and Mayfair

These are two of London's most exclusive neighborhoods, where the homes are fashionable and the shopping is world-class. You can start by walking west from Piccadilly Circus along Piccadilly, a busy street lined with some very English shops (including Hatchards, the booksellers; Swaine, Adeney Brigg, the equestrian outfitters; and Fortnum & Mason, the department store that supplies the Queen's groceries).

㉔ Apsley House. Once known, quite simply, as No. 1, London, this was long celebrated as the best address in town. Built by Robert Adam in the 1770s, this was where the Duke of Wellington lived from the 1820s until his death in 1852. It has been kept as the Iron Duke liked it, his uniforms and weapons, his porcelain and plate, and his extensive art collection, displayed heroically in opulent 19th-century rooms. Unmissable, in every sense, is the gigantic Canova statue of a nude (but fig-leafed) Napoléon Bonaparte, Wellington's archenemy. ⊠ *149 Piccadilly,* ☎ *020/7499–5676.* 🖃 *£4.* ☉ *Tues.–Sun. 11–5.*

㊵ BBC Experience. To celebrate its 75th anniversary, the BBC—the folks who brought you all those wonderful Masterpiece Theater TV shows—has just opened the doors of its own in-house museum. There's an audiovisual show, an interactive section—want to try making your own director's cut of a segment of *EastEnders?*—and, of course, a massive gift shop. This museum will probably be deluged by natives for the first few years—conveniently, admission is on a pre-booked and timed system. ⊠ *Broadcasting House, Portland Pl., W1,* ☎ *0870/603–0304, 01222/55771 outside U.K.* 🖃 *Free.* ☉ *Daily 9:30–5:30.*

Bond Street. Divided into two parts, Old and New (though both are some 300 years old), Bond is the classiest shopping street in London, the home of haute couture, with such famous names as Gucci, Hermès, and Chanel, and costly jewelry from such shops as Asprey, Tiffany, and Cartier.

⑳ Burlington Arcade. This perfectly picturesque covered walkway dates from 1819. Here, shops sell cashmere sweaters, silk scarves, handmade chocolates, and leather-bound books. If not the choice shopping spot it once was, it still makes a great photo-op, particularly if you can snap the uniformed beadle (he ensures that no one runs, whistles, or sings here) on duty. ⊠ *Off Piccadilly.*

㉑ Museum of Mankind. Behind the Royal Academy, this magnificently florid Victorian edifice contains the British Museum's ethnographic collection (though this will soon be transferred to the British Museum when the British Library moves to its new premises in St. Pancras). There are displays on the South Seas, the Arctic, and other regions of the world. ✉ *6 Burlington Gardens,* ☎ *020/7323–8043.* 🎟 *Free.* ☉ *Mon.–Sat. 10–5, Sun. 2:30–6.*

⑲ Royal Academy of Arts. On the north side of Piccadilly, the grand marble pile of **Burlington House** contains the offices of many learned societies and the headquarters of the Royal Academy. The RA, as it is generally known, stages major visiting art exhibitions. Once most famous for its Summer Exhibition (May–Aug.)—a chaotic hodgepodge of works by living and mostly conservative British artists—the RA has now adopted an impressive schedule of temporary art exhibitions that ranks among the most prestigious and cutting-edge in the country; inquire about current calendar of events. ✉ *Burlington House,* ☎ *020/7 439–7438 or 020/7439–4996 (recorded information).* 🎟 *Admission varies according to exhibition.* ☉ *Daily 10–6.*

❼ St. James's Palace. This historic abode has for centuries been a useful royal address and, today, it still is, as it is the current residence of the future King Charles III (if the current Prince of Wales makes it to Westminster Abbey). Although the earliest parts of the lovely brick building date from the 1530s, it had a relatively short career as the center of royal affairs—from the destruction of Whitehall Palace in 1698 until 1837, when Victoria became queen and moved the royal household down the road to Buckingham Palace. Today, the Palace is closed to the public, but your viewfinder will love the picturesque exterior and regimental guard on duty. ✉ *Friary Court, Pall Mall.*

㉒ Wallace Collection. A palatial town house museum, the Wallace is important, exciting, under-visited—and free. As at the Frick Collection in New York, the setting here, Hertford House, is part of the show—built for the Duke of Manchester, and now stuffed with armor, exquisite furniture, and great paintings, including Bouchers, Watteaus, and Fragonard's *The Swing.* Don't forget to smile back at Frans Hals's *Laughing Cavalier* in the Big Gallery. ✉ *Hertford House, Manchester Sq.,* ☎ *020/7935–0687.* 🎟 *Free.* ☉ *Mon.–Sat. 10–5, Sun. 2–5.*

Hyde Park, Kensington, and Beyond

When in need of elbow room, Londoners head for their green "lungs"—Hyde Park and Kensington Gardens. Viewed by natives as their own private backyards, they form an open swath across central London. In and around them are some of London's most noted museums and monuments.

㉙ Albert Memorial. This florid monument of the 19th century commemorates Queen Victoria's much-loved husband, Prince Albert, who died in 1861 at the age of 42. The monument, itself the epitome of high Victorian taste, commemorates the many socially uplifting projects of the prince, among them the Great Exhibition of 1851, whose catalog he is holding. The Memorial, which has been badly eroded by pollution, is currently being restored. It's directly opposite the Royal Albert Hall. ✉ *Kensington Gore.*

㉘ Cheyne Walk. The most beautiful spot in Chelsea—one of London's most arty (and expensive) residential districts—this Thamesside street is adorned with Queen Anne houses and legendary addresses. Author George Eliot died at No. 4 in 1880; Pre-Raphaelite artist Dante Gabriel

Rossetti lived at No. 16. Two other resident artists were James Mc-
Neill Whistler and J.M.W. Turner.

㉓ Hyde Park. Along with the smaller St. James's and Green Parks to the
east, Hyde Park started as Henry VIII's hunting grounds. Nowadays,
it remains a tranquil oasis from urban London—-tranquil, that is, except for Sunday morning, when the soapbox orators take over **Speakers' Corner,** near the northeast corner of the park. Not far away, along
the south side of the park, is **Rotten Row.** It was Henry VIII's royal
path to the hunt—hence the name, a corruption of *route du roi*. It's
still used by the Household Cavalry, the queen's guard. You can see
them leave, in full regalia, plumed helmets and all, at around 10:30,
or await the return of the exhausted ex-guard about noon. ⊠ *Bounded
by the Ring, Bayswater Rd., Park La., and Knightsbridge.*

㉛ Kensington Gardens. More formal than neighboring Hyde Park, Kensington Gardens was first laid out as palace grounds and adjoins Kensington Palace (☞ *below*). George Frampton's 1912 **Peter Pan,** a
bronze of the boy who lived on an island in the Serpentine and never
grew up, overlooks the Long Water. His creator, J. M. Barrie, lived at
100 Bayswater Road, not 500 yards from here. At the **Round Pond,**
you can feed the swans. Nearby is boating and swimming in the **Serpentine,** an S-shape lake. Refreshments can be had at the lakeside tearooms. The **Serpentine Gallery** (☎ 020/7402–6075) holds noteworthy
exhibitions of modern art. ⊠ *Bounded by The Broad Walk, Bayswater Rd., the Ring, and Kensington Rd.*

㉜ Kensington Palace. This has been a royal home since the late 17th century. From the outside it looks less like a palace than a country house,
which it was until William III bought it in 1689. Queen Victoria spent
a less-than-happy childhood at Kensington Palace, Princess Diana a
less-than-happy marriage. Called the "royal ghetto," the palace is
home to many Windsors (they live in a distant section cordoned off to
the public). Kensington Palace's state apartments have been restored
to how they were in Princess Victoria's day. Drop in on the Orangery
here for a very elegant cup of tea. ⊠ *Kensington Gardens,* ☎ *020/7
937–9561.* 🎟 *£5.50.* ☉ *May–Dec., daily 10–3:30.*

㉚ Linley Sambourne House. Stuffed with Victorian and Edwardian antiques,
fabrics, and paintings, this is one of the most charming 19th-century
London houses extant—little wonder it was filmed for Merchant/Ivory's
A Room with A View. During the 1870s this was home to the political
cartoonist Edward Linley Sambourne. ⊠ *18 Stafford Terr.,* ☎ *020/8
994–1019.* 🎟 *£3.* ☉ *Mar.–Oct., Wed. 10–4, Sun. 2–5.*

㉖ Natural History Museum. Housed in an ornate late-Victorian building
with striking modern additions, this museum features displays on such
topics as human biology and evolution, designed to challenge visitors
to think for themselves. ⊠ *Cromwell Rd.,* ☎ *020/7938–9123; 0142/
692–7654 (recorded information).* 🎟 *£6; free weekdays 4:30–5:50
and weekends 5–5:50.* ☉ *Mon.–Sat. 10–6, Sun. 2:30–6.*

㉝ Portobello Road. North of Kensington Gardens is the lively **Notting
Hill** district, full of restaurants and cafés where some of London's most
stylish, trendsetting people gather. The best-known attraction in this
area is Portobello Road, where the lively antiques and bric-a-brac
market is held each Saturday (arrive at 6 AM for the best finds); the
southern end is focused on antiques, the northern end on food, flowers, and secondhand clothes. The street is also full of regular antiques
shops that are open most weekdays. ⊠ *Pembridge Rd., Notting Hill
Gate.*☉ *Antiques market Sat. 6–4.*

㉕ **Science Museum.** The leading national collection of science and technology, this museum has extensive hands-on exhibits on outer space, astronomy, and hundreds of other subjects. ⊠ *Exhibition Rd.,* ☎ *020/7938–8000.* ⌨ *£5.95.* ⊘ *Mon.–Sat. 10–6, Sun. 11–6.*

★ **㉗** **Victoria & Albert Museum.** The V&A, as it is commonly known, originated during the 19th century as a museum of the decorative arts and has extensive collections of costumes, paintings, jewelry, and crafts from every part of the globe. Don't miss the sculpture court, the vintage couture collections, and the great Raphael Room. ⊠ *Cromwell Rd.,* ☎ *020/7938–8500.* ⌨ *£5; free after 4:30, except Wed.* ⊘ *Mon. noon–5:50, Tues.–Sun. 10–5:50; Wed. Late View 4:30–9:30.*

Covent Garden

The Covent Garden district—which lies just to the east of Soho—has gone from a down-at-heels area to one of the busiest, most raffishly enjoyable parts of the city. Continental-style open-air cafés create a very un-English atmosphere, with vintage fashion boutiques, art galleries, and street buskers attracting crowds.

㊱ **Covent Garden.** You could easily spend several hours exploring the block of streets north of the Strand known as Covent Garden. The heart of the area is a former wholesale fruit and vegetable market—made famous as one of Eliza Doolittle's haunts in *My Fair Lady*—established in 1656. **The Piazza,** the Victorian Market Building, is now a vibrant shopping center, with numerous boutiques, crafts shops, and cafés. On the south side of the market building is the **Jubilee market,** with crafts and clothing stalls. The section is anchored by **St. Paul's Church** (☞ *below*) and the **Royal Opera House** (now undergoing extensive renovations; ☞ *below*). For interesting specialty shops, head north of the Market Building. Shops on **Long Acre** sell maps, art books and materials, and clothing; shops on **Neal Street** sell clothes, pottery, jewelry, tea, housewares, and goods from East Asia. ⊠ *Bounded by the Strand, Charing Cross Rd., Long Acre, and Drury La.*

㊴ **Royal Opera House.** Until 2001, the home of the Royal Ballet and the Royal Opera Company will be closed for extensive renovations. These legendary resident troupes will be performing elsewhere (☞ The Arts, *below*). ⊠ *Bow St.*

㊲ **St. Paul's Church.** A landmark of the Covent Garden market area, this 1633 church, designed by Inigo Jones, is known as the Actors' Church. Inside are numerous memorials to theater people. Look for the open-air entertainers performing under the church's portico. ⊠ *Bedford St.*

㊳ **Theatre Museum.** A comprehensive collection of material on the history of the English theater, this museum traces the history not merely of the classic drama but also of opera, music hall, pantomime, and musical comedy. A highlight is the re-creation of a dressing room filled with memorabilia of former stars. ⊠ *Russell St.,* ☎ *020/7836–7891.* ⌨ *£3.50.* ⊘ *Tues.–Sun. 11–7.*

Bloomsbury

Bloomsbury is a semiresidential district to the north of Covent Garden that contains some spacious and elegant 17th- and 18th-century squares. It could be called the intellectual center of London, as both the British Museum and the University of London are here. The area also gave its name to the Bloomsbury Group, a clique of writers and painters who thrived here during the early 20th century.

★ ④ **British Museum.** Known as "Mankind's attic," this fabled museum houses a vast and priceless collection of treasures, including Egyptian, Greek, and Roman antiquities; Renaissance jewelry; pottery; coins; glass; and drawings from virtually every European school since the 15th century. It's best to pick out one section that particularly interests you—to try to see everything would be an overwhelming and exhausting task. Some of the highlights are the **Elgin Marbles,** sculptures that formerly decorated the Parthenon in Athens; the **Rosetta Stone,** which helped archaeologists to interpret Egyptian hieroglyphs; and a copy of the **Magna Carta,** the charter signed by King John in 1215 to which is ascribed the origins of English liberty. ⊠ *Great Russell St.,* ☎ *020/7636–1555; 020/7580–1788 (recorded information).* ☞ *Free.* ☉ *Mon.–Sat. 10–5, Sun. 2:30–6.*

★ ④ **Sir John Soane's Museum.** On the border of London's legal district, this museum, stuffed with antique busts and myriad decorative delights, is an eccentric, smile-inducing 19th-century collection of art and artifacts in the former home of the architect of the Bank of England. ⊠ *13 Lincoln's Inn Fields,* ☎ *020/7405–2107.* ☞ *Free.* ☉ *Tues.–Sat. 10–5.*

The City and South Bank

The City, the commercial center of London, was actually once the site of the great Roman city of Londinium. Since those days, the City has been rebuilt innumerable times and, today, ancient and modern jostle each other elbow to elbow. Several of London's most famous attractions are here, along with the adjacent South Bank area, where Shakespeare's Globe has the starring role.

④ **Barbican Centre.** A vast arts center built by the City of London, the Barbican takes its name from the watchtower that stood here during the Middle Ages. The arts center contains a concert hall, where the London Symphony Orchestra is based, two theaters, an art gallery, a cinema, and several restaurants. The theaters are the London home of the **Royal Shakespeare Company.** ⊠ *Silk St.,* ☎ *020/7638–4141, 020/7 628–0183 tour reservations, 020/7628–3351 RSC backstage tour.* ☞ *Barbican Centre free, gallery £5, conservatory £1.* ☉ *Barbican Centre Mon.–Sat. 9 AM–11 PM, Sun. noon–11; gallery Mon.–Sat. 10–7:30, Sun. noon–7:30; conservatory weekends noon–5:30 when not in use for private function (call first).*

④ **Museum of London.** At **London Wall,** so called because it follows the line of the wall that surrounded the Roman settlement, the Museum of London enables you to get the history of London sorted out—although there's a great deal to sort out: Oliver Cromwell's death mask, Queen Victoria's crinolined gowns, Selfridge's Art-Deco elevator lifts, and the Lord Mayor's Coach are just some of the goodies here. ⊠ *London Wall,* ☎ *020/7600–3699.* ☞ *Free 4:30–5:50.* ☉ *Tues.–Sat. 10–6, Sun. noon–6.*

④ **St. Mary-le-Bow.** This church was rebuilt by Christopher Wren after the Great Fire; it was built again after being bombed during World War II. It is said that to be a true Cockney, you must be born within the sound of Bow bells. The church is a landmark of the **Cheapside** district. This was the marketplace of medieval London (the word *ceap* is Old English for "to barter"), as the street names hereabouts indicate: Milk Street, Ironmonger Lane, and so on. Despite rebuilding, many of the streets still run on the medieval pattern. ⊠ *Cheapside.*

★ ④ **St. Paul's Cathedral.** London's symbolic heart, St. Paul's is Sir Christopher Wren's masterpiece. Its dome—the world's third largest—can be seen from many an angle in other parts of the city. The cathedral was completed in 1710 following the Great Fire. Wren was the architect who was also responsible for designing 50 City parish churches to replace those lost in that disaster. Fittingly, he is buried in the crypt under a simple Latin epitaph, composed by his son, which translates as: "Reader, if you seek his monument, look around you." The cathedral has been the site of many famous state occasions, including the funeral of Winston Churchill in 1965 and the ill-fated marriage of the prince and princess of Wales in 1981. In the ambulatory (the area behind the high altar) is the American Chapel, a memorial to the 28,000 U.S. servicemen and women stationed in Britain during World War II who lost their lives while on active service. The greatest architectural glory of the cathedral is the dome. This consists of three distinct elements: an outer, timber-frame dome covered with lead; an interior dome built of brick and decorated with frescoes of the life of St. Paul by the 18th-century artist Sir James Thornhill; and, in between, a brick cone that supports and strengthens both. There is a good view of the church from the **Whispering Gallery,** high up in the inner dome. The gallery is so called because of its remarkable acoustics, whereby words spoken on one side can be clearly heard on the other, 107 ft away. Above this gallery are two others, both external, from which there are fine views over the City and beyond. ✉ *St. Paul's Churchyard, Paternoster Sq.,* ☎ *020/7 236–4128.* ☼ *Cathedral open for visits Mon.–Sat. 8:30–4:30; ambulatory, crypt, and galleries open Mon.–Sat. 9:30–4:15.*

★ ❹❼ **Shakespeare's Globe.** This spectacular theater is a replica of Shakespeare's open-roof Globe Playhouse (built in 1599; incinerated in 1613), where most of the playwright's great plays premiered. It stands 200 yards from the original, overlooking the Thames. It has been built with the use of authentic Elizabethan materials, down to the first thatch roof in London since the Great Fire. Plays are presented in natural light (and sometimes rain), to 1,000 people on wooden benches in the "bays," plus 500 "groundlings," standing on a carpet of filbert shells and clinker, just as they did nearly 4 centuries ago. The theater season is only from June through September; throughout the year, you can tour the Globe through admission to the **museum** devoted to Shakespeare and his times on the premises. ✉ *New Globe Walk, Bankside (South Bank),* ☎ *020/7928–6406.* ✉ *£5 to museum.* ☼ *Daily 10–5. Call for performance schedule.*

★ ❹❽ **Tower of London.** A guaranteed spine-chiller, this is one of London's most famous sights and one of its most crowded, too. Come as early in the day as possible and head for the Crown Jewels so you can see them before the crowds arrive. The tower served the monarchs of medieval England as both fortress and palace. Every British sovereign from William the Conqueror in the 11th century to Henry VIII in the 16th lived here, and it remains a royal palace, in name at least. The White Tower is the oldest and also the most conspicuous building in the entire complex. Inside, the Chapel of St. John is one of the few unaltered parts. The Royal Armories, England's national collection of arms and armor, occupies the rest of the White Tower.

The **History Gallery,** south of the White Tower, is a walk-through display designed to answer questions about the inhabitants of the tower and its evolution over the centuries. Among other buildings worth seeing is the **Bloody Tower.** The little princes in the tower—the boy-king Edward V and his brother Richard, duke of York, supposedly murdered on the orders of the duke of Gloucester, later crowned Richard III—certainly lived in the Bloody Tower, and may well have died here, too. In the **Wakefield Tower,** Henry VI is alleged to have been murdered in 1471 during England's medieval civil war, the Wars of the Roses. It was a rare honor to be beheaded in private inside the tower; most people were executed outside, on **Tower Hill,** where the rabble could get a much better view.

The **Crown Jewels** are a breathtakingly splendid collection of regalia, precious stones, gold, and silver. The Royal Scepter contains the largest cut diamond in the world. The Imperial State Crown, made for the 1838 coronation of Queen Victoria, contains some 3,000 precious stones, largely diamonds and pearls. The Jewels are housed in the Duke of Wellington's Barracks. Look for the ravens whose presence at the tower is traditional. It is said that if they leave, the tower will fall and England will lose her greatness. ⊠ *Tower Hill,* ☎ *020/7709–0765.* ☜ *£8.50; small additional admission charge to Fusiliers Museum only.* ☉ *Mar.–Oct., Mon.–Sat. 9:30–6:30, Sun. 2–6; Nov.–Feb., Mon.–Sat. 9:30–5. Yeoman Warder guides conduct tours daily from Middle Tower, no charge, but a tip is always appreciated. Subject to weather and availability of guides, tours are conducted about every 30 mins until 3:30 in summer, 2:30 in winter.*

Hampstead

Hampstead is a village within the city, where many famous poets and writers have lived. Today it is a fashionable residential area, with a main shopping street and some rows of elegant 18th-century houses. The heath is one of London's largest and most attractive open spaces.

㉞ Abbey Road Studios. Here, outside the legendary Abbey Road Studios (the facility is closed to the public), is the most famous zebra crossing in the world. Immortalized on the cover of the Beatles' *Abbey Road* album of 1969, this pedestrian crosswalk is a spot beloved to countless Beatlemaniacs and baby boomers, many of whom venture here to leave their signature on the white stucco fence that fronts the adjacent studio facility. Abbey Road is not in Hampstead but in adjacent St. John's Wood, an elegant residential suburb a 10-minute ride on the tube from central London. ⊠ *3 Abbey Rd.*

㉟ Kenwood House. Standing alone in its own landscaped grounds on the north side of the heath is Kenwood House, built during the 17th century and remodeled by Robert Adam at the end of the 18th century. The house contains a collection of superb paintings by such masters as Rembrandt, Turner, Reynolds, Van Dyck, and Gainsborough—and *The Guitar Player,* probably the most beautiful Vermeer in England. Unfortunately, only one grand Adam interior remains. The lovely landscaped grounds provide the setting for symphony concerts in summer. ⊠ *Hampstead La.,* ☎ *020/8348–1286.* ☜ *Free.* ☉ *Easter–Sept., daily 10–6; Oct.–Easter, daily 10–4.*

Greenwich

The historical and maritime attractions at Greenwich, on the Thames, some 8 km (5 mi) east of central London, make it an ideal destination for a day out. You can get to Greenwich by riverboat from Westminster and Tower Bridge piers, by ThamesLine's high-speed river buses, or by train from Charing Cross station. You can also take the Docklands Light Railway from Tower Gateway to Island Gardens and walk a short distance along a pedestrian tunnel under the river.

Cutty Sark. Now in dry dock is the glorious 19th-century clipper ship *Cutty Sark.* ⊠ *King William Walk,* ☎ *020/8858–3445.* ☜ *£3.50.* ☉ *Late-Mar.–Sept., Mon.–Sat. 10–6, Sun. noon–6; Sept.–late-Mar., Mon.–Sat. 10–5, Sun. noon–5.*

National Maritime Museum. A treasure house of paintings, maps, models, and, best of all, ships from all ages, this is a fascinating museum. Don't miss the ornate royal barges. ⊠ *Romney Rd.,* ☎ *020/8858–4422.* ⊠ *£5.* ⊙ *Mon.–Sat. 10–6, Sun. noon–6.*

Old Royal Observatory. Stand astride both hemispheres in the courtyard of the Old Royal Observatory, where the prime meridian—zero degrees longitude—is set. The Observatory is at the top of the hill, behind the National Maritime Museum and Royal Naval College, in **Greenwich Park,** originally a royal hunting ground and today an attractive open space. The Observatory, founded in 1675, has original telescopes and other astronomical instruments on display. ⊠ *Greenwich Park,* ☎ *020/8858–4422.* ⊙ *Mon.–Sat. 10–6, Sun. noon–6.*

DINING

RATINGS

Prices quoted here are per person and include a first course, a main course, and dessert, but not wine or service.

CATEGORY	COST
$$$$	OVER £50
$$$	£35–£50
$$	£25–£35
$	UNDER £25

Bloomsbury

$$ ✕ **Chez Gerard.** This purveyor of steak-*frites* (with french fries) and similarly simple Gallic offerings is reliable, relaxed, and usefully located near Oxford Street. ⊠ *8 Charlotte St.,* ☎ *020/7636–4975. AE, DC, MC, V. Tube: Goodge St.*

$$ ✕ **Museum Street Café.** Convenient for British Museum lunches, and worth a special trip in the evening, the Mediterranean-tinged home cooking (spinach-and-olive tart; char-grilled leg of lamb; Valrhona chocolate cake), and minimalist white-wall decor in this little place are satisfying. ⊠ *47 Museum St.,* ☎ *020/7405–3211. Reservations essential. MC, V. Closed weekends. Tube: Holborn.*

Chelsea

$$$$ ✕ **La Tante Claire.** One of London's best restaurants, La Tante Claire
★ is justly famous for Pierre Koffmann's superb haute cuisine: hot foie gras on shredded potatoes with a sweet wine and shallot sauce or his famous signature dish of pig's trotter stuffed with sweetbreads and wild mushrooms. The set-price lunch is a relative bargain. ⊠ *68 Royal Hospital Rd.,* ☎ *020/7352–6045. Reservations essential 3 wks in advance. AE, DC, MC, V. Closed weekends, 2 wks at Christmas, 10 days at Easter, and 3 wks in Aug.–Sept. Tube: Sloane Sq.*

$$$–$$$$ ✕ **Aubergine.** A table at Aubergine (warning: there are only 14) has
★ been London's toughest reservation to score for almost as long as it's been open, because soccer star-turned-chef Gordon Ramsay has every table gasping in awe at his famous witty cappuccino of white beans with sautéed girolles and truffles, followed by—well, anything at all. Reserve months ahead; go for lunch (£24) if money is an object. ⊠ *11 Park Walk, SW10,* ☎ *020/7352–3449. Reservations essential. AE, DC, MC, V. Closed Sun. No lunch Sat. Tube: South Kensington.*

$$$ ✕ **Chutney Mary.** London's only Anglo-Indian restaurant provides a fantasy version of the British Raj, with colonial cocktails and authentic re-creations of comforting, rich dishes, such as Country Captain (chicken with almonds, raisins, chilis, and spices). ⊠ *535 King's Rd.,* ☎ *020/7351–3113. AE, DC, MC, V. Tube: Fulham Broadway.*

$$ ✕ **Bluebird.** Here's Terence Conran's latest "gastrodome"—supermarket, brasserie, fruit stand, butcher shop, boutique, and café-restaurant, all housed in a snappy King's Road former garage. Go for the synergy and visual excitement—Conran's chefs share a tendency to promise more than they deliver. ✉ *350 King's Rd., SW3,* ☎ *020/7559–1000. Reservations essential. AE, DC, MC, V. Tube: Sloane Sq.*

The City

$$$ ✕ **St. John.** Resembling a stark monks' refectory crossed with an art gallery, this modern British innovator has equally uncompromising menus. Some loathe bone marrow and parsley salad, huge servings of braised pheasant with "black cabbage," or deviled crab, or organ meats any which way, with English puddings and Malmsey wine to follow, but newspaper journalists and swank architects love it. ✉ *26 St John St.,* ☎ *020/7251–0848. Reservations essential. No dinner Sun. Tube: Farringdon.*

Covent Garden

$$$ ✕ **The Ivy.** The epitome of style without pretentiousness, this restau-
★ rant beguiles everybody, including media, literary, and theatrical movers and shakers. The menu's got it all—fish-and-chips, sausage-and-mash, squid-ink risotto, bang-bang chicken, sticky toffee pudding—and all are good. ✉ *1 West St.,* ☎ *020/7836–4751. Reservations essential. AE, DC, MC, V. Tube: Covent Garden.*

$$$ ✕ **Rules.** This is probably the city's most beautiful restaurant—daffodil
★ yellow 19th-century walls, Victorian oil paintings, and hundreds of framed engravings make up the history-rich setting—and certainly one of the oldest (it has been here since 1798). Rules is traditional from soup to nuts, or rather, from venison and Dover sole to trifle and Stilton. There's the odd nod to newer cuisines, but the clientele of expense-accounters and tourists in search of olde London Towne remains. Note there are three floors to this place, with the most opulent salons on the first floor. ✉ *35 Maiden La.,* ☎ *020/7836–5314. AE, DC, MC, V. Tube: Covent Garden.*

$$ ✕ **Christopher's.** It's a palatially good-looking slice of überurban USA, with a vaguely famous face at the neighboring table. Great shrimp, Maryland crab cakes, and steaks, of course. ✉ *18 Wellington St.,* ☎ *020/7 240–4222. AE, DC, MC, V. Tube: Covent Garden.*

$–$$ ✕ **Joe Allen.** This basement restaurant behind the Strand Palace Hotel
★ follows the style of its New York counterpart, is descended on by packs of theatrical types after curtain, and is forever noisy. The menu, too, is straight from the Manhattan parent—Caesar salad, barbecue ribs with black-eyed peas and wilted greens, brownies with ice cream—and it's open late. ✉ *13 Exeter St.,* ☎ *020/7836–0651. Reservations essential. No credit cards. Tube: Covent Garden.*

$ ✕ **Food for Thought.** This is a simple downstairs vegetarian restaurant, with seats for only 50. The menu—stir-fries, casseroles, salads, and dessert—changes daily, and each dish is freshly made. No alcohol is served. ✉ *31 Neal St.,* ☎ *020/7836–0239. Reservations not accepted. No credit cards. Closed 2 wks at Christmas. Tube: Covent Garden.*

Kensington

$$$$ ✕ **Bibendum.** Upstairs in the renovated 1911 Michelin building, this
★ dining extravaganza continues to entice with a menu as Gallic and gorgeous as ever. From the scallops in citrus sauce to the passion-fruit *bavarois* (Bavarian cream), all the dishes are unpretentious but admirably done. The separate Oyster Bar, downstairs, is another way to go. ✉ *81 Fulham Rd.,* ☎ *020/7581–5817. Reservations essential. MC, V. Closed Sun. Tube: South Kensington.*

$$ ★ ✕ **Wódka.** This modern Polish restaurant in a quiet back street serves stylish food to a fashionable group and often has the relaxed atmosphere of a dinner party. Try herring blinis, roast duck with figs and port, and the several flavored vodkas. ⊠ *12 St. Albans Grove,* ☎ *020/7 937–6513. Reservations essential. AE, DC, MC, V. No lunch weekends. Tube: Kensington High St.*

Knightsbridge

$$$ ★ ✕ **Zafferano.** Princess Margaret, Eric Clapton, Joan Collins (she asked that the lights be turned down), and any number stylish folk have flocked to this Belgravia place, London's best exponent of *cucina nuova.* The fireworks are in the kitchen, not in the brick-wall-and-saffron-hued decor, but *what* fireworks: pumpkin ravioli with a splash of Amaretto, *mondeghini ai crostini di risotto* (minced pork wrapped in Savoy cabbage leaves), and monkfish with walnuts. Be sure to book early: even Al Pacino was turned away one night. ⊠ *15 Lowndes St., SW1,* ☎ *020/7 235–5800. Reservations essential. AE, MC, V. Tube: Knightsbridge.*

$–$$ ✕ **The Enterprise.** One of the new luxury breed of gastro-pubs, this is perhaps the chicest of the lot—near Harrods and Brompton Cross, it's filled with decorative types. The menu isn't overly pretty—char-grilled squid stuffed with almonds, entrecôte steak, salmon with artichoke hearts—but the ambience certainly is. ⊠ *35 Walton St., SW3,* ☎ *020/7 584–3148. AE, MC, V. No lunch weekends. Tube: South Kensington.*

$ ✕ **Stockpot.** Speedy service is the mark of this large, jolly restaurant full of students and shoppers. The food is filling and wholesome; try the homemade soups, the Lancashire hot pot, and the apple crumble. Breakfast is also served Monday–Saturday. ⊠ *6 Basil St.,* ☎ *020/7589– 8627. No credit cards. Tube: Knightsbridge.*

Mayfair

$$$$ ★ ✕ **Oak Room.** Bad boy Marco Pierre White enjoys Jagger-like fame from his TV appearances and gossip column reports of his complicated love life and random eruptions of fury. He should stick to his pans, say superchef critics, meaning it literally in some cases. But, hype aside, Marco may be London's greatest chef and now gets to show off in his most spectacular setting yet—all belle epoque soaring ceilings and gilded bits, and palms and paintings. ⊠ *Le Meridien, 21 Piccadilly W1,* ☎ *020/7 734–8000. Reservations essential. Jacket and tie. AE, DC, MC, V. Tube: Piccadilly Circus.*

$$$ ✕ **Criterion.** A spectacular neo-Byzantine palace of gold mosaic, Christo-size turquoise drapes, and white tablecloths, the Criterion is under the aegis of Marco Pierre White, the bigmouthed, bigheaded wunderchef now at the helm of several of London's best restaurants. and features his style of haute-bistro French food: a rich, black squid-ink risotto; intricate assemblies of fish, and delicate salads. ⊠ *Piccadilly Circus,* ☎ *020/7930–0488. AE, DC, MC, V. Tube: Piccadilly Circus.*

$–$$ ✕ **Villandry.** This foodie's paradise just moved to huge new premises— the food hall here is now even larger than the one at Harrods! French pâtés, Continental cheeses, fruit tarts, biscuits, and breads galore are for sale, and if you must indulge but can't wait to take a bite, there's a tearoom café and dining room that both serve exquisite lunches. Twice a month, dinners are offered, but they are among the hardest reservations to book in London. ⊠ *170 Great Portland St., W1,* ☎ *020/7631– 3131. AE, MC, V. Tube: Great Portland St.*

Notting Hill

$$$ ✕ **Clarke's.** There's no choice of dishes at dinner (and only a limited choice at lunch); chef Sally Clarke plans the meal according to what is freshest and best in the market each day. Her style is natural and unfussy West Coast cuisine. ⊠ *124 Kensington Church St.,* ☎ *020/7221–*

9225. *Reservations essential. MC, V. Closed weekends and 2 wks in Aug. Tube: Notting Hill Gate.*

$$$ ✕ **Kensington Place.** Trendy and loud, this ever-popular place features enormous plate-glass windows through which to be seen, and plenty of fashionable food. Try the foie gras with sweet-corn pancake, the rack of lamb, and the baked tamarillo with vanilla ice cream. ✉ *201 Kensington Church St.,* ☎ *020/7727–3184. MC, V. Tube: Notting Hill Gate.*

$$ ✕ **The Cow.** Slightly tucked away in the backwaters of trendy Portobello-land, this is the nicest of a trio of foodie pubs that feed the neighborhood arty hipsters and media stars. The Cow is the child of Tom Conran, son of Sir Terence (who owns half of London's restaurants). It pretends to be a pub in County Derry, serving oysters, crab salad, and other seafood with the beer, and heartier food in the cozy restaurant upstairs. ✉ *89 Westbourne Park Rd.,* ☎ *020/7221–0021. Reservations essential. MC, V. No dinner Sun. Tube: Westbourne Park.*

$$ ✕ **Pharmacy.** London's latest scene-arena, the Pharmacy looks just like its namesake, its wait staff is garbed like hospital orderlies, and even its menu looks fab—but then Damien Hirst, artist extraordinaire, is involved. The menu highlights "comfort food" and ranges from fisherman's pie to spit-roast Landes duck, sauce aigre-doux. Don't you dare leave the bar without ordering a "Cough Syrup." ✉ *150 Notting Hill Gate, W11,* ☎ *020/7221–2442. Reservations essential. AE, MC, V. Tube: Notting Hill Gate.*

$ ✕ **Tootsies.** A useful burger joint characterized by loudish rock and vintage advertisements on the walls, Tootsies serves some of London's better burgers, as well as chili, chicken, BLTs, taco salad, apple pie, fudge cake, and ice cream. There are five other branches. ✉ *120 Holland Park Ave.,* ☎ *020/7229–8567. Reservations not accepted. MC, V. Tube: Holland Park.*

St. James's

$$$$ ✕ **The Ritz.** This Louis XVI marble, gilt, and trompe l'oeil treasure, with its view over Green Park, is known as London's most magnificent dining room. The latest chef retains the French accent and ingredients as rich as the decor, and also offers British specialties. Prix-fixe menus make the check more bearable, but the wine list is pricey. ✉ *Piccadilly,* ☎ *020/7493–8181. Jacket and tie. Reservations essential. AE, DC, MC, V. Tube: Green Park.*

$$$ ✕ **Le Caprice.** Fabulously dark and glamorous, with its black walls and
★ stark white tablecloths, Caprice is a perennial that does nothing wrong, from its kind, efficient, nonpartisan (famous folk eat here often) service to its pan-European menu (salmon fish cake with sorrel sauce; confit of goose with prunes). ✉ *Arlington House, Arlington St.,* ☎ *020/7 629–2239. Reservations essential. AE, DC, MC, V. No lunch Sat. Tube: Green Park.*

Soho

$–$$$ ✕ **Mezzo.** Sir Terence Conran's 700-seater Mezzo isn't only London's biggest; it's the most gigantic restaurant in all of Europe—you could decant most of Soho inside its three levels. Downstairs is Mezzo, where the soaring, glass-walled kitchen abuts a bustling ocean liner of a dining room; here, the food is French-ish, with the usual Conran seafood platters, and there's a nifty jazz trio and dance floor. Upstairs, the "Mezzonine" and bar are informal, and less expensive. Finally, a separate café stays open till the wee hours. ✉ *100 Wardour St.,* ☎ *020/7314–4000. AE, DC, MC, V. Tube: Leicester Sq.*

$ ✕ **Crank's.** This restaurant belongs to a popular vegetarian chain that has weathered the storms of food fashion since the '60s, thanks to a certain worthiness of menu—mixed salads and thick soups; dense, grainy breads; and sugarless cakes. It is self-service, and many branches, though not this one, close at 8 PM. ✉ *8 Marshall St.,* ☎ *020/7437–9431. Reservations not accepted. AE, DC, MC, V. Closed Sun. Tube: Leicester Sq.*

South Bank

\$\$–\$\$\$
★ ✕ **OXO Tower Brasserie and Restaurant.** London finally has a room with a view, and *such* a view. On the eighth floor of the beautifully re-vived OXO Tower Wharf building, near the South Bank Centre, this elegant space has Euro food with this year's trendy ingredients (acorn-fed black pig charcuterie with tomato and pear chutney is one exam-ple). The ceiling slats turn and change from white to midnight blue, but who notices, with St. Paul's dazzling you across the water? ✉ *Bank-side, SE1,* ☎ *020/7803–3888. AE, MC, V. Tube: Waterloo.*

NIGHTLIFE AND THE ARTS

The Arts

For a list of events in the London arts scene, visit a newsstand or book-store to pick up the weekly magazine *Time Out.* The city's evening paper, the *Evening Standard,* carries listings, as do the major Sunday papers; the daily *Independent* and *Guardian;* and, on Friday, *The Times.* The London Tourist Board's *Visitor Call* service (calls cost 49p/min.; ☎ 0891/505440 for what's on this week) also offers listings for theater and other arts events.

BALLET

When its massive renovation program is complete, the Royal Opera House may once again host the **Royal Ballet.** Until 2000, however, the ballet will be performing at the Labatt's Apollo Hammersmith (☎ 020/7304–4000) and the Royal Festival Hall in the South Bank Arts Com-plex (☎ 020/7928–8800): check with the box office of the Royal Opera House (☎ 020/7304–4000) for complete information. The prices are slightly more reasonable than for the opera, but be sure to book well ahead. The **English National Ballet** and visiting companies perform at the Coliseum (☎ 020/7632–8300) but that theater, too, is scheduled for a renovation program lasting several seasons, and resident troupes will be performing elsewhere (call the Coliseum Box Office for further information). **Sadler's Wells Theatre** (☎ 020/7713–6000) hosts regional ballet and international modern dance troupes. Prices here are reasonable.

CONCERTS

Ticket prices for symphony orchestra concerts are still relatively mod-erate—between £5 and £25, although you can expect to pay more to hear big-name artists on tour. If you can't book in advance, arrive half an hour before the performance for a chance at returns.

The London Symphony Orchestra is in residence at the **Barbican Arts Centre** (☎ 020/7638–8891), although other top symphony and cham-ber orchestras also perform here. The **South Bank arts complex** (☎ 020/7928–8800), which includes the **Royal Festival Hall** and the **Queen Elizabeth Hall,** is another major venue for choral, symphonic, and chamber concerts. For less expensive concert going, try the **Royal Albert Hall** (☎ 020/7589–8212) during the summer Promenade sea-son; special tickets for standing room are available at the hall on the night of performance. Note, too, that the concerts have begun to be jumbo-screen broadcast in Hyde Park, but even here a seat on the grass requires a paid ticket. Call 020/7589–82122 for further information. **The Wigmore Hall** (☎ 020/7935–2141) is a small auditorium, ideal for recitals. Inexpensive lunchtime concerts take place all over the city in smaller halls and churches, often featuring string quartets, vocalists, jazz ensembles, and gospel choirs. **St. John's, Smith Square** (☎ 020/7 222–1061), a converted Queen Anne church, is one of the more popular venues. It has a handy crypt cafeteria.

FILM

Most West End cinemas are in the area around Leicester Square and Piccadilly Circus. Tickets average £7.50. Matinees and Monday evenings are cheaper. Cinema clubs screen a wide range of films: classics, Continental, underground, rare, or underestimated masterpieces. A temporary membership fee is usually about £1. One of the best cinema clubs is the **National Film Theatre** (☎ 020/7928–3232), part of the South Bank arts complex.

OPERA

The **Royal Opera House** (☎ 020/7304–4000) ranks alongside the New York Met. It's one of the grandest sights in London, but, unfortunately, as of June 1997, the theater closed for a massive rebuilding program that is scheduled to last another year or two. The resident opera company will be performing at other venues during this period. For the 1998–99 season, most productions should be concentrated in the newly refurbished Sadler's Wells Theatre (☎ 020/7713–6000). For ongoing information check with the box office. The **Coliseum** (☎ 020/7632–8300) is the home of the English National Opera Company; productions are staged in English and are often innovative and exciting. The ticket price range is about £8 to £45. Call the box office for the latest information, as the Coliseum is also scheduled for a major renovation.

THEATER

London's theater life can more or less be divided into three categories: the government-subsidized national companies; the commercial, or "West End," theaters; and the fringe. The **Royal National Theatre Company** (NT) shares the laurels as the top national repertory troupe with the Royal Shakespeare Company. In similar fashion to the latter troupe, the NT presents a variety of plays by writers of all nationalities, ranging from the classics of Shakespeare and his contemporaries to specially commissioned modern works. The NT is based at the South Bank arts complex (box office: ☎ 020/7928–2252). The **Royal Shakespeare Company** (RSC) is based at the Barbican Arts Centre (box office: ☎ 020/7 638–8891). At press time (spring 1998), the RSC announced it had terminated its summer season in London. That's a pity for summer visitors, but they can always book tickets at the spectacular new reconstruction of the famed Elizabethan-era **Globe Theatre** (box office: ☎ 020/7928–6406) on the South Bank, which only offers open-air, late-afternoon performances from June through September.

The **West End theaters** largely stage musicals, comedies, whodunits, and revivals of lighter plays of the 19th and 20th centuries, often starring television celebrities. Occasionally there are more serious productions, including successful productions transferred from the subsidized theaters, such as RSC's *Les Liaisons Dangereuses* and *Les Misérables*. The two dozen or so established **fringe theaters,** scattered around central London and the immediate outskirts, frequently present some of London's most intriguing productions, if you're prepared to overlook occasional rough staging and uncomfortable seating.

Most theaters have an evening performance at 7:30 or 8 daily, except Sunday, and a matinee twice a week (Wednesday or Thursday, and Saturday). Expect to pay from £10 for a seat in the upper balcony and at least £25 for a good seat in the stalls (orchestra) or dress circle (mezzanine)—more for musicals. Tickets may be booked in person at the theater box office; over the phone by credit card; or through ticket agents, such as **First Call** (☎ 020/7497–7941) or **Ticketmaster** (☎ 020/7 344–0055 or 800/775–2525 from the United States). In addition the **SOLT Kiosk** in Leicester Square sells half-price tickets on the day of performance for about 25 theaters; there is a small service charge. Beware of scalpers!

Nightlife

London's night spots are legion; here are some of the best known. For up-to-the-minute listings, buy *Time Out* magazine.

CABARET

The best comedy in town can be found in the big, bright, new-look **Comedy Store** (✉ Haymarket House, Oxendon St., near Piccadilly Circus, ☎ 01426/914433). **Madame Jo Jo's** (✉ 8 Brewer St., ☎ 020/7 287–1414) is possibly the most fun of any London cabaret, with its outrageous, glittering drag shows. The place is luxurious and civilized.

JAZZ CLUBS

Blue Note (✉ 1 Hoxton Sq., ☎ 020/7729–8440), in an out-of-the-way warehouse on the northern edge of the City (the nearest tube is Old Street), is a cool jazz and world-beat club/restaurant that attracts a young crowd. **Ronnie Scott's** (✉ 47 Frith St., ☎ 020/7439–0747) is the legendary Soho jazz club where international performers regularly take the stage.

NIGHTCLUBS

Hanover Grand (✉ 6 Hanover Sq., ☎ 020/7499–7977) is a swank and opulent big West End club, which attracts TV stars and footballers whose exploits here you can later read about in the tabloids. The "Haute Couture" one-nighter takes over on Friday, while Saturday's glam disco "Malibu Stacey" pulls in all those who want to be seen. The lines outside get long, so dress up to impress the bouncers. **Ministry of Sound** (✉ 103 Gaunt St., ☎ 020/7378–6528) is more of an industry than a club, with its own record label, line of apparel, and, of course, DJs. Inside, there are chill-out rooms, dance floors, promotional Sony Playstations, Absolut shot bars—all the club kid's favorite things. If you are one, and you only have time for one night out, make it here. Glitzy **Stringfellows** (✉ 16–19 Upper St. Martin's La., ☎ 020/7240– 5534) has an art deco upstairs restaurant, mirrored walls, and a dazzling light show in the downstairs dance floor.

ROCK

The Forum (✉ 9–17 Highgate Rd., Kentish Town, ☎ 020/7284– 2200), a little out of the way, is a premier venue for medium-to-big acts. **100 Club** (✉ 100 Oxford St., W1, ☎ 020/7636–0933) is a basement dive that's always been there for R&B, rock, jazz, and beer. **The Shepherds Bush Empire** (✉ Shepherds Bush Green, W12, ☎ 020/8740– 7474) is a major venue for largish acts in West London.

SHOPPING

Shopping is one of London's great pleasures. Different areas retain their traditional specialties, but there are also numerous pockets of local shops to explore, and it's fun to seek out the small crafts, antiques, and gift stores, designer-clothing resale outlets, and national department-store chains.

Shopping Districts

Chelsea. Centering on the King's Road, Chelsea was once synonymous with ultrafashion; it still harbors some designer boutiques, plus antiques and home furnishings stores.

Covent Garden. A something-for-everyone neighborhood, Covent Garden has numerous clothing chain stores, stalls selling crafts, and shops selling gifts of every type—bikes, kites, herbs, beads, hats, you name it.

Kensington. This area's main drag, Kensington High Street, is a smaller, classier version of Oxford Street (☞ *below*), with Barkers department store, and a branch of Marks & Spencer at the eastern end. Try Kensington Church Street for expensive antiques, plus a little fashion.

Knightsbridge. Kensington's neighbor, Knightsbridge has Harrods, of course, but also Harvey Nichols, the chicest clothes stop in London, and many expensive designers' boutiques along Sloane Street, Walton Street, and Beauchamp Place.

Mayfair. Bond Street, Old and New, is the elegant lure here, with the hautest of haute couture and jewelry outposts, plus fine art. South Molton Street offers high-price, high-style fashion—especially at Browns— and the tailors of Savile Row are of worldwide repute.

Oxford Street. Crowded and a bit past its prime, Oxford Street is lined with tawdry discount shops. However, Selfridges, John Lewis, and Marks & Spencer are wonderful department stores, and there are interesting boutiques secreted off Oxford Street, just north of the Bond Street tube stop, in little St. Christopher's Place and Gees Court.

Regent Street. Perpendicular to Oxford Street lies this noted shopping avenue—famous for its curving path—with possibly London's most pleasant department store, Liberty's, as well as Hamley's, the capital's toy mecca. Shops around once-famous **Carnaby Street** stock designer youth paraphernalia and at least 57 varieties of T-shirts.

St. James's. The fabled English gentleman buys much of his gear at stores in this area: handmade hats, shirts, and shoes, silver shaving kits, and hip flasks. Here is also the world's best cheese shop, Paxton & Whitfield. Don't expect any bargains in this neighborhood.

Street Markets

Street markets are one aspect of London life not to be missed. Here are some of the more interesting markets:

Bermondsey. Arrive as early as possible for the best treasure—that's what the dealers do. ⊠ *Tower Bridge Rd., SE1.* ⊙ *Fri. 4AM–1 PM. Tube to London Bridge or Bus 15 or 25 to Aldgate and then Bus 42 over Tower Bridge to Bermondsey Sq.*

Camden Lock. The youth center of the world, apparently, it's good for cheap clothes and boots. The canalside antiques, crafts, and junk markets are also picturesque and very crowded. ⊠ *Chalk Farm Rd., NW1.* ⊙ *Shops: Tues.–Sun. 9:30–5:30; stalls: weekends 8–6. Tube or Bus 24 or 29 to Camden Town.*

Camden Passage. The rows of little antiques stalls are a good hunting ground for silverware and jewelry. Stalls open Wednesday and Saturday, but there is also a books and prints market on Thursday. Surrounding shops are open the rest of the week. ⊠ *Islington, N1.* ⊙ *Wed., Sat. 8:30–3. Tube or Bus 19 or 38 to Angel.*

Petticoat Lane. Look for budget-priced leather goods, gaudy knitwear, and fashions, plus cameras, videos, stereos, antiques, books, and bric-a-brac. ⊠ *Middlesex St., E1.* ⊙ *Sun. 9–2. Tube to Liverpool St., Aldgate, or Aldgate East.*

Portobello Market. Saturday is the best day for antiques, though this neighborhood is London's melting pot, becoming more vibrant every year. Find fabulous small shops, the city's trendiest restaurants, and a

Friday and Saturday flea market at the far end. ✉ *Portobello Rd., W11.*
⊘ *Fri. 5 AM–3 PM, Sat. 6 AM–5 PM. Tube or Bus 52 to Notting Hill
Gate or Ladbroke Grove, or Bus 15 to Kensington Park Rd.*

LONDON ESSENTIALS
Arriving and Departing
BY BUS

The **National Express** (✉ Victoria Coach Station, Buckingham Palace
Rd., ☎ 0990/808080) coach service has routes to more than 1,200 major
towns and cities in the United Kingdom. It's considerably cheaper
than the train, although the trips usually take longer. National Express
offers two types of service: ordinary service makes frequent stops for
refreshment breaks (although all coaches have toilet and washroom
facilities and reclining seats); Rapide and Flightlink service has stew-
ardess and refreshment facilities on board. Day returns are available
on both, but booking is advised on the Rapide service.

BY PLANE

International flights to London arrive at either Heathrow Airport, 24
km (15 mi) west of London, or at Gatwick Airport, 43 km (27 mi) south
of the capital. Most flights from the United States go to Heathrow.
Gatwick is London's second gateway. It has grown from a European
airport into an airport that serves 21 scheduled U.S. destinations. A
third, new, state-of-the-art airport, Stansted, is to the east of the city.
It handles mainly European and domestic traffic, although there is a
scheduled service from New York.

Carriers serving Great Britain include **American Airlines** (☎ 800/433–
7300, ☎ 020/8572–5555 in London) to Heathrow, Gatwick; **British
Airways** (☎ 800/247–9297, ☎ 0345/222111 in London) to Heathrow,
Gatwick; **Continental** (☎ 800/231–0856, ☎ 0800/776464 in London)
to Gatwick; **Delta** (☎ 800/241–4141, ☎ 0800/414767 in London) to
Heathrow, Gatwick; **Northwest Airlines** (☎ 800/447–4747, ☎ 0990/
561000 in London) to Gatwick; **United** (☎ 800/241–6522, ☎ 0845/
8444777 in London) to Heathrow; **TWA** (☎ 800/892–4141, ☎ 020/8
814–0707 or 01293/535535 in London) to Gatwick; and **Virgin Atlantic** (☎ 800/862–8621, ☎ 01293/747747 in London) to Heathrow,
Gatwick.

Between the Airport and Downtown. The Piccadilly Line serves
Heathrow (all terminals) with a direct Underground (subway) link. Two
special buses also serve Heathrow: Airbus A1 leaves every 30 minutes
for west and central London and Victoria Station; Airbus A2 goes to
west and north London to Euston and King's Cross Station every 30
minutes. The new Heathrow Express train links the airport with
Paddington station in only 15 minutes.

From Gatwick the quickest way to London is the nonstop rail Gatwick
Express, costing (at press time) £9.50 one-way and taking 30 minutes
to reach Victoria Station. Trains run every 15 minutes from 5:20 AM
to 12:50 AM, then hourly 1:35 AM–4:35 AM. Hourly bus service (6:30
AM to 10 PM) is provided by Flightlink 777 to Victoria Coach Station.
This takes about 90 minutes and costs £7.50 one-way.

Cars and taxis drive into London from Heathrow on M4; the trip can
take more than an hour, depending on traffic. The taxi fare is about
£40, plus tip. From Gatwick the taxi fare is at least £80, plus tip; traffic can be very heavy.

London is served by no fewer than 15 main-line train stations, so be absolutely certain of the station for your departure or arrival. All have Underground stops either in the train station or within a few minutes' walk from it, and most are served by several bus routes. The principal routes that connect London to other major towns and cities are on an InterCity network. Seats can be reserved by phone only with a credit card. You can, of course, apply in person to any British Rail Travel Centre or directly to the station from which you depart.

Fares. The fare structures are slowly changing as the formerly nationalized British Rail is sold off to various independent operators. Generally speaking, it is less expensive to buy a return (round-trip) ticket, especially for day trips not far from London, and you should always inquire at the information office to find out what discount fares are available for your route. You can hear a recorded summary of timetable and fare information to many destinations by calling the appropriate "dial and listen" numbers listed under British Rail in the telephone book. For travel inquiries call 0345/484950.

Below is a list of the major London rail stations and the areas they serve. One central telephone line gets you through to any of the stations: ☎ 0345/484950.

Charing Cross serves southeast England, including Canterbury, Margate, Dover/Folkestone, and ferry ports.

Euston/St. Pancras serves East Anglia, Essex, the Northeast, the Northwest, and North Wales, including Coventry, Stratford-upon-Avon, Birmingham, Manchester, Liverpool, Windermere, Glasgow, and Inverness, northwest Scotland.

King's Cross serves the east Midlands; the Northeast, including York, Leeds, and Newcastle; and north and east Scotland, including Edinburgh and Aberdeen.

Liverpool Street serves Essex and East Anglia.

Paddington serves the south Midlands, west and south Wales, and the west country, including Oxford.

Victoria serves southern England, including Gatwick Airport, Brighton, Dover/Folkestone and ferry ports, and the south coast.

Waterloo serves the southwestern United Kingdom, including Salisbury, Portsmouth, Southampton, and Isle of Wight.

Waterloo International is for the Eurostar to Europe.

Via the Channel Tunnel. If you're combining a trip to Great Britain with stops on the Continent, you can either drive your car onto a Le Shuttle train through the Channel Tunnel (35 minutes from Folkestone to Calais), or book a seat on the Eurostar high-speed train service that zips through the tunnel (3 hours from London's Waterloo International Station to Paris, 3¼ hours from London to Brussels).

Getting Around

London's bus system consists of bright red double- and single-deckers, plus other buses of various colors. Destinations are displayed on the front and back, with the bus number on the front, back, and side. Not all buses run the full length of their route at all times. Some buses are still operated with a conductor whom you pay after finding a seat, but these days you will more often find one-person buses, in which you pay the driver upon boarding.

Buses stop only at clearly indicated stops. Main stops—at which the bus should stop automatically—have a plain white background with a red LT symbol on it. There are also request stops with red signs, a white symbol, and the word REQUEST added; at these you must hail the bus to make it stop. Smoking is not allowed on any bus. Although you can see much of the town from a bus, *don't* take one if you want to get anywhere in a hurry; traffic often slows travel to a crawl, and during peak times you may find yourself waiting at least 20 minutes for a bus and not being able to get on it once it arrives. If you intend to go by bus, ask at a Travel Information Centre for a free bus map.

Fares. Single fares start at 60p for short hops (90p in the central zone). Travelcards (☞ By Underground, *below*) are good for tube, bus, and British Rail trains in the Greater London Zones. There are also a number of bus passes available for daily, weekly, and monthly use, and prices vary according to zones. A photograph is required for weekly or monthly bus passes.

BY CAR

The best advice is to avoid driving in London because of the ancient street patterns and the chronic parking restrictions. One-way streets also add to the confusion.

BY TAXI

London's black taxis are famous for their comfort and for the ability of their drivers to remember the mazelike pattern of the capital's streets. Hotels and main tourist areas have ranks (stands) where you wait your turn to take one of the taxis that drive up. You can also hail a taxi if the flag is up or the yellow FOR HIRE sign is lighted. Fares start at £1.40 and increase by units of 20p per 281 yards or 55.5 seconds until the fare exceeds £8.60. After that, it's 20p for each 188 yards or 37 seconds. Surcharges are a tricky extra, which range from 40p for additional passengers or bulky luggage to 60p for evenings 8 PM until midnight, and until 6 AM on weekends and public holidays—at Christmas it zooms to £2 and there's 40p extra for each additional passenger. Note that fares are occasionally raised from year to year. As for tipping, taxi drivers should get 10%–15% of the tab.

BY UNDERGROUND

Known as "the tube," London's extensive Underground system is by far the most widely used form of city transportation. Trains run both beneath and above ground out into the suburbs, and all stations are clearly marked with the London Underground circular symbol. (A SUBWAY sign refers to an under-the-street crossing.) Trains are all one class; smoking is *not* allowed on board or in the stations.

There are 10 basic lines—all named. The Central, District, Northern, Metropolitan, and Piccadilly lines all have branches, usually taking you to the outlying sections of the city, so be sure to note which branch is needed for your particular destination. Electronic platform signs tell you the final stop and route of the next train, and some signs conveniently indicate how many minutes you'll have to wait for the train to arrive. Begun in the Victorian era, the Underground is still being expanded and improved. The East London line, which runs from Shoreditch and Whitechapel south to New Cross, is due to reopen after major reconstruction in 1998. September 1998 is the latest date for the opening of the Jubilee line extension: This state-of-the-art subway sweeps from Green Park to Southwark, with connections to Canary Wharf and the Docklands and the much hyped Millennium Experience megadome, and on to the east at Stratford.

From Monday through Saturday, trains begin running just after 5 AM; the last services leave central London between midnight and 12:30 AM. On Sunday trains start two hours later and finish about an hour earlier. The frequency of trains depends on the route and the time of day, but normally you should not have to wait more than 10 minutes. A pocket map of the entire tube network is available free from most Underground ticket counters. There should also be a large map on the wall of each platform, and the new computerized database, "Routes," is available at 14 London Transport (LT) Travel Information Centres (☞ *below*).

Fares. For both buses and tube fares, London is divided into six concentric zones; the fare goes up the farther afield you travel. Ask at Underground ticket counters for the LT booklet "Fares and Tickets," which gives all details; after some experimenting you'll soon know which ticket best serves your particular needs. You must buy a ticket before you travel; many types of travel cards can be bought from Pass Agents that display the sign: tobacconists, confectioners, newsagents, and National Railway stations.

Here is a summary of the major ticket categories, but note that these prices are subject to increases. Children (5–10) are usually half price.

Carnet. A convenient book of 10 single tickets to use in central zone 1 only; £10.

Singles and Returns. For one trip between any two stations, you can buy an ordinary single (one-way ticket) for travel anytime on the day of issue; if you're coming back on the same route the same day, then an ordinary return (round-trip ticket) costs twice the single fare. Singles vary in price from 60p for short hops (90p in the central zone) to £3.30 for a six-zone journey—not a good option for the sightseer who wants to make several journeys.

Travelcards. These allow unrestricted travel on the tube, most buses, and British Rail trains in the Greater London zones and are valid weekdays after 9:30 AM, weekends, and all public holidays. They cannot be used on airbuses, night buses, or for certain special services. There are different options available: a **One Day Travelcard** costs £3.50–£4.30; **Weekend Travelcards**, for the two days of the weekend and on any two consecutive days during public holidays, £5.20–£6.40. **Family Travelcards:** one-day ticket for one or two adults with one to four children costs £2.80–£3.40 with one child; extra children cost 60p each—adults do not have to be related to the children or even to each other!

Visitor's Travelcard. These are the best bet for visitors, but they must be bought before leaving home (they're available in both the United States and Canada). They are valid for periods of three, four, or seven days ($25, $32, $49 respectively) and can be used on the tube and virtually all buses and British Rail services in London. All these cards also include a set of money-saving discounts to many of London's top attractions. Apply to travel agents or to **BritRail Travel International** (✉ 1500 Broadway, New York, NY 10036, ☎ 212/382–3737).

For more information there are **LT Travel Information Centres** at the following tube stations: Euston, Hammersmith, King's Cross, Oxford Circus, Piccadilly Circus, St. James's Park, Victoria, and Heathrow (in Terminals 1, 2, and 4); open 7:15 AM–10 PM, with Terminal 4's TIC closing at 3 PM. For information on all London tube and bus times, fares, and so on, dial 020/7222–1234 (24 hours). For travelers with disabilities get the free leaflet, "Access to the Underground," ☎ 020/7918–3312.

Money Matters
CURRENCY

The British unit of currency is the pound sterling, divided into 100 pence (p). Bills are issued in denominations of 5, 10, 20, and 50 pounds (£). Coins are £1, £2, 50p, 20p, 10p, 5p, 2p, and 1p; the 10p and 5p are the size of a quarter and a dime, respectively. Scottish banks issue Scottish currency, of which all coins and notes—with the exception of the £1 notes—are accepted in England. At press time (spring 1998) the pound stood at approximately £.61 to the U.S dollar, £.42 to the Canadian dollar, £.39 to the Australian dollar, and £.33 to the New Zealand dollar.

Traveler's checks are widely accepted in Britain, and many banks, hotels, and shops offer currency-exchange facilities. You will have to pay a £2 commission fee wherever you change them; banks offer the best rates, yet even these fees vary. If you are changing currency, you will have to pay (on top of commission) based on the amount you are changing. In London and other big cities, *bureaux de change* abound, but it definitely pays to shop around: they charge a flat fee and it's often a great deal more than that at other establishments, such as banks. American Express foreign exchange desks do not charge a commission fee on AmEx traveler's checks. Credit cards are universally accepted, too. The most commonly used are MasterCard and Visa.

Telephoning
COUNTRY CODE

When you're dialing overseas, the United Kingdom's country code is 44. When dialing a number in Britain from abroad, drop the initial 0 from the local area code.

Contacts and Resources
EMBASSIES

U.S. Embassy (✉ 24 Grosvenor Sq., W1A 1AE, ☎ 020/7499–9000).

Canadian High Commission (✉ McDonald House, 1 Grosvenor Sq., W1X 0AB, ☎ 020/7258–6600).

EMERGENCIES

Police, fire brigade, or ambulance: ☎ 999. **Late-night pharmacies: Bliss Chemist,** (✉ 5 Marble Arch, W1, ☎ 020/7723–6116) and **Boots** (✉ 44 Piccadilly Circus, W1, ☎ 020/7734–6126; ✉ 151 Oxford St., W1, ☎ 020/7409–2857).

GUIDED TOURS

By Bus. The **Original London Sightseeing Tour** (☎ 020/8877–1722) offers passengers a good introduction to the city from double-decker buses. Tours run daily every 12 minutes or so, departing from Baker Street (Madame Tussaud's), Marble Arch (Speakers' Corner), Piccadilly (Haymarket), or Victoria (Victoria Street). The 21 stops include most of the major sights, such as St. Paul's and Westminster Abbey, and you may hop off to view the sights and then get back on the next bus. Tickets (£12) can be bought from the driver. **The Big Bus Company** (☎ 020/8 944–7810) runs a similar operation with a Red and Blue tour. The Red is a two-hour tour with 18 stops, and the Blue, one hour with 13. Both start from Marble Arch, Speakers' Corner. These tours include stops at such places as St. Paul's Cathedral and Westminster Abbey. Prices and pickup points vary according to the sights visited, but many pickup points are at major hotels. **Evan Evans** (☎ 020/8332–2222) offers good bus tours. Another reputable agency that operates bus tours is **Frames Rickards** (☎ 020/7837–3111).

By Canal. In summer narrow boats and barges cruise London's two canals, the Grand Union and Regent's Canal; most vessels operate on the latter, which runs between Little Venice in the west (the nearest tube is Warwick Ave. on the Bakerloo Line) and Camden Lock (about 200 yards north of Camden Town tube station). **Canal Cruises** (☎ 020/7 485–4433) offers three or four cruises daily from March through October on the *Jenny Wren* and all year on the cruising restaurant *My Fair Lady*. **Jason's Trip** (☎ 020/7286–3428) operates one-way and round-trip narrow-boat cruises on this route. Trips last 1½ hours. The **London Waterbus Company** (☎ 020/7482–2660) operates this route year-round with a stop at London Zoo: trips run daily from April through October, and weekends only from November through March.

By River. All year boats cruise up and down the Thames, offering a different view of the London skyline. In summer (Apr.–Oct.) boats run more frequently than in winter—call to check schedules and routes. For trips from Charing Cross to Greenwich Pier, call **Catamaran Cruisers** (☎ 020/7839–3572) or **Westminster Passenger Boat Services** (☎ 020/7930–4097). **City Cruises** (☎ 020/7488–0344) go from Westminster to the Tower and the Thames Barrier, by **Thames Barrier Cruises** (☎ 020/7930–3373). A **Sail and Rail** ticket combines the modern wonders of Canary Wharf and Docklands development by Docklands Light Railway with the history of the riverside by boat. Tickets are available year-round from Westminster Pier or Tower Gateway (☎ 020/7363–9700). Upstream destinations include Kew, Richmond, and Hampton Court. Most of the launches have a public-address system and provide a running commentary on passing points of interest. Depending upon the destination, river trips may last from one to four hours. For more information call **Tidal Cruises** (☎ 020/7928–9009).

Excursions. LT, Evan Evans, and Frames Rickards (☞ By Bus, *above*) all offer day excursions (some combine bus and boat) to places of interest within easy reach of London, such as Windsor, Hampton Court, Oxford, Stratford-upon-Avon, and Bath. Prices vary and may include lunch and admission prices or admission only. Alternatively, make your own way, cheaply, to many of England's attractions on **Green Line Coaches** (☎ 020/8668–7261).

On Foot. One of the best ways to get to know London is on foot, and there are many guided and themed walking tours from which to choose. **The Original London Walks** (☎ 020/7624–3978), and **City Walks** (☎ 020/7700–6931) are just two of the better-known firms, but your best bet is to peruse the variety of leaflets at a London Tourist Information Centre. The duration of the walks varies (usually one–three hours), and you can generally find one to suit even the most specific of interests—Shakespeare's London, or a Beatles's Magical Mystery Tour, or, even—gasp!—a Jack the Ripper tour.

If you'd rather explore on your own, then the City of London Corporation has laid out a **Heritage Walk** that leads through Bank, Leadenhall, and Monument; follow the trail by the directional stars set into the sidewalks. A map of this walk can be found in *A Visitor's Guide to the City of London,* available from the City Information Centre across from St. Paul's Cathedral. The **Silver Jubilee Walkway** covers 16 km (10 mi) and is marked by a series of silver crowns set into the sidewalks; Parliament Square makes a good starting point. **The Thames Path** is a new National Trail, some 291 km (180 mi) from the river's source in Gloucestershire to the Thames Barrier; for information, call London Docklands Visitor Centre (☎ 020/7512–1111). Several guides offering further walks are available in bookshops. One of the latest and most fascinating is *Secret London* by Andrew Duncan (New Holland).

American Express (✉ 6 Haymarket, SW1, ☎ 020/7930–4411; ✉ 89 Mount St., W1, ☎ 020/7499–4436). **Thomas Cook** (✉ 4 Henrietta St., WC2, ☎ 020/7379–0685; ✉ 1 Marble Arch, W1, ☎ 020/7724–9483).

London Tourist Information Centre (✉ Victoria Station Forecourt). **British Travel Centre** (✉ 12 Regent St., Piccadilly Circus, SW1).

Visitorcall is the London Tourist Board's 24-hour phone service—a premium-rate (39p–49p per minute) recorded information line, with different numbers for theater, events, museums, sports, getting around, and so on. To access the list of options call 0839/123456, or see the separate categories in the telephone directory.

14 Lucerne

As you cruise down the leisurely sprawl of the Vierwaldstättersee, mist rising off the gray waves, mountains—great loaflike masses of forest and stone—looming above the clouds, it's easy to understand how Wagner could have composed his Siegfried Idyll in his mansion beside this lake. This is inspiring terrain, romantic and evocative. When the waters roil up you can hear the whistling chromatics and cymbal clashes of Gioacchino Rossini's thunderstorm from his 1829 opera, Guillaume Tell. It was on this lake, after all, that William Tell—the beloved, if legendary, Swiss national hero—supposedly leapt from the tyrant Gessler's boat to freedom. And it was in a meadow nearby that three furtive rebels and their cohorts swore an oath by firelight and planted the seed of the Swiss Confederation.

EXPLORING LUZERN

Numbers in the margin correspond to points of interest on the Lucerne map.

Luzern's Old Town straddles the waters of the River Reuss where it flows out of the Vierwaldstättersee, its more concentrated section occupying the river's right bank. There are a couple of passes available for discounts for museums and sights in the city. One is a museum pass that costs 25 SF and grants free entry to all museums for one month. If you are staying in a hotel, you may also want to pick up a special visitor's card; once stamped by the hotel, it entitles you to discounts at most museums and other tourist-oriented businesses as well. You can get both passes at the tourist office (*see* Luzern Essentials, *below*).

Altes Rathaus (Old Town Hall). This relic facing the end of a modern bridge, the Rathaus-Steg, was built between 1599 and 1606 in the late-Renaissance style. ✉ *Rathausquai, facing the end of bridge, Rathaus-Steg.*

❶ Am Rhyn-Haus (Am Rhyn House). Also known as the Picasso Museum, the compact Renaissance-style building has an impressive collection of late paintings by Picasso. ✉ *Furreng. 21,* ☎ *041/4101773.* 💶 *6 SF.* ☉ *Apr.–Oct., daily 10–6; Nov.–Mar., daily 11–1 and 2–4.*

❽ Bourbaki-Panorama. An enormous conical wooden structure was created in 1876–1878 as a genuine, step-right-up tourist attraction. Its conical roof covers a sweeping, wraparound epic painting of the French Army of the East retreating into Switzerland at Verrières—a famous episode in the Franco-Prussian War. It is closed for renovations until mid-1999. ✉ *Löwenpl.,* ☎ *041/4109942.* ☉ *May–Sept., daily 9–6; Mar., Apr., and Oct., daily 9–5.*

❺ Franziskanerkirche (Franciscan Church). More than 700 years old, this church retains its 17th-century choir stalls and carved wooden pulpit despite persistent modernization. ✉ *Franziskanerpl., just off Münzg.*

❿ Gletschergarten (Glacier Garden). The bedrock of this 19th-century tourist attraction was excavated between 1872 and 1875 and has been dramatically pocked and polished by Ice Age glaciers. A private museum on the site displays impressive relief maps of Switzerland. ✉ *Denkmalstr. 4,* ☎ *041/4104340.* 💶 *7 SF.* ☉ *May–mid-Oct., daily 8–6; Mar., Apr., and mid-Oct.–mid-Nov., daily 9–5; mid-Nov.–Feb., Tues.–Sat. 10:30–4:30, Sun. 10–5.*

❹ Historisches Museum (Historical Museum). Dating from 1567, this building was an armory and today exhibits city sculptures, Swiss arms, and flags; reconstructed rooms depict rural and urban life. ✉ *Pfisterg. 24,* ☎ *041/2285424.* ☉ *Tues.–Fri. 10–noon and 2–5, weekends 10–5.*

⓫ Hofkirche (Collegiate Church). Founded in 750 as a monastery, this Gothic structure was destroyed by fire in 1633 and rebuilt in late-Renaissance style. The 80-rank organ (1650) is one of Switzerland's finest. ✉ *St. Leodegarstr. 13.*

★ **❻ Jesuitenkirche** (Jesuit Church). Constructed in 1667–78, this Baroque edifice reveals a symmetrical entrance flanked by two onion-dome towers, added in 1893. The vast interior, restored to mint condition, is a rococo explosion of gilt, marble, and epic frescoes. ✉ *Banhofstr., just west of Rathaus-Steg.*

★ **❼ Kapellbrücke** (Chapel Bridge). It snakes diagonally across the water and, when first built during the early 14th century, served as the dividing line between the lake and the river. Its shingled roof and grand stone water tower (now housing a souvenir stand) are to Luzern what the Matterhorn is to Zermatt—but considerably more vulnerable, as was proved by a fire in 1993. Almost 80% of this fragile monument was destroyed, including many of the 17th-century paintings inside; the original 111 gable panels painted by Heinrich Wägmann during the 17th century have been replaced with polychrome copies. The paintings depict scenes from the history of Luzern and Switzerland, legendary exploits of the city's patron saints—St. Leodegar and St. Mauritius, and coats of arms of local patrician families. ✉ *Between*

Lucerne (Luzern)

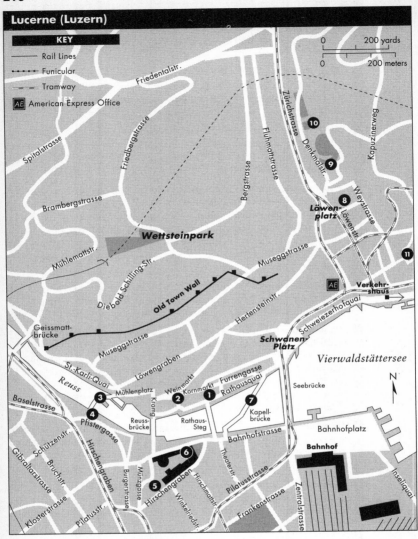

KEY

— Rail Lines

••••• Funicular

⟋⟋ Tramway

⟨AE⟩ American Express Office

0   200 yards

0   200 meters

Friedentalstr.

Friedbergstrasse

Spitalstrasse

Brambergstrasse

Mühlemattstr.

Wettsteinpark

Diebold Schilling-Str.

Bergstrasse

Fluhmattstrasse

Zürichstrasse

Denkmalstr.

Kapuzinerweg

10

9

Weystrasse

Löwen-platz

Löwenstr.

8

11

Museggstrasse

Old Town Wall

Hertensteinstr.

Schweizerhofquai

⟨AE⟩   **Verkehrs-haus**

Geissmatt-brücke

Museggstrasse

Löwengraben

Schwanen-Platz

Seebrücke

Vierwaldstättersee

N

St.-Karli-Quai

Reuss

Baselstrasse

Schützenstr.

Gibraltarstrasse

Klosterstrasse

Pilatusstr.

Bruchstr.

Hirschengraben

Pfistergasse

Mühlenplatz

Kramg.

Reuss-brücke

Rathaus-Steg

Weinmarkt

Kornmarkt

Furrengasse

Rathausquai

3

4

2

1

7

Kapell-brücke

Bahnhofstrasse

6

Münzgasse

Burgerstrasse

Hirschengraben

Hirschmattstr.

5

Winkelriedstr.

Theaterstr.

Pilatusstrasse

Frankenstrasse

Zentralstrasse

Bahnhofplatz

Bahnhof

Inseliquai

Am Rhyn-Haus, **1**

Bourbaki-
Panorama, **8**

Franziskanerkirche, **5**

Gletschergarten, **10**

Historisches
Museum, **4**

Hofkirche, **11**

Jesuitenkirche, **6**

Kapellbrücke, **7**

Löwendenkmal, **9**

Spreuerbrücke, **3**

Weinmarkt, **2**

Seebrücke and Rathaus-Steg bridges, connecting Rathausquai and Bahnhofstr.

★ ❾ **Löwendenkmal** (Lion Monument). The evocative monument commemorates the 760 Swiss guards and their officers who died defending Louis XVI of France at the Tuileries in Paris in 1792. Carved out of a sheer sandstone face by Lucas Ahorn of Konstanz, this 19th-century wonder is a simple image of a dying lion, his chin sagging on his shield, a broken stump of spear in his side. The Latin inscription translates: "To the bravery and fidelity of the Swiss." ⊠ *Denkmalstr.*

❸ **Spreuerbrücke.** This narrow, weathered, all-wood covered bridge dates from 1408. In its center is a lovely 16th century chapel looking back on the Old Town. Its interior gables hold a series of eerie, well-preserved paintings by Kaspar Meglinger of the *Dance of Death*; they date from the 17th century, though their style and inspiration—tracing to the plague that devastated Luzern and all of Europe during the 14th century—are medieval. ⊠ *Between Geissmattbrücke and Reussbrücke bridges, connecting Zeughaus Reuss-Steg and Mühlenpl.*

❷ **Weinmarkt** (Wine Market). One of the loveliest of Luzern's several fountain squares, this former site of the wine market drew visitors from across Europe from the 15th to the 17th century to witness its passion plays. Its Gothic central fountain depicts St. Mauritius, patron saint of warriors, and its surrounding buildings are flamboyantly frescoed in 16th-century style. ⊠ *Sq. just west of Kornmarkt, north of Metzgerrainle.*

Elsewhere in Luzern

★ **Verkehrshaus.** The Swiss Transport Museum is one of Luzern's (if not Switzerland's) greater attractions. Easily reached by steamer, car, or Bus 2, it's almost a world's fair in itself, with a complex of buildings and exhibitions both indoors and out, including dioramas, live demonstrations, an IMAX theater, and a "Swissorama" (360° screen) film about Switzerland. Every mode of transit is discussed, from stagecoaches and bicycles to jumbo jets and space capsules. If you're driving, turn east at the waterfront and follow the signs. ⊠ *Lidostr. 5,* ☎ *041/3704444.* 🎟 *16 SF.* ☉ *Mar.–Oct., daily 9–6; Nov.–Feb., daily 10–5.*

DINING

Because the Swiss are so good at preparing everyone else's dishes, it is sometimes said that they have none of their own, but there definitely is a distinct and characteristic Swiss cuisine. Switzerland produces great cheeses—Gruyère, Emmentaler, Appenzeller, and Vacherin—that form the basis of many dishes. Raclette is cheese melted over a fire and served with potatoes and pickles. Fondue is either a bubbling pot of melted cheeses flavored with garlic and kirsch, into which you dip chunks of bread, or a pot of boiling broth into which you dip various meats. *Rösti* is shredded potato sauteed until golden brown. Other Swiss specialties are *geschnetzeltes Kalbfleisch* (veal bits in cream sauce with mushrooms), Italian-style polenta in the Ticino, and fine game in autumn. A wide variety of Swiss sausages makes for filling, inexpensive meals, and in every region the breads are varied and superb.

Dining options range from luxury establishments to modest cafés, Stübli, and restaurants specializing in local cuisine. In resorts especially, most restaurants are associated with hotels.

MEALTIMES

At home, the main Swiss meal of the day is lunch, followed by a light snack in the evening. Restaurants are open at midday and at night; often limited menus are offered all day. Watch for *Tagesteller* or *Plats du jour* (prix-fixe lunch platters or menus), enabling you to a taste of the best restaurants without paying high à la carte rates.

RATINGS

Prices are per person, including tip and taxes, but not wine and coffee.

CATEGORY	COST
$$$$	over 70 SF
$$$	40 SF–70 SF
$$	20 SF–40 SF
$	under 20 SF

Rooted in the German region of Switzerland and surrounded by farmland, central Switzerland has a native cuisine that's best described as down-home and hearty. Luzern takes pride in its *Kügelipaschtetli*, puff pastry nests filled with tiny veal meatballs, mushrooms, cream sauce, occasionally raisins, and bits of chicken, pork, or sweetbreads. Watch for lake fish such as *Egli* (perch), *Hecht* (pike), *Forelle* (trout), and *Felchen* (whitefish). A Luzern tradition offers them sautéed and sauced with tomatoes, mushrooms, and capers.

$$$$ ✕ **Wilden Mann.** Both dining rooms here—one formal, the other co-
★ zily old-fashioned—are excellent, combining old-style local cooking with French cuisine. The Bürgerstube is all dark beams and family crests, while the Liedertafel dining room has soft candlelight and a vaulted ceiling. In both spots the menus and prices are the same; try the smoked salmon tartare wrapped in Rösti with dill sauce or the duck breast with dandelion honey and balsamic vinegar. ⊠ *Bahnhofstr. 30,* ☎ *041/ 2101666. AE, DC, MC, V.*

$$$ ✕ **Rotes Gatter.** This chic restaurant in the Des Balances hotel has a
★ combination as desirable as it is rare: soigné decor, shimmering river views, and a sophisticated menu with fish dishes such as grilled omble chevalier in vegetable vinaigrette, or the house specialty, fish fondue. There's a more casual, less expensive bistro area as well. ⊠ *Weinmarkt,* ☎ *041/4103010. AE, DC, MC, V.*

$$ ✕ **Galliker.** Step past the ancient facade into an all-wood room roar-
★ ing with local action. Brisk, motherly waitresses serve the dishes Mutti used to make: Fresh *Kutteln* (tripe) in rich white wine sauce with cumin seeds; real *Kalbskopf* (chopped fresh veal head) served with heaps of green onions and warm vinaigrette; and their famous simmered-beef pot-au-feu. ⊠ *Schützenstr. 1,* ☎ *041/2401002. AE, DC, MC, V. Closed Sun., Mon., and 3 weeks in Aug.*

$$ ✕ **Rebstock/Hofstube.** Across from the Hofkirche, this kitchen offers modern, international fare, including rabbit, lamb, and organic vegetarian specialties. The lively bentwood brasserie hums with locals lunching by the bar, while the more formal, old-style restaurant glows with wood and brass under a low-beamed herringbone-patterned ceiling. ⊠ *St. Leodegarpl. 3,* ☎ *041/4103581. AE, DC, MC, V.*

$ ✕ **Pfistern.** One of the architectural focal points of the Old Town waterfront, this floridly decorated former guildhall offers a good selection of moderately priced meals in addition to higher-priced standards. Lake fish and *pastetli* (meat pies made with puff pastry) are good local options. ⊠ *Kornmarkt 4,* ☎ *041/4103650. AE, DC, MC, V.*

NIGHTLIFE AND THE ARTS

For information on its concerts and other performances throughout the year, consult the *Luzern City Guide* published by the city seasonally; it's available at the tourist office (☞ Luzern Essentials, *below*).

The Arts

The Allgemeine Musikgesellschaft Luzern (AML), the local orchestra in residence, offers a season of concerts from October through June. These are held in the **Kunsthaus** (⊠ Frohburgstr. 6, ☎ 041/2103880). Luzern hosts the **International Music Festival** for three weeks in August every year. Performances take place at the Kunsthaus (☎ 041/ 233880). For more information, contact Internationale Musikfestwochen (⊠ Postfach, CH-6002, Luzern, ☎ 041/2103562).

Nightlife

BARS AND LOUNGES

Château Gütsch (⊠ Kanonenstr., ☎ 041/2494141) draws a sedate dinner-and-dancing crowd. The **National Hotel** (⊠ Haldenstr. 4, ☎ 041/ 4190909) serves drinks in both its glossy American-style bar and its imposing lobby lounge. The **Palace Hotel** (⊠ Haldenstr. 10, ☎ 041/ 4100404) has two American-style bars.

CASINO

The most sophisticated nightlife in Luzern is found in the **Casino** (⊠ Haldenstr. 6, ☎ 041/4185656), a turn-of-the-century building on the northern shore by the grand hotels. You can play boule in the Gambling Room (5 SF limit, federally imposed), dance in the **Vegas** club, or have a Swiss meal in **Le Chalet** while watching a folklore display.

FOLKLORE

Nightboat (⊠ Landungsbrücke 6, ☎ 041/3194978) sails nightly May through September at 8:45, offering drinks, meals, and a folklore show. The **Stadtkeller** (⊠ Sternenpl. 3, ☎ 041/4104733) transports you to the Valais Alps for cheese, yodeling, and dirndled dancers.

SHOPPING

Luzern no longer produces embroidery or lace, but you can find Swiss crafts of the highest quality, and watches in all price categories. **Bucherer** (⊠ Schwanenpl., ☎ 041/3697700) represents Piaget and Rolex.

Gübelin (⊠ Schweizerhofquai, ☎ 041/4105142) is the exclusive source for Audemars Piguet, Patek Philippe, and its own house brand. **Ordning & Reda** (⊠ Hertensteinstr. 3, ☎ 041/4109506) is a Swedish stationer whose store is filled with brightly colored, handmade, recycled paper products. At **Sturzenegger** (⊠ Schwanenpl. 7, ☎ 041/4101958), you'll find St.-Gallen-made linens and embroidered niceties.

LUZERN ESSENTIALS

Arriving and Departing

BY CAR

It's easy to reach Luzern from Zürich by road, approaching from the national expressway N3 south, connecting to the N4 via the secondary E41, in the direction of Zug, and continuing on N4 to the city (roads are well-marked). Approaching from the southern St. Gotthard Pass route, or after cutting through the Furka Pass by rail ferry, you'll descend below Andermatt to Altdorf, where a view-stifling tunnel sweeps you through to the shores of the lake and on to the city. Arriving from Basel in the northwest, it's a clean sweep on the N2 into Luzern.

BY PLANE

The nearest international airport is **Kloten** in Zürich (⊠ 54 km/33 mi northeast of Luzern, ☎ 1571060). Swissair flies in most often from the United States and the United Kingdom. Easy rail connections, departing hourly, whisk you on to Luzern within 50 minutes.

BY TRAIN

Luzern functions as a rail crossroads, with express trains connecting hourly from Zürich and every two hours from Geneva, the latter with a change at Bern. For rail information, call the **Swiss Federal Railways** (☎ 1572222).

Getting Around

Luzern's modest scale allows you to explore most of the city easily on foot, but you will want to resort to mass transit to visit such far-flung attractions as the Verkehrshaus (Swiss Transport Museum).

BY BOAT

It's a crime to see this city and the surrounding mountainous region only from the shore; some of its most impressive landscapes can be seen from the deck of one of the cruise ships that ply the Vierwaldstättersee (Lake Luzern). The boats of the Schiffahrtsgesellschaft des Vierwaldstättersees (☎ 041/3676767) operate on a standardized, mass-transit-style schedule, crisscrossing the lake and stopping at scenic resorts and historic sites. The Swiss Pass entitles you to free rides; the Swiss Boat Pass gives you a discount.

BY BUS

The city bus system offers easy access to sights throughout the urban area. If you're staying in a Luzern hotel, you will be eligible for a special **Guest-Ticket,** offering unlimited rides for two days for a minimal fee of 5 SF.

BY TAXI

Given the small scale of the Old Town and the narrowness of most of its streets, taxis can prove a pricey encumbrance.

Contacts and Resources

EMERGENCIES

Police (☎ 117). **Medical, dental, and pharmacy referral** (☎ 111). Auto breakdown: **Tourist Club of Switzerland** (☎ 140); **Swiss Automobile Club** (☎ 041/2100155).

GUIDED TOURS

Orientation. The City Tourist Office (☞ *below*) offers a two-hour guided walking tour of Luzern.

VISITOR INFORMATION

City Tourist Office (⊠ Frankenstr. 1, near the Bahnhof, ☎ 041/4107171). **Tourist information center** (with accommodation service; ⊠ Schweizerhofquai 2). **Central Switzerland Tourism Association** (Verkehrsverband Zentralschweiz, ⊠ Alpenstr. 1, Luzern, ☎ 041/4184080).

15 Madrid

S *mack in the heart of Spain at 2,120 ft above sea level, Madrid is the highest capital in all of Europe. Fittingly, it is also one of Europe's most vibrant cities. Madrileños are vigorous, joyful people, famous for their apparent ability to defy the need for sleep; they embrace their city's cultural offerings and make enthusiastic use of its cafés and bars. If you can match this energy, you'll take in Madrid's museum mile, with more masterpieces per meter than anywhere else in the world; regal Madrid, with its sumptuous palaces and posh boutiques; medieval Madrid, with its dark, narrow lanes, and Madrid after midnight, where today's action is.*

EXPLORING MADRID

Numbers in the margin correspond to points of interest on the Madrid map.

You can see important parts of the city in one day if you stop only to visit the Prado and Royal Palace. Two days should give you time for browsing. You can begin in the Plaza Atocha (Glorieta del Emperador Carlos V), at the bottom of the Paseo del Prado.

★ ❶ **Centro de Arte Reina Sofía** (Queen Sofía Arts Center). Spain's Queen Sofía opened this center in 1986, and it quickly became one of Europe's most dynamic venues—a Spanish rival to Paris's Pompidou Center. A converted hospital, the center houses painting and sculpture, including works by Joan Miró and Salvador Dalí as well as Picasso's *Guernica*, the painting depicting the horrific April 1937 carpet bombing of the Basque country's traditional capital by Nazi warplanes aiding

Franco in the Spanish Civil War. ✉ *Main entrance, C. de Santa Isabel 52,* ☎ *91/467–5062.* 🎫 *Free Sat. 2:30–9 and Sun.* 🕐 *Mon., Wed.– Sat. 10–9; Sun. 10–2:30.*

⓿ **Convento de las Descalzas Reales** (Convent of the Royal Barefoot Nuns). Founded by Juana de Austria, daughter of Charles V, this convent is still in use. Over the centuries, the nuns—daughters of royalty and nobility—have endowed it with an enormous wealth of jewels, religious ornaments, superb Flemish tapestries, and the works of such master painters as Titian and Rubens. A bit off the main track, it's one of Madrid's better-kept secrets. Guided tours in English are led once a day; your ticket includes admission to the nearby, but less interesting, **Convento de la Encarnación.** ✉ *Plaza de las Descalzas,* ☎ *91/559– 7404.* 🕐 *Tues.–Thurs., Sat. 10:30–12:30 and 4–5:30; Fri. 10:30–12:30, and Sun. 11–1:30.*

❼ **Fuente de la Cibeles** (Cybele's Fountain). Cybele, the Greek goddess of fertility and unofficial emblem of Madrid, languidly rides her lion-drawn chariot here, watched over by the mighty Palacio de Comunicaciónes, a splendidly pompous, cathedral-like post office. Fans of the home football team, Real Madrid, used to celebrate major victories by splashing in the fountain, but police now blockade it during big games. The fountain stands in the center of **Plaza de la Cibeles,** one of Madrid's great landmarks, at the intersection of the city's two main arteries. ✉ *Meeting of Castellana and Calle de Alcalá.*

★ ❷ **Museo del Prado** (Prado Museum). On the old cobblestone section of the Paseo del Prado you'll find Madrid's number-one cultural site, one of the world's most important art museums. Plan to spend at least a day here; it takes at least two days to view the museum's treasures properly. Brace yourself for crowds. The greatest treasures—the Velázquez, Murillo, Zurbarán, El Greco, and Goya galleries—are all on the upper floor. Two of the best works are Velázquez's *Surrender of Breda* and his most famous work, *Las Meninas,* awarded a room of its own. The Goya galleries contain the artist's none-too-flattering royal portraits, his exquisitely beautiful *Marquesa de Santa Cruz,* and his famous *Naked Maja* and *Clothed Maja,* for which the 13th duchess of Alba was said to have posed. Goya's most moving works, the *Second of May* and the *Fusillade of Moncloa* or *Third of May,* vividly depict the sufferings of Madrid patriots at the hands of Napoléon's invading troops in 1808. Before you leave, feast your eyes on Hieronymus Bosch's flights of fancy, *Garden of Earthly Delights* and the triptych *The Hay Wagon,* both on the ground floor. ✉ *Paseo del Prado s/n,* ☎ *91/330–2800.* 🎫 *Free Sun.* 🕐 *Tues.–Sat. 9–7, Sun. 9–2.*

❹ **Museo Thyssen-Bornemisza.** Opened in 1992 in the elegantly renovated Villahermosa Palace, this museum has plenty of airy spaces and natural light. The ambitious collection—800 paintings—attempts to trace the history of Western art through examples from each important movement, beginning with 13th-century Italy. Among the museum's gems are the *Portrait of Henry VIII,* by Hans Holbein (purchased from the late Princess Diana's grandfather, who used the money to buy a new Bugatti sports car). Two halls are devoted to the Impressionists and post-Impressionists, with many works by Pissarro as well as Renoir, Monet, Degas, Van Gogh, and Cézanne. The more recent paintings include some terror-filled examples of German expressionism, but these are complemented by some soothing Georgia O'Keeffes and Andrew Wyeths. ✉ *Paseo del Prado 8,* ☎ *91/369–0151.* 🕐 *Tues.–Sun. 10–7.*

★ ⑬ **Palacio Real** (Royal Palace). This magnificent granite-and-limestone pile was begun by Philip V, the first Bourbon king of Spain, who was always homesick for his beloved Versailles and did his best to re-create its opulence and splendor. To judge by the palace's 2,800 rooms, with their lavish rococo decorations, precious carpets, porcelain, timepieces, mirrors, and chandeliers, his efforts were successful. From 1764, when Charles III first moved in, until the coming of the Second Republic and the abdication of Alfonso XIII, in 1931, the Royal Palace proved a very stylish abode for Spanish monarchs; today, King Juan Carlos, who lives in the far less ostentatious Zarzuela Palace outside Madrid, uses it only for official state functions. Allow 1½–2 hours for a visit that includes the Royal Pharmacy and other outbuildings. The **Royal Carriage Museum,** which belongs to the palace, has a separate entrance on Paseo Virgen del Puerto. One of its highlights is the wedding carriage of Alfonso XIII and his English bride, Victoria Eugenia (granddaughter of Queen Victoria), which was damaged by a bomb tossed in the Calle Mayor during the couple's wedding procession in 1906. Another is the chair that carried the gout-stricken Emperor Charles V to his retirement at the remote monastery of Yuste. The museum has been closed for several years for restoration; inquire at the Royal Palace about its reopening. ⊠ *Bailén s/n,* ☏ *91/559–7404.* ☉ *Mon.–Sat. 9:30–5, Sun. 9–3. Closed during official functions.*

★ ⑤ **Parque del Retiro** (Retiro Park). Once a royal retreat, Retiro is Madrid's prettiest park. Visit the beautiful rose garden, **La Rosaleda;** enjoy street musicians and magicians; row a boat around El Estanque; and wander past the park's many statues and fountains. Look particularly at the monumental **statue of Alfonso XII,** one of Spain's least notable kings (though you wouldn't think so from the statue's size), or wonder at the **Monument to the Fallen Angel**—Madrid claims the dubious honor of being the only capital to have a statue dedicated to the Devil. The **Palacio de Velázquez** and the beautiful, glass-and-steel **Palacio de Cristal,** built as a tropical plant house during the 19th century, now host occasional art exhibits. ⊠ *Between C. Alfonso XII and Avda. de Menéndez Pelayo below C. de Alcalá. Daylight hrs.*

⑫ **Plaza de la Villa** (City Square). This plaza's notable cluster of buildings includes some of the oldest houses in Madrid. The **Casa de la Villa,** Madrid's city hall, was built in 1644 and has also served as the city prison and the mayor's home. Its sumptuous salons are occasionally open to the public; ask about guided tours, which are sometimes given in English. An archway joins the Casa de la Villa to the **Casa Cisneros,** a palace built in 1537 for the nephew of Cardinal Cisneros, primate of Spain and infamous inquisitor general. Across the square is the **Torre de Lujanes,** one of the oldest buildings in Madrid; it once imprisoned Francis I of France, archenemy of the Emperor Charles V. ⊠ *C. Mayor between C. Santiago and C. San Nicholas.*

★ ⑪ **Plaza Mayor** (Great Square). Without a doubt the capital's architectural showpiece, the Plaza Mayor was built in 1617–19 for Philip III— the figure astride the horse in the middle. The plaza has witnessed the canonization of saints, the burning of heretics, fireworks, and bullfights, and is still one of Madrid's great gathering places. ⊠ *South of C. Mayor, west of Cava San Miguel.*

⑥ **Puerta de Alcalá** (Alcalá Gate). Built in 1779 for Charles III, the grandiose gateway dominates the Plaza de la Independencia. A customs post once stood beside the gate, as did the old bullring until it was moved to its present site, Las Ventas, in the 1920s. At the turn of the century, the Puerta de Alcalá more or less marked the eastern edge of Madrid. ⊠ *Plaza de la Independencia.*

218

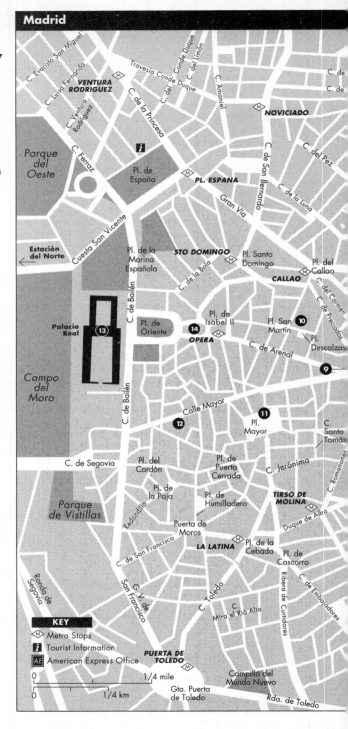

Madrid

C. de Evaristo San Miguel
C. Luisa Fernanda
VENTURA
RODRIGUEZ
C. Ventura Rodriguez
C. Ferraz
Travesía Conde Duque
Conde Duque
C. del Limón
C. Amaniel
C. de la Princesa
NOVICIADO
C. de
C. de
Parque
del
Oeste
Pl. de
España
PL. ESPANA
C. de San Bernardo
C. del Pez
C. de la Luna
Gran Vía
Cuesta San Vicente
Estación
del Norte
Pl. de la
Marina
Española
STO DOMINGO
C. de la Bola
Pl. Santo
Domingo
Pl. del
Callao
CALLAO
C. del Carmen
C. de Preciados
Palacio
Real
13
Pl. de
Oriente
C. de Bailén
14
OPERA
Pl. de
Isabel II
Pl. San
Martín
10
Pl.
Descalzas
C. de Arenal
9
Campo
del
Moro
Calle Mayor
12
11
Pl.
Mayor
C.
Santo
Tomás
C. de Bailén
C. de Segovia
Pl. del
Cordón
Pl. de
Puerta
Cerrada
C. Jerónima
C. Romanones
Pl. de
la Paja
Pl. de
Humilladero
TIRSO DE
MOLINA
Parque
de Vistillas
Redondilla
Puerta de
Moros
Duque de Alba
LA LATINA
Pl. de la
Cebada
Pl. de
Cascorro
C. de San Francisco
Ronda de Segovia
G. V. de San Francisco
C. Toledo
C.
Mira el Río Alto
Ribera de Curtidores
C. de Embajadores
Rda. de Toledo

KEY
Ⓜ Metro Stops
ℹ Tourist Information
AE American Express Office
0   1/4 mile
0   1/4 km

PUERTA DE
TOLEDO
Gta. Puerta
de Toledo
Campillo del
Munda Nuevo

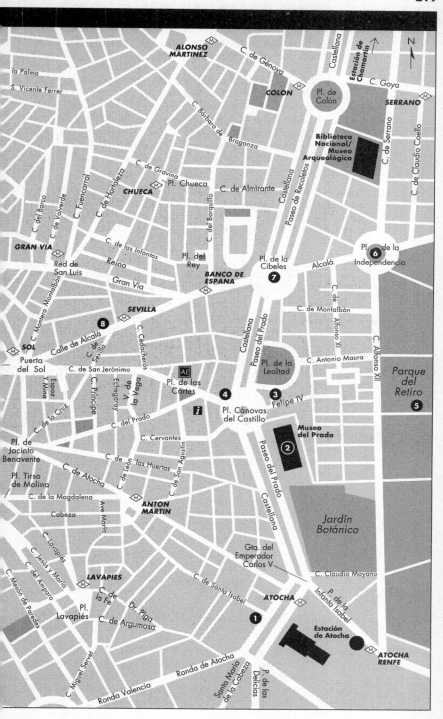

N

ALONSO MARTINEZ

C. de Génova

Castellana

Estación de Chamartín

C. Goya

la Palma

S. Vicente Ferrer

COLON

Pl. de Colón

SERRANO

C. de Serrano

C. de Claudio Coello

C. Bárbara de

Braganza

Biblioteca Nacional/ Museo Arqueológico

C. de Gravina

Pl. Chueca

C. de Almirante

Castellana

Paseo de Recoletos

CHUECA

C. de Hortaleza

C. del Barquillo

C. de las Infantas

Pl. del Rey

Pl. de la Cibeles

Alcalá

Pl. de la Independencia **6**

C. del Barco

C. de Valverde

C. de Fuencarral

GRAN VIA

Reina

Red de San Luis

Gran Vía

BANCO DE ESPAÑA

7

C. de Montalbán

C. de Alfonso XI

SEVILLA

8

Calle de Alcalá

C. de Sevilla

C. Cedaceros

Castellana

Paseo del Prado

C. Antonio Maura

C. Alfonso XII

Parque del Retiro

5

SOL

Puerta del Sol

C. Montera Mamalitos

C. de San Jerónimo

C. Principe

Echegaray

V. de la Vega

AE

Pl. de las Cortes

4

Pl. Cánovas del Castillo

3

Felipe IV

Pl. de la Lealtad

Espoz Y Mina

C. de la Cruz

i

C. Cervantes

Museo del Prado

2

Pl. de Jacinto Benavente

C. del Prado

C. de León

C. de las Huertas

C. de San Agustín

Pl. Tirso de Molina

C. de Atocha

C. de la Magdalena

Cabeza

ANTON MARTIN

Jardín Botánico

Ave María

Gta. del Emperador Carlos V

C. Claudio Moyano

C. Lavapiés

C. Jesús y María

C. del Amparo

C. Mesón de Paredes

LAVAPIES

C. de la Fe

Pl. Lavapiés

Dr. Piga

C. de Argumosa

C. de Santa Isabel

ATOCHA

P. de la Infanta Isabel

Castellana

1

Estación de Atocha

ATOCHA RENFE

C. Miguel Servet

Ronda de Atocha

Ronda Valencia

Santa María de la Cabeza

P. de las Delicias

❾ **Puerta del Sol** (Gate of the Sun). The old gate disappeared long ago, but you're still at the very heart of Madrid here, and indeed the very heart of Spain: kilometer distances for the whole nation are measured from the zero marker in front of the police headquarters. The square was expertly revamped in 1986 and now accommodates both a copy of **La Mariblanca** (a statue that adorned a fountain here 250 years ago) and, at the bottom of Calle Carmen, the much-loved statue of the **bear and strawberry tree**. The Puerta del Sol is inextricably linked with the history of Madrid and of Spain; a half century ago, a generation of literati gathered in Sol's long-gone cafés to thrash out the burning issues of the day. Nearly 200 years ago, the square witnessed the patriots' uprising immortalized by Goya in his painting, *The Second of May.* ⊠ *Meeting of C. Mayor and C. Alcalá.*

❽ **Real Academia de San Fernando** (Royal Academy of St. Ferdinand). Second only to the Prado in the Madrid art stakes, this fine-arts gallery focuses on the masters: Velázquez, El Greco, Murillo, Zurbarán, Ribera, and Goya. ⊠ *Alcalá 13,* ☎ *91/532–1546.* 🖙 *Free weekends.* ☺ *Tues.–Fri. 9–9; Sat.–Mon. 9–2:30.*

❸ **Ritz.** Alfonso II built Madrid's grande dame in 1910, when he realized that his capital had no hotels elegant enough to accommodate his wedding guests. The garden is a wonderfully aristocratic place to lunch in summer. ⊠ *Plaza de Lealtad 5.*

⓮ **Teatro Real** (Royal Theater). This neoclassical theater was built in 1850 and was long a cultural center for *Madrileño* society. Plagued by disasters more recently, including fires, a bombing, and profound structural problems, the house went dark in 1988. Closed for almost a decade for restoration, it reopened to worldwide fanfare in October 1997. Now replete with golden balconies, plush seats, and state-of-the-art stage equipment for operas and ballets, the theater is a modern showpiece with its vintage appeal intact. ⊠ *Plaza de Isabel II.* ☎ *91/516–0606.*

BULLFIGHTING

Madrid's bullfighting season runs from March through October. Fights are held on Sunday and sometimes also on Thursday; starting times vary between 4:30 and 7 PM. The height of taurine spectacle comes with the San Isidro festivals, in May, which usher in three weeks of daily bullfights. The bullring is at **Las Ventas,** formally known as the Plaza de Toros Monumental (⊠ Alcalá 237, ☎ 91/356–2200, metro: Ventas). You can buy your ticket here shortly before the fight or, for a 20% surcharge, at the agencies that line Calle Victoria, just off Carrera San Jerónimo and Puerta del Sol.

DINING

Note that some restaurants in Madrid close for Holy Week.

RATINGS

Spanish restaurants are officially classified from five forks down to one fork, with most places earning two or three forks. In our rating system, prices are per person and include a first course, main course, and dessert, but not wine or tip. Sales tax (IVA) is usually included in the menu price; check the menu for *IVA incluído* or *IVA no incluído.* When it's not included, an additional 7% will be added to your bill. Most restaurants offer a prix-fixe menu called a *menú del día;* however, this is often offered only at lunch, and at dinner tends to be a reheated version of the same. *Menús* are usually the cheapest way to eat; à la carte dining is more expensive. Service charges are never added to your bill; leave around 10%, less in $ restaurants and bars. Major centers such as Madrid, Barcelona, Marbella, and Seville tend to be a bit more expensive.

CATEGORY	COST
$$$$	over 9,000 ptas.
$$$	6,000 ptas.–9,000 ptas.
$$	3,000 ptas.–6,000 ptas.
$	under 3,000 ptas.

$$$$ ✕ **Horcher.** In a luxurious mansion at the edge of Retiro Park, this clas-
★   sic restaurant is renowned for its hearty but elegant fare, served with impeccable style in an intimate dining room. Specialties include wild boar, venison, and roast wild duck with almond croquettes. The star appetizer is lobster salad with truffles. Other dishes, such as stroganoff with mustard, pork chops with sauerkraut, and a chocolate-covered fruit-and-cake dessert called *baumkuchen,* reflect the restaurant's German roots. A wide selection of French and German wines rounds out the menu. ⊠ *Alfonso XII 6,* ☎ *91/522–0731. Reservations essential. AE, DC, MC, V. Closed Sun. No lunch Sat.*

$$$$ ✕ **Viridiana.** The trendiest of Madrid's haute cuisine restaurants, Viridiana is decorated in black and white and has the relaxed atmosphere of a bistro. Iconoclast chef Abraham García creates a new menu every two weeks, dreaming up such varied fare as red onions stuffed with *morcilla* (black pudding); soft flour tortillas wrapped around marinated fresh tuna; and filet mignon in white-truffle sauce. The tangy grapefruit sherbet for dessert is a marvel. ⊠ *Juan de Mena 14,* ☎ *91/531–5222. Reservations essential. AE, MC, V. Closed Sun. and Aug.*

$$$$ ✕ **Zalacaín.** A deep-apricot color scheme, set off by dark wood and gleaming silver, makes this restaurant look like an exclusive villa. Zalacaín introduced nouvelle cuisine to Spain and continues to set the pace after 20 years at the top—splurge on such dishes as prawn salad in avocado vinaigrette, scallops and leeks in Albariño wine, and roast pheasant with truffles. A prix-fixe tasting menu allows you to sample the restaurant's best for about 6,500 ptas. Service is somewhat stuffy. ⊠ *Alvarez de Baena 4,* ☎ *91/561–5935. Reservations essential. AE, DC, V. Closed Sun. and Aug. No lunch Sat.*

$$$ ✕ **El Cenador del Prado.** The Cenador's innovative menu has French
★   and Asian touches, as well as exotic Spanish dishes that rarely appear in restaurants. Dine in a baroque salon or a less-formal, plant-filled conservatory. The house specialty is *patatas a la importancia* (sliced potatoes fried in a sauce of garlic, parsley, and clams); other possibilities include shellfish consommé with ginger ravioli, veal and eggplant in béchamel, or wild boar with prunes. For dessert try the *cañas fritas,* a cream-filled pastry once served only at Spanish weddings. ⊠ *C. del Prado 4,* ☎ *91/429–1561. AE, DC, MC, V. Closed Sun. and Aug. 1–15. No lunch Sat.*

$$$ ✕ **Gure-Etxea.** In the heart of Old Madrid, on the Plaza de Paja, this is one of the capital's most authentic Basque restaurants. The ground-floor dining room is airy, high-ceilinged, and elegant; brick walls line the lower level, giving it a rustic, farmhouse feel. As in the Basque country, you are waited on only by women. Classic dishes include *bacalao al pil-pil* (spicy cod fried in garlic and oil—making the "pil-pil" sound), *rape en salsa verde* (monkfish in garlic-and-parsley sauce), and for dessert *leche frita* (fried custard). On weekdays the lunch menu includes a hearty and inexpensive daily special. ⊠ *Plaza de Paja 12,* ☎ *91/365–6149. AE, DC, V. Closed Sun. and Aug. No lunch Mon.*

$$$ ✕ **La Trainera.** La Trainera is all about fresh seafood—the best money can buy. This informal restaurant, with its nautical decor and maze of

little dining rooms, has reigned as the queen of Madrid's seafood houses for decades. Crab, lobster, shrimp, mussels, and a dozen other types of shellfish are served by weight in *raciones* (large portions). Although many Spanish diners share several plates of these delicacies as their entire meal, the grilled hake, sole, or turbot makes an unbeatable second course. Skip the listless house wine and go for a bottle of Albariño from the cellar. ⊠ *Lagasca 60,* ☎ *91/576–8035. AE, MC, V. Closed Sun. and Aug.*

$$ ✗ **Casa Botin.** Just off the Plaza Mayor, Madrid's oldest and most fa-
★ mous restaurant has been catering to diners since 1725. Its decor and food are traditionally Castilian, as are the wood-fire ovens used for cooking. *Cochinillo asado* and *cordero asado* are the specialties. The restaurant was a favorite of Hemingway's and is somewhat touristy, but it's still fun. Try to get a table in the basement or the upstairs dining room. ⊠ *Cuchilleros 17,* ☎ *91/366–4217. Reservations essential. AE, DC, MC, V.*

$$ ✗ **Casa Vallejo.** With its homey dining room, friendly staff, creative menu, and reasonable prices, this restaurant is a well-kept secret of Madrid's budget gourmets. To start, try the tomato, zucchini, and cheese tart or the artichokes and clams; then move on to duck breast in prune sauce or meatballs made with lamb, almonds, and pine nuts. The fudge-and-raspberry pie is worth a trip in itself. ⊠ *San Lorenzo 9,* ☎ *91/308–6158. Reservations essential. AE, DC, MC, V. Closed Sun. No dinner Mon.*

$$ ✗ **La Gamella.** American-born chef Dick Stephens has created a new
★ reasonably priced menu at this hugely popular spot. The sophisticated rust-red dining room, batik tablecloths, oversize plates, and attentive service remain the same, but much of the nouvelle cuisine has been replaced by more traditional fare, such as chicken in garlic, beef bourguignon, or steak tartare à la Jack Daniels. A few signature dishes—such as sausage-and-red-pepper quiche and, for dessert, bittersweet chocolate pâté—remain, and the lunchtime *menú del día* is a great value at 1,700 ptas. ⊠ *Alfonso XII 4,* ☎ *91/532–4509. AE, DC, MC, V. Closed Sun., Mon., and Aug. 15–31. No lunch Sat.*

$$ ✗ **Nabucco.** Had enough Spanish food for the moment? With pastel-washed walls and subtle lighting from gigantic, wrought-iron candelabras, this pizzeria and trattoria is a trendy but elegant haven in gritty Chueca. Fresh bread sticks and garlic olive oil show up within minutes of your arrival. The spinach, ricotta, and walnut ravioli is heavenly, and this may be the only Italian restaurant in Madrid where you can order (California-style?) barbecued-chicken pizza. Considering the ambience and quality, the bill is a pleasant surprise. ⊠ *Hortaleza 108,* ☎ *91/310–0611. AE, MC, V.*

$$ ✗ **Nicolas.** One of Madrid's hottest restaurants, Nicolas serves updated versions of traditional Spanish classics in a chic brasserie setting, at reasonable prices. Specialties include garlic soup, a stew of garbanzos and baby squid, sea bass with shrimp, and red peppers stuffed with pork. ⊠ *Villalar 4,* ☎ *91/431–7737. AE, DC, MC, V. Closed Sun. and Mon.*

$ ✗ **La Biotika.** A vegetarian's dream, this small, cozy restaurant in the heart of the bar district (just east of Plaza Santa Ana) serves macrobiotic vegetarian cuisine every day of the week. Enormous salads, hearty soups, fresh bread, and creative tofu dishes make dining here a flavorful experience. A small market at the entrance sells macrobiotic groceries. ⊠ *Amor de Dios 3,* ☎ *91/429–0780. No credit cards.*

$ ✗ **Casa Mingo.** Resembling an Asturian cider tavern, Casa Mingo is
★ built into a stone wall beneath the Norte train station. It's a bustling place where the only dishes offered are succulent roast chicken, sausages, and salad, all washed down with endless bottles of *sidra* (hard cider). Normally, you'll share long plank tables with other diners; in summer

small tables appear on the sidewalk. ⊠ *Paseo de la Florida 2,* ☎ *91/ 547–7918. No credit cards.*

NIGHTLIFE AND THE ARTS

The Arts
Details of all cultural events are listed in the daily newspaper *El País* or in the weekly *Guía del Ocio.*

CONCERTS AND OPERA
Madrid's main concert hall is the **Auditorio Nacional de Madrid** (⊠ Príncipe de Vergara 146, ☎ 91/337–0100, metro: Cruz del Rayo). For ballet or opera, catch a performance at the legendary **Teatro Real** (⊠ Plaza de Isabel II, ☎ 91/516-0606), whose splendid facade dominates the Plaza de Oriente. After a lengthy restoration the theater reopened on a grand scale in October 1997 (☞ Exploring, *above*).

FILM
Foreign films are mostly dubbed into Spanish, but movies in English are listed in *El País* or *Guía del Ocio* under "VO" (*versión original*). A dozen or so theaters now show films in English. **Alphaville** (⊠ Martín de los Heroes 14, off Plaza España, ☎ 91/559–3836) and **Cines Renoir** (⊠ Martín de los Heroes 12, off Plaza España, ☎ 91/559–5760) are good bets for VO films. The **Filmoteca** (⊠ Santa Isabel 3, ☎ 91/369–1125) is a city-run institution showing different classic VO films every day.

THEATER
If language is no problem, check out the fringe theaters in Lavapiés and the Centro Cultural de la Villa (☎ 91/575–6080), beneath the Plaza Colón, and the open-air events in Retiro Park. The **Círculo de Bellas Artes** (⊠ Marqués de Casa Riera 2, off Alcalá 42, ☎ 91/531–7700) is a leading theater. The **Teatro Español** (⊠ Príncipe 25 on Plaza Santa Ana, ☎ 91/429–6297) stages Spanish classics. The **Teatro María Guerrero** (⊠ Tamayo y Baus 4, ☎ 91/319–4769), the home of the Centro Dramático Nacional, stages plays by García Lorca. Most theaters have two curtains, at 7PM and 10:30 PM, and close on Monday. Tickets are inexpensive and often easy to come by on the night of the performance.

ZARZUELA
Zarzuela, a combination of light opera and dance that's ideal for non–Spanish speakers, is performed at the **Teatro Nacional Lírico de la Zarzuela** (⊠ Jovellanos 4, ☎ 91/524–5400). The season runs from October through July.

Nightlife
BARS AND CAFÉS
Mesónes. The most traditional and colorful taverns are on Cuchilleros and Cava San Miguel, just west of Plaza Mayor, where you'll find a whole array of *mesónes* with such names as Tortilla, Champiñón, and Boqueron.

Old Madrid. Wander the narrow streets between Puerta del Sol and Plaza Santa Ana—most are packed with traditional tapas bars. The **Cervecería Alemana** (⊠ Plaza Santa Ana 6, ☎ 91/429–7033) is a beer hall founded over 100 years ago by Germans and patronized, inevitably, by Ernest Hemingway. **Los Gabrieles** (⊠ Echegaray 17, ☎ 91/429–6261) has magnificent ceramic decor and becomes something of a disco late at night. For a more tranquil atmosphere try **Viva Madrid** (⊠ Fernández y González 7, ☎ 91/429–3640), a lovely old bar.

Calle Huertas. This street is lined with fashionable bars with turn-of-the-century decor and guitar or chamber music, often live. **La Fídula**

(✉ Calle Huertas 57, ☎ 91/429–2947) is one of the best. **Casa Alberto** (✉ Calle Huertas 18) is a quieter tavern with brick walls, a good selection of draft beers, and tapas in the early evening.

Plaza Santa Bárbara. This area just off Alonso Martínez is packed with fashionable bars and beer halls. Stroll along Santa Teresa, Orellana, Campoamor, or Fernando VI and take your pick. The **Cervecería Santa Bárbara** (☎ 91/319–0449), in the plaza itself, is one of the most colorful, a popular beer hall with a good range of tapas.

Cafés. Madrid has no lack of old-fashioned cafés, with dark-wood counters, brass pumps, marble-top tables, and plenty of atmosphere. **Café Comercial** (✉ Glorieta de Bilbao 7, ☎ 91/521–5655) is a typical spot in the classic style. **Café Gijón** (✉ Paseo de Recoletos 21, ☎ 91/521–5425) is a former literary hangout and the most famous of the old cafés; it's now just one of many terrace cafés that line the Castellana. **Café León** (✉ Alcalá 57) is just up from Cibeles. **El Espejo** (✉ Paseo de Recoletos 31, ☎ 91/308–2347) has art-nouveau decor and an outdoor terrace in summer. For a late-night coffee, or something stronger, stop in at the baroque **Palacio de Gaviria** (✉ Arenal 9, ☎ 91/526–8089), a restored 19th-century palace on a tawdry commercial street. It allegedly once housed an unofficial royal consort.

CABARET

Florida Park (☎ 91/573–7805), in Retiro Park, offers dinner and a show with ballet, flamenco, or Spanish dance; it is open Monday–Saturday from 9:30 PM (shows are at 10:45 PM). **Berlin** (✉ Costanilla de San Pedro 11, ☎ 91/366–2034) opens at 9:30 for a dinner that's tasty by most cabaret standards, followed by a show and dancing until 4 AM. **La Scala** (✉ Rosario Pino 7, ☎ 91/571–4411), in the hotel Meliá Castilla, is Madrid's finest nightclub, with dinner, dancing, cabaret at 8:30 and a second, less expensive show around midnight. Most night tours hit this club.

DISCOS AND NIGHTCLUBS

Nightlife—or *la marcha,* as the Spanish fondly call it—reaches legendary heights in Spain's capital. Smart, trendy dance clubs filled with well-heeled Madrileños are everywhere. For more adventurous exploring, try the scruffy bar district in Malasaña, around the Plaza Dos de Mayo, where smoke-filled hangouts line Calle San Vicente Ferrer, or the notorious haunts of Chueca, where tattoo studios and street-chic boutiques break up the endless alleys of techno and after-hours clubs.

Amadis (✉ Covarrubias 42, under the Luchana Cinema, ☎ 91/446–0036) has telephones on every table, encouraging people to call each other with invitations to dance. You must be over 25 to enter. The well-heeled crowd likes **Archy's** (✉ Marqués de Riscal 11, ☎ 91/308–3162). Salsa has become a fixture in Madrid; check out the most spectacular moves at **Azucar** (Sugar; ✉ Paseo Reina Cristina 7, ☎ 91/501–6107). Madrid's hippest new club is a three-story bar, disco, and cabaret called **Bagelus** (✉ María de Molina 25, ☎ 91/561–6100). **Joy Eslava** (✉ Arenal 11, ☎ 91/366–3733), a downtown disco in a converted theater, is an old standby. **Pacha** (✉ Barceló 11, ☎ 91/466–0137), one of Spain's infamous chain discos, is always energetic. **Siroco** (✉ San Dimas 3, ☎ 91/593–3070) offers two different types of music Tuesday through Saturday: live Spanish pop downstairs, disco and acid jazz upstairs. **Space of Sound** (✉ Plz. Estacion de Chamartin, in the train station, ☎ 91/733-3505) almost fails to qualify as a nightclub: it's open Saturday and Sunday mornings from dawn until noon, full of drag queens and club kids who refuse to let the night end. **Torero** (✉ Cruz 26, ☎

91/523–1129) is for the beautiful people—quite literally: a bouncer allows only those judged *gente guapa* (beautiful people) to enter.

FLAMENCO

Madrid offers an array of flamenco shows. Some are good, but many are aimed at the tourist trade. Dinner tends to be mediocre and over-priced, but it ensures the best seats; otherwise, opt for the show and a *consumición* (drink) only, usually starting around 11 PM and costing 3,000 ptas.–3,500 ptas. **Arco de Cuchilleros** (⊠ Cuchilleros 7, ☎ 91/364–0263) is one of the better and cheaper venues. **Café de Chinitas** (⊠ Torija 7, ☎ 91/559–5135) is reasonably authentic. **Casa Patas** (⊠ Canizares 10, ☎ 91/369–0496) is a major showplace; it offers good, if somewhat touristy, flamenco and tapas to boot, all at reasonable prices. **Corral de la Morería** (⊠ Morería 17, ☎ 91/365–8446) serves dinner à la carte and invites well-known flamenco stars to perform with the resident group. Since the Corral opened its doors in 1956, visiting celebrities such as the late Frank Sinatra and Ava Gardner have left their autographed photos for the walls.

JAZZ CLUBS

The city's best-known jazz venue is **Café Central** (⊠ Plaza de Angel 10, ☎ 91/369–4143). **Café del Foro** (⊠ San Andrés 38, ☎ 91/445–3752) is a friendly club with live music nightly. Another well-known spot is **Clamores** (⊠ Albuquerque 14, ☎ 91/445–7938). **Populart** (⊠ Huertas 22, ☎ 91/429–8407) features blues, Brazilian music, and salsa. Seasonal citywide festivals also present excellent artists; check the local press for listings and venues.

SHOPPING

The main shopping area in central Madrid surrounds the pedestrian streets **Preciados** and **Montera,** off the Gran Vía between Puerta del Sol and Plaza Callao. The **Salamanca** district, just off the Plaza de Colón, bordered roughly by Serrano, Goya, and Conde de Peñalver, is more elegant and expensive; just west of Salamanca, the shops on and around Calle Argensola, just south of Calle Génova, are on their way upmarket. **Calle Mayor** and the streets to the east of **Plaza Mayor** are lined with fascinating old-fashioned stores straight out of the 19th century.

Antiques

The main areas for antiques are the Plaza de las Cortes, the Carrera San Jerónimo, and the Rastro flea market, along the Ribera de Curtidores and the courtyards just off it.

Boutiques

Calle Serrano has the widest selection of smart boutiques and designer fashions—think Prada, Armani, and Donna Karan New York, as well as renowned Spanish designers such as Josep Font-Luz Diaz. Worth special trips are several posh boutiques. **Seseña** (⊠ De la Cruz 23, ☎ 91/531–6840), has outfitted Hollywood stars (and Hillary Rodham Clinton) since the turn of the century. **Sybilla** (⊠ Jorge Juan 12, ☎ 91/578–1322) is the studio of Spain's best-known woman designer, whose fluid dresses and hand-knit sweaters in natural colors and fabrics have made her a favorite with model Helena Christensen. **Adolfo Dóminguez** (⊠ Serrano 96, ☎ 91/576–7053; ⊠ C. Orense, ☎ 91/576–0084), one of Spain's top designers, has several boutiques in Madrid. **Loewe** (⊠ Serrano 26, ☎ 91/577–6056; ⊠ Gran Vía 8, ☎ 91/522–6815) is Spain's most prestigious leather store.

Several upscale shopping centers group a variety of exclusive shops stocked with unusual clothes and gifts: **Galerías del Prado** (⊠ Plaza de las Cortes 7, on the lower level of the Palace Hotel); **Los Jardines de Serrano** (✉ corner of Calle Goya and Claudio Coello); and **Centro Comercial ABC** (✉ Paseo de la Castellana 34). South of the city center an old factory building has been transformed into the ultraslick, government-subsidized **Mercado Puerta de Toledo** (✉ Ronda de Toledo 1). For street-chic fashion closer to medieval Madrid, check out the window displays at the **Madrid Fusión Centro de Moda** (✉ Plaza Tirso de Molina, 15, ☎ 91/369–0018), where up-and-coming Spanish labels like Instinto, Kika, and Extart fill five floors with faux furs, funky jewelry, and the city's most eccentric selection of shoes.

Department Stores

El Corte Inglés (✉ Preciados 3, ☎ 91/532–8100; ✉ Goya 76, ☎ 91/577–7171; ✉ Goya 87, ☎ 91/432–9300; ✉ Princesa 42, ☎ 91/542–4800; ✉ Serrano 47, ☎ 91/432–5490; ✉ La Vaguada Mall, ☎ 91/387–4000; ✉ Parquesur Mall, ☎ 91/558–4400; ✉ Raimundo Fernández Villaverde 79, ☎ 91/556–2300) is Spain's biggest, brightest, and most successful chain store. **Marks & Spencer** (✉ C. Serrano 52, ☎ 91/431–6760), a British department store, specializes in woolen goods, underwear, and gourmet foods.

Food and Flea Markets

The **Rastro,** Madrid's most famous flea market, operates on Sunday from 9 to 2 around the Plaza del Cascorro and the Ribera de Curtidores. A **stamp and coin market** is held on Sunday morning in the Plaza Mayor. Mornings, take a look at the colorful food stalls inside the 19th-century glass-and-steel **San Miguel** market, also near the Plaza Mayor. There's a **secondhand-book market** most days on the Cuesta Claudio Moyano, near Atocha Station.

Gift Ideas

No special crafts are associated with Madrid itself, but traditional Spanish goods are sold in many stores. El Corte Inglés (☞ *above*) stocks a good selection of Lladró **porcelain,** as do several specialty shops on the Gran Vía and the Plaza de España, behind the Plaza Hotel. Department stores stock good displays of **fans,** but for superb examples, try the long-established Casa Diego, in Puerta del Sol. Two stores opposite the Prado on Plaza Cánovas del Castillo, Artesanía Toledana and El Escudo de Toledo, have a wide selection of **souvenirs,** especially Toledo swords, inlaid marquetry ware, and pottery. Carefully selected **handicrafts** from all over Spain—ceramics, furniture, glassware, rugs, embroidery, and more—are sold at **Artespaña** (✉ Hermosilla 14, ☎ 91/435–0221).

MADRID ESSENTIALS

Arriving and Departing

BY BUS

Madrid has no central bus station. Check with the tourist office for departure points for your destination. The **Estación del Sur** (✉ Canarias 17, ☎ 91/468–4200, metro: Palos de la Frontera) serves Toledo, La Mancha, Alicante, and Andalucía. **Auto-Rés** (✉ Plaza Conde de Casal 6, ☎ 91/551–7200, metro: Conde de Casal) serves Extremadura, Cuenca, Salamanca, Valladolid, Valencia, and Zamora. Auto-Rés has a central ticket and information office at Salud 19 (☎ 91/551–7200), just off Gran Vía, near the Hotel Arosa. The Basque country and most of north-central Spain are served by **Auto Continental** (✉ Alenza 20, ☎ 91/533–0400, metro: Ríos Rosas). For Àvila, Segovia, and La Granja, use **Empresa La Sepulvedana** (✉ Paseo de la Florida 11, ☎ 91/530–4800, metro: Norte). **Empresa Herranz** (✉ Calle Fernández de los Ríos s/n, ☎ 91/543–8167, metro: Moncloa) serves El Escorial and the Valley of the Fallen. **La Veloz** (✉ Avda. Mediterraneo 49, ☎ 91/409–7602, metro: Conde de Casal) serves Chinchón.

BY CAR

The main roads are: north–south, the Paseo de la Castellana and Paseo del Prado; east–west, Calle de Alcalá, Gran Vía, and Calle de la Princesa. The M30 ring road circles Madrid, and the M40 is an outer ring road about 12 km (7 mi) further from the city. For Burgos and France, drive north up the Castellana and follow the signs for the N I. For Barcelona, head up the Castellana to Plaza Dr. Marañón, then right onto María de Molina and the N II; for Andalusia and Toledo, head south down Paseo del Prado, then follow the signs to the N IV and N401, respectively. For Segovia, Ávila, and El Escorial, head west along Princesa to Avenida Puerta de Hierro and onto the N VI–La Coruña.

BY PLANE

All international and domestic flights arrive at Madrid's Barajas Airport (☎ 91/305–8343), 16 km (10 mi) northeast of town just off the N II Barcelona highway. For information on arrival and departure times, call **Info-Iberia** (☎ 91/329–5767) or the airline concerned.

Between the Airport and Downtown. Buses leave the national and international terminals every 15 minutes from 5:40 AM to 2 AM for the downtown bus terminal at Plaza de Colón, just off the Paseo de la Castellana. The ride takes about 20 minutes, and the fare at press time (spring 1998) was 450 ptas. Most city hotels are then only a short taxi or metro ride away. The fastest and most expensive route into town is by taxi (usually about 1,500 ptas., but up to 2,000 ptas. plus tip in traffic). Pay the metered amount plus the 350-pta. surcharge and 150 ptas. for each suitcase. By car take the N II (which becomes Avenida de América) into town, then head straight into Calle María de Molina and left on either Calle Serrano or the Castellana.

BY TRAIN

Madrid has three railroad stations. **Chamartín** (✉ Avda. Pío XII), in the northern suburbs beyond the Plaza de Castilla, is the main station, with trains to France and the north (including Barcelona, Ávila, Salamanca, Santiago, and La Coruña). Most trains to Valencia, Alicante, and Andalusia leave from Chamartín but stop at Atocha station as well. **Atocha station** (✉ Glorieta del Emperador Carlos V, southern end of Paseo del Prado) sends trains to Segovia, Toledo, Granada, Extremadura, and Lisbon. A convenient metro stop (Atocha RENFE) connects the Atocha rail station to the city subway system. The old Atocha station, designed by Eiffel, is Madrid's terminal for high-speed AVE service to Córdoba and Seville. **Norte** (or Príncipe Pío; ✉ Paseo de la Florida, above Campo del Moro) serves the residential suburbs.

For all train information call or visit the **RENFE offices** (✉ Alcalá 44, ☎ 91/563–0202 Spanish; 91/328–9020 English, if speaker is available; ◷ weekdays 9:30–8). There's another RENFE office in the International Arrivals Hall at Barajas Airport, or you can purchase tickets at any of the three main stations or from travel agents displaying the blue and yellow RENFE sign.

Getting Around
Madrid is a fairly compact city, and most of the main sights can be visited on foot. If you're staying in one of the modern hotels in northern Madrid, however, off the Castellana, you may need to use the bus or subway. Some rough guidelines: the walk from the Prado to the Royal Palace at a comfortable sightseeing pace, but without stopping, takes around 30 minutes; from Plaza del Callao on Gran Vía to the Plaza Mayor, about 15 minutes.

BY BUS
City buses are red and generally run from 6 AM to midnight (some stop earlier). The flat fare is 130 ptas. Route plans are displayed at *paradas* (bus stops), and a map of the entire system is available from Empresa Municipal de Transportes (EMT) booths on Plaza de la Cibeles, Callao, or Puerta del Sol. You can save money by buying a **Bonobus** (660 ptas.), good for 10 rides, from EMT booths or any tobacco shop.

BY METRO
The metro offers the simplest and quickest means of transport and operates from 6 AM to 1:30 AM. Metro maps are available from ticket offices, hotels, and tourist offices. The flat fare at press time was 130 ptas. a ride; a 10-ride ticket, 660 ptas. Carry some change (5, 25, 50, and 100 ptas.) for the ticket machines, especially after 10 PM; the machines make change and allow you to skip long ticket lines.

BY TAXI
Madrid has more than 18,000 taxicabs, and fares are low by New York or London standards. The meter starts at 170 ptas.; each additional km (½ mi) costs 70 ptas. The average city ride costs about 500 ptas., and there is a surcharge of 150 ptas. between 11 PM and 6 AM and on holidays. A supplemental fare of 150 ptas. applies to trips to the bullring or football matches, and there is an additional charge of 150 ptas. per suitcase. The airport surcharge is 350 ptas. Cabs available for hire display a LIBRE sign during the day and a green light at night. They hold four passengers. Make sure the driver turns the meter on when you start your ride; tip 5%–10% of the fare. To radio a cab call **Tele-Taxi** (☎ 91/445–9008 or 91/448–4259).

Money Matters

CURRENCY
Spain's unit of currency is the peseta (pta.). Bills are worth 10,000, 5,000, 2,000, and 1,000 ptas.; coins are worth 500, 200, 100, 50, 25, 10, 5, and 1 pta. At press time (spring 1998), Europe's currency markets were rather unstable; the Spanish exchange rate was about 150 ptas. to the U.S. dollar, 105 ptas. to the Canadian dollar, and 250 ptas. to the pound sterling.

CURRENCY REGULATIONS
Visitors may take any amount of foreign currency in bills or traveler's checks into Spain, as well as any amount of pesetas. When leaving Spain you may take out only 100,000 ptas. per person in Spanish banknotes and foreign currency up to the equivalent of 500,000 ptas., unless you can prove you declared the excess at customs on entering the country.

Telephoning

COUNTRY CODE
The country code for Spain is 34. When calling Spain from outside the country, do not drop the initial 9 from the regional code.

Contacts and Resources

EMBASSIES
United States (✉ Serrano 75, ☎ 91/577–4000). **Australia** (✉ Paseo de la Castellana 143, ☎ 91/579–0428). **Canada** (✉ Núñez de Balboa 35, ☎ 91/431–4300). **New Zealand** (✉ Plaza de La Lealtad 2, ☎ 91/523–0226). **United Kingdom** (✉ Fernando el Santo 16, ☎ 91/319–0200).

EMERGENCIES
112 is the **general emergency number** in all E.U. nations (akin to 911 in the U.S.). **Police** (emergencies, ☎ 091; Municipal Police, ☎ 092 for towed cars or traffic accidents). **Ambulance** (☎ 061, 91/522–2222 or 91/588–4400). **Emergency clinics:** Hospital 12 de Octubre (☎ 91/

390–8000), La Paz Ciudad Sanitaria (☎ 91/358–2600). **English-speaking doctors:** British-American Medical Unit (☎ 91/435–1823). **Pharmacies:** List of pharmacies open 24 hours (*farmacias de guardia*) published daily in El País.

ENGLISH-LANGUAGE BOOKS

Booksellers (✉ José Abascal 48, ☎ 91/442–8104). **The International Bookshop** (✉ Campomanes 13, ☎ 91/541–7291). **Turner's English Bookshop** (✉ Génova 3, ☎ 91/319–0926).

GUIDED TOURS

Orientation. Julià Tours (✉ Gran Vía 68, ☎ 91/559–9605). **Pullmantur** (✉ Plaza de Oriente 8, ☎ 91/541–1807). **Trapsatur** (✉ San Bernardo 23, ☎ 91/302–6039). All three run the same tours, conducted in Spanish and English. Reserve directly with the offices above, through any travel agent, or through your hotel. Departure points are the addresses above, though you can often arrange to be picked up at your hotel. Tours leave in morning, afternoon, and evening and cover various selections of sites and activities. Trapsatur also runs the Madridvision bus, which makes a one-hour tour of the city with recorded commentary in English. No reservation is necessary; catch the bus in front of the Prado every 1½ hours beginning at 10 AM, from Tuesday through Sunday. There are no buses on Sunday afternoon. A round-trip ticket costs 1,500 ptas., and a two-day pass, 2,200 ptas. If you want a personal tour with a local guide, contact the **Asociación Profesional de Informadores** (✉ Ferraz 82, ☎ 91/542–1214 or 91/541–1221).

Walking and Special-Interest. The **ayuntamiento** (city hall) has a popular selection of Spanish bus and walking tours under the title "Discubre Madrid." Walking tours depart most mornings and visit many hidden corners as well as major sights; options include "Madrid's Railroads," "Medicine in Madrid," "Goya's Madrid," and "Commerce and Finance in Madrid." Schedules are listed in the "Discubre Madrid" leaflet available from the municipal tourist office. Tickets can be purchased at the Patronato de Turismo (✉ C. Mayor 69, ☎ 91/588–2906).

Excursions. Julià Tours, Pullmantur, and **Trapsatur** (☞ *above*) run full- or half-day trips to El Escorial, Ávila, Segovia, Toledo, and Aranjuez, and in summer to Cuenca and Salamanca. Summer weekends, the popular *Tren de la Fresa* (Strawberry Train) takes passengers from the old Delicias Station to Aranjuez (known for its production of strawberries) on a 19th-century train. Tickets can be obtained from RENFE offices (☞ Arriving and Departing by Train, *above*), travel agents, and the Delicias Station (✉ Paseo de las Delicias 61). Other one- or two-day excursions by train are available on summer weekends. Contact RENFE for details.

TRAVEL AGENCIES

American Express (✉ Plaza de las Cortes 2, ☎ 91/322–5445). **Pullmantur,** across the street from the Royal Palace (✉ Plaza de Oriente 8, ☎ 91/541–1807). **Carlson Wagons-Lits** (✉ Paseo de la Castellana 96, ☎ 91/563–1202).

VISITOR INFORMATION

Madrid tourist office (✉ Ground floor, Torre de Madrid, Plaza de España, near Calle de la Princesa, ☎ 91/541–2325) is the best place for comprehensive information. The **Madrid Provincial Tourist Office** (✉ Duque de Medinacelli 2, ☎ 91/429–4951) is also helpful. The **municipal tourist office** (✉ Plaza Mayor 3, ☎ 91/366–5477) is centrally located, but hordes of tourists tend to deplete its stock of brochures. The **airport tourist office** (✉ International Arrivals Hall, Barajas Airport, ☎ 91/305–8656) has a convenient visitors' center.

16 Munich

People who live in other parts of Germany sometimes refer to Munich (München in German) as the nation's "secret capital." Flamboyant, easygoing Munich, city of beer and Baroque, is starkly different from the sometimes stiffly Prussian-influenced Berlin; the gritty and industrial Hamburg; or the hard-headed, commercially driven Frankfurt. This is a city to visit for its good-natured and relaxed charm—Gemütlichkeit, they call it here. Munich is a crazy mix of high culture (witness its world-class opera house and art galleries) and wild abandon (witness the vulgar frivolity of the Oktoberfest). Its citizenry seems determined to perpetuate the lifestyle of the 19th-century king Ludwig I, the Bavarian ruler who brought so much international prestige to his home city after declaring: "I want to make out of Munich a town that does such credit to Germany that nobody knows Germany unless he has seen Munich." He kept his promise with an architectural and artistic renaissance—before abdicating in the wake of a wild romance with an Irish-born dancing girl, Lola Montez.

EXPLORING MUNICH

Numbers in the margin correspond to points of interest on the Munich map.

Munich is unique among German cities because it has no identifiable, homogeneous Old Town center. The historic heart of the city is a quiet courtyard unknown to most tourists, while clusters of centuries-old buildings that belong to Munich's origins are often separated by postwar developments of sometimes singular ugliness.

★ ⓳ **Alte Pinakothek** (Old Picture Gallery). This major art gallery contains some of the world's most celebrated old master paintings, including works by Dürer, Rembrandt, Rubens, and Murillo. Built by Leo von Klenze at the beginning of the 19th century to house Ludwig I's collections, the towering brick edifice is also an architectural treasure in its own right. After extensive renovations, the museum reopened in late 1997 and now displays its treasures in the high style they deserve. ✉ *Barestr. 27,* ☎ *089/238–05215.* ⊙ *Wed., Fri., and weekends 9–5; Tues. and Thurs. 9–8.*

⓼ **Altes Rathaus** (Old Town Hall). The 1474 medieval building has a fine assembly room used for official functions. Its tower provides a satisfyingly atmospheric setting for a little toy museum. ✉ *Marienpl.,* ☎ *089/233–22347.* ⊙ *Daily 10–5:30.*

★ ⓽ **Asamkirche** (Asam Church). Some consider the Asamkirche a preposterously overdecorated jewel box; others find it one of Europe's finest late-Baroque churches. It was built around 1730 by the Asam brothers—Cosmas Damian and Egid Quirin—next door to their home, the Asamhaus. They dedicated it to St. John Nepomuk, a 14th-century monk. Inside, there is a riot of decoration: frescoes, statuary, rich rosy marble, billowing stucco clouds, and gilding everywhere. ✉ *Sendlingerstr.* ⊙ *Daily 9–5:30.*

❸ **Bürgersaal.** Behind the modest facade of this unassuming building is an unusual split-level interior. The main Oberkirche (upper level) consists of a richly decorated Baroque oratory. The Unterkirche (lower level) is a cryptlike chapel containing the tomb of the courageous Jesuit priest Rupert Mayer, an outspoken opponent of the Nazis. ✉ *Neuhauserstr. 14,* ☎ *089/223–884.* ⊙ *Oberkirche: Mon.–Sat. 11–1, Sun. 9–12:30; Unterkirche: Mon.–Sat. 6:30 AM–7 PM, Sun. 7–7.*

⓱ **Englischer Garten** (English Garden). Count Rumford, a refugee from the American War of Independence, designed this seemingly endless park (5 km/3 mi long and more than ½ km/¼ mi wide). He was born in England, but it wasn't his English ancestry that determined the park's name as much as its open, informal nature, a style favored by 18th-century English aristocrats. Here you can rent boats, relax in beer gardens (the most famous is at the foot of a Chinese Pagoda), ride your bike (or ski in winter), or simply stroll. Ludwig II loved to wander incognito along the English Garden's serpentine paths. A large section of the park right behind the **Haus der Kunst**(☞ *below*) has been designated a nudist area. ✉ *Bordering the eastern side of Schwabing.*

⓯ **Feldherrnhalle** (Hall of Generals). This local open-air hall of fame was modeled on the 14th-century Loggia dei Lanzi in Florence. During the '30s and '40s it was a key Nazi shrine, marking the site of Hitler's abortive rising, or putsch, which took place in 1923. All who passed it had to give the Nazi salute. ✉ *South end of Odeonspl.*

★ ❺ **Frauenkirche** (Church of Our Lady). This soaring Gothic redbrick masterpiece has two incongruous towers topped by onion-shape domes,

232

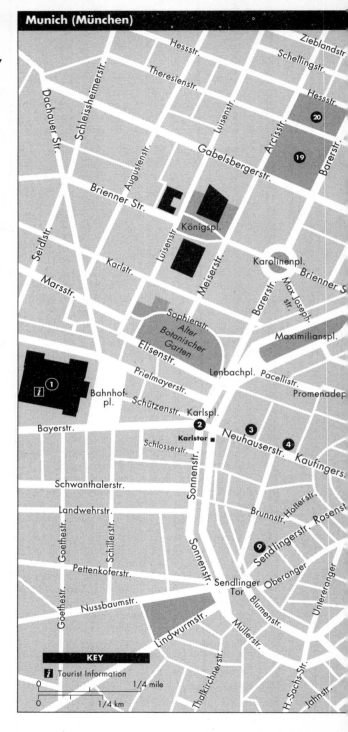

Munich (München)

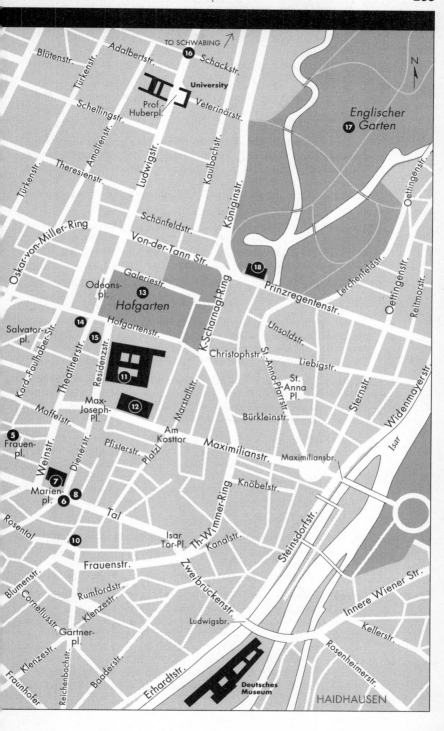

symbols of the city (perhaps because they resemble brimming beer mugs, cynics claim). The church was built between 1474 and 1494, and the towers were added in 1524–2l. The cathedral's interior is stark. The crypt houses the tombs of numerous Wittelsbachs, the family that ruled Bavaria for 7 centuries until forced to abdicate in 1918. ⊠ *Frauenpl.*, ☎ *089/290–0820.*

❶ Hauptbahnhof (Main Train Station). It contains the city tourist office, with maps and helpful information on events around town. ⊠ *Bayerstr.*, ☎ *089/239–1256.*

❶⑧ Haus der Kunst (House of Art). Munich's leading modern art gallery is housed in one of the city's few remaining Nazi-era monuments, opened officially in 1938 by Hitler himself. The gallery contains some outstanding 20th-century art, including works by Kandinsky and Klee. ⊠ *Prinzregentenstr. 1,* ☎ *089/2112–7137.* ⊘ *Tues., Wed., Fri., and weekends 10–5, Thurs. 10–8.*

❶③ Hofgarten (Royal Garden). Two sides of the pretty, formal garden that was once part of the royal palace grounds are bordered by arcades designed in the 19th century by the royal architect Leo von Klenze. ⊠ *Hofgartenstr., north of the Residenz.*

❷ Karlsplatz (Charles Square). Known locally as Stachus, this busy intersection has one of Munich's most popular fountains, a circle of water jets that cool city shoppers and office workers on hot summer days. The semicircle of yellow-front buildings that backs the fountain, with their high windows and delicate cast-iron balconies, gives the area a southern, almost Mediterranean, air. ⊠ *At the meeting point of Sonnenstr., Bayerstr., Schützenstr., Luisenstr., Prielmayerstr., and Neuhauserstr.*

★ **❻ Marienplatz** (Square of Our Lady). Surrounded by shops, restaurants, and cafés, this square is named after the 1638 gilt statue of the Virgin Mary that has been watching over it for nearly 4 centuries. ⊠ *Bordered by Kaufingerstr., Rosenstr., Weinstr., and Dienerstr.*

❹ Michaelskirche (St. Michael's Church). One of the most magnificent Renaissance churches in Germany, this spacious and handsome structure is decorated throughout in plain white stucco. It was built during the late 16th century for the Jesuits and was closely modeled on Il Gesù, the Jesuit church in Rome. ⊠ *Neuhauserstr. 6,* ☎ *089/551–99257.* ⊘ *Mon.–Wed., Fri., Sat. 8:30–7, Thurs. 8:30–9, Sun. 6 AM–10 PM. Guided tours Wed. at 2.*

❶② Nationaltheater (National Theater). Constructed at the beginning of the 19th century and twice destroyed, this neo-Classical opera house with state-of-the-art facilities is the home of the world-famous Bavarian State Opera and Ballet companies. ⊠ *Maximilianstr. 1,* ☎ *089/218–51920.*

❷⓪ Neue Pinakothek (New Picture Gallery). The original art gallery that King Ludwig I built to house his "modern" collections (meaning, of course, 19th-century works) was destroyed during World War II and replaced by a new exhibition hall in 1981. The low, brick structure— some have compared it to a Florentine palazzo—is a superb, skylit setting for one of the finest collections of European 19th-century paintings and sculpture in the world. ⊠ *Barerstr. 29, near Königspl.,* ☎ *089/238–05195.* ⊘ *Wed., Fri., and weekends 10–5; Tues., Thurs. 10–8.*

❼ Neues Rathaus (New City Hall). Munich's present city hall was built between 1867 and 1908 in the fussy, turreted, neo-Gothic style so beloved by King Ludwig II. At 9 AM and 11 AM daily (also May–Oct. at 5 PM and 9 PM), the Glockenspiel, or chiming clock, in the central tower swings into action with two tiers of dancing and jousting figures. An elevator whisks visitors to an observation point near the top of one of the towers. ⊠ *Marienpl.,* ☎ *089/2331.* ⊘ *Tower Apr.–Oct., Mon.–Thurs. 9–4, Fri. 9–1.*

⑪ **Residenz** (Royal Palace). This mighty yet somber palace dating from the 14th century was the home of the Wittelsbach dukes for more than 3 centuries. Its main attractions are the glittering Schatzkammer, or treasury, and glorious Rococo theater. ⊠ *Max-Joseph-Pl. 3,* ☎ *089/290–671.* ⊘ *Treasury: Tues.–Sun. 10–4:30. Cuvilliés Theater: Mon.–Sat. 2–5, Sun. 10–5.*

⑯ **Siegestor** (Victory Arch). The monument has Italian origins—it was modeled on the Arch of Constantine in Rome—and was built to honor the achievements of the Bavarian army during the Wars of Liberation (1813–15). ⊠ *At start of Leopoldstr.*

⑭ **Theatinerkirche** (Theatine Church). This handsome, yellow-stucco church was built for the Theatine monks in the mid-17th century, though its striking facade, with twin eye-catching domes, was added only in the following century. The interior is austerely white. ⊠ *Theatinerstr. 22,* ☎ *089/221–650.* ⊘ *Daily 7–7.*

★ ⑩ **Viktualienmarkt** (Food Market). The city's open-air market (*Viktualien* is an old German word for vittles, or food) has a wide range of produce—German and international goods, Bavarian beer, and French wines—making it a feast for the eyes as well as the stomach. ⊠ *Southeast of Marienpl. via Tal or Rindermarkt.* ⊘ *Mon.–Sat. 7–6:30.*

Munich Environs

KZ–Gedenkstätte Dachau (Dachau Concentration Camp Memorial). Although the 1,200-year-old town of Dachau attracted hordes of painters and artists from the mid-19th century until World War I, it is now best known as the site of Germany's first concentration camp. From its opening in 1933 until its capture by American soldiers in 1945, the camp held more than 206,000 political dissidents, Jews, homosexuals, clergy, and other "enemies" of the Nazis; more than 32,000 prisoners died here. Photographs, contemporary documents, the few remaining cell blocks, and the grim crematorium create a somber and moving picture of the vicious living and working conditions at the camp. The town of Dachau is a 20-minute ride from Marienplatz on the S-2 suburban railway line. To get to the concentration camp site take Bus 722 from the train station to Robert-Boschstrasse and walk along Alte Römerstrasse for 100 yards, or board Bus 720 and get off at Ratiborer Strasse. ⊠ *Alte Römerstr. 75,* ☎ *08121/1741.* 🎫 *Free.* ⊘ *Tues.–Sun. 9–5; documentary (in English) shown at 11:30 and 3:30.*

Olympiapark (Olympic Park). The undulating circus-tent-like roofs that cover the stadia built for the 1972 Olympic Games are unobtrusively tucked away in what is now known as Olympiapark on the northern edge of Schwabing. The roofs are made of translucent tiles that glisten in the midday sun and act as amplifiers for visiting rock bands. Train tours of the park run throughout the day from March through November. Take the elevator up the 960-ft Olympia Tower for a view of the city and the Alps; there's also a revolving restaurant near the top. Take the U-bahn 3 to the park. ⊠ *U-bahn 3 to northern edge of Schwabing,* ☎ *089/306–72414.* ⊘ *Main stadium: daily 9–4:30. Tower: daily 9 AM–midnight.*

Schloss Nymphenburg (Nymphenburg Palace). The summer palace of the Wittelsbachs stands magnificently in its own park in the western suburb of Nymphenburg. The oldest parts date from 1664, but construction continued for more than 100 years, the bulk of the work undertaken during the reign of Max Emmanuel between 1680 and 1730. The interiors are exceptional, especially the **Festsaal** (Banqueting Hall), a rococo masterpiece in green and gold. The **Schönheits Galerie** (Gallery of Beauties) contains more than 100 portraits of women who had caught the eye of Ludwig I. The rococo **Amalienburg** (Hunting Lodge) on the grounds was built by François Cuvilliés, architect of the theater in Munich's **Residenz** (☞ *above*). The palace also contains the **Marstallmuseum** (Museum of Royal Carriages), a sleigh that belonged to Ludwig II among the opulently decorated vehicles, and, on the floor above, the **Nymphenburger Porzellan** (Nympenburg Porcelain Gallery) with examples of the porcelain produced here between 1747 and the 1920s. The **Museum Mensch und Natur** (Museum of Man and Nature) in the north wing concentrates on the history of humans, the variety of life on Earth, and our place in the environment. ⊠ *U-bahn 1 from Hauptbahnhof to Rotkreuzpl., then pick up Tram 12, heading for Amalienburg,* ☎ *089/ 179–080.* ☉ *Apr.–Sept., Tues.–Sun. 9–12:30 and 1:30–5; Oct.–Mar., Tues.–Sun. 10–12:30 and 1:30–4; gardens daily year-round.*

DINING

The range of dining experiences in Germany is vast: everything from high priced nouvelle cuisine to plenty of sausages. Seek out local restaurants if atmosphere and regional specialties are your priority. Beer restaurants in Bavaria, *Apfelwein* (alcoholic apple cider) taverns in Frankfurt, and *Kneipen*—the pubs-cum-local-cafés on the corner—in Berlin nearly always offer the best value and atmosphere. But throughout the country you'll find *Gaststätten, Gasthäuser,* and/or *Gasthöfe*—local inns— where atmosphere and regional specialties are always available. Likewise, just about every town will have a *Ratskeller,* a cellar restaurant in the town hall, where exposed beams, huge fireplaces, sturdy tables, and immense portions are the rule.

The natural accompaniment to German food is either beer or wine. Munich is the beer capital of Germany, though there's no part of the country where you won't find the amber nectar. Say *"Helles"* or *"Export"* if you want light beer; *"Dunkles"* if you want dark beer. In Bavaria try the sour but refreshing beer brewed from wheat, called *Weissbier.*

Germany is also a major producer of wine, and much of it is of superlative quality. Try the house wine in most restaurants or an earthenware pitcher of cold Mosel wine. If you want something more expensive, remember that all wines are graded in one of three basic categories: *Tafelwein* (table wine); *Qualitätswein* (fine wine); and *Qualitätswein mit Prädikat* (top-quality wine).

MEALTIMES
Breakfast, served from 6:30 to 10 (in some cafés and Kneipen, until as late as 2 or 4 PM), is often a substantial meal, with cold meats, cheeses, rolls, and fruit. Many city hotels offer Sunday brunch, and the custom is rapidly catching on. Lunch is served from around 11:30 (especially in rural areas) to around 2; dinner is generally from 6 until 9:30, or earlier in some quiet country areas. Big-city hotels and popular restaurants serve later. Lunch tends to be the main meal, a fact reflected in the almost universal appearance of a lunchtime *Tageskarte,* or suggested menu; try it if you want maximum nourishment for minimum outlay.

RATINGS
The following chart gives price ranges for restaurants in the western part of Germany. Food prices in the former East Germany are still somewhat unstable, although in the bigger cities many of the better-quality restau-

rants already mimic rates in western Germany. Bills in simple restaurants in country areas of the eastern region still come well below DM 35. Prices are per person and include a first course, main course, dessert, and tip and 10% tax.

CATEGORY	COST
$$$$	over DM 100
$$$	DM 75–DM 100
$$	DM 50–DM 75
$	under DM 50

Munich claims some of Europe's best chefs, purveyors of French nouvelle cuisine in some of the most noted—and pricey—restaurants in Germany. For local cuisine, Munich's wood-paneled, flagstone beer restaurants and halls serve food as sturdy as the large measure of beer that comes to your table almost automatically. Münchners love to eat just as much as they love to drink their beer, and the range of food is as varied and rich as the local breweries' output.

$$$$ ✕ **Königshof.** On the second floor of the postwar Königshof Hotel and
★ overlooking the Karlstor at the northern entrance to the pedestrian-only center, the Königshof is without doubt Munich's most opulent restaurant. The neo-Baroque style includes ceiling frescoes, subdued chandelier lighting, and heavy drapery. Nouvelle cuisine is served—breast of goose with truffles, for example, or veal in basil cream and mushroom sauce. ✉ *Karlspl. 25,* ☎ *089/551–36142. AE, DC, MC, V.*

$$$ ✕ **Lenbach.** Michael Käfer's latest spectacular addition to the restaurant scene is not for the shy: Guests enter the vast dining area along a floor-lit catwalk. Britain's number-one restaurant designer, Sir Terence Conran, was given a 100-year-old city palace to work on and clearly had a ball. The high, vaulted ceilings, marble pillars, art nouveau wrought-iron and rich stucco were blended with Conran's typical minimalist decoration, all under the general theme of the "Seven Deadly Sins." The seafood is outstanding and is a feature of a daily buffet in the chandelier-hung main lobby. The bar, by the way, is Munich's longest. ✉ *Ottostr. 6,* ☎ *089/549–1300. Jacket and tie. AE, MC, V.*

$$$ ✕ **Preysing Keller.** The food here is light and sophisticated but with
★ recognizably Teutonic touches. The over-restored restaurant is in a 16th-century cellar. It's the food, the extensive wine list, and the perfect service that make this place special. ✉ *Innere-Wiener-Str. 6,* ☎ *089/458–45260. Reservations essential. No credit cards. Closed Sun.*

$$–$$$ ✕ **Dukatz.** Join the Munich literati and glitterati in the severely intellectual surroundings of the *Literaturhaus* (House of Literature). The restaurant hums with talk of publishing contracts and literary gossip. Its excellent cuisine combines traditional German with a light Gallic touch: lamb's tripe melting in a rich champagne sauce, for instance, or stuffed pig's trotters with truffles. The light and airy café-bar has a pile of American and British daily papers. ✉ *Salvatorpl. 1,* ☎ *089/291–9600. Reservations essential. No credit cards. Closed Sun. dinner.*

$$ ✕ **Augustiner Keller.** This 19th-century establishment is the flagship beer restaurant of one of Munich's oldest breweries, Augustiner. The decor of the two baronial hall-like rooms emphasizes wood—from the refurbished parquet floors to the wooden barrels from which the beer is drawn. Bavarian specialties such as *Tellerfleisch*—cold roast beef with lashings of horseradish, served on a big wooden board—fill the daily menu. ✉ *Arnulfstr. 52,* ☎ *089/594–393. AE, DC, MC, V.*

$$ ✕ **Bamberger Haus.** This historic villa on the edge of Schwabing's Luitpold Park has a rambling, vaulted beer-cellar and a slightly faded upstairs dining room. You dine beneath crystal chandeliers and under the gaze of Baroque statuary. Some of the vegetarian dishes on the imaginative menu, such as finely prepared vegetables au gratin, are incredibly cheap and filling. ✉ *Brunnerstr. 2,* ☎ *089/308–8966. AE, MC, V.*

$$ ✕ **Dürnbräu.** A fountain plays outside this picturesque old Bavarian inn. Inside, it's crowded and noisy. Expect to share a table; your fellow diners will range from business sorts to students. The food is resolutely traditional. Try the cream of spinach soup and the boiled beef. ✉ *Dürnbräug. 2,* ☎ *089/222–195. AE, DC, MC, V.*

$$ ✕ **Grüne Gans.** This small, chummy restaurant near the Viktualienmarkt is popular with local entertainers, whose photographs clutter the walls. International fare with regional German influences dominates the menu. Try the chervil cream soup, followed by calves' kidneys in tarragon sauce. ✉ *Am Einlass 5,* ☎ *089/266–228. Reservations essential. No credit cards. Closed lunch and Sun.*

$$ ✕ **Weinhaus Neuner.** Originally a seminary, this early 18th-century building houses Munich's oldest surviving wine hostelry, in the Neuner family since 1852. The high-ceiling dining rooms are lined with dark oak paneling. Look for the herb-filled pork fillets with noodles, and veal with Morchela mushroom sauce. ✉ *Herzogspitalstr. 8,* ☎ *089/260– 3954. Reservations essential. AE, DC, MC. Closed Sun. and holidays.*

$ ✕ **Altes Hackerhaus.** This upscale beer restaurant on one of Munich's
★ ritziest shopping streets is full of bric-a-brac and mementos that hark back to its origins as a medieval brewery. Since 1570, beer has been brewed or served here at the birthplace of one of the city's largest breweries—Hacker-Pschorr. Duck into one of the cozy little rooms and choose from the selection of hearty soups, then try a plate of *Käsespätzle* (egg noodles with melted cheese). ✉ *Sendlingerstr. 14,* ☎ *089/260– 5026. AE, DC, MC, V.*

$ ✕ **Brauhaus zur Brez'n.** This hostelry bedecked in the blue and white of the Bavarian flag spreads over three floors. Everyone from local business lunchers to hungry night owls chooses from a big all-day menu of traditional roasts, to be washed down with a choice of three draft beers. ✉ *Leopoldstr. 72,* ☎ *089/390–092. No credit cards.*

$ ✕ **Franziskaner.** Vaulted archways, cavernous rooms interspersed with intimate dining areas, bold blue frescoes on the walls, and long wooden tables create a spic-and-span medieval atmosphere. Besides the late-morning *Weisswurst* (a delicate white sausage), look for *Ochsenfleisch* (boiled ox meat) and dumplings. ✉ *Perusastr. 5,* ☎ *089/231–8120. Reservations not accepted. AE, DC, MC, V.*

$ ✕ **Hofbräuhaus.** The cavernous, smoky, stone vaults of the Hofbräuhaus contain crowds of singing, shouting, swaying beer drinkers. If you're not here solely to drink, try the Bavarian food in the more subdued upstairs restaurant, where the service is not so brusque. It's between Marienpl. and Maximilianstrasse. ✉ *Platzl 9,* ☎ *089/221– 676. Reservations not accepted. MC, V.*

$ ✕ **Hundskugel.** History practically oozes from the crooked walls at this tavern, Munich's oldest, which dates from 1440. Order *Spanferkel*— roast suckling pig—if it's on the menu; this is simple Bavarian fare at its best. ✉ *Hotterstr. 18,* ☎ *089/264–272. No credit cards. Closed Sun.*

$ ✕ **Pfälzer Weinprobierstube.** A warren of stone-vault rooms of vari-
★ ous sizes, wooden tables, glittering candles, dirndl-clad waitresses, and a vast range of wines provide a backdrop for food that's reliable rather than spectacular. Local specialties predominate. ✉ *Residenzstr. 1,* ☎ *089/225–628. Reservations not accepted. No credit cards.*

NIGHTLIFE AND THE ARTS

The Arts

Details of concerts and theater performances are available from the "Vorschau" or "Monatsprogramm" booklets obtainable at most hotel reception desks. Some hotels will make ticket reservations; otherwise book tickets at the two kiosks on the concourse below Marienplatz, or use one of the ticket agencies in the city center: **Max Hieber Konzertkasse** (✉ Liebfrauenstr. 1, ☎ 089/290–08014) or the **Residenz Bücherstube** (✉ Residenzstr. 1, ☎ 089/220–868 concert tickets only).

CONCERTS

Munich's Philharmonic Orchestra performs in Germany's biggest concert hall, the **Gasteig Cultural Center** (✉ Rosenheimerstr. 5, ☎ 089/5481–8181). Tickets can be purchased at the box office. The Bavarian Radio Orchestra also performs Sunday concerts here. In summer, concerts are held at Schloss Nymphenburg and in the open-air interior courtyard of the Residenz (☞ Exploring Munich, *above*).

DANCE

The ballet company of the Bavarian State Opera performs at the **Nationaltheater** (✉ Maximilianstr. 11, ☎ 089/2185–1920). Ballet productions are also staged at the attractive late-19th-century **Staatstheater am Gärtnerplatz** (✉ Gärtnerpl. 3, ☎ 089/201–6767).

OPERA

Munich's Bavarian State Opera company is world famous, and tickets for major productions in its permanent home, the **Nationaltheater** (✉ Maximilianstr. 11, ☎ 089/2185–1920), are difficult to obtain; the box office takes reservations one week in advance only. Book far in advance through the tourist office (☞ Visitor Information, *below*) for the annual opera festival held in July and August.

THEATER

The Bavarian state-supported Residenz Theater (Royal Theater), concentrates on the classics. The Kammerspiele is financed mostly by the city government. More than 20 other theater companies (some of them performing in basements) are to be found throughout the city. Regular English-language productions, featuring the American Drama Group Europe, are staged at the **Theater an der Leopoldstrasse** (✉ Leopoldstr. 17, ☎ 089/380–14032) or in the auditorium of **America House** (Amerikahaus; ✉ Karolinenpl. 3, ☎ 089/552–5370). The English-language productions are also staged from time to time at the **Theater im Karlshof** (✉ Karlstr. 43, ☎ 089/596–611).

Nightlife

BARS, CABARET, NIGHTCLUBS

Schumann's (✉ Maximilianstr. 36, ☎ 089/229–268) has a shabby New York bar look, but the clientele is Munich chic. **Käfers am Odeonsplatz** (✉ Odeonspl. 3, ☎ 089/290–7530) attracts a similarly smart and contact-happy crowd. Munich's media types have turned the **Alter Simpl** (✉ Turkenstr. 57, ☎ 089/272–3083) into an unofficial press club. **O'Reilly's Irish Cellar Pub** (✉ Maximilianstr. 29, ☎ 089/292–311) serves genuine Irish Guinness. Great Caribbean cocktails and a powerful Irish-German Black and Tan (Guinness and strong German beer) are served at the English nautical-style **Pusser's** bar (✉ Falkenturmstr. 9, ☎ 089/220–500). The **Havana** (✉ Herrnstr. 3, ☎ 089/291–884) does its best to look like a run-down Cuban dive, drawing a chic clientele. At the **Wunderbar** (✉ Hochbrückenstr. 3, ☎ 089/295–118) on Tuesday nights telephones are installed on the tables and at the bar, and the place hums like a stygian switchboard.

Munich has a spectacular new disco center: the **Kunstpark Ost** (⊠ Grafingerstr. 6, ☎ 089/490–72113), a former pasta factory with 13 "entertainment areas," including several discos and music bars. Discos abound in the side streets off **Freilitzschstrasse,** surrounding Münchener Freiheit in Schwabing. Tops of the lot (quite literally) is the **Skyline** (⊠ Münchner Freiheit, ☎ 089/333–131), at the top of the Hertie department store building Münchner Freiheit. The **Nachtcafe** (⊠ Maximilianspl. 5, ☎ 089/595–900), is open all night on weekends. At **Maximilian's** (⊠ Maximilianspl. 16, ☎ 089/223–252), the chic crowd packs a throbbing cellar into the early hours. **P1** (⊠ Haus der Kunst, Prinzregentenstr. 1, ☎ 089/294–252) is the queen of them all, a place to see and be seen, with a series of tiny dance floors and a great sound system.

The **Unterfahrt** (⊠ Kirchenstr. 96, ☎ 089/448–279), in Munich's latest "quartier Latin," Haidhausen, has traditional and mainstream jazz. Munich's longest-established jazz haunt, the **Podium** (⊠ Wagnerstr. 1, ☎ 089/399–482), has taken to offering rock music as well as traditional jazz; it's packed nightly.

SHOPPING

Antiques

Blumenstrasse, Ottostrasse, Türkenstrasse, and Westenriederstrasse all have antiques shops. The open-air **Auer Dult fairs** sell antiques; they're held on Mariahilfplatz at the end of April, July, and October (Streetcar 25).

Department Stores

Most of the city's major department stores are along Maffeistrasse, Kaufingerstrasse, and Neuhauserstrasse. **Hertie** (⊠ Bahnhofpl. 7, ☎ 089/55120) is the largest and, some claim, the best department store in the city; it has a stylish delicatessen with champagne bar and bistro. **Kaufhof** has two central Munich stores (⊠ Karlspl. 2, opposite Hertie, ☎ 089/51250; ⊠ corner of Marienpl., ☎ 089/231–851); both offer a wide range of goods in the middle price range. **Karstadt** (⊠ Neuhauserstr. 18, ☎ 089/290–230) is a high-class department store, with a very wide range of Bavarian arts and crafts.

Gift Ideas

Munich is a city of beer, and beer mugs and coasters make an obvious gift to take home. Many shops specialize in beer-related souvenirs, but **Ludwig Mory** (⊠ Marienpl. 8, ☎ 089/224–542) is about the best. Munich is also the home of the famous **Porzellan Manufaktur Nymphenburg** (Nymphenburg Porcelain Factory; ⊠ corner of Odeonspl. and Briennerstr., ☎ 089/282–428; ⊠ Nördliche Schlossrondell 8, in front of Schloss Nymphenburg, ☎ 089/1791–9710).

Shopping Districts

Munich has an immense **central shopping area,** 2 km (1 mi) of pedestrian streets stretching from the train station to Marienplatz and north to Odeonsplatz. The two main streets here are Neuhauserstrasse and Kaufingerstrasse. For **upscale shopping** Maximilianstrasse, Residenzstrasse, and Theatinerstrasse are unbeatable and contain a fine array of classy and tempting stores. **Schwabing,** north of the university, has several of the city's most intriguing and offbeat shopping streets—Schellingstrasse and Hohenzollernstrasse are two to try.

MUNICH ESSENTIALS

Arriving and Departing

BY BUS

Munich has no central bus station. Long-distance buses arrive at and depart from the north side of the train station on Arnulfstrasse.

BY CAR

From the north (Nürnberg, Frankfurt), leave the autobahn at the Schwabing exit and follow the STADTMITTE signs. The autobahn from Stuttgart and the west ends at Obermenzing; again, follow the STADT-MITTE signs. The autobahns from Salzburg and the east, from Garmisch and the south, and from Lindau and the southwest all join up with the city beltway, the Mittlerer Ring. The city center is well posted.

BY PLANE

Munich's **Franz Josef Strauss (FJS) Airport,** named for a former state premier, is 28 km (17 mi) northeast of the city center.

Between the Airport and Downtown. The S-8 and S-1 **S-bahn** (suburban train lines) link FJS Airport with the city's main train station (Hauptbahnhof). Trains depart in both directions every 10 minutes from 3:55 AM to 12:55 AM daily. Intermediate stops are made at the Ostbahnhof (good for hotels located east of the River Isar) and city-center stations such as Marienplatz. The 38-minute trip costs DM 10.80 if you purchase a multi-use strip ticket (☞ Getting Around, *below*) and use 8 strips; otherwise an ordinary one-way ticket is DM 12.80 per person. A tip for families: Up to five people (maximum of two adults) can travel to or from the airport for only DM 24 after 9 AM by buying a Tageskarte (☞ Getting Around, *below*).

Bus service is slower and more expensive (DM 15) than the S-bahn; only use it if you're carrying a great deal of luggage. A **taxi** will cost between DM 80 and DM 100. If you are **driving** from the airport into the city, follow the MÜNCHEN autobahn signs to A92 and A9. Once on the A92, watch carefully for the signs to Munich; a relatively high number of motorists miss the sign and end up headed toward Stuttgart.

BY TRAIN

All long-distance services arrive at and depart from the main train station, the Hauptbahnhof. Trains to and from destinations in the Bavarian Alps usually use the adjoining Starnbergerbahnhof. For information on train times call 089/19419. For tickets and information go to the station or to the ABR travel agency on Bahnhofplatz.

Getting Around

BY PUBLIC TRANSPORTATION

Downtown Munich is only about 1.6 km (1 mi) square, so it can easily be explored on foot. Other areas—Schwabing, Nymphenburg, the Olympiapark—are best reached on the efficient and comprehensive **public transportation network,** which incorporates buses, streetcars, U-bahn (subways), and S-bahn (suburban trains). Tickets are good for the entire network, and you can break your trip as many times as you like using just one ticket, provided you travel in one direction within a given period of time. If you plan to make only a few trips, buy *Streifenkarten* (strip tickets)—blue for adults, red for children. At press time (spring 1998), an 11-strip ticket cost DM 15. All tickets must be validated by time, punching them in the automatic machines at station entrances and on all buses and streetcars.

The best buy is the *Tageskarte* (all-day ticket): Up to two adults and three children can use this ticket for unlimited journeys between 9 AM and the end of the day's service (about 2 AM). It costs DM 12 for the

inner zone, which covers central Munich. A Tageskarte for the entire
system, extending to the Starnbergersee and Ammersee, costs DM 24.
Holders of a Eurail Pass, a Youth Pass, an InterRail Card, or a DB Tourist
Card travel free on all S-bahn trains.

BY TAXI

Munich's cream-color taxis are numerous. Hail them in the street or
call 089/21610 or 089/19410. Rates start at DM 5 and rise by DM
2.20 per km (about DM 4 per mi). There are additional charges of DM
2 if a taxi is ordered by telephone and DM 1 per piece of luggage. Plan
to pay about DM 13 for a short trip within the city.

Contacts and Resources

CONSULATES

United States (⊠ Königinstr. 5, ☎ 089/28880). **Canadian** (⊠ Tal 29, ☎
089/290–650). **United Kingdom** (⊠ Bürkleinstr. 10, ☎ 089/211–090).

EMERGENCIES

Police (☎ 110). **Fire Department and Paramedical Aid** (☎ 112). **Ambulance and emergency medical attention** (☎ 089/19222). **Dentist** (☎
089/723–3093). **Pharmacies: Internationale Ludwigs-Apotheke** (⊠
Neuhauserstr. 11, ☎ 089/260–3021); **Europa-Apotheke** (⊠ Schützenstr. 12, near the Hauptbahnhof, ☎ 089/595–423).

ENGLISH-LANGUAGE BOOKSTORES

The **Anglia English Bookshop** (⊠ Schellingstr. 3, ☎ 089/283–642).
Hugendubel (⊠ Marienpl. 22, ☎ 089/22890; ⊠ Karlspl. 3, ☎ 089/
552–2530).

GUIDED TOURS

Orientation. City bus tours are operated by **Panorama Tours** (⊠ Arnulfstr. 8, ☎ 089/591–504). Tours run daily and take in the city center, the Olympiapark, and Schloss Nymphenburg. Departures are at
10 AM and 2:30 PM (and 11:30 AM in midsummer) from outside the
Hertie department store across from the Hauptbahnhof, the main
train station. The cost ranges from DM 15 to DM 27 per person.

Walking and Cycling. Münchner Stadtrundgänge has a Central Munich walking tour that starts daily at 9:30 at the Mariensäule column
in the center of the Marienplatz; cost: DM 10. **Radius Touristik** (⊠ Arnulfstr. 3, opposite platforms 30–36 in the Hauptbahnhof main concourse, ☎ 089/596–113) has bicycle tours from May through the
beginning of October at 10:15 and 2; cost, including bike rental: DM
15. **City Hopper Touren** (☎ 089/272–1131) tours of the city, including bike rentals, cost DM 40 per person in a group of two to DM 20
for larger groups. **Mike's Bike Tours** (☎ 089/651–4275) organizes tours
of the city by English-speaking guides daily March through November, starting from the Altes Rathaus at 11:30 and 4. The DM 28 cost
includes bike rental and, in fine weather, a beer-garden stop.

Excursions. Panorama Tours (⊠ Arnulfstr. 8, ☎ 089/591–504) organizes bus trips to most leading tourist attractions outside the city, including the "Royal Castles Tour" (Schlösserfahrt) of "Mad" King
Ludwig's dream palaces; cost: DM 75.

TRAVEL AGENCIES

American Express (⊠ Promenadepl. 6, ☎ 089/290–900). **ABR** (☎ 089/
12040), the official Bavarian travel, has outlets all over Munich.

VISITOR INFORMATION

Rathaus (⊠ City Hall on Marienpl., ☎ 089/233–30273). **Hauptbahnhof**
(Main Train Station, ⊠ Bahnhofpl. 2, next to ABR travel agency, ☎
089/233–30256). **Franz Josef Strauss Airport** (☎ 089/9759–2815).

17 Paris

*I*f there's a problem with a trip to Paris, it is the embarrassment of riches that faces you. A city of vast, noble perspectives and winding, hidden streets, Paris remains a combination of the pompous and the intimate. Whether you've come looking for sheer physical beauty, cultural and artistic diversions, world-famous dining and shopping, history, or simply local color, you will find it here in abundance.

EXPLORING PARIS

Numbers in the margin correspond to points of interest on the Paris map.

Paris is a compact city. With the exceptions of the Bois de Boulogne and Montmartre, you can easily walk from one sight to the next. The city is divided in two by the River Seine, with two islands (Ile de la Cité and Ile St-Louis) in the middle. The south—or Left—Bank has a more intimate, bohemian flavor than the haughtier Right Bank. The east–west axis from Châtelet to the Arc de Triomphe, via the rue de Rivoli and the Champs-Elysées, is the principal thoroughfare for sightseeing and shopping on the Right Bank.

A special **Carte Musées et Monuments** pass, allowing access to most Paris museums and monuments, can be obtained from museums or major métro stations (one-day pass, 70 frs; three days, 140 frs; five days, 200 frs). Note, however, that this pass may only be useful to you if you plan to see a lot of museums in the allotted days.

If time is a problem, try to get in several "musts": Explore Notre-Dame and the Latin Quarter; head to place de la Concorde and enjoy the vista from the Champs-Elysées to the Louvre; then take a boat along the Seine for a waterside rendezvous with the Eiffel Tower. You could finish off with dinner in Montmartre and consider it a day well spent.

From the Arc de Triomphe to the Louvre

❶ Arc de Triomphe (Triumphal Arch). This 164-ft arch was planned by Napoléon to celebrate his military successes. Yet when Empress Marie-Louise entered Paris in 1810, it was barely off the ground. Napoléon had been dead for 15 years when the Arc de Triomphe was finished in 1836. The arch looms over place Charles-de-Gaulle, referred to by Parisians as **L'Étoile** (The Star), one of Europe's most chaotic traffic circles. Short of a death-defying dash, your only way to get over to the Arc de Triomphe is to take the pedestrian underpass. France's Unknown Soldier is buried beneath the archway; the flame is rekindled every evening at 6:30. Halfway up the arch is a small museum devoted to its history. ✉ *Pl. Charles-de-Gaulle,* ☎ *01–43–80–31–31.* ⊙ *Daily 10–5:30; Oct.–Easter, daily 10–5. Closed public holidays. Métro, RER: Charles-de-Gaulle–Étoile.*

❹ Champs-Elysées. The cosmopolitan pulse of Paris beats strongest along this gracefully sloping, 2-km (1¼-mi) avenue, originally laid out in the 1660s by André Le Nôtre as a garden sweeping away from the Tuileries. There isn't much sign of that pastoral past these days, as you stroll by the cafés, restaurants, airline offices, car showrooms, movie theaters, and chic arcades that occupy its upper half. *Métro: George-V, Franklin-D.-Roosevelt, Champs-Elysées–Clemenceau.*

❺ Grand Palais (Grand Palace). This so-called palace was built for the World Exhibition of 1900 and now houses temporary exhibitions. Unfortunately the main hall, with its Art Nouveau iron banisters and striking glass roof, is closed for renovation until the end of the century; but you can still visit the **Palais de la Découverte** (Palace of Discovery), with scientific and mechanical exhibits and a **planetarium.** ✉ *Av. Winston-Churchill,* ☎ *01–44–13–17–17.* ⊙ *Palais de la Découverte: Tues.–Sat. 9:30–6, Sun. 10–7. Métro: Franklin-D.-Roosevelt.*

⓱ Jardin des Tuileries (Tuileries Garden). This enormous formal garden is lined with trees, ponds, and statues. Standing guard on either side as you arrive from place de la Concorde are two museums, the **Musée Jeu de Paume** and the **Musée de l'Orangerie** (☞ *below*), identical buildings erected during the mid-19th century. At the far end of the Tuileries, leading toward the Louvre, is the **Arc du Carrousel,** a dainty triumphal arch erected more quickly (1806–08) than its big brother at the far end of the Champs-Elysées. *Métro: Concorde.*

★ ⓲ Louvre. Once a royal palace, now the world's largest and most famous museum, the Louvre has been given fresh purpose by a decade of expansion, renovation, and reorganization, symbolized by I. M. Pei's daring glass pyramid that now serves as the entrance to both the museum and an underground shopping arcade, the **Carrousel du Louvre.**

The Louvre was begun as a fortress around 1200, but the earliest parts still in use date from the 1540s. Building was a regular process until the reign of Napoléon III in the 1860s. Then, the Louvre was even larger; a wing facing the Tuileries Gardens was razed by rampaging revolutionaries during the bloody Paris Commune of 1871.

Pei's new Louvre has emerged less cramped and more rationally organized. Yet its sheer variety can intimidate. The main tourist attraction is Leonardo da Vinci's *Mona Lisa* (known in French as *La Joconde*), painted in 1503. It's smaller than you might have imagined, kept behind glass, and invariably encircled by a mob of tourists. Turn your attention instead to some less-crowded rooms and galleries nearby, where Leonardo's fellow Italians are strongly represented: Fra Angelico, Giotto, Mantegna, Raphael, Titian, and Veronese. El Greco, Murillo, and Velázquez lead the Spanish; Van Eyck, Rembrandt, Frans Hals, Bruegel, Holbein, and Rubens underline the achievements of northern European art. English paintings are highlighted by works of Lawrence, Reynolds, Gainsborough, and Turner. Highlights of French painting include works by Poussin, Fragonard, Chardin, Boucher, and Watteau—together with David's *Coronation of Napoléon,* Géricault's *Raft of the Medusa,* and Delacroix's *Liberty Guiding the People.*

Famous statues include the soaring *Victory of Samothrace,* the celebrated *Venus de Milo,* and the realistic Egyptian *Seated Scribe.* New rooms for ancient Persian, Arab, and Greek art were opened in 1997. Also be sure to inspect the Gobelin tapestries, the Crown Jewels (including the 186-carat Regent diamond), and the 9th-century bronze statuette of Emperor Charlemagne. ✉ *Palais du Louvre,* ☎ *01–40–20–53–17 for information.* ☉ *Mon. and Wed. 9 AM–9:45 PM, Thurs.–Sun. 9–6. Métro: Palais Royal.*

❾ Musée du Jeu de Paume. Home to the Impressionists before their move to the Musée d'Orsay across the Seine, the Jue de Paume (literally, palm game—a forerunner of tennis) Museum is now an airy, austere, white-walled center for contemporary art. ✉ *Pl. de la Concorde,* ☎ *01–42–60–69–69.* ☉ *Tues. noon–9:30, Wed.–Fri. noon–7, weekends 10–7. Métro: Concorde.*

❽ Musée de l'Orangerie (Orangery Museum). This museum bordering the Jardins des Tuileries contains fine early 20th-century French works by Monet (including some of his *Water Lilies*), Renoir, Marie Laurencin, and others. ✉ *Pl. de la Concorde,* ☎ *01–42–97–48–16.* ☉ *Wed.–Mon. 9:45–5:15.*

❻ Petit Palais (Little Palace). Directly opposite the main entrance to the Grand Palais, and built at the same time (1900), this building is now home to an attractively presented collection of French paintings and furniture from the 18th and 19th centuries. ☉ *Tues.–Sun. 10–5:40,* ☎ *01–42–65–12–73. Métro: Champs-Elysées–Clemenceau.*

❼ Place de la Concorde. Flanked by elegant neoclassical buildings, this huge square is often choked with traffic and perhaps at its most scenic come nightfall. Over 1,000 people, including Louis XVI and Marie-Antoinette, were guillotined here in the early 1790s. The obelisk, a gift from the viceroy of Egypt, originally stood at Luxor and was erected here in 1833. *Métro: Concorde.*

From the Eiffel Tower to Pont de l'Alma

㊼ Hôtel des Invalides. The Invalides, soaring above expansive if hardly manicured lawns, was founded by Louis XIV in 1674 to house wounded (or "invalid") war veterans. Although only a few old soldiers live here today, the military link remains in the form of the **Musée de l'Armée**—a vast, though musty military museum with a collection of arms, armor, and uniforms. The **Musée des Plans-Reliefs** contains a fascinating collection of scale models of French towns, dating from the days of military architect Vauban in the 17th century. The Invalides, itself, is an outstanding Baroque ensemble, designed by Bruand and Hardouin-Mansart. Its church, the **Église du Dôme**, possesses the city's most elegant dome as well as the tomb of Napoléon. ✉ *Esplanade des Invalides,* ☎ *01–44–42–37–67.* ☉ *Daily 10–6 (Oct.–Mar. 10–5). Métro: Latour-Maubourg.*

㊿ Musée d'Art Moderne de la Ville de Paris (City of Paris Museum of Modern Art). Both temporary exhibits and a permanent collection of top-quality 20th-century art can be found at this modern art museum.

Paris

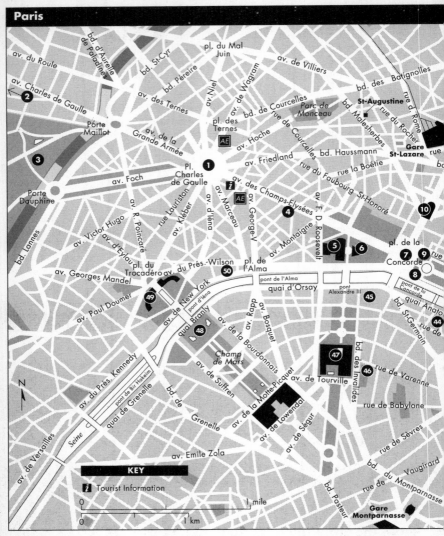

KEY

i Tourist Information

0 ———————— 1 mile

0 ———————— 1 km

Place des Vosges, **24**
Sacré-Coeur, **14**
St-Eustache, **20**
St-Germain-
des-Prés, **43**
St-Paul–
St-Louis, **33**
St-Sulpice, **42**
La Sorbonne, **38**
Tour Eiffel
(Eiffel Tower), **48**
Val de Grâce, **40**

It takes over, chronologically speaking, where the Musée d'Orsay leaves off. ⊠ *11 av. du Président-Wilson,* ☎ *01–53–67–40–00.* 🖾 *27 frs.* ⊘ *Tues.–Sun. 10–5:30, Wed. 10–8:30. Métro: Iéna.*

㊾ Palais de Chaillot (Chaillot Palace). This honey-color, Art Deco culture center facing the Seine, perched atop tumbling gardens with sculpture and fountains, was built in the 1930s. It houses three museums: the **Musée des Monuments Français** (French Monuments Museum), whose painstaking replicas of statues and archways form an excellent introduction to French medieval architecture; the **Musée de la Marine** (Maritime Museum), with a salty collection of seafaring paraphernalia; and the **Musée de l'Homme** (Museum of Mankind), an anthropology museum with an array of prehistoric artifacts. ⊠ *Pl. du Trocadéro.* ⊘ *Daily 10–5. Métro: Trocadéro.*

㊽ Tour Eiffel (Eiffel Tower). What is now the worldwide symbol of Paris nearly became 7,000 tons of scrap-iron when its concession expired in 1909. Only its potential use as a radio antenna saved the day. Architect Gustave Eiffel, whose skill as an engineer earned him renown as a builder of iron bridges, created his Tower for the World Exhibition of 1889. Restoration in the 1980s didn't make the elevators any faster—long lines are inevitable unless you come in the evening (when every girder is lit in glorious detail)—but decent shops and two good restaurants were added. The view from 1,000 ft up will enable you to appreciate the city's layout and proportions. ⊠ *quai Branly,* ☎ *01–44–11–23–23.* 🖾 *On foot, 14 frs; by elevator, 20–57 frs, depending on the level.* ⊘ *July–Aug., daily 9 AM–midnight; Sept.–June, Sun.–Thurs. 9 AM–11 PM, Fri., Sat. 9 AM–midnight. Métro: Bir-Hakeim, RER: Champ-de-Mars.*

The Faubourg St-Honoré

⑩ Église de la Madeleine. With its uncompromising array of columns, this church, known as La Madeleine, looks more like a Greek temple. The only natural light inside comes from three shallow domes; the walls are richly but harmoniously decorated, with plenty of gold glinting through the murk. The church was designed in 1814 but not consecrated until 1842, after futile efforts to turn the site into a train station. ⊠ *Pl. de la Madeleine.* ⊘ *Mon.–Sat. 7:30–7, Sun. 8–7. Métro: Madeleine.*

⑲ Palais-Royal (Royal-Palace). This former royal palace, built in the 1630s and now occupied by the Ministry of Culture, has a charming garden bordered by arcades and boutiques, discreetly tucked away in the heart of Paris. Not so discreet are Daniel Buren's sawn-off candy-stripe columns in the adjacent courtyard, commissioned by Socialist Culture Minister Jack Lang in the 1980s. ⊠ *Entrance on pl. André-Malraux. Métro: Palais-Royal.*

⑯ Place Vendôme. This rhythmically proportioned example of 17th-century urban architecture is one of the world's most opulent squares. Top jewelers compete for attention with the limousines and supermodels that draw up outside the Ritz Hotel. The square's central pillar was made from the melted bronze of 1,200 cannons captured by Napoléon at the Battle of Austerlitz in 1805. That's Napoléon at the top, disguised as a Roman emperor. *Métro: Tuileries.*

⑳ St-Eustache. This colossal church, also known as the Cathedral of Les Halles, was erected between 1532 and 1637, and testifies to the stylistic transition between Gothic and Classical architecture. ⊠ *2 rue du Jour. Métro: Les Halles, RER: Châtelet–Les Halles.*

The Grand Boulevards

⑫ **Grands Magasins** (Department Stores). Paris's most venerable department stores can be found behind the Opéra: **Galeries Lafayette** has an elegant turn-of-the-century glass dome; **Au Printemps** has an excellent view from its rooftop cafeteria. ⊠ *Bd. Haussmann. Métro: Havre-Caumartin.*

㉑ **Les Halles.** Since the city's much-lamented central glass-and-iron market halls were torn down during the late '60s, the area has been transformed into a trendy—albeit slightly seedy—shopping complex, Le Forum des Halles, with an extensive topiary garden basking in the shadow of the nearby **Bourse du Commerce** (Commercial Exchange) and bulky church of **St-Eustache** (☞ Faubourg St-Honoré, *above*). *Métro/RER: Les Halles.*

⑪ **Opéra Garnier.** The original Paris opera house was the flagship building of the Second Empire (1851–70), and its design mirrors the period's flaunt-it philosophy. Architect Charles Garnier fused elements of neoclassical architecture—bas-reliefs on facades and columns—in an exaggerated combination imbued with as much subtlety as a Wagnerian cymbal crash. You can visit the lavishly upholstered auditorium, with its delightful ceiling painted by Marc Chagall in 1964. The stage is the largest in the world, accommodating up to 450 players. ⊠ *Pl. de l'Opéra,* ☎ *01–47–42–07–02.* ☉ *Daily 10–5. Métro: Opéra.*

The Marais and the Bastille

㉗ **Bercy.** This colorful district, tucked away on the Right Bank of the Seine, south of the Gare de Lyon in the 12ᵉ arrondissement and opposite the new national library, was for centuries filled with warehouses storing wine from the provinces. The old warehouses have been replaced by the **Parc de Bercy,** a witty, state-of-the art garden. The mighty glass wall of the new **Ministère des Finances** (Finance Ministry) looms up at one end, beyond the sloping, grass-walled **Palais Omnisports** indoor stadium. Nearby, Frank Gehry's quirky, cubistic former **American Center** sounds a mournful note; it closed in 1996 for lack of funds. ⊠ *rue de Bercy. Métro: Bercy.*

㉒ **Centre Pompidou** (Pompidou Center). The futuristic, funnel-top Pompidou Center—known to Parisians as Beaubourg, after the surrounding district—was built in the mid-1970s and named in honor of former French president Georges Pompidou (1911–74). The Center was soon attracting over 8 million visitors a year—five times more than intended. Hardly surprising, then, that it was soon showing signs of fatigue. In 1996 the government stepped in and took drastic action: shutting the Center until December 1999 and embarking on top-to-bottom renovation. A canvas teepee has been erected on the sloping esplanade in front of the Center, with a battery of computer screens to outline its future plans. Alongside you can visit the **Atelier Brancusi** (Brancusi's Studio), four reconstituted glass-fronted rooms of Romanian-born sculptor Constantin Brancusi, crammed with smooth, stylized works from throughout his career. ⊠ *Pl. Georges-Pompidou,* ☎ *01–44–78–12–33.* ☉ *Atelier Brancusi: Wed.–Mon. noon–10. Métro: Rambuteau.*

㉖ **Cimetière du Père-Lachaise** (Father Lachaise Cemetery). Cemeteries may not be your idea of the ultimate attraction, but this one is the largest and most interesting in Paris. It forms a veritable necropolis with cobbled avenues and tombs competing in pomposity and originality. Leading incumbents include Frédéric Chopin, Marcel Proust, Jim Morrison, Edith Piaf, and Gertrude Stein. Get a map at the entrance and track them down. ⊠ *Entrances on rue des Rondeaux, bd. de Ménilmontant,* *and rue de la Réunion.* ⊙ *Apr.–Sept., daily 8–6; Oct.–Mar., daily 8– 5. Métro: Père-Lachaise, Gambetta, Philippe-Auguste.*

㉞ Hôtel de Ville (City Hall). Overlooking the Seine, the City Hall has only been the office of the mayor since 1977—when the seat was first created in Paris. The square in front of the Hôtel de Ville was once the site of public executions. During the Commune of 1871, the Hôtel de Ville was burned to the ground. Today's exuberant building, based closely on the 16th-century Renaissance original, went up between 1874 and 1884. ⊠ *Pl. de l'Hôtel-de-Ville.* ⊙ *For special exhibitions. Métro: Hôtel-de-Ville.*

★ **㉓ Musée Picasso** (Picasso Museum). The Hôtel Salé, an elegant mansion in the heart of the Marais, was comprehensively restored by the French government in the 1980s to receive an extensive collection of little-known paintings, drawings, and engravings donated to the state by Picasso's heirs in lieu of death duties. ⊠ *5 rue Thorigny,* ☎ *01–42–71–25– 21.* ⊙ *Wed.–Mon. 9:30–6. Métro: Chemin-Vert.*

㉕ Place de la Bastille. Nothing remains of the fortress stormed at the outbreak of the French Revolution, but just to mislead you, there's a soaring gilt-edge column, topped by the figure of Liberty, commemorating Parisians killed . . . in the long-forgotten uprising of 1830. Also on the square is the modern, glass-fronted **Opéra de la Bastille** (Bastille Opera) opened in 1989 in commemoration of the Revolution's bicentennial. Rather more appealing is the **Viaduc des Arts** (Arts Viaduct) that leads off down avenue Daumesnil: a disused railway viaduct converted into boutiques below and a walkway on top. *Métro: Bastille.*

★ **㉔ Place des Vosges.** Built in 1605, this is the oldest square in Paris. Its harmonious proportions, soft pink brick, and cloisterlike arcades give it an aura of calm. In the far corner is the **Maison de Victor Hugo** (Victor Hugo House), containing souvenirs of the great poet's life and many of his surprisingly able paintings and ink drawings. ⊠ *Maison de Victor Hugo: 6 pl. des Vosges.* ⊙ *Tues.–Sun. 10–5:45. Métro: St-Paul.*

㉝ St-Paul–St-Louis. This stately Baroque church in the Marais (1627–41) has one of the city's earliest domes, and a compelling, if melodramatic, vision of *Christ on the Mount of Olives* (1826) high up in the north transept, by a youthful Delacroix. ⊠ *Rue St-Antoine. Métro: St-Paul.*

The Islands and the Latin Quarter

㉛ Arènes de Lutèce (Lutèce Arena). This Gallo-Roman arena was rediscovered only in 1869; it has since been landscaped and excavated to reveal parts of the original amphitheater, but remains one of the lesser-known points of interest in Paris. ⊙ *During daylight hrs. Métro: Monge.*

㉙ Bibliothèque François-Mitterrand (François Mitterrand Library). The last of late president Mitterrand's grand building projects opened in early 1997. Architect Dominique Perault's controversial design features four soaring 24-story L-shape towers (meant to resemble open books) around a stunning interior courtyard—sunk beneath ground level. ⊠ *11 quai François-Mauriac,* ☎ *01–53–79–53–79.* ⊙ *Tues.–Sat. 10– 7, Sun. noon–6. Métro: Quai de la Gare.*

㊱ La Conciergerie. This former prison has a superb vaulted 14th-century hall, the **Salles des Gens d'Armes** (Hall of the Men-at-Arms), that often hosts temporary exhibitions. The **Tour de l'Horloge** (Clock Tower) near the entrance on the quai de l'Horloge has a clock that has been ticking off time since 1370. ⊠ *Entrance on quai de l'Horloge.* ⊙ *Daily 9:30–6:30 (Oct.–Mar. 10–5). Métro: Cité.*

32 **Ile St-Louis** (St-Louis Island). The city's second and smaller island, barely 650 yards long, was developed as an upscale property venture during the 17th century, and remains largely residential. From its eastern tip you can admire the curving glass facade of Jean Nouvel's Institut du Monde Arabe (Insitute of the Arab World) on the Left Bank. *Métro: Pont-Marie.*

30 **Jardin des Plantes** (Botanical Garden). Established here since the 17th century, Paris's Botanical Garden has a zoo, an aquarium, a maze, an alpine garden, hothouses, and several natural history museums: the **Musée Entomologique** (insects); the **Musée Paléontologique** (fossils and prehistoric animals); and the **Musée Minéralogique** (minerals). Don't miss the **Grande Galerie de l'Évolution** (Great Hall of Evolution) for its mind-blowing collection of stuffed and mounted animals (some now extinct). ✉ *36 rue Geoffroy-St-Hilaire.* ⊙ *Museums: Wed.–Mon. 9–11:45 and 1–4:45. Grande Galerie de l'Évolution: Wed.–Mon. 10–5, Thurs. 10–10. Métro: Monge.*

37 **Musée National du Moyen-Age** (National Museum of the Middle Ages). This museum, housed in the Hôtel de Cluny, is devoted to the late Middle Ages and Renaissance. Look for the *Lady with the Unicorn* tapestries and the beautifully displayed medieval statues. The gardens contain remnants of Roman baths. ✉ *6 pl. Paul-Painlevé,* ☎ *01–53–73–78–00.* ⊙ *Wed.–Mon. 9:30–5:45. Métro: Cluny–La Sorbonne.*

35 **Notre-Dame.** Notre-Dame Cathedral, Paris's historic and geographic heart, has been a place of worship for more than 2,000 years; the present building is the fourth on this site. It was begun in 1163, making it one of the earliest Gothic cathedrals, but wasn't finished until 1345. The facade seems perfectly proportioned until you notice that the north (left) tower is wider than the south. The interior is at its lightest and least cluttered in the early morning. Bay-by-bay cleaning is gradually revealing the original honey color of the stone. Window space is limited and filled with shimmering stained glass; the circular rose windows in the transept are particularly delicate. The 387-step climb up the towers is worth the effort for a perfect view of the famous gargoyles and the heart of Paris. ✉ *Pl. du Parvis.* ⊙ *Cathedral: daily 10–5. Treasury (religious and vestmental relics): Mon.–Sat. 10–6, Sun. 2–6. Métro: Cité.*

39 **Panthéon.** This Temple to the Famous started life as a church; its huge dome recalls that of St-Paul's in London, but dates from nearly a century later (1758–89). Since the Revolution, the crypt has contained the remains of such national heroes as Voltaire, Rousseau, and Zola. The austere interior is ringed with Puvis de Chavannes's late-19th-century frescoes, relating the life of Geneviève, patron saint of Paris. ✉ *Pl. du Panthéon,* ☎ *01–43–54–34–51.* ⊙ *Daily 10–5:30. Métro: Cardinal-Lemoine.*

38 **La Sorbonne.** Students at Paris's ancient university—one of the oldest in Europe—used to listen to lectures in Latin, which explains why the surrounding area is known as the Quartier Latin (Latin Quarter). You can visit the main courtyard and peek into the lecture halls if they're not in use. The Baroque chapel is only open during exhibitions. ✉ *Rue de la Sorbonne. Métro: Cluny–La Sorbonne.*

Ste-Chapelle (Holy Chapel). This chapel was built by St-Louis (Louis IX) in the 1240s to house the Crown of Thorns he had just bought from Emperor Baldwin of Constantinople. The building's lead-covered wood spire, rebuilt in 1854, rises 246 ft. The somewhat garish lower chapel is less impressive than the upper one, whose walls consist of little else but dazzling 13th-century stained glass. ✉ *In the Palais de Justice.* ⊙ *Daily 9:30–6:30 (Oct.–Mar. 10–5). Métro: Cité.*

40 Val de Grâce. This domed church was designed by François Mansart and Jacques Lemercier, and erected in 1645–67 (after the Sorbonne church but before the Invalides). Its two-tier facade, with capitals and triangular pedestals, was inspired by the Counter-Reformation Jesuit architectural style, found more often in Rome than in Paris. ⊠ *1 pl. Alphonse-Laveran. RER: Port-Royal.*

From Orsay to St-Germain

41 Jardin du Luxembourg (Luxembourg Garden). Paris's most famous Left Bank park has tennis courts, colorful flower beds, tree-lined alleys, and a large pond (with toy boats for hire alongside). The **Palais du Luxembourg** (Luxembourg Palace), built by Queen Maria de' Medici at the beginning of the 17th century in answer to Florence's Pitti Palace, houses the French Senate and is not open to the public. *Métro: Odéon; RER: Luxembourg.*

★ **44 Musée d'Orsay** (Orsay Museum). This museum is one of Paris's star attractions, thanks to its imaginatively housed collections of the arts (mainly French) spanning the period 1848–1914. Exhibits take up three floors, but your immediate impression may be of one single, vast hall. This is not surprising: The museum was originally built in 1900 as a train station. The chief artistic attraction is its Impressionist collection. Other highlights include Art Nouveau furniture, a faithfully restored Belle Epoque restaurant, and a model of the Opéra quarter beneath a glass floor. ⊠ *1 rue Bellechasse,* ☎ *01–40–49–48–14.* ☼ *Tues., Wed., Fri., Sat. 10–5:30; Thurs. 10–9:30; Sun. 9–5:30. Métro: Solférino; RER: Musée d'Orsay.*

46 Musée Rodin (Rodin Museum). The splendid, 18th-century Hôtel Biron makes a gracious setting for the sculpture of Auguste Rodin (1840–1917). There's also a pretty garden filled with Rodin sculptures and hundreds of rosebushes. ⊠ *77 rue de Varenne,* ☎ *01–47–05–01–34.* ☼ *Tues.–Sun. 10–5. Métro: Varenne.*

45 Palais Bourbon. The 18th-century home of the **Assemblée Nationale** (French National Legislature) is only open during temporary exhibitions, but its colonnaded facade, commissioned by Napoléon, is a handsome sight across the Seine from place de la Concorde. ⊠ *Pl. du Palais-Bourbon. Métro: Assemblée Nationale.*

43 St-Germain-des-Prés. The oldest church in Paris was first built to shelter a relic of the true cross, brought back from Spain in AD 542. The chancel was enlarged and the church consecrated by Pope Alexander III in 1163 (the church tower dates from this period). ⊠ *Pl. St-Germain-des-Prés.* ☼ *Weekdays 8–7:30, weekends 8 AM–9 PM. Métro: St-Germain-des-Prés.*

42 St-Sulpice. Stand back and admire the impressive 18th-century facade of this enormous 17th-century church, known as the Cathedral of the Left Bank. The unequal, unfinished towers strike a quirky, fallible note at odds with the chillingly impersonal interior, embellished only by the masterly wall paintings by Delacroix—notably *Jacob and the Angel*—in the first chapel on the right. ⊠ *Pl. St-Sulpice. Métro: St-Sulpice.*

Montmartre

13 Place du Tertre. This folksy, tumbling square is the hub of Montmartre, humming most of the time with tourists and would-be painters. Its old-time charm is best appreciated over breakfast, before they all arrive. The understated facade of **St-Pierre de Montmartre** emerges sleepily around one corner of the square, as the bombastic bell-tower of the Sacré-Coeur belts out a morning call behind. *Métro: Anvers.*

⑭ **Sacré-Coeur.** If you start at the Anvers métro station and head up rue de Steinkerque (full of budget clothing shops), you will be greeted by the most familiar and spectacular view of the Sacré-Coeur, perched proudly atop the Butte Montmartre. The basilica was built in a bizarre, mock-Byzantine style between 1876 and 1910; although no favorite with aesthetes, it has become a major Paris landmark. It was constructed as an act of national penitence after the disastrous Franco-Prussian War of 1870—a Catholic show of strength at a time of bitter church-state conflict. ⊠ *Pl. du Parvis-du-Sacré-Coeur. Métro: Anvers.*

On the Fringe

🐚 ❸ **Bois de Boulogne.** Class and style have been associated with "Le Bois" (The Wood) ever since it was landscaped into an upper-class playground by Haussmann in the 1850s. The attractions of this sprawling 2,200-acre wood include cafés, restaurants, racetracks, gardens, waterfalls, and two lakes. An inexpensive ferry crosses frequently to the idyllic island in the larger of the lakes, the **Lac Inférieur,** and rowboats can be rented nearby. Fairground stalls, a folly, a small zoo, and a miniature railway await youngsters at the **Jardin d'Acclimatation** (Zoo/Amusement Park). ⊠ *Jardin d'Acclimatation: bd. des Sablons,* ☎ *01–40–67– 90–82.* ☉ *Daily 10–6. Métro: Les Sablons, Porte-Maillot.*

㉘ **Bois de Vincennes.** This less touristy east Paris counterweight to the Bois de Boulogne has a zoo, a racetrack, and an extensive flower garden, the **Parc Floral.** You can also rent rowboats here and take them out to the two islands in **Lac Daumesnil** or to the three in **Lac des Minimes.** In addition, you can visit the **Château de Vincennes,** an imposing, high-walled castle surrounded by a dry moat and dominated by a 170-ft keep. It contains a replica of the Ste-Chapelle on Ile de la Cité. ⊠ *Château de Vincennes: av. de Paris; Parc Floral: rte. de la Pyramide.* ☉ *Château daily 10–5; park daily 9:30–5. Métro: Château de Vincennes.*

❷ **La Défense.** If you're interested in modern architecture, you'll be stimulated by the variety of skyscrapers clustered around the sculpture-littered plaza in this contemporary suburb, just west of Paris. The most famous building is the **Grande Arche,** a huge hollow cube crowning the famous vista that extends from the Louvre via the Arc de Triomphe. Tubular glass elevators whisk you to the top. ☉ *Grande Arche: daily 10–5. Métro: Grande Arche de La Défense.*

🐚 ⑮ **Parc de la Villette** (La Villette Park). This 130-acre site in northeast Paris has been imaginatively landscaped, with sweeping lawns, playground, moats, canopied walkways, and brightly painted pavilions. Chief attractions are the spherical **Géode** cinema; the iron and glass **Grande Halle** (Big Hall) arts center; the **Cité de la Musique** (Music Center), with its outstanding collection of musical instruments; and the **Cité des Sciences et de l'Industrie** (Industry and Science Museum), which tries to do for science and industry what the Pompidou Center does for modern art. ⊠ *221 av. Jean-Jaures, 30 av. Corentin-Cariou. Museums closed Mon. Métro: Porte de Pantin, Porte de la Villette.*

DINING

RATINGS

Prices are per person and include a first course, main course, and dessert plus tax (20.6%) and service (which are always included in displayed prices), but not wine.

CATEGORY	COST
$$$$	over 600 frs
$$$	300 frs–600 frs
$$	175 frs–300 frs
$	under 175 frs

Left Bank

$$$ ✕ **Le Violon d'Ingres.** Christian Constant, former head chef of the Hôtel
★ Crillon, has created a hit with his own well-heeled bistro. The regu-
larly revised menu may include such dishes as cream of pumpkin soup
with sheep's cheese, and guinea hen on a bed of diced turnips. ⊠ *135
rue St-Dominique,* ☎ *01–45–44–15–05. Reservations essential. AE,
DC, MC, V. Closed weekends. Métro: École-Militaire.*

$$ ✕ **Campagne et Provence.** On the quai across from Notre-Dame, this
pleasant little restaurant serves Provençal cuisine including grilled John
Dory with preserved fennel, and peppers stuffed with cod and eggplant.
⊠ *25 quai de la Tournelle, 5ᵉ,* ☎ *01–43–54–05–17. MC, V. Closed
Sun. No lunch Sat., Mon. Métro: Maubert-Mutualité.*

$$ ✕ **Philippe Detourbe.** Sample Detourbe's spectacular food at remark-
★ ably good prices amid black lacquer, mirrors, and Burgundy velvet up-
holstery. The menu of contemporary French cooking changes with every
meal. ⊠ *8 rue Nicolas Charlet, 15ᵉ,* ☎ *01–42–19–08–59. Reserva-
tions essential. MC, V. Closed Sun. No lunch Sat. Métro: Pasteur.*

$–$$ ✕ **Au Bon Accueil.** Book a table at this popular bistro as soon as you
get to town. The excellent *cuisine du marché* (menu based on what's
in the markets that day) has made it a hit, as have the delicious, homemade desserts. ⊠ *14 rue de Montessuy, 7ᵉ,* ☎ *01–47–05–46–11. Reservations essential. MC, V. Closed Sun. Métro, RER: Pont l'Alma.*

$ ✕ **Le Bouillon Racine.** Originally a *bouillon,* a Parisian soup restaurant
popular at the turn of the century, this two-story place is now a delightfully renovated Belle Epoque oasis with a good Franco-Belgian menu.
⊠ *3 rue Racine, 6ᵉ,* ☎ *01–44–32–15–60. Reservations essential. AE,
MC, V. Closed Sun. Métro: Odéon.*

$ ✕ **Chantairelle.** Not only is delicious south-central Auvergne cuisine
served at this restaurant, but the owners also offer a full regional experience. Hence the decor: recycled barn timbers and essential oils dif-
fusing local scents. The food is hearty and the portions copious. ⊠ *17
rue Laplace, 5ᵉ,* ☎ *01–46–33–18–59. MC, V. Closed Sun. No lunch
Sat. Métro: Maubert-Mutualité.*

$ ✕ **Le Terroir.** A jolly crowd of regulars makes this little bistro festive.
The solidly classical menu includes an assortment of salads, and calves'
liver, or monkfish with saffron. ⊠ *11 bd. Arago, 13ᵉ,* ☎ *01–47–07–
36–99. AE, MC, V. Closed Sun. No lunch Sat. Métro: Les Gobelins.*

Right Bank

$$$$ ✕ **Le Grand Véfour.** Luminaries from Napoléon to Colette to Jean
Cocteau frequented this intimate and sumptuous address under the arcades of the Palais-Royal. Chef Guy Martin impresses with his unique
blend of such sophisticated yet rustic dishes as roast lamb in a juice of
herbs. ⊠ *17 rue Beaujolais, 1ᵉʳ,* ☎ *01–42–96–56–27. Reservations
essential 1 wk in advance. Jacket and tie. AE, DC, MC, V. Closed weekends and Aug. Métro: Palais-Royal.*

$$$$ ✕ **Guy Savoy.** Top chef Guy Savoy's other five bistros have not distracted
★ him too much from his handsome luxury restaurant near the Arc de
Triomphe. The oysters in aspic, and grilled pigeon reveal the magnitude
of his talent. ⊠ *18 rue Troyon, 17ᵉ,* ☎ *01–43–80–40–61. AE, MC,
V. Closed Sun. No lunch Sat. Métro: Charles de Gaulle–Étoile.*

$$$$ ✕ **Pierre Gagnaire.** Legendary chef Pierre Gagnaire's cooking is at once
★   intellectual and poetic—unexpected tastes and textures are brought to-
       gether in a sensational experience. The only drawback is the amateurish
       service and the puzzlingly brief wine list. ⊠ *6 rue de Balzac, 8ᵉ,* ☎ *01–
       44–35–18–25. Reservations essential. AE, DC, MC, V. Closed Sun.
       Métro: Charles-de-Gaulle–Etoile.*

$$$ ✕ **Le Cercle Ledoyen.** For about 250 francs a dinner—wine included—
       you can sample renowned chef Ghislaine Arabian's northern French
       cuisine at this luxury brasserie. The handsome, curved dining room with
       a view of the surrounding park is a pleasure year-round, and the
       terrace is a special treat in warm weather. ⊠ *1 av. Dutuit, 8ᵉ,* ☎ *01–
       47–42–23–23. AE, DC, MC, V. Closed Sun. Métro: Champs-Elysées–
       Clemenceau.*

$$ ✕ **Chardenoux.** A bit off the beaten path but well worth the effort,
       this cozy neighborhood bistro with etched-glass windows, dark bent-
       wood furniture, and a long zinc bar attracts a cross-section of savvy
       Parisians. The traditional cooking is first-rate, from the delicious foie
       gras salad to the veal chop with morels. ⊠ *1 rue Jules-Valles, 11ᵉ,* ☎
       01–43–71–49–52. AE, V. Closed weekends, Aug. Métro: Charonne.

$$ ✕ **Chez Georges.** The traditional bistro cooking is good—herring,
       sole, kidneys, steak, and *frîtes* (fries)—but the atmosphere is better. A
       wood-paneled entry leads you to an elegant and unpretentious dining
       room where one long, white-clothed stretch of table lines the mirrored
       walls. ⊠ *1 rue du Mail, 2ᵉ,* ☎ *01–42–60–07–11. AE, DC, MC, V.
       Closed Sun. and Aug. Métro: Sentier.*

$$ ✕ **Le Repaire de Cartouche.** Near the Cirque d'Hiver in the Bastille, this
★   split-level, '50s-style bistro with dark-wood decor is the latest good-value
       sensation in Paris. Young chef Rodolphe Paquin is a creative and im-
       peccably trained cook who does a stylish take on earthy French regional
       dishes. ⊠ *99 rue Amelot, 11ᵉ,* ☎ *01–47–00–25–86. AE, MC, V. Reser-
       vations essential. Closed Sun., dinner Mon. Métro: Filles du Calvaire.*

$–$$ ✕ **Chez Michel.** If you're willing to go out of your way for excellent
       food at fair prices, even if the decor and the neighborhood are drab,
       then this place is for you. Chef Thierry Breton pulls a stylish crowd
       with his wonderful cuisine du marché and dishes from his native Brit-
       tany, including lasagna stuffed with chèvre cheese. ⊠ *10 rue Belzunce,
       10ᵉ,* ☎ *01–44–53–06–20. Reservations essential. MC, V. Closed
       Sun., Mon. No lunch Sat. Métro: Gare du Nord.*

$ ✕ **Le Moi.** At this superb Vietnamese restaurant near the Opéra, sam-
       ple *nems* (deep-fried mini spring rolls); steamed dumplings; and chicken,
       beef, and seafood salads enlivened with lemongrass and lemon basil.
       Service is prompt and friendly. ⊠ *5 rue Danou, 1ᵉʳ,* ☎ *01–47–03–
       92–05. MC, V. Closed Sun. No lunch Sat. Métro: Opéra.*

NIGHTLIFE AND THE ARTS

Look for the weekly magazines *Pariscope, L'Officiel des Spectacles,*
and *Figaroscope,* which contain detailed entertainment listings. The
Paris Tourist Office has a **24-hour English-language hot line** (☎ 01–
49–52–53–56) with information about weekly events. Buy tickets at
the place of performance; otherwise, try hotels or such travel agencies
as **Paris-Vision** (⊠ 1 rue Auber, 9ᵉ, ☎ 01–40–06–01–00, métro
Opéra). Tickets for most concerts can be bought at **FNAC** (⊠ 1–5 rue
Pierre Lescot, Forum des Halles, 1ᵉ, ☎ 01–40–41–40–00, métro
Châtelet–Les Halles). Half-price tickets for many same-day theater performances are available at the **Kiosques Théâtre** (⊠ across from 15 pl.
de la Madeleine, métro Madeleine, and in front of the Gare Montparnasse at ⊠ pl. Raoul Dautry, 14ᵉ, métro Montparnasse-Bienvenue).
It's open Tuesday–Sunday 12:30–7:30; expect a line.

The Arts

Getting a ticket for an opera or ballet performance is not always easy and may require luck, preplanning, or a well-connected hotel receptionist. Beware of scalpers: Counterfeit tickets have been known to be sold. Inexpensive organ or chamber music concerts proliferate in churches throughout the city.

CLASSICAL MUSIC AND OPERA

Following are other venues for fine orchestral concerts and recitals: **Cité de la Musique** (⌧ parc de la Villette, 221 av. Jean-Jaurès, 19ᵉ, ☎ 01–44–84–44–84, métro Porte de Pantin); **Salle Pleyel** (⌧ 252 rue du Faubourg-St-Honoré, 8ᵉ, ☎ 01–45–61–53–00, métro Ternes); and the **Théâtre des Champs-Elysées** (⌧ 15 av. Montaigne, 8ᵉ, ☎ 01–49–52–50–50, métro Alma-Marceau). The **Opéra de la Bastille** (⌧ pl. de la Bastille, 12ᵉ, ☎ 08–36–69–78–68, métro Bastille) has replaced the 19th-century Opéra Garnier as the main Paris operatic venue since opening in 1989.

DANCE

Opéra Garnier (⌧ pl. de l'Opéra, 9ᵉ, ☎ 08–36–69–78–68, métro Opéra), the "old Opéra," now concentrates on dance: In addition to being the home of the well-reputed Paris Ballet, it also bills a number of major foreign troupes. The **Théâtre de la Ville** (⌧ 2 pl. du Châtelet, 4ᵉ, métro Châtelet and 31 rue des Abbesses, 18ᵉ, métro Abbesses, ☎ 01–42–74–22–77 for both) is the place for contemporary dance.

FILM

There are hundreds of movie theaters in Paris, and some of them, especially in such principal tourist areas as the Champs-Elysées, Les Halles, Odéon and the boulevard des Italiens near the Opéra, run English films marked *"version originale"* (v.o., i.e., not dubbed). Admission is around 40–50 francs, with reduced rates on Monday. Classics and independent films often play in Latin Quarter theaters. Movie fanatics should check out the **Cinémathèque Française** (⌧ 42 bd. de Bonne-Nouvelle, 10ᵉ, ☎ 01–47–04–24–24, métro Bonne-Nouvelle), where classic French and international films are shown Wednesday–Sunday.

THEATER

There is no Parisian equivalent to Broadway or the West End, although a number of theaters line the grand boulevards between the Opéra and République. Shows are mostly in French. The **Comédie Française** (⌧ pl. André-Malraux, 1ᵉʳ, ☎ 01–44–58–15–15, métro Palais-Royal) performs distinguished classical drama by Racine, Molière, and Corneille. The **Théâtre de la Huchette** (⌧ 23 rue de la Huchette, 5ᵉ, ☎ 01–43–26–38–99, métro St-Michel) is a tiny venue where Ionesco's short plays make a deliberately ridiculous mess of the French language. The **Théâtre de l'Odéon** (⌧ pl. de l'Odéon, 6ᵉ, ☎ 01–44–41–36–36, métro Odéon) has made pan-European theater its primary focus.

Nightlife

BARS AND CLUBS

The hottest area at the moment is around Ménilmontant. Nightlife is still hopping in and around the Bastille, and the Left Bank has a bit of everything. The Champs-Elysées is making a comeback, though the clientele remains predominantly foreign. Gay and lesbian bars and clubs are mostly concentrated in the Marais (especially around rue Ste-Croix-de-la-Bretonnerie) and include some of the most happening addresses in the city.

If you want to dance the night away, the best addresses are the trendy **Les Bains** (⌧ 7 rue du Bourg-l'Abbé, 3ᵉ, ☎ 01–48–87–01–80, métro Etienne-Marcel); super chic **Le Cabaret** (⌧ 68 rue Pierre-Charron, 8ᵉ,

☎ 01–42–89–44–14, métro Franklin-D.-Roosevelt); and the predominantly gay **Queen** (✉ 102 av. des Champs-Elysées, 8ᵉ, ☎ 01–53–89–08–90, métro George V).

Barfly (✉ 49–51 av. George V, 8ᵉ, ☎ 01–53–67–84–60, métro George V) has its followers among the business and fashion crowd who come to this place to see and be seen. **Buddha Bar** (✉ 8 rue Boissy d'Anglas, 8ᵉ, ☎ 01–53–05–90–00, métro Concorde) has a spacious mezzanine bar that overlooks the dining room where cuisines, east and west, meet somewhere in California. **Café Charbon** (✉ 109 rue Oberkampf, 11ᵉ, ☎ 01–43–57–55–13, métro St-Maur/Parmentier) is a beautifully restored 19th-century café, whose trend-setting clientele chats to jazz in the background.

La Champmeslé (✉ 4 rue Chabanais, 2ᵉ, ☎ 01–42–96–85–20, métro Bourse) is the hub of lesbian nightlife with a dusky back room reserved exclusively for women. **China Club** (✉ 50 rue de Charenton, 12ᵉ, ☎ 01–43–43–82–02, métro Ledru-Rollin) has three floors of bars and a restaurant with lacquered furnishings and a colonial Orient theme. **Le Moloko** (✉ 26 rue Fontaine, 9ᵉ, ☎ 01–48–74–50–26, métro Blanche) is a popular, smoky, late-night bar with several rooms, a mezzanine, and a small dance floor.

CABARET

Paris's cabarets are household names, shunned by Parisians and beloved of foreign tourists, who flock to the shows. You can dine at many of them; prices range from 200 francs (simple admission plus one drink) to more than 800 francs (dinner plus show). **Crazy Horse** (✉ 12 av. George V, 8ᵉ, ☎ 01–47–23–32–32, métro Alma-Marceau) is one of the best-known clubs for pretty dancers and raunchy routines. **Lido** (✉ 116 bis av. des Champs-Elysées, 8ᵉ, ☎ 01–40–76–56–10, métro George-V) stars the famous Bluebell Girls; the owners claim that no show in Las Vegas rivals it for special effects. **Moulin Rouge** (✉ pl. Blanche, 18ᵉ, ☎ 01–46–06–00–19, métro Blanche), the old favorite at the foot of Montmartre, mingles the Doriss Girls, a horse, and the cancan in an extravagant spectacle.

JAZZ CLUBS

The French take jazz seriously, and Paris is one of the great jazz cities of the world. For nightly schedules consult the specialty magazines *Jazz Hot* or *Jazz Magazine*. Nothing gets going till 10 or 11 PM, and entry prices vary widely from about 40 francs to over 100 francs.

The **New Morning** (✉ 7 rue des Petites-Ecuries, 10ᵉ, ☎ 01–45–23–51–41, métro Château-d'Eau) is a premier spot for serious fans of avant-garde jazz, folk, and world music; decor is spartan, the mood reverential. The greatest names in French and international jazz have been playing at **Le Petit Journal** (✉ 71 bd. St-Michel, 5ᵉ, ☎ 01–43–26–28–59, RER Luxembourg) for decades. Sundays are devoted to the blues. **Le Petit Opportun** (✉ 15 rue des Lavandières-Ste-Opportune, 1ᵉʳ, ☎ 01–42–36–01–36, métro Châtelet), in a converted bistro, sometimes features top-flight American soloists with French backup.

ROCK CLUBS

Lists of upcoming concerts are posted on boards in the FNAC stores. Following are the best places to catch big French and international stars: **Palais Omnisports de Paris-Bercy** (✉ rue de Bercy, 12ᵉ, ☎ 01–44–68–44–68, métro Bercy); and **Zenith** (✉ Parc de la Villette, 19ᵉ, ☎ 01–42–08–60–00, métro Porte-de-Pantin). For emerging talent and lesser known groups, try : **Bataclan** (✉ 50 bd. Voltaire, 11ᵉ, ☎ 01–47–00–30–12, métro Oberkampf); or **Elysée Montmartre** (✉ 72 bd. Rochechouart, 18ᵉ, ☎ 01–44–92–45–45, métro Anvers).

SHOPPING

Antiques
Antiques dealers proliferate in the **Carré Rive Gauche** (⊠ between St-Germain-des-Prés and the Musée d'Orsay). There are also several antiques dealers around the **Drouot** auction house (⊠ corner of rue Rossini and rue Drouot, 9ᵉ, métro Richelieu-Drouot) near the Opéra . The **Louvre des Antiquaires** (⊠ pl. du Palais-Royal, 1ᵉʳ, métro Palais-Royal) is a stylish shopping mall devoted primarily to antiques. At the **Village Suisse** (⊠ 78 av. de Suffren, 15ᵉ, métro La Motte–Picquet-Grenelle), near the Champ de Mars, over 100 dealers are grouped together.

Boutiques
Only Milan can compete with Paris for the title of Capital of European Chic. The top designer shops are found on **avenue Montaigne, rue du Faubourg-St-Honoré,** and **place des Victoires.** The areas surrounding **St-Germain-des-Prés** on the Left Bank is a mecca for small specialty shops and boutiques, and has recently seen an influx of the elite names in haute couture. Scores of trendy boutiques can be found in the **Bastille** and **Les Halles.** Between the pre-Revolution mansions and tiny kosher food stores that characterize the **Marais** are numerous gift shops and clothing stores. The streets to the north of the Marais, close to the Arts-et-Métiers métro stop, are historically linked to the cloth trade, and some shops sell garments at wholesale prices. Also search for bargains along the streets around the foot of Montmartre, or in the designer discount shops (Cacharel, Rykiel, Dorotennis) along **rue d'Alésia** in Montparnasse.

Department Stores
Au Bon Marché (⊠ 22 rue de Sèvres, 7ᵉ, métro Sèvres-Babylone) is the leading department store on the Left Bank. **Au Printemps** (⊠ 64 bd. Haussmann, 9ᵉ, métro Havre-Caumartin) is perhaps the most famous Paris department store; its distinctive narrow domes add an Art Nouveau touch to boulevard Haussmann. **Galeries Lafayette** (⊠ 40 bd. Haussmann, 9ᵉ, métro Chaussée-d'Antin) has a comprehensive array of fashionable goods beneath its shimmering turn-of-the-century glass cupola. **La Samaritaine** (⊠ 19 rue de la Monnaie, 1ᵉʳ, métro Pont-Neuf) occupies several buildings near the Louvre; building No. 2 is an airy Art Nouveau emporium overlooking the Seine.

Food and Flea Markets
Every *quartier* (neighborhood) has at least one open-air food market. Sunday morning till 1 PM is usually a good time to go; they are likely to be closed Monday. The **Marché aux Puces de St-Ouen** (métro Porte de Clignancourt), just north of Paris, is one of Europe's largest flea markets; it's open Saturday–Monday. Best bargains are to be had early in the morning. There are also smaller flea markets at the **Porte de Vanves** and **Porte de Montreuil** (weekends only).

Gift Ideas
Old prints are sold by *bouquinistes* (secondhand booksellers) in stalls along the banks of the Seine. **Guerlain** (⊠ 47 rue Bonaparte, 6ᵉ, métro Mabillon) sells legendary French perfumes. The **Musée des Arts Décoratifs** (⊠ 107 rue de Rivoli, 1ᵉʳ, métro Palais-Royal) has state-of-the-art home decorations. **Le Cave Augé** (⊠ 116 bd. Haussmann, 8ᵉ, métro St-Augustin) is one of the best wine shops in Paris. **Fauchon** (⊠ 30 pl. de la Madeleine, 8ᵉ, métro Madeleine) is an upscale grocery with regional specialty foods, herbs, and pâtés. **Hédiard** (⊠ 21 pl. de la Madeleine, 8ᵉ, métro Madeleine) is a super-deluxe delicatessen with a wide choice of French specialties.

PARIS ESSENTIALS

Arriving and Departing

BY BUS

Long-distance bus journeys within France are uncommon, which may be why Paris has no central bus depot. But if you do need to take a bus in France, contact **Eurolines** (✉ 28 av. du Général-de-Gaulle, Bagnolet, ☎ 01–49–72–51–51).

BY CAR

In a country as highly centralized as France, it is no surprise that expressways converge on the capital from every direction: A1 from the north (225 km/140 mi to Lille); A13 from Normandy (225 km/140 mi to Caen); A4 from the east (499 km/310 mi to Strasbourg); A10 from the southwest (579 km/360 mi to Bordeaux); and A7 from the Alps and Riviera (466 km/290 mi to Lyon). Each connects with the *périphérique*, the beltway. Exits are named by "porte" (gateway) and are not numbered. The "Périphe" can be fast—but gets very busy; try to avoid it between 7:30 and 10 AM and between 4:30 and 7:30 PM.

BY PLANE

International flights arrive at either **Charles de Gaulle Airport** (also called Roissy), 24 km (15 mi) northeast of Paris, or at **Orly Airport,** 16 km (10 mi) south of the city. Both airports have two terminals.

Between the Airport and Downtown. Both airports have their own train stations from which you can take the **RER** to Paris. The advantages of this are speed, price (47 frs to Paris from Roissy, 57 frs from Orly on the shuttle-train Orlyval), and the RER's direct link with the métro system. The disadvantage is having to lug your bags around. **Taxi** fares from both airports to Paris range from 150 to 250 francs, with a 6-franc surcharge per bag. The **Paris Airports Service** takes you by eight-passenger van to your destination in Paris from de Gaulle: 140 francs (one person) or 170 francs (two); Orly: 110 francs (one), 130 francs (two), less for groups. You need to book at least two days in advance (there are English-speaking clerks); call ☎ 33–1/49–62–78–78 or fax ⒡ 33–1/49–62–78–79.

From Roissy **Air France Buses** (open to all) leave every 15 minutes from 5:40 AM to 11 PM. The fare is 55 francs and the trip takes from 40 minutes to 1½ hours during rush hour. You arrive at the Arc de Triomphe or Porte Maillot, on the Right Bank by the Hôtel Concorde-Lafayette. From Orly, buses operated by Air France leave every 12 minutes from 6 AM to 11 PM and arrive at the Air France terminal near Les Invalides on the Left Bank. The fare is 40 francs, and the trip takes between 30 and 60 minutes, depending on traffic. Alternatively, the **Roissybus**, operated by Paris Transport Authority (RATP), runs directly to and from rue Scribe, by the Opéra, every 15 minutes and costs 45 francs. RATP also runs the **Orlybus** to and from Denfert-Rochereau and Orly every 15 minutes for 30 francs; the trip takes around 35 minutes.

BY TRAIN

Paris has five international stations: **Gare du Nord** (for northern France, northern Europe, and England via Calais or the Channel Tunnel); **Gare de l'Est** (for Strasbourg, Luxembourg, Basel, and central Europe); **Gare de Lyon** (for Lyon, Marseille, the Riviera, Geneva, and Italy); **Gare d'Austerlitz** (for the Loire Valley, southwest France, and Spain); and Gare St-Lazare (for Normandy and England via Dieppe). The **Gare Montparnasse** serves western France (mainly Nantes and Brittany) and is the terminal for the TGV Atlantic service from Paris to Bordeaux. For train information call ☎ 08–36–35–35–35 . You can

Paris Métro

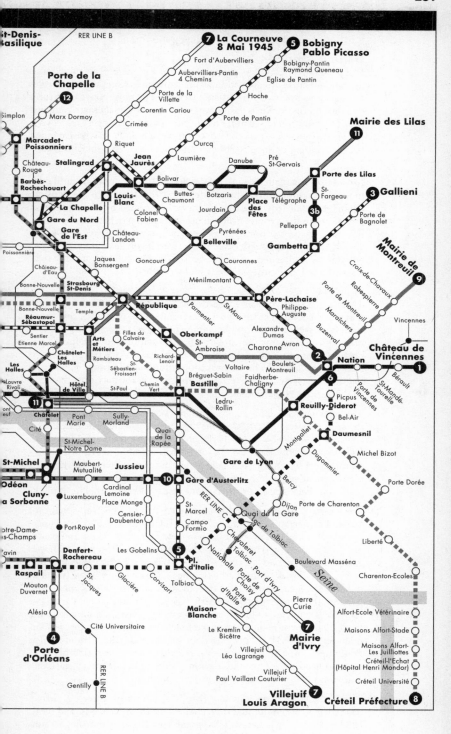

reserve tickets at any Paris station regardless of the destination. Go to the Grandes Lignes counter for travel within France or to the Billets Internationaux desk if you're heading out of France.

Getting Around

Paris is relatively small as capital cities go, and most of its prize monuments and museums are within walking distance of one another. A river cruise is a pleasant way to get an overview. The most convenient form of public transportation is the métro; buses are a slower alternative, though they do allow you to see more of the city. Taxis are not very expensive, but are not always so easy to find. Car travel within Paris is best avoided because finding parking is difficult and there is often a lot of traffic.

BY BUS

Most buses run from around 6 AM to 8:30 PM; some continue until midnight. Noctambus (night buses) operate from 1 AM to 6 AM between Châtelet and nearby suburbs. They can be stopped by hailing them at any point on their route. You can use your métro tickets on the buses, or you can buy a one-ride ticket on board. You need to show weekly/monthly/special tickets to the driver; if you have individual tickets, state your destination and be prepared to punch one or more tickets in the red and gray machines on board the bus.

BY MÉTRO

There are 13 métro lines crisscrossing Paris and the nearby suburbs, and you are seldom more than a five-minute walk from the nearest station. It is essential to know the name of the last station on the line you take, since this name appears on all signs within the system. A connection (you can make as many as you please on one ticket) is called a *correspondance*. At junction stations illuminated orange signs bearing the names of each line terminus appear over the corridors that lead to the various correspondances.

The métro runs from 5:30 AM to 1:15 AM. Some lines and stations in the seedier parts of Paris are a bit risky at night—in particular, Line 2 (Porte-Dauphine–Nation) and the northern section of Line 13 from St-Lazare to St-Denis/Asnières. The long, bleak corridors at Jaurès and Stalingrad are a haven for pickpockets and purse snatchers. But the Paris métro is relatively safe, as long as you don't walk around with your wallet in your back pocket or travel alone (especially women) late at night.

The métro connects at several points in Paris with RER trains that race across Paris from suburb to suburb: RER trains are a sort of supersonic métro and can be great time-savers. All métro tickets and passes are valid for RER and bus travel within Paris. Métro tickets cost 8 francs each, though a *carnet* (10 tickets for 48 frs) is a far better value. If you're staying for a week or more, the best deal is the *coupon jaune* (weekly) or *carte orange* (monthly) ticket, sold according to zone. Zones 1 and 2 cover the entire métro network (75 frs per week or 243 frs per month). If you plan to take a suburban train to visit monuments in the Ile-de-France, you should consider a four-zone ticket (Versailles, St-Germain-en-Laye; 131 frs per week) or a six-zone ticket (Rambouillet, Fontainebleau; 181 frs per week). For these weekly or monthly tickets, you need a pass (available from train and major métro stations), and you must provide a passport-size photograph.

Alternatively there are one-day (Mobilis) and two-, three-, and five-day (Paris Visite) unlimited travel tickets for the métro, bus, and RER. Unlike the coupon jaune, which is good from Monday morning to Sunday evening, the latter are valid starting any day of the week and give you admission discounts to a limited number of museums and tourist attractions. The prices are 30, 85, 120, and 170 francs for Paris only;

100, 175, 245, and 300 francs for the suburbs, including Versailles, St-Germain-en-Laye, and Disneyland Paris.

Access to métro and RER platforms is through an automatic ticket barrier. Slide your ticket in flat and pick it up as it pops up farther along. Keep your ticket; you'll need it again to leave the RER system. Sometimes green-clad métro authorities will ask to see it when you enter or leave the station: Be prepared—they aren't very friendly, and they will impose a large fine if you do not show them your ticket.

BY TAXI

There is no standard vehicle or color for Paris taxis. Daytime rates (7 to 7) within Paris are about 2.80 francs per km (½ mi), and nighttime rates are around 4.50 francs, plus a basic charge of 13 francs. Rates outside the city limits are about 40% higher. Ask your hotel or restaurant to call for a taxi, since cruising cabs can be hard to find. There are numerous taxi stands, but you have to know where to look. Taxis seldom take more than three people at a time.

Money Matters

CURRENCY

The unit of French currency is the franc, subdivided into 100 centimes. Bills are issued in denominations of 50, 100, 200, and 500 francs (frs); coins are 5, 10, 20, and 50 centimes and 1, 2, 5, 10, and 20 francs. The small, copper-color 5-, 10-, and 20-centime coins have considerable nuisance value, but they can be used for tips in bars and cafés. International credit cards and traveler's checks are widely accepted throughout France, except in rural areas. At press time (spring 1998), the U.S. dollar bought 6 francs, the Canadian dollar 4.13 francs, the pound sterling 9.7 francs, the Australian dollar 3.8 francs, and the New Zealand dollar 3.2 francs.

Telephoning

French phone numbers have 10 digits. All phone numbers have a two-digit prefix determined by zone: Paris and the Ile de France, 01; the northwest, 02; the northeast, 03; the southeast, 04; and the southwest, 05.

COUNTRY CODE

The country code for France is 33 and for Monaco 337. To call France from the United States, dial 011 (for all international calls), then dial 33 (the country code), and the number in France, minus any initial 0. To dial France from the United Kingdom, dial 00–33, then dial the number in France, minus any initial 0.

Contacts and Resources

EMBASSIES

Canada (✉ 35 av. Montaigne, 8ᵉ, ☎ 01–44–43–29–00, métro Franklin-D.-Roosevelt, ☾ weekdays 8:30–11). **United Kingdom** (✉ 35 rue du Faubourg-St-Honoré, 8ᵉ, ☎ 01–44–51–31–00, métro Madeleine, ☾ weekdays 9:30–12:30 and 2:30–5). **United States** (✉ 2 rue St-Florentin, 1ᵉʳ, ☎ 01–43–12–22–22 in English or ☎ 01–43–12–23–47 in emergencies, métro Concorde, ☾ weekdays 9–3).

EMERGENCIES

Ambulance (☎ 15 for emergencies or 01–15 or 43–78–26–26). **Police** (☎ 17). Automatic phone booths can be found at various main crossroads for use in police emergencies (Police-Secours) or for medical help (Services Médicaux). **Dentist** (☎ 01–43–37–51–00, ☾ 24 hrs). **Doctor** (☎ 01–47–07–77–77).

Hospitals: American Hospital (✉ 63 bd. Victor-Hugo, Neuilly, ☎ 01–47–45–71–00); **British Hospital** (✉ 3 rue Barbès, Levallois-Perret, ☎ 01–47–58–13–12).

Pharmacies: Dhéry (✉ Galerie des Champs, 84 av. des Champs-Elysées, ☎ 01–45–62–02–41; ⊘ 24 hrs); **Pharmacie des Arts** (✉ 106 bd. Montparnasse, 6ᵉ, ☎ 01–43–35–44–88; ⊘ until midnight).

ENGLISH-LANGUAGE BOOKSTORES
Most newsstands in central Paris sell *Time, Newsweek,* and the *International Herald Tribune,* as well as the English dailies. Some English-language bookstores include: **W. H. Smith** (✉ 248 rue de Rivoli); **Brentano's** (✉ 37 av. de l'Opéra); and **Shakespeare & Co.** (✉ rue de la Bûcherie).

GUIDED TOURS
Bicycling Tours: Paris à Vélo (✉ 37 bd Bourdon, 4ᵉ, ☎ 01–48–87–60–01) organizes three-hour cycling tours around Paris and rents bikes for 80 francs a day.

Boat Tours: Boat rides along the Seine are a must if it's your first time in Paris. The price for a 60-minute trip is usually around 40 francs. Boats depart in season every half hour from 10:30 to 5 (less frequently in winter). The **Bateaux Mouches** leave from the Pont de l'Alma, at the bottom of avenue George-V. The **Vedettes du Pont-Neuf** set off from the square du Vert-Galant on the western edge of the Ile de la Cité.

Bus Tours: Bus tours of Paris provide a good introduction to the city. Tours usually start from the tour company's office and are generally given in double-decker buses with either a live guide or tape-recorded commentary. They last two to three hours and cost about 150 francs. Tour operators also have a variety of theme tours (historic Paris, modern Paris, Paris by night) that last from 2½ hours to all day and cost up to 390 francs. **Cityrama** (✉ 147 rue St-Honoré, 1ᵉʳ, ☎ 01–44–55–61–00) is one of the largest bus operators in Paris. For an intimate tour of the city, Cityrama also runs minibus excursions that pick you up and drop you off at your hotel. **Paris Vision** (✉ 214 rue de Rivoli, 1ᵉʳ, ☎ 01–42–60–31–25) is another large bus tour operator.

Excursions: Cityrama and **Paris Vision** (☞ Bus Tours, *above*) organize half- and full-day trips to Chartres, Versailles, Fontainebleau, the Loire Valley, and Mont-St-Michel at a cost of between 195 and 950 francs.

Personal Guides: Tours of Paris or the surrounding areas by limousine or minibus for up to seven passengers for a minimum of three hours can be organized. The cost starts at about 250 francs per hour. Contact **International Limousines** (✉ 182 bd. Pereire, 17ᵉ, ☎ 01–53–81–14–14) or **Paris Bus** (✉ 22 rue de la Prévoyance, Vincennes, ☎ 01–43–65–55–55).

Walking Tours: Numerous special-interest tours concentrate on historical or architectural topics. Most are in French and cost between 40 and 60 francs. Details are published in the weekly magazines *Pariscope* and *L'Officiel des Spectacles* under the heading "Conférences."

TRAVEL AGENCIES
American Express (✉ 11 rue Scribe, 75009 Paris, ☎ 01–47–77–77–07). **Wagons-Lits** (✉ 32 rue du Quatre-Septembre, 75002 Paris, ☎ 01–44–94–20–67).

VISITOR INFORMATION
The **Paris Tourist Office** (✉ 127 av. des Champs-Elysées, ☎ 01–49–52–53–54; 01–49–52–53–56 for recorded information in English) is open daily 9–8. It has branches at all mainline train stations except Gare St-Lazare.

18 Prague

Poets, philosophers, and the Czech-in-the-street have long sung the praises of Praha (Prague), also referred to as the "Golden City of a Hundred Spires." Like Rome, Prague is built on seven hills, which slope gently or tilt precipitously down to the Vltava (Moldau) River. The riverside location, enhanced by a series of graceful bridges, makes a great setting for two of the city's most notable features: its extravagant, fairy-tale architecture and its memorable music.

It was under Karel IV (Charles IV), during the 14th century, that Prague first became the seat of the Holy Roman Empire—virtually the capital of Western Europe—and acquired its distinctive Gothic imprint. At times you'll need to look quite hard for this medieval inheritance; it's still here, though, under the overlays of graceful Renaissance and exuberant Baroque.

Prague escaped serious wartime damage, but it didn't escape neglect. During the last decade, however, artisans and their workers have restored dozens of the city's historic buildings with care and sensitivity.

EXPLORING PRAGUE

Shades of the five medieval towns that combined to form Prague linger in the divisions of its historic districts. On the flat eastern shore of the Vltava River are three areas arranged like nesting boxes: **Josefov** (the old Jewish Quarter) within **Staré Město** (Old Town) within **Nové Město** (New Town). **Malá Strana** (the Lesser Quarter) and **Hradčany** (Castle District) perch along the river's hillier west bank. Spanning the Vltava is **Karlův most** (the Charles Bridge), which links the Old Town to the Lesser Quarter; everything within the historic center can be reached on foot in a half hour or less from here.

Nové Město and Staré Město (New Town and Old Town)

Numbers in the margin correspond to points of interest on the Prague map.

⓫ **Betlémská kaple** (Bethlehem Chapel). The martyr and national hero Jan Hus thundered his humanitarian teachings from the chapel pulpit during the early 15th century. The structure was reconstructed in the 1950s, but the little door through which Hus came to the pulpit is original, as are some of the inscriptions on the wall. ⊠ *Betlémské nám.* ⊙ *Apr.–Sept. daily 9–6; Oct.–Mar. daily 9–5.*

❸ **Celetná ulice.** Medieval kings set off along this street on their way to their coronation at Prague Castle. The **Royal Route** includes this street, passing the Gothic spires of the Týn Church in Old Town Square; it then crosses Charles Bridge and goes up to the castle. As you explore the route, you can study every variety of Romanesque, Gothic, Renaissance, and Baroque architecture.

❿ **Clam-Gallas palác** (Clam-Gallas Palace). Squatting on a constricted site in the heart of the Old Town is this pompous Baroque palace, designed by the great Viennese architect J. B. Fischer von Erlach. All the sculptures, including the Titans that struggle to support the two doorways, are the work of one of the great Bohemian Baroque artists, Matthias Braun. Take a peek inside at the superb staircase. ⊠ *Husova 20.*

❹ **Dům U černé Matky Boží** (House of the Black Madonna). This Cubist building adds a decided jolt to the architectural styles along Celetná ulice. In the second decade of this century, several leading Czech architects boldly applied Cubism's radical reworking of visual space to structures. The Black Madonna, designed by Josef Gočár, is unflinchingly modern yet topped with an almost Baroque tile roof. ⊠ *Celetná ul. (at Ovocný trh).* ⊙ *Tues.–Sun. 10–6.*

❷ **Na Příkopě.** Once part of the moat surrounding the Old Town, this street is now an elegant (in places) pedestrian mall. It leads from the bottom of Wenceslas Square to the **Obecní dům** (Municipal House), Prague's most lavish Art Nouveau building, which reopened in 1997 after a controversial, two-year refurbishment. A bridge links it to the Prašná brána (Powder Tower), a 19th-century neo-Gothic restoration of the medieval original. ⊠ *Nám. Republiky.*

★ ❺ **Staroměstské náměstí** (Old Town Square). The old commercial center of the Old Town is now a remarkably harmonious hub—architecturally beautiful and relatively car-free and quiet. Looming over the center, the twin towers of **Kostel Panny Marie před Týnem** (the Church of the Virgin Mary before Týn) still look forbidding even though their grimy stones have been cleaned and Disneyesque lighting has been installed in the spires. The large Secession-style **sculptural group** in the square's center commemorates the martyr Jan Hus, whose followers completed the Týn Church during the 15th century. The white Baroque **Kostel svatého Mikuláše** (Church of St. Nicholas) is tucked into the square's northwest angle. It was built by Kilian Ignatz Dientzenhofer, co-architect also of the Lesser Quarter's church of the same name. Every hour, mobs converge on the famous Clock Tower of the **Staroměstská radnice** (Old Town Hall) as the clock's 15th-century mechanism activates a procession that includes the 12 Apostles. Note the skeleton figure of Death that tolls the bell.

8 **Staronová synagóga** (Old-New Synagogue). A small congregation still attends the little Gothic Old-New Synagogue, one of Europe's oldest surviving houses of Jewish prayer. Men are required to cover their heads upon entering; skull caps can be bought for a small fee at the door. ⊠ *Červená at Pařížská.* ⊙ *Sun.–Thurs. 9–5, Fri. 9–2.*

★ **9** **Starý židovský hřbitov** (Old Jewish Cemetery). The crowded cemetery is part of **Josefov**, the former Jewish quarter. Here, ancient tombstones lean into one another; below them, piled layer upon layer, are thousands of graves. Many gravestones—they date from the mid-14th to the late 17th centuries—are carved with symbols indicating the name, profession, and attributes of the deceased. If you visit the tomb of the 16th-century scholar Rabbi Löw, you may see scraps of paper covered with prayers or requests stuffed into the cracks. In legend the rabbi protected Prague's Jews with the help of a *golem,* or artificial man; today he still receives appeals for assistance. ⊠ *Entrance at Pinkas Synagogue, Široká 3.*

1 **Václavské náměstí** (Wenceslas Square). In the Times Square of Prague hundreds of thousands voiced their disgust for the Communist regime in November 1989 at the outset of the "Velvet Revolution." The "square" is actually a broad boulevard that slopes down from the **Národní muzeum** (National Museum) and the equestrian **statue of St. Václav** (Wenceslas).

6 **Expozice Franze Kafky** (Franz Kafka's birthplace). Since the 1989 revolution, Kafka's popularity has soared, and the works of this German Jewish writer are now widely available in Czech. A small museum in the house displays photos, editions of Kafta's books, and other memorabilia. (Kafka's grave lies in the overgrown New Jewish Cemetery at the Želivského Metro stop.) ⊠ *U radnice 5.* ⊙ *Tues.–Fri. 10–6, Sat. 10–5.*

7 **Židovské muzeum (Jewish Museum).** The rich exhibits in the Josefov's Pinkas Synagogue, Maisel Synagogue, Klaus Synagogue, and Ceremonial Hall, along with the Old Jewish Cemetery, make up the museum. Jews, forced to fulfill Adolf Hitler's plan to document the lives of the people he was trying to exterminate, gathered the collections. They include ceremonial objects, textiles, and displays covering the history of Bohemia's and Moravia's Jews. The interior of the Pinkas Synagogue is especially poignant, as it is painted with the names of 77,297 Jewish Czechs killed during World War II. Communists closed the building and allowed it to decay; now, however, the lists have been restored. *Museum ticket offices:* ⊠ *U starého hřbitova 3a and Široká 3.* ⊙ *Sun.–Fri. 9–6 (9–4 in winter; last tour of cemetery at 3 in winter). Closed Sat. and religious holidays.*

Karlův most and Malá Strana (Charles Bridge and the Lesser Quarter)

14 **Chrám svatého Mikuláše** (Church of St. Nicholas). Designed by the late-17th-century Dientzenhofer architects, father and son, this edifice is widely considered the most beautiful example of the Bohemian Baroque, an

Prague (Praha)

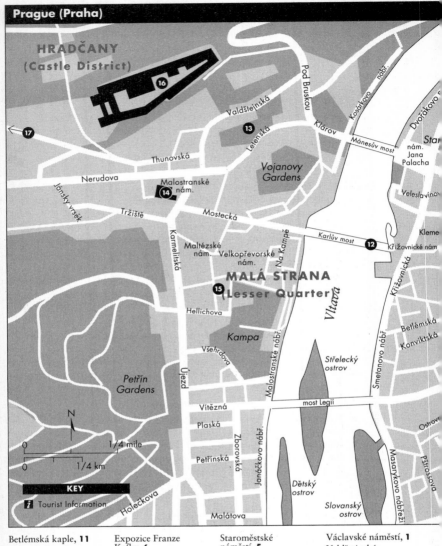

HRADČANY (Castle District)

Pod Bruskou
Kosárkovo nábř.
Dvořákovo
Valdštejnská
Klárov
Mánesův most
Stat
nám. Jana Palacha
Thunovská
Letenská
Vojanovy Gardens
Nerudova
Malostranské nám.
Veleslavíno
Jánský vršek
Tržiště
Mostecká
Karmelitská
Karlův most
Kleme
Maltézské nám.
Velkopřevorské nám.
Na Kampě
Křižovnické nám
MALÁ STRANA (Lesser Quarter)
Křižovnická
Hellichova
Vltava
Kampa
Betlémská
Konvíktská
Všehrdova
Malostranské nábř.
Střelecký ostrov
Petřín Gardens
Újezd
Smetanovo nábř.
Vítězná
most Legií
Plaská
Ostrov
Zborovská
Janáčkovo nábř.
Pstrossova
Petřínská
Masarykovo nábřeží
Dětský ostrov
Slovanský ostrov
Holečkova
Malátova

N

0 ——— 1/4 mile
0 ——— 1/4 km

KEY

i Tourist Information

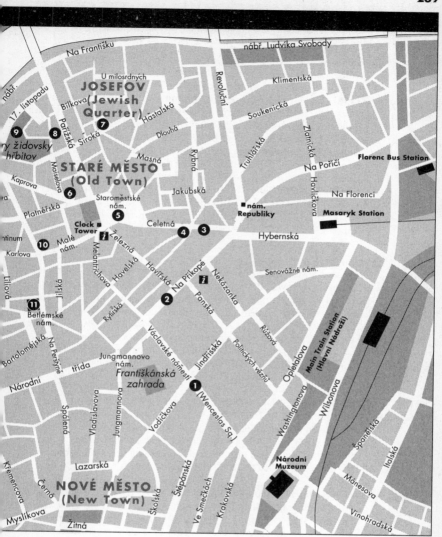

Na Františku

nábř. Ludvíka Svobody

U milosrdných

JOSEFOV
Bílkova **(Jewish**
Quarter) Haštalská

Klimentská

Soukenická

17. listopadu

nábř.

7

Pařížská Široká

Dlouhá

Zlatnická

Truhlářská

Na Poříčí

Florenc Bus Station

9

8

ry židovský
hřbitov

Masná

Rybná

Na Florenci

Kaprova

STARÉ MĚSTO
(Old Town)

Jakubská

Havlíčkova

Masaryk Station

Maiselova

6

Staroměstské
nám.

■ **nám.**
Republiky

Platnéřská

5

Celetná

Karlova

Clock
Tower

i

4

3

Hybernská

tinum

10

Malé
nám.

Železná

Melantrichova

Havelská

Havířská

Na Příkopě

Senovážné nám.

Iliová

Rytířská

i

Nekázanka

2

Panská

11

Betlémské
nám.

Bartolomějská

Na Perštýně

třída

Jungmannovo
nám.

Václavské náměstí

Jindřišská

Politických vězňů

Růžová

Opletalova

Main Train Station
(Hlavní Nádraží)

Národní

Františkánská
zahrada

1

Washingtonova

Wilsonova

Spálená

Vladislavova

Jungmannova

Vodičkova

[Wenceslas Sq.]

Španělská

Kremencova

Lazarská

Školská

Štěpánská

Ve Smečkách

Krakovská

Národní
Muzeum

Italská

Mánesova

Černá

NOVÉ MĚSTO
(New Town)

Myslíkova

Žitná

Vinohradská

architectural style that flowered in Prague after the turbulence of the Counter-Reformation. On clear days you can enjoy great views from the tower. ⊠ *Malostranské nám.* ⊘ *Daily 9–4 (9–6 in summer).*

★ ⑫ **Karlův most** (Charles Bridge). As you stand on this statue-lined stone bridge, unsurpassed in grace and setting, you see views of Prague that would be familiar to its 14th-century builder Peter Parler and to the artists who started adding the 30 sculptures during the 17th century. Today, nearly all the sculptures on the bridge are fakes—skillful copies of the originals, which have been taken indoors to escape the polluted air. Still, examine the 12th on the left (starting from the Old Town side of the bridge), which depicts St. Luitgarde (Matthias Braun sculpted the original, circa 1710), and the 14th on the left, in which a Turk guards suffering saints (F. M. Brokoff sculpted the original, circa 1714). The eighth on the right side, a bronze of John of Nepomuk, marks the spot where in 1393 King Václav IV's men hurled the saint's tortured corpse into the river. The bridge itself is a gift to Prague from the Holy Roman Emperor Charles IV. ⊠ *Between Mostecká ul. on Mala Strana side and Karlova ul. on Old Town side.*

⑮ **Malá Strana** (Lesser Quarter). One of Prague's most intriguing neighborhoods, the "Little Town" lolls indolently below Prague Castle. Two events, above all, made possible the quarter's aristocratic architectural visage: the fire of 1541 and the expulsions of Czech nobles and townspeople defeated in the Protestant rebellion against the Catholic Hapsburgs in 1620. Each of these catastrophes cleared the way for extensive rebuilding and new construction of palaces and gardens. On Malostranské náměstí (Lesser Quarter Square), you'll find the **Church of St. Nicholas** (☞ Chrám svatého Mikuláše, *above*). ⊠ *Bordered by Pražský hrad, Petřín Hill, Vítězná ul.*

OFF THE **Villa Bertramka** While in Prague Mozart liked to stay at the secluded es-
BEATEN PATH tate of his friends the Dušeks. The house is now a small museum packed with Mozart memorabilia. From Karmelitská ulice in Malá Strana, take Tram 12 south to the Anděl Metro station; walk down Plzeňská ulice a few hundred yards, and take a left at Mozartova ulice. ⊠ *Mozartova ul. 169, Smíchov,* ☎ *02/543893.* ⊘ *Daily 9:30–6.*

⑬ **Valdštejnská zahrada** (Wallenstein Gardens). This is one of the most elegant of the many sumptuous Lesser Quarter gardens. During the 1620s the Hapsburgs' victorious commander, Czech nobleman Albrecht of Wallenstein, demolished a wide swath of existing structures in order to build his oversize palace with its charming walled garden. A covered outdoor stage of late-Renaissance style dominates the western end. ⊠ *Entrance at Letenská 10.* ▧ *Free.* ⊘ *May–Sept., daily 9–7.*

Pražský hrad and Hradčany (Prague Castle and the Castle District)

⑰ **Loreta.** This Baroque church and shrine are named for the Italian town to which angels supposedly transported the Virgin Mary's house from Nazareth to save it from the infidel. The glory of its fabulous treasury is the monstrance, the *Sun of Prague*, with its 6,222 diamonds. Arrive on the hour to hear the 27-bell carillon. ⊠ *Loretánské nám. 7.* ⊘ *Tues.– Sun. 9–noon and 1–4:30.*

★ ⑯ **Pražský hrad** (Prague Castle). From its narrow hilltop, the monumental castle complex has witnessed the changing fortunes of the city for more than 1,000 years. The castle's physical and spiritual core, **Chrám svatého Víta** (St. Vitus Cathedral), took from 1344 to 1929 to build, so you can trace in its lines architectural styles from high Gothic to

Art Nouveau. The eastern end, mostly the work of Peter Parler, builder
of the Charles Bridge, is a triumph of Bohemian Gothic. "Good King"
Wenceslas (in reality a mere prince, later canonized) has his own chapel
in the south transept, dimly lit and decorated with fine medieval wall
paintings. Four silver angels hover over the tomb of St. John of Nepomuk, whose statue adorns many a Central European bridge, including the Charles Bridge. Note the fine 17th-century carved wooden panels
on either side of the chancel. The left-hand panel shows a view of the
castle and town in November 1620 as the defeated Czech Protestants
flee into exile. The three easternmost chapels house tombs of Czech
princes and kings of the 11th to the 13th centuries, while Charles IV
and Rudolf II lie in the crypt, the former in a bizarre modern sarcophagus.

Behind St. Vitus's, don't miss the miniature houses of **Zlatá ulička**
(Golden Lane). Its name, and the apocryphal tale of how Holy Roman
Emperor Rudolf II used to lock up alchemists here until they transmuted
lead into gold, may come from the gold-beaters who once lived here.
Knightly tournaments often accompanied coronation ceremonies in the
Královský palác (Royal Palace), next to the cathedral, hence the broad
Riders' Staircase leading up to the grandiose **Vladislavský sál** (Vladislav
Hall), with its splendid late-Gothic vaulting and Renaissance win-
dows. Oldest of all the castle's buildings, though much restored, is the
complex of **Bazilika svatého Jiří** (St. George's Basilica and Convent).
The basilica's cool Romanesque lines hide behind a glowing salmon-
color Baroque facade. The ex-convent houses a superb collection of
Bohemian art from medieval religious sculptures to Baroque paintings.
The castle **ramparts** afford glorious vistas of Prague's fabled hundred
spires rising above the rooftops. ☒ *Main castle ticket office in Second
Courtyard.* ▩ *Tickets valid 3 days; admits visitors to cathedral, Royal
Palace, and St. George's Basilica (but not convent gallery) and Pow-
der Tower:* ☞ *Nové Město and Staré Město (New Town and Old Town),
above.* ☉ *Daily 9–5 (9–4 in winter); castle gardens, Apr.–Oct.*

DINING

Eating out is important to Prague residents, so restaurants are well at-
tended. Make reservations whenever possible.

RATINGS
Prices are reasonable by American standards, even in some of the
more expensive restaurants. Czechs don't normally go for three-course
meals, and the following prices apply only if you're having a first
course, main course, and dessert (prices are per person, excluding
wine and tip).

CATEGORY	PRAGUE	OTHER AREAS
$$$$	over 1,440 Kč	over 1,260 Kč
$$$	900 Kč–1,440 Kč	720 Kč–1,260 Kč
$$	540 Kč–900 Kč	360 Kč–720 Kč
$	under 540 Kč	under 360 Kč

$$$$ ✕ **Jewel of India.** Although generally Asian cooking is not Prague's
forte, here is a spot worth seeking out for Northern Indian tandooris
and other moderately spiced specialties, including some vegetarian
dishes. The decor is luxurious without being stuffy, with rich colors
and thick carpeting. ☒ *Pařížská 20, Staré Město,* ☎ *02/2481–1010.
Reservations essential. AE, MC, V.*

$$$$ ✕ **La Perle de Prague.** This French restaurant, which opened in 1996,
★ continues to be one of Prague's most glamorous spots. The location
doesn't hurt: atop the love-it-or-hate-it "Fred and Ginger" building,

co-designed by Frank Gehry, whose two contrasting wings swoop and sway toward one another like a dancing couple. The nouvelle cuisine Parisian dishes are excellent: superb soups, young rabbit in mustard sauce, sea bream à la Badiane, and tournedos de boeuf with Bearnaise sauce. For dessert, there is a chocolate plate to die for (an assortment of tiny treats—tartelettes, ice cream, and so on—served in a fanciful style). ⊠ *Raší Building, Rašínovo nábřeží 80 (at Resslova),* ☎ *02/2198–4160. Reservations essential. AE, DC, MC, V.*

$$$$ ✕ **Opera Grill.** Though called a grill, this is a stylish little restaurant,
★ complete with antique Meissen candelabra and such Czech specialties as *svíčková* (beef in a delectable cream sauce with a hint of lemon) and roast duck with dumplings. ⊠ *K. Světlé 35, Staré Město,* ☎ *02/265–508. Reservations essential. AE, MC, V. Dinner only.*

$$$$ ✕ **U Zlaté Hrušky.** Careful restoration has returned this restaurant to its original 18th-century style. It specializes in Moravian wines, which are well matched with fillet steaks and goose liver. ⊠ *Nový Svět 3, Hradčany,* ☎ *02/2051–5356. Reservations essential. AE, V.*

$$$ ✕ **U Mecenáše.** This wine restaurant manages to be both medieval and elegant despite the presence of an ancient gallows. Try to get a table in the back room. The chef specializes in thick, juicy steaks, served with a variety of sauces. ⊠ *Malostranské nám. 10, Malá Strana,* ☎ *02/533–881. Reservations essential. AE, MC, V. Dinner only.*

$$$ ✕ **U Modré Kachničky.** The exuberant, eclectic decor is as attractive
★ as the Czech and international dishes served, which include steaks, duck, and game in the autumn, and Bohemian trout and carp specialties. ⊠ *Nebovidská 6, Malá Strana,* ☎ *02/5732–0308. Dinner reservations essential. AE, V.*

$$ ✕ **La colline oubliée.** In "The Forgotten Hill," savor authentic *brik* (spicy ratatouille or ground meat in pastry) and *amekful* (flavorful vegetables and steamed grain), as well as all-you-can eat couscous served by charming waiters from North Africa. You may even be whisked into the kitchen for a sample of the offerings. The decor in this intimate restaurant is bright and cheerful, as is the music; the Old Town location is ideal, just off Pařížská street. ⊠ *Elišky Krásnohorské 11, Staré Město,* ☎ *02/232–9522. AE, V.*

$$ ✕ **Oscar's.** You can enjoy juicy barbecued ribs in Prague at this spacious and informal basement restaurant tucked inside the elegant Tynsky Court (just off Old Town Square). Huge portions of burgers, nachos, salads, hearty sandwiches, and potato skins help distract diners from the restaurant's cute but kitschy theme, which highlights Academy Award–winning movies in everything from decor to names of sandwiches. ⊠ *Týnský dvur, Týn 1, Staré Město,* ☎ *02/2489–5404. AE, MC, V.*

$$ ✕ **Palffy palác.** The faded charm of an old-world palace makes this a
★ lovely, romantic spot for a meal. Very good continental cuisine is served with elegance that befits the surroundings. Try the potatoes au gratin or chicken stuffed with goat cheese. Surprisingly, brunches here are not worth the price. Dining is also possible on the terrace in summer. ⊠ *Valdštejnská 14, Malá Strana,* ☎ *02/5731–2243. AE, MC, V.*

$$ ✕ **Pezinok.** You'll get good, filling Slovak fare at this relaxed, no-frills restaurant behind Národní třída in the New Town. The homemade sausage, accompanied by hearty wine, is excellent. ⊠ *Purkyňova 4, Nové Město,* ☎ *02/291–996. AE, MC, V.*

$$ ✕ **U Lorety.** You can hear the carillon from neighboring Loreta church in this otherwise quiet spot. The service here is discreet but attentive, the tables are private, and the food is consistently good. Venison and steak are specialties. ⊠ *Loretánské nám. 8, Hradčany,* ☎ *02/5732–0073. No credit cards.*

$–$$ ✕ Novoměstský pivovar. Always packed with out-of-towners and locals alike, this microbrewery-restaurant is a maze of rooms, some painted in mock-medieval style, others decorated with murals of Prague street scenes. Pork knuckle *(vepřové koleno)* is a favorite dish. The beer is the cloudy, fruity, fermented style exclusive to this venue. ✉ *Vodičkova 20, Prague 1,* ☎ *02/2423–3533. AE, MC, V.*

$ ✕ Bohemia Bagel. Okay, it's not New York, but the American-owned and child-friendly Bohemia Bagel still serves a good assortment of fresh bagels from raisin-walnut to "supreme" with all kinds of spreads and toppings. The thick soups are among the best in Prague for the price, and the bottomless cups of coffee (from gourmet blends) are a further draw. The casual setting makes it a popular choice for weekend brunches, too. ✉ *Újezd 16, Malá Strána,* ☎ *02/531–002. No credit cards.*

$ ✕ Česká hospoda v Krakovské. Right off Wenceslas Square, this clean pub noted for its excellent traditional fare is the place to try Bohemian duck: It's cooked just right and offered at an excellent price. Pair it with cold Krušovice beer. ✉ *Krakovská 20, Nové Město,* ☎ *02/2221–0204. No credit cards.*

$ ✕ Slávia kavárna. ★ This legendary hangout for the best and brightest of the Czech arts world—from composer Bedřich Smetana and poet Jaroslav Seifert to then-dissident Václav Havel—is back in business after real-estate wrangles held it hostage for most of the '90s. Its Art Deco decor is a perfect backdrop for people-watching, and the vistas (the river and Prague Castle on one side, the National Theater on the other) are a compelling reason to linger over an espresso. Although the Slávia is principally a café, you can also order a light meal here. ✉ *Smetanovo nábřeží 1012/2, Nové Městoď,* ☎ *02/2422–0957. No credit cards.*

$ ✕ U Zlatého Tygra. This crowded hangout is the last of a breed of authentic Czech pivnice. The smoke and stares preclude a long stay, but it's still worth a visit for such pub staples as ham and cheese plates or roast pork. The service is surly, but the beer is good. ✉ *Husova 17, Staré Město,* ☎ *02/2422–9020. Reservations not accepted. No credit cards.*

$ ✕ Vltava. In this riverside retreat you'll find classic Bohemian fish dishes, served in big portions. Try the simple preparations—like carp or trout sautéed in butter with slivered almonds. ✉ *On quay below Rašínovo nábřeží, near Palackého Bridge,* ☎ *02/294–964. No credit cards.*

NIGHTLIFE AND THE ARTS

The Arts

Prague's cultural life is one of its top attractions—and its citizens like to dress up for it and participate; performances can be booked far ahead. You can get a monthly program of events from the PIS (☞ Visitor Information, *below*), Čedok (☞ Visitor Information, *below*), or hotels. The English-language newspaper *The Prague Post* carries detailed entertainment listings. The main ticket agencies are **Bohemia Ticket International** (✉ Salvátorská 6, ☎ 02/2422–7832) and **Ticketpro** (☎ 02/2481–4020, credit card orders accepted). For major concerts, opera, and theater, it's much cheaper to buy tickets at the box office.

CONCERTS

Performances are held in many palaces and churches. Too often, programs lack originality (how many different ensembles can play the *Four Seasons* at once?), but the settings are lovely and the acoustics can be superb. Concerts at the **churches of St. Nicholas** in both the Old Town Square and the Lesser Quarter are especially enjoyable. At **St. James's**

Church on Malá Stupartská (Old Town) cantatas are performed amid a flourish of Baroque statuary. At the Prague Castle's **Garden on the Ramparts,** music in summer comes with a view.

The excellent Czech Philharmonic plays in the intimate, lavish Dvořák Hall in the **Rudolfinum** (⊠ Nám. Jana Palacha, ☎ 02/2489–3111). The lush home of the Prague Symphony, **Smetana Hall,** reopened in 1997 along with the rest of the Obecní dům building (⊠ Nám. Republiky 5, ☎ 02/2200–2336).

OPERA AND BALLET

Opera is of an especially high standard in the Czech Republic. One of the main venues in the grand style of the 19th century is the beautifully restored **National Theater** (⊠ Národní třída 2, ☎ 02/2421–5001). The **State Opera of Prague** (⊠ Wilsonova 4, ☎ 02/265–353; formerly the Smetana Theater) is another historic site for opera lovers. The **Theater of the Estates** (⊠ Ovocný trh 1, ☎ 02/2421–5001) hosts opera, ballet, and theater performances. Mozart conducted the premiere of *Don Giovanni* here.

PUPPET SHOWS

This traditional form of Czech entertainment, generally adaptations of operas performed to recorded music, has been given new life thanks to productions at the **National Marionette Theater** (⊠ Žatecká 1, ☎ 02/232–4565).

THEATER

Theater thrives in the Czech Republic. A dozen or so professional companies play in Prague to packed houses. Nonverbal theater abounds as well, notably "black theater," a melding of live acting, mime, video, and stage trickery that, despite signs of fatigue, continues to draw crowds. The popular **Archa Theater** (⊠ Na Poříčí 26, ☎ 02/232–8800) offers avant-garde and experimental theater, music, and dance and hosts world-class visiting ensembles, including the Royal Shakespeare Company. **Laterna Magika** (Magic Lantern; ⊠ Národní třída 4, ☎ 02/2491–4129) is one of the more established producers of black theater extravaganzas.

Nightlife

DISCOS AND CABARET

Discos catering to a young crowd blast sound onto lower Wenceslas Square. Corona Club and Latin Café (⊠ Novotného lávká, ☎ 02/2108–2357) has Latin, Gypsy, and other dance-friendly music. A classier act, where the newest dance music plays, is the ever-popular **Radost FX** (⊠ Bělehradská 120, Prague 2, ☎ 02/251–210).

JAZZ AND ROCK CLUBS

Jazz clubs are a Prague institution, although foreign customers keep them in business. Excellent Czech groups play the tiny **AghaRTA** (⊠ Krakovská 5, ☎ 02/2221–1275); arrive well before the 9 PM show time to get a seat with a sight line. **Malostranská Beseda** (⊠ Malostranské nám. 21, ☎ 02/539–024) is a funky hall for rock, jazz, and folk. **Reduta** (⊠ Národní třída 20, ☎ 02/2491–2246), the city's best-known jazz club for three decades, features mostly local talent. Hip locals congregate at **Roxy** (⊠ Dlouhá 33, ☎ 02/2481–0951) for everything from punk to funk to New Age tunes.

SHOPPING

Many of the main shops are in and around Old Town Square and Na Příkopě, as well as along Celetná ulice and Pařížská. On the Lesser Quarter side, Nerudova has the densest concentration of shops.

Department Stores

The biggest department store is **Kotva** (⊠ Nám. Republiky 8), which grows flashier and more expensive every year. **Bílá Labut'** (⊠ Na poříčí 23) and **Tesco** (⊠ Národní třída 26) are good-value options.

Specialty Shops

Dila addresses include: Shops specializing in Bohemian crystal, porcelain, ceramics, and antiques abound in Old Town and Malá Strana, and on Golden Lane at Prague Castle. (Every other shop sells these items in the main tourist areas.) Look for the name **Dílo** (⊠ Melantrichova 17, Old Town; Mostecká 17, Malá Strana) for glass and ceramic sculptures, prints, and paintings by local artists. **Lidová Řemesla** (⊠ Jilská 22, Old Town; Nerudova 23, Malá Strana) (folk art) shops in the Old Town stock wooden toys, elegant blue-and-white textiles, and gingerbread Christmas ornaments. **Moser** (⊠ Na Příkopě 12) is the source for glass and porcelain.

SIDE TRIPS

The castle and spa region of Bohemia or the history-drenched villages of Moravia make excellent (and convenient) excursions from Prague. Buses or trains link the capital with every corner of the Bohemian region; transportation to towns in Moravia takes longer (three hours or more from the capital) but is also dependable.

Bohemia's Spas and Castles

The Bohemian countryside is a restful world of gentle hills and thick woods. It is especially beautiful during fall foliage season or in May, when the fruit trees that line the roads are in blossom. Two of the most famous of the Czech Republic's scores of spas lie in such settings: Karlovy Vary (Karlsbad) and Mariánské Lázně (Marienbad). During the 19th and early 20th centuries, European royalty and aristocrats came to ease their overindulged bodies (or indulge them even more!) at these spas.

South Bohemia, a country of lonely castles, green hills, and quiet fish ponds, is peppered with exquisite medieval towns, many of which are undergoing much-needed rehabilitation. In such towns as Tábor, the Hussite reformist movement was born during the early 15th century, sparking a series of religious conflicts that engulfed all of Europe. Countering the Hussites from Český Krumlov was the powerful Rožmberk family, who scattered castles over the countryside and created lake-size "ponds" in which to breed highly prized carp, still the focus of a Czech Christmas dinner.

Praguers love to spend weekends in the **Berounka Valley.** Two magnificent castles, Karlštejn and Křivoklát, rise up over the river.

Karlštejn, less than an hour from Prague off Route E50 (direction Beroun), is an admirable restoration of the 14th-century castle built by Charles IV. It protects the crown jewels of the Holy Roman Empire, housed in the castle's stunning **Kaple svatého kříže** (Chapel of the Holy Rood). The chapel is filled with 128 Gothic paintings and 2,000 dazzling gems. ⊠ *Karlštejn,* ☎ *0311/684–617.* ☉ *Nov.–Mar., Tues.– Sun. 9–noon and 1–4 (Apr. and Oct. 1–5; May, June, and Sept. 1– 6; July and Aug. 1–7).*

The main attractions of **Křivoklát** are its glorious woodlands, a favorite royal hunting ground in times past. The castle is about an hour from Prague. ⊠ *Křivoklát.* ☉ *Apr.–May and Sept.–Dec., Tues.–Sun. 9–4; June–Aug., Tues.–Sun. 9–6.*

KARLOVY VARY

★ Karlovy Vary, or Karlsbad, was named for the Holy Roman Emperor Charles IV. While he was in pursuit of a deer during a hunt, the animal supposedly led him to the main spring of Vřídlo. Over the years the spa attracted not only many of the crowned heads and much of the blue blood of Europe, but also leading musicians and writers. Confident bourgeois architecture in a deep, forested valley makes it an indisputably picturesque town. The waters from the spa's 12 springs are uniformly foul-tasting: Sip them while nibbling rich Karlovy Vary *oplatky* (wafers), then resort to the "13th spring," Karlovy Vary's tangy herbal liqueur known as Becherovka. Karlovy Vary is about two hours from Prague by car on route E48.

MARIÁNSKÉ LÁZNĚ

The sanatoriums and colonnades of Mariánské Lázně (Marienbad) are impressively arrayed around an oblong park; it's not hard to conjure up visions of Chopin or Goethe retreating here from the comparatively noisy Karlovy Vary. Nowadays, the town has one of the Czech Republic's best golf courses and hosts a PGA European Tour event. Mariánské Lázně is about three hours from Prague, on Route 21 off Route E50.

ČESKÝ KRUMLOV

★ Once the main seat of the Rožmberks, Bohemia's noblest family, Český Krumlov, about four hours from Prague on Route 159 from Route E55, is an enchanting town with its imposing **Renaissance Castle** (✉ Hrad, ☎ 0337/711465; ☉ Apr., Oct. 9–4; May–Aug. 8–5; Sept. 9–5) complete with romantic elevated walkways, a round, pastel-hued tower, and an 18th-century theater that still hosts performances. The Vltava River snakes through the town, which has steeply stacked steps on either bank linking various levels and twisting narrow lanes that converge on **Náměstí Svornosti,** the Old Town's main square. A number of notable Renaissance houses add an air of formality to the overall effect of this exquisite place. The **Egon Schiele Center (Mezinárodní kulturní centrum Egona Schieleho)** exhibits the work of the painter Schiele, a frequent visitor to the town, and other 20th-century artists. ✉ *Široká 70–72,* ☎ *0337/61349, or 0337/61352.* ☉ *Daily 10–6 (11–5 in low season).*

TÁBOR

After Jan Hus's death at the stake in 1415, his proto-Protestant followers established an egalitarian commune on a fortified bluff above the Lužnice river. Jan Žižka, a one-eyed general, led the zealots of Tábor, (1½ hr from Prague on Route E55) and shaped them into Europe's most feared army. The town itself became a weapon of defense: Its twisting streets were designed to confuse the enemy. A labyrinth of tunnels and cellars below the town served both as living quarters and as a link with the outer defenses. The story is told in the **Husitské muzeum** (Hussite Museum) just off Žižkovo náměstí. ✉ *Křivkova 31.* ☉ *Apr.–Nov. 8:30– 4 (in winter on request).*

Moravian Towns

Moravia, with its peaceful villages and small towns, is the easternmost of the historic Czech Lands, sharing a lightly populated border with Bohemia. About three hours southeast of Prague on Route 406 (from E50 and 19) is the tiny village of Telč, one of the most beautiful towns in an area with stiff competition. Farther southeast, limestone crags tower over the sleepy town of Mikulov.

MIKULOV

A former center of Jewish life and learning in the Hapsburg empire, Mikulov (about 4 hr southeast of Prague on Route 620 off E55) now bears few traces of its scholarly past. Today, the town is known for its wine making. If your visit coincides with the grape harvest in October, head for the hills surrounding the town—tradition dictates that a knock on the door of a private *sklípek* (wine cellar) will lead to a tasting session. The town's Baroque-and-Gothic **Zámek Mikulov** (château) contains a wine-making museum where you can see a 22,000-gallon wine cask from 1643. ☏ *0625/2255.* ☉ *Apr.–Oct., Tues.–Sun. 9–4.*

OLOMOUC

Amid the farmlands and industrial centers of middle Moravia, Olomouc, three hours from Prague on Route 462 off E50, comes as an unexpected joy. The city retains its rambling Old Town, partially circled by high brick fortifications. The Renaissance town hall and the tall, impossibly ornate Trinity column compete for attention on **Horní náměstí,** the main square. At the eastern end of the Old Town are the neo-Gothic **Dóm svatého Václava** (Cathedral of St. Wenceslas, ✉ Václavské nám.) and a ruined 12th-century **palace** (✉ Dómská ul.) with an exquisite row of Romanesque stone windows.

TELČ

It is a surprise to come upon trim little Telč, with its neat, formal architecture, nestled in such bucolic countryside. Only the Renaissance facades, each fronted by arcades and topped with rich gables, are visible, and although they are colorful, cute, and well maintained, often the buildings behind them are falling apart. The Renaissance theme carries over to the **Zámek Telč** (château), whose architecture and decoration form a rare pre-Baroque example of stylistic unity. ☏ *066/962–943.* ☉ *Apr.–Oct., Tues.–Sun. 9–4.*

PRAGUE ESSENTIALS

Arriving and Departing

BY BUS

The Czech bus network **(CHAD)** operates from a station (✉ Křižíkova 4, ☏ 02/1034) near the main train station. Take Metro B or C to Florenc.

BY PLANE

All international flights arrive at Prague's Ruzyně Airport, about 20 km (12 mi) from downtown. For arrival and departure times, call 02/367–814.

Between the Airport and Downtown. The private Cedaz minibus shuttle links the airport and Náměstí Republiky, a downtown square near the Old Town. Shuttles run every 30–60 minutes between 5:30 AM and 9 PM daily. The trip costs 90 Kč one-way and takes about 30 minutes. The cheapest way to get into Prague is by regular Bus 119; the cost is 12 Kč, but you'll need to change to the subway at the Dejvická station to reach the center. By taxi, expect to pay 500 Kč.

BY TRAIN

The main station for international and domestic routes is Hlavní Nádraží (✉ Wilsonova ul.), not far from Wenceslas Square. Some international trains arrive at and depart from Nádraží Holešovice (✉ Vrbenského ul.), on the same Metro line (C) as the main station. Call 02/2422–4200, 02/2461–4030, or 02/2461–4031 for domestic and international schedules for both stations.

Getting Around

BY CAR

In the center of the city parking meters with green stripes let you park up to six hours; an orange stripe indicates a two-hour parking limit. Avoid the blue-marked spaces, which are reserved for local residents.

(Parking boots may be attached to offending vehicles.) There is an underground lot on Alšovo nábřeží, near Old Town Square.

BY PUBLIC TRANSPORT
Public transportation is a bargain. *Jízdenky* (tickets) can be bought at hotels, newsstands, and from dispensing machines in Metro stations. Transport passes for unlimited use of the system for one day (70 Kč) up to 15 days (280 Kč) are sold at some newsstands and at the windows marked DP or *Jízdenky* in the main Metro stations. Be sure to validate your pass by signing it where indicated. A basic 12-Kč ticket allows one hour's travel, with unlimited transfers (90 minutes on weekends and between 8 PM and 5 AM weekdays) on the Metro, tram, and bus network within the city limits. Cheaper 8-Kč tickets are good for a tram or bus ride up to 15 minutes without transferring, or 30 minutes on the Metro including transfers between lines; on the Metro, though, you cannot travel more than four stops from your starting point. For the Metro punch the ticket in the station before getting onto the escalators; for buses and trams punch the ticket inside the vehicle.

Subway. Prague's three modern Metro lines are easy to use and relatively safe. They provide the simplest and fastest means of transportation, and most new maps of Prague mark the routes. The Metro runs from 5 AM to midnight, seven days a week.

Tram and Bus. Trams are often more convenient than the Metro for short hops. Most bus lines connect outlying suburbs with the nearest Metro station. Trams 50–59 and buses numbered 500 and above run all night after the Metro shuts down.

BY TAXI
Each of Prague's countless taxi operators is allowed to set its own fares; the rates should be posted on the cab doors. The average basic charge is 20–30 Kč and per-kilometer rates range from 15 Kč to 30 Kč. Taxi scams are common. Avoid taxi stands in heavily touristed areas. Instead, order them in advance by telephone. Two established firms with telephone dispatchers are **AAA** (☎ 02/1080) and **Profitaxi** (☎ 02/1035). Some larger hotels have their own fleets, which are a little more expensive.

Money Matters
CURRENCY
The unit of currency in the Czech Republic is the crown, or *koruna* (plural *koruny*), written as Kč, and divided into 100 *haléřů* (hellers). There are bills of 20, 50, 100, 200, 500, 1,000, and 5,000 koruny and coins of 10, 20, and 50 hellers and 1, 2, 5, 10, 20, and 50 koruny. At press time (spring 1998), the rate of exchange was 32 Kč to the U.S. dollar, 23 Kč to the Canadian dollar, 54 Kč to the pound sterling, 21 Kč to the Australian dollar, and 18 Kč to the New Zealand dollar. Banks and ATMs give the best rates. Banks and private exchange outlets, which litter Prague's tourist routes, charge either a set fee or a percentage of the transaction or both, and for small transactions (US$100 or less) the charge at a bank may be more than you would pay for the same transaction at a private exchange outlet. It's wise to compare. The koruna is fully convertible and can be purchased outside the country and changed into other currencies, but you should keep your receipts and convert your koruny before you leave the country just to be sure.

Telephoning
To use a public phone buy a phone card at a newsstand or tobacconist. Cards cost 100 Kč for 50 units or 190 Kč for 100 units. To place a call lift the receiver, insert the card, and dial.

Contacts and Resources

EMBASSIES AND CONSULATE

United States (⊠ Tržiště 15, Malá Strana, ☎ 02/5732–0663). **Canadian** (⊠ Mickiewiczova 6, Hradčany, ☎ 02/2431–1108). **United Kingdom** (⊠ Thunovská 14, Malá Strana, ☎ 02/5732–0355). **Australian Consulate** (The Honorary Consulate and Trade Commission of Australia, ⊠ Na Ořechovce 38,☎ 02/2431–0071, 02/2431–0743).

EMERGENCIES

Police (☎ 158). **Ambulance** (☎ 155). **Foreigners' Department of Na Homolce Hospital** (weekdays ☎ 02/5292–2146, evenings and weekends ☎ 02/5292–2191 or 02/5721–1111). **First Medical Clinic of Prague** (☎ 02/292–286, 02/2421–6200; 24-hr emergency ☎ 02/0601–225050, mobile phone). **American Medical Center** (☎ 02/807–756, weekdays). Be prepared to pay in cash for medical treatment, whether you are insured or not. **24-Hour Pharmacies** (⊠ Lékárna U Anděla, ☎ 02/537–039; ⊠ Lékárna U svaté Ludmily, ☎ 02/2423–7207).

ENGLISH-LANGUAGE BOOKSTORES

Globe Bookstore and Coffeehouse (⊠ Janovského 14, Prague 7). **U Knihomola** (⊠ Mánesova 79, Prague 2). **Knihkupectví U černé Matky Boží** (⊠ Celetná ul. at Ovocný trh; good for hiking maps and atlases; go downstairs). **Big Ben Bookshop** (⊠ Malá Štupartská 5, Prague 1).

GUIDED TOURS

Excursions. Čedok's (☞ Visitor Information, *below*) one-day tours out of Prague include excursions to the lovely medieval town of Kutná Hora, the unusual sandstone formations of the "Bohemian Paradise" region, famous spa towns and castles, wineries, and the Terezín ghetto.

Orientation. Čedok offers a daily three-hour tour of the city, starting at 10 AM from the Čedok (☎ 02/231–8255) offices at Na Příkopě 18 and Pařížská 6. From April through October, the organization also operates an afternoon tour, starting at 2. Both tours cost about 500 Kč. **Martin-Tour** (☎ 02/2421–2473) offers a similar tour departing from Náměstí Republiky and three other Old Town points four times daily. **PIS** (☎ 02/2448–2018, 02/264–020) arranges guided tours at its Na Příkopě and Old Town Square locations.

Personal Guides. Contact Čedok (☞ Visitor Information, *below*) or PIS(☞ Visitor Information, *below*) to arrange a personal walking tour of the city. Prices start at around 400 Kč per hour.

Special-Interest. For cultural tours call Čedok (☞ Visitor Information, *below*). These include visits to the Jewish quarter, performances of folk troupes, Laterna Magika (☞ Nightlife and the Arts, *above*), opera, and concerts. Shalom (☎ 02/2481–2325) specializes in tours of the Jewish quarter.

TRAVEL AGENCIES

American Express (⊠ Václavské nám. 56, ☎ 02/2421–9992, FAX 02/2221–1131). **Thomas Cook** (⊠ Národní třída 28, ☎ 02/2110–5276).

VISITOR INFORMATION

The main **Čedok** office (⊠ Na Příkopě 18, near Wenceslas Sq., ☎ 02/2419–7111; other branches at Rytířská 16 and Pařížská 6). **Prague Information Service** (PIS; ⊠ Na Příkopě 20 and Staroměstské náměstí [Old Town Square] 22, ☎ 02/2448–2018, 02/264020).

The English-language weekly, *The Prague Post,* lists current events and entertainment programs.

The **Czech Tourist Authority** (✉ Národní třída 37, ☏ FAX 02/2421–1458) provides information on tourism outside Prague. Tourist bureaus are also found in: **Český Krumlov** (✉ Čedok, Latrán 79, ☏ 0337/711–406, 711–607; ✉ Infocentrum, Nám. Svornosti 1, ☏ 0337/711–183). **Karlovy Vary** (✉ Ul. Dr. Bechera 21–23, ☏ 017/22281). **Mariánské Lázně** (✉ Infocentrum, Hlavní 47, ☏ 0165/5330, 0165/5892, 0165/3757). **Mikulov** (✉ Regional Tourist Center, Námtřiida 32, ☏ 0625/2855). **Olomouc** (✉ Horní nám, ☏ 068/551–3385). **Tábor** (✉ Žižkovo nám., ☏ 0361/252–385). **Telč** (✉ Town hall, Nám. Zachariáše z Hradce 10, ☏ 066/962–233).

19 Rome

Antiquity is taken for granted in Rome, where successive ages have piled the present on top of the past—building, layering, and overlapping their own particular segments of Rome's 2,500 years of history to form a remarkably varied urban complex. Most of the city's major sights are in the fairly small centro (center). At its heart lies ancient Rome, site of the Foro Romano and Colosseo. It was around this core that the other sections of the city grew up through the ages: medieval Rome, which covered the horn of land that pushes the Tiber toward the Vatican and extended across the river into Trastevere; and Renaissance Rome, which was erected upon medieval foundations and extended as far as the Vatican, with beautiful villas created in what were then the outskirts of the city.

EXPLORING ROME

Numbers in the margin correspond to points of interest on the Rome map.

The layout of the centro is highly irregular, but several landmarks serve as orientation points to identify the areas that most visitors come to see: The Colosseo (Colosseum), the Pantheon and Piazza Navona, the Basilica di San Pietro (St. Peter's Church), the Scalinata di Piazza di Spagna (Spanish Steps), and Villa Borghese. You'll need a good map to find your way around; newsstands offer a wide choice. Energetic sightseers will walk a lot, a much more pleasant way to see the city now that some traffic has been barred from the centro during the day; others might choose to take taxis, buses, or the Metro. If you are in Rome during a hot spell, do as the Romans do: Start out early in the morning, have a light lunch and a long siesta during the hottest hours, then resume sightseeing in the late afternoon and end your evening with a leisurely meal outdoors, refreshed by cold Frascati wine and the *ponentino*, the cool evening breeze.

Ancient Rome

➐ Arco di Costantino (Arch of Constantine). The best-preserved of Rome's triumphal arches, this 4th-century BC monument is covered with reliefs depicting Constantine's victory over Maxentius at the Milvian Bridge. Just before this battle in AD 312, Constantine had a vision of a cross in the heavens and heard the words: "In this sign thou shalt conquer." The victory led not only to the construction of this majestic marble arch but also to a turning point in the history of Christianity: Soon afterward a grateful Constantine decreed that it was a lawful religion and should be tolerated throughout the empire. ⊠ *Piazza del Colosseo at end of Via di San Gregorio.*

➋ Campidoglio (Capitol Square). In the square on the Capitoline Hill, the majestic ramp and beautifully proportioned piazza are the handiwork of Michelangelo (1475–1564), who also worked on the three palaces, two of which house the Capitoline Museums. Palazzo Senatorio, at the center, is still the ceremonial seat of Rome's city hall; it was built over the Tabularium, where ancient Rome's state archives were kept. The statue at the center of the square is a copy of an ancient Roman bronze of Marcus Aurelius (AD 120–180). ⊠ *Piazza del Campidoglio.*

★ ➏ Colosseo (Colosseum). Massive and majestic, this ruin is ancient Rome's most famous monument, inaugurated in AD 80 with a program of games and shows that lasted 100 days. On opening day alone some 5,000 wild animals perished in the arena. The Colosseum could hold more than 50,000 spectators; it was faced with marble, decorated with stuccos, and had an ingenious system of awnings to provide shade. Try to see it both in daytime and at night, when yellow floodlights make it a magical sight. The Colosseum, by the way, takes its name from a colossal, 118-ft statue of Nero that stood nearby. Some sections of the amphitheater may be closed during ongoing restorations. ⊠ *Piazza del Colosseo,* ☎ *06/ 7004261.*☉ *Mon.–Sat. 9–2 hrs before sunset, Sun. 9–1.*

➎ Foro Romano (Roman Forum). In the valley below the Campidoglio, what was once a marshy hollow important only as a crossroads and marketplace, became the political, commercial, and social center of Rome, containing public meeting halls, shops, and temples. As Rome declined, these monuments lost their importance and were eventually destroyed by fire or the invasions of barbarians. Rubble accumulated (though much of it was carted off later by medieval home builders as construction material), and the site reverted to marshy pastureland; sporadic excavations began at the end of the 19th century. You don't really have to try to make sense of the mass of marble fragments scattered over the area of the Roman Forum. Just consider that 2,000 years ago this was the center of the Mediterranean world. Wander down the **Via Sacra** and climb the **Colle Palatino** (Palatine Hill), where the emperors had their palaces and where 16th-century cardinals strolled in elaborate Italian gardens. From the belvedere you have a good view of the **Circo Massimo** (Circus Maximus). ⊠ *Entrances to Via Sacra on Via dei Fori Imperiali and Piazza Santa Maria Nova; entrances to Palatine on Via Sacra and Via di San Gregorio,* ☎ *06/6990110.*▨ *Entry to Via Sacra free.* ☉ *Mon.– Sat. 9–2 hrs before sunset, Sun. 9–1.*

❸ Musei Capitolini (Capitoline Museums). The **Museo Capitolino** and **Palazzo dei Conservatori,** the palaces flanking Palazzo Senatorio on the Campidoglio, form a single museum holding some fine classical sculptures, including the gilded bronze equestrian statue of Marcus Aurelius that once stood on the pedestal in the piazza, as well as the *Dying Gaul,* the *Capitoline Venus,* and a fascinating series of portrait busts of ancient philosophers and emperors. In the courtyard of Palazzo dei Conservatori on the right of the piazza, you can use the mammoth fragments of a colossal statue of the emperor Constantine (c.280–336) as amusing props for snapshots. Inside you will find splendidly frescoed salons still used for municipal ceremonies, as well as sculptures and paintings. ⊠ *Piazza del Campidoglio,* ☎ *06/67102071.* 🎫 *Free last Sun. of month.* ⏱ *Tues.–Sat. 9–7, Sun. 9–6:45.*

❶ Piazza Venezia. Considered the geographical heart of the city, the square is dominated by the enormous marble monument honoring the first king of unified Italy, Victor Emmanuel II (1820–1878), which is a rhetorical 19th-century counterpart of another Rome landmark, the Colosseum. ⊠ *Square at intersection of Via del Corso, Via del Plebiscito, and Via dei Fori Imperiali.*

❹ Santa Maria dell'Aracoeli. The 13th-century church on the Campidoglio can be reached by a long flight of steep stairs or, more easily, by way of the stairs on the far side of the Museo Capitolino. Stop in to see the medieval pavement, the Renaissance gilded ceiling that commemorates the victory of Lepanto, and the Pinturicchio frescoes. ⊠ *Piazza Aracoeli.*

❽ Terme di Caracalla (Baths of Caracalla). The scale of the towering ruins of ancient Rome's most beautiful and luxurious public baths hint at their past splendor. Inaugurated by Caracalla in 217, the baths were used until the 6th century. An ancient version of a swank athletic club, the baths were open to all, though men and women used them separately; citizens could bathe, socialize, and exercise in huge pools and richly decorated halls and libraries. ⊠ *Via delle Terme di Caracalla.* ⏱ *Apr.–Sept., Tues.–Sat. 9–6, Sun.–Mon. 9–1; Oct.–Mar., Tues.– Sat. 9–3, Sun.–Mon. 9–1.*

Piazzas and Fountains

⑭ Fondazione Keats-Shelley Memorial (Keats and Shelley Memorial House). To the right of the Spanish Steps is the house where Keats (1795–1821) died; the building is now a museum of Keats memorabilia and it also houses a library of works by Romantic authors. ⊠ *Piazza di Spagna 26,* ☎ *06/6784235.* ⏱ *June–Sept., weekdays 9–1 and 3–6; Oct.–May, weekdays 9–1 and 2:30–5:30.*

★ ⑮ Fontana di Trevi (Trevi Fountain). A spectacular fantasy of mythical sea creatures and cascades of splashing water, this fountain is one of Rome's Baroque greats. The fountain as you see it was completed in the mid-1700s, but there had been a drinking fountain on the site for centuries. Pope Urban VIII almost sparked a revolt when he slapped a tax on wine to cover the expenses of having the fountain repaired. Legend has it that visitors must toss a coin into the fountain to ensure their return to Rome. ⊠ *Piazza di Trevi.*

⑲ Galleria Borghese (Borghese Gallery). At the northeast corner of Villa Borghese, a park studded with pines and classical statuary, is this gallery created by Cardinal Scipione Borghese in 1613 as a showcase for his fabulous collection of ancient sculpture. One of the noteworthy additions to the collections over the centuries, the reclining statue of Pauline Borghese by Canova continues to seduce visitors. Among some extraordinary works by Bernini (1598–1680), the unforgettable *Apollo*

284

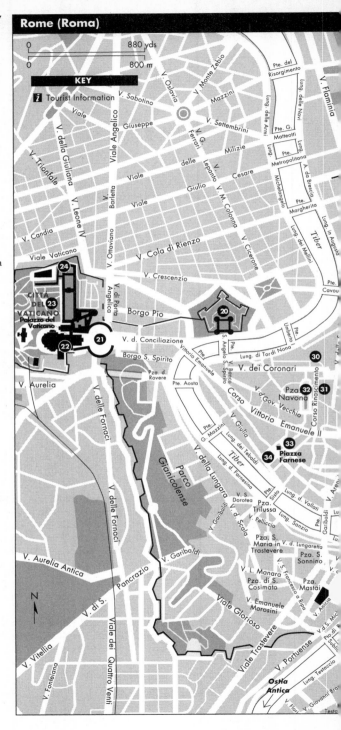

Rome (Roma)

⑪

Viale delle Belle Arti

V. Ulisse Aldrovandi

Zoological Gardens

V. P. Raimondi

Botanical Gardens

Viale dell' Uccelliera

⑲

V. P. Canonica

Vle. G. Washington

Villa Borghese

⑩

V. d. Museo Borghese

Pincio

V. d. Magnolie

V. Pinciana

⑨

Vle G. d'Annunzio

Villa Medici

Viale del Muro Torto

Porta Pinciana

V. P. Pinciana

Corso d'Italia

Pza. Fiume

Pza. Alessandria

Ple. di Porta Pia

V. di Ripetta

V. del Babuino

V. Trinità d. Monti

Galoppatoio

V. Pio Pinciana

V. Campania

V. Romagna

V. Piave

V. Nomentana

V. Vittoria

Trinità dei Monti

⑫ ⑬

⑭

V. Ludovisi

Vitt. Veneto

V. Piemonte

V. Sallustiana

V. XX Settembre

V. Goito

V. Palestro

Viale del Policlinico

Pza. Augusto Imperatore

V. Tomacelli

V. Condotti

V. F. Crispi

V. Due Macelli

V. Sistina

⑱

V. Veneto

V. Bissolati

Quintino Sella

V. Cernaia

V. Volturno

V. Goeta

V. Vicenza

Viale Castro Pretorio

Pza. Colonna

V. Vittoria

V. Tritone

MONTE QUIRINALE

⑯

V. Barberini

⑰

ℹ

Pza. d. Repubblica

V. Torino

V. Nazionale

Napoli

Stazione Termini

V. Marsala

V. Castro Pretorio

Viale Pretoriano

V. del Corso

⑮

V. d. Scuderie

Giardini del Quirinale

V. Quattro Fontane

V. A. Depretis

V. G. Amendola

V. Giovanni Giolitti

V. IV Novembre

Palazzo del Quirinale

Milano

V. d. S. Maria Maggiore

Sta. Maria Maggiore

V. F. Turati

V. Pr. Umberto

㉙

㉘

V. d. Plebiscito

㉗ V. C. Battisti

V. d. Serpenti

Panisperna

V. d. S. Maria Maggiore

V. Carlo Alberto

V. Napoleone III

V. Pr. Eugenio

㉖

Pza. Venezia

①

V. Cavour

MONTE VIMINALE

Quattro Cantoni

V. d. Statuto

V. Conte Verde

V. Emanuele Filiberto

Manzoni

Vittoriano

V. dei Fori Imperiali

V. Giovanni Lanza

V. Mecenate

㉕

④

MONTE CAPITOLINO

② ③

V. Cavour

MONTE ESQUILINO

V. d. Monte Oppia

V. Ruggero Bonghi

Viale

Pte. Fabricio

⑤

Foro Romano

⑥

Viale del Monte Oppia

V. d. Domus Aurea

V. Labicana

V. Claudia

V. S. Giovanni in Laterano

S. Giovanni in Laterano

Pza. Giovanni XXIII

V. di Pietro

Palazzo dei Conservatori

⑦

V. d. Cenci

V. di S. Gregorio

Pza. SS. Giovanni e Paolo

V. di S. Stefano Rotondo

V. di S. Erasmo

V. d. Amba Aradam

V. Magna Grecia

㉟

Pte.

MONTE PALATINO

MONTE CELIO

Pza. di Pta. Capena

V. d. Navicella

Pza. di Porta Metronia

Tiber

COLLE AVENTINO

V. dei Cerchi

Circo Massimo

V. del Circo Massimo

Ple. Romolo e Remo

V. delle Terme Caracalla

Pza. di Porta Metronia

V. Gallia

V. S. Sabina

V. S. A. Magno

S. Prisca

Viale Aventino

MONTE AVENTINO

Pza. Albania

Parco di Porta Capena

⑧

Pza. d. Emporio

V. M. Gelsomini

V. d. Porta Latina

V. Pannonia

and Daphne shows how the artist transformed marble into flesh and foliage. The picture collection is no less impressive, with works by Caravaggio (1573–1610), Raphael (1483–1520), and Titian (c.1488–1576). ⊠ *Piazzale Scipione Borghese, Villa Borghese,* ☎ 06/8548577. *Reservations essential.* ☎ 06/84241607. ⊙ *Tues.–Sat. 9–7, Sun. 9–1.*

⑪ **Museo Etrusco di Villa Giulia** (Etruscan Museum of Villa Giulia). Pope Julius III built this gracious Renaissance villa as a summer retreat. It now holds a world-class museum where you can delve into the world of the Etruscans, who inhabited Italy in pre-Roman times and have left fascinating evidence of their relaxed, sensual lifestyle. You'll observe smiles as enigmatic as that of the Mona Lisa on deities and other figures in terracotta, bronze, and gold. Ask especially to see the Castellani collection of ancient jewelry (and copies) hidden away on the upper floor. And see the full-scale replica of an Etruscan temple in the garden. ⊠ *Piazza di Villa Giulia 9,* ☎ 06/3201951. ⊙ *Tues.–Sat. 9–7, Sun. 9–2.*

⑰ **Palazzo Barberini** (Barberini Palace). Rome's most splendid 17th-century palace houses the **Galleria Nazionale di Arte Antica.** Its gems include Raphael's *Fornarina* and many other fine paintings, some lavishly frescoed ceilings, and a charming suite of rooms decorated in 1782 on the occasion of the marriage of a Barberini heiress. ⊠ *Via delle Quattro Fontane 13,* ☎ 06/4814591. ⊙ *Tues.–Sat. 9–7, Sun. 9–1.*

⑯ **Piazza Barberini.** This busy crossroads has two fountains by Bernini: the jaunty **Fontana del Tritone** (Triton) in the middle of the square and the **Fontana delle Api** (Bees) at the corner of Via Veneto. Decorated with the heraldic Barberini bees, this latter shell-shape fountain bears an inscription that was immediately regarded as an unlucky omen by the superstitious Romans, for it erroneously stated that the fountain had been erected in the 22nd year of the reign of Pope Urban VIII, who commissioned it, whereas in fact the 21st anniversary of his election was still some weeks away. The wrong numeral was hurriedly erased, but to no avail: Urban died eight days before the beginning of his 22nd year as pontiff. ⊠ *Square at intersection of Via del Tritone, Via Vittorio Veneto, and Via Barberini.*

⑨ **Piazza del Popolo.** Designed by neoclassic architect Giuseppe Valadier in the early 1800s, this square is one of the largest and airiest in Rome. The 3,000-year-old obelisk in the middle was brought to Rome from Egypt by the emperor Augustus, and it once stood in the Circus Maximus. ⊠ *Square at southern end of Via Flaminia and northern end of Via del Corso.*

⑫ **Piazza di Spagna** (Spanish Square). The square is the heart of Rome's chic shopping district and a popular rendezvous spot, especially for the young people who throng the Spanish Steps on evenings and weekend afternoons. In the center of the elongated square, at the foot of the Spanish Steps, is Bernini's Fontana della Barcaccia (Old Boat), around which passersby cool themselves on hot summer nights. ⊠ *Southern end of Via del Babuino and northern end of Via Due Macelli.*

⑱ **Santa Maria della Concezione.** In the crypt under the main Capuchin church skeletons and scattered bones of some 4,000 dead Capuchin monks are arranged in odd decorative designs, a macabre practice peculiar to the Baroque age. ⊠ *Via Veneto 27,* ☎ 06/462850. ☒ *Free (donations encouraged).* ⊙ *Daily 9–noon and 3–6.*

⑩ **Santa Maria del Popolo.** This medieval church rebuilt by Bernini in Baroque style is rich in art; the pièces de résistance: two stunning Caravaggios in the chapel to the left of the main altar. You'll find it tucked away in the corner of Piazza del Popolo next to the monumental Renaissance city gate. ⊠ *Piazza del Popolo.*

★ ⑬ **Scalinata di Piazza di Spagna** (Spanish Steps). The 200-year-old stair-case got its name from the Spanish Embassy to the Holy See (the Vatican), though the staircase was built with French funds in 1723, as the approach to the French church of **Trinità dei Monti** at the top of the steps. The steps are banked with blooming azaleas from mid-April to mid-May. ⊠ *Piazza di Spagna and Piazza Trinità dei Monti.*

Castel Sant'Angelo and the Vatican

★ ㉒ **Basilica di San Pietro** (St. Peter's Basilica). In all of its staggering grandeur and magnificence, St. Peter's Basilica is best appreciated as the lustrous background for ecclesiastical ceremonies thronged with the faithful. The original basilica was built during the early 4th century AD by the emperor Constantine, above an earlier shrine that supposedly marked the burial place of St. Peter. After more than a thousand years, the old basilica was so decrepit it had to be torn down. The task of building a new, much larger one took almost 200 years, and employed the architectural geniuses of Alberti (1404–72), Bramante (1444–1514), Raphael, Peruzzi, Antonio Sangallo the Younger (1483–1546), and Michelangelo, who died before the dome he had planned could be completed. The structure was finally finished in 1626.

Among the most famous works of art is Michelangelo's *Pietà* (1498), seen in the first chapel on the right just as you enter the basilica. Michelangelo carved four statues of the Pietà; this one is the earliest and best known, two others are in Florence, and the fourth, the *Rondanini Pietà,* is in Milan. At the end of the central aisle is the bronze statue of St. Peter, its foot worn by centuries of reverent kisses. The bronze throne above the altar in the apse was created by Bernini to contain a simple wood-and-ivory chair once believed to have belonged to St. Peter. Bernini's bronze baldachin over the papal altar was made with metal stripped from the portico of the Pantheon at the order of Pope Urban VIII, one of the powerful Roman Barberini family. His practice of plundering ancient monuments for material with which to carry out his grandiose schemes inspired the famous quip, *"Quod non fecerunt barbari, fecerunt Barberini"* ("What the barbarians didn't do, the Barberini did").

As you stroll up and down the aisles and transepts, observe the fine mosaic copies of famous paintings above the altars, the monumental tombs and statues, and the fine stucco work. Stop at the **Treasury** (Historical Museum), which contains some priceless liturgical objects. ⊠ *Historical Museum entrance in the Sacristy .* ☉ *Apr.–Sept., daily 9–6:30; Oct.–Mar., daily 9–5:30.*

The entrance to the so-called **Grotte Vaticane** (Vatican Grottoes), crypts containing chapels and the tombs of various popes, is in one of the huge piers at the crossing. It's best to leave this visit for last, as the crypt's only exit takes you outside the church. It occupies the area of the original basilica, over the necropolis, the ancient burial ground where evidence of what may be St. Peter's burial place has been found. ⊠ *Vatican Grottoes entrance at piers at the crossing.* ▱ *Free.* ☉ *Apr.–Sept., daily 7–6; Oct.–Mar., daily 7–5.*

To see the roof and dome of the basilica, take the elevator or climb the stairs in the courtyard near the exit from the Vatican Grottoes. From the roof you can climb a short interior staircase to the base of the dome for an overhead view of the basilica's interior. Then, only if you are in good shape should you attempt the very long, strenuous, and claustrophobic climb up the narrow stairs to the balcony of the lantern atop the dome, where you can look down on the Vatican Gardens and out across all of Rome. ⊠ *Entrance in courtyard to the left as you leave the basilica.* ⊙ *Apr.–Sept., daily 8–6; Oct.–Mar., daily 8–5.*

Free 60-minute tours of St. Peter's Basilica are offered in English daily (usually starting about 10 AM and 3 PM, and at 2:30 PM Sun.) by volunteer guides. They start at the information desk under the basilica portico. At the Ufficio Scavi (☞ *below*) you can book special tours of the necropolis. Note that entry to St. Peter's, the Vatican Museums, and the Gardens is barred to those wearing shorts, miniskirts, sleeveless T-shirts, and otherwise revealing clothing. Women can cover bare shoulders and upper arms with scarves; men should wear full-length pants or jeans. ⊠ *Piazza San Pietro,* ☏ *06/69884466.* ⊙ *Apr.–Sept., daily 7–7; Oct.–Mar., daily 7–6. Necropolis (left beyond Arco delle Campane entrance to Vatican),* ☏ *06/69885318. Apply a few days in advance to Ufficio Scavi, or try in morning for the same day. Office hrs Mon.–Sat. 9–5; closed Sun.*

㉑ Castel Sant'Angelo (Sant'Angelo Castle). Transformed into a formidable fortress, this castle was originally built as the tomb of Emperor Hadrian (AD 76–138) in the 2nd century AD. In its early days it looked much like the Augusteo (Tomb of Augustus), which still stands in more or less its original form across the river. Hadrian's Tomb was incorporated into the city's walls and served as a military stronghold during the barbarian invasions. According to legend it got its present name in the 6th century, when Pope Gregory the Great, passing by in a religious procession, saw an angel with a sword appear above the ramparts to signal the end of the plague that was raging. Enlarged and fortified, the castle became a refuge for the popes, who fled to it along the Passetto, an arcaded passageway that links it with the Vatican.

Inside the castle you see ancient corridors, medieval cells, and Renaissance salons, a museum of antique weapons, courtyards piled with stone cannonballs, and terraces with great views of the city. There's a pleasant bar with outdoor tables. The highest terrace of all, under the bronze statue of the legendary angel, is the one from which Puccini's heroine Tosca threw herself to her death. **Ponte Sant'Angelo,** the ancient bridge spanning the Tiber in front of the castle, is decorated with lovely Baroque angels designed by Bernini. ⊠ *Lungotevere Castello 50,* ☏ *06/68300183.* ⊙ *Daily 9–7. Closed 2nd and 4th Tues. of month.*

㉓ Giardini Vaticani (Vatican Gardens). The attractively landscaped gardens can be seen in a two-hour tour that shows you a few historical monuments, fountains, and the lovely 16th-century house of Pius IV designed by Pirro Ligorio, as well as the Vatican's mosaic school. Vistas from within the gardens give you a different perspective of the basilica itself. *Tickets:* ⊠ *Information office, on left side of St. Peter's Square,* ☏ *06/69884466.* ⊙ *Mon.–Sat. 8:30–7. Garden tour:* ▨ *16,000 lire.* ⊙ *Mon., Tues., and Thurs.–Sat. 10 AM.*

㉔ Musei Vaticani (Vatican Museums). The accumulated collections of humanity's artistic history are housed here, from the Egyptians to the present, boasting such masterpieces as Michelangelo's frescoes in the Sistine Chapel. The collections cover nearly 8 km (5 mi) of displays, so if you are visiting St. Peter's and the museums on the same day, save yourself the 15-minute walk between the two by taking the shuttle bus (2,000 lire) that operates during museum opening hours, except on Wednesday. The ride gives you a glimpse of the Giardini Vaticani (☞ *above*). Posters at the museum entrance plot out a choice of four color-coded itineraries; the shortest takes about 90 minutes, the longest more than four hours, depending on your rate of progress. No matter
★ which tour you take, it will include the famed **Cappella Sistina** (Sis-

tine Chapel). In 1508 Pope Julius II commissioned Michelangelo to paint the more than 10,000 square ft of the chapel's ceiling. For four years Michelangelo dedicated himself to painting in the fresco technique, over fresh plaster, and the result was a masterpiece. Cleaning has removed centuries of soot and revealed the original and surprisingly brilliant colors of the ceiling and the *Last Judgment.* You can try to avoid the tour groups by going early or late, allowing yourself enough time before the closing hour. In peak season the crowds definitely detract from your appreciation of this outstanding artistic achievement. To make sense of the figures on the ceiling, buy an illustrated guide or rent an audio guide. A pair of binoculars also helps.

Some of the highlights that might be of interest on your first tour are the reorganized Egyptian collection and the *Laocoön,* the *Belvedere Torso,* which inspired Michelangelo, and the *Apollo Belvedere.* The Raphael Rooms are decorated with masterful frescoes, and there are more of Raphael's works in the *Pinacoteca* (Picture Gallery). At the Quattro Cancelli, near the entrance to the Picture Gallery, a rather spartan cafeteria provides basic refreshments. ⊠ *Viale Vaticano,* ☎ *06/ 69883041.* 🎟 *Free last Sun. of the month.* ⊙ *Easter wk and mid-Mar.– Oct., weekdays 8:45–3:45, Sat. 8:45–12:45; Nov.–mid-Mar., Mon.– Sat. 8:45–12:45. Last Sun. of the month 8:45–12:45. Closed Sun., except last Sun. of the month.*

㉑ **Piazza San Pietro** (St. Peter's Square). Completed in 1667, the vast, oval-shape square in front of St. Peter's basilica opens at the western end of Via della Conciliazione, the broad avenue created by Mussolini's architects by razing blocks of old houses. This opened up a vista of the basilica, giving the eye time to adjust to its mammoth dimensions, and thereby spoiling the effect Bernini sought. He enclosed his huge square in the embrace of mammoth quadruple colonnades. Look for the stone disks in the pavement halfway between the fountains and the obelisk. From these points the colonnades seem to be formed of a single row of columns all the way around. The square was designed to accommodate crowds, and it has held up to 400,000 people at one time. At noon on Sunday when he is in Rome, the pope appears at his third-floor study window in the **Palazzo Vaticano,** to the right of the basilica, to bless the crowd in the square.

Since the Lateran Treaty of 1929, Vatican City has been an independent and sovereign state, which covers about 108 acres and is surrounded by thick, high walls. Its gates are watched over by the Swiss Guards, who still wear the colorful dress uniforms designed by Michelangelo. Sovereign of this little state is John Paul II, 264th pope of the Roman Catholic Church. For many visitors a **papal audience** is the highlight of a trip to Rome. Mass audiences take place on Wednesday morning in a modern audience hall (capacity 7,000) off the left-hand colonnade or in St. Peter's Square. Tickets are necessary, but you can also see the Pope when he appears at the window of the Vatican Palace to bless the crowd in the square below at noon on Sunday. He also blesses the public on summer Sundays when he's at the papal residence at Castel Gandolfo (☞ Guided Tours *in* Rome Essentials, *below*). For audience tickets write or fax well in advance indicating the date you prefer, language you speak, and hotel in which you will stay. Or, apply for tickets in person on the Monday or Tuesday before the Wednesday audience. ⊠ *Prefettura della Casa Pontificia, 00120 Vatican City,* ☎ *06/69883017,* 𝖥𝖠𝖷 *06/69885863.* ⊙ *Mon. and Tues. 9–1.*

Old Rome

㉝ Campo dei Fiori (Field of Flowers). This square is the site of a crowded and colorful daily morning market. The hooded bronze figure brooding over the piazza is philosopher Giordano Bruno, who was burned at the stake here for heresy. ⊠ *Piazza Campo dei Fiori.*

㉖ Chiesa del Gesù. This huge 16th-century church is a paragon of the Baroque style and the tangible symbol of the power of the Jesuits, who were a major force in the Counter-Reformation in Europe. Its interior gleams with gold and precious marbles, and it has a fantastically painted ceiling that flows down over the pillars, merging with painted stucco figures to complete the three-dimensional illusion. ⊠ *Piazza del Gesù.*

㉕ Fontana delle Tartarughe (Turtles). This pretty 16th-century bronze fountain by Giacomo della Porta (the turtles were added probably by Bernini in 1658) is in the heart of Rome's former Jewish Ghetto, a neighborhood with medieval inscriptions and friezes on the old buildings on Via Portico d'Ottavia, and the remains of the Teatro di Marcello (Theater of Marcello), a theater built by Julius Caesar to hold 20,000 spectators. ⊠ *Piazza Mattei.*

㉗ Galleria Doria Pamphili. You can visit this rambling palazzo, still the residence of a princely family, to view the gallery housing the family's art collection and also some of the magnificently furnished private apartments. ⊠ *Piazza del Collegio Romano 2, near Piazza Venezia,* ☎ *06/6797323.* ⊙ *Fri.–Wed. 10–5; guided tours of private apartments mornings only.*

㉟ Isola Tiberina (Tiberina Island). Built in 62 BC, Rome's oldest bridge, the **Ponte Fabricio,** links the Ghetto neighborhood on the Tiber's left bank to this little island, home to the city hospital and the church of San Bartolomeo. The island has been dedicated to healing ever since a temple to Aesculapius was erected here in 291 BC. **Ponte Cestio** links the island with the Trastevere section on the right bank.

OFF THE **Ostia Antica** – (Ancient Ostia). The well-preserved Roman port city of
BEATEN PATH Ostia Antica, near the sea, is a parklike archaeological site analogous with Pompeii and much easier to get to from Rome. There's a regular train service from the Ostiense Station (Piramide Metro stop). ⊠ *Via dei Romagnoli, Ostia Antica,* ☎ *06/5651405.* ⊙ *Daily 9–1 hr before sunset.*

㉚ Palazzo Altemps. A 15th-century patrician dwelling, the palace has been beautifully restored and is now a showcase for the sculpture collection of the Museo Nazionale Romano. Informative labels in English make it easy to appreciate such famous sculptures as the amazingly intricate carved reliefs on the *Ludovisi Sarcophagus* and the *Galata,* representing the heroic death of a barbarian warrior. ⊠ *Piazza Sant'Apollinare 46,* ☎ *06/6833759.* ⊙ *Tues.–Sun. 10–5.*

㉞ Palazzo Farnese. Now the French Embassy, one of the most beautiful of Rome's many Renaissance palaces dominates Piazza Farnese, where Egyptian marble basins from the Terme di Caracalla have been transformed into fountains. ⊠ *Piazza Farnese.*

㉙ Pantheon. Originally built in 27 BC by Augustus's general Agrippa and totally rebuilt by Hadrian in the 2nd century AD, this is one of Rome's finest, best-preserved, and perhaps least appreciated ancient monuments. You don't have to look far past the huge columns of the portico and the original bronze doors to find the reason for its astounding architectural harmony: the diameter of the soaring dome is exactly equal to the height of the walls. The hole in the ceiling is intentional: the oculus at the apex of the dome signifies the "all-seeing eye of heaven." In ancient times the entire interior was encrusted with rich decorations of gilt bronze and marble that were plundered by later emperors and popes. ⊠ *Piazza della Rotonda.* ⊙ *Mon.–Sat. 9–6:30, Sun. 9–1.*

★ ㉜ **Piazza Navona.** This elongated 17th-century piazza traces the oval form of the underlying Circus of Diocletian. At the center Bernini's lively **Fontana dei Quattro Fiumi** (Four Rivers) is a showpiece. The four statues represent rivers in the four corners of the world: the Nile, with its face covered in allusion to its then unknown source; the Ganges; the Danube; and the River Plate, with its hand raised. And here we have to give the lie to the legend that this was Bernini's mischievous dig at Borromini's design of the facade of the church of **Sant'Agnese in Agone,** from which the statue seems to be shrinking in horror. The fountain was created in 1651; work on the church's facade began a year or two later. The piazza dozes in the morning, when little groups of pensioners sun themselves on the stone benches and children pedal tricycles around the big fountain. In the late afternoon the sidewalk cafés fill up for the aperitif hour, and in the evening, especially in good weather, the piazza comes to life with a throng of street artists, vendors, tourists, and Romans out for their evening *passeggiata* (promenade). ⊠ *North of Corso Vittorio Emanuele and west of Corso Rinascimento.*

㉛ **San Luigi dei Francesi.** The clergy of San Luigi considered Caravaggio's roistering and unruly lifestyle scandalous enough, but his realistic treatment of sacred subjects—seen in three paintings in the last chapel—was just too much for them. They rejected his first version of the altarpiece and weren't particularly happy with the other two works either. Thanks to the intercession of Caravaggio's patron, an influential cardinal, they were persuaded to keep them—a lucky thing, since they are now recognized to be among the artist's finest paintings. Have a few hundred-lire coins handy for the light machine. ⊠ *Via della Dogana Vecchia.* ⊙ *Fri.–Wed. 7:30–12:30 and 3:30–7, Thurs. 7:30–12:30.*

㉘ **Santa Maria sopra Minerva.** Rome's only major Gothic church takes its name from the temple of Minerva over which it was built. Inside there are some beautiful frescoes by Filippo Lippi (1457–1504); outside there is a charming elephant by Bernini with an obelisk on its back. ⊠ *Piazza della Minerva.*

DINING

There is an abundance of restaurants in Rome, generally serving various Italian regional cuisines. The most expensive restaurants usually offer interpretations of Italian and international specialties with a flourish of linen and silver, followed up by a whopping *conto* (check). If you want typical Italian cooking and lower prices, try a more moderately priced ristorante or a trattoria, usually a smallish and unassuming, often family-run place. Fast-food places, many with Italian fare, and Chinese restaurants are proliferating in Rome. During August many restaurants close for vacation.

RATINGS

Prices are per person and include first course, main course, dessert or fruit, and house wine, where available.

CATEGORY	COST
$$$$	over 120,000 lire
$$$	70,000 lire–120,000 lire
$$	40,000 lire–70,000 lire
$	under 40,000 lire

$$$$ ✕ **La Pergola.** High atop Monte Mario, the Cavalieri Hilton (☞
★ *below*) rooftop restaurant commands sweeping views onto the city below.
The warmly elegant dining room has trompe l'oeil ceilings, handsome
wood paneling, and large windows. Celebrated Wunder-chef Heinz Beck
is a skilled technician, and brings Rome its finest example of Mediterranean *alta cucina* (haute cuisine). ⊠ *Cavalieri Hilton, Via Cadlolo 101,*
☎ *06/3509221. Reservations essential. Jacket and tie. AE, DC, MC,*
V. Closed Sun.–Mon. No lunch.

$$$$ ✕ **La Rosetta.** In 1992 chef-owner Massimo Riccioli took the nets and
★ fishing gear off the classic cherry-wood walls of his parents' trattoria
to create what is widely known as the place to go in Rome to eat first-
rate fish. Start with *ricci di mare* (sea urchins), *vongole veraci* (sautéed
clams), or a variety of delicately marinated fish; move on to perfectly
grilled seafood or a poached fillet. Desserts (made in house) are worth
saving room for. ⊠ *Via della Rosetta 9,* ☎ *06/6861002. Dinner reser-*
vations essential. AE, DC, MC, V.

$$$ ✕ **Checchino dal 1887.** Literally carved out of a hillside made of pot-
sherds from Roman times, Checchino serves the most traditional
Roman cuisine—carefully prepared and served without fanfare—in a
clean, sober environment. The slaughterhouses of the Testaccio quar-
ter are long gone, but you can still try the variety of meats that make
up the soul of Roman cooking, including *trippa* (tripe), and *coratella*
(sweetbreads). There's also plenty to choose from for those uninter-
ested in innards. Desserts are very good. ⊠ *Via di Monte Testaccio 30,*
☎ *06/5746318. AE, DC, MC, V. Closed Mon., Aug., and during*
Christmas. No dinner Sun.

$$$ ✕ **Da Checco er Carettiere.** Maybe this is what all Italian restaurants
once looked like: an aging doorman, garlic braids hanging from the
ceiling, black-and-white photos in small frames lining the wood-paneled walls. At this third-generation, family-run Trastevere institution
you'll find all the Roman standards, solidly prepared with good-qual-
ity ingredients, plus plenty of local vegetables and an unusually good
selection of fish. ⊠ *Via Benedetta 10,* ☎ *06/5817018. AE, DC, MC,*
V. Closed Mon. No dinner Sun.

$$–$$$ ✕ **Dal Bolognese.** This classic restaurant is a trendy choice for a
leisurely lunch between sightseeing and shopping. An array of contemporary paintings decorates the dining room but the real attraction
is the lovely piazza—prime people-watching real estate. As the name
of the restaurant promises, the cooking here adheres to the hearty tradition of Bologna, with delicious homemade *tortellini in brodo* (filled
pasta in broth), fresh pastas in creamy sauces, and *bollito misto* (steam-
ing trays of boiled meats). ⊠ *Piazza del Popolo 1,* ☎ *06/3611426. AE,*
MC, V. Closed Mon. and Aug.

$$ ✕ **Colline Emiliane.** Behind an opaque glass facade not far from Piazza
Barberini are a couple of plain dining rooms, where you are served light
homemade pastas, *tortelli di zucca* (pumpkin-filled ravioli), and meats
ranging from *giambonetto di vitello*(roast veal) to *cotoletta alla bolo-
gnese* (fried veal cutlet with cheese and prosciutto). Family-run, it's quiet
and soothing. ⊠ *Via San Nicolò da Tolentino 26,* ☎ *06/4818564. Reser-*
vations essential. AE, DC, MC, V. Closed Sun. and Aug.

$$ ✕ **Il Cardinale.** This serene little restaurant turns out fanciful, light-
ened-up Roman fare, beautifully presented on king-size plates. Oil paint-
ings and enlarged old photos of Roman landmarks are hung against

golden damask wall coverings, and chairs and couches are covered in a pretty floral print. The menu speaks of composed salads, vegetable soups, and such pastas as *vermicelli cacio e pepe* (pasta with pecorino cheese and black pepper) or *ravioli di borragine* (ravioli filled with borage leaves), and various vegetable *sformati* (flans). ⊠ *Via delle Carceri 6,* ☎ *06/6869336. AE, DC, MC, V. Closed Sun.*

$$ ✕ **Myosotis.** Myosotis is the sequel to a successful restaurant on the
★ outskirts of town run by the Marsilis. The menu rides that delicate line between tradition and innovation, focusing more on the freshness and quality of the ingredients than on elaborate presentation. Fresh pasta gets special attention: it's rolled out by hand to order for the *stracci alla delizia di mare* (pasta with seafood). There's a wide choice of fish, meat, and seasonal veggies to choose from. ⊠ *Via della Vaccarella 3/ 5,* ☎ *06/2053943. Closed Mon. and 2 wks in Aug. AE, DC, MC, V.*

$$ ✕ **Papá Baccus.** Italo Cipriani, owner of Rome's best Tuscan restaurant, takes his meat as seriously as any Tuscan, using real Chianina beef for the house special, *bistecca alla fiorentina* (grilled, thick bone-in steak). Cipriani brings many ingredients from his home town in northern Tuscany. Try the sweet and delicate prosciutto from Pratomagno. The welcome here is warm, the service excellent. ⊠ *Via Toscana 36,* ☎ *06/42742808. AE, DC, MC, V. Closed Sun., 2 wks in Aug., and during Christmas. No lunch Sat.*

$–$$ ✕ **Antico Arco.** Run by three friends with a passion for wine and fine
★ food, the Antico Arco has quickly won the hearts of Roman foodies with great invention and moderate prices. Particularly good are such starters as *sformato di finocchi in salsa d'arancia* (fennel flan with orange sauce) and such second courses as *petto d'anatra con salsa di lamponi* (duck breast with raspberry sauce). Don't miss dessert. ⊠ *Piazzale Aurelio 7,* ☎ *06/5815274. Closed Mon. No lunch Tues.–Sat. AE, DC, MC, V.*

$ ✕ **Dal Toscano.** The hallmarks of this great family-run Tuscan trattoria
★ ria near the Vatican are friendly and speedy service, an open wood-fired grill, and such classic dishes as *ribollita* (a dense bread and vegetable soup), and the prized bistecca alla fiorentina. Wash it all down with a strong Chianti. All desserts are yummy and homemade. ⊠ *Via Germanico 58,* ☎ *06/39725717. DC, MC, V. Closed Mon., Aug., and 2 wks in Dec.*

$ ✕ **Dar Poeta.** Romans drive across town for great pizza from this neighborhood joint in Trastevere. Maybe it's the dough—it's made from a secret blend of flours reputed to be easier to digest than the crust of the competition. For dessert try the unusual calzone with Nutella and ricotta. ⊠ *Vicolo del Bologna 45,* ☎ *06/5880516. Reservations not accepted. AE, MC, V. Closed Mon. No lunch.*

$ ✕ **Il Simposio di Costantini.** At the classiest wine bar in town—wrapped in wrought-iron vines, wood paneling, and velvet—choose from about 30 wines in *degustazione* (available by the glass) or order a bottle from a list of over a thousand Italian and foreign labels sold in the shop next door. Food is appropriately fancy: marinated and smoked fish, composed salads, fine salami and cured meats (classical and wild), terrines and pâtes, and stellar cheeses. ⊠ *Via Appia Antica 139,* ☎ *06/7880494. AE, MC, V. Closed Thurs.*

$ ✕ **L'Osteria dell'Ingegno.** This trendy *enoteca* (wine bar), infused with a hip modern decor and happening groove, seems almost out of place among the ruins of the old town. The short menu—a sampling of simple dishes that emphasize fine ingredients—changes weekly. Service is fast. ⊠ *Piazza di Pietra 45,* ☎ *06/6780662. AE, D, MC, V. Closed Sun.*

$ ✕ **Perilli.** A bastion of authentic Roman cooking and trattoria charm since 1911 (the decor has changed very little), this is the place to go to try *rigatoni con pajata* (rigatoni with baby veal's intestines)—if you're into that sort of thing. Otherwise the carbonara and *all'ama-*

triciana (spicy tomato sauce with pancetta) are classics. The house wine is a golden nectar from the Castelli Romani. ⊠ *Via Marmorata 39,* ☎ *06/5742415. No credit cards. Closed Wed.*

NIGHTLIFE AND THE ARTS

You will find information on scheduled events and shows at EPT and municipal tourist offices or booths. The biweekly booklet "Un Ospite a Roma," free from concierges at some hotels, is another source of information, as is "Wanted in Rome," published on Wednesday, available at newsstands. There are listings in English in the back of the weekly "Roma c'è" booklet, with handy bus information for each listing; it is published on Thursday and sold at newsstands. If you want to go to the opera, the ballet, or a concert, it's best to ask your concierge to get tickets for you. They are sold at box offices only, just a few days before performances.

The Arts

CONCERTS

The main concert hall is the **Accademia di Santa Cecilia** (⊠ Via della Conciliazione 4, ☎ 06/68801044). There are many concerts year-round; look for posters or for schedules in the publications mentioned above.

FILM

The only English-language movie theater in Rome is the **Pasquino** (⊠ Vicolo del Piede, just off Piazza Santa Maria in Trastevere, ☎ 06/5803622). The program is listed in Rome's daily newspapers. Several other movie theaters show films in English on certain days of the week; the listings in "Roma c'è" are reliable.

OPERA

The opera season runs from November or December through May, and performances are staged in the **Teatro dell'Opera** (⊠ Via del Viminale, ☎ 06/4817003; toll-free in Italy 167016665). From May through August, the spectacular performances are held in the open air. After having been evicted from the ancient ruins of the Terme di Caracalla, performances have been held temporarily in Villa Pepoli, a parklike area adjacent to the ruins of the baths. Tickets go on sale at the opera box office two days in advance.

Nightlife

Rome's "in" nightspots change like the flavor of the month, and many fade into oblivion after a brief moment of glory. The best places to find an up-to-date list are the weekly entertainment guide "Trovaroma," published each Thursday in the Italian daily *La Repubblica,* and "Roma c'è," the weekly guide sold at newsstands.

BARS

Jacket and tie are in order in the elegant **Blue Bar** (⊠ Via dei Soldati 25, ☎ 06/6864250) of the Hostaria dell'Orso. One of the grandest places for a drink in well-dressed company is **Le Bar** (⊠ Via Vittorio Emanuele Orlando 3, ☎ 06/482931) of Le Grand Hotel. **Jazz Club** (⊠ Via Zanardelli 12, ☎ 06/6861990), near Piazza Navona, is an upscale watering hole. **Flann O'Brien** (⊠ Via Napoli 29, ☎ 06/4880418), one of a plethora of pubs that now monopolize the bar scene in Rome, has the feel of a good Irish pub but also serves a decent cappuccino. **Trinity College** (⊠ Via del Collegio Romano 6, near Piazza Venezia, ☎ 06/6786472) has two floors of Irish pub trappings, with plenty o' gift of the gab and music until 2 AM.

Testaccio's three-floor **The Saint** (⊠ Via Galvani 46, ☎ 06/5747945) has two discos designated "Paradiso" and "Inferno" (Heaven and Hell). You might spot an American celeb at **Gilda** (⊠ Via Mario dei Fiori 97, ☎ 06/6784838), with a disco, piano bar, and live music. It's closed Monday and jackets are required. Just as exclusive is **Bella Blu** (⊠ Via Luciani 21, ☎ 06/3230490), a Parioli club that caters to Rome's thirtysomething elite.

MUSIC CLUBS

For the best live music, including jazz, blues, rhythm and blues, African, and rock, go to **Big Mama** (⊠ Vicolo San Francesco a Ripa 18, ☎ 06/5812551). Live performances of jazz, soul, and funk by leading musicians draw celebrities to **Alexanderplatz** (⊠ Via Ostia 9, in the Vatican area, ☎ 06/39742171). The music starts about 10 PM, and you can have supper while you wait.

WINE BARS

Informal enoteche (wine bars) are popular with Romans who like to burn the midnight oil but don't dig disco music. They usually serve light meals or snacks. **Spiriti** (⊠ Via Sant'Eustachio 5, ☎ 06/6892499), near the Pantheon, serves light lunches at midday and is open until 1:30 AM. At family-run **Trimani Wine Bar** (⊠ Via Cernaia 37/b, ☎ 06/4469630), you can sample some great wines at the counter or with a light, fixed-price meal at an upstairs table. **Il Simposio di Costantini** (⊠ Via Appia Antica 139, near the Vatican, ☎ 06/7880494), wrapped in wrought iron vines, wood paneling, and velvet, offers about 30 wines by the glass.

SHOPPING

Via Condotti, directly across from the Spanish Steps, and the streets running parallel to Via Condotti, as well as its cross streets, form the most elegant and expensive shopping area for clothes and accessories in Rome. Lower-price fashions may be found on display at shops on **Via Frattina** and **Via del Corso.** Romans in the know do much of their shopping along **Via Cola di Rienzo** and **Via Nazionale.** For prints browse among the stalls at **Piazza Fontanelle Borghese** or stop in at the shops in the Pantheon area. For minor antiques **Via dei Coronari** and other streets in the Piazza Navona area are good. The most prestigious antiques dealers are situated in **Via del Babuino** and its environs. The open-air markets at **Campo dei Fiori** and in many neighborhoods throughout the city provide an eyeful of great local color.

ROME ESSENTIALS

Arriving and Departing

BY PLANE

Rome's principal airport is **Aeroporto Leonardo da Vinci** usually known as **Fiumicino** (⊠ 29 km/18 mi southeast of Rome, ☎ 06/65953640 for flight information). The smaller **Ciampino** (⊠ on the edge of Rome, ☎ 06/794941 for flight information) is used as an alternative by international and domestic lines, especially for charter flights.

Between the Airport and Downtown. To get to downtown Rome from **Fiumicino** you have a choice of two trains. Ask at the airport (at EPT or train information counters) which one takes you closest to your hotel. The nonstop Airport–Termini express takes you directly to Track 22 at Termini Station, Rome's main train terminal, well served by taxis and the hub of Metro (subway) and bus lines. The ride to Termini takes

30 minutes; departures are hourly, beginning at 7:50 AM, with the final departure at 10:05 PM. Tickets cost 13,000 lire. The other airport train (FM1) runs to Tiburtina station in Rome and beyond to Monterotondo, a suburban town to the east. The main stops in Rome are at the Trastevere, Ostiense, and Tiburtina stations. At each of these you can find taxis and bus and/or Metro connections to various parts of Rome. This train runs from 6:35 AM to 12:15 AM, with departures every 20 minutes. The ride to Tiburtina takes 40 minutes. Tickets cost 7,000 lire. For either train you buy your ticket at an automatic vending machine (you need Italian currency). There are ticket counters at some stations (Termini Track 22, Trastevere, Tiburtina). Remember to **date-stamp your ticket in one of the yellow machines near the track.**

A taxi to or from Fiumicino costs about 70,000 lire, including supplements. At a booth inside the terminal you can hire a four- or five-passenger car with driver for a little more. If you decide to take a taxi, use only the yellow or the newer white cabs, which must wait outside the terminal; make sure the meter is running. Gypsy cab drivers solicit your business as you come out of customs; they're not reliable, and their rates may be rip-offs. **Ciampino** is connected with the Anagnina Station of the Metro A by bus (runs every half hour). A taxi between Ciampino and downtown Rome costs about 35,000 lire.

BY TRAIN

Termini Station is Rome's main train terminal, although the Tiburtina, Ostiense, and Trastevere stations serve some long-distance trains, many commuter trains, and the FM1 line to Fiumicino Airport. For train information call ☎ 06/4775, ☎ 1478/88088 toll free, or try the English-speaking personnel at the Information Office in Termini, or at any travel agency. Tickets and seats can be reserved and purchased at travel agencies bearing the FS (Ferrovie dello Stato) emblem. Tickets can be purchased up to two months in advance. Short-distance tickets are also sold at tobacconists and ticket machines in the stations.

Getting Around
Rome's integrated Metrebus transportation system includes buses and trams (ATAC), Metro and suburban trains and buses (COTRAL), and some other suburban trains (FS) run by the state railways. A ticket valid for 75 minutes on any combination of buses and trams and one admission to the Metro costs 1,500 lire (time-stamp your ticket when boarding the first vehicle; you're supposed to stamp it again if you board another vehicle just before the ticket runs out, but few do). Tickets are sold at tobacconists, newsstands, some coffee bars, automatic ticket machines in Metro stations, some bus stops, and at ATAC and COTRAL ticket booths. A BIG tourist ticket, valid for one day on all public transport, costs 6,000 lire. A weekly ticket (Settimanale, also known as CIS) costs 24,000 lire and can be purchased only at ATAC and Metro booths.

BY BICYCLE

Pedaling through Villa Borghese, along the Tiber, and through city center when traffic is light is a pleasant way to see the sights, but remember: Rome is hilly. Rental concessions are at the Piazza di Spagna and Piazza del Popolo Metro stops, and at Largo San Silvestro and Largo Argentina. You will also find rentals at Viale della Pineta and Viale del Bambino on the Pincio. **I Bike Rome** (✉ underground parking lot Sector III at Villa Borghese, ☎ 06/3225240) leases bikes. **St. Peter's Motor Rent** (✉ Via di Porta Castello 43, near St. Peter's, ☎ 06/6875714) also rents bikes.

BY BUS

Orange ATAC (☎ 06/46954444) city buses (and a few streetcar lines) run from about 6 AM to midnight, with night buses (indicated N) on some lines. When entering a bus, remember to board at the rear and exit at the middle. Bus lines 117 and 119, with compact electric vehicles, makes a circuit of limited but scenic routes in downtown Rome. They can save you from a lot of walking, and you can get on and off as you please.

BY CAR

If you come by car, put it in a parking space (and note that parking in central Rome is generally either metered or prohibited) or a garage, and use public transportation. If you plan to drive into or out of the city, take time to study your route, especially on the GRA (Grande Raccordo Anulare, a beltway that encircles Rome and funnels traffic into the city, not always successfully). The main access routes to Rome from the north are the A1 autostrada from Florence and Milan, and the Aurelia highway (SS 1) from Genoa. The principal route to or from points south, such as Naples, is the A2 autostrada.

BY METRO

The Metro is the easiest and fastest way to get around, but the network has limited stops. It opens at 5:30 AM, and the last train leaves each terminal at 11:30 PM. Metro A runs from the eastern part of the city to Termini Station and past Piazza di Spagna and Piazzale Flaminio to Ottaviano-S. Pietro, near St. Peter's and the Vatican museums. Metro B serves Termini, the Colosseum, and Tiburtina Station (where the FM1 Fiumicino Airport train stops).

BY MOPED

You can rent a moped or scooter and mandatory helmet at **Scoot-a-Long** (✉ Via Cavour 302, ☎ 06/6780206). **St. Peter Moto** (✉ Via di Porta Castello 43, ☎ 06/6875714) also rents equipment.

BY TAXI

Taxis wait at stands and, for a small extra charge, can also be called by telephone. The meter starts at 4,500 lire; there are supplements for service after 10 PM, on Sunday and holidays, and for each piece of baggage. Use the yellow or the newer white cabs only, and be very sure to check the meter. To call a cab dial ☎ 06/3570, 06/5551, 06/4994, or 06/88177.

Money Matters

CURRENCY

The unit of currency in Italy is the lira (plural, lire). There are bills of 1,000, 2,000, 5,000, 10,000, 50,000, 100,000, and 500,000 lire (impossible to change, except in banks); coins are worth 50, 100, 200, and 500 lire. In 1999 the euro will be used as a banking currency, but the lire will still be the currency in use on a day-to-day basis. At press time (spring 1998) the exchange rate was about 1,798 lire to the U.S. dollar, 1,266 lire to the Canadian dollar, and 2,943 lire to the pound sterling.

When your purchases run into hundreds of thousands of lire, beware of being shortchanged, a dodge that is practiced at ticket windows, toll booths, and cashiers' desks, as well as in shops and even in banks. *Always count your change before you leave the counter.* Always carry some smaller-denomination bills for sundry purchases; you're less likely to be shortchanged, and you won't have to face the eye-rolling dismay of cashiers reluctant to change large-denomination bills.

Credit cards are generally accepted in shops and hotels, but may not always be welcome in restaurants, so always look for card logos displayed in windows or ask when you enter to avoid embarrassing situations. When you wish to leave a tip beyond the 15% service charge that is usually included with your bill, leave it in cash rather than adding it to the credit card slip.

Telephoning

COUNTRY CODE
The country code for Italy is 39.

Contacts and Resources

EMBASSIES
United States (✉ Via Veneto 121, ☎ 06/46741). **Canadian** (✉ Via Zara 30, ☎ 06/445981). **United Kingdom** (✉ Via Venti Settembre 80a, ☎ 06/4825441).

EMERGENCIES
Police (☎ 113). **Ambulance** (☎ 1188 or 06/5510) Say "Pronto Soccorso" and be prepared to give your address. **Doctor** and **dentist: Salvator Mundi Hospital** (☎ 06/588961). **Rome American Hospital** (☎ 06/22551). **Pharmacies** are open 8:30–1 and 4–8. Some stay open all night, and all open Sunday on a rotation system; a notice of the pharmacies open in the neighborhood is posted at each pharmacy.

ENGLISH-LANGUAGE BOOKS
Economy Book and Video Center (✉ Via Torino 136, ☎ 06/4746877). **Anglo-American Bookstore** (✉ Via della Vite 102, ☎ 06/6795222). **Corner Bookstore** (✉ Via del Moro 48, Trastevere, ☎ 06/5836942).

GUIDED TOURS
Excursions. Most operators offer half-day excursions to Tivoli to see the Villa d'Este's fountains and gardens; Appian Line's and CIT's half-day tours to Tivoli also include Hadrian's Villa and its impressive ancient ruins. Most operators have all-day excursions to Assisi, to Pompeii and/or Capri, and to Florence. For do-it-yourself excursions to Ostia Antica and other destinations, pick up information at the EPT information offices (☞ *below*).

Orientation. Three-hour tours in air-conditioned buses with English-speaking guides cover Rome with four separate itineraries: "Ancient Rome," "Classic Rome," "Christian Rome," and the "Vatican Museums and Sistine Chapel." Most tours cost about 53,000 lire, though the Vatican Museums tour is about 60,000 lire. **American Express** (☎ 06/67641) tours depart from Piazza di Spagna. **CIT** (☎ 06/47941) depart from Piazza della Repubblica. **Appian Line** (☎ 06/4884151) picks up sightseers at their hotels. Though operators and names change, there is usually some kind of bus tour following a continuous circle route through the city center, stopping at important sites where you can get on and off at will. Check with the EPT for the name of the current operator and schedules. The least expensive organized bus tour (three hours) on the special 110 bus is run by **ATAC,** the municipal bus company. Book tours for about 15,000 lire at the ATAC information booth in front of Termini Station. There is at least one tour daily, departing at 2:30 (3:30 in summer).

Papal Audience. You can make your own arrangements (at no cost) to attend a public papal audience in the Vatican or to be at the Sunday blessing at the Pope's summer residence at Castel Gandolfo. Tour operators will make the arrangements for you, for a price. **CIT** (☎ 06/47941). **Appian Line** (✉ Via Barberini 109, ☎ 06/4884151). **Carrani** (✉ Via V. E. Orlando 95, ☎ 06/4880510).

Walking. Secret Walks (⊠ Viale Medaglie d'Oro 127, 00136 Rome, ☎ 06/39728728 and 06/39728728) conducts small groups on theme walks led by English-speaking city experts; they can also arrange excursions. **Scala Reale** (⊠ Via Varese 52, 00185 Rome, ☎ 06/44700898) also has English-language tours. For more information contact city tourist offices.

TRAVEL AGENCIES

American Express (⊠ Piazza di Spagna 38, ☎ 06/67641). **CIT** (⊠ Piazza della Repubblica 64, ☎ 06/47941). **CTS** (youth and budget travel, discount fares; ⊠ Via Genova 16, ☎ 06/46791; ☎ 06/4679271 for information).

VISITOR INFORMATION

EPT (Rome Provincial Tourist) main office (⊠ Via Parigi 5, 00185, ☎ 06/48899253; ⊠ Termini Station; ⊠ Fiumicino Airport). **City tourist information booths** (⊠ Largo Goldoni, corner of Via Condotti; Via del Corso in the Spanish Steps area; Via dei Fori Imperiali, opposite the entrance to the Roman Forum; Via Nazionale, at Palazzo delle Esposizioni; Piazza Cinque Lune, off the north end of Piazza Navona).

20 Stockholm

Stockholm stands on 14 islands surrounded by water so clean that you can fish and swim in the heart of the city. This cultivated, civilized city has many parks, squares, and wide streets, providing welcome calm in what has become a bustling metropolis. Modern glass and steel buildings abound in the city center, but you are seldom more than a five-minute walk from twisting, medieval streets and water views.

The first written mention of Stockholm dates from 1252, when a powerful regent named Birger Jarl built a fortified castle here. This strategic position, where the fresh waters of Lake Mälaren meet the brackish Baltic Sea, prompted King Gustav Vasa to take over the city in 1523, and King Gustavus Adolphus to make it the heart of an empire a century later.

During the Thirty Years' War (1618–48), Sweden became an important Baltic trading state, and the city gained a reputation as a commercial center. But by the beginning of the 18th century, Swedish influence had begun to wane, and Stockholm's development slowed. It did not pick up again until the Industrial Revolution, when the hub of the city moved north from the Gamla Stan (Old Town) area.

EXPLORING STOCKHOLM

Numbers in the margin correspond to points of interest on the Stockholm map.

Stockholm's main attractions are concentrated in a relatively small area, and the city itself can be explored in just a few days. If you have only limited time in Stockholm, give priority to a tour of Stockholm's Gamla Stan (Old Town), a labyrinth of narrow medieval streets, alleyways, and quiet squares on the island just south of the city center. Be sure to visit the large island of Djurgården. Although it's only a short walk from the city center, the most pleasant way to approach it is by ferry from Skeppsbron, in Gamla Stan.

⑪ **Gröna Lund Tivoli.** Stockholm's only amusement park is a family favorite, with traditional rides and new attractions on the waterfront each season. ⊠ *Djurgårdsv.,* ☎ *08/6707600.* ⊙ *Late Apr.–early Sept. Prices and hours are subject to change; call ahead.*

⑭ **Historiska Museet** (Historical Museum). The museum houses some remarkable gold and silver treasures dating from the Swedish Viking era. ⊠ *Narvav. 13–17,* ☎ *08/7839400.* ⊙ *Tues.–Sun. 11–5, Thurs. 11–8. Closed Mon.*

★ ⑧ **Junibacken.** This fairy-tale house lets you travel in small carriages through the world of children's book writer Astrid Lindgren, creator of the irrepressible character Pippi Longstocking. ⊠ *Galärvarsv.,* ☎ *08/6600600.* ⊙ *Daily 10–6.*

★ ③ **Kungliga Slottet** (Royal Palace). Visit at noon and watch the time-honored, yet now superfluous changing of the smartly dressed guards. You can wander at will into the palace courtyard and the building itself. The **Livrustkammaren** (Royal Armory), has an outstanding collection of weaponry and royal regalia. The **Skattkammaren** (Treasury) houses the Swedish crown jewels, including the regalia used for the coronation of King Erik XIV in 1561. You can also visit the **Representationsvånengen** (State Apartments), where the king swears in each successive government. ⊠ *Gamla Stan,* ☎ *08/6664466.* 🎫 *SKr 35 daytime, SKr 40 evening, not including coupons or passes for rides.* ⊙ *Late Apr.–early Sept. Prices and hrs subject to change; call ahead.*

⑦ **Kungsträdgården** (King's Garden). Originally built as a royal kitchen garden, this was turned into a public park in 1562. In summer you can watch people playing open-air chess with giant chess pieces. In winter the park has a skating rink. ⊠ *Between Hamng. and the Royal Opera in the city center.*

⑥ **National Museet** (National Museum). The works of important old masters, including Rembrandt, and those of many Swedish artists line the walls here. ⊠ *Södra Blasieholmshamnen,* ☎ *08/6664250.* ⊙ *Wed., Fri.–Sun. 11–5, Tues., Thurs. 11–8.*

⑬ **Nordiska Museet** (Nordic Museum). The museum shows how Swedes have lived during the past 500 years. On permanent display are peasant costumes, folk art, and items from the Sami (Lapp) culture. On the ground floor, there's a delightful "village life" play area. ⊠ *Djurgårdsv. 6–16,* ☎ *08/6664600.* ⊙ *Tues.–Sun. 11–5.*

② **Riddarholms kyrkan** (Riddarholm Church). A host of Swedish kings are buried in this magnificent sanctuary, a Greyfriars monastery dating from 1270. ⊠ *Riddarholmen, Gamla Stan,* ☎ *08/4026000.* ⊙ *June–Aug., Mon.–Sat. 11–4, Sun. noon–4; May and Sept., Wed. and weekends noon–3.*

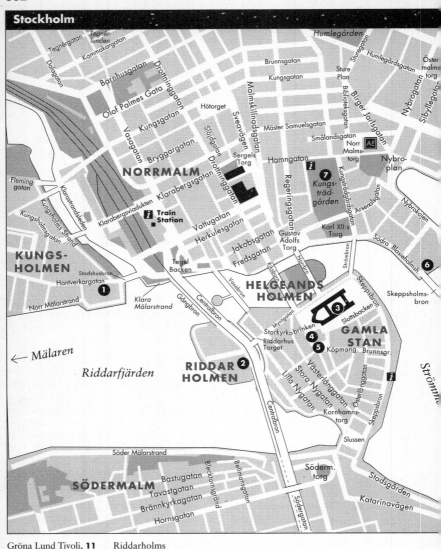

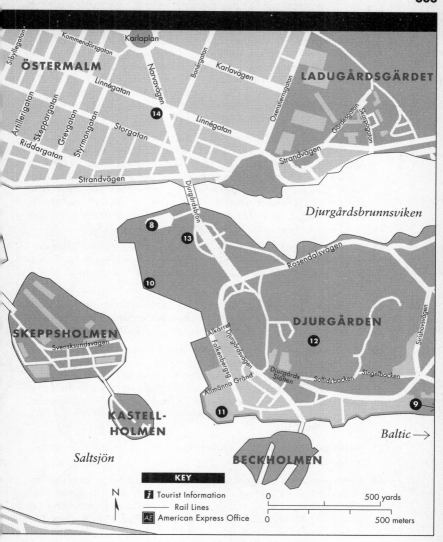

ÖSTERMALM

Sibyllegatan
Kommendörsgatan
Karlaplan
Artillerigatan
Skeppargatan
Grevgatan
Riddargatan
Styrmangatan
Storgatan
Linnégatan
Narvavägen
Banérgatan
Karlavägen

14

Linnégatan

LADUGÅRDSGÄRDET

Oxenstiernsgatan
Gärdesgatan
Storgatan

Strandvägen

Strandvägen

Djurgårdsbron

Djurgårdsbrunnsviken

8

13

Rosendalsvägen

10

SKEPPSHOLMEN
Svensksundsvägen

DJURGÅRDEN

12

Alkärret
Djurgårdsvägen
Falkenbergsg.
Allmänna Gränd
Djurgårds-Slätten
Solliddsbacken
Singelbacken
Sirishovsvägen

9

11

Baltic →

KASTELL-
HOLMEN

BECKHOLMEN

Saltsjön

KEY

N

i Tourist Information
— Rail Lines
AE American Express Office

0   500 yards

0   500 meters

★ ❀ ⑫ **Skansen.** More than 150 reconstructed traditional buildings from all over Sweden and a variety of handicraft displays and demonstrations form this large, open-air folk museum. There is a zoo, with native Scandinavian lynxes, wolves, and elks, as well as an aquarium and an old-style *tivoli* (amusement park). Snack kiosks and a nicer restaurant make it easy to spend a whole day. ⊠ *Djurgårdsslätten 49–51,* ☎ *08/ 4428000.* ⊡ *Sept.–Apr., SKr 30 weekdays, SKr 40 weekends; May– Aug., SKr 50.* ⊙ *Sept.–Apr., daily 9–5; May–Aug., daily 9 AM–10 PM. Prices and hours subject to change; call ahead.*

★ ❶ **Stadshuset** (City Hall). Architect Ragnar Östberg's ornate 1923 facade is a Stockholm landmark. Lavish mosaics adorn the walls of the **Gyllene Salen** (Golden Hall), and the **Prinsens Galleri** (Prince's Gallery) holds a collection of large murals by Prince Eugen, brother of King Gustav V. Take the elevator halfway up, then climb the rest of the way to the top of the 348-ft tower for a magnificent view of the city. ⊠ *Hantverkarg. 1,* ☎ *08/50829000.* ⊙ *Tours: daily at 10 and noon; also at 11 and 2 in summer. Tower: May–Sept., daily 10–4:30.*

❹ **Storkyrkan** (Cathedral). In this 15th-century Gothic cathedral in central Gamla Stan, you will find the *Parhelion,* a painting of Stockholm dating from 1520, the oldest in existence. ⊠ *Trångsund 1,* ☎ *08/ 7233000.*

❺ **Stortorget.** Danish King Christian II ordered a massacre in this square in 1520 that triggered a revolt and the founding of the sovereign state of Sweden. ⊠ *Gamla Stan, just southwest of Kungliga Slottet.*

★ ❿ **Vasamuseet.** The 17th-century warship *Vasa* sank ignominiously in Stockholm Harbor on its maiden voyage in 1628 because it was not carrying sufficient ballast. Forgotten for centuries, the largely intact vessel was recovered from the sea in 1961 and now stands sentinel over the harbor in this striking museum; the museum also has film presentations and displays. ⊠ *Galärvarvet,* ☎ *08/6664800.* ⊙ *Thurs.–Tues. 10–5, Wed. 10–8.*

Västerlånggatan. The main street of Gamla Stan brims with boutiques and antiques shops.

❾ **Waldemarsudde.** Once the summer residence of Prince Eugen, this museum offers an important collection of Nordic paintings dating from 1880 to 1940, as well as the prince's own works. ⊠ *Prins Eugens väg 6,* ☎ *08/6622800.* ⊡ *SKr 50.* ⊙ *June–Aug., Wed. and Fri.–Sun. 11– 5, Tues. and Thurs. 11–8; Sept.–May, Tue.–Sun. 11–4. Prices and hrs subject to change; call ahead.*

Elsewhere in Stockholm

You can admire the world's largest display of water lilies at the **Bergianska Botaniska Trädgården** (Bergianska Botanical Garden), north of the city center. There are plants from all over the world at the **Victoria House.** ⊠ *Frescati,* ☎ *08/162853.* ⊡ *Free to park.* ⊙ *Greenhouse daily 11– 5; herbal garden daily 8–5; Victoria House May–Sept., daily 11-5; park always open.*

Just shy of 508 ft, the **Kaknästornet** (the Kaknäs TV Tower) on Gärdet is the tallest structure in Scandinavia. From its top you have a magnificent view of the city and the surrounding archipelago. Facilities include a cafeteria, restaurant, and gift shop. ⊠ *Ladugårdsgärdet, Bus 69 from Sergels Torg,* ☎ *08/7892435.* ⊙ *10–9 year-round.*

DINING

Traditional Swedish restaurants are giving way to myriad international culinary influences. Fast-food outlets abound, but there is an impressive range of eateries—from top-class establishments to less expensive places for lunch or a snack—to suit even the most fickle palates and every budget.

Restaurants all over the country specialize in *husmanskost* (home cooking), based on traditional Swedish recipes. Sweden is world famous for its *smörgåsbord,* a word now internationally used as a synonym for diversity. This tempting buffet of hot and cold dishes, usually with a strong emphasis on seafood, notably herring, has something to tickle all taste buds. You can usually find an authentic smörgåsbord, and eat as much as you wish, for SKr 200–300. Hotels sometimes serve a smörgåsbord-style breakfast, often included in the room price.

MEALTIMES

Swedes eat early. Lunch is served from 11 AM, and outside the main cities restaurants often close at 9 PM or don't even open for dinner. In the large cities there are plenty of places to eat, although it is advisable to make reservations at the more popular establishments, especially on weekends.

RATINGS

Prices are per person and include a first course and main course, but no drinks. Service charges and *moms* (value-added tax) are included in the check, but it is common to tip 5%–10%.

CATEGORY	COST
$$$$	OVER SKR 350
$$$	SKR 250–SKR 350
$$	SKR 120–SKR 250
$	UNDER SKR 120

Stockholm has one of the highest densities of restaurants per capita in Europe. Lunch is generally served between 11 and 2; if you're looking for value dining, make lunch your big meal.

$$$$ ✕ **Operakällaren.** One of Stockholm's best-known traditional restaurants is found in the elegant Opera House. With both Scandinavian and Continental cuisine on its menu, it is famed for its smörgåsbord, available from June 1st, with seasonal variations, through Christmas. In summertime you can dine on the veranda. ⊠ *Operahuset, Jakobs Torg 2,* ☎ *08/6765801. AE, DC, MC, V. Main dining room closed July.*

$$$$ ✕ **Ulriksdals Värdshus.** Top-notch service, a beautiful location—in a castle park on the outskirts of town—and a noteworthy Swedish and international menu highlighting a lunchtime smörgåsbord all make this worth a splurge. Built in 1868, the restaurant was once a country inn, and it hasn't lost a bit of its country hospitality. ⊠ *Ulriksdals Slottspark, Solna,* ☎ *08/850815. AE, DC, MC, V. No dinner Sun.*

$$$$ ✕ **Videgård.** One of Stockholm's best restaurants offers delicious, orig-
★ inal meat and fish dishes. The decor is subtly modern and the staff well versed with the contents of the varied menu. ⊠ *Regeringsg. 111,* ☎ *08/4116153. AE, DC, MC, V.*

$$$ ✕ **Clas på Hörnet.** Just outside the city center, this small, intimate es-
★ tablishment occupies the ground floor of a restored 200-year-old town house, now a hotel. It serves international and Swedish cuisine. ⊠ *Surbrunnsg. 20,* ☎ *08/165136. AE, DC, MC, V. Closed July.*

$$$ ✕ **Den Gyldene Freden.** Once a favorite haunt of Stockholm's artists
★ and composers, this restaurant, dating from 1722, has an Old Town

ambience. Every Thursday, the Swedish Academy meets for lunch on the second floor. The menu offers a tasteful combination of French and Swedish cuisines. ⊠ *Österlångg. 51*, ☎ *08/249760. AE, DC, MC, V. Closed Sun. and July. No lunch except Sat.*

$$$ ✕ **Il Conte.** A warm, Italian-style restaurant close to Stockholm's most elegant avenue, Strandvägen, Il Conte has delicious Italian dishes and wines served by an attentive staff. The restaurant is tastefully decorated to create an alluring, refined atmosphere. ⊠ *Grevg. 9*, ☎ *08/6612628. Reservations essential. AE, DC, MC, V. Call for closing dates.*

$$$ ✕ **Stallmästaregården.** This historic inn with an attractive courtyard
   ★ and garden sits in Haga Park, just north of Norrtull, about 15 minutes by car or slightly longer by bus from the city center. In summer fine French and Swedish cuisine is served in the courtyard overlooking Brunnsviken lake. ⊠ *Norrtull, near Haga, Bus 52 to Stallmästaregården.* ☎ *08/6101300. AE, DC, MC, V. Closed Sun.*

$$$ ✕ **Wedholms Fisk.** You can only get fresh fish and shellfish at this open, high-ceiling restaurant near Berzelli Park, across from the Royal Dramatic Theater. The tartare of salmon and the grilled sole are noteworthy, and portions are generous. The Scandinavian artwork on display is part of the owner's personal collection. ⊠ *Nybrokajen 17*, ☎ *08/6117874. AE, DC, MC, V. Closed Sun. and July.*

$$ ✕ **Calle P.** Palm leaves function as plates at this trendy restaurant, which
   ★ has an unusual menu of exotic dishes. On the edge of a small park, it draws a younger crowd for people-watching and music. ⊠ *Berzelli Park*, ☎ *08/6782120. AE, DC, MC, V. Closed Sun.*

$$ ✕ **Eriks Bakficka.** A favorite among locals, Eriks is a block from elegant Strandvägen and a few steps down from street level. The restaurant serves a wide variety of Swedish dishes; the pub section has a lower-priced menu. The same owner operates Eriks in Gamla Stan, one of Stockholm's most exclusive restaurants. ⊠ *Frederikshovsg. 4*, ☎ *08/6601599. AE, DC, MC, V. Closed July.*

$$ ✕ **Gondolen.** Suspended under the gangway of the Katarina elevator at Slussen square, Gondolen has a magnificent view over the harbor, Mälaren, and the Baltic. The cuisine is international with a range of prix-fixe menus available. ⊠ *Stadsgården 6*, ☎ *08/6417090. AE, DC, MC, V. Closed Sun.*

$$ ✕ **Martini.** This Italian restaurant is a great place to eat; patrons line up for a seat in summer, when the terrace is open. The main restaurant is below street level, but light colors and a bustling atmosphere make it cheerful. ⊠ *Norrmalmst. 4*, ☎ *08/6798220. AE, DC, MC, V.*

$$ ✕ **Nils Emil.** Frequented by members of the Swedish royal family, this elegant but unpretentious restaurant is noted for its delicious Swedish cuisine and generous helpings. Paintings of the Stockholm archipelago decorate the walls. ⊠ *Folkungag. 122, Södermalm*, ☎ *08/6407209. Reservations essential. AE, DC, MC, V. Closed July. No lunch Sat.*

$$ ✕ **Sturehof.** Opened before the turn of the century, Sturehof is one of Sweden's oldest fish restaurants. It has a refurbished (1996) bistro/pub, but the nautically inspired ambience of the main restaurant has been preserved. ⊠ *Stureplan 2*, ☎ *08/6798750. AE, DC, MC, V.*

$ ✕ **Örtagården.** One floor up from Östermalms Saluhall market is this attractive, vegetarian buffet of soups, salads, hot dishes, and homemade bread plus a 5-SKr bottomless cup of coffee—in a turn-of-the-century atmosphere. ⊠ *Nybrog. 31*, ☎ *08/6621728. AE, MC, V.*

NIGHTLIFE AND THE ARTS

The Arts

Stockholm's theater and concert season runs from September through May, so you won't find many big-name artists in summer except during the Stockholm Water Festival in August. For a list of events, pick up the free booklet *Stockholm This Week,* available from hotels and tourist information offices. For tickets to theaters and shows try **Biljettdirekt** at Sweden House (☞ Visitor Information *in* Stockholm Essentials, *below*) or any **post office.**

CONCERTS

The city's main concert hall is **Konserthuset** (⊠ Hötorget 8, ☎ 08/102110), home of the Stockholm Philharmonic Orchestra. Also look in the local press for events at **Berwaldhallen** (⊠ Strandv. 69, ☎ 08/7845000). In summer many city parks have free concerts; listings appear in the "Events" section of *Stockholm This Week.*

FILM

English and American films predominate, screened with the original soundtrack and Swedish subtitles. Programs are listed in the local evening newspapers, although movie titles are usually given in Swedish. **Filmstaden Sergel** (⊠ Hötorget, ☎ 08/7896060) has 18 cinemas under one roof. Most cinemas take reservations over the phone, and the latest releases may well be sold out. The city's annual **Stockholms Filmfestival** is held in early November, screening new and classic films from all over the world.

OPERA

Operan (the Royal Opera House; ⊠ Jakobs Torg 2, ☎ 08/248240) lies just across the water from Slottet. The season runs from mid-August to early June and offers world-class performances. The exquisite **Drottningholms Slottsteater** (Drottningholm Court Theater, ⊠ Drottningholm, ☎ 08/6608225) offers opera, ballet, and orchestral music from May to early September; the original 18th-century stage machinery is still used in these productions. Drottningholm, the royal residence, is reached by subway and bus or by special theater-bus (which leaves from the Grand Hotel or opposite the Central Train Station). Boat tours run here in summer (☞ Contacts and Resources *in* Stockholm Essentials, *below*).

THEATER

Stockholm has some 20 theaters. **Kungliga Dramatiska Teatern** (Dramaten: the Royal Dramatic Theater, ⊠ Nybroplan, ☎ 08/6670680), with great gilded statues at Nybroplan, stages international productions in Swedish. **Vasa Teatern** (⊠ Vasag. 19–21, ☎ 08/102363) offers whimsical Swedish comedies. Musicals are presented regularly at several city theaters. Productions by the **English Theatre Company** are occasionally staged at various venues in Stockholm; check the local press for details.

Nightlife

CABARET

Stockholm's biggest nightclub, **Börsen** (⊠ Jakobsg. 6, ☎ 08/7878500), has high-quality Swedish and international cabaret. **Wallmans Salonger** (⊠ Teaterg. 3, ☎ 08/6116622) offers an unforgettable cabaret experience; reservations are essential.

BARS AND NIGHTCLUBS

Café Opera (⊠ Operahuset, Gustav Adolfs Torg, ☎ 08/4110026) is a favorite meeting place of the suit and tie set; at the waterfront end of Kungsträgården, it has the longest bar in town, plus dining, roulette, and dancing after midnight. Royalty and other dignitaries mingle at **Riche** (⊠ Birger Jarlsg. 4, ☎ 08/6117022); the grand bar's pedigree stretches back to 1893. **Birger Bar** (⊠ Birger Jarlsg. 5, ☎ 08/6797210) is a bar, eatery (Italian), and night club. The **Clipper Club** at the Hotel Reisen (⊠ Skeppsbron 12–14, ☎ 08/223260) is a hot spot. Not to be forgotten is the renovated restaurant/bar **Berns' Salonger** (⊠ Berzelli Park 9, ☎ 08/6140550); the Red Room, on the second floor, is where playwright August Strindberg once held court. **Sture Compagniet** (⊠ Stureg. 4, ☎ 08/6117800) is good for drinking and dancing. **Mushrooms** (⊠ Berzelli Park) is the bar for trendy night owls.

Pubs now abound in Stockholm. Watch for happy hour when drinks are cheap. **Limerick** (⊠ Tegnérg. 10, ☎ 08/6734398) is a favorite Hibernian spot. Irish beer enthusiasts rally at **Dubliner** (⊠ Smålandsg. 8, ☎ 08/6797707). **The Tudor Arms** (⊠ Grevg. 31, ☎ 08/6602712) is just as popular as when it opened in the '70s.

DANCING

Penny Lane (⊠ Birger Jarlsg. 29, ☎ 08/201411) pulls in all ages with music from the '70s. **Karlson & Co** (⊠ Kungsg. 56, ☎ 08/203339) is a pub, restaurant, and nightclub. **Bäckahästen** (⊠ Kungsg. 56, ☎ 08/4115180) is lively on weekends.

JAZZ CLUBS

Fasching (⊠ Kungsg. 63, ☎ 08/216267) is Stockholm's largest, with a varied jazz and soul offering. **Stampen** (⊠ Stora Nyg. 5, ☎ 08/205793) runs out of seats early; reservations are useful.

SHOPPING

Department Stores

NK (⊠ Hamng. 18–20, ☎ 08/7628000) is a high-class galleria. **PUB** (⊠ Hötorget, ☎ 08/239915) has 42 boutiques. **Åhléns City** (⊠ Klarabergsg. 50, ☎ 08/246000) is a traditional department store.

Food and Flea Markets

One of the largest flea markets in northern Europe, the **Loppmarknaden,** is held in the parking garage of the Skärholmen shopping center, a 20-minute subway ride from downtown. (SKr 10 on weekends; weekdays 11–6, Saturday 9–3, and Sunday 10–3). Beware of pickpockets. For a real Swedish food market with such specialties as marinated salmon and reindeer try **Östermalms Saluhall** (⊠ at Hötorget; Mon. 10–6, Tues. 9–6, and Sat. 9–3; from late June through Aug., the Sat. market is open 9–2). Another good bet is **Hötorgshallen** (⊠ at Hötorget; ⊙ Aug.–Apr., Mon.–Thur. 10–6, Fri. 10–6:30, and Sat. 10–4, and May–July, weekdays 10–6 and Sat. 10–1), under Filmstaden Sergel (☞ Film *in* Nightlife and the Arts, *above*).

Gift Ideas

Stockholm shops have the best in Swedish design and elegance. The choice and price of Swedish and international brand name items, particularly glass, porcelain, furs, jewelry, and leather goods, makes a day's shopping a must.

Glassware

For the best buys try **Nordiska Kristall** (⊠ Kungsg. 9, ☎ 08/104372). **Gustavsbergs Fabriksbod** (⊠ Odelbergs Väg 13, Gustavsberg, ☎ 08/57035655) just outside the city is a factory shop of quality. **Duka** (⊠ Sveav. 24/26, ☎ 08/104530) specializes in crystal as well as porcelain.

Handicrafts

A good center for all kinds of Swedish wood and metal handicrafts is **Svensk Hemslöjd** (⊠ Sveav. 44, ☎ 08/232115). For elegant home furnishings and timeless fabrics, try **Svenskt Tenn** (⊠ Strandv. 5A, ☎ 08/6701600), best known for its selection of designer Josef Franck's furniture and fabrics. **Svenskt Hantwerk** (⊠ Kungsg. 55, ☎ 08/214726) has Swedish folk costumes and handicraft souvenirs from different parts of Sweden.

Shopping Districts

Shop till you drop means hitting the stores along **Hamngatan** with a vengeance. The **Gamla Stan** area is best for antiques shops, bookshops, and art galleries. **Sturegallerian** (⊠ Stureg.) is an elegant covered shopping gallery on the site of the former public baths at Stureplan.

SIDE TRIPS

★ Skärgården

You could sail forever among the 24,000 islands of Stockholm's Skärgården (archipelago). But if you don't have a boat, then purchase the Båtluffarkortet (Inter-Skerries Card, ⊠ SKr 250) from early June to mid-August, which gives you 16 days' unlimited travel on Waxholmsbolaget (Waxholm Steamship Company) boats. Get the card at Excursion Shop at Sweden House or at the Waxholm Steamship Company terminal (☞ Stockholm Essentials, *below*).

Fjäderholmarna

ᘓ The group of four islands known as Fjäderholmarna (the Feather Islets) lies only 20 minutes by boat from the city center. They were formerly a restricted military zone but are now a haven of restaurants, cafés, a museum depicting life in the archipelago, an aquarium with many species of Baltic marine life, handicraft studios, shops, and a pirate-ship playground. Boats leave from Slussen, Strömkajen, and Nybroplan (Apr. 29–Sept. 17); contact the **Strömma Canal Company** (☎ 08/4117023) or Fjäderholmarna information (☎ 08/7180100).

Mariefred

★ In Mariefred, on the southern side of Lake Mälaren about 64 km (40 mi) from Stockholm, **Gripsholm Slott** (Gripsholm Castle), with its drawbridge and four massive round towers, is one of Sweden's most romantic castles. Following the destruction of a castle from the 1380s, King Gustav Vasa built the present structure in 1577. It now houses the state portrait collection, some 3,400 paintings. ☎ *0159/10194.* ⊙ *Apr.–Sept., Tues.–Sun. 10–3; Oct.–Mar., weekends noon–3.*

An unforgettable boat journey on the recently restored vintage steamer *Mariefred,* the last coal-fired ship on Lake Mälaren, is the best way to get to Gripsholm, but you can also take the train. ⊠ *Boat departs quay next to City Hall,* ☎ *08/6698850.* ⊠ *SKr 160 round-trip.* ⊙ *Mid-June–late Aug., Tues.–Sun. 10 AM (returns 4:30).*

Skokloster

Built by the Swedish field marshal Carl Gustav Wrangel, **Skokloster Slott** (Skokloster Palace) contains many of his trophies from the Thirty Years' War. The palace, about 70 km (44 mi) from Stockholm in Skokloster, also displays one of the largest private collections of arms in the world, as well as some magnificent Gobelin tapestries. Next door to the palace is a **motor museum** housing Sweden's largest collection of vintage cars and motorcycles. ☎ *018/386077.* ⊙ *May–Aug. 11–4 daily, Sept. and Oct. weekdays 1–2, Sat. and Sun. 1–4.*

Skokloster is easily reached by boat. The route follows the narrow inlets of Lake Mälaren along the "Royal Waterway." It stops at **Sigtuna,** an ancient trading center. You can get off the boat here to visit the town, which has medieval ruins and an 18th-century town hall. For boat information contact the **Strömma Canal Company.** ⊠ *Boats depart from Stadshusbron (City Hall Bridge,* ☎ *08/4117023).* ⊠ *SKr 165 round-trip.* ⊙ *Early June–mid.-Aug. Tues.–Thurs. and weekends.*

STOCKHOLM ESSENTIALS

Arriving and Departing

BY BUS

All major bus lines arrive at the **Cityterminalen** (⊠ Next to the train station). Bus tickets are also sold at the railroad reservations office.

BY CAR

One of the two main access routes from the west and south is the **E20** main highway from Göteborg The other is the **E4** from Helsingborg, continuing as the main route to Sundsvall, the far north, and Finland. All routes to the CENTRUM (city center) are well marked.

BY PLANE

International flights arrive at **Arlanda Airport** (⊠ 40 km/25 mi north of the city). For information on arrival and departure times, call the individual airlines.

Between the Airport and Downtown. The airport is linked to Stockholm by a major highway. Buses depart for **Cityterminalen** from the international and domestic terminals every 10–15 minutes between 6:30 AM and 11 PM. The ride costs SKr 60 per person. A bus-taxi package is available from the bus driver at prices ranging from SKr 160 per person to SKr 220; additional passengers in a group pay only the bus portion of the fare. Ask the bus driver for details. For bus information call the **Stockholm Transit Authority** (SL; ☎ 08/6001000). A **taxi** directly from the airport will cost around SKr 345 (be sure to ask the driver if he offers a "fixed-price" airport-to-city rate before you get into the taxi). Look for Taxi Stockholm and Taxi Kurir cabs and ask the cab line attendant for help. Illegal taxis abound. The **SAS limousine service** operates a shared taxi service at SKr 263 per person to any point in greater Stockholm. Limousine rental is SKr 616. The moms will be deducted if the limousine is booked ahead of time through a travel agent in connection with an international arrival.

BY TRAIN

Both long distance and commuter trains arrive at Stockholm Central Station on Vasagatan, a main boulevard in the heart of the city. For train information and ticket reservations 6 AM–11 PM, call 020/757575 (recorded message, wait for assistance). There is a ticket and information office at the station where you can make reservations. Automatic ticket-vending machines are also available.

Getting Around

Maps and timetables for all city transportation networks are available from the **Stockholm Transit Authority** (SL) information desks (⊠ Sergels Torg; Stockholm Central Station; Slussen in Gamla Stan; information ☎ 08/6001000).

Stockholmskortet (the Stockholm card) grants unlimited transportation on city subway, bus, and rail services, and free admission to 70 museums and several sightseeing trips. The card costs SKr 199 for 24 hours, SKr 398 for two days, and SKr 498 for three days. It is available at the tourist information centers at Sweden House, Kaknästornet (TV tower; ☞ Visitor Information, *below*), and at Hotellcentralen at the central train station.

BY BOAT

Waxholmsbolaget (Waxholm Steamship Company) terminal (⊠ Strömkajen, in front of Grand Hotel, ☎ 08/6795830). **Strömma Kanal**

Stockholm Environs

Tärnsjö
N
Heby 72
Sala
Uppsala Norrtälje
55 E4 76 276
70 Skokloster Slott
Sigtuna
Västerås Enköping E18
Mälaren Vaxholm
Gustavsberg
Strängnäs Södertälje ★ Stockholm
Eskilstuna Gripsholm Slott Mariefred
E3 Ornö
225
57 Utö
56 Nynäshamn
Katrineholm E4 Baltic Sea
53
55 Nyköping
Norrköping Öxelösund
Bråviken

0 20 miles
0 30 km

Bolaget (Strömma Canal Company; ✉ boats depart from Stadshus-
bron/City Hall Bridge, ☎ 08/4117023).

BY BUS AND SUBWAY

The SL operates both the bus and subway systems. Tickets for the two
networks are interchangeable. The subway system, known as T-banan
(*T* stands for tunnel), is the easiest and fastest way to get around. Station entrances are marked with a blue T on a white background. Trains
run frequently between 5 AM and 2 AM. The comprehensive bus network serves out-of-town points of interest, such as Waxholm, with its
historic fortress, and Gustavsberg, with its porcelain factory. In greater
Stockholm there are a number of night-bus services.

Bus and subway fares are based on zones, starting at SKr 14, good for
travel within one zone, such as downtown, for one hour. You pay more
if you travel in more than one zone. Single tickets are available at station ticket counters, but it is cheaper to buy the **SL Tourist Card,** which
is valid on buses and the subway and also gives free admission to a
number of sights and museums (though not as many as the Stockholmskortet). It can be purchased at Pressbyrån newsstands and SL information desks and costs SKr 60 for 24 hours or SKr 120 for 72 hours.
Also available from the Pressbyrån newsstands are SKr 95 coupons,
good for at least 10 bus or subway rides in the central zone.

BY TAXI

Typically, a trip of 10 km (6 mi) will cost SKr 97 between 9 AM and 4
PM on weekdays, SKr 107 on weekday nights, and SKr 114 on weekends. Call **Taxi Stockholm** (☎ 08/150000), **Taxikurir** (☎ 08/300000),
or **Taxi 020** (☎ 020/939393).

BY TRAIN

SL runs commuter trains from Stockholm Central Station to a number of nearby locales, including Nynäshamn, a departure point for fer-

ries to the island of Gotland. Trains also run from the Slussen station to the fashionable seaside resort of Saltsjöbaden.

Contacts and Resources

EMBASSIES

Unietd States (⊠ Strandv. 101, ☎ 08/7835300). **Canadian** (⊠ Tegelbacken 4, ☎ 08/4533000). **United Kingdom** (⊠ Skarpög. 6–8, ☎ 08/6719000). **Australian** (⊠ Sergelstorg 12, ☎ 08/61323900).

EMERGENCIES

Police (☎ 08/4010000; 112, emergencies only). **Ambulance** (☎ 112). **Doctor** (Medical Care Information, ☎ 08/6449200). **Private clinic** (⊠ City Akuten, ☎ 08/4122960). **Dentist** (8 AM–9 PM, ☎ 08/6541117, 9 PM–8 AM, ☎ 08/6449200). **24-hour Pharmacy** (C. W. Scheele, ☎ 08/4548130).

ENGLISH-LANGUAGE BOOKSTORES

Akademibokhandeln (⊠ Mäster Samuelsg. 32, ☎ 08/6136100).

GUIDED TOURS

Boat. Take a trip through the **archipelago** with one of Waxholm Steamship Company and Strömma Kanal Bolaget's (Strömma Canal Company's) ships (☞ Getting Around, *above*). Trips range from one to three hours each way. One-day excursions include Waxholm, Utö, Sandhamn, and Möja. Conventional sightseeing tours include a one-hour **city tour** run by Strömma Kanal Bolaget and leaving from the Nybroplan quay every hour on the half hour between 10:30 and 5:30 in summer. Don't miss the boat trip to the 17th-century palace of **Drottningholm.** Trips depart every hour on the hour from 10 to 4 and at 6 PM during the summer from City Hall Bridge (Stadshusbron). Other trips go from Stadshusbron to the ancient towns of **Sigtuna and Vaxholm.** By changing boats you can continue to Uppsala to catch the train back to Stockholm. Information is available from the Strömma Canal Company (☞ Getting Around, *above*) or the Stockholm Tourist Centre at Sweden House (☞ Visitor Information, *below*).

Orientation. More than 35 different tours—by foot, boat, bus, or a combination of these—are available throughout the summer. Some take only 30 minutes, others an entire day. A 90-minute coach tour, costing SKr 120, runs daily. Tickets are available from the Excursion Shop at Sweden House (☞ Visitor Information, *below*).

Personal Guides. Guide Centralen (⊠ Sweden House, Hamng. 27, Box 7542, 103 93, ☎ 08/7892496) at the Stockholm Information Service offers individual guides and group bookings.

Special-Interest. Special-interest tours in the Stockholm area include spending a weekend at a cabin in the archipelago, renting a small fishing or sailing boat, visiting the Gustavsberg porcelain factory, and more. Call the Tourist Centre at Sweden House (☞ Visitor Information, *below*) for details.

TRAVEL AGENCY

American Express (⊠ Birger Jarlsg. 1, ☎ 08/6795200, FAX 08/6116214).

VISITOR INFORMATION

Stockholm Tourist Centre (⊠ Sweden House, Kungsträdgården, Hamng. 27, ☎ 08/7892490). **Stockholm Information Service** (⊠ Sweden House, Excursion Shop, Box 7542, 103 93, ☎ 08/7892415). **Stockholm Central Station** (⊠ Vasag., ☎ 020757575). **City Hall** (summer only) (⊠ Hantverkarg. 1, ☎ 08/50829000). **Kaknästornet** (TV Tower; ⊠ Ladugårdsgärdet, ☎ 08/7892435). **Fjäderholmarna** (☎ 08/7180100).

21 Venice

V enice—La Serenissima, the Most Serene—
is disorienting in its complexity, an extraordinary labyrinth of narrow streets
and waterways, opening now and again onto an
airy square or broad canal. The majority of its magnificent palazzi are slowly crumbling; though this
sounds like a recipe for a down-at-the-heels slum,
somehow in Venice the shabby, derelict effect is
magically transformed into one of supreme beauty
and charm, rather than horrible urban decay. The
place is romantic, especially at night when the
lights from the vaporetti and the stars overhead pick
out the gargoyles and arches of the centuries-old
facades. For hundreds of years Venice was the unrivaled mistress of trade between Europe and the
Orient, and the staunch bulwark of Christendom
against the tide of Turkish expansion. Though the
power and glory of its days as a wealthy city-
republic are gone, the art and exotic aura remain.

EXPLORING VENICE

*Numbers in the margin correspond to points of interest on the Venice
map.*

To enjoy the city you will have to come to terms with the crowds of
day-trippers, who take over the center around San Marco from May
through September. Hot and sultry in summer, Venice is much more

welcoming in early spring and late fall. Romantics like it in the winter, when prices are much lower, the streets are often deserted, and the sea mists impart a haunting melancholy to the *campi* (squares) and canals. Piazza San Marco is the pulse of Venice, but after joining with the crowds to visit the Basilica di San Marco and the Doge's Palace, strike out on your own and just follow where your feet take you—you won't be disappointed.

San Marco, Dorsoduro, and San Polo

★ **❸ Basilica di San Marco** (St. Mark's Basilica). Half Christian church, half Middle Eastern mosque, this building was conceived during the 11th century to hold the relics of St. Mark the Evangelist, the city's patron saint. Its richly decorated facade is surmounted by copies of four famous gilded bronze horses (the originals are in the basilica's upstairs museum). Inside, golden mosaics cover walls and vaults, lending an extraordinarily exotic aura. Be sure to see the **Pala d'Oro,** an eye-filling 10th-century altarpiece in gold and silver studded with precious gems and enamels. From the atrium climb the steep stairway to the museum: The bronze horses alone are worth the effort. ⊠ *Piazza San Marco. Basilica:* ☉ *Mon.–Sat. 9:30–5:30 (Oct.–Apr. until 5), Sun. 2–5:30 (Oct.–Apr. until 5).* ▨ *Free. Pala d'Oro and Treasury:* ☎ *041/5225205.* ☉ *same as basilica, last entry 30 min before closing. Gallery and Museum:* ☉ *same as basilica, last entry 30 min before closing.*

★ **❺ Campanile di San Marco** (St. Mark's Bell Tower). This bell tower is a reconstruction of the 1,000-year-old tower that collapsed one morning in 1912, practically without warning. For a pigeon's-eye view of Venice, you can now take the elevator up to the top of this bell tower. Fifteenth-century clerics found guilty of immoral acts were suspended in wooden cages from the tower, sometimes to live on bread and water for as long as a year, sometimes to die of starvation and exposure. Look for them in Carpaccio's paintings of the square that hang in the Accademia. ⊠ *Piazza San Marco,* ☎ *041/5224064.* ☉ *June–Sept., daily 9:30–7, Oct.–May, daily 9:30–3:45. Closed 2 wks Jan.*

❻ Collezione Peggy Guggenheim. The late heiress's exceptional modern art collection—with works by Picasso, Kandinsky, Ernst, Pollock, and Motherwell—is housed in the incomplete Palazzo Venier dei Leoni. ⊠ *Calle San Cristoforo, 701 Dorsoduro,* ☎ *041/5206288.* ☉ *Wed.–Mon. 11–6.*

★ **❼ Galleria dell'Accademia** (Accademia Gallery). Hanging in this museum is unquestionably the most extraordinary collection of Venetian art in the world. Works range from 14th-century Gothic to the Golden Age of the 15th and 16th centuries, including oils by Giovanni Bellini (1430–1516), Giorgione (1477–1511), Titian, and Tintoretto (1518–94), and superb later works by Veronese (1528–88) and Tiepolo (1696–1770). ⊠ *Campo della Carità, Dorsoduro,* ☎ *041/5222247.* ☉ *Mon.–Sat. 9–7, Sun. 9–2.*

❷ Museo Correr. Upstairs here you will find an eclectic collection of historical objects and a picture gallery of fine 13th- to 17th-century paintings. ⊠ *Piazza San Marco, Ala Napoleonica,* ☎ *041/5225625.* ☉ *Apr.–Oct., daily 9–5; Nov.–Mar., daily 9–7, last entry 1 hr before closing.*

★ **❹ Palazzo Ducale** (Doge's Palace). During Venice's heyday, this was the epicenter of its great empire. More than just a palace, it was a combination White House, Senate, Supreme Court, torture chamber, and prison. The building's exterior is striking; the lower stories consist of two rows of fragile-seeming arches, while above rests a massive pink-and-white marble wall whose solidity is barely interrupted by its six great Gothic windows. The interior is a maze of vast halls, monumental staircases, secret corridors, and sinister prison cells. The palace is filled with frescoes, paintings, and a few examples of statuary by some of the Renaissance's greatest artists. Don't miss the famous view from the balcony, overlooking the piazza and St. Mark's Basin and the church of San Giorgio Maggiore across the lagoon. ⊠ *Piazzetta San Marco,* ☎ *041/5224951.* ☉ *Apr.–Oct., daily 9–7; Nov.–Mar., daily 9–5. Last entry 1½ hrs before closing time.*

★ **①** **Piazza San Marco.** In the most famous piazza in Venice, pedestrian traffic jams clog the surrounding byways and even pigeons have to fight for space. Despite the crowds, San Marco is the logical starting place from which to explore the city. The short side of the square opposite the Basilica of San Marco is known as the Ala Napoleonica, a wing built by order of Napoléon to complete the much earlier palaces on either side of the square, enclosing it to form what he called "the most beautiful drawing room in all of Europe."

⑨ **Santa Maria Gloriosa dei Frari.** This vast, soaring Gothic brick church known simply as I Frari contains a number of the most sumptuous, important pictures in Venice. Paradoxically, as the principal church of the Franciscans it is austere in design, suitably reflecting the order's vows of poverty. Chief among the works are the magnificent Titian altarpiece, the immense *Assumption of the Virgin* over the main altar. Titian was buried here at the ripe old age of 88, the only one of 70,000 plague victims to be given a personal church burial. ⊠ *Campo dei Frari, San Polo,* ☎ *041/5222637.* ☉ *Mon.–Sat. 9–noon and 3–6, Sun. 3–6.*

⑧ **Scuola Grande di San Rocco** (School of St. Rocco). In the 1500s Tintoretto embellished the school with more than 50 canvases; they are an impressive sight, dark paintings aglow with figures hurtling dramatically through space amid flashes of light and color. The *Crucifixion* in the Albergo (the room just off the great hall) is held to be his masterpiece. ⊠ *Campo di San Rocco, San Polo,* ☎ *041/5234864.* ☉ *Nov.–Mar., weekdays 10–1 and weekends 10–4; Apr.–Oct., daily 9–5:30.*

North of San Marco and Ponte Rialto

★ **⑬** **Ponte Rialto** (Rialto Bridge). Street stalls hung with scarves and gondolier's hats signal the heart of Venice's shopping district. Cross over the bridge, and you'll find yourself on the edge of the famous market. Try to visit the Rialto market (☉ Tues.–Sat. mornings; fish market closed Mon.) when it's in full swing, with fruit and vegetable vendors hawking their wares in a cacophony of sights and sounds. Not far beyond is the fish market, where you'll probably find sea creatures you've never seen before (and possibly won't want to see again). Ruga San Giovanni and Ruga del Ravano, beside the market, will bring you face to face with scores of shops. Start from the Salizzada San Giovanni side of the bridge.

⑪ **Santa Maria dei Miracoli.** Perfectly proportioned and sheathed in marble, the church embodies all the classical serenity of the early Renaissance. The interior of this late-15th-century building is decorated with marble reliefs by the church's architect, Pietro Lombardo, and his son Tullio. ⊠ *Campo dei Miracoli.* ☎ *041/5235293.* ☉ *Mon.–Sat. 10–5:30 and Sun. 3–6.*

⑩ **Santa Maria Formosa.** This graceful white marble church built by Mauro Coducci in 1492, was grafted onto 11th-century foundations. Inside is a hodgepodge of Renaissance and Baroque styles. A small vegetable market bustles in the square weekday mornings. ⊠ *Campo*

316

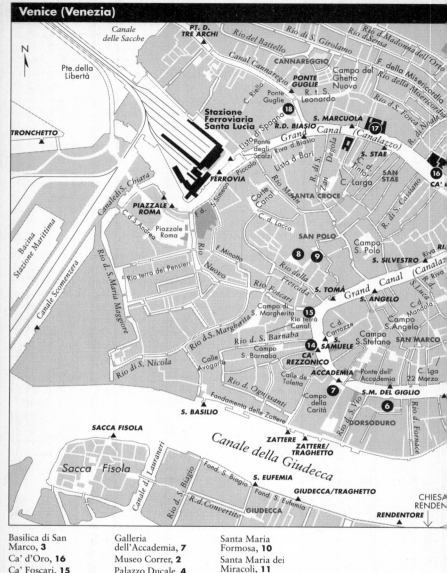

Venice (Venezia)

Basilica di San
Marco, **3**

Ca' d'Oro, **16**

Ca' Foscari, **15**

Ca' Rezzonico, **14**

Campanile di San
Marco, **5**

Collezione Peggy
Guggenheim, **6**

Galleria
dell'Accademia, **7**

Museo Correr, **2**

Palazzo Ducale, **4**

Palazzo Labia, **18**

Palazzo Vendramin
Calergi, **17**

Piazza San Marco, **1**

Ponte Rialto, **13**

Santa Maria
Formosa, **10**

Santa Maria dei
Miracoli, **11**

Santa Maria
Gloriosa dei Frari, **9**

Santi Giovanni e
Paolo, **12**

Scuola Grande di
San Rocco, **8**

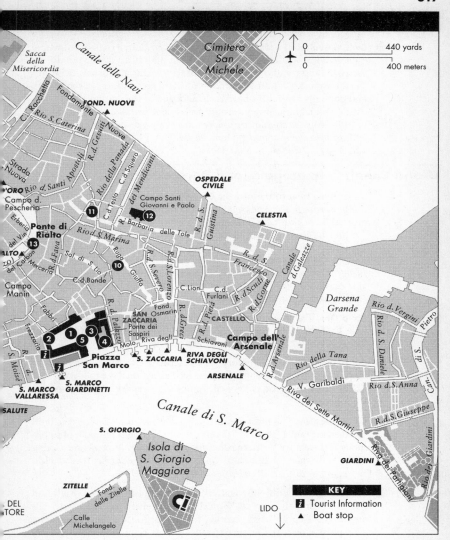

Sacca della Misericordia

Canale delle Navi

Cimitero San Michele

0   440 yards
0   400 meters

Racchetta
Fondamenta

FOND. NUOVE

C. Rio S. Caterina

Stroda Nuova

R. d. Gesuiti Nuove

R. d. Santi Apostoli

C. d. Testa

C. d. Squero

dei Mendicanti

'ORO

Campo d. Pescheria

Rio d. Santi

Erberia

del Vin

Ponte di Rialto

C. d. Tela

R. della Panada

Campo Santi Giovanni e Paolo

OSPEDALE CIVILE

CELESTIA

11

12

R. Barbaria

delle Tole

R. d. S.

Giustina

R. d. S.

R. d. S. Francesco

Canale d. Galeazze

ALTO

13

ZO

del Carbon

Merceria

Rio d. S. Marina

Sal. di S. Lio

R. d. Fava

10

Rigo Giuffa

R. d. S. Severo

C. Lion

C. d. Furlani

R. d. Scudi

R. d. Gorne

Darsena Grande

Rio d. Vergini

Campo Manin

Fabbri

R. d. Bande

Fond. Osmarin

R. d. Greci

R. d. Pietà

CASTELLO

R. d. S.

Rio d. S. Daniele

Trezaria

SAN ZACCARIA

Ponte dei Sospiri

Molo

Riva degli

Campo dell' Arsenale

R. d. Arsenale

R. d. S. Anna

Cannaregio

di S. Pietro

2 **1** **3**

5 **4**

i

i

PIAZZA San Marco

S. ZACCARIA

Schiavoni

RIVA DEGLI SCHIAVONI

Rio della Tana

V. Garibaldi

R. d. S. Giuseppe

S. MARCO VALLARESSA

S. MARCO GIARDINETTI

ARSENALE

SALUTE

Riva dei Sette Martiri

Canale di S. Marco

S. GIORGIO

Isola di S. Giorgio Maggiore

Riva dei partigiani

GIARDINI

Rio dei Giardini

ZITELLE

Fond. delle Zitelle

DEL TORE

Calle Michelangelo

LIDO

KEY

i   Tourist Information

▲   Boat stop

Santa Maria Formosa, ☎ *041/5234645.* 🎫 *Free.* ⊙ *Mon.–Sat. 10–5, Sun. 2–5.*

⑫ **Santi Giovanni e Paolo.** A massive Dominican church of Santi Giovanni e Paolo—known in the slurred Venetian dialect as San Zanipolo—is the twin (and rival) of the Franciscan Santa Maria Gloriosa dei Frari. The church is a kind of pantheon of the doges (25 are buried here), and contains a wealth of artwork. Outside in the campo stands Verrocchio's magnificent equestrian monument of **Bartolomeo Colleoni** (1400–75) who fought for the Venetian cause during the mid-1400s. ⊠ *Campo San Giovanni e Paolo,* ☎ *041/5237510.* 🎫 *Free.* ⊙ *Mon.–Sat. 8–12:30 and 3–6, Sun. 3–6.*

Grand Canal, Cannareggio, and Dorsoduro

Set off on a boat tour along the **Grand Canal,** which serves as Venice's main thoroughfare. The canal winds in the shape of a backwards S for more than 3½ km (2 mi) through the heart of the city, past some 200 Gothic and Renaissance palaces. Your vaporetto tour will give you an idea of the opulent beauty of the palaces and a peek into the side streets and tiny canals where the Venetians go about their daily business. ⊠ *Just off Piazzetta di San Marco (the square in front of the Doge's Palace) you can catch Vaporetto 1 at either the San Marco or San Zaccaria landing stages (on Riva degli Schiavoni).*

⑯ **Ca' d'Oro.** The most flowery palace on the canal now houses the Galleria Franchetti. ⊠ *Galleria Franchetti, Calle della Ca' d'Oro, 3933 Cannaregio,* ☎ *041/5238790.* ⊙ *Daily 9–2.*

⑮ **Ca' Foscari.** This 15th-century Gothic structure was once the home of Doge Foscari, who was unwillingly deposed and died the following day! Today it's the headquarters of Venice's university. ⊠ *Fondamenta Ca'Foscari.*

★ ⑭ **Ca' Rezzonico.** The most spectacular palace in all of Venice was built between the mid-17th and 18th centuries and is now a museum of sumptuous 18th-century Venetian paintings and furniture. At press time (spring 1998) only the first floor was open. ⊠ *Fondamenta Pedrocco, 3136 Dorsoduro,* ☎ *041/2410100.* ⊙ *Sat.–Thurs. 10–4.*

⑱ **Palazzo Labia.** Within the walls of this sumptuous palazzo you'll find the prettiest ballroom in Venice, magnificently adorned with Giambattista Tiepolo's 18th-century frescoes of Anthony and Cleopatra. This palace, once the home of Venice's most ostentatiously rich family, is now the Venetian headquarters of RAI, Italy's National Broadcasting Corporation, which occasionally hosts concerts in the Tiepolo ballroom. ⊠ *Campo San Geremia, near the train station,* ☎ *041/5242812.* 🎫 *Free ballroom only Mon., Thurs., and Fri. 3–4.*

⑰ **Palazzo Vendramin Calergi.** This opulent Renaissance structure is noted as the place Wagner (1813–83) died. It's also the winter home of the municipal casino. ⊠ *2040 Cannaregio, 30133.* ☎ *041/5297111.*

Elsewhere in Venice

Torcello. Discover the Venetian equivalent of World's End on this magical island in the Venetian lagoon. Settled 1,500 years ago and a thriving city during the Byzantine era, the island is now deserted, but art lovers still make pilgrimages to it because of its two great 11th-century churches. The cathedral of **Santa Maria Assunta** has a world-famous mosaic of the Virgin. Locanda Cipriani, a restaurant favored by Hemingway and the Duke of Windsor, still lures gourmands. Katharine Hepburn and Rossanzo Brazzi fell in love during a picnic on Torcello in the film classic *Summertime.* ⊠ *Take Vaporetto 12 from Fondamente Nuove.*

DINING

Venetians love seafood, and it figures prominently on most restaurant menus, sometimes to the exclusion of meat dishes. Fish is generally expensive, however, and you should bear this in mind when ordering: The price given on menus for fish as a main course is often per 100 grams, not the total cost of what you are served, which could be two or three times that amount. City specialties also include pasta e fagioli, risotto, and the delicious *fegato alla veneziana* served with grilled polenta.

RATINGS

Prices are per person and include first course, main course, dessert or fruit, and house wine, where available.

CATEGORY	COST
$$$$	over 120,000 lire
$$$	70,000 lire–120,000 lire
$$	40,000 lire–70,000 lire
$	under 40,000 lire

$$$$ ★ ✕ **Grand Canal.** The Hotel Monaco and Grand Canal's restaurant is a favorite among Venetians, who enjoy the sunny canal-side terrace, with views across the mouth of the Grand Canal to Giorgio Maggiore, and the cozy dining room in winter. Chef Fulvio De Santa turns out well-prepared Venetian seafood specialties, such as *scampi alla Ca' d'Oro* (shrimp in cognac sauce, served with rice), and savory meats. Pasta is made fresh daily on the premises, as is the marinated smoked salmon. ⊠ *Hotel Monaco and Grand Canal, Calle Vallaresso 1325, San Marco,* ☎ *041/5200211. Jacket required. AE, DC, MC, V.*

$$$$ ✕ **La Caravella.** La Caravella is reminiscent of an old Venetian sailing ship's dining saloon, with lots of authentic touches, and has a pretty garden courtyard used during summer. The menu is long and slightly intimidating, though the highly competent maître d' will advise you well. The *granseola* (crab) is marvelous in any of several versions. ⊠ *Calle Larga XXII Marzo 2397, San Marco,* ☎ *041/5208901. AE, DC, MC, V.*

$$$–$$$$ ✕ **Al Mondo Novo.** In this fish restaurant you can get *cape sante* (pilgrim scallops) and *cape longhe* (razor clams), risotto and pasta dishes, charcoal-grilled fish, and a less-expensive tourist menu. ⊠ *Salizzada San Lio, 5409 Castello,* ☎ *041/5200698. AE, MC, V.*

$$$–$$$$ ✕ **Da Arturo.** The tiny Da Arturo is a refreshing change from the numerous seafood restaurants of which Venetians are so fond. The cordial proprietor prefers, instead, to offer varied and delicious seasonal vegetable and salad dishes, or tasty, tender and generous meat courses like *braciola alla veneziana* (pork chop schnitzel with vinegar). ⊠ *Calle degli Assassini 3656, San Marco,* ☎ *041/5286974. Reservations essential. No credit cards. Closed Sun. and 4 wks in Aug.*

$$$–$$$$ ✕ **Fiaschetteria Toscana.** Once the storehouse of a 19th-century wine merchant from Tuscany, this popular restaurant has long been a favorite of Venetians and visitors from terra firma. Courteous, cheerful waiters serve such specialties as *rombo* (turbot) with capers, an exceptionally good *pasta alla buranella* (pasta with shrimp, au gratin), and zabaglione. ⊠ *Campo San Giovanni Crisostomo, 5719 Cannaregio,* ☎ *041/5285281. AE, DC, MC, V. Closed Tues. and 4 wks in July and Aug.*

$$$–$$$$ ★ ✕ **Osteria Da Fiore.** Long a favorite with Venetians, Da Fiore has been discovered by tourists, so reservations are imperative. It's known for its excellent seafood dinners, which might include such specialties as *pasticcio di pesce* (fish pie) and *seppioline* (little cuttlefish). Not easy to find, it's just off Campo San Polo. ⊠ *Calle dello Scaleter 2202, San*

Polo, ☎ 041/721308. *Reservations essential. AE, DC, MC, V. Closed Sun., Mon., first 3 wks in Aug.*

$$$ ✕ **Al Covo.** This small osteria changes its menu according to the day's bounty—mostly local seafood caught just hours before. Cesare Benelli and his American wife, Diane, insist on only the freshest ingredients and claim to not use butter or animal fats. Try the *zuppa di pesce* (fish broth) followed by the fish of the day either grilled, baked, or steamed. ⊠ *Campiello della Pescaria 3968, Castello,* ☎ *041/5223812. No credit cards. Closed Wed. and Thurs., 1 wk in Aug., and 1 month between Dec. and Jan.*

$$$ ✕ **Locanda Montin.** Peggy Guggenheim used to wine and dine the greatest artists of the 20th century here. Since those days, Montin has become more of an institution, less a bohemian hangout. Service can be erratic, but crowds still pack the place to enjoy the *rigatoni ai quattro formaggi* (rigatoni with four cheeses, mushrooms, and tomato) and antipasto Montin. ⊠ *Fondamenta di Borgo, 1147 Dorsoduro,* ☎ *041/5227151. AE, DC, MC, V. Jan. 7–26, closed Tues. dinner and Wed.; closed 15 days in Aug.*

$$ ✕ **Vini da Gigio.** An attractive, friendly, and family-run establishment, this trattoria is found on the quayside of a canal, just off the Strada Nuova. Customers appreciate the affable service and tasty homemade pasta, fish, and meat dishes, and good draft wine. The barroom is pleasant and casual for lunch. ⊠ *Fondamenta de la Chiesa, 3628A Cannaregio,* ☎ *041/5285140. AE, DC, MC, V. Closed Mon., 2 wks in Jan.–Feb., and 2 wks in Aug. No dinner Sun.*

$ ✕ **L'Incontro.** This trattoria has a faithful clientele drawn in by good food (excellent meat, but no fish) at reasonable prices. Menu choices include freshly made Sardinian pastas, juicy steaks, wild duck, boar, and (with advance notice) roast suckling pig. L'Incontro is between San Barnaba and Campo Santa Margherita. ⊠ *Rio Terrá Canal, 3062A Dorsoduro,* ☎ *041/5222404. MC, V. Closed Mon., 2 wks in Jan. and 2 wks. in Aug.*

NIGHTLIFE AND THE ARTS

The Arts

The **Biennale,** a cultural institution, organizes many events throughout the year, including the film festival, which begins at the end of August. The big Biennale international art exhibition, usually held from mid-June to the end of September, has been held since 1993 on odd-numbered years at the **Giardini di Castello** (Castello Gardens).

CONCERTS

Regular concerts are held at the Pietà Church, with an emphasis on Vivaldi, and at San Stae and San Barnaba. Concerts, sometimes free, are also held by visiting choirs and musicians in other churches. For information on these often impromptu events, ask at the APT office and look for posters on walls and in restaurants and shops. **Kele e Teo Agency** (⊠ Ponte dei Bareteri, 4930 San Marco, ☎ 041/5208722, FAX 041/5208913) handles tickets for many musical events. You can often get them at **Box Office** (⊠ Calle Loredan 4127, off Salizzada San Luca, ☎ 041/988369), too.

OPERA

Because of the devastating fire that destroyed **Teatro La Fenice** in January 1996, opera and concert performances were rescheduled in various venues. Although plans are being made to restore the building, performances are not forecast to recommence until the year 2000. Check with the APT (☞ Visitor Information *in* Venice Essentials, *below*) for current performances.

Nightlife

The Martini Scala Club (✉ Calle del Cafetier, 2077 San Marco, ☎ 041/5224121) is an elegant piano bar with a restaurant. Tunes start at 10 PM and go until the wee hours; it's closed Tuesday. For dancing try the **Disco Club Piccolo Mondo** (✉ 1056 Dorsoduro, ☎ 041/5200371), near the Accademia Gallery. **Fiddler's Elbow** (✉ Strada Nuova, Cannaregio 3847, ☎ 041/5239930) offers all the typical trappings of an Irish pub: gab, grub, and frothy Guinness.

SHOPPING

At **La Scialuppa** (✉ Calle delle Saoneri, 2695 San Polo) you'll find hand-carved wooden models of gondolas and their graceful oar locks known as *forcole*. **Norelene** (✉ Calle della Chiesa 727, in Dorsoduro, near the Guggenheim) has stunning hand-painted fabrics that make wonderful wall hangings or elegantly styled jackets and chic scarves. **Venetia Studium** (✉ Calle Larga XXII Marzo, 2430 San Marco) is famous for Fortuny-inspired lamps, furnishings, clothes, and accessories.

Glass

There's a lot of cheap Venetian glass for sale; if you want something better, try **l'Isola** (✉ Campo San Moisè 1468, near Piazza San Marco), where Carlo Moretti's chic, contemporary designs are on display. **Domus** (✉ Fondamenta dei Vetrai, Murano) has a good selection of glass and is on the island of Murano.

Shopping Districts

Le Mercerie, along with the Frezzeria and Calle dei Fabbri are some of Venice's busiest streets, which lead off from Piazza San Marco (☞ Ponte Rialto *in* Exploring Venice, *above*).

VENICE ESSENTIALS

Arriving and Departing

BY CAR

If you bring a car to Venice, you will have to pay for a garage or parking space during your stay. Warning: Do not be waylaid by illegal con artists often wearing fake uniforms who may try to flag you down and offer to arrange parking and hotels. Continue on until you reach the automatic ticket machines.

Parking at **Piazzale Roma** (✉ Autorimessa Comunale, end of S11 road) costs between 15,000 and 25,000 lire. The private **Garage San Marco** (✉ Piazzale Roma, end of S11 road) costs between 34,000 and 46,000 lire per 24 hours, depending on the size of the car. To reach the privately run **Tronchetto** parking area, follow the signs to turn right before Piazzale Roma. Parking here costs 25,000 lire per 24 hours. (Do not leave valuables in the car. There is a left-luggage office, open daily 8–8, next to the Pullman Bar on the ground floor of the municipal garage at Piazzale Roma.) The AVA (☞ Visitor Information, *below*) has arranged a discount of around 5,000 lire per day for hotel guests who use the official Tronchetto parking facility. Ask for a voucher on checking into your hotel. Present the voucher at Tronchetto when you pay the parking fee.

A vaporetto (No. 82) runs from Tronchetto to Piazzale Roma and Piazza San Marco (also to the Lido in summer). In thick fog or when tides are extreme, a bus runs instead to Piazzale Roma, where you can pick up a vaporetto.

Aeroporto Marco Polo (✉ 10 km/6 mi northeast of Venice on the mainland, flight information ☎ 041/2609260).

Between the Airport and Downtown. The most direct way is by the **Cooperativa San Marco** (✉ just off Piazza San Marco, ☎ 041/5222303) launch, with regular scheduled service throughout the day, until midnight; it takes about an hour to get to the landing, stopping at the Lido on the way, and the fare is 17,000 lire per person, including bags. Blue **ATVO** buses make the 25-minute trip in to Piazzale Roma, where the road to Venice terminates; the cost is 5,000 lire. From Piazzale Roma visitors will most likely have to take a vaporetto to their hotel (☞ Getting Around, *below*). **Water taxis** (slick high-power motorboats called *motoscafi*) should cost about 87,000 lire. **Land taxis** are available, running the same route as the buses; the cost is about 60,000 lire.

Make sure your train goes all the way to the **Stazione Ferroviaria Santa Lucia** (✉ Venice's northwest corner; ☎ 1478/88088 toll free). Some trains leave passengers at the **Stazione Ferroviaria Venezia-Mestre** (✉ on the mainland; ☎ 1478/880880 toll free). All trains traveling to and from Santa Lucia stop at Mestre, so to get from Mestre to Santa Lucia, or vice versa (a 10-minute trip), take the first available train, remembering there is a *supplemento* (extra charge) for traveling on Intercity, Eurocity, and Eurostar trains, and that if you board one of these trains without having paid in advance for this part of the trip, you are subject to a hefty fine. Since most tourists arrive in Venice by train, tourist services are conveniently located at Santa Lucia, including an **APT** information booth (☎ 041/5298727) and baggage depot. If you need a hotel room, the station has an **AVA** booth (☞ *below*). Directly outside the train station are the main vaporetto landing stages; from here, vaporetti can transport you to your hotel's general neighborhood. Be prepared with advance directions from the hotel and a good map.

Getting Around

First-time visitors find that getting around Venice presents some unusual problems: The complexity of its layout (the city is made up of more than 100 islands, all linked by bridges); the bewildering unfamiliarity of waterborne transportation; the apparently illogical house numbering system and duplication of street names in its six districts; and the necessity of walking whether you enjoy it or not. It's essential to have a good map showing all street names and water bus routes; buy one at any newsstand.

If you mustn't leave Venice without treating yourself to a gondola ride, take it in the quiet of the evening when the churning traffic on the canals has died down and at high tide, the palace windows are illuminated, and the only sounds are the muted splashes of the gondolier's oar. Make sure he understands that you want to see the *rii*, or smaller canals, as well as the Grand Canal. There's supposed to be a fixed minimum rate of about 120,000 lire for 50 minutes, and a nighttime supplement of 30,000. Come to terms with your gondolier *before* stepping into his boat.

Few tourists know about the two-man gondolas that ferry people across the Grand Canal at various fixed points. It's the cheapest and shortest gondola ride in Venice, and it can save a lot of walking. The fare is 700 lire, which you hand to one of the gondoliers when you get on. Look for TRAGHETTO signs.

BY VAPORETTO

ACTV water buses run the length of the Grand Canal and circle the city. There are several lines, some of which connect Venice with the major and minor islands in the lagoon. The fare is 4,500 lire on all lines. A 24-hour tourist ticket costs 15,000 lire, a three-day ticket 30,000 lire, and a seven-day ticket 55,000 lire; these are especially worthwhile if you are planning to visit the islands. ACTV information is available by calling ☎ 041/5287886, daily from 7:30 AM–8 PM. Free timetables are available at the ticket office at Piazzale Roma. Timetables are posted at every landing stage, but there is not always a ticket booth operating. After 9 PM, tickets are available on the boats, but you must immediately inform the controller that you need a ticket. For this reason it may be useful to buy a *blocchetto* (book of tickets) in advance. Landing stages are clearly marked with name and line number, but check before boarding, particularly with the 52 and 82, to make sure the boat is going in your direction.

Line 1 is the Grand Canal local, calling at every stop, and continuing via San Marco to the Lido. (It takes about 45 minutes from the station to San Marco.) **Line 52** runs from the railway station to San Zaccaria via Piazzale Roma and Zattere, and continues to the Lido. **Line 52/** (note the difference) goes along the same route but makes stops along the Giudecca instead of Zattere and continues to Fondamente Nuove (where boats leave for the islands of the northern Lagoon) and Murano. **Line 82** runs in a loop from San Zaccaria to Giudecca, Zattere, Piazzale Roma, the train station, Rialto, (with fewer stops along the Grand Canal than Line 1), and back to San Zaccaria (and out to the Lido in the afternoon).

BY WATER TAXI

Motoscafi, or taxis, are excessively expensive, and the fare system is as complex as Venice's layout. A minimum fare of about 50,000 lire gets you nowhere, and you'll pay three times as much to get from one end of the Grand Canal to the other. *Always agree on the fare before starting out.* It's probably worth considering taking a water taxi only if you are traveling in a small group.

ON FOOT

This is the only way to reach many parts of Venice, so wear comfortable shoes. Invest in a good map that names all the streets, and count on getting lost more than once.

Money Matters

CURRENCY

The unit of currency in Italy is the lira (plural, lire). There are bills of 1,000, 2,000, 5,000, 10,000, 50,000, 100,000, and 500,000 lire (impossible to change, except in banks); coins are worth 50, 100, 200, and 500 lire. In 1999 the euro will be used as a banking currency, but the lire will still be the currency in use on a day-to-day basis. At press time (spring 1998) the exchange rate was about 1,798 lire to the U.S. dollar, 1,266 lire to the Canadian dollar, and 2,943 lire to the pound sterling.

When your purchases run into hundreds of thousands of lire, beware of being shortchanged, a dodge that is practiced at ticket windows, toll booths, and cashiers' desks, as well as in shops and even in banks. *Always count your change before you leave the counter.* Always carry some smaller-denomination bills for sundry purchases; you're less likely to be shortchanged, and you won't have to face the eye-rolling of cashiers reluctant to change large bills.

Credit cards are generally accepted in shops and hotels, but may not always be welcome in restaurants, so always look for card logos displayed in windows or ask when you enter to avoid embarrassing situations. When you wish to leave a tip beyond the 15% service charge that is usually included with your bill, leave it in cash rather than adding it to the credit card slip.

Telephoning

COUNTRY CODE

The country code for Italy is 39.

Contacts and Resources

CONSULATES

United Kingdom (✉ Campo della Carità 1051, Dorsoduro, ☎ 041/5227207). There is no U.S. or Canadian consular service in Venice. The nearest consulates are in Milan.

EMERGENCIES

Police (☎ 113). **Carabinieri** (☎ 112). **Ambulance** (☎ 118). **Doctor** (emergency room, Venice's hospital, ☎ 041/5230000). **Red Cross First Aid Station** (✉ Piazza San Marco 55, near Caffè Florian, ☎ 041/52286346).

Pharmacies are open weekdays 9–12:30 and 3:45–7:30; Saturday 9–12:45; a notice telling where to get late-night and Sunday service is posted outside every pharmacy. **Farmacia Italo-Inglese** (✉ Calle della Mandola, ☎ 041/5224837). **Farmacia Internazionale** (✉ Calle Larga XXII Marzo, ☎ 041/5222311).

GUIDED TOURS

Excursions. The **Cooperativa San Marco** (✉ just off San Marco, ☎ 041/5222303) organizes tours of the islands of Murano, Burano, and Torcello departing daily at 9:30 and 2:30 from the landing stage in front of Giardini Reali near Piazza San Marco; tours last about 3½ hours and cost about 25,000 lire. However, tours tend to be annoyingly commercial and emphasize glass factory showrooms where you are pressured to buy, often at higher than standard prices. **American Express** (✉ Salizzada San Moisè, 1471 San Marco, ☎ 041/5200844, FAX 041/5229937) books a day trip to Padova by boat along the Brenta River, with stops at three Palladian villas. The tours run three days a week from March to November; the cost is about 120,000 lire per person, and bookings need to be made the day before.

Orientation. American Express (☞ *above*) and other operators offer two-hour walking tours of the San Marco area, taking in the basilica and the Doge's Palace. The cost is about 36,000 lire, including admission. From April 25 through November 15, American Express offers an afternoon walking tour that ends with a short gondola ride (about 40,000 lire).

Personal Guides. American Express (☞ *above*) can provide guides for walking or gondola tours of Venice, or cars with driver and guide for excursions on the mainland. Pick up a list of licensed guides and their rates from the main **APT** office (✉ Calle dell'Ascensione 71C, ☎ 041/5226356, FAX 041/5298730).

Special-Interest. Some tour operators offer group gondola rides with a serenade. The cost is about 40,000 lire. During the summer free guided tours of the Basilica di San Marco are offered by the Procuratoria; information is available at a desk in the atrium of the church. From June through August there are several tours daily, except Sunday, and some tours are in English, including one at 11 AM.

American Express (⊠ Salizzada San Moisè 1471, ☎ 041/5200844, FAX 041/5229937). **Wagons-Lits Turismo** (⊠ Piazzetta dei Leoncini 289, ☎ 041/5223405, FAX 041/5228508).

Main APT (⊠ Calle dell'Ascensione 71C, Palazzetto Selva off Piazza San Marco, ☎ 041/5226356 or 041/5298730, FAX 041/5230399; ⊙ Mon.–Sat. 9:40–3:20). **APT booths** (⊠ Santa Lucia Station, ☎ 041/5298727, ⊙ daily 8:10–6:50; ⊠ on the Lido, Gran Viale S. M. Elisabetta 6A, ☎ 041/5265721, FAX 041/5298720; ⊙ summer only).

AVA (Venetian Hoteliers Association, ⊠ train station, ☎ 041/715016 or 1678/43006; ⊙ daily 8 AM–9 PM). Satellite locations at airport, Municipal parking garage, and Piazzale Roma.

22 Vienna

V ienna has been characterized as an "old dowager of a town"—an Austro-Hungarian empress, don't forget, widowed in 1918 by the Great War. It's not just the aristocratic and courtly atmosphere, with monumental doorways and facades of former palaces at every turn. Nor is it just that Vienna (Wien in German) has a higher proportion of middle-aged and older citizens than any other city in Europe, with a concomitant air of stability, quiet, and respectability. Rather, it's this factor—combined with a love of music; a discreet weakness for rich food (especially cakes); an adherence to old-fashioned and formal forms of address; a high, if unadventurous, regard for the arts; and a gentle mourning for lost glories—that preserves the stiff elegance of Old World dignity.

EXPLORING VIENNA

Numbers in the margin correspond to points of interest on the Vienna map.

Most main sights are in the inner zone, the oldest part of the city, encircled by the Ring, once the course of the city walls and today a broad tree-lined boulevard. Carry a ready supply of AS10 coins; many places of interest have coin-operated tape-recording machines that provide English commentaries. As you wander around, train yourself to look upward; some of the most memorable architectural delights are found on upper stories and along roof lines. Note that addresses throughout the chapter ending with "-strasse" or "-gasse" (both meaning "street") are abbreviated "str." or "g." respectively (Augustiner-strasse will be "Augustinerstr."; Dorotheergasse will be "Dorotheerg.").

The Heart of Vienna

❶ Albertina. Some of the greatest Old Master drawings—including Dürer's legendary *Praying Hands*—are housed in this unassuming building, home to the world's largest collection of drawings, sketches, engravings, and etchings. Dürer leads the list, but there are many other highlights, including works by Rembrandt, Michelangelo, and Correggio. The building is undergoing restoration and at press time (spring 1998) the collection is being housed in the Akademiehof, possibly for the next two years. The Akademiehof is across from the Secession (the building with the gold cabbage-shape ball on top). The closest U-bahn stop is Karlsplatz. Entrance to the collection is at Makartplatz 3. ✉ *Augustinerstr. 1,* ☎ *01/534–830.* ⊙ *Tues.–Fri. 10–6, weekends 10–4; may be closed in July and Aug.*

❸ Augustinerkirche (St. Augustine's Church). The interior of this 14th-century church has undergone restoration; while much of the earlier Baroque ornamentation was removed in the 1780s, the gilt organ ornamentation and main altar remain as visual sensations. This was the court church; the Hapsburg rulers' hearts are preserved in a chamber here. The Augustinerkirche is a favorite on Sunday, when the 11 AM mass is sung in Latin. The church is on Josefsplatz, where much of Graham Greene's great spy story *The Third Man* was filmed (specifically in and around the **Palais Pallavicini** across the street). ✉ *Josefspl.*

⓲ Donner Brunnen (Donner Fountain). Marking the center of Neuer Markt square since 1739, this fountain is a Baroque showpiece, adorned with florid sculpted figures. The characters represent the main rivers that flow into the Danube. Empress Maria Theresa thought the figures were scandalously underclad and wanted them removed. ✉ *Neuer Markt.*

㉕ Freud Museum. The original famous couch is gone (there's a replica), but the apartment in which Sigmund Freud developed modern psychology and treated his first patients is otherwise generally intact. Other rooms include a reference library. ✉ *Bergg. 19,* ☎ *01/319–1596.* ⊙ *July–Sept., daily 9–6, Oct.–June, daily 9–4.*

★ ❻ Hofburg (Imperial Palace). This centerpiece of Imperial Vienna is actually a vast complex comprising numerous buildings, courtyards, and must-sees. Start with the magnificent domed entry—**Michaelertor** (St. Michael's Gate), or the principal gateway to the Hofburg, named for the church diagonally opposite—and go through the courtyards to the vast grassy plaza, Heldenplatz (Hero's Square), on the front. The palace complex, with sections dating from the 13th through 18th centuries, includes the ☞ **Augustinerkirche**, the ☞ **Nationalbibliothek**—its central room is one of the most spectacular Baroque showpieces anywhere—and the ☞ **Hofburgkapelle**, home to the Vienna Boys Choir. Here, too, are the famous ☞ **Spanische Reitschule**—where the Lipizzaners go through their paces—and three fascinating museums: ☞ **Hofsilber-und Tafelkammer Museum**, the ☞ **Schauräume in der Hofburg**, and the ☞ **Schatzkammer**. The complex also houses the office of the federal presidency, a glittering chandelier-lit convention center, an elegant multipurpose hall (Redoutensaal), and private apartments as well as lesser government offices. The complex of the Hofburg is centered around the ☞ **Neue Berg** palace. ✉ *Hofburg; main streets circling the complex are the Opernring, Augustinerstr., Schauflerg., and Dr. Karl Renner-Ring Str.*

❾ Hofburgkapelle (Court Chapel). Home to the renowned Vienna Boys Choir, this Gothic chapel dates to 1449. You'll need tickets to hear the

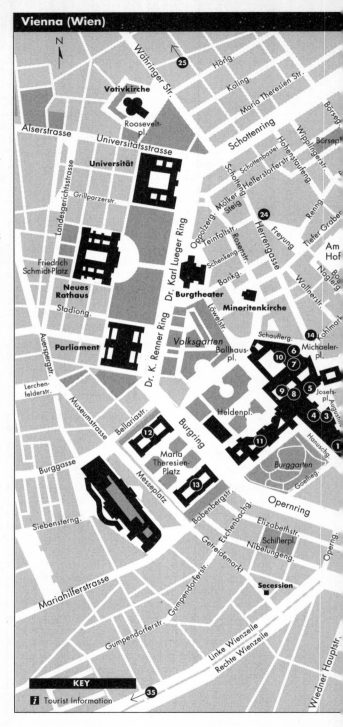

Vienna (Wien)

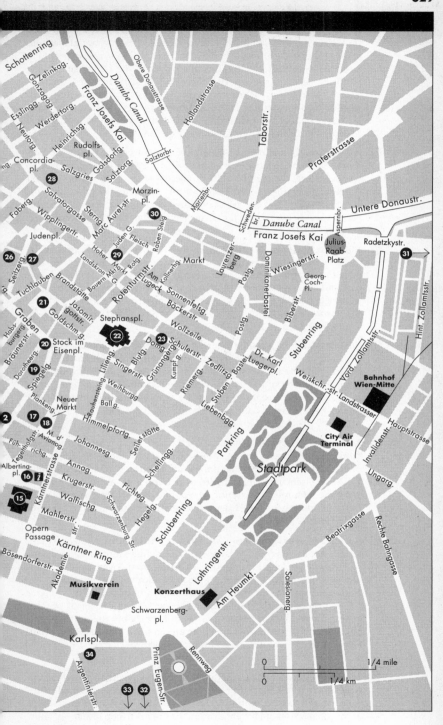

Schottenring

G. Zelinkag.

Gonzagag.

Esslingg.

Neutorg.

Werdertorg.

Concordia-pl.

Heinrichsg.

Rudolfs-pl.

Franz Josefs Kai

Obere Donaustrasse

Danube Canal

Salztorbr.

Hollandstrasse

Taborstr.

Praterstrasse

ng.

Faberg.

Judenpl.

Salzgries

Salvatorgasse

Wipplingertr.

Goldorfg.

Salztorg.

Sterng.

Marc Aurel-str.

Morzin-pl.

28

30

Untere Donaustr.

Schweden-br.

Danube Canal

Franz Josefs Kai

Julius-Raab-Platz

Radetzkystr.

31

26

27

Seilerg.

g.

Tuchlauben

Graben

21

Jasomir-gottsfr.

Goldschm.-g.

Habs-burgerg.

Bräunerstr.

Dorotheerg.

20

19

Spiegelg.

Plankeng.

Brandstätte

Landskron

Hoher Mkt

Bauern Mkt

Markt

Rabensteig

Juden G.

Fleisch

Rotenturmstr.

Wildpret Mkt Brdg.

Lugeck

Bäckerstr.

Sonnenfelsg.

Am Kolnerhg.

Wollzeile

Wiesingerstr.

Postg.

Dominikanerbastei

Biberstr.

Laurenzer-berg

Georg-Coch-Pl.

Stubenring

29

Stephanspl.

22

23

Schulerstr.

Domg.

Blutg.

Grünangerg.

Kumpfg.

Zedlitzg.

Riemerg.

Singerstr.

Lilleng.

2

17

18

Füh.-richg.

Kegelthofsfr.

Avianog.

Neuer Markt

Ball g.

Himmelpfortg.

M. d'

Johannesg.

Weihburgg.

Seilerstätte

Stuben Bastei

Liebenbgg.

Dr. Karl Luegerpl.

Weiskirch.-str.

Landstrasser

Vord. Zollamtstr.

Hint. Zollamtstr.

Bahnhof Wien-Mitte

Albertina-pl.

16

15

Kärntnerstrasse

Annag.

Krugerstr.

Walfischg.

Mahlerstr.

Schwarzenberg Str.

Fichteg.

Hegelg.

Schellingg.

Scheurleg.

Parkring

Schubertring

Stadtpark

City Air Terminal

Hauptstrasse

Invalidenstr.

Ungarg.

Opern Passage

Kärntner Ring

Bösendorferstr.

Akademie-

str.

Karlspl.

34

Argentinierstr.

Lothringerstr.

Am Heumkt.

Salesianerg.

Beatrixgasse

Rechte Bahngasse

Musikverein

Konzerthaus

Schwarzenberg-pl.

33

32

Prinz Eugen-Str.

Rennweg

0   1/4 mile

0   1/4 km

angelic boys sing mass (alas, you can hear them but, due to the chapel layout, not see them) at 9:15 AM on Sunday mid-September through June; tickets are available from travel agencies at a substantial markup, at the chapel itself from 5 PM Friday (queue up by 4:30 and expect long lines), or by writing two months in advance to the Hofmusikkapelle, Hofburg, Schweizerhof, A-1010 Vienna. The City Tourist Office (☞ Visitor Information *in* Vienna Essentials, *below*) can sometimes help with ticket applications. Limited standing room is available for free; get to the chapel by at least 8:30 AM on Sunday for a shot at a spot. ⊠ *Hofburg, Schweizer Hof,* ☎ *01/533–9927,* FAX *01/533–9927–75.*

★ ➓ **Hofsilber-und Tafelkammer Museum** (Court Silver and Tableware Museum). See how royalty dined in this brilliant showcase of imperial table settings. Little wonder Marie Antoinette—who, as a child of Maria Theresa, grew up in Schloss Schönbrunn (☞ *below*)—got a taste for extreme luxury. You can get a combined ticket, which includes the imperial apartments around the corner. ⊠ *Burghof inner court, Michaelertrakt,* ☎ *01/533–7570.* ۝ *Daily 9–4:30.*

➒ **Jüdisches Museum der Stadt Wien** (Jewish Museum). Housed in the former Eskeles town palace, the city's Jewish Museum offers permanent and changing exhibits that portray the richness of the Jewish culture and heritage that contributed so much to Vienna and Austria. Go to the top floor to view the staggering warehouse collection of Judaica. ⊠ *Dorotheerg. 11,* ☎ *01/535–0431.* ۝ *Sun.–Wed. and Fri. 10–6, Thurs. 10–9.*

➐ **Kapuzinerkirche** (Capuchin Church). The ground-level church is nothing unusual, but the basement crypt holds the imperial vault known as the **Kaisergruft,** the final resting place of many sarcophagi of long-dead Hapsburgs. The oldest tomb is that of Ferdinand II; it dates from 1633. The most recent one is that of Empress Zita, widow of the last of the kaisers, who died in 1989. ⊠ *Neuer Markt 1,* ☎ *01/512–6853–12.* ۝ *Daily 9:30–4.*

★ ➍ **Karlskirche** (St. Charles' Church). The classical Baroque facade and dome flanked by vast twin columns instantly identify the Karlskirche, one of the city's best-known landmarks. The church was built around 1715 by Fischer von Erlach. Its oval interior is surprisingly small, given the monumental exterior. The ceiling has airy frescoes, while the Baroque altar is adorned with a magnificent sunburstlike array of gilded shafts. ⊠ *Karlspl.*

★ ⓭ **Kunsthistorisches Museum** (Art History Museum). Cranach, Titian, Canaletto, Rubens, and Velázquez. . . . A definite must-see, this is one of the world's finest art museums. A spectacular foyer staircase leads you to rooms filled with some of the most adored paintings anywhere. Most celebrated is the incomparable collection of paintings by Pieter Bruegel the Elder, the 16th-century Netherlandish master of peasant genre scenes. His *Hunters in the Snow* is probably the most famous painting in Austria. Elsewhere in the museum are important Egyptian, Greek, Etruscan, and Roman exhibits. ⊠ *Maria-Theresien-Pl.,* ☎ *01/525–240.* ۝ *Tues.–Sun. 10–6, Thurs. 10–9.*

⓮ **Looshaus** (Loos Building). Tellingly located opposite the Baroque-era Michaelertor (☞ Hofburg, *above*), this famed monument of 20th-century architecture, built in 1911 and designed by Adolf Loos, stands at the intersection of Herrengasse and Kohlmarkt. Step inside—it's now a bank—to see the remarkable restoration of the foyer. Outside, it's no more than a simple stucco-and-glass structure, but architectural historians point to it as one of the earliest "modern" buildings—with style determined by function—in Europe. ⊠ *Michaelerpl. 3.*

㉓ **Mozart Errinerungsräume** (Mozart Memorial Rooms). A commemorative museum now occupies the small apartment in the house on a narrow street just east of St. Stephen's cathedral where Mozart lived from 1784 to 1787. It was here that the composer wrote *The Marriage of Figaro* (hence the nickname Figaro House), and, some claim, spent the happiest years of his life. Fascinating Mozart memorabilia are on view, but, unfortunately, displayed in an inappropriately modern fashion. ✉ *Domg. 5,* ☎ *01/513–6294.*☺ *Tues.–Sun. 9–12:15 and 1–4:30.*

㉜ **Museum des 20 Jahrhunderts** (Museum of the 20th Century). The building that housed the Austrian pavilion at the Brussels World's Fair now contains a small but extremely tasteful modern art collection along with changing exhibits and art-related events. It is southward across the Gürtel from the Upper Belvedere of Schloss Belvedere (☞ *below*). ✉ *Schweizer Garten,* ☎ *01/799–69–000.* ☺ *Tues.–Sun. 10–6.*

★ ❹ **Nationalbibliothek** (National Library). The focus here is on the stunning Baroque central hall—one of Europe's most magnificently decorated spaces. There's usually a special display of rare books or related art. Don't overlook the fascinating collection of globes on the third floor. ✉ *Josefspl. 1. Library:* ☎ *01/534–100.* ☺ *Hours vary, but are generally May–Oct., Mon.–Sat. 10–4; Jan.–Feb., Mon.–Sat. 10–2; Mar.–Apr. and Nov.–Dec., Mon.–Sat. 10–noon, Sun. and holidays 10–1. Globe museum:* ☎ *01/534–10–297.* ☺ *Mon.–Wed. and Fri. 11–noon, Thurs. 2–3.*

⑫ **Naturhistorisches Museum** (Natural History Museum). The twin building opposite the art-filled Kunsthistorisches Museum (☞ *above*) houses ranks of assorted showcased stuffed animals, but such special collections as butterflies are better presented. There are dinosaur skeletons, of course. Here also is the Venus of Willendorf, a 25,000-year-old statuette discovered in Lower Austria. ✉ *Maria-Theresien-Pl.,* ☎ *01/521–770.* ☺ *Wed.–Mon. 9–6; in winter, first floor only, Wed.–Mon. 9–3.*

⑪ **Neue Burg** (New Wing of the Imperial Palace). This ponderously ornate 19th-century edifice—Hitler announced the annexation of Austria from its balcony in 1938—now houses a series of museums, ranging from musical instruments (Beethoven's piano) to weapons (tons of armor) to the ethnological collections of the Museum für Völkerkunde (Montezuma's headdress) and Ephesus (classical antiquity) museums. ✉ *Heldenpl. 1,* ☎ *01/521–770.* ☺ *Wed.–Mon. 10–6. Ethnological Museum:* ☺ *Wed.–Mon. 10–4.*

⑳ **Pestsäule** (Plague Column). Shooting up from the middle of the broad Graben Square like a geyser of whipped cream touched with gold, this heavily ornate Baroque-era column commemorates the Black Death of the plague epidemic of 1697. ✉ *Graben.*

㉑ **Peterskirche.** (St. Peter's Church). This Baroque jewel just off the Graben was erected by Johann Lukas von Hildebrandt in about 1730, and has what is probably the city's most theatrical interior. The pulpit is especially fine, with a highly ornate canopy, but florid and swirling decoration is everywhere. Many of the decorative elements are based on the tent form, a motif suggested by the encampment of Turkish forces beyond the city walls during the great siege of Vienna at the end of the 17th century. ✉ *Peterspl., just off the Graben.*

⑯ **Sacher Hotel.** Behind the Opera is Vienna's enduring plush red-and-gilt monument to the fin de siècle. Take a look into the grandly historic ground-floor complex—a veritable maze of gilded lobbies and bars. Who can pay a call and resist ordering up a slice of the original Sachertorte—the ultimate chocolate cake—in the hotel's noted café? ⊠ *Phil-harmonikerstr. 4,* ☎ *01/514–56–0.*

★ ⑧ **Schatzkammer** (Imperial Treasury). An almost overpowering display includes the magnificent crown jewels, the imperial crowns, the treasure of the Order of the Golden Fleece, regal robes, and other secular and ecclesiastical treasures. The imperial crown of the Holy Roman Empire is over 1,000 years old. This is one of the world's greatest collections of imperial regalia. ⊠ *Hofburg, Schweizer Hof,* ☎ *01/533–7931.* ⊘ *Wed.–Mon. 10–6.*

⑦ **Schauräume in der Hofburg** (Imperial Apartments). These rooms were the crystal-bedecked and tapestry-draped residence of Emperor Franz Josef and Empress Elisabeth. Among the exhibits is the exercise equipment used by the beautiful empress. Here, too, is the dress she was wearing when she was stabbed to death in 1898 by a demented Italian anarchist on the shore of Lake Geneva; the dagger marks are visible. State reception rooms are included in the tour. A combined admission with the Hofsilber-und Tafelkammer (Court Silver and Tableware Museum; ☞ *above*) is available. ⊠ *Michaelerpl. 1 entrance is under the Michaelertor dome (☞ above) from Michaelerpl.,* ☎ *01/533–7570.* ⊘ *Daily 9–4:30 (Thurs. until 9).*

★ ⑤ **Spanische Reitschule** (Spanish Riding School). Probably the most famous interior in Vienna, the riding arena of the Spanish Riding School—wedding-cake white and crystal-chandeliered—is where the beloved white Lippizaner horses train and perform dressage when they are not stabled in stalls across the Reitschulgasse to the east side of the school. Due to renovations, the school entrance has been moved temporarily from Josefsplatz to the main courtyard next to the Swiss Gate, beyond the Michaelertor rotunda dome; when renovations are done, the main entrance will be moved back, so double-check. For performance schedules and tickets, write to the Spanische Reitschule (⊠ Hofburg, A-1010, Vienna) *at least* three months in advance. There are generally full performances on Sunday at 10:45 AM from March through June, and from September into October. There are no performances in July and August. Evening performances are occasionally given on Wednesday at 7. The AmEx office sometimes has a few last-minute tickets, but expect a 22% service charge. Tickets for the few short training performances on Saturday morning at 10 are available only from ticket offices and travel agencies; a list of these agencies is available from the Austrian National Tourist Office. You can watch the 10 AM–noon training sessions Tuesday–Saturday during much of the performance season; tickets for these training sessions are available only at the door. ⊠ *Michaelerpl. 1, Hofburg,* ☎ *01/533–9032,* ℻ *01/535–0186.* ▨ *AS250–AS900, standing room AS200, Sat. morning training session with music AS250, other morning training sessions AS100.* ⊘ *Mar.–June and Sept.–mid-Dec; closed tour wks.*

⑮ **Staatsoper** (State Opera House). Considered one of the best opera houses in the world, the Staatsoper is a focus of Viennese social life as well. The house was almost totally destroyed in the last days of World War II (only the walls and front foyers were saved), but rebuilt in its present simpler elegance and reopened in 1955. Tickets for seats can be expensive and scarce, but one of the very best bargains in Vienna are the Staatsoper standing-room tickets, available for each performance at delightfully affordable prices—as low as AS50 ($4)! Backstage tours also are available: The tour schedule for the day is usually posted beside the door under the right front arcade, on the Kärntnerstrasse side (depending on the activities inside, there are usually tours at 2 and 3 PM). The repertory schedule here is one of the most ambitious in Europe; as many as four different operas are performed in a single week during the September–June season. ⊠ *Opernring 2,* ☎ *01/514–4429–69.*

★ ㉒ **Stephansdom** (St. Stephen's Cathedral). The towering Gothic spires and gaudy 19th-century tile roof of the city's central landmark still dominate the skyline. The oldest parts of the structure are the 13th-century entrance, the soaring **Riesentor** (Great Entry), and the Heidentürme (Heathens' Towers). Inside, the church is mysteriously shadowy, filled with an array of monuments, tombs, sculptures, paintings, and pulpits. Despite extensive wartime damage—and numerous Baroque additions—the atmosphere seems authentically medieval. Climb the 343 steps of the south tower—Alte Steffl (Old Stephen) as the Viennese call it—for a stupendous view over the city. An elevator goes up the north tower to the Pummerin, a 22-ton bell cast in part from cannons captured from the Turks in 1683. If you take a 30-minute tour of the crypt, you can see the copper jars in which the entrails of the Hapsburgs are carefully preserved. ⊠ *Stephanspl.,* ☎ *01/5155–2526.* ☉ *Catacombs (guided tour only): Mon.–Sat. 10, 11, 11:30, 2, 2:30, 3:30, 4, 4:30; Sun. and holidays 2, 2:30, 3:30, 4, 4:30. North tower: Apr.–Sept., daily 9–6, Oct.–Mar., daily 8–5. South tower: daily 9–5:30.*

☝ ❷ **Theater Museum.** Housed in the noted 18th-century Palais Lobkowitz—Beethoven was a regular visitor here—this museum covers the history of theater in Vienna and the rest of Austria. A children's museum in the basement—alas, open only by appointment—is reached by a slide! ⊠ *Lobkowitzpl. 2,* ☎ *01/512–8800–0.* ☉ *Tues.–Sun. 10–5.*

Other Corners of Vienna

㉖ **Am Hof.** The Kirche am Hof (Church of the Nine Choirs of Angels is its complete name, on the east side of Am Hof) is only one feature of this remarkable square, whose name simply translates as "at court." Most of the Baroque overlay both inside and out on the massive church dates from the 1600s. The somewhat dreary interior is curiously reminiscent of those of many Dutch churches. In the northeast corner of the square check out what is possibly the most ornate fire station in the world. You'll find an open-air antiques market in the square on Thursday and Friday in summer and frequent seasonal markets at other times. ⊠ *Bounded by Tiefer Graben to the west, Nagelrg. to the south, and Seitzerg. to the west.*

㉙ **Hoher Markt.** This ancient cobblestone square with its imposing central monument celebrating the betrothal of Mary and Joseph sits atop **Roman ruins** (⊠ Hoher Markt 3, ☎ 01/535–5606), remains of the 2nd-century Roman legion encampment. On the north side of Hoher Markt is the amusing **Anker-Uhr,** a clock that marks the hour with a parade of moving figures. The figures are identified on a plaque at the lower left of the clock; it's well worth passing by at noon to catch the show.

㉛ **Hundertwasserhaus** (Hundertwasser House). This famous structure is a masterpiece envisioned by artist Friedenreich Hundertwasser—an astonishing apartment complex marked by turrets, towers, unusual windows, and uneven floors. The nearby **KunstHaus Wien** (Vienna House of Art; ⊠ KunstHaus Wien, Untere Weissgerberstr. 13, ☎ 01/712–0491) is an art museum designed by the artist; it offers a floor of Hundertwasser plus changing exhibits of other modern works. ⊠ *Kegelg. and Köweng.* ☉ *Daily 10–7.*

㉘ **Maria am Gestade** (St. Mary's on the Bank). When built around 1400, this was a church for fishermen from the nearby canal, hence the name. Note the arched stone doorway and the ornate carved stone latticework "folded hands" spire. ⊠ *Salvatorg./Passauer Pl.*

③⓪ **Ruprechtskirche** (St. Rupert's Church). Vienna's oldest church, dating from the 11th century, is small, damp, dark, and—unfortunately—usually closed. ✉ *Ruprechtspl.*

★ ③③ **Schloss Belvedere** (Belvedere Palace). On a rise overlooking the city, this Baroque-era palace is one of the showpieces of Vienna. It was commissioned by Prince Eugene of Savoy and built by Johann Lukas von Hildebrandt in 1721–22. The palace consists of two separate buildings, one at the foot of the hill and the other at the top. The lavish gardens are among the finest showpieces of the Baroque style in landscaping found anywhere. The Upper Belvedere houses a gallery of 19th- and 20th-century Viennese art, featuring works by Klimt (including his world-famous painting *The Kiss*), Kokoschka, Schiele, Waldmüller, and Makart; the Lower Belvedere has a Baroque museum together with exhibits of Austrian art of the Middle Ages. Take Streetcar D toward the Südbahnhof to reach the Belvedere. ✉ *Prinz-Eugen-Str. 27,* ☎ *01/795-570.* ⏲ *Tues.–Sun. 10–5.*

★ ③⑤ **Schloss Schönbrunn** (Schönbrunn Palace). The Versailles of Vienna, this magnificent Baroque residence has grandly formal gardens, and was built for the Hapsburgs between 1696 and 1713. The palace was originally conceived to top the hill behind the present palace, but the scheme was too costly and plans were changed, putting the palace on the lower ground and capping the hill with that touch of architectural genius, the Gloriette. The complex has been a summer residence for personages including Maria Theresa and Napoléon. Kaiser Franz Josef I was born and died here. His "office" (kept as he left it in 1916) is a touching reminder of his Spartan life. In contrast, other rooms are filled with truly spectacular imperial elegance. Six-year-old Mozart played here in the Hall of Mirrors for Maria Theresa and the court. The ornate reception areas are still used for state occasions. A guided tour leading through more than 40 of the palace's 1,441 rooms is the best way to see inside the palace (you can take a tour of just 20 rooms, but since the most dazzling salons start at No. 21, opt for the full tour). Other rooms are occasionally open independent of tours. Ask to see the **Berglzimmer,** ornately decorated ground-floor rooms generally not included in tours. To get to the palace, take the U4 subway line from the city center; it's an easy ride and just five stops from Karlsplatz. ✉ *Schönbrunner Schlosstr.,* ☎ *01/81113.* 🎟 *AS140 with guided tour; AS110 without tour (40 rooms).* ⏲ *Nov.–Mar., daily 8:30–4:30; Apr.–Oct., daily 8:30–5.*

☾ Once on the grounds of the Schönbrunn Palace, don't overlook the **Tiergarten** (zoo). It's Europe's oldest menagerie, established in 1752 to amuse and educate the court. It houses an extensive assortment of animals; the original Baroque enclosures now serve as viewing pavilions, with the animals housed in effective, modern settings. ☎ *01/877-9294.* ⏲ *Nov.–Jan., daily 9–4:30; Feb. and Oct., daily 9–5; Mar., daily 9–5:30; Apr., daily 9–6; May–Sept., daily 9–6:30.*

Pathways lead up through the formal gardens to the famous **Gloriette,** an 18th-century Baroque folly on the rise behind Schloss Schönbrunn built so that palace residents could enjoy superb views of the city. There's a café inside. ⏲ *Daily 9–5.*

☾ The **Wagenburg** (Imperial Coach Collection), near the entrance to the palace grounds, displays splendid examples of bygone conveyances, from ornate children's sleighs to the grand carriages built to carry the coffins of deceased emperors in state funerals. ☎ *01/877-3244.* 🎟 *AS30.* ⏲ *Apr.–Oct., daily 9–6; Nov.–Mar., Tues.–Sun. 10–4.*

If you have time, wander the grounds to discover the **Schöner Brunnen** (Beautiful Fountain) for which the Schönbrunn Palace is named; the re-created but convincing massive **Römische Ruinen** (Roman Ruins); the great glass **Palmenhaus** (Palmery), with its orchids and exotic plants; and the **Schmetterlinghaus** (Butterfly House), alive with unusual butterflies. *Palm House: ⊠ Nearest entrance Hietzing, ☎ 01/877–5087–406. ☉ May–Sept., daily 9:30–5:30; Oct.–Apr., daily 9:30–4:30. Butterfly House:☎ 01/877–5087–421. ☉ May–Sept., daily 10–4:30; Oct.–Apr., daily 10–3.*

㉔ **Schottenkirche, Museum im Schottenstift** (Scottish Church and Museum). Despite its name, the monks who founded this church around 1177 were actually Irish, not Scots. The present imposing building dates from the mid-1600s. In contrast to the plain exterior, the interior bubbles with cherubs and angels. The Benedictines have set up a small but worthwhile museum of mainly religious art, including a late-Gothic winged altarpiece removed from the church when the interior was given a Baroque overlay. The museum entrance is in the courtyard. *⊠ Freyung 6, ☎ 01/534–98–600. ☉ Thurs.–Sat. 10–5, Sun. noon–5.*

㉗ **Uhrenmuseum** (Clock Museum). Tucked away on several floors of a lovely Renaissance structure is an amazing collection of clocks and watches. Try to be there when the hundreds of clocks strike the noon hour. *⊠ Schulhof 2, ☎ 01/533–2265. ☉ Tues.–Sun. 9–4:30.*

Vienna Environs

Wienerwald (Vienna Woods). You can reach a small corner of the legendary Vienna Woods by streetcar and bus: Take a streetcar or the U-2 subway line to Schottentor/University and, from there, Streetcar 38 (Grinzing) to the end of the line. To get into the woods, change in Grinzing to Bus 38A. This will take you to the Kahlenberg, which provides a superb view out over the Danube and the city. You can take the bus or hike to the Leopoldsberg, the promontory over the Danube from which Turkish invading forces were repulsed during the 16th and 17th centuries. Grinzing itself is a village out of a picture book. Unfortunately, much of the wine offered in its wine taverns, or Heuriger, is less than enchanting. For better wine and ambience, try the area around Pfarrplatz and Probusgasse in Hohe Warte—Streetcar 37, Bus 39A— or the suburb of Nussdorf—Streetcar D.

DINING

In recent years Vienna, once a culinary backwater, has produced a new generation of chefs willing to slaughter sacred cows and create a *Neue Küche,* a new Vienna cuisine. The movement is well past the "less is more" stage that nouvelle cuisine traditionally demands (and to which most Viennese vociferously objected), relying now on lighter versions of the old standbys and clever combinations of such traditional ingredients as liver pâtés and sour cream.

In a first-class restaurant you will pay as much as in most other Western European capitals. But you can still find good food at refreshingly low prices in the simpler restaurants, particularly at neighborhood *Gasthäuser* (rustic inns) in the suburbs. Remember if you eat your main meal at noon (as the Viennese do), you can take advantage of the luncheon specials available at most restaurants and in cafés.

RATINGS

Prices are per person and include appetizer and a main course, usually with salad, and a small beer or glass of wine. Meals in the top price categories will include a dessert or cheese with coffee. Prices include taxes and service (but adding another 3%–5% to the bill as a tip is customary).

CATEGORY	COST
$$$$	over AS800
$$$	AS500–AS800
$$	AS200–AS500
$	under AS200

$$$$ ★ ✕ **Korso.** A veritable gourmet temple, Korso has a sumptuous setting with elegant paneling and velvet and gold accents. For aficionados of the new Vienna cuisine, the decor is almost as delicious as the house specialties. Chef Reinhard Gerer produces exquisite variations on such Austrian standards as pork and beef by borrowing accents from Asian traditions. Sample the delicate Styrian lamb or fillet of venison. ⊠ *Kärtner Ring 1,* ☎ *01/515–16–546. Reservations essential. Jacket and tie. AE, DC, MC, V. Closed 3 wks in Aug. No lunch Sat.*

$$$$ ★ ✕ **Le Siècle.** Most diners come for the pampered elegance and the variety of seafood, flown in fresh daily. Tempting items on the ever-changing menu might include marinated salmon with a dill mustard sauce to start, followed by a lightly fried turbot fillet with white asparagus and artichoke and truffle mousse. Desserts, such as the delicate citrus fruit terrine, are inspired and steer away from traditional heavy cakes and strudels. ⊠ *Radisson/SAS Palais Hotel, Parkring 16,* ☎ *01/515–17–3440. Reservations essential. Jacket and tie. AE, DC, MC, V.*

$$$ ✕ **Do & Co.** The spectacular setting at the top of the modern Haas-Haus building smack in the middle of Stephansplatz would make this worthwhile for the view alone, but the food is also excellent and varied, with a nouvelle-Oriental slant featuring fragrant, tangy wok creations. For heartier appetites there are numerous meat choices, with the combination king crab and Uruguayan steak being most popular. There is also a fantastic, though pricey, sushi bar at lunchtime. In the evenings, book a table by the window so you can see the sunset over the spires of St. Stephen's, and in warm weather, ask for a table outside on the balcony. ⊠ *In Haas–Haus, Stephanspl. 12,* ☎ *01/535–3969. Reservations essential. Jacket and tie. AE, DC, MC, V.*

$$$ ★ ✕ **Fadinger.** Near the *Börse* (the Vienna Stock Exchange), this unpretentious restaurant serves some of the best nouvelle Austrian cuisine in the city. The widely varied menu includes light-as-a-feather fish dishes, such as salmon in a crisp potato crust, as well as hearty, but never heavy, meat courses. The *Zwiebelrostbraten,* skirt steak topped with crisp fried onions, is outstanding. ⊠ *Wipplingerstr. 29,* ☎ *01/533–4341. Reservations essential. No credit cards. Closed weekends.*

$$$ ✕ **Zu ebener Erde und erster Stock.** Ask for a table upstairs in this tiny, utterly charming original Biedermeier house, which serves excellent Austrian fare plus international specialties; the downstairs space is good for snacks. ⊠ *Burgg. 13,* ☎ *01/523–6254. Reservations essential. Jacket and tie. AE, V. Closed Sun.–Mon. and late July–late Aug. No lunch Sat.*

$$ ✕ **Bei Max.** The decor is somewhat bland, but the tasty Carinthian specialties—*Käsnudeln* and *Fleischnudeln* (cheese and meat ravioli) in particular—keep this friendly restaurant packed. ⊠ *Landhausg. 2 at Herreng.,* ☎ *01/533–7359. No credit cards. Closed weekends, last wk in July, first 3 wks in Aug.*

$$ ✕ **Figlmüller.** Known for its gargantuan schnitzel, which is so large it overflows the plate, Figlmüller is always packed with diners sharing benches and long tables. Food choices are limited and everything is à la carte. The small enclosed "greenhouse" in the passageway entry is more popular than the inside rooms. ⊠ *Wollzeile 5 (passageway from Stephansdom),* ☎ *01/512–6177. No credit cards. Closed Aug.*

$$ ✕ **Lebenbauer.** This is Vienna's premier vegetarian restaurant and it
★ even has a no-smoking room, rare in this part of Europe. Specialties
include *Hirsegröstl* (millet hash with pumpkin seeds in an oyster mush-
room sauce) and gluten-free pasta with smoked salmon and shrimp in
a dill cream sauce. ⊠ *Teinfaltstr. 3, near the Freyung,* ☎ *01/533–55–560.
AE, DC, MC, V.* ⊙ *Weekdays 11–3 and 5–10 , Sat. 11–2. Closed Sat.
evening, Sun., and first two weeks of Aug.*

$$ ✕ **Livingstone.** If you're homesick for a hamburger and fries, this is
★ the place to go. Buns are homemade and the Austrian beef is of the
finest quality. But if the tropical-colonial setting straight out of a 1940s
Bogart movie makes you want to try something more adventurous—
such as pasta with smoked tofu, tiger shrimp, and squash, and green
chili peppers in a garlic-ginger sesame oil sauce—you won't be disappointed. ⊠ *Zelinkag. 4, near the Börse,* ☎ *01/533–3393. AE, DC,
MC, V. No lunch.*

$$ ✕ **Melker Stiftskeller.** This is one of the city's half-dozen genuine
Weinkeller (cellar wine taverns). The food selection is limited but
good, featuring *Stelze* (crisp roasted pig's knuckle). ⊠ *Schotteng. 3,*
☎ *01/533–5530. MC, V. Closed Sun. No lunch.*

$$ ✕ **Neu Wien.** As the name says, this is a taste of the new Vienna. The
vaulted interior is enlivened by cheeky modern art. The eclectic menu
changes frequently, but look for the herbed goat cheese salad with basil
oil dressing; *Zanderfilet,* a crisp pike perch with a cream beet sauce;
or veal with tagliatelle in a truffle sauce. ⊠ *Bäckerstr. 5, near St.
Stephen's,* ☎ *01/512–0999. Reservations essential. MC, V. Closed weekends in summer. No lunch.*

$ ✕ **Gigerl.** It's hard to believe you're right in the middle of the city at
★ this imaginative and charming wine restaurant that serves hot and cold
buffets. The rooms are small and cozy but may get smoky and noisy
when the place is full—which it usually is. The food is typical of wine
gardens on the fringes of the city: roast meats, casserole dishes, cold cuts,
salads. The wines are very good. The surrounding narrow alleys and
ancient buildings add to the charm of the outdoor tables in summer. ⊠
Rauhensteing. 3, ☎ *01/513–4431. AE, DC, MC, V. No lunch Sun.*

$ ✕ **Königsbacher bei der Oper.** The space is intimate and tables are close,
★ but portions are generous and the daily special (listed for the week)
could be anything from roast pork to a ham-and-noodle casserole. Shaded
outdoor tables are delightful in summer. ⊠ *Walfischg. 5,* ☎ *01/513–
1210. No credit cards. Closed Sun. No dinner Sat.*

$ ✕ **Spatzennest.** This is simple, hearty Viennese cooking at its best, served
★ on a quaint, cobblestone, pedestrian street in Old Vienna. Tasty dishes
include schnitzel and roast chicken with spaetzle prepared with sliv-
ers of ham and melted cheese. It's especially delightful in summer, when
tables are set outside. It can be smoky indoors. ⊠ *Ulrichspl. 1, near
the Volkstheater,* ☎ *01/520–1659. No credit cards. Closed Fri.–Sat.*

NIGHTLIFE AND THE ARTS

The Arts

MUSIC

Most classical concerts are held in one of two places. The **Konzerthaus**
(⊠ Lothringerstr. 20, ☎ 01/712–4686, ticket window 01/712–1211,
FAX 01/712–2872) is one. The **Musikverein** (⊠ Dumbastr. 3, ☎ 01/505–
86–8194, FAX 01/505–8681–94) is the other. Tickets can be bought at
their box offices or ordered by phone (AE, DC, MC, V). Pop concerts
are scheduled from time to time at the **Austria Center** (⊠ Am Huber-
tusdamm 6, U-1 subway to Vienna International Center stop, ☎ 01/
236–9150). Tickets to various musical events are sold through **Vienna
Ticket Service** (☎ 01/588–850, FAX 01/588–3033) and the Salettl

gazebo ticket office (☎ 01/588–8581), which is open daily 10–7, on Kärntnerstrasse next to the Staatsoper (State Opera House). At the same office, same-day half-price tickets to many musical events—*but not the Staatsoper, Volksoper, or symphony concerts*—go on sale at 2 PM.

THEATER AND OPERA

Check the monthly program published by the city; posters also show opera and theater schedules. The **Staatsoper,** one of world's great opera houses, features major stars in its almost-nightly original-language performances. The **Volksoper** offers lighter operas, operettas, and musicals, all in German. Performances at the **Burgtheater** and **Akademietheater** are also in German. Tickets for the Staatsoper, the Volksoper, and the Burg and Akademie theaters are available at the central ticket office to the left rear of the Staatsoper (Bundestheaterkassen, Hanuschg. 3, 01/514–44–2959, 01/514–44–2969; weekdays 8–6, weekends and holidays 9–noon). Tickets go on sale a month before performances. Unsold tickets can be obtained at the evening box office. Plan to be there at least one hour before the performance; students can buy remaining tickets at lower prices, so they are usually out in force. Tickets can be ordered three weeks or more in advance in writing (or by fax) or a month in advance from anywhere in the world by phone (01/513–1513). Standing room tickets for the Staatsoper are a great bargain.

Theater is offered in English at **Vienna's English Theater** (⊠ Josefsg. 12, ☎ 01/402–1260).The **International Theater** (⊠ Porzellang. 8, ☎ 01/319–6272) also has performances in English.

Nightlife

The central district for nightlife in Vienna is nicknamed the **Bermuda-Dreieck** (Bermuda Triangle). Centered around Judengasse/Seitenstettengasse, next to St. Ruprecht's, a small Romanesque church, the area is jammed with everything from good bistros to jazz clubs.

CABARETS

Most cabarets are expensive and unmemorable. One leading option is **Casanova** (⊠ Dorotheerg. 6, ☎ 01/512–9845), which emphasizes striptease. Another popular cabaret is **Moulin Rouge** (⊠ Walfischg. 11, ☎ 01/512–2130).

CAFÉS

A quintessential Viennese institution, the coffeehouse, or café, is club, pub, and bistro all rolled into one. To savor the atmosphere of the coffeehouses you must take your time: Set aside an afternoon, a morning, or at least a couple of hours, and settle down in one of your choice. There is no need to worry about overstaying your welcome, even over a single small cup of Mokka—although in some of the more opulent coffeehouses, this cup of coffee can cost as much as a meal.

Alte Backstube (⊠ Lange Gasse 34, ☎ 01/406–1101; AE, MC, V), in a gorgeous Baroque house—with a café in front and restaurant in back— was once a bakery and is now a museum as well. **Café Central** (⊠ Herreng. 14,☎ 01/535–41–760) is where Stalin and Trotsky played chess; in the Palais Ferstel, it's one of Vienna's most beautiful cafés. **Cafe Landtmann** (⊠ Dr. Karl Leuger Str. 4, ☎ 01/532–0621), next to the dignified Burgtheater, with front-row views of the Ringstrasse, was reputedly Freud's favorite café. In May they offer a tempting selection of fresh strawberry tortes. A 200-year-old institution, **Demel** (⊠ Kohlmarkt 14, ☎ 01/535–17–170) is the *grande dame* of Viennese cafés. Order a melange, brought with milk on the side in a dainty creamer, to go along with their Senegal torte, a scrumptious hazelnut cake. The elegant front rooms have more atmosphere than the airy modern atrium and are now reserved as no-smoking rooms. **Gerstner** (⊠ Kärntnerstr. 15,

☎ 01/496–377) is in the heart of the bustling Kärntnerstrasse, and one of the more modern Viennese cafés. Popular here is the Bruegel torte, a marzipan pastry especially concocted for their branch in the Kunsthistorisches Museum. **Museum** (✉ Friedrichstr. 6, ☎ 01/586–5202), with its original interior by the architect Adolf Loos, draws a mixed crowd and has lots of newspapers. **The Sacher** (✉ Philharmonikerstr. 4, ☎ 01/514–560) is hardly a typical Vienna café; more a shrine to plush gilt and marzipan, it's both a must-see and a must-eat. The world's ultimate chocolate cake is served here.

DISCOS

Atrium (✉ Schwarzenbergpl. 10, ☎ 01/505–3594) is open Thursday through Sunday and draws a lively young crowd. **Queen Anne** (✉ Johannesg. 12, ☎ 01/512–0203) is central, popular, and always packed. The **U-4** (✉ Schönbrunnerstr. 222, ☎ 01/815–8307) ranks high among the young set. **P 1** (✉ Rotg. 9, ☎ 01/535–9995) is another spot for the MTV crowd. Live bands, dancing, and snacks are offered at **Chattanooga** (✉ Graben 29A, ☎ 01/533–50–000).

NIGHTCLUBS

A casual '50s atmosphere pervades the popular **Café Volksgarten** (✉ Burgring 1, ☎ 01/533–0518), in the city park of the same name; tables are set outdoors in summer. The more formal **Eden Bar** (✉ Lilieng. 2, ☎ 01/512–7450) is considered one of Vienna's classiest nightspots; don't expect to be let in unless you're dressed to kill.

WINE TAVERNS

For a traditional Viennese night out, head to one of the city's atmospheric *Heuriger,* or wine taverns, some of which date from as far back as the 12th century. You can often have full meals at these taverns, but the emphasis is mainly on drinking. The **Melker Stiftskeller** (☞ Dining, *above*) is one of the friendliest and most typical. Another wine-tavern option is the **Augustinerkeller** (✉ Augustinerstr. 1, ☎ 01/533–1026), open at lunchtime as well as evenings, in the same building as the Albertina collection. The **Esterházykeller** (✉ Haarhof 1, ☎ 01/533–3482), in a particularly mazelike network of rooms, has excellent wines. The **Zwölf Apostelkeller** (✉ Sonnenfelsg. 3, ☎ 01/512–6777), near St. Stephen's has rooms that are down, down, down underground.

SHOPPING

Boutiques

Famous name brands are found along the **Kohlmarkt** and **Graben** and their respective side streets, and the side streets off **Kärntnerstrasse.**

Folk Costumes

The main resource for exquisite Austrian *Trachten* (native dress) is **Loden-Plankl** (✉ Michaelerpl. 6, ☎ 01/533–8032).

Food and Flea Markets

The **Naschmarkt** (foodstuffs market; ✉ Between the Rechte and LinkeWienzeile; ⊙ weekdays 6 AM–mid-afternoon, Sat. 6–1) is a sensational open-air market offering specialties from around the world. The **Flohmarkt** (flea market) operates year-round beyond the Naschmarkt (subway U-4 to Kettenbrückeng.; Sat. 8–4) and is equally fascinating. An **Arts and Antiques Market** with better offerings operates on Saturday (2–6) and Sunday (10–6) alongside the Danube Canal near the Salztorbrücke. From late spring to early fall, check Am Hof square for antiques and collectibles on Thursday and Friday. Also look for the seasonal markets in Freyung Square opposite Palais Fersteal.

Shopping Districts

Many tourists first gravitate to **Kärntnerstrasse,** lined with luxury boutiques and large emporiums. Running neck and neck in popularity with the Kärntnerstrasse shopping avenue, however, is **Mariahilfer Strasse,** where the Viennese do much of their in-town shopping in the many department and specialty stores.

VIENNA ESSENTIALS

Arriving and Departing

BY CAR

Main access routes are the expressways to the west and south (Westautobahn A1, Südautobahn A2). Routes leading to the downtown area are marked ZENTRUM.

BY PLANE

All flights use Schwechat Airport (☎ 01/711–10–2231), about 16 km (10 mi) southwest of Vienna.

Between the Airport and Downtown. Buses leave the airport for the city air terminal, Wien-Mitte Landstrasse Hauptstrasse (✉ Am Stadtpark, ☎ 01/580–03–3369), by the Hilton, on every half hour from 5 to 6:30 AM and every 20 minutes from 6:50 AM to 11:30 PM; after that, buses depart every hour until 5 AM. The S7 train (called the *Schnellbahn*) shuttles every half hour between the airport and the Landstrasse/Wien–Mitte (city center) and Wien–Nord (north Vienna) stations; the fare is AS34 and it takes about 35 minutes. Follow the picture signs of a train to the basement of the airport. Buses also run every hour (every half hour on weekends and holidays Apr.–Sept.) from the airport to the Westbahnhof (West Train Station) and the Südbahnhof (South Train Station). Be sure you get on the right bus! The one-way fare for all buses is AS70. A taxi from the airport to downtown Vienna costs about AS350–AS450; agree on a price in advance. Cabs (legally) do not meter this drive, as airport fares are more or less fixed (legally again) at about double the meter fare. The cheapest cab service is C+K Airport Service (☎ 01/1731, 01/689–6969), charging a set price of AS270. C+K will also meet your plane at no extra charge if you let them know in advance.

BY TRAIN

Vienna has four train stations. The principal station, the Westbahnhof, is for trains to and from Linz, Salzburg, and Innsbruck, and to and from Germany, France, and Switzerland. The Südbahnhof is for trains to and from Graz, Klagenfurt, Villach, and Italy. The Franz-Josefs-Bahnhof, or Nordbahnhof, is for trains to and from Prague, Berlin, and Warsaw. Go to the Wien–Mitte/Landstrasse Hauptstrasse station for local trains to and from the north of the city. Budapest trains use both the Westbahnhof and Südbahnhof, and Bratislava trains both Wien–Mitte and the Südbahnhof, so check.

Getting Around

Vienna is fairly easy to explore on foot; as a matter of fact, much of the heart of the city—the area within the Ring—is a pedestrian zone. Public transportation is comfortable, convenient, and frequent, though not cheap. **Tickets for buses, subways, and streetcars** are available in subway stations and from dispensers on buses and streetcars. Tickets in multiples of five are sold at cigarette shops—look for the sign TABAK-TRAFIK—or at the window marked VORVERKAUF at such central stations as Karlsplatz or Stephansplatz. A block of five tickets costs AS85, a single ticket AS20. If you plan to use public transportation frequently, get a **24-hour ticket** (AS50), a **three-day tourist ticket** (AS130), or an

eight-day ticket (AS265). Tariffs could be slightly higher in 1999. Maps and information in English are available at the Stephansplatz, Karlsplatz, and Praterstern U-bahn stations.

The Vienna Card, available for AS180 at tourist and transportation information offices and most hotels, will give you unlimited travel for 72 hours on city buses, streetcars, and the subway, reductions on selected museum entry fees, plus tips and discounts on various attractions and selected shopping throughout the city.

BY BICYCLE

Vienna has hundreds of kilometers of marked cycle routes, including reserved routes through the center of the city. Paved cycling routes parallel the Danube. For details, get the city brochure on cycling. Bicycles can be rented at a number of locations and can be taken on the Vienna subway (with the exception of the U-6 line) year-round all day Sunday and holidays, from 9 to 3, and after 6:30 on weekdays, and, from May through September, after 9 AM Saturday. You'll need a half-fare ticket for the bike (☞ By Subway, *below*).

BY BUS OR STREETCAR

Inner-city buses are numbered 1A through 3A and operate weekdays until about 7:40 PM, Saturday until 7 PM. Reduced fares are available for these routes (buy a **Kurzstreckenkarte;** it allows you four trips for AS34) as well as designated shorter stretches (roughly two to four stops) on all other bus and streetcar lines. Streetcars and buses are numbered or lettered according to route, and they run until about midnight. Night buses marked *N* follow 22 special routes every half hour between 12:30 AM and 4:30 AM. Get a route plan from any of the public transport or VORVERKAUF offices. The fare is AS25, payable on the bus unless you have a 24-hour, three-day, or eight-day ticket; then you need only pay an AS10 supplement. The central terminus is Schwedenplatz. Streetcars 1 and 2 run the circular route around the Ring, clockwise and counterclockwise, respectively.

BY CAR

Unless you know your way around the city, a car is more of a nuisance than a help. The center of the city is a pedestrian zone. Drive on the right. Seat belts are compulsory in front. Children under 12 must sit in the back, and smaller children must have a restraining seat. Speed limits are as posted; otherwise, 130 kph (80 mph) on expressways, 100 kph (62 mph) on other main roads, 50 kph (31 mph) in built-up areas. Some city areas have speed limits of 30 kph (19 mph). The right-of-way is for those coming from the right (especially in traffic circles) unless otherwise marked.

City on-street parking is a problem. Observe signs; tow-away is expensive. In winter, overnight parking is forbidden on city streets with streetcar lines. Overnight street parking in districts I, VI, VII, VIII, and IX is restricted to residents with stickers; check before you leave a car on the street, even for a brief period.

All vehicles using the autobahn (divided, mostly limited-access main highways, including the main highway from Vienna airport to the city) must display an autobahn-Vignette toll sticker on the inside of the windshield (to apply, contact the **ÖAMTC/Österreichischer Automobil-, Mororrad- und Touringclub,** ✉ Schubertring 3, A-1010, Vienna, ☎ 01/711–997).

BY SUBWAY

Subway (U-bahn) lines—stations are marked with a huge blue U—are designated U-1, U-2, U-3, U-4, and U-6, and are clearly marked and

color-coded. Trains run daily until about 12:30 AM. Additional services
are provided by fast suburban trains, the S-bahn, indicated by a stylized blue *S* symbol. Both are tied into the general city fare system.

Cabs can be flagged on the street if the FREI (free) sign is lit. You can
also dial 60160, 31300, or 40100 to request one. All rides around town
are metered. The initial fare is AS35, but expect to pay AS80–AS100
for an average city ride. There are additional charges for luggage, and
a surcharge of AS16 is added at night, on Sunday, and for telephone
orders. Tip the driver AS5–AS8 by rounding up the fare.

Money Matters
CURRENCY
The unit of currency is the Austrian schilling (AS), divided into 100
groschen. There are AS20, 50, 100, 500, 1,000, and 5,000 bills; AS1,
5, 10, and 20 coins; and 1-, 2-, 5-, 10-, and 50-groschen coins. The
1-, 2-, and 5-groschen coins are rare, and the AS20 coins are unpop-
ular, though useful for some cigarette machines. The 500- and 100-
schilling notes look similar; confusing the two can be an expensive
mistake. At press time (spring 1998), the exchange rate was AS12.5
to the dollar, AS8.9 to the Canadian dollar, and AS21 to the pound
sterling. You may bring in any amount of either foreign currency or
schillings and take out any amount with you.

Exchange traveler's checks at a bank, a post office, or the American Express office to get the best rate. All charge a small commission; some smaller
banks or "change" offices may give a poorer rate *and* charge a higher
fee. All change offices at airports and at main train stations in major cities
cash traveler's checks. In Vienna, bank-operated change offices with extended hours are found on Stephansplatz and at the main rail stations.
The Bank Austria machines on Stephansplatz and at Kärntnerstrasse 51
(to the right of the Opera) and at the Raiffeisenbank on Kohlmarkt (at
Michaelerplatz) change bills from other currencies into schillings, but
rates are poor and a hefty commission is automatically deducted.

Telephoning
COUNTRY CODE
The country code for Austria is 43. When dialing an Austrian number
from abroad, drop the initial 0 from the local area code.

Contacts and Resources
EMBASSIES
U.S. embassy (✉ Boltzmanng. 16, ☎ 01/31339); **consulate** (✉ Garten-
baupromenade, Parkring 12A, in the Marriott building, ☎ 01/31339).
Canadian embassy (✉ Laurenzerberg 2, on the 3rd floor of Haupt-
post building complex, ☎ 01/531–3801). **U.K. embassy and consulate** (✉ Jauresg. 10, near Schloss Belvedere, ☎ 01/71613–5151 for
embassy and consulate).

EMERGENCIES
Police (☎ 133). **Ambulance** (☎ 144). **Doctor:** ask your hotel, or in an
emergency, phone your embassy or consulate (☞ *above*). **Pharmacies:**
in city center, open weekdays 8–6, Saturday 8–noon; in neighborhoods,
weekdays 8–noon, 2–6. In each neighborhood, one pharmacy
(Apotheke) in rotation is open all night and weekends; the address is
posted on each area pharmacy.

ENGLISH-LANGUAGE BOOKSTORES
Big Ben Bookshop (✉ Serviteng. 4a, ☎ 01/319–6412). **British Book-
shop** (✉ Weihburgg. 24–26, ☎ 01/512–19–450). **Shakespeare & Co.**
(✉ Sterng. 2, ☎ 01/535–5053).

GUIDED TOURS

Guided walking tours in English are available almost daily and include such topics as "Jewish Vienna." There are also tours that will take you to cultural events and nightclubs, and there are daytime bus trips to the Danube Valley, Salzburg, and Budapest, among other spots. Check with the City Tourist Office (☞ Visitor Information, *below*) or your hotel for details.

The following are city orientation tours. **Vienna Sightseeing Tours** (☎ 01/712–46–830) offers a short highlights tour or a lengthier one to the Vienna Woods, Mayerling, and other sights near Vienna. Tours start in front of or beside the Staatsoper (State Opera House) on the Operngasse. **Cityrama** (☎ 01/533–4373) provides city tours with hotel pickup; tours assemble opposite the Inter-Continental Hotel (⊠ Johannesg. 28). **CityTouring Vienna** (☎ 01/894–14–170), with hotel pickup, starts from the city air terminal behind the Hilton Hotel (⊠ Am Stadtpark). Prices are similar, but find out whether you will visit or just drive past Schönbrunn and Belvedere palaces and whether admission fees are included.

TRAVEL AGENCIES

American Express (⊠ Kärntnerstr. 21–23, ☎ 01/515–400). **Österreichisches Verkehrsbüro** (Austrian Travel Agency; ⊠ Opernring 3–5, ☎ 01/588–000). **Ökista** (⊠ Reichstratstr. 13, next to the Rathaus, ☎ 01/402–1561).

VISITOR INFORMATION

City Tourist Office (⊠ Kärntnerstr. 38, behind the Staatsoper ; ⊘ Daily 9–7).

NOTES

NOTES

NOTES

NOTES

NOTES

NOTES

NOTES

NOTES

NOTES

NOTES

NOTES